American International Law Cases

AMERICAN INTERNATIONAL LAW CASES

1783-1968

Collected and Edited
by
FRANCIS DEAK
Visiting Professor of International Law
Rutgers — Camden Law School

Volume I
International Law in General

This volume may be cited as
1 AILC

1971 / OCEANA PUBLICATIONS, INC. / DOBBS FERRY, NEW YORK

©Copyright 1971 by Oceana Publications, Inc.

Library of Congress Catalog Card Number: 78-140621

Series International Standard Book Number (ISBN): 0-379-20075-9

Volume I International Standard Book Number (ISBN): 0-379-20076-7

This volume may be cited as *I AILC*

Manufactured in the United States of America

Advisory Committee

Professor R. R. Baxter, *Chairman*

Professor Alona E. Evans

Judge Philip C. Jessup

Professor Oliver J. Lissitzyn

Professor Myres S. McDougal

Dr. Oscar Schachter

FOREWORD

The approach of the two hundredth anniversary of the independence of the United States makes this an appropriate time to take stock of the multiplicity of decisions of United States courts bearing on questions of international law. The judgments of these courts are scattered through so many series of reports and so many volumes that many of them may be lost to sight. Americans and non-Americans alike who may be interested in pursuing these cases may be pardoned for their bewilderment in the face of this mass of material, to which existing indices and digests give only limited guidance. The publication of *American International Law Cases* will make this rich source of international law readily accessible to judges, practitioners, and scholars.

The size of the United States and the extraordinary range of its international contacts have had much to do with the frequency with which its courts have had to deal with international questions. Beyond this, the relation established between international law and municipal law under the constitutional law of the United States has led to the frequent invocation of international law in the courts of this country. Article VI, clause 2 of the United States Constitution makes treaties, together with the Constitution and statutes, "the supreme Law of the Land." Similarly, customary international law "is part of our law, and must be ascertained and administered by the courts of justice of appropriate jurisdiction, so often as questions of right depending upon it are duly presented for their determination."[1] This incorporation of conventional and customary international law into the law of the United States has had the beneficial effect of harmonizing the decisions of courts of the United States with the international duties and obligations of this country in many, if not in all, cases. For the courts are under certain constraints of municipal law which can lead to decisions in which primacy is not given to international law, for example, under the rule that in the event of a conflict between a treaty and a later statute, the statute, being later in time, prevails for the purposes of internal law.

In those cases in which treaties and customary international law are applied in municipal courts, there is often reason to be cautious about accepting the resulting statements of law as sound evidence of public international law. Incorporation not infrequently has a distorting effect on the law, and more especially on treaties.

There are in the United States, as in all countries, instances in which national interpretations of international law may not accord with those entertained in other states. The national understanding of the law relating to the immunities of foreign states and that concerning jurisdiction over extraterritorial activities may in certain respects set the law of the United States apart from the views on these questions of international law held in other states. These are probably less cases of national bias than of differing lines of decision in the courts of various countries.

A commingling of issues of international law and of municipal law may often be discerned in American cases. As one examines the cases on jurisdiction, for example, one is often hard put to determine whether the courts are applying a prohibitory rule of international law or, on the other hand, exercising a rule of national self-restraint or a presumption about Congressional intention regarding the territorial application of a statute. It is by no means clear whether cases dealing with the treatment of enemy or enemy-tainted property or enemy interests in neutral property in time of war purport to apply constraints imposed by international law or are merely applications of the United States Trading With the Enemy Act. And although the *Sabbatino* case[2] seems ultimately to turn on constitutional issues concerning the relations of the executive and legislative branches of Government, this matter is by no means free from doubt, and considerations of domestic and international law are closely intermingled in the opinions rendered by the various justices.

When dealing with the interpretation of treaties, courts – especially those not having much experience of litigation of an international character – often approach questions of construction in exactly the same way that they would go about interpreting statutes of the United States. Once a treaty norm is incorporated in municipal law, not under the general principle enunciated in the Constitution but by transformation into statutory form, the problem of determining whether the court is applying municipal or international law becomes the more difficult. And the very attempt to preserve treaties from the impact of possibly conflicting statutes may lead to a subtle distortion of the interpretation of the treaty in order to make it consistent with the statute.

Because international law and treaties do form part of the law of the United States, judges take judicial notice of them as they do of the statutes, regulatory material, and cases of various jurisdictions of the United States. There have been eras in which the presence on a court of a judge or judges skilled in international law has led to highly learned and perceptive opinions, drawing heavily upon the sources and evidence of international law and in turn contributing materially to the corpus of that law. But other courts betray a lack of expertise in international law in their approach to international issues, and these opinions must be discounted accordingly. The municipal law of the United States does not provide any general way for courts to obtain special guidance on questions of customary international law and on the interpretation of treaties, although courts have sometimes relied upon statements furnished by the Department of State about the force and meaning of treaties. A procedure whereby domestic courts might be able to refer questions to the International Court, by analogy to the reference of questions to the Court of Justice of the European Communities under Article 177 of the Treaty of Rome establishing the European Economic Community,[3] could lead to a more informed application of international law in the municipal courts of the United States and of other countries.

It is of course true that the law that emerges from the decision of any court may be influenced by the very process of submitting the dispute to adjudication. This phenomenon is visible not only in municipal courts, such as those of the United States, but in international tribunals as well. A stipulation of the governing law in the compromis establishing an international arbitral tribunal or the waiver of defenses, such as failure to exhaust local remedies, may skew the law enunciated by the tribunal in its decision. It should therefore be evident that American cases bearing on questions of international law must be read in context and with an understanding of the relation between international law and municipal law in the United States. The superficial generalization that treaties and international law are part of the law of the United States obscures a highly complex symbiosis.

Much gratitude is owed to Professor Deák for the initiative and learning that he has displayed in sifting through an enormous amount of case-law in order to provide us with the important cases on international law that are displayed in this volume and those that are to follow. They will take their place beside Professor Parry's *British International Law Cases* as an authoritative guide to the case-law of another important common law jurisdiction.

R. R. Baxter

Cambridge, Mass.
27 January 1971

Footnotes

[1] The Paquete Habana, 175 U.S. 677,700 (1900).
[2] Banco Nacional de Cuba v. Sabbatino, 376 U.S. 398 (1964)
[3] Signed March 25, 1957, 294 U.N.T.S. 3, 109.

INTRODUCTION

In conceiving the project of a collection of American cases dealing with issues of public international law spanning nearly 200 years, the editor was inspired by years of browsing through hundred of volumes of federal and state court reports which revealed a great number of decisions seldom if ever cited. He also concluded that the various standard sources for digests of judicial decisions and other aids useful though they are, are not adequate guides for those wishing to appraise in depth the contribution made by the American judiciary to the development of international law. That contribution, in the aggregate, is highly impressive. It is fair to say that of the three coordinate branches of the United States Government, the judiciary has done far the most for the interpretation, the application and the growth of international law. In our Constitution, direct references to international law are few. Congress is given power to define and punish offenses against the law of nations; and treaties, concluded with the advice and consent of the Senate, are equated with the Constitution and with Acts of Congress as the supreme law of the land. But there is no provision for the general primacy of international law over domestic law in the case of conflict between the two such as can be found in some more recent constitutions, or in amendments to them (e.g., the 1958 French Constitution and the 1953 amendments to the Netherland Constitution). The resolution of such conflicts was left to the courts, and, on the whole, they have done a fairly good job in handling this problem.

As compared to the role of the judiciary in the development of international law, the contributions of the executive and, particularly, the legislative branches of the Federal Government can hardly be characterized as distinguished. True, the executive, which under the Constitution has primary (in some respect, exclusive) responsibility for the conduct of international relations, has been consistent in giving at least lip service to the need for respect for international law. In some instances, it has taken praiseworthy initiatives, as for instance, in our early recognition that a neutral has duties as well as rights; in promoting and practicing resort to arbitration for the settlement of international disputes; in declaring the "Open Door" policy with regard to China; in concluding a number of bilateral conciliation and arbitration agreements (the so-called "Bryan Treaties"); in actively participating in the formulation of the 1928 Pact for the Renunciation of War as an Instrument of National Policy (the so-called "Kellogg-Briand Pact"), even though it has been honored more in the breach than in the observance; the non-recognition doctrine announced by Secretary of State Stimson; and the United States leadership in the establishment of the United Nations.

In listing the contributions of the Executive Branch to the development of international law, reference should be made to the vast accumulation of material contained in diplomatic notes (many of them published in *Papers Relating to the Foreign Relations of the United States* and, more recently in the *Department of State Bulletin,* and in the opinions of the Attorney General and of the Legal Adviser of the Department of State. It should be noted that those documents supplied much of the material for the International Law Digests successively compiled by Wharton, Moore, Hackworth and White. These Digests pioneered in a new approach to the dissemination of international law. They inspired a number of governments to make known to the public in general, and especially to international law scholars, their position on questions of international law, as the United States has done.

On the other hand, the interest of Congress in international law has been generally marginal, and not always constructive. In the early history of the Republic, in the first half of the 19th century, Congress was relatively active in supporting and approving executive initiative, (although the House was often obstreperous with regard to commercial treaties). In more recent times, its role has generally been that of critic and, often of a negative character. The Senate Committee on Foreign Relations — which spearheads Congressional participation in the conduct of foreign affairs — has sometimes distinguished itself by constructive consideration and endorsement of Executive proposals. Often, however, its handling of treaties has, to say the least, been negative — indeed harmful. The crippling amendments to the Treaty of Versailles which precluded United States membership in the League of Nations, doubtless contributed to the weakness and ineffectiveness of the organization, and to the gradual deterioration of the European scene, and led ultimately to World War II. The so-called "Connally Reservation" to the United States acceptance of the compulsory jurisdiction of the International Court of Justice initiated a series of similar crippling amendments by other States, rendering the clause for all practical purposes wholly ineffective. It must take a share of responsibility for the increasingly infrequent resort to that Court. (In fairness, it should be pointed out that four Presidents have urged repeal of the Connally Reservation, but the Senate has turned a deaf ear thus far to these recommendations). We also may mention the fact that senatorial action on important multilateral conventions is often dilatory for reasons varying from pressure of domestic interest groups to sheer indifference. The United States had let 45 years slip by without ratifying the Geneva Protocol prohibiting Chemical and Bacteriological Warfare and has yet to become a party to the Genocide Convention and the Vienna Convention of 1961 on Diplomatic Relations.

It is from this background that the editor thought it useful to make readily available the significant contribution of the American judiciary to the growth of international law and thus to put in perspective what the United States has done in this area where the more easily available record of Executive and Legislative actions is likely to give a somewhat distorted picture.

Another reason for undertaking this task was my belief that the availability of American decisions in a single collection might be welcomed by universities and public libraries and, particularly, by institutions abroad where the thousands of volumes of American court reports, among which hundreds of international law cases are scattered, are not readily available. Moreover, the American experience in the course of nearly two centuries — during which the United States, starting as a newly independent developing nation grew into one of the world's great powers — may be of special interest for recently independent states, and may serve as a useful tool in their own search for the position to take toward international law rules. This belief was greatly strengthened by the enthusiastic reception given to the *British International Law Cases,* edited by the distinguished British scholar, Professor Clive Parry, and by the wide use made of the *International Law Reports,* currently edited by another British scholar, Mr. Elihu Lauterpacht, Q.C., in succession to his father, Judge Sir Hersch Lauterpacht.

A few explanatory words concerning the procedure followed in the selection, organization, and annotation of this collection are called for.

(1) *Selection of cases.* Although all published federal and state decisions involving questions of public international law have been reviewed, not every decision is printed in this collection. The editor omitted cases which do not contain any real discussion of international law, those which refer to international law but are decided on some other ground, and those which rest on the authority of a prior decision. On the other hand, opinions which do not openly invoke international law rules but obviously apply such rules in deciding the issue have been included. Significant concurring and dissenting opinions are of course reproduced.

The collection is confined to decisions of law courts, federal and state, including the Court of Claims, the Court of Customs and Patent Appeals, and the United States Court of Military Appeals. Decisions of regulatory agencies, although often involving international law issues, have not been covered. It is my hope that a collection of such decisions will be made available in the near future. A single exception to this exclusionary policy is the reproduction of the opinion of the Federal Communication Commission in the case of the *International Monetary Fund v. All American Cable,* included in Chapter VII, Section 1; this regulatory agency opinion explores in depth the status of international organizations in contemporary international law.

(2) *Structure.* The present organization of the selected cases into chapters, sections, and subsections was devised, after considerable experimentation, to facilitate the location of relevant material. While the traditional classification of international law topics has been followed, allowance has been made for the expansion of international law into new areas. Further, some deference has been paid to the school of thought which should like to treat international law in terms of factual problems. In adopting the present organization, the editor proceeded on the assumption that the collection should be made as useful as possible for readers unfamiliar with the technical terminology of common law jurisdictions by making it possible for them to find the relevant decisions under traditional headings.

In each chapter and section, cases are grouped in three parts: first United States Supreme Court decisions, second, decisions of lower federal courts and, third, state court decisions. In each part, the arrangement is chronological. In a few instances, the editor has departed from this arrangement. Where opinions written in various stages of litigation appeared to be of sufficient importance to justify reprinting all or several of the opinions, they are published together, irrespective of chronology or the level of the judiciary. In the great majority of cases, only the decision of the highest court is reproduced. In a few instances, where the lower court's decision contained a helpful analysis of international law, both decisions are published.

(3) *Cross-references.* Many decisions involve more than one topic of international law. For instance, the status of aliens is almost always determined by a treaty of commerce or a consular convention, and cases on such questions frequently involve the consul's authority to intervene on behalf of nationale of his country. Hence, such a case may properly be placed either in the section on Aliens, or in the Treaty chapter, or in the section on Consular Authority. Again, extraditon cases invariably depend on the interpretation and application of extradition treaties. Such cases could be placed with equal justification either in the Treaty chapter or in the Extradition section. Various alternative ways of resolving this problem were considered. Excessive size and the probability of confusion prevented the reproduction of these multiple issue cases in each of the relevant chapters or sections. The possibility of breaking up such multiple issue cases and reproducing only the relevant part of the opinion

under the appropriate chapter or section heading was also considered. In fact, this procedure has been adopted in some of the leading
casebooks. Nevertheless, the editor concluded that this would not be
a satisfactory solution. After much thought, it was decided that each
decision would be printed only at one place — namely in the chapter
or section dealing with the topic which appeared to the editor to be
the principal or primary focus of the court — and that the case would
be referred to in other relevant chapters or sections by its name and
citation only. The editor is aware that his judgment as to the focus of
the opinion might not be shared by all.

(4) *Editor's Notes.* These are designed to identify precisely the
treaties cited and relied on in the opinion. Especially in earlier cases
courts cited treaties without adequately indentifying them. Also,
they were inconsistent in giving the date of the treaty involved.
Sometimes they use the date of signature, at other times the date of
ratification or coming into force. There is no uniformity in the citation of sources. Sometimes courts cite the page where the treaty
begins and at other times the page where the particular article applicable to the case appears. The editor's notes endeavor to give full and
uniform information about the treaty involved (except when such
information is fully set forth in the opinion). The title of the treaty,
the date of signature, alternative citations to the Statutes at Large, to
the Malloy collection, to the more recent United States Treaties
(UST), and Treaties and International Agreements Series (TIAS); and
where available to League of Nations Treaty Series (LNTS) and
United Nations Treaty Series (UNTS) are all set out. In some instances, the editor's notes also cites cases not printed which, in
identical or similar fact situations and on the authority of the principal case printed, contain identical conclusions.

(5) *Acknowledgements.* The editor wishes to express his appreciation for the generous assistance he had from several quarters. The
Editor wishes, first, to express his appreciation to members of the
Advisory Committee who assisted him in planning the scope of these
volumes and who helped to solve some of the problems that arose in
the course of completing this work. The distinguished members of
the Advisory Group are listed on the title page.

A grant from the Carnegie Endowment of International Peace not
only facilitated but also expedited the preparation of the material
published; and I wish to record my gratitude for this grant.

The West Publishing Company generously gave permission for the
reproduction of Federal Court decisions available only in the Federal
Reporter and Federal Supplement series, and of State court decisions
(when not available in official State reports) published in its National
Reporter series.

My thanks are due to the Librarians of Rugers Law School — that is my colleagues, Professors Albert P. Blaustein and Arno Liivak — and to the library staff, who gave continuous assistance in my research. I also had sustained support from the secretaries of the Dean's office who willingly undertook the thankless task of xeroxing thousands of pages of decisions and typing hundreds of editor's notes. I also wish to thank the Columbia Law School Library for permission to use its facilities.

Several of my students at Rutgers Law School helped in my research during the last three years. My special thanks are due to Mr. J. Robert Steelman who worked with me during the academic year 1969-1970. His enthusiastic and highly competent assistance in completing the selection of cases and in checking the accuracy of citations greatly expedited the preparation of the collection for publication.

Last, but not least, I wish to thank Oceana Publications for its interest in this project from the outset, and for the efforts of its staff to resolve numerous and difficult technical problems of production created by the somewhat unusual character of the material and its organization.

Despite guidance and assistance from several quarters, the editor is solely responsible for the content and organization of this collection. It is his hope that it will be, whatever its short-comings, a useful tool for scholars and students of international law.

Francis Deák
Visiting Professor of
International Law
Rutgers-Camden Law School

January 15, 1971

TABLE OF CONTENTS FOR THE COLLECTION

Each volume will have a Table of Contents covering the material included in that volume. A complete Table of Contents, with volume and page numbers, will be printed upon completion of the collection.

Foreword by Professor R. R. Baxter
Introduction
Table of Abbreviations (for each vol.)
Table of Cases (for each vol.)

SECTION I. INTERNATIONAL LAW IN GENERAL

(1) Nature, Sources and Application
(2) Subjects of International Law - States as International Persons

  (a) Sovereignty, Independence, Equality
  (b) Recognition of States, Governments, Belligerency
  (c) Continuity: State and Governmental Succession
  (d) Effect of Change of Sovereignty

(3) Relation of International and Domestic Law
    (see also infra. V. (2))

SECTION II. CONTROL OF RESOURCES

State Territory

(1) Acquisition and Loss (Cession, Annexation, Prescription, Acquiescence, Occupation)
(2) Boundaries: Rivers, Lakes, Bays, Inland and Territorial Waters

SECTION VIII. WAR, BELLIGERENCY AND NEUTRALITY

TABLE OF CONTENTS OF VOLUME I

A consolidated Table of Contents will be published in the last volume of the collection.

LIST OF ABBREVIATIONS IN VOLUME I

A consolidated List of Abbreviations will be printed in the last volume of this collection.

U.S.	United States Supreme Court Reports (Official edition)
S.Ct.	United States Supreme Court Reports (West Publishing Co. edition)
Fed.Cas.	Federal Cases. U. S. Courts of Appeals and District Courts (formerly Circuit Courts) decisions, 1789-1879, 31 volumes, published by the West Publishing Co.
Fed.	Federal Reporter. U.S. Courts of Appeals and District Court Decisions, 1878-1924, 300 volumes (West Publishing Co.)
F.2d.	Federal Reporter, 2d. series, U.S. Courts of Appeals and District Court Decisions, 1924-1932, volumes 1-60. U.S. Courts of Appeals decisions since 1932, beginning volume 61. (West Publishing Co.)
F.Supp.	Federal Supplement, U.S. District Courts decisions since 1932. (West Publishing Co.)
1st., 2d., 3d. etc. Cir.	Numbered Circuits of U.S. Courts of Appeals. (These are divided into ten numbered Circuits and the U.S. Court of Appeals for the District of Columbia)
Ct.Cl.	Court of Claims
C.C.P.A.	Court of Customs and Patent Appeals

Ky.	Kentucky Reports, Decisions of the Supreme Court of Kentucky
Misc.2d.	New York Miscellaneous Reports, 2d. series, since 1955. (Decisions of courts of original jurisdiction.)
Pa.St.	Pennsylvania State Reports. (Decisions of the State Appellate Courts)
So.	Southern Reporter, 1886-1941 (West Publishing Co. edition) Selected decisions of southern state courts.
Stat.	United States Statutes at large (Session Laws of the United States)
LNTS	League of Nations Treaty Series
Malloy	Treaties, Conventions, International Acts, Protocols and Agreements between the United States of America and other Powers, 1776-1909. Edited by William M. Malloy. 2 vols. (Washington: Government Printing Office, 1910.)
Trentwith	Treaties, Conventions, International Acts, Protocols and Agreements between the United State of America and other Powers, 1923-1937. Vol. 4 compiled by Edward J. Trentwith. (Washington: Government Printing Office, 1938).

TABLE OF CASES - VOL. I

Each volume will have a Table of Cases covering the material included in that volume. A consolidated Table of Cases will be printed upon completion of the collection. The names of cases and page numbers underlined below indicate that the case is only cited with reference to subsequent chapters or sections where the opinion is printed; or cases only cited in editorial notes.

I. INTERNATIONAL LAW IN GENERAL

(1). NATURE, SOURCES AND APPLICATION.

Thirty Hogshead of Sugar v. Boyle
13 U. S. (9 Cranch) 191 (1815)

MARSHALL, *Ch. J.* delivered the opinion of the Court as follows:

The island of Santa Cruz, belonging to the kingdom of Denmark, was subdued, during the late war, by the arms of his Britannic majesty. Adrian Benjamin Bentzon, an officer of the Danish government, and a proprietor of land therein, withdrew from the island on its surrender, and has since resided in Denmark. The property of the inhabitants being secured to them, he still retained his estate in the island under the management of an agent, who shipped thirty hogsheads of sugar, the produce of that estate, on board a British ship, to a commercial house in London, on account and risk of the said A. B. Bentzon. On her passage, she was captured by the American privateer, the Comet, and brought into Baltimore, where the vessel and cargo were libelled as enemy property. A claim for these sugars was put in by Bentzon; but they were condemned with the rest of the cargo; and the sentence was affirmed in the Circuit Court. The Claimant then appealed to this Court.

Some doubt has been suggested whether Santa Cruz, while in the possession of Great Britain, could properly be considered as a British island. But for this doubt there can be no foundation. Although acquisitions made during war are not considered as permanent until confirmed by treaty, yet to every commercial and belligerent purpose, they are considered as a part of the domain of the conqueror, so long as he retains the possession and government of them. The island of Santa Cruz, after its capitulation, remained a British island until it was restored to Denmark.

Must the produce of a plantation in that island, shipped by the proprietor himself, who is a Dane residing in Denmark, be considered as British, and therefore enemy property?

30 HHDS.   In arguing this question, the counsel for the Clai-
OF SUGAR mants has made two points.
  v.
BOYLE   1. That this case does not come within the rule ap-
&OTHERS. plicable to shipments from an enemy country, even as
————·——— laid down in the British Courts of admiralty.

2. That the rule has not been rightly laid down in
those Courts, and consequently will not be adopted in this.

1. Does the rule laid down in the British Courts of
admiralty embrace this case?

It appears to the Court that the case of the Phœnix
is precisely in point. In that case a vessel was captured in a voyage from Surinam to Holland, and a part
of the cargo was claimed by persons residing in Germany, then a neutral country, as the produce of their
estates in Surinam.

The counsel for the captors considered the law of the
case as entirely settled. The counsel for the Claimants did not controvert this position. They admitted
it; but endeavored to extricate their case from the general principle by giving it the protection of the treaty
of Amiens. In pronouncing his opinion, sir William
Scott lays down the general rule thus: " Certainly
" nothing can be more decided and fixed, as the princi-
" ple of this Court and of the Supreme Court, upon
" very solemn arguments, than that the possession of
" the soil does impress upon the owner the character of
" the country, as far as the produce of that plantation
" is concerned, in its transportation to any other coun-
" try, whatever the local residence of the owner may
" be. This has been so repeatedly decided, both in this
" and the superior Court, that it.is no longer open to
" discussion. · No question can be made on the point of
" law, at this day."

Afterwards, in the case of the *Vrow Anna Catharina,*
sir William Scott lays down the rule, and states its reason. " It cannot be doubted," he says, " that there are
transactions so radically and fundamentally national as
to impress the national character, independent of peace
or war, and the local residence of the parties. The

produce of a person's own plantation in the colony of 30 HHDS.
the enemy, though shipped in time of peace, is liable to OF SUGAR
be considered as the property of the enemy, by reason *v.*
that the proprietor has incorporated himself with the BOYLE
permanent interests of the nation as a holder of the soil, &OTHERS.
and is to be taken as a part of that country, in that particular transaction, independent of his own personal residence and occupation."

This rule laid down with so much precision, does
not, it is contended, embrace Mr. Bentzon's claim, because he has not " incorporated himself with the perma-
" nent interests of the nation." He acquired the property while Santa Cruz was a Danish colony, and he
withdrew from the island when it became British.

This distinction does not appear to the Court to be a
sound one. The identification of the national character
of the owner with that of the soil, in the particular transaction, is not placed on the dispositions with which he
acquires the soil, or on his general character. The acquisition of land in Santa Cruz binds him, so far as
respects that land, to the fate of Santa Cruz, whatever
its destiny may be. While that island belonged to Denmark, the produce of the soil, while unsold, was, according to this rule, Danish property, whatever might be the
general character of the particular proprietor. When
the island became British, the soil and its produce,
while that produce remained unsold, were British.

The general commercial or political character of Mr.
Bentzon could not, according to this rule, affect this
particular transaction. Although incorporated, so far
as respects his general character, with the permanent
interests of Denmark, he was incorporated, so far as
respected his plantation in Santa Cruz, with the permanent interests of Santa Cruz, which was, at that time,
British; and though as a Dane, he was at war with
Great Britain, and an enemy, yet, as a proprietor of
land in Santa Cruz, he was no enemy: he could ship
his produce to Great Britain in perfect safety.

The case is certainly within the rule as laid down in
the British Courts. The next enquiry is: how far will
that rule be adopted in this country?

30 HHDS.
OF SUGAR
v.
BOYLE
&OTHERS.
——————

The law of nations is the great source from which we derive those rules, respecting belligerent and neutral rights, which are recognized by all civilized and commercial states throughout Europe and America. This law is in part unwritten, and in part conventional. To ascertain that which is unwritten, we resort to the great principles of reason and justice : but, as these principles will be differently understood by different nations under different circumstances, we consider them as being, in some degree, fixed and rendered stable by a series of judicial decisions. The decisions of the Courts of every country, so far as they are founded upon a law common to every country, will be received, not as authority, but with respect. The decisions of the Courts of every country show how the law of nations, in the given case, is understood in that country, and will be considered in adopting the rule which is to prevail in this.

Without taking a comparative view of the justice or fairness of the rules established in the British Courts, and of those established in the Courts of other nations, there are circumstances not to be excluded from consideration, which give to those rules a claim to our attention that we cannot entirely disregard. The United States having, at one time, formed a component part of the British empire, *their* prize law was our prize law. When we separated, it continued to be our prize law, so far as it was adapted to our circumstances and was not varied by the power which was capable of changing it.

It will not be advanced, in consequence of this former relation between the two countries, that any obvious misconstruction of public law made by the British Courts, will be considered as forming a rule for the American Courts, or that any recent rule of the British Courts is entitled to more respect than the recent rules of other countries. But a case professing to be decided on ancient principles will not be entirely disregarded, unless it be very unreasonable, or be founded on a construction rejected by other nations.

The rule laid down in the Phœnix is said to be a recent rule, because a case solemnly decided before the lords commissioners in 1783, is quoted in the margin as its authority. But that case is not suggested to have been determined contrary to former practice or former opinions. Nor do we perceive any reason for supposing it to be contrary to the rule of other nations in a similar case.

30 HHDS.
OF SUGAR
v.
BOYLE
& OTHERS.

The opinion that ownership of the soil does, in some degree, connect the owner with the property, so far as respects that soil, is an opinion which certainly prevails very extensively. It is not an unreasonable opinion. Personal property may follow the person any where; and its character, if found on the ocean, may depend on the domicil of the owner. But land is fixed. Wherever the owner may reside, that land is hostile or friendly according to the condition of the country in which it is placed. It is no extravagant perversion of principle, nor is it a violent offence to the course of human opinion to say that the proprietor, so far as respects his interest in this land, partakes of its character; and that the produce, while the owner remains unchanged, is subject to the same disabilities. In condemning the sugars of Mr. Bentzon as enemy property, this Court is of opinion that there was no error, and the sentence is affirmed with costs.

———o*c———

United States v. Smith
18 U.S. (5 Wheaton) 153 (1820)

The act of the 3d of March, 1819, c. 76. s. 5. referring to the law of nations for a definition of the crime of piracy, is a constitutional exercise of the power of Congress to define and punish that crime.
The crime of piracy is defined by the law of nations with reasonable certainty.
Robbery, or forcible depredation, upon the sea, *animo furandi*, is piracy by the law of nations, and by the act of Congress.

THIS was an indictment for piracy against the prisoner Thomas Smith, before the Circuit Court of

1820.
U. States
v.
Smith.

Virginia, on the act of Congress, of the 3d of March, 1819, c. 76.[a]

The jury found a special verdict as follows : " We, of the jury, find, that the prisoner, Thomas Smith, in the month of March, 1819, and others, were part of the crew of a private armed vessel, called the Creollo, (commissioned by the government of Buenos Ayres, a colony then at war with Spain,) and lying in the port of Margaritta ; that in the month of March, 1819, the said prisoner and others of the crew mutinied, confined their officer, left the vessel, and in the said port of Margaritta, seized by violence a vessel called the Irresistible, a private armed vessel, lying in that port, commissioned by the government of Artigas, who was also at war with Spain ; that the said prisoner and others, having so possessed themselves of the said vessel, the Irresistible, appointed their officers, proceeded to sea on a cruize, without any documents or commission whatever ; and while on that cruize, in the month of April, 1819, on the high seas, committed the offence charged in the indictment, by the plunder and robbery of the Spanish vessel therein mentioned. If the plunder and robbery aforesaid be piracy under the act of the Congress of the United States, entitled, ' An act to protect the commerce of the

a Which provides, (s. 5.) " That if any person or persons whatsoever, shall, on the high seas, commit the crime of piracy, *as defined by the law of nations*, and such offender or offenders shall afterwards be brought into, or found in, the United States, every such offender or offenders shall, upon conviction thereof, before the Circuit Court of the United States for the District into which he or they may be brought, or in which he or they shall be found, be punished with death."

United States, and punish the crime of piracy,' then we find the said prisoner guilty ; if the plunder and robbery, above stated, be not piracy under the said act of Congress, then we find him, not guilty."

The Circuit Court divided on the question, whether this be piracy as defined by the law of nations, so as to be punishable under the act of Congress, of the 3d of March, 1819, and thereupon the question was certified to this Court for its decision.

Mr. Justice STORY delivered the opinion of the court. The act of Congress upon which this indictment is founded provides, "that if any person or persons whatsoever, shall, upon the high seas, commit the crime of piracy, as defined by the law of nations, and such offender or offenders shall be brought into, or found in the United States, every such offender or offenders shall, upon conviction thereof, &c. be punished with death."

The first point made at the bar is, whether this enactment be a constitutional exercise of the authority delegated to Congress upon the subject of piracies. The constitution declares, that Congress shall have power " to define and punish piracies and felonies committed on the high seas, and offences against the law of nations." The argument which has been urged in behalf of the prisoner is, that Congress is bound to define, in terms, the offence of piracy, and is not at liberty to leave it to be ascertained by judicial interpretation. If the argument be well founded, it seems admitted by the counsel that it equally applies to the 8th section of the act of Congress of 1790, ch. 9. which declares, that robbery and murder committed on the high seas shall be deemed piracy ; and yet, notwithstanding a

1820.

U. States
v.
Smith

Feb. 25th.

series of contested adjudications on this section, no doubt has hitherto been breathed of its conformity to the constitution.

In our judgment, the construction contended for proceeds upon too narrow a view of the language of the constitution. The power given to Congress is not merely "to define and punish piracies;" if it were, the words " to define," would seem almost superfluous, since the power to punish piracies would be held to include the power of ascertaining and fixing the definition of the crime. And it has been very justly observed, in a celebrated commentary, that the definition of piracies might have been left without inconvenience to the law of nations, though a legislative definition of them is to be found in most municipal codes.[a] But the power is also given "to define and punish felonies on the high seas, and offences against the law of nations." The term " felonies," has been supposed in the same work, not to have a very exact and determinate meaning in relation to offences at the common law committed within the body of a county. However this may be, in relation to offences on the high seas, it is necessarily somewhat indeterminate, since the term is not used in the criminal jurisprudence of the admiralty in the technical sense of the common law.[b] Offences, too, against the law of nations, cannot, with any accuracy, be said to be completely ascertained and defined in any public code recognised by the common consent of nations. In respect, therefore, as well to felonies on the high seas as to offences against the law of nations, there is a peculiar fitness in giving the power to define as well as to punish ; and there is not the slightest reason to doubt that this consideration had very great weight in producing the phraseology in question.

But supposing Congress were bound in all the cases included in the clause under consideration to define the offence, still there is nothing which restricts it to a mere logical enumeration in detail of all the facts constituting the offence. Congress may as well define by using a term of a known and determinate meaning, as by an express enumeration of all the particulars included in that term. That is certain which is by necessary reference made certain. When the act of 1790 declares, that any person who shall commit the crime of robbery, or murder, on the high seas, shall be deemed a pirate, the crime is not less clearly ascertained than it would be by using the definitions of these terms as they are found in our treatises of the common law. In fact, by such a reference, the definitions are necessarily included, as much as if they stood in the text of the act. In respect to murder, where " malice aforethought" is of the essence of the offence, even if the common law definition were quoted in express terms, we should still be driven to deny that the definition was perfect, since the meaning of " malice aforethought" would remain to be gathered from the common law. There would then be no end to our difficulties, or our definitions, for each would involve some terms which might still require some new explanation. Such a construction of the constitution is, therefore, wholly inadmissible. To define piracies, in the sense of the constitution, is merely to enumerate the crimes which shall constitute piracy; and this may be done either by a reference to crimes having a technical

The crime of piracy is constitutionally defined by Congress, in an act referring to the law of nations for a definition of that crime.

a *The Federalist, No.* 42. *p.* 276.
b See 3 *Inst.* 112. *Hawk. P. C. ch.* 37. *Moore,* 576.

name, and determinate extent, or by enumerating the acts in detail, upon which the punishment is inflicted.

Definition of piracy by the law of nations, and the act of Congress.It is next to be considered, whether the crime of piracy is defined by the law of nations with reasonable certainty. What the law of nations on this subject is, may be ascertained by consulting the works of jurists, writing professedly on public law; or by the general usage and practice of nations; or by judicial decisions recognising and enforcing that law. There is scarcely a writer on the law of nations, who does not allude to piracy as a crime of a settled and determinate nature; and whatever may be the diversity of definitions, in other respects, all writers concur, in holding, that robbery, or forcible depredations upon the sea, *animo furandi*, is piracy. The same doctrine is held by all the great writers on maritime law, in terms that admit of no reasonable doubt.[a] The common law, too, recognises and punishes piracy as an offence, not against its own municipal code, but as an offence against the law of nations, (which is part of the common law,) as an offence against the universal law of society, a pirate being deemed an enemy of the human race. Indeed, until the statute of 28th of Henry VIII. ch. 15. piracy was punishable in England only in the admiralty as a civil law offence; and that statute, in changing the jurisdiction, has been universally admitted not to have changed the nature of the offence.[b] Sir Charles Hedges, in his charge at the Admiralty sessions, in the case of Rex v. Dawson, (5 *State Trials*,) declared in emphatic terms, that "piracy is

a Santerna, (*lib.* 4. *note* 50.) for instance, says, "Inter piratam et latronem, non sit alia differentia, nisi quia pirata depredator est in mari et potest dici fur et latro maris, quia latrocinium et furtum sicut fit in terra, sic fit in mari." And Emerigon, (1 *Emerig. Assur. ch.* 12. *s.* 29. *p.* 523.) "La piraterie est un brigandage sur mer. Le Brigandage, sur terre est appellé vol ou rapine." So Straccha "Piratae sunt latrones maritimi."

b *Hawk. P. C. ch.* 37. *s.* 2.   3 *Inst.* 112.

only a sea term for robbery, piracy being a robbery committed within the jurisdiction of the admiralty." Sir Leoline Jenkins, too, on a like occasion, declared that " a robbery, when committed upon the sea, is what we call piracy ;" and he cited the civil law writers, in proof. And it is manifest from the language of Sir William Blackstone,[a] in his comments on piracy, that he considered the common law definition as distinguishable in no essential respect from that of the law of nations. So that, whether we advert to writers on the common law, or the maritime law, or the law of nations, we shall find that they universally treat of piracy as an offence against the law of nations, and that its true definition by that law is robbery upon the sea. And the general practice of all nations in punishing all persons, whether natives or foreigners, who have committed this offence against any persons whatsoever, with whom they are in amity, is a conclusive proof that the offence is supposed to depend, not upon the particular provisions of any municipal code, but upon the law of nations, both for its definition and punishment. We have, therefore, no hesitation in declaring, that piracy, by the law of nations, is robbery upon the sea, and that it is sufficiently and constitutionally defined by the fifth section of the act of 1819.

The special verdict in this case contains sufficient facts upon which to pronounce the prisoner guilty of piracy.

Another point has been made in this case, which is, that the special verdict does not contain sufficient facts upon which the Court can pronounce that the

1820.

U. States
v.
Smith.

prisoner is guilty of piracy. We are of a different opinion. The special verdict finds that the prisoner is guilty of the plunder and robbery charged in the indictment; and finds certain additional facts from which it is most manifest that he and his associates were, at the time of committing the offence, freebooters upon the sea, not under the acknowledged authority, or deriving protection from the flag or commission of any government. If, under such circumstances, the offence be not piracy, it is difficult to conceive any which would more completely fit the definition.

It is to be certified to the Circuit Court, that upon the facts stated, the case is piracy, as defined by the law of nations, so as to be punishable under the act of Congress of the 3d of March, 1819.[a]

a To show that piracy is defined by the law of nations, the following citations are believed to be sufficient :[1]

Grotius (*lib*. 3. *c*. 3. *s*. 1.) says, " Supra dicere incepimus justum bellum apud probos auctores dici saepe, non ex causa unde oritur, neque ut alias ex rerum gestarum magnitudine, sed ob peculiares quosdam juris effectus. Quale autem sit hoc bellum optime intelligitur ex hostium definitione apud Romanos jurisconsultos : *Hostes sunt, qui nobis, aut quibus nos publice bellum decernimus ; cœteri* LATRONES *aut* PRÆDONES *sunt, ait Pomponius* (*Dig*. *Lib*. 50. *tit*. 16. *l*. 118.) *nec aliter Ulpianus,* (*Dig. lib*. 49. *tit*. 15. *l*. 24.) *hostes sunt, quibus bellum publice populus Romanus decrevit, vel ipsi populo Romano ; cœteri* LATRUNCULI *vel* PRÆDONES *appellantur. Et ideo, qui à latronibus captus est servus latronum non est, nec postliminium illi, necessarium est. Ab hostibus autem captus ; puta à Germanis et Parthis et servus est hostium, et postliminio statum pristinum recuperat. Et Paulus,* (*Dig. lib*. 49. *tit*. 15. *l*. 19. *s*. 2.) *À piratis aut latronibus capti liberi permanent. Accedat illud Ulpiani ; in civilibus dissentionibus quamvis sœpe per eas respublica lœdatur, non ta-*

Mr. Justice LIVINGSTON dissented. In a case affecting life, no apology can be necessary for expres-

1820.

U. States
v.
Smith.

men in exitium reipublicæ contenditur ; qui in alterutras partes discedent, vice hostium non sunt eorum, inter quos jura captivitatum aut postliminiorum fuerint ; et ideo captos, et venundatos, posteaque manumissos placuit supervacuo repetere a principe ingenuitatem, quam nulla captivitate amiserant. (*Dig. lib. 49. tit. 15. l. 321. s. 2.*")

Grotius adds, (*s. 2.*) " Illud tantum notandum, sub exemplo populi Romani quemvis intelligi, qui in civitate summum imperium habeat."

Again, he says, (*s. 2.*) " Non autem statim respublica aut civitas esse desinit, si quid admittat injustum, etiam communiter ; nec coetus PIRATARUM aut LATRONUM civitas est, etiamsi forte æqualitatem quandam inter se servent, sine qua nullus coetus posset consistere. Nam hi criminis causa sociantur ; illi etsi interdum delicto non vacant juris tamen fruendi causa sociati sunt, et exteris jus reddunt, si non per omnia secundum jus naturæ, quod multos apud populos ex parte quasi obliteratum alibi ostendimus, certe secundum pacta cum quibus que inita, aut secundum mores."

Again, he says, (*s. 2.*) " A latronibus captos capientium non fieri, supra dicentem audivimus Ulpianum. Idem captos à Germanos ait libertatem amittere. Atqui apud Germanos latrocinia, quæ extra civitatis cujusque fines fiebant, nullam habebant infamiam, quæ verba sunt Cæsaris, etc. Idem alibi Cattos nobilem Germaniæ populum latrocinia agitasse dicit. Apud eundem Garamantes latrociniis facunda gens ; sed gens tamen. Illyrici sine discrimine maris proedas agere soliti ; *de iis tamen triumphus fuit ; Pompeio de piratis non fuit. Tantum discrimen est inter populum quantumvis sceleratum et inter eos, qui, cum populus non sint, sceleris causa coïunt.*"

Again, he says, (*lib. 3. c. 9. s. 16.*) " Eae vexo res quæ intra presidia perductæ nondum sunt, quanquam ab hostibus occupatæ, ideo postliminii non egent, quia dominum nondum mutarunt, ex gentium jure. Et quæ *piratæ* aut *latrones* nobis eripuerunt non opus habent postliminis, ut Ulpianus et Javolenus

1820.

U. States
v.
Smith.

sing my dissent from the opinion which has just been delivered.

responderunt ; quia *jus gentium* illis non concessit ut jus domini mutare possint, &c. Itaque res ab illis captæ ubicunque reperiunter vindicari possunt, nisi quod ex naturali jure alibi censuimus ei qui suo sumtu possessionem rei adeptus est tantum esse reddendum, quantum dominus ipse ad rem recuperandam libenter impensurus fuerat."

And (*id. s.* 17.) " Potest tamen lege civili aliud constitui ; sicuti lege Hispanica naves a piratis captæ eorum fiunt, qui eas eripiunt piratis ; neque enim iniquum est, ut privata res publicæ utilitati cedat, presertim in tanta recuperandi difficultate. Sed lex talis non obstabit exteris, quo minus res suas vindicent."

Again ; he says, (*lib.* 2. *c.* 17. *s.* 20.) " Ex neglectu tenuntur reges ac magistratus, qui ad inhibenda *latrocinia* et *piraticam* non adhibent ea quae possunt ac debent remedia ; quo nomine damnati olim ab Amphictionibus Scyrii. Quae potestatem predarum in maris ex hoste agendarum per codicillos plurimis dedissent, et eorum nonnulli res amicorum rapuissent, desertaque patriae mari vagarentur ac ne revocati quidem redirent, an rectores eo nomine tenerentur, aut quod malorum hominum usiessent opera, aut quod cautionem non exigissent. Dixi eos in nihil amplius teneri, quam ut noxios, si reperiri possent, punirent, aut dederent; *praeterea in bona raptorum jus reddi curarent.*"

Again ; he says, (*Id. c.* 18. *s.* 2, 3.) " *Piratae* et *latrones* qui civitatem non faciunt, *jure gentium* niti non possunt, &c. Sed interdum tales qui sunt jus legationis nanciscuntur fide data, ut olim fugitivi in saltu Pyrenaeo."

Again ; (*lib.* 3. *c.* 13. *s.* 15.) " Repudiandus ergo Cicero (*De Offic. lib.* 3. *cap.* 29.) cum ait perjurium nullum esse predonibus pactum pro capite pretium non adservatur, nec si juratum quidem sit ; quia *pirata* non sit ex perduellium numero desinitus, sed communis hostis omnium, eum quo nec fides esse debeat, nec jus jurandum commune, &c. Atque sicut in jure gentium constituto differe hostem a pirata verum est, et a nobis infra ostendetur ; ita hic ea differentia locum habere non potest,

The only question of any importance in this case is, whether the act of the 3d of March, 1819, be a

ubi, etsi personae jus deficiat cum Deo negotium est ; qua de causa juramentum voti nomine nuncupatur. Neque id quod sumit Cicero verum est, nullum esse cum praedone juris societatem. Nam depositum ex ipso gentium jure reddendum latroni, si dominus non apparet recte Tryphonino responsum est."

These passages abundantly show the opinion of Grotius, that piracy by the law of nations is the same thing as piracy by the civil law ; and though he no where defines the crime, in precise terms, yet there seems to be no doubt as to what he understood to be comprehended in that crime. *Piratae, latrones, prædones*, are used to denote the same class of offenders ; the first term being generally applied to robbers or plunderers on the sea, and the others to robbers or plunderers on land.

The terms are, indeed, convertible in many instances in the civil law. Thus, in the title, De Lege Rhodia de Jactu, (*Dig. lib*. 14. *tit*. 2. *s*. 3.) it is said, " Si navis a *piratis* redempta sit, Servius, Osilius, Labeo, omnes conferre debere aiunt. Quod vero *praedones* abstulerint, cum perdere cujus fuerit, nec conferendum ei qui suas merces redimerit."

Bynkershoek, (*Quæst. Jur. Pub. lib. c.* 17.) treating on the subject of piracy, says, " interest scire qui *piratae* ac *latrones* sunt, nam ab his capta dominium non mutant neque adeo postliminio egent. Sic docet ratio ; sic auctoritas juris in *l*. 19. *s*. 2. *l*. 24. and *l*. 27. de Capt. et Postlim. rev. (*Dig. lib*. 49. *tit*. 15.) et sic ex pactis quarandam gentium supra probavi. Non est igitur ut addam auctoritates *Grotii de Jure B. et. P. l*. 3. *c*. 9. *s*. 16. *Alberici Gentilis de jure belli lib*. 1. *c*. 4. *Zoucheii de Jure feciali, p*. 2. *s*. 8. *qu*. 15., aliorumque plurium in eandem sententiam. *Qui autem nullius principis auctoritate sive mari sive terra*, RAPIUNT, PIRATARUM PRAEDONUMQUE *vocabulo intelliguntur*."

Azuni (*Part* 2. *c*. 5. *s*. 3.) says, " A pirate is one who roves the sea in an armed vessel without any commission or passport from any prince or sovereign state, solely on his own authority,

constitutional exercise of the power delegated to Congress of " defining and punishing piracies ?"

and for the purpose of seizing by force, and appropriating to himself without discrimination, every vessel he may meet. For this reason pirates have always been compared to robbers. The only difference between them is, that the sea is the theatre of action for the one, and the land for the other." (*s.* 11.) "Thus, as pirates are the enemies of the human race, piracy is justly re-garded as a crime against the universal laws of society, and is every where punished with death. As they form no national body, as they have no right to arm, nor make war, and on ac-count of their indiscriminate plunder of all vessels are consi-dered only as public robbers, every nation has a right to pur-sue, and exterminate them, without any declaration of war. For these reasons it is lawful to arrest them, in order that they may undergo the punishment merited by their crimes." (*s.* 12.) " Pirates having no right to make conquests, cannot, therefore, acquire any lawful property in what they take ; for the law of nations does not authorize them to deprive the true owner of his property, who always retains the right of reclaiming it wherever it may be found. Thus, by the principles of common law, as well as the law of nature, at whatever period, or in whatever manner, things taken by a pirate may be recovered, they return again to their former owners, who lose none of their rights by such unjust usurpation." (See *Azuni, part.* 2. *c.* 5. *art.* 3. *p.* 351. 361. *Mr. Johnson's translation.*)

Lord Bacon, in his dialogue *De Bello Sacro* says, " Indubi-tatum semper fuit, bellum contra *piratas* juste geri posse per na-tionem quamcumque, licet ab iis minime infestatam et læsam, &c. &c. Vera enim causa hujus rei haec est, quod *piratæ com-munes humani generis hostes sint* ; quos idcirco omnibus na-tionibus persequi incumbit, non tam propter metus proprios quam *respectu fœderis inter homines sociales.* Sicut enim quæ-dam sunt fœdera inscriptis et in tractatus redacta contra hostes particulares inita ; ita naturalis et tacita confœderatio inter

The act declares, that any person who shall commit on the high seas the crime of piracy as *defined by the*

omnes homines intercedit contra communes societatis humanæ hostes." (10 *Bac. Works,* 313, 314. *edit.* 1803.)

Martens, in his Essay on Privateers, Captures and Recaptures, (*c.* 1. *s.* 1.) says, " L'armateur differe du *Pirate,* (1.) Le premier est muni d'une commission ou de lettres de marque du souverain, dont le pirate est destitué. (2.) L'armateur suppose le cas d'une guerre, (ou du moins celui de represailles,) le pirate pille au sein de la paix comme au milieu de la guerre. (3.) L'armateur s'oblige d'observer les ordonnances et les instructions qui lui ont été données, et de n'attaquer qu'en consequence de celles ci de l'ennemi, et ceux des vaisseaux neutres qui font un commerce illicite, le pirate pille indistinctement les vaisseaux de toutes les nations, sans observer même les loix de la guerre."

Rutherforth (*Inst. b.* 2. *c.* 9. *s.* 9. *p.* 481.) speaking with reference to the law of nations, says, " All wars of a nation against its external enemies are not public wars. To make a war a public one, both the contending parties must be public persons ; that is, it must be a war of one nation against another, &c. Where a nation makes war upon *pirates* or *other robbers,* though these are external enemies, the war will be a mixed one ; it is public on one side, because a nation or public person is one of the parties ; but it is private on the other side, because the parties on this side are private persons, who act together occasionally, and are not united into a civil society. A *band of robbers* or a *company of pirates* may in fact be united to one another by compact, &c. But they are still, by the law of nature, only a number of unconnected individuals ; and consequently, in the view of the law of nations they are not considered as a collective body or public person. For the compact by which they unite themselves is void, because the matter of it is unlawful, &c. &c. The common benefit which a *band of robbers* or a *company of pirates* propose to themselves consists in doing harm to the rest of mankind."

1820.

U. States
v.
Smith.

law of nations, shall be punished with death. The special power here given to define piracy, can be at-

Woodeson, (*Lect.* 34. *vol.* 2. 422.) treating on captures at sea, after stating that the law of nations is part of the laws of England, and that captures at sea may happen either by pirates, or by way of reprisal, or as prize of war, says, " *Piracy, according to the law of nations, is incurred by depredations on or near the sea, without authority from any prince or State.*" He then quotes the opinion of Sir Leoline Jenkins with approbation, that it is piracy, not only when a man robs without any commission at all, but when, having a commission, he despoils those with whom he is not warranted to fight or meddle, such as are de legantia vel amicitia of the prince or state which hath given him his commission. He then adds : " But according to the judgments of our domestic tribunals, a bare assault without taking or pillaging something away does not constitute the crime, though Molloy pretends, that by the law of nations it is otherwise. Yet it does not seem necessary that any person should be on board the pillaged vessel." " If these violations of property be perpetrated by any national authority, they are the commencement of a public war ; if without that sanction, they are *acts of piracy.*" He then proceeds to state several cases which had arisen in the Admiralty of England, and sums up his remarks as follow : " The foregoing particulars are the more deserving of consideration, because it seems agreed that when a piratical taking is ascertained, it becomes a clear and indisputable consequence that there is no transmutation of property. No right to the spoil vests in the piratical captor ; no right is derivable from them to any recaptors in prejudice of the original owners. These *piratical seizures* being wholly unauthorized, and highly criminal by *the law of nations*, there is no pretence for devesting the dominion of the former proprietor. This principle, therefore, ' a piratis et latronibus capta dominium non mutant,' is the received opinion of ancient civilians and more modern writers, on general jurisprudence. The same doctrine was maintained in our Courts of Common Law long antecedent to the great cultivation and improvements made in the science of the law of na-

tributed to no other cause, than to the uncertainty which it was known existed on this subject in the

1820.

U. States
v.
Smith.

tions. And he remarks in a note, (*p.* 427. note *n.*) "I have looked into the indictment against Luke Ryan, tried at the Admiralty Sessions, March, 1782, for piracy, and who is alleged to have had a Dutch commission. He was indicted not *for piracy generally by the law of nations*, but for that, being a natural born subject, he piratically, &c. against the form of the statute." From the whole scope of Mr. Woodeson's observations on the subject of piracy, it is very clear that he considered piracy, as punishable by the law of the admiralty, to be no other than piracy by the law of nations. The definition of piracy, and Mr. Woodeson's comments are cited with approbation by Mr. Gwillim in his late edition of Bacon's Abridgment. (5 *Bac. Abr.* 310. *edit.* 1807. London.)

Burlamaqui (*Part.* 2. *c.* 7. *s.* 41.) says : "Lastly, as to the wars of *robbers and pirates*, if they do not produce the effects above-mentioned, (transmutation of property on capture,) nor give to those pirates a right of appropriating what they have taken, it is *because they are robbers and enemies of mankind*, and, consequently, persons whose acts of violence are manifestly unjust, which authorizes all nations to treat them as enemies."

Thus far, the authorities cited are such as profess to treat of piracy *in terms* according to the law of nations, the notion of which was manifestly derived from the civil law, " on which," as Sir William Scott observes, (The Maria, 1 *Rob.* 340.) "great part of the law of nations is founded." Indeed, in the law of England, it is treated altogether as a *civil law* offence, and referred to that law for its definition and punishment. Piracies and depredations at sea, are capital offences by the civil law. (5 *Bac. Abr. Piracy*, 311. *Edit. ubi supra*, 3 *Inst.* 112. *Hawk. P. C. c.* 37. 2 *East, P. C.* 796. 4 *Bl. Comm.* 72.) The commentaries of the common law writers on the subject of piracy will be more fully considered hereafter.

Let us now advert to the definitions of the civil law and maritime writers.

law of nations, and which it must have been the intention of the framers of the constitution to remove,

In the Novels (*Nov.* 134. *tit.* 17. *c.* 13.) it is declared, " *Pro furto* autem nolumus omnino quodlibet membrum abscindi, aut mori; sed aliter eum castigari. *Fures* autem vocamus *qui occulte et sine armis* hujusmodi delinquunt. *Eos vero, qui violenter aggrediuntur aut cum armis aut sine armis in domibus aut itineribus* aut IN MARI *poenis eos legalibus subdi jubemus.*"

Calvinus, in his *Lexicon Juridicum*, says : " *Piratae* dicuntur *praedatores marini ;* sic dicti vel a pirata, qui prius maria infestavit, vel a Graeco πιρανω, id est, transeo, quod conspecta insula in illam transirent, jam praedaturi. Hinc piratica ars est, quam exercent." In the French *Code des Prises*, (*Edition of M. Dufriche Foulaines, Paris,* 1804, *tom.* 1. *p.* 6.) the editor says : " Le pirate est celui qui parcourt les mers avec une batiment armè sans commission ou patente d'aucune etat, dans la vue exclusive de s'approprier tous les navires *par la force.* La piraterie est un assassinat ; *tout puissance doit faire arreter et juger* des pareils brigands, et en purger la terre." Emerigon (*Assur. tom.* 1. *c.* 12. *s.* 28. *p.* 523.) says : " Les Pirates sont ceux qui courent les mers sans commission d'aucun Prince ni Etat souverain pour *depreder* les vaisseaux qu'ils rencontrent." " Les Ennemis sont ceux, qui autorisés par un prince, on etat souverain font la guerre dans la forme établie par le droit des gens ; au lieu que les Pirates sont de simples particuliers qui *depredent* le premier navire qu'ils recontrent." " Les hostilités se commettent de nation á nation ; au lieu que la piraterie est un *brigandage qui s'exerce sur mer* par gens sans aveu, et *d'une maniere furtive.*" " Les pirates sont ennemis du genre humain." " La piraterie, on le *brigandage sur mer,* est un delit contre la loi universelle des societies," &c. And Emerigon fortifies his opinion on this subject, by citations from the civil law, from other maritime writers, and from Blackstone's Commentaries. It is plain, therefore, that he considered piracy as defined in the civil law, the maritime law, and the common law of England, as the same crime.

by conferring on the national legislature the power which has been mentioned.   It was well known to

Bouchard (cited in 1 *Emerigon, c. 12. s. 28. p.* 527.) " Les pirates n'ont pas le droit des armes.   Ce sont des *voleurs* et assassins, qui ne forme pas un corps d'etat.   Ennemis des toutes les nations contre lesquelles ils exercent indistinctement leurs brigandages, toutes les nations sont en droit de courir sus, et de les exterminer sans declaration de guerre."

M. Bonnemant, in his edition of the Chevalier De Habreu's treatise on maritime captures, (*edit.* 1802, *Paris, part.* 1. *c.* 1. *s.* 5. *p.* 15. *note*,) says, " les pirates sont ceux dont la navigation, les actions et les entreprises ne sont autorisées ni avoneés par aucune puissance, qui agissent sur la propriété publique et particulière contre le vœu de toutes les nations."   And De Habreu himself (as translated by M. Bonnemant, *Part* 2. *c.* 6. *s.* 1. *p.* 100, 101.) says, " Selon la définition de la prise, il paroît que le droit d'armer en course n'appartient qu'à ceux qui sont ennemis autorisés, appellés, en Latin, *hostes*.   D'ou il s'ensuit que les *brigands* et les *pirates* sont exclus de ce droit ; qu'ils ne peuvent prétendre aux privilèges que les loix de la guerre accorde aux ennemis, et qu'au contraire ils méritent d'être punis rigoureusement comme les malfaiteurs, et qu'on est autorisé à se saisir de tous leurs biens."   " De tous les tems les pirates ont été regardés comme des voleurs publics et des perturbateurs de la paix.   C'est pour cela qu'il est libre à quiconque s'en saisit de leur ôter la vie sans se rendre coupable d'injustice.   La prejudice qu'ils causent à la tranquillité publique, á la liberté du commerce, et à la sûreté de la navigation, a fait que toutes les nations se sont accordées à les poursuivre et à les punir avec la plus grande rigueur."

Ferriere (*Dict. du Droit. art. Pirates*) says, " Pirates sont des corsaires, ecumeurs de mer, qui font des courses sur mer sans aveu ni autorité du Prince ou du Souverain."

In the Encyclopedie des Sciences, &c. (*Edit.* 1765, *art. Pirate*,) it is said, " On donne ce nom (Pirate) à *des bandits*, qui

the members of the Federal Convention, that in treatises on the law of nations, or in some of them at

maitres d'une vaisseau vont *sur mer attaquer les vaisseaux* mar-
chands pour *les piller et les voler*."

Valin (*Traité des Prises, c.* 3. *s.* 2. *p.* 29.) says, " Or la
peine des *pirates* ou *forbans* est celle du dernier supplice, sui-
vant l'opinion commune ; parceque ce sont des ennemis de-
clarés de la societé, *des violateurs* de la foi publique and *du droit
des gens, des voleurs publiques à main armé et à force ouverte*."

Straccha says, (*De Naut. Part.* 3. *n.* 30.) " Inter Piratam
et Latronem nulla alia est differentia nisi quia *Pirata deprae-
dator est in mari*."

Casaregis (*Disc.* 64. *n.* 4.) says, " Proprie pirata ille discitur
qui sine patentibus alicujus principis ex propria tantum et privata auctoritate per mare discurrit *depredendi causâ*."

Dr. Brown (2 *Civ. and Adm. Law*, 461, 462.) says, " Piracy
is *depredation* without authority from any Prince or State, or
transgression of authority by *despoiling* beyond its warrant."
" *Unlawful depredation* is of the essence of piracy."

Beawes (*Lex Mercatoria art. Piracy, p.* 250.) says, " A pirate is a *sea thief*, or an enemy of human kind, also aims at en-
riching himself by *marine robberies* committed either by force,
fraud, or surprise, on merchants or other traders at sea."

Molloy (*b.* 1. *c.* 4. *s.* 1.) says, " A pirate is a *sea thief*, or
hostis humani generis, who, for to enrich himself either by surprise, or open force, sets upon merchants or others trading at
sea, ever spoiling their lading, if by possibility they can get the
mastery."

Marshall (*Insur. c.* 12. *s.* 11. *p.* 556.) says, " The crime of
piracy or *robbery on the high seas*, is an offence against the *universal law of society*."

It is also said in 16 Viner's Abridgment, (*art. Pirate and
Piracy, A. p.* 556.) and in Cowell's Interpreter, (*Pirate*,) " A
pirate is now taken for one who maintains himself by *pillage
and robbery at sea*."

Comyn's (*Dig. Admiralty, E.* 3.) defines piracy thus : " Piracy is when a man commits *robbery upon the sea*;" and he
cites as authority, 3 *Inst.* 113. and 1 Sir *Leol. Jenk.* 94.

least, definitions of piracy might be found; but it must have been as well known to them that there

1820.

U. States
v.
Smith.

Lord Coke says, (3 *Inst.* 113. *Co. Litt.* 391.) " This word pirate, in Latin, pirata, from the Greek word πειρατης, which again comes from πειραν a transcendo mare, of roving upon the sea; and, therefore, in English, is called a rover and *robber upon the sea.*"

Sir Leoline Jenkins, in his charge at the admiralty sessions in 1668, says : " You are, therefore, to inquire of *all pirates* and *sea rovers*, they are in the law *hostes humani generis*, enemies, not of one nation, or of one sort of people only, but of all mankind. They are outlawed as I may say, by the laws of all nations; that is, out of the protection of all princes, and of all laws whatsoever. Every body is commissioned, and is to be armed against them as rebels and traitors to subdue and root them out. That which is called *robbing upon the highway, the same being done upon the water, is called piracy.* Now, robbery as it is distinguished from thieving or larceny, implies not only the actual taking away of my goods, while I am, as we say, in peace, but, also, the putting me in fear by taking them by force and arms, out of my hands, or in my sight and presence. When this is done upon the sea, without a lawful commission of war or reprisals, it is downright piracy." *Vol.* 1. *p.* 86.

Again; in another charge, he says, (*vol.* 1. *p.* 94.) " The next sort of offences pointed at in the statute [28 Hen. VIII. ch. 15.] are robberies; and a robbery, when it is committed upon the sea, is what we call piracy. A robbery, when it is committed upon the land, does imply three things, 1. That there be a violent assault; 2. That a man's goods be actually taken from his person or possession; 3. That he who is despoiled be put in fear thereby. When this is done upon the sea, when one or more persons enter on board a ship with force and arms, and those in the ship have their ship carried away by violence, or their goods taken away out of their possession, and are put in fright by the assault, this is piracy; and he that does so is a pirate or a robber within the statute."

was not such a coincidence on this subject, as to render a reference to that code a desirable or safe mode

The statute of Henry VIII. here referred to, does not contain any description of piracy. Before that statute, piracy was only cognizable by the civil law in the Admiralty Court. But the statute gave the High Commission Court (created by that statute) jurisdiction of " all treasons, felonies, *robberies*, murders, and confederacies committed in, or on the sea," &c. The term *piracy* is not found in the statute, and it is only as a *robbery* upon the sea that the High Commission Court has jurisdiction of piracy. . Sir Leoline Jenkins, therefore, refers to the civil law definition of the offence of *piracy;* for it is agreed on all sides, that the statute of Henry VIII. has not altered the nature of the offence. (See 1 *Hawk. P. C. b.* 1. *c.* 37.)

Targa (as I find him quoted by his Spanish translator, *Gison, Reflex. c.* 61. *De los Corsarios o Pyratas,* for the original is not before me) says, " Esta (depredacion) se comete de dos modos, o por causa de guerra declarada entre dos naciones, &c. o por modo *de hurto violento como Ladrones del Mar* y como *hacen los robos en terra los salteadores de caminos;* y esto se compuela con la authentica del Derecho Civil, (*a*) que distingue la pyrateria del robo," &c. Again; " A los *pyratas* como tambien a los *salteadores de camino,* enemigos comunes, opresores de la libertad y comercio, y como a *violadores del derecho de las gentes,* puede qualquiera oponerse y los ministros y subditos del principe pueden perseguir los y prender los aunque sea fuera del dominio y se hayan refugiado a los estados confinantes, sin que per esso quede violada la jurisdiccion ; y presas que sean, se pendran en poder de la justicia de aquel Principe en cuyo estado han sido cogidos." Again ; " Y assi concluyo, diciendo, que deben todos guardarse en el mar de Pyratas, y en la tierra de Ladrones ; y *todo aquel,* que en el mar, playa, puerto, ò otro seño de mar, ò rio navigable, *roba ò apresa,* ya sea amigo, esto es, enemigo no declarado, y tambien los paysanos, ò enemigos propriamente tales, ò con patente, estandarte, ò sin el, ò con *engano,* ò *fuerza, siempre es pyrata.*"

a Dig. lib. 49. *tit.* 15. *l.* 19. *s.* 2.

of proceeding in a criminal, and especially in a capital case.   If it had been intended to adopt the defi-

Citations from civilians and maritime writers to the same effect might be multiplied ; but they would unnecessarily swell
this note.   It remains only to notice the doctrines which have
been held by the tribunals of Great Britain, and asserted by
her common law writers on the subject of piracy.

Hawkins (*P. C. b.* 1. *c.* 37.) says, " A pirate at the common
law is a person who commits any of those acts of piracy, *robbery and depredation upon the high seas*, which, if committed
upon land, would have amounted to felony there." ·

From the terms of this definition, (if it may be so called,) it
might be supposed, that by piracy *at the common law*, something
was meant peculiar to that law, and not piracy by the civil law,
or the law of nations.   But that was certainly not the meaning
of the writer.   For it is perfectly well settled, that piracy is no
felony at common law, being *out of its jurisdiction;* and before
the statute of 28 Henry VIII. c. 15. it was only punishable by
the *civil law*.   That statute, however, does not (as has been
already stated) alter the nature of the offence in this respect ;
and, therefore, a pardon of all felonies generally, does not extend to it.   (2 *East's P. C.* 796.   1 *Hawk. c.* 37. *s.* 6. 8. 10.
1 *Hale*, 354.   2 *Hale*, 18.   3 *Inst.* 112.)   And it was also determined in Rex v. Morphes, (*Salk.* 85.) that " no attainder for
piracy wrought corruption of blood, *for it was no offence at
common law.* (2 *East's P. C.* 796.   Co. *Litt.* 391. *a.*)   The
intention of Hawkins must have been to use the phrase " at
the common law" in its most comprehensive sense ; in which
sense the *law of nations* itself is a part of the common law ;
since all offences against the law of nations are punishable by
the criminal jurisprudence of England.

Blackstone, in the Commentaries, (4 *Comm.* 71. 73.) evidently
proceeds upon this notion.   He says, " The crime of piracy,
or *robbery and depredation* upon the high seas, is an offence
against the *universal law of society*, a pirate being, according to
Sir Edward Coke, *hostis humani generis.*"   He goes on to re-

nition or definitions of this crime, so far as they were
to be collected from the different commentators on

mark, that every community hath a right to punish it, for it is
a war against all mankind.   He then gives the definition of piracy by Hawkins, as the definition of the common law; and
then states the several statutes made in England on the subject
of piracy, concluding thus: " These are the principal cases
in which the *statute* law of England interposes *to aid and enforce the law of nations as a part of the common law*, by inflict-
ing an adequate punishment for offences against that universal
law committed by private persons."

The state trials for piracy in the reign of William III. are
entitled to great consideration, both from the eminent talents
of the Judges who constituted the tribunal, and the universal approbation of the legal principles asserted by them.   It is, also,
worthy of remark, that in none of these indictments was there
any averment that the prisoners were British subjects; and
most of them were for piracies committed on foreign subjects
and vessels.   They were all framed as indictments at common
law, or for general piracy, without reference to any British
statute.

In Rex v. Dawson and others, (8 *William* III. 1696.   5 *State
Trials*, 1 *edit.* 1742.) the Court was composed of Sir Charles
Hedges, Judge of the High Court of Admiralty, (as President,)
Lord Chief Justice Holt, Lord Chief Justice Treby, Lord Chief
Baron Ward, Mr. Justice Rookby, Mr. Justice Turton, Mr.
Justice Eyre, Mr. Baron Powis, and Doctors Lane, King, and
Cook, (Civilians.)   Sir Charles Hedges delivered the charge
to the grand jury, and among other things, directed them as
follows : " Now piracy is only a *sea term* for robbery, *piracy
being a robbery committed within the jurisdiction of the Admiralty*.   If any man be assaulted within that jurisdiction, and his
ship or goods violently taken away without legal authority, this
is *robbery and piracy*.   If the mariners of a ship shall violently
dispossess the master, and afterwards carry away the ship itself,
or any of the goods, or tackle, apparel or furniture, with a fe-

this code, with all the uncertainty and difficulty attending a research for that purpose, it might as well

1820.

U. States
v.
Smith.

lonious intention, in any place where the Lord Admiral hath, or pretends to have, jurisdiction, this is also robbery and piracy. The intention will, in these cases, appear, by considering the end for which the fact is committed, and the end will be known, if the evidence show you what hath been done. The King of England hath not only an empire or sovereignty over the British seas for the punishment of piracy, *but in concurrence with other Princes and States, an undoubted jurisdiction and power in the most remote parts of the world. If any person, therefore, native or foreigner,* Christian or Infidel, Turk or Pagan, *with whose country we are in amity, trade or correspondence, shall be robbed or spoiled,* in the narrow or *other seas, whether the Mediterranean, Atlantic, or Southern, or any branches thereof, either on this or the other side of the line,* IT IS A PIRACY, *within the limits of your inquiry, and cognizable by this Court.*" It seems impossible to doubt, that Sir Charles Hedges here understood piracy to be punishable *by all nations,* as a crime *against the law of nations,* and that its true definition is the same in the civil and common law, as in the law of nations, viz. robbery upon the seas ; and that, as such, it was punishable by the British Courts in virtue of their general concurrent jurisdiction on the seas.

In Rex v. Dawson and others, there were several indictments. 1. The first was for piracy in robbing and plundering the ship Gunsway, *belonging to the Great Mogul and his subjects,* in the Indian seas. 2. The second for piracy, in forcibly seizing and feloniously taking, stealing, and carrying away a merchant ship called the Charles 2d. *belonging to certain of his majesty's subjects unknown,* on the high seas, about three leagues from the Groyne in Spain. 3. The third was for piracy *on two Danish ships.* 4. The fourth for piracy *on a Moorish ship.* Dawson pleaded guilty ; and the other prisoners not guilty, and were upon trial convicted, and all sentenced to death accordingly. It appeared in evidence that the prisoners were part of the crew of the Charles the 2d, and rose upon her near

at once have been adopted as a standard by the constitution itself.   The object, therefore, of referring

the Groyne, and afterwards ran away with her, and committed
the piracies.   The Solicitor General, in stating the case to the
jury, said, "They (the prisoners) are arraigned for a very
high crime, a robbery upon the seas."   "These are crimes
against the law of nations, and worse than robbery on land."
Lord Chief Justice Holt, in delivering the charge to the jury,
said, " that there was a piracy committed on the ship Charles
is most apparent by the evidence that hath been given ; that is,
a force was put upon the master, and some of the seamen on
board her, who because they would not agree to go on a piratical expedition, had liberty to depart and be set ashore, &c.
&c.   So that I must tell you beyond all contradiction, the *force
put upon the captain*, and taking away this ship, called the
Charles 2d, is piracy."
   On the trial of Kidd and others for piracy, &c. in 13th of
William III, 1713, (5 *State Trials, edit.* 1742.) there were
several indictments.   1. The first was against William Kidd
for the murder of one W. Moore, on the high seas, near the
coast of Malabar, in a vessel called the Adventure Galley,
of which Kidd was commander.   2. The second was against
all the prisoners for piracy in seizing and running away with a
certain merchant ship called the Quedash Merchant, then being
a ship of certain persons to the jurors unknown, (not stated to be
British subjects,) upon the high seas about ten leagues from
Cutsheen in the East Indies.   In fact, the vessel and cargo appeared by the evidence to belong to Armenian merchants, and
then on a voyage from Bengal to Surat.   Lord Chief Baron Ward,
in charging the jury on this indictment. said, " the crime charged
upon them (the prisoners) is *piracy*, that is, *seizing and taking
this ship and the goods in it piratically and feloniously.   This ship
belonged to people in amity with the king of England*."   " If this
was a capture on the high seas, and these were the goods of
persons in amity with the king, and had no FRENCH PASS, then
it is a plain piracy ; and if you believe the witnesses, here is

its definition to Congress was, and could have been no other than, to enable that body, to select from sources it might think proper, and then to declare, and with reasonable precision to define, what act or acts should constitute this crime; and having done

the taking of the goods and ship of persons in amity, and converting them to their own use. Such a taking as this would be *felony*; and *being at sea*, it *will be piracy.*" The prisoners were convicted and sentenced to death. There were four other indictments, three for piracy on Moorish ships, and one for piracy on a Portuguese ship; and all the prisoners were convicted and sentenced. Mr. Justice Turton, in charging the jury on one of these indictments, said, " pirates are called hostes humani generis, the enemies to all mankind."

The case of Rex v. Green (4 *Anne*, 1704. 5 *State Trials*, 573. *edit.* 1742.) was a libel or indictment in the Court of Admiralty in Scotland for piracy, manifestly treated both in the libel and the arguments as a crime against the law of nations, and as such, also against the law of Scotland.

In Erskine's Institutes of the law of Scotland, in treating of the crime of piracy, the author says, " piracy is that particular kind of robbery which is committed on the seas." (*Ersk. Inst. b.* 4. *tit.* 4. *s.* 65.) He had in the preceding section, (64.) declared that, " robbery is truly a species of theft; for both are committed on the property of another, and with the same view of getting gain; but robbery is aggravated by the *violence* with which it is attended." The definition of both these crimes seems not at all different from that of the common law.

The foregoing collection of doctrines, extracted from writers on the civil law, the law of nations, the maritime law, and the common law, in the most ample manner confirms the opinion of the Court in the case in the text; and it is with great diffidence submitted to the learned reader to aid his future researches in a path, which, fortunately for us, it has not been hitherto necessary to explore with minute accuracy.

so, to annex to it such punishment as might be thought proper. Such a mode of proceeding would be consonant with the universal practice in this country, and with those feelings of humanity which are ever opposed to the putting in jeopardy the life of a fellow-being, unless for the contravention of a rule which has been previously prescribed, and in language so plain and explicit as not to be misunderstood by any one. Can this be the case or can a crime be said to be defined, even to a common intent, when those who are desirous of information on the subject are referred to a code, without knowing with any certainty, where it is to be found, and from which even those to whom it may be accessible, can with difficulty decide, in many cases, whether a particular act be piracy or not? Although it cannot be denied that some writers on the law of nations do declare what acts are deemed piratical, yet it is certain, that they do not all agree; and if they did, it would seem unreasonable to impose upon that class of men, who are the most liable to commit offences of this description, the task of looking beyond the written law of their own country for a definition of them. If in criminal cases every thing is sufficiently certain, which by reference may be rendered so, which was an argument used at bar, it is not perceived why a reference to the laws of China, or to any other foreign code, would not have answered the purpose quite as well as the one which has been resorted to. It is not certain, that on examination, the crime would not be found to be more accurately defined in the code thus referred to, than in any writer on the law of nations; but the objection to the reference in both cases is the same; that it is the duty of Congress to incorporate into their own statutes a definition in *terms*, and not to refer the citizens of the United States for rules of conduct to the statutes or laws of any foreign country, with which it is not to be presumed that they are acquainted. Nor does it make any difference in this case, that the law of nations forms part of the law of every civilized country. This may be the case to a certain extent; but as to criminal cases, and as to the offence of piracy in particular, the law of nations could not be supposed of itself to form a rule of action; and, therefore, a reference to it in this instance, must be regarded in the same light, as a reference to any other foreign code. But, it is said, that murder and robbery have been declared to be punishable by the laws of the United States, without any definition of what act or acts shall constitute either of these offences. This may be; but both murder and robbery, with arson, burglary, and some other crimes, are defined by writers on the common law, which is part of the law of every State in the Union, of which, for the most obvious reasons, no one is allowed to allege his ignorance in excuse for any crime he may commit. Nor is there any hardship in this, for the great body of the community have it in their power to become acquainted with the criminal code under which they live; not so when acts which constitute a crime are to be collected from a variety of writers, either in different languages, or under the disadvantage of translations, and from a code with whose provisions even profes-

1820.

U. States
v.
Smith.

sional men are not always acquainted.   By the same clause of the constitution, Congress have power to punish offences against the law of nations, and yet it would hardly be deemed a fair and legitimate execution of this authority, to declare, that all offences against the law of nations, without defining any one of them, should be punished with death.   Such mode of legislation is but badly calculated to furnish that precise and accurate information in criminal cases, which it is the duty, and ought to be the object, of every legislature to impart.

Upon the whole, my opinion is, that there is not to be found in the act that definition of piracy which the constitution requires, and that, therefore, judgment on the special verdict ought to be rendered for the prisoner.

CERTIFICATE.   This cause came on to be heard on the transcript of the record of the Circuit Court of the United States for the district of Virginia, and on the question on which the Judges of that Court were divided in opinion, and was argued by counsel. On consideration whereof, this Court is of opinion, that the offence charged in the indictment in this case, and found by the jury to have been committed by the prisoner, amounts to the crime of piracy, as defined by the law of nations, so as to be punishable under the act of Congress, entitled, " an act to protect the commerce of the United States, and punish the crime of piracy."   All which is ordered to be certified to the Circuit Court for the district of Virginia.[a]

a *Vide* APPENDIX, Note IV. for the new act of Congress on the subject of piracy, passed May 15, 1820.

The Antelope
23 U.S. (10 Wheaton) 66 (1825)

APPEAL from the Circuit Court of Georgia.

These cases were allegations filed by the Vice-
Consuls of Spain and Portugal, claiming certain
Africans as the property of subjects of their nation. The material facts were as follows : A privateer, called the Colombia, sailing under a Vene-
zuelean commission, entered the port of Baltimore
in the year 1819; clandestinely shipped a crew
of thirty or forty men; proceeded to sea, and
hoisted the Artegan flag, assuming the name of
the Arraganta, and prosecuted a voyage along
the coast of Africa ; her officers and the greater
part of her crew being citizens of the United
States. Off the coast of Africa she captured an
American vessel, from Bristol, in Rhode Island,
from which she took twenty-five Africans ; she
captured several Portuguese vessels, from which
she also took Africans ; and she captured a Spanish vessel, called the Antelope, in which she
also took a considerable number of Africans.
The two vessels then sailed in company to the
coast of Brazil, where the Arraganta was wrecked,
and her master, Metcalf, and a great part of his
crew, made prisoners ; the rest of the crew, with
the armament of the Arraganta, were transferred
to the Antelope, which, thus armed, assumed the
name of the General Ramirez, under the command of John Smith, a citizen of the United
States ; and on board this vessel were all the

1825.

The Antelope.

Africans, which had been captured by the privateer in the course of her voyage. This vessel,
thus freighted, was found hovering near the coast
of the United States, by the revenue cutter,
Dallas, under the command of Captain Jackson,
and finally brought into the port of Savannah for
adjudication. The Africans, at the time of her
capture, amounted to upwards of two hundred
and eighty. On their arrival, the vessel, and the
Africans, were libelled, and claimed by the Portuguese and Spanish Vice-Consuls reciprocally.
They were also claimed by John Smith, as captured *jure belli*. They were claimed by the United States, as having been transported from foreign parts by American citizens, in contravention to the laws of the United States, and as entitled to their freedom by those laws, and by the
law of nations. Captain Jackson, the master of
the revenue cutter, filed an alternative claim for
the bounty given by law, if the Africans should
be adjudged to the United States; or to salvage, if
the whole subject should be adjudged to the Portuguese and Spanish Consuls.

The Court dismissed the libel and claim of
John Smith. They dismissed the claim of the
United States, except as to that portion of the
Africans which had been taken from the Ameri-
can vessel. The residue was divided between
the Spanish and Portuguese claimants.

No evidence was offered to show which of the
Africans were taken from the American vessel,
and which from the Spanish and Portuguese;
and the Court below decreed, that, as about one
third of them died, the loss should be averaged

among these three different classes ; and that sixteen should be designated, by lot, from the whole
number, and delivered over to the Marshal, according to the law of the United States, as being
the fair proportion of the twenty-five, proved to
have been taken from an American vessel.

Mr. Chief Justice MARSHALL delivered the
opinion of the Court, and, after stating the
case, proceeded as follows :

In prosecuting this appeal, the United States
assert no property in themselves. They appear
in the character of guardians, or next friends, of
these Africans, who are brought, without any act
of their own, into the bosom of our country, insist on their right to freedom, and submit their
claim to the laws of the land, and to the tribunals of the nation.

The Consuls of Spain and Portugal, respectively, demand these Africans as slaves, who
have, in the regular course of legitimate commerce, been acquired as property by the subjects
of their respective sovereigns, and claim their
restitution under the laws of the United States.

In examining claims of this momentous importance ; claims in which the sacred rights of liberty
and of property come in conflict with each other ;
which have drawn from the bar a degree of talent
and of eloquence, worthy of the questions that
have been discussed ; this Court must not yield to
feelings which might seduce it from the path of
duty, and must obey the mandate of the law.

That the course of opinion on the slave trade
should be unsettled, ought to excite no surprise.
The Christian and civilized nations of the world,

1825.

The Antelope.

March 18*th*.

How far the
slave trade is
contrary to the
law of nature,
and nations.

with whom we have most intercourse, have all been engaged in it. However abhorrent this traffic may be to a mind whose original feelings are not blunted by familiarity with the practice, it has been sanctioned in modern times by the laws of all nations who possess distant colonies, each of whom has engaged in it as a common commercial business which no other could rightfully interrupt. It has claimed all the sanction which could be derived from long usage, and general acquiescence. That trade could not be considered as contrary to the law of nations which was authorized and protected by the laws of all commercial nations; the right to carry on which was claimed by each, and allowed by each.

The course of unexamined opinion, which was founded on this inveterate usage, received its first check in America; and, as soon as these States acquired the right of self-government, the traffic was forbidden by most of them. In the beginning of this century, several humane and enlightened individuals of Great Britain devoted themselves to the cause of the Africans; and, by frequent appeals to the nation, in which the enormity of this commerce was unveiled, and exposed to the public eye, the general sentiment was at length roused against it, and the feelings of justice and humanity, regaining their long lost ascendency, prevailed so far in the British parliament as to obtain an act for its abolition. The utmost efforts of the British government, as well as of that of the United States, have since been assiduously employed in its suppression. It has been denounced by both in terms of great severity, and those concerned in it are subjected to the heaviest penalties which law can inflict. In addition to these measures operating on their own people, they have used all their influence to bring other nations into the same system, and to interdict this trade by the consent of all.

Public sentiment has, in both countries, kept pace with the measures of government; and the opinion is extensively, if not universally entertained, that this unnatural traffic ought to be suppressed. While its illegality is asserted by some governments, but not admitted by all; while the detestation in which it is held is growing daily, and even those nations who tolerate it in fact, almost disavow their own conduct, and rather connive at, than legalize, the acts of their subjects; it is not wonderful that public feeling should march somewhat in advance of strict law, and that opposite opinions should be entertained on the precise cases in which our own laws may control and limit the practice of others. Indeed, we ought not to be surprised, if, on this novel series of cases, even Courts of justice should, in some instances, have carried the principle of suppression farther than a more deliberate consideration of the subject would justify.

The *Amedie*, (1 *Acton's Rep.* 240.) which was an American vessel employed in the African trade, was captured by a British cruiser, and condemned in the Vice Admiralty Court of Tortola.

1825.

The Antelope.

An appeal was prayed; and Sir William Grant, in delivering the opinion of the Court, said, that the trade being then declared unjust and unlawful by Great Britain, " a claimant could have no right, upon principles of universal law, to claim restitution in a prize Court, of human beings carried as his slaves. He must show some right that has been violated by the capture, some property of which he has been dispossessed, and to which he ought to be restored. In this case, the laws of the claimant's country allow of no right of property such as he claims. There can, therefore, be no right of restitution. The consequence is, that the judgment must be affirmed."

The *Fortuna* (1 *Dodson's Rep.* 81.) was condemned on the authority of the *Amedie,* and the same principle was again affirmed.

The *Diana* (1 *Dodson's Rep.* 95.) was a Swedish vessel, captured with a cargo of slaves, by a British cruiser, and condemned in the Court of Vice Admiralty at Sierra Leone. This sentence was reversed on appeal, and Sir William Scott, in pronouncing the sentence of reversal, said, " the condemnation also took place on a principle which this Court cannot in any manner recognise, inasmuch as the sentence affirms, ' that the slave trade, from motives of humanity, hath been abolished by most civilized nations, *and is not, at the present time, legally authorized by any.'* This appears to me to be an assertion by no means sustainable." The ship and cargo were restored, on the principle that the trade was allowed by the laws of Sweden.

The principle common to these cases is, that the legality of the capture of a vessel engaged in the slave trade, depends on the law of the country to which the vessel belongs. If that law gives its sanction to the trade, restitution will be decreed; if that law prohibits it, the vessel and cargo will be condemned as good prize.

1825.

The Antelope.

This whole subject came on afterwards to be considered in the *Louis*, (2 *Dodson's Rep.* 238.) The opinion of Sir William Scott, in that case, demonstrates the attention he had bestowed upon it, and gives full assurance that it may be considered as settling the law in the British Courts of Admiralty as far as it goes.

The *Louis* was a French vessel, captured on a slaving voyage, before she had purchased any slaves, brought into Sierra Leone, and condemned by the Vice Admiralty Court at that place. On an appeal to the Court of Admiralty in England, the sentence was reversed.

In the very full and elaborate opinion given on this case, Sir William Scott, in explicit terms, lays down the broad principle, that the right of search is confined to a state of war. It is a right strictly belligerent in its character, which can never be exercised by a nation at peace, except against professed pirates, who are the enemies of the human race. The act of trading in slaves, however detestable, was not, he said, " the act of freebooters, enemies of the human race, renouncing every country, and ravaging every country, in its coasts and vessels, indiscriminately." It was not piracy.

1825.

The Antelope.

He also said, that this trade could not be pronounced contrary to the law of nations. " A Court, in the administration of law, cannot attribute criminality to an act where the law imputes none. It must look to the legal standard of morality; and, upon a question of this nature, that standard must be found in the law of nations, as fixed and evidenced by general, and ancient, and admitted practice, by treaties, and by the general tenor of the laws and ordinances, and the formal transactions of civilized states ; and, looking to those authorities, he found a difficulty in maintaining that the transaction was legally criminal."

The right of visitation and search being strictly a belligerent right, and the slave trade being neither piratical, nor contrary to the law of nations, the principle is asserted and maintained with great strength of reasoning, that it cannot be exercised on the vessels of a foreign power, unless permitted by treaty. France had refused to assent to the insertion of such an article in her treaty with Great Britain, and, consequently, the right could not be exercised on the high seas by a British cruiser on a French vessel.

" It is pressed as a difficulty," says the Judge, " what is to be done, if a French ship, laden with slaves, is brought in ? I answer, without hesitation, restore the possession which has been unlawfully devested ; rescind the illegal act done by your own subject, and leave the foreigner to the justice of his own country."

This reasoning goes far in support of the proposition, that, in the British Courts of admiralty, the vessel even of a nation which had forbidden the slave trade, but had not conceded the right of search, must, if wrongfully brought in, be restored to the original owner.   But the Judge goes farther, and shows, that no evidence existed to prove that France had, by law, forbidden that trade. Consequently, for this reason, as well as for that previously assigned, the sentence of condemnation was reversed, and restitution awarded.

1825.

The Antelope.

In the United States, different opinions have been entertained in the different Circuits and Districts; and the subject is now, for the first time, before this Court.

The question, whether the slave trade is prohibited by the law of nations has been seriously propounded, and both the affirmative and negative of the proposition have been maintained with equal earnestness.

That it is contrary to the law of nature will scarcely be denied.   That every man has a natural right to the fruits of his own labour, is generally admitted; and that no other person can rightfully deprive him of those fruits, and appropriate them against his will, seems to be the necessary result of this admission.   But from the earliest times war has existed, and war confers rights in which all have acquiesced.   Among the most enlightened nations of antiquity, one of these was, that the victor might enslave the vanquished.   This, which was the usage of all, could not be pronounced repugnant to the law of nations, which is certainly to be tried by the test of neral usage. That which has received the assent of all, must be the law of all.

Slavery, then, has its origin in force ; but as the world has agreed that it is a legitimate result of force, the state of things which is thus produced by general consent, cannot be pronounced unlawful.

Throughout Christendom, this harsh rule has been exploded, and war is no longer considered as giving a right to enslave captives. But this triumph of humanity has not been universal. The parties to the modern law of nations do not propagate their principles by force ; and Africa has not yet adopted them. Throughout the whole extent of that immense continent, so far as we know its history, it is still the law of nations that prisoners are slaves. Can those who have themselves renounced this law, be permitted to participate in its effects by purchasing the beings who are its victims ?

Whatever might be the answer of a moralist to this question, a jurist must search for its legal solution, in those principles of action which are sanctioned by the usages, the national acts, and the general assent, of that portion of the world of which he considers himself as a part, and to whose law the appeal is made. If we resort to this standard as the test of international law, the question, as has already been observed, is decided in favour of the legality of the trade. Both Europe and America embarked in it ; and for nearly two centuries, it was carried on without opposition, and without censure. A jurist could not say, that a practice thus supported was illegal, and that those engaged in it might be punished, either personally, or by deprivation of property.

In this commerce, thus sanctioned by universal assent, every nation had an equal right to engage. How is this right to be lost? Each may renounce it for its own people; but can this renunciation affect others?

No principle of general law is more universally acknowledged, than the perfect equality of nations. Russia and Geneva have equal rights. It results from this equality, that no one can rightfully impose a rule on another. Each legislates for itself, but its legislation can operate on itself alone. A right, then, which is vested in all by the consent of all, can be devested only by consent; and this trade, in which all have participated, must remain lawful to those who cannot be induced to relinquish it. As no nation can prescribe a rule for others, none can make a law of nations; and this traffic remains lawful to those whose governments have not forbidden it.

If it is consistent with the law of nations, it cannot in itself be piracy. It can be made so only by statute; and the obligation of the statute cannot transcend the legislative power of the state which may enact it.

If it be neither repugnant to the law of nations, nor piracy, it is almost superfluous to say in this Court, that the right of bringing in for adjudication in time of peace, even where the vessel belongs to a nation which has prohibited the trade,

1825.

The Antelope.

1825.

The Antelope.

cannot exist. The Courts of no country execute the penal laws of another; and the course of the American government on the subject of visitation and search, would decide any case in which that right had been exercised by an American cruiser, on the vessel of a foreign nation, not violating our municipal laws, against the captors.

It follows, that a foreign vessel engaged in the African slave trade, captured on the high seas in time of peace, by an American cruiser, and brought in for adjudication, would be restored.

The general question being disposed of, it remains to examine the circumstances of the particular case.

The Spanish claim.

The Antelope, a vessel unquestionably belonging to Spanish subjects, was captured while receiving a cargo of Africans on the coast of Africa, by the Arraganta, a privateer which was manned in Baltimore, and is said to have been then under the flag of the Oriental republic. Some other vessels, said to be Portuguese, engaged in the same traffic, were previously plundered, and the slaves taken from them, as well as from another vessel then in the same port, were put on board the Antelope, of which vessel the Arraganta took possession, landed her crew, and put on board a prize master and prize crew. Both vessels proceeded to the coast of Brazil, where the Arraganta was wrecked, and her captain and crew either lost or made prisoners.

The Antelope, whose name was changed to the General Ramirez, after an ineffectual attempt to sell the Africans on board at Surinam, arrived off the coast of Florida, and was hovering on that coast, near that of the United States, for several days. Supposing her to be a pirate, or a vessel wishing to smuggle slaves into the United States, Captain Jackson, of the revenue cutter Dallas, went in quest of her, and finding her laden with slaves, commanded by officers who were citizens of the United States, with a crew who spoke English, brought her in for adjudication.

She was libelled by the Vice Consuls of Spain and Portugal, each of whom claim that portion of the slaves which were conjectured to belong to the subjects of their respective sovereigns; which claims are opposed by the United States on behalf of the Africans.

In the argument, the question on whom the *onus probandi* is imposed, has been considered as of great importance, and the testimony adduced by the parties has been critically examined. It is contended, that the Antelope, having been wrongfully dispossessed of her slaves by American citizens, and being now, together with her cargo, in the power of the United States, ought to be restored, without farther inquiry, to those out of whose possession she was thus wrongfully taken. No proof of property, it is said, ought to be required. Possession is in such a case evidence of property.

Conceding this as a general proposition, the counsel for the United States deny its application to this case. A distinction is taken between

1825.

The Antelope.

On whom the *onus probandi* is thrown in this case.

men, who are generally free, and *goods*, which are always property. Although, with respect to the last, possession may constitute the only proof of property which is demandable, something more is necessary where men are claimed. Some proof should be exhibited that the possession was legally acquired. A distinction has been also drawn between Africans unlawfully taken from the subjects of a foreign power by persons acting under the authority of the United States, and Africans first captured by a belligerent privateer, or by a pirate, and then brought rightfully into the United States, under a reasonable apprehension that a violation of their laws was intended. Being rightfully in the possession of an American Court, that Court, it is contended, must be governed by the laws of its own country; and the condition of these Africans must depend on the laws of the United States, not on the laws of Spain and Portugal.

Had the Arraganta been a regularly commissioned cruiser, which had committed no infraction of the neutrality of the United States, her capture of the Antelope must have been considered as lawful, and no question could have arisen respecting the rights of the original claimants. The question of prize or no prize belongs solely to the Courts of the captor. But, having violated the neutrality of the United States, and having entered our ports, not voluntarily, but under coercion, some difficulty exists respecting the extent of the obligation to restore, on the mere proof of former possession, which is imposed on this government.

If, as is charged in the libels of both the Consuls, as well as of the United States, she was a pirate, hovering on the coast with intent to introduce slaves in violation of the laws of the United States, our treaty requires that property rescued from pirates shall be restored to the Spanish owner on his making proof of his property.

Whether the General Ramirez, originally the Antelope, is to be considered as the prize of a commissioned belligerent ship of war unlawfully equipped in the United States, or as a pirate, it seems proper to make some inquiry into the title of the claimants.

In support of the Spanish claim, testimony is produced, showing the documents under which the Antelope sailed from the Havana on the voyage on which she was captured ; that she was owned by a Spanish house of trade in that place ; that she was employed in the business of purchasing slaves, and had purchased and taken on board a considerable number, when she was seized as prize by the Arraganta.

Whether, on this proof, Africans brought into the United States, under the various circumstances belonging to this case, ought to be restored or not, is a question on which much difficulty has been felt. It is unnecessary to state the reasons in support of the affirmative or negative answer to it, because the Court is divided on it, and, consequently, no principle is settled. So much of the decree of the Circuit Court as di-

1825.

The Antelope.

rects restitution to the Spanish claimant of the Africans found on board the Antelope when she was captured by the Arraganta, is affirmed.

There is some difficulty in ascertaining their number. The libel claims one hundred and fifty as belonging to Spanish subjects, and charges that one hundred or more of these were on board the Antelope. Grondona and Ximenes, Spanish officers of the Antelope before her capture, both depose positively to the number of one hundred and sixty-six. Some deduction, however, is to be made from the weight of Grondona's testimony, because, he says, in one of his depositions, that he did not count the slaves on the last day when some were brought on board, and adds, that he had lost his papers, and spoke from memory, and from the information he had received from others of the crew, after his arrival in the Havana. Such of the crew as were examined, concur with Grondona and Ximenes as to numbers.

The depositions of the Spanish witnesses on this point, are opposed by those of John Smith, the Captain of the General Ramirez, and William Brunton, one of the crew of the Arraganta, who was transferred to the Antelope.

John Smith deposes, that ninety-three Africans were found on board the Antelope when captured, which he believes to have been Spanish property. He also says, that one hundred and eighty-three were taken out of Portuguese vessels.

William Brunton deposes, that more slaves

were taken out of the Portuguese ship than were 1825. in any other, and that ninety odd were represent- ~~~ ed by the crew to have been on board the Ante- The Antelope. lope when she was captured.

If, to the positive testimony of these witnesses, we add the inference to be drawn from the statement of the libel, and the improbability that so large a number of Africans as are claimed could have been procured, under the circumstances in which the Antelope was placed, between the 13th, when she was liberated by the first pirate who seized her, and the 23d, when she was finally captured, we are rather disposed to think the weight of testimony is in favour of the smaller number. But supposing perfect equality in this respect, the decision ought, we think, to be against the claimant.

Whatever doubts may attend the question whether the Spanish claimants are entitled to restitution of all the Africans taken out of their possession with the Antelope, we cannot doubt the propriety of demanding ample proof of the extent of that possession. Every legal principle which requires the plaintiff to prove his claim in any case, applies with full force to this point; and no countervailing consideration exists. The *onus probandi*, as to the number of Africans which were on board when the vessel was captured, unquestionably lies on the Spanish libellants. Their proof is not satisfactory beyond ninety-three. The individuals who compose this number must be designated to the satisfaction of the Circuit Court.

1825.

The Antelope.

The Portuguese claim.

We proceed next to consider the libel of the Vice-Consul of Portugal. It claims one hundred and thirty slaves, or more, " all of whom, as the libellant is informed and believes," are the property of a subject or subjects of his Most Faithful Majesty; and although " the rightful owners of such slaves be not at this time individually and certainly known to the libellant, he hopes and expects soon to discover them."

John Smith, and William Brunton, whose depositions have already been noticed, both state, that several Africans were taken out of Portuguese vessels; but neither of them state the means by which they ascertained the national character of the vessels they had plundered. It does not appear that their opinions were founded on any other fact than the flag under which the vessels sailed. Grondona, also, states the plunder of a Portuguese vessel, lying in the same port, and engaged in the same traffic with the Antelope when she was captured; but his testimony is entirely destitute of all those circumstances which would enable us to say, that he had any knowledge of the real character of the vessel, other than was derived from her flag. The cause furnishes no testimony of any description, other than these general declarations, that the proprietors of the Africans now claimed by the Vice-Consul of Portugal, were the subjects of his king; nor is there any allusion to the individuals to whom they belong. These vessels were plundered in March, 1820, and the libel was filed in August of the same year. From that time to this, a period of more than five years, no subject of the crown of Portugal has appeared to assert his title to this property, no individual has been designated as its probable owner.   This inattention to a subject of so much real interest, this total disregard of a valuable property, is so contrary to the common course of human action, as to justify serious suspicion that the real owner dares not avow himself.

1825.

The Antelope.

That Americans, and others, who cannot use the flag of their own nation, carry on this criminal and inhuman traffic under the flags of other countries, is a fact of such general notoriety, that Courts of admiralty may act upon it.   It cannot be necessary to take particular depositions, to prove a fact which is matter of general and public history.   This long, and otherwise unaccountable absence, of any Portuguese claimant, furnishes irresistible testimony, that no such claimant exists, and that the real owner belongs to some other nation, and feels the necessity of concealment.

An attempt has been made to supply this defect of testimony, by adducing a letter from the secretary to whose department the foreign relations of Portugal are supposed to be intrusted, suggesting the means of transporting to Portugal those slaves which may be in the possession of the Vice-Consul, as the property of his fellow subjects.   Allow to this document all the effect which can be claimed for it, and it can do no more than supply the want of an express power from the owners of the slaves to receive them. It cannot be considered as ascertaining the owners, or as proving their property.

The difficulty, then, is not diminished by this paper. These Africans still remain unclaimed by the owner, or by any person professing to know the owner. They are rightfully taken from American citizens, and placed in possession of the law. No property whatever in them is shown. It is said, that possession, in a case of this description, is equivalent to property. Could this be conceded, who had the possession? From whom were they taken by the Arraganta? It is not alleged that they are the property of the crown, but of some individual. Who is that individual? No such person is shown to exist, and his existence, after such a lapse of time, cannot be presumed.

The libel, which claims them for persons entirely unknown, alleges a state of things which is *prima facie* evidence of an intent to violate the laws of the United States, by the commission of an act which, according to those laws, entitles these men to freedom. Nothing whatever can interpose to arrest the course of the law, but the title of the real proprietor. No such title appears, and every presumption is against its existence.

We think, then, that all the Africans, now in possession of the Marshal for the District of Georgia, and under the control of the Circuit Court of the United States for that District, which were brought in with the Antelope, otherwise called the General Ramirez, except those which may be designated as the property of the Spanish claimants, ought to be delivered up to the United States, to be disposed of according to law. So much of the sentence of the Circuit Court as is contrary to this opinion, is to be reversed, and the residue affirmed.

1825.

The Antelope.

DECREE. This cause came on to be heard, &c.; On consideration whereof, this Court is of opinion, that there is error in so much of the sentence and decree of the said Circuit Court, as directs the restitution to the Spanish claimant of the Africans in the proceedings mentioned, in the ratio which one hundred and sixty-six bears to the whole number of those which remained alive at the time of pronouncing the said decree; and also in so much thereof, as directs restitution to the Portuguese claimant; and that so much of the said decree ought to be reversed, and it is hereby reversed and annulled. And this Court, proceeding to give such decree as the said Circuit Court ought to have given, doth DIRECT and ORDER, that the restitution to be made to the Spanish claimant, shall be according to the ratio which ninety-three (instead of one hundred and sixty-six) bears to the whole number, comprehending as well those originally on board the Antelope, as those which were put on board that vessel by the Captain of the Arraganta. After making the apportionment according to this ratio, and deducting from the number the rateable loss which must fall on the slaves to which the Spanish claimants were originally entitled, the

residue of the said ninety-three are to be delivered to the Spanish claimant, on the terms in the said
decree mentioned ; and all the remaining Africans are to be delivered to the United States, to
be disposed of according to law ; and the said
decree of the said Circuit Court is, in all things
not contrary to this decree, affirmed.

———

United States v. Brig Malek Adhel
43 U.S. (2 Howard) 209 (1844)

Mr. Justice STORY delivered the opinion of the court.

This is an appeal from a decree of the Circuit Court of the United
States for the district of Maryland, sitting in admiralty, and affirming
a decree of the District Court rendered upon an information *in rem*,
upon a seizure brought for a supposed violation of the act of the 3d of
March, 1819, ch. 75, (ch. 200,) to protect the commerce of the United
States, and to punish the crime of piracy. The information originally contained five counts, each asserting a piratical aggression and
restraint on the high seas upon a different vessel : one, the Madras,
belonging to British subjects ; another, the Sullivan, belonging to
American citizens ; another, the Emily Wilder, belonging to American citizens ; another, the Albert, belonging to British subjects ; and
another upon a vessel whose name was unknown, belonging to
Portuguese subjects ; and this last count contained also an allegation
of a piratical depredation. The Malek Adhel and cargo were claimed by the firm of Peter Harmony and Co., of New York, as their
property, and the answer denied the whole gravamen of the information. At the hearing in the District Court, the vessel was condemned
and the cargo acquitted, and the costs were directed to be a charge
upon the property condemned. An appeal was taken by both parties
to the Circuit Court ; and upon leave obtained, two additional counts
were there filed, one alleging a piratical aggression, restraint, and
depredation upon a vessel belonging to Portuguese subjects, whose
name was unknown, in a hostile manner and with intent to destroy

and plunder the vessel, in violation of the law of nations; and another alleging an aggression by discharge of cannon and restraint upon a British vessel called the Alert, or the Albert, in a hostile manner, and with intent to sink and destroy the same vessel, in violation of the law of nations. Upon the hearing of the cause in the Circuit Court, the decree of the District Court was affirmed; and from that decree an appeal has been taken by both parties to this court.

It was fully admitted in the court below, that the owners of the brig and cargo never contemplated or authorized the acts complained of; that the brig was bound on an innocent commercial voyage from New York to Guayamas, in California; and that the equipments on board were the usual equipments for such a voyage. It appears from the evidence that the brig sailed from the port of New York on the 30th of June, 1840, under the command of one Joseph Nunez, armed with a cannon and ammunition, and with pistols and daggers on board. The acts of aggression complained of, were committed at different times under false pretences, and wantonly and wilfully without provocation or justification, between the 6th of July, 1840, and the 20th of August, 1840, when the brig arrived at Bahia; where, in consequence of the information given to the American consul by the crew, the brig was seized by the United States ship Enterprize, then at that port, and carried to Rio Janeiro, and from thence brought to the United States.

The general facts are fully stated in a deposition of one John Myers, the first mate of the Malek Adhel; and his testimony is corroborated by the other evidence in the cause, in its main outlines and details. The narrative, although long, cannot be better given than in his own words. He says, among other things, " On Tuesday, the 30th of June," [Here the judge read a part of the evidence of Myers, which is set forth in the statement of the case by the reporter.]

Now upon this posture of the case, it has been contended, 1st. That the brig was not an armed vessel in the sense of the act of Congress of 1819, ch. 75, (ch. 200.) 2. That the aggressions, restraints, and depredations disclosed in the evidence were not piratical within the sense of the act. 3. That if the case in both respects is brought within the scope of the act, still neither the brig nor the cargo are liable to condemnation, because the owners neither participated in nor authorized the piratical acts, but are entirely innocent thereof. 4. That if the brig is so liable to condemnation, the cargo is not, either under the act of Congress or by the law of nations.

We shall address ourselves accordingly to the consideration of each of these grounds of defence. The act of 1819, ch. 75, (ch. 200,) provides, in the first section, that the President is authorized and requested to employ the public armed ships of the United States with suitable instructions "in protecting the merchant ships of the United States and their crews from piratical aggressions and depredations." By the second section the commanders of such armed vessels are authorized "to subdue, seize, take, and send into any port of the United States any armed vessel or boat, or any vessel or boat the crew whereof shall be armed, and which shall have attempted or committed any piratical aggression, search, restraint, depredation, or seizure upon any vessel of the United States, or of the citizens of the United States, or upon any other vessel," &c. By the third section it is provided "that the commander and crew of any merchant vessel owned wholly or in part by a citizen thereof, may oppose and defend against any aggression, search, restraint, depredation, or seizure, which shall be attempted upon such vessel, or upon any other vessel owned as aforesaid by the commander or crew of any other armed vessel whatsoever, not being a public armed vessel of some nation in amity with the United States, and may subdue and capture the same," &c. Then comes the fourth section, (upon which the five counts of the original information are founded,) which is as follows, "That whenever any vessel or boat from which any piratical aggression, search, restraint, depredation, or seizure shall have been first attempted or made, shall be captured and brought into any port of the United States, the same shall and may be adjudged and condemned to their use and that of the captors, after due process and trial in any court having admiralty jurisdiction, and which shall be holden for the district into which such captured vessel shall be brought; and the same court shall thereupon order a sale and distribution thereof accordingly, and at their discretion." The fifth section declares, that any person who shall on the high seas commit the crime of piracy as defined by the law of nations, shall, upon conviction thereof, be punished with death.

Such are the provisions of the act of 1819, ch. 75, (ch. 200.) And it appears to us exceedingly clear, that the Malek Adhel is an "armed vessel" within the true intent and meaning of the act. No distinction is taken, or even suggested in the act, as to the objects, or purposes, or character of the armament, whether it be for offence or defence, legitimate or illegitimate. The policy as well as the words of the act equally extend to all armed vessels which commit the unlawful acts specified therein. And there is no ground, either of principle or authority, upon which we are at liberty to extract the present case from the operation of the act.

The next question is whether the acts complained of are piratical within the sense and purview of the act. The argument for the claimants seems to suppose, that the act does not intend to punish any aggression, which, if carried into complete execution, would not amount to positive piracy in contemplation of law. That it must be mainly, if not exclusively, done *animo furandi*, or *lucri causa*; and that it must unequivocally demonstrate that the aggression is with a view to plunder, and not for any other purpose, however hostile or atrocious or indispensable such purpose may be. We cannot adopt any such narrow and limited interpretation of the words of the act; and in our judgment it would manifestly defeat the objects and policy of the act, which seems designed to carry into effect the general law of nations on the same subject in a just and appropriate manner. Where the act uses the word "piratical," it does so in a general sense; importing that the aggression is unauthorized by the law of nations, hostile in its character, wanton and criminal in its commission, and utterly without any sanction from any public authority or sovereign power. In short, it means that the act belongs to the class of offences which pirates are in the habit of perpetrating, whether they do it for purposes of plunder, or for purposes of hatred, revenge, or wanton abuse of power. A pirate is deemed, and properly deemed, *hostis humani generis*. But why is he so deemed? Because he commits hostilities upon the subjects and property of any or all nations, without any regard to right or duty, or any pretence of public authority. If he wilfully sinks or destroys an innocent merchant ship, without any other object than to gratify his lawless appetite for mischief, it is just as much a piratical aggression, in the sense of the law of nations, and of the act of Congress, as if he did it solely and exclusively for the sake of plunder, *lucri causa* The law looks to it as an act of hostility, and being committed by a vessel not commissioned and engaged in lawful warfare, it treats it as the act of a pirate, and of one who is emphatically *hostis humani generis*. We think that the aggressions established by the evidence bring the case completely within the prohibitions of the act; and if an intent to plunder were necessary to be established, (as we think it is not,) the acts of aggression and hostility and plunder committed on the

Portuguese vessel are sufficient to establish the fact of an open although petty plunderage.

Besides, the argument interprets the act of Congress as though it contained only the word " depredation," or at least coupled aggression and depredation as concurrent and essential circumstances to bring the case within the penal enactment of the law. But the act has no such limitations or qualifications. It punishes any piratical aggression or piratical search, or piratical restraint, or piratical seizure, as well as a piratical depredation. Either is sufficient. The search or restraint may be piratical although no plunder follows, or is found worth carrying away. What Captain Nunez designed under his false and hollow pretences and excuses it may not be easy to say, with exact confidence or certainty. It may have been to train his crew to acts of wanton and piratical mischief, or to seduce them into piratical enterprises. It may have been from a reckless and wanton abuse of power, to gratify his own lawless passions. It could scarcely have been from mental hallucinations; for there was too much method in his mad projects to leave any doubt that there was cunning and craft and worldly wisdom in his course, and that he meditated more than he chose to explain to his crew. They never suspected or accused him of insanity, although they did of purposes of fraud.

The next question is, whether the innocence of the owners can withdraw the ship from the penalty of confiscation under the act of Congress. Here, again, it may be remarked that the act makes no exception whatsoever, whether the aggression be with or without the co-operation of the owners. The vessel which commits the aggression is treated as the offender, as the guilty instrument or thing to which the forfeiture attaches, without any reference whatsoever to the character or conduct of the owner. The vessel or boat (says the act of Congress) from which such piratical aggression, &c., shall have been first attempted or made shall be condemned. Nor is there any thing new in a provision of this sort. It is not an uncommon course in the admiralty, acting under the law of nations, to treat the vessel in which or by which, or by the master or crew thereof, a wrong or offence has been done as the offender, without any regard whatsoever to the personal misconduct or responsibility of the owner thereof. And this is done from the necessity of the case, as the only adequate means of suppressing the offence or wrong, or insuring an indemnity to the injured party. The doctrine also is familiarly applied to cases of smuggling and other misconduct under our revenue laws; and has been applied to other kindred cases, such as cases arising on embargo and non-intercourse acts. In short, the acts of the master and crew, in cases of this sort, bind the interest of the owner of the ship, whether he be innocent or guilty ; and he impliedly submits to whatever the law denounces as a forfeiture attached to the ship by reason of their unlawful or wanton wrongs. In the case of the United States *v.* The Schooner Little Charles, 1 Brock. Rep. 347, 354, a case arising under the embargo laws, the same argument which has been addressed to us, was upon that occasion addressed to Mr. Chief Justice Marshall. The learned judge, in reply, said : " This is not a proceeding against the owner ; it is a proceeding against the vessel for an offence committed by the vessel ; which is not the less an offence, and does not the less subject her to forfeiture because it was committed without the authority and against the will of the owner. It is true that inanimate matter can commit no offence. But this body is animated and put in action by the crew, who are guided by the master. The vessel acts and speaks by the master. She reports herself by the master. It is therefore not unreasonable that the vessel should be affected by this report." The same doctrine was held by this court in the case of the Palmyra, 12 Wheat. R. 1, 14, where referring to seizures in revenue causes, it was said : " The thing is here primarily considered as the offender, or rather the offence is primarily attached to the thing ; and this whether the offence be *malum prohibitum* or *malum in re.* The same thing applies to proceeding *in rem* or seizures in the Admiralty." The same doctrine has been fully recognised in the High Court of Admiralty in England, as is sufficiently apparent from the Vrow Judith, 1 Rob. R. 150 ; the Adonis, 5 Rob. R. 256 ; the Mars, 6 Rob. R. 87, and indeed in many other cases, where the owner of the ship has been held bound by the acts of the master, whether he was ignorant thereof or not.(a)

The ship is also by the general maritime law held responsible for the torts and misconduct of the master and crew thereof, whether arising from negligence or a wilful disregard of duty ; as for example, in cases of collision and other wrongs done upon the high seas or elsewhere within the admiralty and maritime jurisdiction, upon the general policy of that law, which looks to the instrument itself, used as the means of the mischief, as the best and surest pledge for the compensation and indemnity to the injured party.

(a) See 3 Wheaton's Rep., Appendix, p. 37 to p. 40.

The act of Congress has therefore done nothing more on this point than to affirm and enforce the general principles of the maritime law and of the law of nations.

The remaining question is, whether the cargo is involved in the same fate as the ship. In respect to the forfeiture under the act of 1819, it is plain that the cargo stands upon a very different ground from that of the ship. Nothing is said in relation to the condemnation of the cargo in the fourth section of the act; and in the silence of any expression of the legislature, in the case of provisions confessedly penal, it ought not to be presumed that their intention exceeded their language. We have no right to presume that the policy of the act reached beyond the condemnation of the offending vessel.

The argument, then, which seeks condemnation of the cargo, must rely solely and exclusively for its support upon the sixth and seventh counts, founded upon the law of nations and the general maritime law. So far as the general maritime law applies to torts or injuries committed on the high seas and within the admiralty jurisdiction, the general rule is, not forfeiture of the offending property; but compensation to the full extent of all damages sustained or reasonably allowable, to be enforced by a proceeding therefor in rem or in personam. It is true that the law of nations goes in many cases much farther, and inflicts the penalty of confiscation for very gross and wanton violations of duty. But, then, it limits the penalty to cases of extraordinary turpitude or violence. For petty misconduct, or petty plunderage, or petty neglect of duty, it contents itself with the mitigated rule of compensation in damages. Such was the doctrine recognised by this court in the case of the Marianna Flora, 11 Wheat. R. 1, 40, where an attempt was made to inflict the penalty of confiscation for an asserted (but not proved) piratical or hostile aggression. Upon that occasion, the court said: "The other count" (which was similar to those now under our consideration) "which seeks condemnation on the ground of an asserted hostile aggression, admits of a similar answer. It proceeds upon the principle that, for gross violations of the law of nations on the high seas, the penalty of confiscation may be properly inflicted upon the offending property. Supposing the general rule to be so in ordinary cases of property taken in delicto, it is not, therefore, to be admitted, that every offence, however small, however done under a mistake of rights, or for purposes wholly defensive, is to be visited with such harsh punishments. Whatever may be the case, where a gross, fraudulent, and unprovoked attack is made by one vessel upon another upon the sea, which is attended with grievous loss or injury, such effects are not to be attributed to lighter faults or common negligence. It may be just in such cases to award to the injured party full compensation for his actual loss and damage; but the infliction of any forfeiture beyond this does not seem to be pressed by any considerations derived from public law." And the court afterwards added : "And a piratical aggression by an armed vessel sailing under the regular flag of any nation, may be justly subjected to the penalty of confiscation for such a gross breach of the law of nations. But every hostile attack in a time of peace is not necessarily piratical. It may be by mistake or in necessary self-defence, or to repel a supposed meditated attack by pirates. It may be justifiable, and then no blame attaches to the act ; or it may be without any just excuse, and then it carries responsibility in damages. If it proceed farther, if it be an attack from revenge or malignity, from a gross abuse of power, and a settled purpose of mischief, then it assumes the character of a private unauthorized war, and may be punished by all the penalties which the law of nations can properly administer;" that is, (as the context shows,) confiscation and forfeiture of the offending vessel.

Now, it is impossible to read this language and not to feel that it directly applies to the present case. In the first place, it shows, that the offending vessel may by the law of nations, in the case supposed of an attack from malignity, from a gross abuse of power, and a settled purpose of mischief, be justly subjected to forfeiture. But it is as clear that the language is solely addressed to the offending vessel and was not intended as of course to embrace the cargo, even if it belonged to the same owner, and he did not participate in or authorize the offensive aggression. For the court afterwards, in another part of the case, where the subject of the cargo was directly under consideration said, "But the second count" (founded on the law of nations) " embraces a wider range ; and if it had been proved in its aggravated extent, it does not necessarily follow that the cargo ought to be exempted. That is a question which would require grave deliberation. It is in general true that the act of the master does not bind the innocent owner of the cargo ; but the rule is not of universal application. And where the master is also agent and the owner of the cargo, or both ship and cargo belong to the same person, a distinction may, perhaps, arise in the principle of decision." So that the court studiously avoided giving a conclusive opinion upon this point. Looking to the authorities upon this subject, we shall find that the cargo is not generally deemed to be involved in the same confiscation as the ship, unless the owner thereof co-operates in or authorizes the unlawful act. There are exceptions founded in the policy of nations, and as it were the necessities of enforcing belligerent rights against fraudulent evasions, where a more strict rule is enforced and the cargo follows the fate of the ship. But these exceptions stand upon peculiar grounds, and will be found, upon a close examination, to be consistent with, and distinguishable from, the general principle above suggested. Many of the authorities upon this subject have been cited at the bar, and others will be found copiously collected in a note in the appendix to the 2d vol. of Wheat. Rep. p. 37—40.

The present case seems to us fairly to fall within the general principle of exempting the cargo. The owners are confessedly innocent of all intentional or meditated wrong. They are free from any imputation of guilt, and every suspicion of connivance with the master in his hostile acts and wanton misconduct. Unless, then, there were some stubborn rule, which, upon clear grounds of public policy, requred the penalty of confiscation to extend to the cargo, we should be unwilling to enforce it. We know of no such rule. On the contrary, the act of Congress, pointing out, as it does, in this very case, a limitation of the penalty of confiscation to the vessel alone, satisfies our minds that the public policy of our government in cases of this nature is not intended to embrace the cargo. It is satisfied by attaching the penalty to the offending vessel, as all that public justice and a just regard to private rights require. For these reasons, we are of opinion that the decrees condemning the vessel and restoring the cargo, rendered in both the courts below, ought to be affirmed.

There remains then, only the consideration of the costs, whether the courts below did right in making them exclusively a charge upon the proceeds of the condemned property. Costs in the admiralty are in the sound discretion of the court; and no appellate court should ordinarily interfere with that discretion, unless under peculiar circumstances. Here, no such circumstances occur. The matter of costs is not *per se* the proper subject of an appeal; but it can be taken notice of only incidentally as connected with the principal decree, when the correctness of the latter is directly before the court. In the present case the cargo was acquitted, and there is no ground to impute any fault to it. If it had been owned by a third person, there would have been no reason for mulcting the owner in costs, under circumstances like the present, where it was impracticable to separate the cargo from the vessel by any delivery thereof, unless in a foreign port, and no peculiar cause of suspicion attached thereto. Its belonging to the same owner might justify its being brought in and subjected to judicial examination and inquiry, as a case where there was probable cause for the seizure and detention. But there it stopped. The innocence of the owner has been fully established; the vessel has been subjected to condemnation, and the fund is amply sufficient to indemnify the captors for all their costs and charges. We see no reason why the innocent cargo, under such circumstances, should be loaded with any cumulative burdens.

Upon the whole, we are all of opinion that the decree of the Circuit Court ought to be, and it is affirmed, without costs.

ORDER.

This cause came on to be heard on the transcript of the record from the Circuit Court of the United States for the District of Maryland, and was argued by counsel. On consideration whereof, It is now here ordered, adjudged, and decreed by this court, that the decree of the said Circuit Court in this cause be, and the same is hereby affirmed, without costs.

The Scotia
81 U.S. (14 Wallace) 170 (1872)

APPEAL from the Circuit Court for the Southern District of New York, in a case of collision between the American ship Berkshire and the British steamer Scotia, by which the ship was sunk and totally lost.

On the 9th of January, 1863, a British order in council, authorized by virtue of the Merchant Shipping Amendment Act of July 29th, 1862 (25 and 26 Victoria), made a body of "Regulations for preventing collisions at sea." Among these were "Rules concerning lights," and "Steering and sailing rules."

In the first class were these:

LIGHTS FOR STEAMSHIPS.

ART. 3. Sea-going steamships when under way shall carry—

(*a*) At the foremast head, a bright white light . . . of such a character as to be visible on a dark night, with a clear atmosphere, at a distance of at least five miles.

(*b*) On the starboard side a green light, &c., visible on a dark night, with a clear atmosphere, at a distance of at least two miles.

(*c*) On the port side a red light, &c., visible on a dark night, with a clear atmosphere, at a distance of at least two miles.

(*d*) The said green and red side-lights shall be fitted with inboard screens, projecting at least three feet forward from the light so as to prevent these lights being seen across the bow.

LIGHTS FOR SAILING SHIPS.

ART. 6. Sailing vessels under way . . . shall carry the same lights as steamships under way, *with the exception of the white masthead lights, which they shall never carry.*

In the steering and sailing rules was this one—

SAILING SHIP AND SHIP UNDER STEAM.

If two ships, one of which is a sailing ship and the other a steamship are proceeding in such directions as to involve risk of collision, the steamship shall keep out of the way of the sailing ship.

All these regulations, as originally promulgated by Great Britain, were made applicable to all ships, whatever their nationality, within the limits of British jurisdiction, and to British and French ships whether within British jurisdiction or not. The Merchant Shipping Amendment Act, in virtue of which these regulations were passed, provided also that whenever it should be made to appear to the British government, that the government of any foreign country was willing that these regulations should apply to the ships of such country, when beyond the limits of British jurisdiction, Her Britannic Majesty might, by order in council, direct that such regulations should apply to the ships of such foreign country, whether within British jurisdiction or not.

On the 29th April, 1864,* the Congress of the United States passed *its* " act fixing certain rules and regulations for preventing collisions on the water," and these rules as respects sea-going vessels being, to all intents, identical with those above quoted from the British act, the British government regarded the act of Congress as an expression by our government, that it was willing that the British regulations should apply to our ships when beyond the limits of British jurisdiction. The British government accordingly, by order in council, directed that the regulations should apply to all sea-going vessels of the United States, whether within British jurisdiction or not.

The governments of various other countries soon also manifested their willingness that the British regulations should apply to their ships respectively, when beyond the limits of British jurisdiction; and orders in council accordingly directed that such regulations should apply to the ships of such countries respectively, whether within British jurisdiction or not. The countries referred to were Austria, the Argentine Republic, Belgium, Brazil, Bremen, Chili, Denmark proper, the Republic of the Equator, France, Greece, Hamburg, Hanover, the Hawaiian Islands, Hayti, Italy, Lubeck, Mecklenburg - Schwerin, Morocco, the Netherlands, Norway, Oldenburg, Peru, Portugal, Prussia, the Roman States, Russia, Schleswig, Spain, Sweden, Turkey, Uruguay. These orders in council were published at various dates, from January 13th, 1863, to February 6th, 1866. All countries named except Denmark, Greece, the Hawaiian Islands, Schleswig, and the United States, adopted the regulations in 1863.

With these various statutes and orders in existence, the Scotia, a British steamer of the Cunard line, steering west by north one-half north, was sailing about midnight on the 8th of April, 1867, near mid-ocean, from Liverpool towards New York. Her lookouts were properly set, and her lights rightly stationed, that is to say, a white light was at her mast-

---

* 13 Stat. at Large, 58.

head, a green light on her starboard or right side, and a red
light on her port or left side; all burning brightly.

Sailing at the same hour, equally about mid-ocean, the
Berkshire, a sailing ship belonging to the American marine,
was on her voyage from New Orleans to Havre, and with a
wind free, blowing from about south-southwest, was pursuing
a course southeast by east one-half east, as indicated by the
following diagram.   The courses of the two vessels thus intersected at an angle of exactly one point.

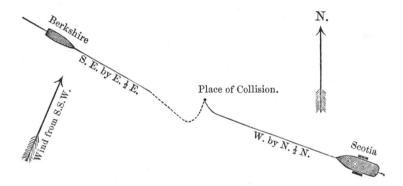

The Berkshire had no colored lights anywhere; nor any
light but a white light, and this was at her bow, fastened to
her anchor-stock, and raised about four feet above her deck.
Of course, if the Scotia should mistake this light for a light
fastened on the *masthead* of the Berkshire, she would infer
from its apparent proximity to the water that the Berkshire
was far off.

The Scotia was first seen from the Berkshire bearing one
point or so off the ship's port bow, at a distance apparently
of five or six miles.   Then the steamer's white masthead
light only was seen.

Immediately on her sighting the steamer, which was at
most from fifteen to twenty minutes before the collision, her
mate gave an order to luff, and she did luff, so as to head
more into the wind.   The effect of this was to make her go
further to the south and thus diverge farther from the course
of the steamer.   She continued in this new direction ten or

fifteen minutes, when, moving at the rate at which it was proved that the vessels were moving, she could not have been more than one or two miles from the Scotia. Her helm was then suddenly put to starboard, then steadied for a brief period, then put hard a-starboard and kept there, thus pointing her directly across the bow of the approaching vessel. By keeping her helm hard a-starboard she was made to change her course constantly. The diagram on the preceding page may perhaps assist the reader's comprehension. The dotted lines represent the Berkshire's movements.

Before she bore away the red light of the steamer was seen by her wheelsman, and probably by her lookout, if not indeed by her master.

The Scotia saw the white light on the Berkshire in due time, and first saw it off her port bow, from one to two points. Seeing a white light, the deck officer of the Scotia took the vessel for a steamer, and from the proximity of the light to the water inferred that she was far off; coming in fact just above the horizon, and accounting for the non-appearance of the usual colored lights because he supposed that they had not come up to view.* He thus not only supposed the Berkshire to be a steamer, but judged that the supposed steamer was at a much greater distance than it was in fact. As already signified, the location of the light warranted the supposition, and its color gave no indication that it was on a sailing vessel. After its discovery the ship's light opened on the steamer's port bow; how much it opened was a matter somewhat agitated by the witnesses and the counsel, though this court considered that matter immaterial, because if it receded at all it indicated that there was then no danger of collision without some change of course, and consequently no necessity to take measures to avoid one. The weight of the evidence was that the ship had not then turned her course northward, but if she had it was still proved that her light opened on the Scotia's port side, after

---

* The "Rules concerning Lights," it will be remembered, see *supra*, pp. 171-2, requires the white light of steamers to be such as shall be visible **five** miles off; while the colored lights need be visible but two miles off.

it was first seen, and before the steamer's course was changed. Soon after, and because of the ship's change of course, her light began to close in on the steamer's bow, and then for the first time was there any apparent danger of collision. Then the Scotia's helm was immediately ported, then hard ported, and observing that the ship's light still closed in, orders were given, in quick succession, to half-speed, slow, reverse, and back, but notwithstanding these orders, which were all promptly obeyed, the vessels came together in the position indicated on the diagram, and the Berkshire with her cargo went right down in mid-ocean.

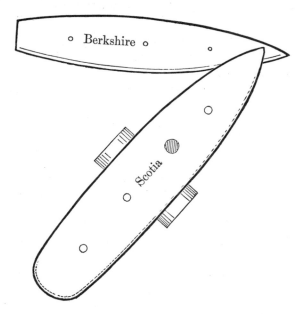

The owners of the Berkshire, one Sears and others, now for themselves and the owners of the cargo, filed their libel in the District Court at New York, to recover the loss sustained by the collision. The libel charged, of course, that the collision occurred through the fault of the Scotia. The District Court decreed for the respondents. The view of that court was, that courts of admiralty were now required to take judicial notice of the existence of the British orders in council, and of the fact that so numerous maritime states had accepted them; that so general an adoption by such states of one rule had made a rule and usage of the sea; that by this rule and usage—in other words, by the law of the sea as it existed at the time of the collision—the Berkshire was bound to exhibit colored lights, and colored lights alone; and that as she had not done so, she had no remedy. The decree, therefore, was, that the libel be dismissed; and the Circuit Court affirming this decree, the case was now here for review.

Mr. Justice STRONG delivered the opinion of the court.

It is plain that had the ship continued on her course after she first saw the steamer's bright light, there could have been no collision. And, still more, had she not afterwards and when near the steamer put her helm to starboard she would have been out of all danger. Even when she first sighted the Scotia she had passed the point at which her course and that of the steamer intersected. This is a necessary sequence from the facts that the angle between the courses of the two vessels was exactly one point, and that the light of the steamer, when first seen, bore from a point to a point and a half off her port bow. Besides, when the ship was first seen from the steamer, her bearing, it is clearly proved, was from a point to two points off the steamer's port bow. Such a bearing was impossible unless the ship had already crossed the line of the Scotia's course, and passed the point at which the vessels could have come together unless one or the other had taken a new direction. They must have passed with a wide berth between had the ship made no change of her helm, or had she kept her luff in obedience to the mate's order. But by putting her helm hard a-starboard she was made to change her course constantly till the collision occurred. Even before she bore away the red light of the steamer was seen by her wheelsman, and probably by her lookout, if not indeed by her master, doubtless in time even then to escape harm. Had it not been then for the unfortunate order of the master to starboard her helm, and bear away before the wind, this case could not have arisen.

It must, however, be conceded that this, of itself, is not sufficient to excuse the Scotia, if she failed to adopt such precautions as were in her power, and were necessary to avoid a collision. Meeting a sailing vessel proceeding in such a direction as to involve risk, it was her duty to keep out of the way, and nothing but inevitable accident, or the conduct and movements of the ship, can repel the presumption that she was negligent, arising from the fact of collision. But this duty of the steamer implies a correlative obligation of the ship to keep her course, and to do nothing to mislead. Nor is a steamer called to act, except when she is approaching a vessel in such a direction as to involve risk of collision. She is required to take no precautions when there is no apparent danger.

Was, then, the Scotia in fault? If she was, the fault must have been either that she did not change her helm sooner, or that she ported, or that she was unjustifiably late in slackening her speed and reversing her engines. No other fault is imputed to her. We have already said that she was not bound to take any steps to avoid a collision until danger of collision should have been apprehended, and we think there was no reason for apprehension until the ship's light was seen closing in upon her. Assuming for the present that she had no right to conclude that the light was on a steamer and to manœuvre accordingly, and, therefore, that it was her duty to keep out of the way, it is still true that all her duty at first was to watch the light in order to discover certainly what it was, and to observe its course and notice whether it crossed her own course. It is not the law that a steamer must change her course, or must slacken her speed the instant she comes in sight of another vessel's light, no matter in what direction it may be. With such a rule navigation cannot be conducted. Nor is such a rule necessary to safety. It is, therefore, no fault that, seeing the ship's light off her port bow, apparently at a distance of several miles, the Scotia continued on her course without slackening her speed, until that light began to close in upon her. Then she ported her helm, the obvious effect of which was to take her farther away from the approaching vessel. Then she slowed her engines, stopped and backed, until, at the time when the collision took place, she had almost, if not entirely, ceased to move through the water. Had she starboarded, instead of porting, the movement would have turned her toward the Berkshire, and apparently would have rendered collision more probable. Of the propriety of her slowing her engines, stopping, and backing, there can be no doubt. If, now, it be considered that she had been misled by the nature and location of the light on the Berkshire, which indicated that the ship was at a much greater distance than she was in fact; that consequently the peril came upon her suddenly, leaving short time for deliberation, and if it be considered that she had been brought into this extremity, first, by the ill-judged and causeless change of the ship's course, and, second, by the persistent effort of the ship's master to cross her bow after he had seen her red light, and discovered certainly that she was a steamer, it would be unjust to impute to her as a fault that she did what she ought to have done, had the approaching vessel been in fact a steamer, and that which at all events seemed most likely to avoid a collision. Certainly it was not her fault that she did not know the Berkshire to be a sailing vessel. And in all human probability the measures taken by her to avoid a collision would have been successful if they had not been counteracted by the constant veering of the Berkshire, with her helm kept hard a-starboard.

Independently, therefore, of any statutory regulations, and looking to the facts with reference to the old maritime law alone, as it was before any modern legislation, we think the Scotia was not chargeable with fault.

But we think the Scotia had a right to conclude that the Berkshire was a steamer rather than a sailing vessel, and that, when first seen, she was at the distance of four or five miles, instead of being near at hand. Such was the information given her by the ship's white light, fastened as it was to the anchor-stock on deck, and no watchfulness could have enabled her to detect the misrepresentation until it was too

late. Both vessels were moving under similar regulations.
The Berkshire was an American ship, belonging to the mercantile marine, and she was required by the act of Congress
of April 29th, 1864, to carry green and red lights, which she
did not carry, and she was forbidden to carry the white
light, which she did carry.   By exhibiting a white light, she,
therefore, held herself forth as a steamer, and by exhibiting
it from her deck, instead of from her masthead, she misrep-
resented her distance from approaching vessels.   It is clear
the Scotia would have been justified in taking her for·a
steamer had she been known to be an American ship.   But
it is insisted on behalf of the appellants that, inasmuch as
the act of Congress is a mere municipal regulation, obligatory as a statute only upon American vessels, the Scotia, a
British steamer, cannot avail herself of it to fault an American ship, or to justify her own conduct.   Waiving for the
moment consideration of the question whether this position
is well taken, it is yet true that the Berkshire was under the
statute, though on the high seas, and that the Scotia was
subject to and sailing under similar regulations (the British
orders in council of January 9th, 1863); that the collision
happened in the known path of vessels navigating between
the United States and Great Britain, and that there was a
reasonable probability that vessels in that path would be
either American or British, and would, therefore, carry the
lights prescribed by the laws of those countries.   The
steamer might well, therefore, in the absence of knowledge,
act upon that probability, and in the emergency into which
she had been brought, might, without fault, apply the rule
of navigation common to the ships of both countries.

But, to return to the question, we think that independently of the act of Congress, considered as a mere municipal regulation, the Berkshire was bound to show a green
light on her starboard, and a red light on her port side,
without exhibiting any white light; and that the Scotia may
set up in defence her failure to carry such green and red
lights, as also the fact that she did improperly show a white
light.   And we think that her breach of duty in these re-

spects misled the officers of the steamer, and caused them
to act on the assumption that she was a steamer, and therefore under obligation to pass on the port side. If so, the
collision was solely due to the fault of the ship. We rest
this conclusion not solely, or mainly, upon the ground that
the navigation laws of the United States control the conduct of foreign vessels, or that they have, as such, any extraterritorial authority, except over American shipping. Doubtless they are municipal regulations, yet binding upon American vessels, either in American waters or on the high seas.
Nor can the British orders in council control our vessels,
though they may their own. We concede also that whether
an act is tortious or not must generally be determined by
the laws of the place where the act was committed. But
every American vessel, outside of the jurisdiction of a foreign
power, is, for some purposes at least, a part of the American
territory, and our laws are the rules for its guidance. Equally
true is it that a British vessel is controlled by British rules
of navigation. If it were that the rules of the two nations
conflicted, which would the British vessel, and which would
the American, be bound to obey? Undoubtedly the rule
prescribed by the government to which it belonged. And
if, in consequence, collision should ensue between an American and a British vessel, shall the latter be condemned in an
American court of admiralty? If so, then our law is given
an extra-territorial effect, and is held obligatory upon British
ships not within our jurisdiction. Or might an American
vessel be faulted in a British court of admiralty for having
done what our statute required? Then Britain is truly not
only mistress of the seas, but of all who traverse the great
waters. It is difficult to see how a ship can be condemned
for doing that which by the laws of its origin, or ownership,
it was required to do, or how, on the other hand, it can
secure an advantage by violation of those laws, unless it is
beyond their domain when upon the high seas. But our
navigation laws were intended to secure the safety of life
and property, as well as the convenience of commerce.
They are not in terms confined to the regulation of shipping
in our own waters. They attempt to govern a business that

is conducted on every sea. If they do not reach the conduct of mariners in its relation to the ships and people of other nations, they are at least designed for the security of the lives and property of our own people. For that purpose they are as useful and as necessary on the ocean as they are upon inland waters. How, then, can our courts ignore them in any case? Why should it ever be held that what is a wrong when done to an American citizen, is right if the injured party be an Englishman?

But we need not affirm that the Berkshire was under obligation to show colored lights, or to refrain from showing a white light, merely because of an act of Congress, nor need we affirm that the Scotia can protect herself by setting up the ship's violation of that act. Nor is it necessary to our conclusions that the British rules in regard to lights are the same as ours, though that is an important consideration. We are not unmindful that the English courts of admiralty have ruled that a foreigner cannot set up against a British vessel, with which his ship has collided, that the British vessel violated the British mercantile marine act, on the high seas, for the reason, as given, that the foreigner was not bound by it, inasmuch as it is beyond the power of Parliament to make rules applicable to foreign vessels outside of British waters. This decision was made in 1856, in the case of *The Zollverein*.* A similar rule was asserted also in *The Dumfries*,† decided the same year; in *The Saxonia*,‡ decided in the High Court of Admiralty in 1858, and by the Privy Council in 1862. The same doctrine was laid down in 1858, in the case of *Cope* v. *Doherty*,§ and in *The Chancellor*,‖ decided in 1861. All these decisions were made before the passage of the Merchant Shipping Amendment Act, which took effect on the 1st day of June, 1863. By that act the same rules in regard to lights and movements of steamers and sailing vessels on the high seas were adopted as those which were prescribed by the act of Congress of

---

* 1 Swabey, 96.   † Ib. 63.   ‡ 1 Lushington, 410.
§ 4 Kay & Johnson, 367; 2 De Gex & Jones, 626.
‖ 4 Law Times, 627.

1864, and by the same act it was provided that the government of any foreign state might assent to the regulations, and consent to their application to the ships of such state, and that thereupon the Queen, by order in council, might direct that such regulations should apply to ships of such foreign state when within or without British jurisdiction. The act further provided that whenever an order in council should be issued applying any regulation made under it to the ships of any foreign country, such ships should in all cases arising in British courts be deemed to be subject to such regulations, and for the purpose thereof be treated as British ships. Historically, we know that before the close of the year 1864, nearly all the commercial nations of the world had adopted the same regulations respecting lights, and that they were recognized as having adopted them. These nations were the following: Austria, the Argentine Republic, Belgium, Brazil, Bremen, Chili, Denmark, Ecuador, France, Great Britain, Greece, Hamburg, Hanover, Hawaii. Hayti, Italy, Lubeck, Mecklenburg-Schwerin, Morocco, Netherlands, Norway, Oldenburg, Peru, Portugal, Prussia, Roman States, Russia, Schleswig, Spain, Sweden, Turkey, United States, and Uruguay—almost every commercial nation in existence.* Had this libel then been filed in a British court, the Berkshire must have been found solely in fault, because her white light and her neglect to exhibit colored lights signalled to the Scotia that she was a steamer, and directed the Scotia to do exactly what she did.

It must be conceded, however, that the rights and merits of a case may be governed by a different law from that which controls a court in which a remedy may be sought. The question still remains, what was the law of the place where the collision occurred, and at the time when it occurred. Conceding that it was not the law of the United States, nor that of Great Britain, nor the concurrent regulations of the two governments, but that it was the law of the sea, was it the ancient maritime law, that which existed before the commercial nations of the world adopted the regulations of 1863 and 1864, or the law changed after those

---

* See Holt's Rule of the Road, page 2.

regulations were adopted? Undoubtedly, no single nation can change the law of the sea. That law is of universal obligation, and no statute of one or two nations can create obligations for the world. Like all the laws of nations, it rests upon the common consent of civilized communities. It is of force, not because it was prescribed by any superior power, but because it has been generally accepted as a rule of conduct. Whatever may have been its origin, whether in the usages of navigation or in the ordinances of maritime states, or in both, it has become the law of the sea only by the concurrent sanction of those nations who may be said to constitute the commercial world. Many of the usages which prevail, and which have the force of law, doubtless originated in the positive prescriptions of some single state, which were at first of limited effect, but which when generally accepted became of universal obligation. The Rhodian law is supposed to have been the earliest system of marine rules. It was a code for Rhodians only, but it soon became of general authority because accepted and assented to as a wise and desirable system by other maritime nations. The same may be said of the Amalphitan table, of the ordinances of the Hanseatic League, and of parts of the marine ordinances of Louis XIV. They all became the law of the sea, not on account of their origin, but by reason of their acceptance as such. And it is evident that unless general assent is efficacious to give sanction to international law, there never can be that growth and development of maritime rules which the constant changes in the instruments and necessities of navigation require. Changes in nautical rules have taken place. How have they been accomplished, if not by the concurrent assent, express or understood, of maritime nations? When, therefore, we find such rules of navigation as are mentioned in the British orders in council of January 9th, 1863, and in our act of Congress of 1864, accepted as obligatory rules by more than thirty of the principal commercial states of the world, including almost all which have any shipping on the Atlantic Ocean, we are constrained to regard them as in part at least, and so far as relates to these vessels, the laws of the sea, and as having been the law at the time when the collision of which the libellants complain took place.

This is not giving to the statutes of any nation extra-territorial effect. It is not treating them as general maritime laws, but it is recognition of the historical fact that by common consent of mankind, these rules have been acquiesced in as of general obligation. Of that fact we think we may take judicial notice. Foreign municipal laws must indeed be proved as facts, but it is not so with the law of nations.

The consequences of this ruling are decisive of the case before us. The violation of maritime law by the Berkshire in carrying a white light (to say nothing of her neglect to carry colored lights), and her carrying it on deck instead of at her masthead, were false representations to the Scotia. They proclaimed that the Berkshire was a steamer, and such she was manifestly taken to be. The movements of the Scotia were therefore entirely proper, and she was without fault.

DECREE AFFIRMED, WITH COSTS.

United States v . ARJONA
120 U .S . 479; 7 Sup . Ct . 628 (1887)

INDICTMENT under the act of May 16, 1884, 23 Stat. 22, to prevent and punish the counterfeiting within the United States of notes, bonds, and other securities of foreign governments. The court below certified a Division in Opinion on several points. The case is stated in the opinion of the court.

MR. CHIEF JUSTICE WAITE delivered the opinion of the court.

This is an indictment containing three counts against Ramon Arjona, for violations of §§ 3 and 6, of the act of May 16, 1884, c. 52, 23 Stat. 22, " to prevent and punish the counterfeiting within the United States of notes, bonds, and other securities of foreign Governments." The first and second counts were found under § 6 of the statute, and the third under § 3.

The statute makes the following things criminal:

1. SEC. 1. Forging or counterfeiting within the United States, with intent to defraud, "any bond, certificate, obligation, or other security of any foreign Government, issued or put forth under the authority of such foreign Government, or any treasury note, bill, or promise to pay issued by such foreign Government, and intended to circulate as money either by law, order, or decree of such foreign Government."

2. SEC. 2. Knowingly, and with intent to defraud, uttering, passing or putting off in payment or negotiation, within the United States, any forged or counterfeit bonds, &c., such as are described in § 1.

3. SEC. 3. Falsely making, forging or counterfeiting within the United States, with intent to defraud, or knowingly assisting therein, "any bank note or bill issued by a bank or other corporation of any foreign country, and intended by the law or usage of such foreign country to circulate as money, such bank or corporation being authorized by the laws of such country."

4. SEC. 4. Knowingly uttering, passing, putting off or tendering in payment, within the United States, with intent to defraud, any such false or counterfeited bank note or bill as is mentioned in § 3, whether forged or counterfeited in the United States or not.

5. SEC. 5. Having in possession any forged or counterfeit instruments mentioned in the preceding sections, with intent to utter, pass, or put them off, or to deliver them to others, with the intent that they may be uttered or passed.

6. SEC. 6. Having in possession "any plate, or any part thereof, from which has been printed or may be printed any counterfeit note, bond, obligation, or other security, in whole or in part, of any foreign Government, bank, or corporation, except by lawful authority;" or using such plate, or knowingly permitting or suffering "the same to be used, in counterfeiting such foreign obligations, or any part thereof;" or engraving, or causing or procuring to be engraved, or assisting "in engraving, any plate in the likeness or similitude of any plate designed for the printing of the genuine issues of the obligations of any foreign Government, bank, or corporation;" or printing, photographing, or in any other manner making,

executing, or selling, or causing "to be printed, photographed, made, executed, or sold," or aiding "in printing, photographing, making, executing, or selling any engraving, photograph, print, or impression in the likeness of any genuine note, bond, obligation, or other security, or any part thereof, of any foreign Government, bank, or corporation;" or bringing "into the United States . . . any counterfeit plate, engraving, photograph, print, or other impressions of the notes, bonds, obligations, or other securities of any foreign Government, bank, or corporation."

The first count of the indictment charges Arjona with having "in his control and custody a certain metallic plate from which there might then and there be printed in part a counterfeit note in the likeness and similitude in part of the notes theretofore issued by a foreign bank, to wit, the bank known as El Banco del Estado de Bolivar, which said bank was then and there a bank authorized by the laws of a foreign state, to wit, the state of Bolivar, said state being then and there one of the states of the United States of Columbia."

In the second count, he is charged with having caused and procured "to be engraved a certain metallic plate in the likeness and similitude of a plate designated for the printing of the genuine issues of the obligations of a foreign bank, that is to say, of the bank notes of the bank known as El Banco del Estado de Bolivar, the same being then and there a bank authorized by the laws of a foreign state, to wit, the state of Bolivar, said state being then and there one of the states of the United States of Columbia."

In the third count, the charge is that he, "unlawfully and with intent to defraud, did cause and procure to be falsely made a certain note in the similitude and resemblance of the notes theretofore issued by a bank of a foreign country, to wit, the bank known as El Banco del Estado de Bolivar, the same being then and there a bank authorized by the laws of one of the states of the United States of Columbia, that is to say, the state of Bolivar, and the notes issued by the said bank being then and by the usage of the said state of Bolivar intended to circulate as money."

To this indictment a demurrer was filed, and the judges holding the court have certified that at the hearing the following questions arose, upon which their opinions were opposed:

1. Whether the third section of the statute is constitutional.

2. Whether the sixth section is constitutional so far as it relates to "foreign banks and corporations."

3. Whether the counterfeiting within the United States of the notes of a foreign bank or corporation can be constitutionally made by Congress an offence against the law of nations.

4. Whether the obligations of the law of nations, as referred to in the Constitution of the United States, include the punishment of counterfeiting the notes of a foreign bank or corporation, or of having in possession a plate from which may be printed counterfeits of the notes of foreign banks or corporations, as mentioned in the third and sixth sections, "unless it appear or is alleged in the indictment that the notes of said foreign bank or corporation are the notes or money of issue of a foreign Government, prince, potentate, state, or power."

5. Whether, if there is power to "so define the law of nations" as to include the offences mentioned in the third and sixth sections, it is not necessary, in order "to define" the offence, that it be declared in the statute itself "to be an offence against the law of nations."

6. Whether the indictment is sufficient in law.

The fourth of the questions thus stated embraces the 4th, 5th, 6th, 7th, and 8th of those certified, and the fifth embraces the 9th and 10th.

Congress has power to make all laws which shall be necessary and proper to carry into execution the powers vested by the Constitution in the Government of the United States, Art. I, sec. 8, clause 18; and the Government of the United States has been vested exclusively with the power of representing the nation in all its intercourse with foreign countries. It alone can "regulate commerce with foreign nations," Art. I, sec. 8, clause 3; make treaties and appoint ambassadors and other public ministers and consuls. Art. II, sec. 2, clause 2. A state is expressly prohibited from entering into any "treaty, alliance, or confederation." Art. I, sec. 10, clause 1. Thus all official intercourse between a state and foreign nations is prevented, and exclusive authority for that purpose given to the United States. The national government is in this way made responsible to foreign nations for all violations by the United States of their international obligations, and because of this, Congress is expressly authorized " to define and punish . . . offences against the law of nations." Art. I, sec. 8, clause 10.

The law of nations requires every national government to use " due diligence " to prevent a wrong being done within its own dominion to another nation with which it is at peace, or to the people thereof; and because of this the obligation of one nation to punish those who within its own jurisdiction counterfeit the money of another nation has long been recognized. Vattel, in his Law of Nations, which was first printed at Neuchâtel in 1758, and was translated into English and published in England in 1760, uses this language: " From the principles thus laid down, it is easy to conclude, that if one nation counterfeits the money of another, or if she allows and protects false coiners who presume to do it, she does that nation an injury." [1] When this was written money was the chief thing of this kind that needed protection, but still it was added: " There is another custom more modern, and of no less use to commerce than the establishment of coin, namely, *exchange*, or the traffic of bankers, by means of which a merchant remits immense sums from one end of the world to the other, at very trifling expense, and, if he pleases, without risk. For the same reason that sovereigns are obliged to protect commerce, they are obliged to support this custom, by good laws, in which every merchant, whether citizen or foreigner, may find security. In general, it is equally the interest ,and duty of every nation to have wise and equitable commercial laws

---

[1] § 108. Des principes que nous venons d'établir, il est aisé de conclure, que si une Nation contrefait la monnaie d'une autre, ou si elle souffre et protége les faux-monnayeurs qui osent l'entreprendre, elle lui fait injure.

established in the country." [2] Vattel, Law of Nations, Phil. ed. 1876, Book I, chap. 10, pages 46, 47. In a note by Mr. Chitty in his London edition of 1834 it is said: "This is a sound principle, which ought to be extended so as to deny effect to any fraud upon a foreign nation or its subjects." Id. 47, note 50.

This rule was established for the protection of nations in their intercourse with each other. If there were no such intercourse, it would be a matter of no special moment to one nation that its money was counterfeited in another. Its own people could not be defrauded if the false coin did not come among them, and its own sovereignty would not be violated if the counterfeit could not under any circumstances be made to take the place of the true money. But national intercourse includes commercial intercourse between the people of different nations. It is as much the duty of a nation to protect such an intercourse as it is any other, and that is what Vattel meant when he said: "For the same reason that sovereigns are obliged to protect commerce, they are obliged to support this custom;" "namely, *exchange*, or the traffic of bankers, by means of which a merchant remits immense sums from one end of the world to the other," "by good laws, in which every merchant, whether citizen or foreigner, may find security."

In the time of Vattel certificates of the public debt of a nation, government bonds, and other government securities, were rarely seen in any other country than that in which they were put out. Banks of issue were not so common as to need special protection for themselves or the public against forgers and counterfeiters elsewhere than at home, and the great

---

[2] Il est un autre usage plus moderne, et non moins utile au commerce que l'établissement de la monnaie: c'est le *change*, ou le négoce des banquiers, par le moyen duquel un marchand remet d'un bout du monde à l'autre des sommes immenses, presque sans frais, et, s'il le veut, sans péril. Par la même raison que les souverains doivent protéger le commerce, ils sont obligés de soutenir cet usage par de bonnes lois, dans lesquelles tout marchand, étranger ou citoyen, puisse trouver sa sûreté. En général, il est également de l'intérêt et du devoir de toute Nation, d'établir chez elle de sages et justes lois de commerce.

corporations, now so numerous and so important, established by public authority for the promotion of public enterprises, were almost unknown, and certainly they had not got to be extensive borrowers of money wherever it could be had at home or abroad on the faith of their *quasi* public securities. Now, however, the amount of national and corporate debt and of corporate property represented by bonds, certificates, notes, bills, and other forms of commercial securities, which are bought and sold in all the money markets of the world, both in and out of the country under whose authority they were created, is something enormous.

Such being the case, it is easy to see that the same principles that developed, when it became necessary, the rule of national conduct which was intended to prevent, as far as might be, the counterfeiting of the money of one nation within the dominion of another, and which, in the opinion of so eminent a publicist as Vattel, could be applied to the foreign exchange of bankers, may, with just propriety, be extended to the protection of this more recent custom among bankers of dealing in foreign securities, whether national or corporate, which have been put out under the sanction of public authority at home, and sent abroad as the subjects of trade and commerce. And especially is this so of bank notes and bank bills issued under the authority of law, which, from their very nature, enter into and form part of the circulating medium of exchange — the money — of a country. Under such circumstances, every nation has not only the right to require the protection, as far as possible, of its own credit abroad against fraud, but the banks and other great commercial corporations, which have been created within its own jurisdiction for the advancement of the public good, may call on it to see that their interests are not neglected by a foreign government to whose dominion they have, in the lawful prosecution of their business, become to some extent subjected.

No nation can be more interested in this question than the United States. Their money is practically composed of treasury notes or certificates issued by themselves, or of bank bills issued by banks created under their authority and subject to their control. Their own securities, and those of the states, the cities, and the public corporations, whose interests abroad they alone have the power to guard against foreign national neglect, are found on sale in the principal money markets of Europe. If these securities, whether national, municipal, or corporate, are forged and counterfeited with impunity at the places where they are sold, it is easy to see that a great wrong will be done to the United States and their people. Any uncertainty about the genuineness of the security necessarily depreciates its value as a merchantable commodity, and against this international comity requires that national protection shall, as far as possible, be afforded. If there is neglect in that, the United States may, with propriety, call on the proper government to provide for the punishment of such an offence, and thus secure the restraining influences of a fear of the consequences of wrong doing. A refusal may not, perhaps, furnish sufficient cause for war, but it would certainly give just ground of complaint, and thus disturb that harmony between the governments which each is bound to cultivate and promote.

But if the United States can require this of another, that other may require it of them, because international obligations are of necessity reciprocal in their nature. The right, if it exists at all, is given by the law of nations, and what is law for one is, under the same circumstances, law for the other. A right secured by the law of nations to a nation, or its people, is one the United States as the representatives of this nation are bound to protect. Consequently, a law which is necessary and proper to afford this protection is one that Congress may enact, because it is one that is needed to carry into execution a power conferred by the Constitution on the Government of the United States exclusively. There is no authority in the United States to require the passage and enforcement of such a law by the states. Therefore the United States must have the power to pass it and enforce it themselves, or be unable to perform a duty which they may owe to another nation, and which the law of nations has imposed on them as part of their international obligations. This, however, does not prevent a state from providing for the punishment of the same thing; for here, as in the case of counterfeiting the coin of the United States, the act may be an offence against the authority of a state as well as that of the United States.

Again, our own people may be dealers at home in the public or *quasi* public securities of a foreign government, or of foreign banks or corporations, brought here in the course of our commerce with foreign nations, or sent here from abroad for sale in the money markets of this country. As such they enter into and form part of the foreign commerce of the country. If such securities can be counterfeited here with impunity, our own people may be made to suffer by a wrong done which affects a business that has been expressly placed by the Constitution under the protection of the government of the United States.

It remains only to consider those questions which present the point whether, in enacting a statute to define and punish an offence against the law of nations, it is necessary, in order "to define" the offence, that it be declared in the statute itself to be "an offence against the law of nations." This statute defines the offence, and if the thing made punishable is one which the United States are required by their international obligations to use due diligence to prevent, it is an offence against the law of nations. Such being the case, there is no more need of declaring in the statute that it is such an offence than there would be in any other criminal statute to declare that it was enacted to carry into execution any other particular power vested by the Constitution in the Government of the United States. Whether the offence as defined is an offence against the law of nations depends on the thing done, not on any declaration to that effect by Congress. As has already been seen, it was incumbent on the United States as a nation to use due diligence to prevent any injury to another nation or its people by counterfeiting its money, or its public or *quasi* public securities. This statute was enacted as a means to that end, that is to say, as a means of performing a duty which had been cast on the United States by the law of nations, and it was clearly appropriate legislation for that purpose. Upon its face, therefore, it defines an offence against the law of nations as clearly as if Congress had in express terms so declared.

Criminal statutes passed for enforcing and preserving the neutral relations of the United States with other nations were passed by Congress at a very early date; June 5, 1794, c. 50, 1 Stat. 381; June 14, 1797, c. 1, 1 Stat. 520; March 3, 1817, c. 58, 3 Stat. 370; April 20, 1818, c. 88, 3 Stat. 447: and those now in force are found in Title LXVII of the Revised Statutes. These all rest on the same power of Congress that is here invoked, and it has never been supposed they were invalid because they did not expressly declare that the offences there defined were offences against the law of nations.

If there is anything more in the eleventh question certified than has been already disposed of in answering the others, it is too broad and indefinite for our consideration under the rules which have been long established regulating the practice on a certificate of division.

All the questions certified, except the eleventh, are answered in the affirmative, and as to that, no special answer will be made.

The Chinese Exclusion Case
130 U.S. 581; 9 S. Ct. 623 (1889)

For opinion see <span navigation>infra I (2) (a)

The Paquete Habana
175 U.S. 677; Sup. Ct. 290 (1900)

MR. JUSTICE GRAY delivered the opinion of the court.

These are two appeals from decrees of the District Court of the United States for the Southern District of Florida, condemning two fishing vessels and their cargoes as prize of war.

Each vessel was a fishing smack, running in and out of Havana, and regularly engaged in fishing on the coast of Cuba; sailed under the Spanish flag; was owned by a Spanish subject of Cuban birth, living in the city of Havana; was commanded by a subject of Spain, also residing in Havana; and her master and crew had no interest in the vessel, but were entitled to shares, amounting in all to two thirds, of her catch, the other third belonging to her owner. Her cargo consisted of fresh fish, caught by her crew from the sea, put on board as they were caught, and kept and sold alive. Until stopped by the blockading squadron, she had no knowledge of the existence of the war, or of any blockade. She had no arms or ammunition on board, and made no attempt to run the blockade after she knew of its existence, nor any resistance at the time of the capture.

The Paquete Habana was a sloop, 43 feet long on the keel, and of 25 tons burden, and had a crew of three Cubans, including the master, who had a fishing license from the Spanish Government, and no other commission or license. She left Havana March 25, 1898; sailed along the coast of Cuba to Cape San Antonio at the western end of the island, and there fished for twenty-five days, lying between the reefs off the cape, within the territorial waters of Spain; and then started back for Havana, with a cargo of about 40 quintals of live fish. On April 25, 1898, about two miles off Mariel, and eleven miles from Havana, she was captured by the United States gunboat Castine.

The Lola was a schooner, 51 feet long on the keel, and of 35 tons burden, and had a crew of six Cubans, including the master, and no commission or license. She left Havana April 11, 1898, and proceeded to Campeachy Sound off Yucatan, fished there eight days, and started back for Havana with a cargo of about 10,000 pounds of live fish. On April 26, 1898, near Havana, she was stopped by the United States steamship Cincinnati, and was warned not to go into Havana, but was told that she would be allowed to land at Bahia Honda. She then changed her course, and put for Bahia Honda, but on the next morning, when near that port, was captured by the United States steamship Dolphin.

Both the fishing vessels were brought by their captors into Key West. A libel for the condemnation of each vessel and

her cargo as prize of war was there filed on April 27, 1898;
a claim was interposed by her master, on behalf of himself
and the other members of the crew, and of her owner; evidence was taken, showing the facts above stated; and on
May 30, 1898, a final decree of condemnation and sale was
entered, "the court not being satisfied that as a matter of
law, without any ordinance, treaty or proclamation, fishing
vessels of this class are exempt from seizure."

Each vessel was thereupon sold by auction; the Paquete
Habana for the sum of $490; and the Lola for the sum of
$800.   There was no other evidence in the record of the
value of either vessel or of her cargo.

We are then brought to the consideration of the question
whether, upon the facts appearing in these records, the fishing smacks were subject to capture by the armed vessels of
the United States during the recent war with Spain.

By an ancient usage among civilized nations, beginning
centuries ago, and gradually ripening into a rule of international law, coast fishing vessels, pursuing their vocation of
catching and bringing in fresh fish, have been recognized as
exempt, with their cargoes and crews, from capture as prize
of war.

This doctrine, however, has been earnestly contested at the
bar; and no complete collection of the instances illustrating
it is to be found, so far as we are aware, in a single published
work, although many are referred to and discussed by the
writers on international law, notably in 2 Ortolan, Règles
Internationales et Diplomatie de la Mer, (4th ed.) lib. 3, c. 2,
pp. 51–56; in 4 Calvo, Droit International, (5th ed.) §§ 2367–
2373; in De Boeck, Propriété Privée Ennemie sous Pavillon
Ennemi, §§ 191–196; and in Hall, International Law, (4th.
ed.) § 148.   It is therefore worth the while to trace the history of the rule, from the earliest accessible sources, through
the increasing recognition of it, with occasional setbacks, to
what we may now justly consider as its final establishment in
our own country and generally throughout the civilized world.

The earliest acts of any government on the subject, mentioned in the books, either emanated from, or were approved by, a King of England.

In 1403 and 1406, Henry IV issued orders to his admirals and other officers, entitled " Concerning Safety for Fishermen — *De Securitate pro Piscatoribus*." By an order of October 26, 1403, reciting that it was made pursuant to a treaty between himself and the King of France; and for the greater safety of the fishermen of either country, and so that they could be, and carry on their industry, the more safely on the sea, and deal with each other in peace; and that the French King had consented that English fishermen should be treated likewise; it was ordained that French fishermen might, during the then pending season for the herring fishery, safely fish for herrings and all other fish, from the harbor of Gravelines and the island of Thanet to the mouth of the Seine and the harbor of Hautoune. And by an order of October 5, 1406, he took into his safe conduct, and under his special protection, guardianship and defence, all and singular the fishermen of France, Flanders and Brittany, with their fishing vessels and boats, everywhere on the sea, through and within his dominions, jurisdictions and territories, in regard to their fishery, while sailing, coming and going, and, at their pleasure, freely and lawfully fishing, delaying or proceeding, and returning homeward with their catch of fish, without any molestation or hindrance whatever; and also their fish, nets, and other property and goods soever; and it was therefore ordered that such fishermen should not be interfered with, provided they should comport themselves well and properly, and should not, by color of these presents, do or attempt, or presume to do or attempt, anything that could prejudice the King, or his kingdom of England, or his subjects.   8 Rymer's Foedera, 336, 451.

The treaty made October 2, 1521, between the Emperor Charles V and Francis I of France, through their ambassadors, recited that a great and fierce war had arisen between them, because of which there had been, both by land and by sea, frequent depredations and incursions on either side, to the grave detriment and intolerable injury of the innocent subjects of each; and that a suitable time for the herring fishery was at hand, and, by reason of the sea being beset by the enemy, the fishermen did not dare to go out, whereby the subject of their industry, bestowed by heaven to allay the hunger of the poor, would wholly fail for the year, unless it were otherwise provided — *quo fit, ut piscaturæ commoditas, ad pauperum levandam famem a cœlesti numine concessa, cessare hoc anno omnino debeat, nisi aliter provideatur.* And it was therefore agreed that the subjects of each sovereign, fishing in the sea, or exercising the calling of fishermen, could and might, until the end of the next January, without incurring any attack, depredation, molestation, trouble or hindrance soever, safely and freely, everywhere in the sea, take herrings and every other kind of fish, the existing war by land and sea notwithstanding; and further that, during the time aforesaid, no subject of either sovereign should commit, or attempt or presume to commit, any depredation, force, violence, molestation or vexation, to or upon such fishermen, or their vessels, supplies, equipments, nets and fish, or other goods soever truly appertaining to fishing. The treaty was made at Calais, then an English possession. It recites that the ambassadors of the two sovereigns met there at the earnest request of Henry VIII, and with his countenance, and in the presence of Cardinal Wolsey, his chancellor and representative. And towards the end of the treaty it is agreed that the said King and his said representative, " by whose means the treaty stands concluded, shall be conservators of the agreements therein, as if thereto by both parties elected and chosen." 4 Dumont, Corps Diplomatique, pt. 1, pp. 352, 353.

The herring fishery was permitted, in time of war, by French and Dutch edicts in 1536. Bynkershoek, Quæstiones Juris Publicæ, lib. 1, c. 3 ; 1 Emerigon des Assurances, c. 4, sect. 9 ; c. 12, sect. 19, § 8.

France, from remote times, set the example of alleviating the evils of war in favor of all coast fishermen. In the compilation entitled Us et Coutumes de la Mer, published by Cleirac in 1661, and in the third part thereof, containing " Maritime or Admiralty Jurisdiction — *la Jurisdiction de la*

Marine ou d'Admirauté — as well in time of peace as in time of war," article 80 is as follows : "The admiral may in time of war accord fishing truces — *tresves pescheresses* — to the enemy and to his subjects ; provided that the enemy will likewise accord them to Frenchmen." Cleirac, 544. Under this article, reference is made to articles 49 and 79 respectively of the French ordinances concerning the Admiralty in 1543 and 1584, of which it is but a reproduction. 4 Pardessus, Collection de Lois Maritimes, 319 ; 2 Ortolan, 51. And Cleirac adds, in a note, this quotation from Froissart's Chronicles : " Fishermen on the sea, whatever war there were in France and England, never did harm to one another ; so they are friends, and help one another at need — *Pescheurs sur mer, quelque guerre qui soit en France et Angleterre, jamais ne se firent mal l'un à l'autre ; ainçois sont amis, et s'aydent l'un à l'autre au besoin.*"

The same custom would seem to have prevailed in France until towards the end of the seventeenth century. For example, in 1675, Louis XIV and the States General of Holland, by mutual agreement, granted to Dutch and French fishermen the liberty, undisturbed by their vessels of war, of fishing along the coasts of France, Holland and England. D'Hauterive et De Cussy, Traités de Commerce, pt. 1, vol. 2, p. 278. But by the ordinances of 1681 and 1692 the practice was discontinued, because, Valin says, of the faithless conduct of the enemies of France, who, abusing the good faith with which she had always observed the treaties, habitually carried off her fishermen, while their own fished in safety. 2 Valin sur l'Ordonnance de la Marine, (1776) 689, 690 ; 2 Ortolan, 52 ; De Boeck, § 192.

The doctrine which exempts coast fishermen with their vessels and cargoes from capture as prize of war has been familiar to the United States from the time of the War of Independence.

On June 5, 1779, Louis XVI, our ally in that war, addressed a letter to his admiral, informing him that the wish he had always had of alleviating, as far as he could, the hardships of war, had directed his attention to that class of his subjects which devoted itself to the trade of fishing, and had no other means of livelihood; that he had thought that the example which he should give to his enemies, and which could have no other source than the sentiments of humanity which inspired him, would determine them to allow to fishermen the same facilities which he should consent to grant; and that he had therefore given orders to the commanders of all his ships not to disturb English fishermen, nor to arrest their vessels laden with fresh fish, even if not caught by those vessels; provided they had no offensive arms, and were not proved to have made any signals creating a suspicion of intelligence with the enemy; and the admiral was directed to communicate the King's intentions to all officers under his control. By a royal order in council of November 6, 1780, the former orders were confirmed; and the capture and ransom, by a French cruiser, of *The John and Sarah*, an English vessel, coming from Holland, laden with fresh fish, were pronounced to be illegal. 2 Code des Prises, (ed. 1784) 721, 901, 903.

Among the standing orders made by Sir James Marriott, Judge of the English High Court of Admiralty, was one of April 11, 1780, by which it was "ordered, that all causes of prize of fishing boats or vessels taken from the enemy may be consolidated in one monition, and one sentence or interlocutory, if under fifty tons burden, and not more than six in number." Marriott's Formulary, 4. But by the statements of his successor, and of both French and English writers, it appears that England, as well as France, during the American Revolutionary War, abstained from interfering with the coast fisheries. *The Young Jacob and Johanna*, 1 C. Rob. 20; 2 Ortolan, 53; Hall, § 148.

In the treaty of 1785 between the United States and Prussia, article 23, (which was proposed by the American Commissioners, John Adams, Benjamin Franklin and Thomas Jefferson, and is said to have been drawn up by Franklin,) provided that, if war should arise between the contracting parties, "all women and children, scholars of every faculty, cultivators of the earth, artisans, manufacturers and fishermen, unarmed and inhabiting unfortified towns, villages or places, and in general all others whose occupations are for the common subsistence and benefit of mankind, shall be allowed to continue their respective employments, and shall not be molested in their persons; nor shall their houses or goods be burnt or otherwise destroyed, nor their fields wasted, by the armed force of the enemy, into whose power, by the events of war, they may happen to fall; but if anything is necessary to be taken from them for the use of such armed force, the same shall be paid for at a reasonable price." 8 Stat. 96; 1 Kent Com. 91 note; Wheaton's History of the Law of Nations, 306, 308. Here was the clearest exemption from hostile molestation or seizure of the persons, occupations, houses and goods of unarmed fishermen inhabiting unfortified places. The article was repeated in the later treaties between the United States and Prussia of 1799 and 1828. 8 Stat. 174, 384. And Dana, in a note to his edition of Wheaton's International Law, says: "In many treaties and decrees, fishermen catching fish as an article of food are added to the class of persons whose occupation is not to be disturbed in war." Wheaton's International Law, (8th ed.) § 345, note 168.

Since the United States became a nation, the only serious interruptions, so far as we are informed, of the general recognition of the exemption of coast fishing vessels from hostile capture, arose out of the mutual suspicions and recriminations of England and France during the wars of the French Revolution.

In the first years of those wars, England having authorized the capture of French fishermen, a decree of the French National Convention of October 2, 1793, directed the executive power "to protest against this conduct, theretofore without example; to reclaim the fishing boats seized; and, in case of refusal, to resort to reprisals." But in July, 1796, the Committee of Public Safety ordered the release of English fishermen seized under the former decree, "not considering them as prisoners of war." *La Nostra Segnora de la Piedad*, (1801) cited below; 2 De Cussy, Droit Maritime, 164, 165; 1 Massé, Droit Commercial, (2d ed.) 266, 267.

On January 24, 1798, the English Government, by express order, instructed the commanders of its ships to seize French and Dutch fishermen with their boats. 6 Martens, Recueil des Traités, (2d ed.) 505 ; 6 Schoell, Histoire des Traités, 119 ; 2 Ortolan, 53. After the promulgation of that order, Lord Stowell (then Sir William Scott) in the High Court of Admiralty of England condemned small Dutch fishing vessels as prize of war. In one case, the capture was in April, 1798, and the decree was made November 13, 1798. *The Young Jacob and Johanna*, 1 C. Rob. 20. In another case, the decree was made August 23, 1799. *The Noydt Gedacht*, 2 C. Rob. 137, note.

For the year 1800, the orders of the English and French governments and the correspondence between them may be found in books already referred to. 6 Martens, 503 – 512; 6 Schoell, 118 – 120 ; 2 Ortolan, 53, 54. The doings for that year may be summed up as follows : On March 27, 1800, the French government, unwilling to resort to reprisals, reënacted the orders given by Louis XVI in 1780, above mentioned, prohibiting any seizure by the French ships of English fishermen, unless armed, or proved to have made signals to the enemy. On May 30, 1800, the English government, having received notice of that action of the French government, revoked its order of January 24, 1798. But, soon afterwards, the English government complained that French fishing boats had been made into fireboats at Flushing, as well as that the French government had impressed, and had sent to Brest, to serve in its flotilla, French fishermen and their boats, even those whom the English had released on condition of their not serving; and on January 21, 1801, summarily revoked its last order, and again put in force its order of January 24, 1798. On February 16, 1801, Napoleon Bonaparte, then First Consul, directed the French commissioner at London to return at once to France, first declaring to the English government that its conduct, "contrary to all the usages of civilized nations, and to the common law which governs them, even in time of war, gave to the existing war a character of rage and bitterness which destroyed even the relations usual in a loyal war," and

" tended only to exasperate the two nations, and to put off the term of peace;" and that the French government, having always made it "a maxim to alleviate as much as possible the evils of war, could not think, on its part, of rendering wretched fishermen victims of a prolongation of hostilities, and would abstain from all reprisals."

On March 16, 1801, the Addington Ministry, having come into power in England, revoked the orders of its predecessors against the French fishermen; maintaining, however, that " the freedom of fishing was nowise founded upon an agree- ment, but upon a simple concession;" that "this concession would be always subordinate to the convenience of the moment," and that "it was never extended to the great fishery, or to commerce in oysters or in fish." And the free- dom of the coast fisheries was again allowed on both sides. 6 Martens, 514; 6 Schoell, 121; 2 Ortolan, 54; Manning, Law of Nations, (Amos ed.) 206.

Lord Stowell's judgment in *The Young Jacob and Johanna*, 1 C. Rob. 20, above cited, was much relied on by the counsel for the United States, and deserves careful consideration.

The vessel there condemned is described in the report as " a small Dutch fishing vessel taken April, 1798, on her return from the Dogger bank to Holland;" and Lord Stowell, in delivering judgment, said: "In former wars, it has not been usual to make captures of these small fishing vessels; but this rule was a rule of comity only, and not of legal decision; it has prevailed from views of mutual accommodation between neighboring countries, and from tenderness to a poor and industrious order of people. In the present war there has, I presume, been sufficient reason for changing this mode of treatment, and, as they are brought before me for my judg- ment, they must be referred to the general principles of this court; they fall under the character and description of the last class of cases; that is, of ships constantly and exclusively employed in the enemy's trade." And he added: "It is a farther satisfaction to me in giving this judgment to observe that the facts also bear strong marks of a false and fraudulent transaction."

Both the capture and condemnation were within a year after the order of the English government of January 24, 1798, instructing the commanders of its ships to seize French and Dutch fishing vessels, and before any revocation of that order. Lord Stowell's judgment shows that his decision was based upon the order of 1798, as well as upon strong evidence of fraud. Nothing more was adjudged in the case.

But some expressions in his opinion have been given so much weight by English writers, that it may be well to examine them particularly. The opinion begins by admitting the known custom in former wars not to capture such vessels — adding, however, "but this was a rule of comity only, and not of legal decision." Assuming the phrase "legal decision" to have been there used, in the sense in which courts are accustomed to use it, as equivalent to "judicial decision," it is true that, so far as appears, there had been no such decision on the point in England. The word "comity" was apparently used by Lord Stowell as synonymous with courtesy or good will. But the period of a hundred years which has since elapsed is amply sufficient to have enabled what originally may have rested in custom or comity, courtesy or concession, to grow, by the general assent of civilized nations, into a settled rule of international law. As well said by Sir James Mackintosh: "In the present century a slow and silent, but very substantial mitigation has taken place in the practice of war; and in proportion as that mitigated practice has received the sanction of time, it is raised from the rank of mere usage, and becomes part of the law of nations." Discourse on the Law of Nations, 38; 1 Miscellaneous Works, 360.

The French prize tribunals, both before and after Lord Stowell's decision, took a wholly different view of the general question. In 1780, as already mentioned, an order in council of Louis XVI had declared illegal the capture by a French cruiser of *The John and Sarah*, an English vessel, coming from Holland, laden with fresh fish. And on May 17, 1801, where a Portuguese fishing vessel, with her cargo of fish, having no more crew than was needed for her management, and for serving the nets, on a trip of several days, had been captured in April, 1801, by a French cruiser, three leagues off the coast of Portugal, the Council of Prizes held that the capture was contrary to "the principles of humanity, and the maxims of international law," and decreed that the vessel, with the fish on board, or the net proceeds of any that had been sold, should be restored to her master. *La Nostra Segnora de la Piedad*, 25 Merlin, Jurisprudence, Prise Maritime, § 3, art. 1, 3; *S. C.* 1 Pistoye et Duverdy, Prises Maritimes, 331; 2 De Cussy, Droit Maritime, 166.

The English government, soon afterwards, more than once unqualifiedly prohibited the molestation of fishing vessels employed in catching and bringing to market fresh fish. On May 23, 1806, it was "ordered in council, that all fishing vessels under Prussian and other colors, and engaged for the purpose of catching fish and conveying them fresh to market, with their crews, cargoes and stores, shall not be molested on their fishing voyages and bringing the same to market; and that no fishing vessels of this description shall hereafter be molested. And the Right Honorable the Lords Commissioners of His Majesty's Treasury, the Lords Commissioners of the Admiralty and the Judge of the High Court of Admiralty are to give the necessary directions herein as to them may respectively appertain." 5 C. Rob. 408. Again, in the order in council of May 2, 1810, which directed that "all vessels which shall have cleared out from any port so far under the control of France or her allies as that British vessels may not freely trade thereat, and which are employed in the whale fishery, or other fishery of any description, save as hereinafter excepted, and are returning or destined to return either to the port from whence they cleared, or to any other port or place at which the British flag may not freely trade, shall be captured, and condemned together with their stores and cargoes, as prize to the captors," there were excepted "vessels employed in catching and conveying fish fresh to market, such vessels not being fitted or provided for the curing of fish." Edw. Adm. appx. L.

Wheaton, in his Digest of the Law of Maritime Captures and Prizes, published in 1815, wrote: "It has been usual in maritime wars to exempt from capture fishing boats and their cargoes, both from views of mutual accommodation between neighboring countries, and from tenderness to a poor and industrious order of people. This custom, so honorable to the humanity of civilized nations, has fallen into disuse; and it is remarkable that both France and England mutually reproach each other with that breach of good faith which has finally abolished it." Wheaton on Captures, c. 2, § 18.

This statement clearly exhibits Wheaton's opinion that the custom had been a general one, as well as that it ought to remain so. His assumption that it had been abolished by the differences between France and England at the close of the last century was hardly justified by the state of things when he wrote, and has not since been borne out.

During the wars of the French Empire, as both French and English writers agree, the coast fisheries were left in peace. 2 Ortolan, 54; De Boeck, § 193; Hall, § 148. De Boeck quaintly and truly adds, "and the incidents of 1800 and of 1801 had no morrow — *n'eurent pas de lendemain.*"

In the war with Mexico in 1846, the United States recognized the exemption of coast fishing boats from capture. In proof of this, counsel have referred to records of the Navy Department, which this court is clearly authorized to consult upon such a question. *Jones* v. *United States*, 137 U. S. 202; *Underhill* v. *Hernandez*, 168 U. S. 250, 253.

By those records it appears that Commodore Conner, commanding the Home Squadron blockading the east coast of Mexico, on May 14, 1846, wrote a letter from the ship Cumberland, off Brazos Santiago, near the southern point of Texas, to Mr. Bancroft, the Secretary of the Navy, enclosing a copy of the commodore's "instructions to the commanders of the vessels of the Home Squadron, showing the principles to be observed in the blockade of the Mexican ports," one of which was that "Mexican boats engaged in fishing on any part of the coast will be allowed to pursue their labors unmolested;" and that on June 10, 1846, those instructions were approved by the Navy Department, of which Mr. Bancroft was still the head, and continued to be until he was appointed Minister to

England in September following. Although Commodore Conner's instructions and the Department's approval thereof do not appear in any contemporary publication of the Government, they evidently became generally known at the time, or soon after; for it is stated in several treatises on international law (beginning with Ortolan's second edition, published in 1853) that the United States in the Mexican War permitted the coast fishermen of the enemy to continue the free exercise of their industry. 2 Ortolan, (2d ed.) 49 note; (4th ed.) 55; 4 Calvo, (5th ed.) § 2372; De Boeck, § 194; Hall, (4th ed.) § 148.

As qualifying the effect of those statements, the counsel for the United States relied on a proclamation of Commodore Stockton, commanding the Pacific Squadron, dated August 20, 1846, directing officers under his command to proceed immediately to blockade the ports of Mazatlan and San Blas on the west coast of Mexico, and saying to them, " All neutral vessels that you may find there you will allow twenty days to depart; and you will make the blockade absolute against all vessels, except armed vessels of neutral nations. You will capture all vessels under the Mexican flag that you may be able to take." Navy Report of 1846, pp. 673, 674. But there is nothing to show that Commodore Stockton intended, or that the Government approved, the capture of coast fishing vessels.

On the contrary, General Halleck, in the preface to his work on International Law or Rules Regulating the Intercourse of States in Peace and War, published in 1861, says that he began that work, during the war between the United States and Mexico, " while serving on the staff of the commander of the Pacific Squadron " and " often required to give opinions on questions of international law growing out of the operations of the war." Had the practice of the blockading squadron on the west coast of Mexico during that war, in regard to fishing vessels, differed from that approved by the Navy Department on the east coast, General Halleck could hardly have failed to mention it, when stating the prevailing doctrine upon the subject as follows :

"Fishing boats have also, as a general rule, been exempted from the effects of hostilities. As early as 1521, while war was raging between Charles V and Francis, ambassadors from these two sovereigns met at Calais, then English, and agreed that, whereas the herring fishery was about to commence, the subjects of both belligerents, engaged in this pursuit, should be safe and unmolested by the other party, and should have leave to fish as in time of peace. In the war of 1800, the British and French governments issued formal instructions exempting the fishing boats of each other's subjects from seizure. This order was subsequently rescinded by the British government, on the alleged ground that some French fishing boats were equipped as gunboats, and that some French fishermen, who had been prisoners in England, had violated their parole not to serve, and had gone to join the French fleet at Brest. Such excuses were evidently mere pretexts, and, after some angry discussions had taken place on the subject, the British restriction was withdrawn, and the freedom of fishing was again allowed on both sides. French writers consider this exemption as an established principle of the modern law of war, and it has been so recognized in the French courts, which have restored such vessels when captured by French cruisers." Halleck, (1st ed.) c. 20, § 23.

That edition was the only one sent out under the author's own auspices, except an abridgment, entitled Elements of International Law and the Law of War, which he published in 1866, as he said in the preface, to supply a suitable text-book for instruction upon the subject, "not only in our colleges, but also in our two great national schools — the Military and Naval Academies." In that abridgment, the statement as to fishing boats was condensed, as follows: "Fishing boats have also, as a general rule, been exempted from the effects of hostilities. French writers consider this exemption as an established principle of the modern law of war, and it has been so recognized in the French courts, which have restored such vessels when captured by French cruisers." Halleck's Elements, c. 20, § 21.

In the treaty of peace between the United States and Mexico in 1848 were inserted the very words of the earlier treaties with Prussia, already quoted, forbidding the hostile molestation or seizure in time of war of the persons, occupations, houses or goods of fishermen. 9 Stat. 939, 940.

Wharton's Digest of the International Law of the United States, published by authority of Congress in 1886 and 1887, embodies General Halleck's fuller statement, above quoted, and contains nothing else upon the subject. 3 Whart. Int. Law Dig. § 345, p. 315; 2 Halleck, (Eng. eds. 1873 and 1878) p. 151.

France, in the Crimean War in 1854, and in her wars with Austria in 1859 and with Germany in 1870, by general orders, forbade her cruisers to trouble the coast fisheries, or to seize any vessel or boat engaged therein, unless naval or military operations should make it necessary. Calvo, § 2372; Hall, § 148; 2 Ortolan, (4th ed.) 449; 10 Revue de Droit International, (1878) 399.

Calvo says that in the Crimean War, "notwithstanding her alliance with France and Italy, England did not follow the same line of conduct, and her cruisers in the Sea of Azof destroyed the fisheries, nets, fishing implements, provisions, boats, and even the cabins, of the inhabitants of the coast." Calvo, § 2372. And a Russian writer on Prize Law remarks that those depredations, "having brought ruin on poor fishermen and inoffensive traders, could not but leave a painful impression on the minds of the population, without impairing in the least the resources of the Russian government." Katchenovsky, (Pratt's ed.) 148. But the contemporaneous reports of the English naval officers put a different face on the matter, by stating that the destruction in question was part of a military measure, conducted with the coöperation of the French ships, and pursuant to instructions of the English admiral "to clear the seaboard of all fish stores, all fisheries and mills, on a scale beyond the wants of the neighboring population, and indeed of all things destined to contribute to the maintenance of the enemy's army in the Crimea;" and that the property destroyed consisted of large fishing establishments and storehouses of the Russian government, numbers of heavy launches, and enormous quantities of nets and gear, salted fish, corn and other provisions, intended for the supply of the Russian army.   United Service Journal of 1855, pt. 3, pp. 108–112.

Since the English orders in council of 1806 and 1810, before quoted, in favor of fishing vessels employed in catching and bringing to market fresh fish, no instance has been found in which the exemption from capture of private coast fishing vessels, honestly pursuing their peaceful industry, has been denied by England, or by any other nation.   And the Empire of Japan, (the last State admitted into the rank of civilized nations,) by an ordinance promulgated at the beginning of its war with China in August, 1894, established prize courts, and ordained that " the following enemy's vessels are exempt from detention " — including in the exemption " boats engaged in coast fisheries," as well as " ships engaged exclusively on a voyage of scientific discovery, philanthropy or religious mission."   Takahashi, International Law, 11, 178.

International law is part of our law, and must be ascertained and administered by the courts of justice of appropriate jurisdiction, as often as questions of right depending upon it are duly presented for their determination.   For this purpose, where there is no treaty, and no controlling executive or legislative act or judicial decision, resort must be had to the customs and usages of civilized nations; and, as evidence of these, to the works of jurists and commentators, who by years of labor, research and experience, have made themselves peculiarly well acquainted with the subjects of which they treat. Such works are resorted to by judicial tribunals, not for the speculations of their authors concerning what the law ought to be, but for trustworthy evidence of what the law really is. *Hilton* v. *Guyot*, 159 U. S. 113, 163, 164, 214, 215.

Wheaton places, among the principal sources of international law, " Text-writers of authority, showing what is the approved usage of nations, or the general opinion respecting their mutual conduct, with the definitions and modifications introduced by general consent."   As to these he forcibly observes: " Without wishing to exaggerate the importance of these writers, or to substitute, in any case, their authority for the principles of reason, it may be affirmed that they are generally impartial in their judgment. They are witnesses of the sentiments and usages of civilized nations, and the weight of their testimony increases every time that their authority is invoked by statesmen, and every year that passes without the rules laid down in their works being impugned by the avowal of contrary principles." Wheaton's International Law, (8th ed.) § 15.

Chancellor Kent says: " In the absence of higher and more authoritative sanctions, the ordinances of foreign States, the opinions of eminent statesmen, and the writings of distinguished jurists, are regarded as of great consideration on questions not settled by conventional law. In cases where the principal jurists agree, the presumption will be very great in favor of the solidity of their maxims ; and no civilized nation, that does not arrogantly set all ordinary law and justice at defiance, will venture to disregard the uniform sense of the established writers on international law." 1 Kent Com. 18.

It will be convenient, in the first place, to refer to some leading French treatises on international law, which deal with the question now before us, not as one of the law of France only, but as one determined by the general consent of civilized nations.

" Enemy ships," say Pistoye and Duverdy, in their Treatise on Maritime Prizes, published in 1855, "are good prize. Not all, however ; for it results from the unanimous accord of the maritime powers that an exception should be made in favor of coast fishermen. Such fishermen are respected by the enemy, so long as they devote themselves exclusively to fishing." 1 Pistoye et Duverdy, tit. 6, c. 1, p. 314.

De Cussy, in his work on the Phases and Leading Cases of the Maritime Law of Nations — *Phases et Causes Célèbres du Droit Maritime des Nations* — published in 1856, affirms in the clearest language the exemption from capture of fishing boats, saying, in lib. 1, tit. 3, § 36, that " in time of war the freedom of fishing is respected by belligerents ; fishing boats are considered as neutral ; in law, as in principle, they are not subject either to capture or to confiscation ; " and that in lib. 2, c. 20, he will state " several facts and several decisions which prove that the perfect freedom and neutrality of fishing boats are not illusory." 1 De Cussy, p. 291. And in the chapter referred to, entitled *De la Liberté et de la Neutralité Parfaite de la Pêche*, besides references to the edicts and decisions in France during the French Revolution, is this general statement: "If one consulted only positive international law" — *le droit des gens positif* — (by which is evidently meant international law expressed in treaties, decrees or other public acts, as distinguished from what may be implied from custom or usage,) "fishing boats would be subject, like all other trading vessels, to the law of prize; a sort of tacit agreement among all European nations frees them from it, and several official declarations have confirmed this privilege in favor of 'a class of men whose hard and ill rewarded labor, commonly performed by feeble and aged hands, is so foreign to the operations of war.'" 2 De Cussy, 164, 165.

Ortolan, in the fourth edition of his *Règles Internationales et Diplomatie de la Mer*, published in 1864, after stating the general rule that the vessels and cargoes of subjects of the enemy are lawful prize, says: "Nevertheless, custom admits an exception in favor of boats engaged in the coast fishery; these boats, as well as their crews, are free from capture and exempt from all hostilities. The coast fishing industry is, in truth, wholly pacific, and of much less importance, in regard to the national wealth that it may produce, than maritime commerce or the great fisheries. Peaceful and wholly inoffensive, those who carry it on, among whom women are often seen, may be called the harvesters of the territorial seas, since they confine themselves to gathering in the products thereof; they are for the most part poor families who seek in this calling hardly more than the means of gaining their livelihood." 2 Ortolan, 51. Again, after observing that there are very few solemn public treaties which make mention of the immunity of fishing boats in time of war, he says: "From another point of view, the custom which sanctions this immunity is not so general that it can be considered as making an absolute international rule; but it has been so often put in practice, and, besides, it accords so well with the rule in use, in wars on land, in regard to peasants and husbandmen, to whom coast fishermen may be likened, that it will doubtless continue to be followed in maritime wars to come." 2 Ortolan, 55.

No international jurist of the present day has a wider or more deserved reputation than Calvo, who, though writing in French, is a citizen of the Argentine Republic, employed in its diplomatic service abroad. In the fifth edition of his great work on international law, published in 1896, he observes, in § 2366, that the international authority of decisions in particular cases by the prize courts of France, of England, and of the United States, is lessened by the fact that the principles on which they are based are largely derived from the internal legislation of each country ; and yet the peculiar character of maritime wars, with other considerations, gives to prize jurisprudence a force and importance reaching beyond the limits of the country in which it has prevailed. He therefore proposes here to group together a number of particular cases proper to serve as precedents for the solution of grave questions of maritime law in regard to the capture of private property as prize of war. Immediately, in § 2367, he goes on to say : "Notwithstanding the hardships to which maritime wars subject private property, notwithstanding the extent of the recognized rights of belligerents, there are generally exempted, from seizure and capture, fishing vessels." In the next section he adds : "This exception is perfectly justiciable — *Cette exception est parfaitement justiciable*" — that is to say, belonging to judicial jurisdiction or cognizance. Littré, Dict. *voc.* Justiciable ; *Hans* v. *Louisiana*, 134 U. S. 1, 15. Calvo then quotes Ortolan's description, above cited, of the nature of the coast fishing industry ; and proceeds to refer, in detail, to some of the French precedents, to the acts of the French and English governments in the times of Louis XVI and of the French Revolution, to the position of the United States in the war with Mexico, and of France in later wars, and to the action of British cruisers in the Crimean War. And he concludes his discussion of the subject, in § 2373, by affirming the exemption of the coast fishery, and pointing out the distinction in this regard between the coast fishery and what he calls the great fishery, for cod, whales or seals, as follows: "The privilege of exemption from capture, which is generally acquired by fishing vessels plying their industry near the coasts, is not extended in any country to ships employed on the high sea in what is called the great fishery, such as that for the cod, for the whale or the sperm whale, or for the seal or sea calf. These ships are, in effect, considered as devoted to operations which are at once commercial and industrial — *Ces navires sont en effet considérés comme adonnés à des opérations à la fois commerciales et industrielles.*" The distinction is generally recognized. 2 Ortolan, 54; De Boeck, § 196; Hall, § 148. See also *The Susa*, 2 C. Rob. 251; *The Johan*, Edw. Adm. 275, and appx. L.

The modern German books on international law, cited by the counsel for the appellants, treat the custom, by which the vessels and implements of coast fishermen are exempt from seizure and capture, as well established by the practice of nations. Heffter, § 137; 2 Kaltenborn, § 237, p. 480; Bluntschli, § 667; Perels, § 37, p. 217.

De Boeck, in his work on Enemy Private Property under Enemy Flag — *de la Propriété Privée Ennemie sous Pavillon Ennemi* — published in 1882, and the only continental treatise cited by the counsel for the United States, says in § 191: "A usage very ancient, if not universal, withdraws from the right of capture enemy vessels engaged in the coast fishery. The reason of this exception is evident; it would have been too hard to snatch from poor fishermen the means of earning their bread." "The exemption includes the boats, the fishing implements and the cargo of fish." Again, in § 195: "It is to be observed that very few treaties sanction in due form this immunity of the coast fishery." "There is, then, only a custom. But what is its character? Is it so fixed and general that it can be raised to the rank of a positive and formal rule of international law?" After discussing the statements of other writers, he approves the opinion of Ortolan (as expressed in the last sentence above quoted from his work) and says that, at bottom, it differs by a shade only from that formulated by Calvo and by some of the German jurists, and that "it is more exact, without ignoring the imperative character of the humane rule in question — *elle est plus exacte, sans méconnaître le caractère impératif de la règle d'humanité dont il s'agit.*" And, in § 196, he defines the limits of the rule as follows: "But the immunity of the coast fishery must be limited by the reasons that justify it. The reasons of humanity and of harmlessness — *les raisons d'humanité et d'innocuité* — which militate in its favor do not exist in the great fishery, such as the cod fishery; ships engaged in that fishery devote themselves to truly commercial operations, which employ a large number of seamen. And these same reasons cease to be applicable to fishing vessels employed for a warlike purpose, to those which conceal arms, or which exchange signals of intelligence with ships of war; but only those taken in the fact can be rigorously treated; to allow seizure by way of prevention would open the door to every abuse, and would be equivalent to a suppression of the immunity."

Two recent English text-writers, cited at the bar, (influenced by what Lord Stowell said a century since,) hesitate to recognize that the exemption of coast fishing vessels from capture has now become a settled rule of international law. Yet they both admit that there is little real difference in the views, or in the practice, of England and of other maritime nations; and that no civilized nation at the present day would molest coast fishing vessels, so long as they were peaceably pursuing their calling, and there was no danger that they or their crews might be of military use to the enemy. Hall, in § 148 of the fourth edition of his Treatise on International Law, after briefly sketching the history of the positions occupied by France and England at different periods, and by the United States in the Mexican War, goes on to say: "In the foregoing facts there is nothing to show that much real difference has existed in the practice of the maritime countries. England does not seem to have been unwilling to spare fishing vessels so long as they are harmless, and it does not appear that any State has accorded them immunity under circumstances of inconvenience to itself. It is likely that all nations would now refrain from molesting them as a general rule, and would capture them so soon as any danger arose that they or their crews might be of military use to the enemy; and it is also likely that it is impossible to grant them a more distinct exemption." So T. J. Lawrence, in § 206 of his Principles of International Law, says: "The difference between the English and the French view is more apparent than real; for no civilized belligerent would now capture the boats of fishermen plying their avocation peaceably in the territorial waters of their own State; and no jurist would seriously argue that their immunity must be respected if they were used for warlike purposes, as were the smacks belonging to the northern ports of France when Great Britain gave the order to capture them in 1800."

But there are writers of various maritime countries, not yet cited, too important to be passed by without notice.

Jan Helenus Ferguson, Netherlands Minister to China, and previously in the naval and in the colonial service of his country, in his Manual of International Law for the Use of Navies, Colonies and Consulates, published in 1882, writes: "An exception to the usage of capturing enemy's private vessels at sea is the coast fishery." "This principle of immunity from capture of fishing boats is generally adopted by all maritime powers, and in actual warfare they are universally spared so long as they remain harmless." 2 Ferguson, § 212.

Ferdinand Attlmayr, Captain in the Austrian Navy, in his Manual for Naval Officers, published at Vienna in 1872 under the auspices of Admiral Tegetthoff, says: "Regarding the capture of enemy property, an exception must be mentioned, which is a universal custom. Fishing vessels which belong to the adjacent coast, and whose business yields only a necessary livelihood, are, from considerations of humanity, universally excluded from capture." 1 Attlmayr, 61.

Ignacio de Negrin, First Official of the Spanish Board of Admiralty, in his Elementary Treatise on Maritime International Law, adopted by royal order as a text-book in the Naval Schools of Spain, and published at Madrid in 1873, concludes his chapter "Of the lawfulness of prizes" with these words: "It remains to be added that the custom of all civilized peoples excludes from capture, and from all kind of hostility, the fishing vessels of the enemy's coasts, considering this industry as absolutely inoffensive, and deserving, from its hardships and usefulness, of this favorable exception. It has been thus expressed in very many international conventions, so that it can be deemed an incontestable principle of law, at least among enlightened nations." Negrin, tit. 3, c. 1, § 310.

Carlos Testa, Captain in the Portuguese Navy and Professor in the Naval School at Lisbon, in his work on Public International Law, published in French at Paris in 1886, when discussing the general right of capturing enemy ships, says : " Nevertheless, in this, customary law establishes an exception of immunity in favor of coast fishing vessels. Fishing is so peaceful an industry, and is generally carried on by so poor and so hardworking a class of men, that it is likened, in the territorial waters of the enemy's country, to the class of husbandmen who gather the fruits of the earth for their livelihood. The examples and practice generally followed establish this humane and beneficent exception as an international rule, and this rule may be considered as adopted by customary law and by all civilized nations." Testa, pt. 3, c. 2, in 18 Bibliothèque International et Diplomatique, pp. 152, 153.

No less clearly and decisively speaks the distinguished Italian jurist, Pasquale Fiore, in the enlarged edition of his exhaustive work on Public International Law, published at Paris in 1885–6, saying : " The vessels of fishermen have been generally declared exempt from confiscation, because of the eminently peaceful object of their humble industry, and of the principles of equity and humanity. The exemption includes the vessel, the implements of fishing, and the cargo resulting from the fishery. This usage, eminently humane, goes back to very ancient times ; and although the immunity of fishery along the coasts may not have been sanctioned by treaties, yet it is considered to-day as so definitely established, that the inviolability of vessels devoted to that fishery is proclaimed by the publicists as a positive rule of international law, and is generally respected by the nations. Consequently, we shall lay down the following rule : (a) Vessels belonging to citizens of the enemy State, and devoted to fishing along the coasts, cannot be subject to capture. (*b*) Such vessels, however, will lose all right of exemption, when employed for a warlike purpose. (*c*) There may, nevertheless, be subjected to capture vessels devoted to the great fishery in the ocean, such as those employed in the whale fishery, or in that for seals or sea calves." 3 Fiore, § 1421.

This review of the precedents and authorities on the subject appears to us abundantly to demonstrate that at the present day, by the general consent of the civilized nations of the world, and independently of any express treaty or other public act, it is an established rule of international law, founded on considerations of humanity to a poor and industrious order of men, and of the mutual convenience of belligerent States, that coast fishing vessels, with their implements and supplies, cargoes and crews, unarmed, and honestly pursuing their peaceful calling of catching and bringing in fresh fish, are exempt from capture as prize of war.

The exemption, of course, does not apply to coast fishermen or their vessels, if employed for a warlike purpose, or in such a way as to give aid or information to the enemy; nor when military or naval operations create a necessity to which all private interests must give way.

Nor has the exemption been extended to ships or vessels employed on the high sea in taking whales or seals, or cod or other fish which are not brought fresh to market, but are salted or otherwise cured and made a regular article of commerce.

This rule of international law is one which prize courts, administering the law of nations, are bound to take judicial notice of, and to give effect to, in the absence of any treaty or other public act of their own government in relation to the matter.

Calvo, in a passage already quoted, distinctly affirms that the exemption of coast fishing vessels from capture is perfectly justiciable, or, in other words, of judicial jurisdiction or cognizance. Calvo, § 2368. Nor are judicial precedents wanting in support of the view that this exemption, or a somewhat analogous one, should be recognized and declared by a prize court.

By the practice of all civilized nations, vessels employed only for the purposes of discovery or science are considered as exempt from the contingencies of war, and therefore not subject to capture. It has been usual for the government sending out such an expedition to give notice to other powers; but it is not essential. 1 Kent Com. 91, note; Halleck, c. 20, § 22; Calvo, § 2376; Hall, § 138.

In 1813, while the United States were at war with England, an American vessel, on her voyage from Italy to the United States, was captured by an English ship, and brought into Halifax in Nova Scotia, and, with her cargo, condemned as lawful prize by the Court of Vice Admiralty there. But a petition for the restitution of a case of paintings and engravings, which had been presented to and were owned by the Academy of Arts in Philadelphia, was granted by Dr. Croke, the judge of that court, who said: " The same law of nations, which prescribes that all property belonging to the enemy shall be liable to confiscation, has likewise its modifications and relaxations of that rule. The arts and sciences are admitted, amongst all civilized nations, as forming an exception to the severe rights of warfare, and as entitled to favor and protection. They are considered not as the peculium of this or of that nation, but as the property of mankind at large, and as belonging to the common interests of the whole species." And he added that there had been " innumerable cases of the mutual exercise of this courtesy between nations in former wars." *The Marquis de Somerueles*, Stewart Adm. (Nova Scotia) 445, 482.

In 1861, during the War of the Rebellion, a similar decision was made, in the District Court of the United States for the Eastern District of Pennsylvania, in regard to two cases of books belonging and consigned to a university in North Carolina. Judge Cadwalader, in ordering these books to be liberated from the custody of the marshal, and restored to the agent of the university, said: " Though this claimant, as the resident of a hostile district, would not be entitled to restitution of the subject of a commercial adventure in books, the purpose of the shipment in question gives to it a different character. The United States, in prosecuting hostilities for the restoration of their constitutional authority, are compelled incidentally to confiscate property captured at sea, of which the proceeds would otherwise increase the wealth of that district. But the United States are not at war with literature in that part of their territory." He then referred to the decision in Nova Scotia, and to the French decisions upon cases of fishing vessels, as precedents for the decree which he was about to pronounce; and he added that, without any such precedents, he should have had no difficulty in liberating these books. *The Amelia*, 4 Philadelphia, 417.

In *Brown* v. *United States*, 8 Cranch, 110, there are expressions of Chief Justice Marshall which, taken by themselves, might seem inconsistent with the position above maintained of the duty of a prize court to take judicial notice of a rule of international law, established by the general usage of civilized nations, as to the kind of property subject to capture. But the actual decision in that case, and the leading reasons on which it was based, appear to us rather to confirm our position. The principal question there was whether personal property of a British subject, found on land in the United States at the beginning of the last war with Great Britain, could lawfully be condemned as enemy's property, on a libel filed by the attorney of the United States, without a positive act of Congress. The conclusion of the court was "that the power of confiscating enemy property is in the legislature, and that the legislature has not yet declared its will to confiscate property which was within our territory at the declaration of war." 8 Cranch, 129. In showing that the declaration of war did not, of itself, vest the executive with authority to order such property to be confiscated, the Chief Justice relied on the modern usages of nations, saying: "The universal practice of forbearing to seize and confiscate debts and credits, the principle universally received that the right to them revives on the restoration of peace, would seem to prove that war is not an absolute confiscation of this property, but simply confers the right of confiscation;" and again: "The modern rule then would seem to be that tangible property belonging to an enemy, and found in the country at the commencement of war, ought not to be immediately confiscated; and in almost every commercial treaty an article is inserted stipulating for the right to withdraw such property." 8 Cranch, 123, 125. The decision that enemy property on land, which by the modern usage of nations is not subject to capture as prize of war, cannot be condemned by a prize court, even by direction of the executive, without express authority from Congress, appears to us to repel any inference that coast fishing vessels, which are exempt by the general consent of civilized nations from capture, and which no act of Congress or order of the President has expressly authorized to be taken and confiscated, must be condemned by a prize court, for want of a distinct exemption in a treaty or other public act of the Government.

To this subject, in more than one aspect, are singularly applicable the words uttered by Mr. Justice Strong, speaking for this court: "Undoubtedly, no single nation can change the law of the sea. That law is of universal obligation, and no statute of one or two nations can create obligations for the world. Like all the laws of nations, it rests upon the common consent of civilized communities. It is of force, not because it was prescribed by any superior power, but because it has been generally accepted as a rule of conduct. Whatever may have been its origin, whether in the usages of navigation, or in the ordinances of maritime States, or in both, it has become the law of the sea only by the concurrent sanction of those nations who may be said to constitute the commercial world. Many of the usages which prevail, and which have the force of law, doubtless originated in the positive prescriptions of some single State, which were at first of limited effect, but which, when generally accepted, became of universal obligation." "This is not giving to the statutes of any nation extra-territorial effect. It is not treating them as general maritime laws; but it is recognition of the historical fact that by common consent of mankind these rules have been acquiesced in as of general obligation. Of that fact, we think, we may take judicial notice. Foreign municipal laws must indeed be proved as facts, but it is not so with the law of nations." *The Scotia*, 14 Wall. 170, 187, 188.

The position taken by the United States during the recent war with Spain was quite in accord with the rule of international law, now generally recognized by civilized nations, in regard to coast fishing vessels.

On April 21, 1898, the Secretary of the Navy gave instructions to Admiral Sampson, commanding the North Atlantic Squadron, to "immediately institute a blockade of the north coast of Cuba, extending from Cardenas on the east to Bahia Honda on the west." Bureau of Navigation Report of 1898, appx. 175. The blockade was immediately instituted accordingly. On April 22, the President issued a proclamation, declaring that the United States had instituted and would maintain that blockade, "in pursuance of the laws of the United States, and the law of nations applicable to such cases." 30 Stat. 1769. And by the act of Congress of April 25, 1898, c. 189, it was declared that the war between the United States and Spain existed on that day, and had existed since and including April 21. 30 Stat. 364.

On April 26, 1898, the President issued another proclamation, which, after reciting the existence of the war, as declared by Congress, contained this further recital: "It being desirable that such war should be conducted upon principles in harmony with the present views of nations and sanctioned by their recent practice." This recital was followed by specific declarations of certain rules for the conduct of the war by sea, making no mention of fishing vessels. 30 Stat. 1770. But the proclamation clearly manifests the general policy of the Government to conduct the war in accordance with the principles of international law sanctioned by the recent practice of nations.

On April 28, 1898, (after the capture of the two fishing vessels now in question,) Admiral Sampson telegraphed to the Secretary of the Navy as follows: "I find that a large number of fishing schooners are attempting to get into Havana from their fishing grounds near the Florida reefs and coasts. They are generally manned by excellent seamen, belonging to the maritime inscription of Spain, who have already served in the Spanish navy, and who are liable to further service. As these trained men are naval reserves, have a semi-military character, and would be most valuable to the Spaniards as artillerymen, either afloat or ashore, I recommend that they should be detained prisoners of war, and that I should be authorized to deliver them to the commanding officer of the army at Key West." To that communication the Secretary of the Navy, on April 30, 1898, guardedly answered: "Spanish fishing vessels attempting to violate blockade are subject, with crew, to capture, and any such vessel or crew considered likely to aid enemy may be detained." Bureau of Navigation Report of 1898, appx. 178. The Admiral's despatch assumed that he was not authorized, without express order, to arrest coast fishermen peaceably pursuing their calling; and the necessary implication and evident intent of the response of the Navy Department were that Spanish coast fishing vessels and their crews should not be interfered with, so long as they neither attempted to violate the blockade, nor were considered likely to aid the enemy.

The Paquete Habana, as the record shows, was a fishing sloop of 25 tons burden, sailing under the Spanish flag, running in and out of Havana, and regularly engaged in fishing on the coast of Cuba. Her crew consisted of but three men, including the master; and, according to a common usage in coast fisheries, had no interest in the vessel, but were entitled to two thirds of her catch, the other third belonging to her Spanish owner, who, as well as the crew, resided in Havana. On her last voyage, she sailed from Havana along the coast of Cuba, about two hundred miles, and fished for twenty-five days off the cape at the west end of the island, within the territorial waters of Spain; and was going back to Havana, with her cargo of live fish, when she was captured by one of the blockading squadron, on April 25, 1898. She had no arms or ammunition on board; she had no knowledge of the blockade, or even of the war, until she was stopped by a blockading vessel; she made no attempt to run the blockade, and no resistance at the time of the capture; nor was there any evidence whatever of likelihood that she or her crew would aid the enemy.

In the case of the Lola, the only differences in the facts were that she was a schooner of 35 tons burden, and had a crew of six men, including the master; that after leaving Havana, and proceeding some two hundred miles along the coast of Cuba, she went on, about a hundred miles farther, to the coast of Yucatan, and there fished for eight days; and that, on her return, when near Bahia Honda, on the coast of Cuba, she was captured, with her cargo of live fish, on April 27, 1898. These differences afford no ground for distinguishing the two cases.

Each vessel was of a moderate size, such as is not unusual in coast fishing smacks, and was regularly engaged in fishing on the coast of Cuba. The crew of each were few in number, had no interest in the vessel, and received, in return for their toil and enterprise, two thirds of her catch, the other third going to her owner by way of compensation for her use. Each vessel went out from Havana to her fishing ground, and was captured when returning along the coast of Cuba. The cargo of each consisted of fresh fish, caught by her crew from the sea, and kept alive on board. Although one of the vessels extended her fishing trip across the Yucatan Channel and fished on the coast of Yucatan, we cannot doubt that each was engaged in the coast fishery, and not in a commercial adventure, within the rule of international law.

The two vessels and their cargoes were condemned by the District Court as prize of war; the vessels were sold under its decrees; and it does not appear what became of the fresh fish of which their cargoes consisted.

Upon the facts proved in either case, it is the duty of this court, sitting as the highest prize court of the United States, and administering the law of nations, to declare and adjudge that the capture was unlawful, and without probable cause; and it is therefore, in each case,

Ordered, that the decree of the District Court be reversed, and the proceeds of the sale of the vessel, together with the proceeds of any sale of her cargo, be restored to the claimant, with damages and costs.

Mr. Chief Justice Fuller, with whom concurred Mr. Justice Harlan and Mr. Justice McKenna, dissenting.

The District Court held these vessels and their cargoes liable because not "satisfied that as a matter of law, without any ordinance, treaty or proclamation, fishing vessels of this class are exempt from seizure."

This court holds otherwise, not because such exemption is to be found in any treaty, legislation, proclamation or instruction, granting it, but on the ground that the vessels were exempt by reason of an established rule of international law applicable to them, which it is the duty of the court to enforce.

I am unable to conclude that there is any such established international rule, or that this court can properly revise action which must be treated as having been taken in the ordinary exercise of discretion in the conduct of war.

It cannot be maintained "that modern usage constitutes a rule which acts directly upon the thing itself by its own force, and not through the sovereign power." That position was disallowed in *Brown* v. *The United States*, 8 Cranch, 110, 128, and Chief Justice Marshall said : "This usage is a guide which the sovereign follows or abandons at his will. The rule, like other precepts of morality, of humanity and even of wisdom, is addressed to the judgment of the sovereign ; and although it cannot be disregarded by him without obloquy, yet it may be disregarded. The rule is, in its nature, flexible. It is subject to infinite modification. It is not an immutable rule of law, but depends on political considerations which may continually vary."

The question in that case related to the confiscation of the property of the enemy on land within our own territory, and it was held that property so situated could not be confiscated without an act of Congress. The Chief Justice continued : "Commercial nations, in the situation of the United States, have always a considerable quantity of property in the possession of their neighbors. When war breaks out, the question, what shall be done with enemy property in our country, is a question rather of policy than of law. The rule which we apply to the property of our enemy, will be applied by him to the property of our citizens. Like all other questions of policy, it is proper for the consideration of a department which can modify it at will; not for the consideration of a department which can pursue only the law as it is written. It is proper for the consideration of the legislature, not of the executive or judiciary."

This case involves the capture of enemy's property on the sea, and executive action, and if the position that the alleged rule *proprio vigore* limits the sovereign power in war be rejected, then I understand the contention to be that, by reason of the existence of the rule, the proclamation of April 26 must be read as if it contained the exemption in terms, or the exemption must be allowed because the capture of fishing vessels of this class was not specifically authorized.

The preamble to the proclamation stated, it is true, that it was desirable that the war "should be conducted upon principles in harmony with the present views of nations and sanctioned by their recent practice," but the reference was to the intention of the Government "not to resort to privateering, but to adhere to the rules of the Declaration of Paris;" and the proclamation spoke for itself. The language of the preamble did not carry the exemption in terms, and the real question is whether it must be allowed because not affirmatively withheld, or, in other words, because such captures were not in terms directed.

These records show that the Spanish sloop Paquete Habana "was captured as a prize of war by the U. S. S. Castine" on April 25, and "was delivered" by the Castine's commander "to Rear Admiral Wm. T. Sampson, (commanding the North Atlantic Squadron,)" and thereupon "turned over" to a prize master with instructions to proceed to Key West.

And that the Spanish schooner Lola "was captured as a prize of war by the U. S. S. Dolphin," April 27, and "was delivered" by the Dolphin's commander "to Rear Admiral Wm. T. Sampson, (commanding the North Atlantic Squadron,)" and thereupon "turned over" to a prize master with instructions to proceed to Key West.

That the vessels were accordingly taken to Key West and there libelled, and that the decrees of condemnation were entered against them May 30.

It is impossible to concede that the Admiral ratified these captures in disregard of established international law and the proclamation, or that the President, if he had been of opinion that there was any infraction of law or proclamation, would not have intervened prior to condemnation.

The correspondence of April 28, 30, between the Admiral and the Secretary of the Navy, quoted from in the principal opinion, was entirely consistent with the validity of the captures.

The question put by the Admiral related to the detention as prisoners of war of the persons manning the fishing schooners " attempting to get into Havana." Non-combatants are not so detained except for special reasons. Sailors on board enemy's trading vessels are made prisoners because of their fitness for immediate use on ships of war. Therefore the Admiral pointed out the value of these fishing seamen to the enemy, and advised their detention. The Secretary replied that if the vessels referred to were " attempting to violate blockade " they were subject " with crew " to capture, and also that they might be detained if " considered likely to aid enemy." The point was whether these crews should be made prisoners of war. Of course they would be liable to be if involved in the guilt of blockade running, and the Secretary agreed that they might be on the other ground in the Admiral's discretion.

All this was in accordance with the rules and usages of international law, with which, whether in peace or war, the naval service has always been necessarily familiar.

I come then to examine the proposition " that at the present day, by the general consent of the civilized nations of the world, and independently of any express treaty or other public act, it is an established rule of international law, founded on considerations of humanity to a poor and industrious order of men, and of the mutual convenience of belligerent States, that coast fishing vessels, with their implements and supplies, cargoes and crews, unarmed, and honestly pursuing their peaceful calling of catching and bringing in of fresh fish, are exempt from capture as prize of war."

This, it is said, is a rule "which prize courts, administering the law of nations, are bound to take judicial notice of, and to give effect to, in the absence of treaty or other public act of their own government."

At the same time it is admitted that the alleged exemption does not apply "to coast fishermen or their vessels, if employed for a warlike purpose, or in such a way as to give aid or information to the enemy; nor when military or naval operations create a necessity to which all private interests must give way;" and further that the exemption has not "been extended to ships or vessels employed on the high sea in taking whales or seals, or cod or other fish which are not brought fresh to market, but are salted or otherwise cured and made a regular article of commerce."

It will be perceived that the exceptions reduce the supposed rule to very narrow limits, requiring a careful examination of the facts in order to ascertain its applicability; and the decision appears to me to go altogether too far in respect of dealing with captures directed or ratified by the officer in command.

But were these two vessels within the alleged exemption? They were of twenty-five and thirty-five tons burden respectively. They carried large tanks, in which the fish taken were kept alive. They were owned by citizens of Havana, and the owners and the masters and crew were to be compensated by shares of the catch. One of them had been two hundred miles from Havana, off Cape San Antonio, for twenty-five days, and the other for eight days off the coast of Yucatan. They belonged, in short, to the class of fishing or coasting vessels of from five to twenty tons burden, and from twenty tons upwards, which, when licensed or enrolled as prescribed by the Revised Statutes, are declared to be vessels of the United States, and the shares of whose men, when the vessels are employed in fishing, are regulated by statute. They were engaged in what were substantially commercial ventures, and the mere fact that the fish were kept alive by contrivances for that purpose — a practice of considerable antiquity — did not render them any the less an article of trade than if they had been brought in cured.

I do not think that, under the circumstances, the considerations which have operated to mitigate the evils of war in respect of individual harvesters of the soil can properly be invoked on behalf of these hired vessels, as being the implements of like harvesters of the sea. Not only so as to the owners but as to the masters and crews. The principle which exempts the husbandman and his instruments of labor, exempts the industry in which he is engaged, and is not applicable in protection of the continuance of transactions of such character and extent as these.

In truth, the exemption of fishing craft is essentially an act of grace, and not a matter of right, and it is extended or denied as the exigency is believed to demand.

It is, said Sir William Scott, "a rule of comity only, and not of legal decision."

The modern view is thus expressed by Mr. Hall : " England does not seem to have been unwilling to spare fishing vessels so long as they are harmless, and it does not appear that any State has accorded them immunity under circumstances of inconvenience to itself. It is likely that all nations would now refrain from molesting them as a general rule, and would capture them so soon as any danger arose that they or their crews might be of military use to the enemy ; and it is also likely that it is impossible to grant them a more distinct exemption."

In the Crimean War, 1854–5, none of the orders in council, in terms, either exempted or included fishing vessels, yet the allied squadrons swept the Sea of Azof of all craft capable of furnishing the means of transportation, and the English admiral in the Gulf of Finland directed the destruction of all Russian coasting vessels, not of sufficient value to be detained as prizes, except " boats or small craft which may be found empty at anchor, and not trafficking."

It is difficult to conceive of a law of the sea of universal obligation to which Great Britain has not acceded. And I am not aware of adequate foundation for imputing to this country the adoption of any other than the English rule.

In his Lectures on International Law at the Naval Law College the late Dr. Freeman Snow laid it down that the exemption could not be asserted as a rule of international law. These lectures were edited by Commodore Stockton and published under the direction of the Secretary of the Navy in 1895, and, by that department, in a second edition, in 1898, so that in addition to the well-known merits of their author they possess the weight to be attributed to the official imprimatur. Neither our treaties nor settled practice are opposed to that conclusion.

In view of the circumstances surrounding the breaking out of the Mexican War, Commodore Conner, commanding the Home Squadron, on May 14, 1846, directed his officers, in respect of blockade, not to molest " Mexican boats engaged exclusively in fishing on any part of the coast," presumably small boats in proximity to the shore; while on the Pacific coast Commodore Stockton in the succeeding August ordered the capture of " all vessels under the Mexican flag."

The treaties with Prussia of 1785, 1799 and 1828, and of 1848 with Mexico, in exempting fishermen, " unarmed and inhabiting unfortified towns, villages or places," did not exempt fishing vessels from seizure as prize; and these captures evidence the convictions entertained and acted on in the late war with Spain.

It is needless to review the speculations and repetitions of the writers on international law. Ortolan, De Boeck and others admit that the custom relied on as consecrating the immunity is not so general as to create an absolute international rule; Heffter, Calvo and others are to the contrary. Their lucubrations may be persuasive, but are not authoritative.

In my judgment, the rule is that exemption from the rigors of war is in the control of the Executive. He is bound by no immutable rule on the subject. It is for him to apply, or to modify, or to deny altogether such immunity as may have been usually extended.

Exemptions may be designated in advance, or granted according to circumstances, but carrying on war involves the infliction of the hardships of war at least to the extent that the seizure or destruction of enemy's property on sea need not be specifically authorized in order to be accomplished.

Being of opinion that these vessels were not exempt as matter of law, I am constrained to dissent from the opinion and judgment of the court; and my brothers Harlan and McKenna concur in this dissent.

On January 29, 1900, the court, in each case, on motion of the Solicitor General in behalf of the United States, and after argument of counsel thereon, and to secure the carrying out of the opinion and decree according to their true meaning and intent, ordered that the decree be so modified as to direct that the damages to be allowed shall be compensatory only, and not punitive.

In re Henfield
11 Fed. Cas. 1099, No. 6360 (D. Pa., 1793)

A charge delivered by the Honourable JOHN JAY, Esquire, Chief Justice of the United States, to the grand jury impannelled for the court of the United States, holden for the Middle circuit in the district of Virginia, at the capitol in the city of Richmond, on the 22d day of May, 1793.[1]

[1] This prosecution, which has been referred to frequently in the subsequent reports as the earliest case on the subject of the common law jurisdiction of the federal courts, and which was considered of so much importance by General Washington, as to justify a special meet-

Gentlemen of the Grand Jury: That citizens and nations should [so] use their own as not to injure others, is an ancient and excellent maxim; and is one of those plain precepts of common justice, which it is the interest of all, and the duty of each to obey, and that not only in the use they may make of their property, but also of their liberty, their power and other blessings of every kind.

To restrain men from violating the rights of society and of one another; and impartially to give security and protection to all, are among the most important objects of a free government. I say a free government, because in those that are not free, these objects being in certain respects secondary to others are less regarded, and less perfectly provided for. Where the conduct of the citizens is regulated by the laws made by themselves and for their common benefit, and ex-

ecuted by men deriving authority from, and responsible to them, the most regular and exact obedience to those laws is to be expected, required and rendered. By their constitution and laws, the people of the United States have expressed their will, and their will so expressed, must sway and rule supreme in our republic. It is in obedience to their will, and in pursuance of their authority, that this court is now to dispense their justice in this district; and they have made it your duty, gentlemen, to inquire whether any and what infractions of their laws have been committed in this district, or on the seas, by persons in or belonging to it. Proceed, therefore, to inquire accordingly, and to present such as either have, or shall come to your knowledge. That you may perceive more clearly the extent and objects of your inquiries, it may be proper to observe, that the laws of the United States admit of be-

---

ing of congress, and by Mr. Jefferson as to require a distinct explanation to the British government, is now for the first time reported. The charges of Chief Justice Jay and Judge Wilson, it is true, were printed by the government for the purpose of explaining abroad the position of the United States, but they have never yet been presented to the professional eye. Fortunately, however, among the papers of the late Mr. Rawle, who, as district attorney, conducted the prosecution; and those of Mr. Duponceau, who, with Mr. Sergeant and Mr. Ingersoll, were counsel for the defence, the editor has been enabled to discover notes which give an almost complete report of the case. The causes which led to it are best given by the following letters, which were obtained from the same source, and which are now for the first time published:

Mr. Hammond to Mr. Jefferson.

The undersigned, his Britannic Majesty's Minister Plenipotentiary to the United States of America, has the honour of informing the Secretary of State, that he has received intelligence from his Majesty's Consul, at Charleston, South Carolina, that two privateers have been fitted out from that port under French commissions. They carry six small guns, and are navigated by forty or fifty men, who are, for the most part, citizens of the United States. One of these privateers left the harbour of Charleston on the 18th ult., and the other was on the 22d ready to depart.

The undersigned does not deem it necessary to enter into any reasoning upon these facts, as he conceives them to be breaches of that neutrality which the United States profess to observe, and direct contraventions of the proclamation which the president issued upon the 22d of last month. Under this impression, he doubts not that the executive government of the United States, will pursue such measures as to its wisdom may appear the best calculated for repressing such practices in future, and for restoring to their rightful owners any captures which these particular privateers may attempt to bring into any of the ports of the United States.　　　　Geo. Hammond.

Philadelphia, 8th May, 1793.

The Secretary of State.

Norfolk, May 5, 1793.

Sir: We have taken the liberty, considering it a duty, to give you information of two schooner boats, cruizing off our capes, as privateers, under French commissions, who are daily chasing vessels bound in and out, to the great prejudice of our trade, and contrary to the

law of nations to be chasing and boarding vessels within our territories. One of these vessels is called the Sans Culotte, and commanded by a Mr. Farre, the other called the Eagle; they are about the size of the largest pilot boats, and rigged as they are, mounting four carriage guns each, and fitted from Charleston. By reference to Captain Tucker's report, you will find how the Sans Culotte is manned; and from report of negro Caesar, the pilot, the Eagle has but one Frenchman on board her, the others Americans and Englishmen. One of these vessels belonged to Mr. Hooper, of Cambridge, in Maryland. Mr. Hooper is gone with Captain Tucker's vessel to that place, where his father lives, and Captain Tucker says, he understood she was to be laid up in some creek thereabouts. From the circumstances of erasing the name out of her stern, it appears as if some fraud was intended. We are, with the greatest respect, &c.,

Thos. Newton. Jr.
Wm. Lindsay.

Captain Lindsay, of the schooner Greyhound, in twenty-three days from Jamaica, reports that he arrived here the 4th inst. That on the day before, about half past 11 o'clock, a. m., he fell in with the pilot boat Ranger, of Hampton, belonging to Mr. Latimer, who hailed him and asked what vessel he commanded, to which he replied, the Greyhound of Norfolk, (Captain Lindsay having erased the name of the port he belonged to, and substituted Norfolk,) and added, that he was from St. Eustatius, upon which Mr. Latimer gave information to a small schooner privateer, at not more than twenty-four yards from them, and not a half mile from Cape Henry: by this deception, Captain Lindsay supposes, he escaped being taken.

Captain Tucker, of the schooner Eunice of New Providence, reports that he was, on the 29th last month, taken by a privateer schooner, called the Sans Culotte, commanded by Captain Farre, in the latitude 36, in 27 fathom water. That after being in possession of the privateer, the name of his schooner was erased from the stern, and a Mr. Hooper, of Cambridge, in the state of Maryland, was put on board as prize master, and he understood she was to be carried there and laid up in some creek, and that Mr. Hooper was to go to Philadelphia on some business. That whilst he was prisoner, both the privateer and the prize came into Hampton Road, and lay in Hawkin's Hole part of two days and two nights, and then sailed out on a cruise. He says that a Major-General, of New England, was on board the privateer, and acted as a marine officer, and a lieutenant in the absence of Mr. Hooper.

Mr. Hooper owned the schooner Eagle, and

ing classed under three heads of descriptions. 1st. All treaties made under the authority of the United States. 2d. The laws of nations. 3dly. The constitution, and statutes of the United States.

Treaties between independent nations, are contracts or bargains which derive all their force and obligation from mutual consent and agreement; and consequently, when once fairly made and properly concluded, cannot be altered or annulled by one of the parties, without the consent and concurrence of the other. Wide is the difference between treaties and statutes—we may negotiate and make contracts with other nations, but we can neither legislate for them, nor they for us; we may repeal or alter our statutes, but no nation can have authority to vacate or modify treaties at discretion. Treaties, therefore, necessarily become the supreme law of the land, and so they are very properly de-

plied from this to Georgia and Charleston as a packet. She was fitted originally from Cambridge. From every circumstance, Captain Tucker was of opinion, they would take vessels in the Bay of Chesapeake, as they lay along side one all night, but she proved to be an American vessel.

Mr. Jefferson to Mr. Rawle, Enclosing the Above.

Philadelphia, May 15, 1793.

Sir: By the enclosed papers, you will perceive, there is reason to believe that certain citizens of the United States, have engaged in committing depredations on the property and commerce of some of the nations at peace with the United States. I have it in charge to express to you the desire of the government, that you would take such measures for apprehending and prosecuting them as shall be according to law. I am not able to point out to you the individuals against whom suggestions have been made, but take the liberty of referring you to Mr. Deblois and Mr. Sharpe Delany, who may give you information on the subject. I am, with great esteem, sir, your most obedient and most humble servant,   Th. Jefferson.
Mr. Rawle.

Mr. Rawle to Mr. Baker.

Sir: I have received information that a citizen of the United States, named Gideon Henfield, late of Salem, Massachusetts, has arrived at this port in the quality of an officer of a privateer, lately fitted out in Charleston, So. Carolina, on board a British vessel, taken as prize by the said privateer.

As I have received orders to prosecute, in every instance, those who commit breaches of the neutrality, declared to exist on the part of the United States, during the present war between the European powers; it is my duty to request, that you will be pleased to summon Mr. Lewis Deblois to appear before you, and if he verifies the above information upon oath, to issue your warrant for apprehending the said Gideon Henfield, in order that he may be dealt with according to law.

Yours, &c.,   W. Rawle.
17 May, 1793.

The following paper was certified from the department of state to be used on the trial:

Marine Francaise.—Liberté, Egalité.—Au nom de la République Francaise.

Le Conseil Exécutif provisoire de la République Francaise permet, par les présentes, à

clared to be by the sixth article of the constitution. Whenever doubts and questions arise relative to the validity, operation or construction of treaties, or of any articles in them, those doubts and questions must be settled according to the maxims and principles of the laws of nations applicable to the case. The peace, prosperity, and reputation of the United States, will always greatly depend on their fidelity to their engagements; and every virtuous citizen (for every citizen is a party to them) will concur in observing and executing them with honour and good faith; and that, whether they be made with nations respectable and important, or with nations weak and inconsiderable, our obligation to keep our faith results from our having pledged it, and not from the character or description of the state or people, to whom, neither impunity nor the right of retaliation can sanctify perfidy; for although

—— de faire armer et équipper en guerre un —— nommé le —— du port de —— tonneaux, ou environ, actuellement au port de ——, avec tel nombre de canons, boulets, et telle quantité de poudres, plombs, et autres munitions de guerre et vivres qu'il jugera nécessaire pour le mettre en état de courir sur les pirates, forbans, gens sans aveu, et généralement sur tous les ennemis de la République Francaise, en quelque lieu qu'il pourra les rencontrer, de les prendre et amener prisonniers avec leurs navires, armes, et autres objets dont ils seront saisis, à la charge, par ledit —— de se conformer aux Ordonnances de la Marine, aux Lois décrétées par les Représentans du Peuple Francais, et notamment à l'article IV. de la Loi du 31 Janvier, concernant le nombre d'hommes devant former son équipage, de faire enregistrer les présentes Lettres au Bureau des Classes du lieu de son départ, d'y déposer un rôle, signé et certifié du lui, contenant les noms et surnoms, âge, lieu de naissance et demeure des gens de son équipage, et à son retour, de faire son rapport pardevant l'Officier chargé de l'Administration des lasses, de ce qui se sera passé pendant son Voyage.

Le Conseil Exécutif provisoire requiert tous Peuples, amis et allies de la République Francaise et leurs agens, de donner audit —— toute assistance, passage et retraite en leurs ports avec sondit vaisseau et les prises qu'il aura pu faire, offrant d'en user de même en pareilles circonstances. Mande et ordonne aux Commandans des Bâtimens de l'Etat, de laisser librement passer ledit —— avec son vaisseau et ceux qu'il aura pu prendre sur l'ennemi, et de lui donner secours et assistance.

Ne pourront, les présentes, servir que pour —— mois seulement, à compter de la date de leur enregistrement.

En foi de quoi le Conseil Exécutif provisoire de la République, a fait signer les présentes Lettres par le Ministre de la Marine, et y a fait apposer le sceau de la République.

Donné à Paris le —— jour du mois d —— mil sept cent —— l'an —— de la République Francaise.

Nul. (Signé) Monyes, (L. S.)
Par le Ministre de la Marine.
Pour servir remodel.
(Signé.) Cottrau.

Department of State, to wit: I hereby certify, that the aforegoing is one of the blank forms of commissions, issued by the French Republic, communicated to me officially by the Minister of France. In testimony whereof, I have caused my seal of office to be hereto affixed. Given under my hand, this first day of June, 1793.   Th. Jefferson.

perfidy may deserve chastisement, yet it can never merit imitation.

2. As to the laws of nations—they are those laws by which nations are bound to regulate their conduct towards each other, both in peace and war. Providence has been pleased to place the United States among the nations of the earth, and therefore, all those duties, as well as rights, which spring from the relation of nation to nation, have devolved upon us. We are with other nations, tenants in common of the sea—it is a highway for all, and all are bound to exercise that common right, and use that common highway in the manner which the laws of nations and treaties require. On this occasion, it is proper to observe to you, gentlemen, that various circumstances and considerations now unite in urging the people of the United States to be particularly exact and circumspect in observing the obligation of treaties, and the laws of nations, which, as has been already remarked, form a very important part of the laws of our nation. I allude to the facts and injunctions specified in the president's late proclamation; it is in these words: "Whereas, it appears that a state of war exists between Austria, Prussia, Sardinia, Great Britain, and the United Netherlands of the one part, and France of the other, and the duty and interest of the United States, require that they should with sincerity and good faith, adopt and pursue a conduct friendly and impartial towards the belligerent powers: I have, therefore, thought fit by these presents, to declare the disposition of the United States to observe the conduct aforesaid towards these powers respectively, and to exhort and warn the citizens of the United States, carefully to avoid all acts and proceedings whatsoever, which may in any manner tend to contravene such disposition. I do hereby make known, that whosoever of the citizens of the United States, shall render himself liable to punishment or forfeiture, under the law of nations, by committing, aiding, or abetting hostilities against any of the said powers, or by carrying to them those articles which are deemed contraband, by the modern usage of nations, will not receive the protection of the United States against such punishment or forfeiture; and further, that I have given instructions to those officers to whom it belongs, to cause prosecutions to be instituted against all persons who shall within the cognizance of the courts of the United States, violate the law of nations, with respect to the powers at war, or any of them."

By this proclamation, authentic and official information is given to the citizens of the United States:—That war actually exists between the nations mentioned in it: That they are to observe a conduct friendly and impartial towards the belligerent powers: That offenders will not be protected, but on the contrary, prosecuted and punished. The law of nations, considers those as neutral nations "who take no part in the war, remaining friends to both parties, and not favouring the arms of one to the detriment of the other;" and it declares that a "nation, desirous safely to enjoy the conveniences of neutrality, is in all things to show an exact impartiality between the parties at war; for should he, when under no obligation, favour one to the detriment of the other, he cannot complain of being treated as an adherent and confederate of his enemy, of which no nation would be the dupe if able to resent it." The proclamation is exactly consistent with and declaratory of the conduct enjoined by the law of nations. It is worthy of remark that we are at peace with all these belligerent powers not only negatively in having war with none of them, but also in a more positive and particular sense by treaties with four of them.

By the first article of our treaty with France it is stipulated that "there shall be a firm, inviolable and universal peace, and true and sincere friendship between his Most Christian Majesty, his heirs and successors, and the United States; and between the countries, islands, cities and towns situate under the jurisdiction of his Most Christian Majesty and of the United States, and the people and inhabitants of every degree, without exception of persons or places." By the first article of our treaty with the United Netherlands, it is stipulated that "there shall be a firm, inviolable and universal peace, and sincere friendship between their High Mightinesses, the Lords and States General of the United Netherlands and the United States of America, and between the subjects and inhabitants of the said parties, and between the countries, islands and places situate under the jurisdiction of the said United Netherlands and the United States of America, their subjects and inhabitants of every degree, without exception of persons or places." The definitive treaty of peace with Great Britain begins with great solemnity, in the words following: "In the name of the most holy and undivided Trinity." By the seventh article of this treaty it is stipulated that "there shall be a firm and perpetual peace between his Britannic Majesty and the United States, and between the subjects of the one and the citizens of the other." By the first article of our treaty with Prussia it is stipulated that "there shall be a firm, inviolable and universal peace and sincere friendship between his Majesty, the King of Prussia, his heirs, successors and subjects on the one part, and the United States of America and their citizens on the other, without exception of persons or places."

By the laws of nations, the United States, as a neutral power, are bound to observe the line of conduct indicated by the proclamation towards all the belligerent powers, and that although we may have no treaties with them. But with respect to France, the United Netherlands, Great Britain and Prussia, the before-mentioned articles in our treaties with them, create additional obligations, to wit: all those obligations which result from express compact and from national faith, mutually, explicitly and solemnly pledged. Surely no engagements can be more wise and virtuous than those whose direct object is to maintain peace and to preserve large portions of the human race from the complicated evils incident to war. While the people of other nations do no violence or injustice to our citizens, it would certainly be criminal and wicked in our citizens, for the sake of plunder, to do violence and injustice to any of them. The president, therefore, has with great propriety declared "that the duty and interest of the United States require that they should, with sincerity and good faith, adopt and pursue a conduct friendly and impartial towards the belligerent powers." A celebrated writer on the law of nations very justly observes that "as nature has given to man the right of using force only when it becomes necessary for their defence, and the preservation of their rights, the inference is manifest that since the establishment of political societies, a right so dangerous in its exercise no longer remains with private persons, except in those kind of rencontres, where society cannot protect or defend them. In the bosom of society, public authority decides all differences of the citizens, represses violence and checks the impulse of revenge. It woud be too dangerous to give every citizen the liberty of doing himself justice against foreigners, as every individual of a nation might involve it in a war, and how could peace be preserved between nations if it was in the power of every man to disturb it? A right of so great moment, the right of judging whether a nation has a real cause of complaint, whether its case allows of using force, and having recourse to arms; whether prudence admits, and whether the welfare of the state demands it; this right," he says, "can only belong to the body of the nation, or to the sovereign its representative. It is doubtless one of those without which there can be no salutary government." It is on these and similar principles that whoever shall render himself liable to punishment or forfeiture, under the law of nations, by committing, aiding or abetting hostilities forbidden by his country, ought to lose the protection of his country against such punishment or forfeiture. But this is not all, it is not sufficient that a nation should only withdraw its protection from such offenders, it ought also to prosecute and punish them. The same writer very justly remarks that "the nation or sovereign ought not to suffer the citizens to do any injury to the subjects of another state, much less to offend the state itself; and that not only because no sovereign ought to permit those who are under his command to violate the precepts of the law of nature which forbids all injuries, but also because nations ought to respect each other, to ab-

stain from all abuse, from all injury, and, in a word, from everything that may be of prejudice to others. If a sovereign who might keep his subjects within the rules of justice and peace, suffers them to injure a foreign nation, either in its body or its members, he does no less injury to that nation than if he injured them himself. In short, the safety of the state and that of human society require this attention from every sovereign. If you let loose the reins of your subjects against foreign nations, these will behave in the same manner to you, and instead of that friendly intercourse which nature has established between all men we should see nothing but one nation robbing another." The respect which every nation owes to itself imposes a duty on its government to cause all its laws to be respected and obeyed, and that not only by its proper citizens, but also by those strangers who may visit and occasionally reside within its territories. There is no principle better established than that all strangers admitted into a country, are, during their residence, subject to the laws of it; and if they violate the laws they are to be punished according to the laws; the design of pains and penalties being to render the laws respected and to maintain order and safety. Hence, it follows that the subjects of belligerent powers are bound, while in this country, to respect the neutrality of it, and are punishable in common with our own citizens for violations of it, within the limits and jurisdiction of the United States. It is to be remembered, that every nation is, and ought to be, perfectly and absolutely sovereign within its own dominions, to the entire exclusion of all foreign power, interference and jurisdiction, whether attempted by a foreign prince, or by his subjects, with or without his order. "It is a manifest consequence of the liberty and independence of nations, that all of them have a right to be governed as they think proper, and that none have the least authority to interfere in the government of another state. Of all the rights that can belong to a nation, sovereignty is doubtless the most precious, and that which others ought the most scrupulously to respect, if they would not do it an injury." These are general principles—the laws to which they apply are numerous, and need not be particularized in detail—on the present occasion, it will be sufficient to lead your attention to one or two, which will serve to explain the reason and extent of these principles. "The right of levying soldiers is a sovereign right belonging only to the nation. No foreign power can lawfully exercise it without permission, nor without previous permission can such attempts be otherwise regarded, than as improper interferences with the sovereignty of the country; on this head the law of nations is explicit. It declares, That the right of levying soldiers belongs solely to the nation: this important power is the appendage of the sovereign; it makes a part of the supreme prerogative. No person is to enlist soldiers in a foreign country without the permission of the sovereign. They who undertake to enlist soldiers in a foreign country, without the sovereign's permission, or alienate the subjects of another, violate one of the most sacred rights both of the prince and the state; it is a crime punished with great severity in every policied state. Foreign recruiters are hanged immediately, and very justly, as it is not to be presumed, that their sovereign ordered them to commit the crime; and if he did, they ought not to have obeyed his order, their sovereign having no right to command what is contrary to the law of nature; usually they who have practised seduction only are severely punished. But if it appears that they acted by order of the sovereign, such a proceeding in a foreign sovereign is justly considered as an injury, and as a sufficient cause for declaring war against him, unless he condescends to make suitable reparation."

From the observations which have been made, this conclusion appears to result, viz.: That the United States are in a state of neutrality relative to all the powers at war, and that it is their duty, their interest, and their disposition to maintain it: that, therefore, they who commit, aid, or abet hostilities against these powers, or either of them, offend against the laws of the United States, and ought to be punished; and consequently, that it is your duty, gentlemen, to inquire into and present all such of these offences, as you shall find to have been committed within this district. What acts amount to committing or aiding, or abetting hostilities, must be determined by the laws and approved practice of nations, and by the treaties and other laws of the United States relative to such cases. I doubt the expediency of anticipating such cases, and endeavouring now to distinguish acts which do, from others which do not, involve the criminality in question. Singular cases may arise.—If, in the course of your inquiries, you should experience difficulties, the attorney general and, if necessary, the court, will assist you.

Before I dismiss this subject, it cannot be improper to remark, that a state of neutrality leaves us perfectly at liberty to exercise every humane, benevolent, and friendly office towards the powers at war and their subjects; and to continue our usual commerce with them, excepting only those offices and that kind of trade, which may be designed and calculated to give to one party a military preponderancy to the detriment of the others. While we contemplate with anxiety and regret the desolation and distress which a war so general and so inflamed will probably spread over more than one country, let us with becoming gratitude wisely estimate and cherish the peace, liberty, and safety with which the Divine Providence has been pleased so liberally to bless us. By the favour of Heaven, we this day enjoy a degree of prosperity unknown to any other nation in the world—let it be among our enjoyments to render our happiness instrumental in alleviating the misfortunes to which many have already been, and more will yet be, reduced by those national contentions—in a word—let us be faithful to all—kind to all—but let us also be just to ourselves.

The people of the United States have exhibited too many proofs of virtue and intelligence, to leave room to doubt their continuing to be so guided by their usual integrity and good sense—but in every nation individuals will always be found who, impelled by avarice or ambition, or by both, will not hesitate to gratify those passions at the expense of the blood and tears even of those who are free from blame. Such men are to be restrained only by fear of punishment. There is, however, another consideration connected with the subject which merits much attention. It is natural in all contests, even for the best men, to take sides, and wish success to one party in preference to the other; our wishes and partialities becoming inflamed by opposition, often cause indiscretions, and lead us to say and to do things that had better have been omitted. It is not certain that the irritability of the belligerent powers, combined with some indiscretions on our part, will not involve us in war with some of them. Prudence directs us to look forward to such an event, and to endeavour not only to avert, but also to be prepared for it. Among our preparations, there can be none more important than union and harmony among ourselves. It is very desirable, that such an event do not find us divided into parties, and particularly into parties in favour of either foreign nation. Should this be the case, our situation would be dangerous as well as disgraceful. While blessed with union in sentiments and measures relative to national objects, we shall have little fear; and, therefore, it is sincerely to be wished that our citizens will cheerfully and punctually do their duty to every other nation, but at the same time carefully avoid becoming partisans of any of them. There is not a history of any nation which does not record the mischiefs they experienced from such parties, and they rarely present us with an instance of a nation being conquered and subjugated, without the detestable aid of its own degenerate or deluded citizens. Nothing is more certain than, that if such parties should arise among the people, they will find their way into every department of government, and carry distrust and discord with them—dark and dreary would then be the prospect before us, and we should in vain look for the speedy return of those happy days, when the government was peacefully, wisely and prosperously administered, under the care and auspices of a patriot, in whom the United States have by repeated unanimity in their suffrages, manifested a degree of confidence, no less reputable to their own wisdom and virtue than to his. But, if neither integrity nor prudence on our part should prove sufficient to shield us from war, we may then meet it with fortitude, and a firm dependence on the Divine protection; whenever it shall become impossible to preserve peace by avoiding offences, it will be our duty to refuse to purchase it by sacrifices and humiliations, unworthy of a free and magnanimous people, either to demand or submit to. The subject presented by the proclamation, appeared to me to be highly interesting, and I thought it useful to treat it with much plainness, as well as latitude. I was aware that I was treading on delicate ground; but as the path of my duty led over it, it was incumbent on me to proceed.

On the third branch of the laws of the United States, viz: their constitution and statutes, I shall be concise. Here, also, one great unerring principle, viz: the will of the people, will take the lead. The people of the United States, being by the grace and favour of Heaven, free, sovereign and independent, had a right to choose the form of national government which they should judge most conducive to their happiness and safety. They have done so, and have ordained and established the one which is specified in their great and general compact or constitution—a compact deliberately formed, maturely considered, and solemnly adopted and ratified by them. There is not a word in it but what is employed to express the will of the people; and what friend of his country, and the liberties of it, will say that the will of the people is not to be observed, respected and obeyed? To this general compact every citizen is a party, and consequently, every citizen is bound by it. To oppose the operation of this constitution and of the government established by it, would be to violate the sovereignty of the people, and would justly merit reprehension and punishment. The statutes of the United States, constitutionally made, derive their obligation from the same source, and must bind accordingly. Happy would it be for mankind, and greatly would it promote the cause of liberty and the equal rights of men, if the free and popular government which from time to time may result, should be so constructed, so balanced, so organized and administered, as to be evidently and eminently productive of a higher and more durable degree of happiness than any of the other forms. It is not sufficient to tell men by a bill of rights, that they are free, that they have equal rights, and that they are entitled to be protected in them; men will not believe they are really free, while they experience oppression—they do not think their title to equal rights realized until they enjoy them; nor will they esteem that a good government, whatever may be its name, which does not uniformly, impartially and effectually protect them. The more free the people are, the more strong and efficient ought their government to be, and for this plain reason, that it is a more arduous task to make and keep up the fences of law and justice about twenty rights than about five or six; and because it is more difficult to fence against and restrain men who are unfettered, than men who are in yokes and chains. Being a free people, we are governed only by laws, and those of our own making—these laws are rules for regulating the conduct of individuals, and are established according to, and in pursuance of that contract which each citizen has made with the rest, and all with each. He is not a good citizen who violates his contract with society; and when society execute their laws, they do no more than what is necessary to constrain individuals to perform that contract, on the due operation and observance of which the common good and welfare of the community depend; for the object of it is to secure to every man what belongs to him, as a member of the nation; and by increasing the common stock of property, to augment the value of his share in it. Most essentially, therefore, is it the duty and interest of us all, that the laws be observed, and irresistibly executed. I might now proceed to call your attention to certain statutes which merit particular attention, and it would not be difficult to place them in points of view, in which their importance to the public would appear in strong lights— but having already detained you so long, and these subjects not being new to you, I will forbear enlarging on them on the present occasion. The manner in which you are to fulfil the duties now incumbent on you, is specified in the oath you have taken. The experience of ages commends the institution of grand juries; it has merited and received constant encomiums, and I trust, gentlemen, that your conduct on this and similar occasions, will afford new proofs of its utility and excellence.[2]

(The charge of Judge Wilson, President of a Special Federal Court for Pennsylvania to the Grand Jury; the indictment returned by the Grand Jury, and the proceeding at the trial leading to a verdict of not guilty are omitted.)

[2] This charge, though not delivered to the particular grand jury by whom the bill against Henfield was found, was prepared for the purpose of settling the law generally as applying to the class of offenders, of whom Henfield was one, and in this light it is here introduced.

Editor's Note. The treaties of the U.S. cited by Chief Justice Jay in his charge to the Grand Jury were: the Treaty of Amity and Commerce with France, February 6, 1778 (8 Stat. 12; 1 Malloy, p. 468) (which was terminated by Congress on July 7, 1798;) the Treaty of Amity and Commerce with the Netherlands; October 8, 1782 (8 Stat. 32; 2 Malloy, p. 1233); the Definitive Treaty of Peace with Great Britain, September 3, 1783 (8 Stat. 80; 1 Malloy, p. 586); and the Treaty of Amity and Commerce with Prussia, September 10, 1785 (8 Stat. 84; 2 Malloy, p. 1497).

Jones v. Walker
13 Fed. Cas. 1059, No. 7507 (C.C.Va., 1803)
For opinion see infra V (1)

Johnson et al. v. Twenty-One Bales, Etc.
13 Fed. Cas. 855, No. 7417 (C.C., N.Y. 1814)

VAN NESS, District Judge. This case will first be considered as it is disclosed by the ship's papers, and the preparatory examinations, and then will be examined the defence arising out of the further proof that was ordered and produced. It appears by the papers that the property in question was laden on board the ship Mary and Susan, at Liverpool, in England, some time in the month of July, 1812. That the Mary and Susan is an American registered vessel, and that she sailed from Liverpool on the 16th July, 1812, on a voyage to New York, with these goods on board, and under a charter party to John Richardson, styling himself an "English merchant, residing in Liverpool." That she had a license on board, obtained from the British government, to protect her against capture by British cruisers. That at the time of her departure, information of the hostilities existing between the United States and Great Britain had not reached England. That on the 3d September, 1812, she was captured as a prize by the privateer Tickler, and brought into the port of New York. The position in which she was taken is not ascertained with precision. It is differently stated in the preparatory examinations which have been read, varying from eighteen to thirty miles south of the lighthouse. It is also in evidence, that John

Richardson, the person in whose behalf these goods are claimed, is a native subject of the king of Great Britain, but a naturalized citizen of the United States. The national character of Mr. Richardson is the principal ground on which this cause must be decided; but before I proceed to consider that, to examine the effect of his naturalization here, and of his subsequent residence in England, with the explanation given of it, by the further proof which was ordered and produced, I wish to dispose of some other questions which were first raised as principal grounds of defence, in a preceding cause, and also relied on in this.

It has been insisted, that this property was confided to the faith of the government, because laden on board an American vessel before the commencement of hostilities, and proceeding to its destined port in ignorance of that event. 2d. That it was captured within the territorial waters of the United States; thus under the protection of the government, and not subject to be made prize. 3d. That it was exempt from capture, because proceeding in an American vessel, and under the American flag.

In examining the points which have been stated, it will be necessary to advert to some general principles of the law of nations. In doing this, it will not be requisite to notice particularly its divisions into necessary, voluntary, conventional, customary or positive. The law of nations, without defining or developing its divisions more minutely, may be stated to be the law of nature, rendered applicable to political societies, and modified, in progress of time, by the tacit or express consent, by the long-established usages and written compacts of nations: usages and compacts become so general that every civilized people ought to recognize and adopt their principles. A principle which is deducible from natural reason, and firmly established by the primitive law of war, the general law of nations, in which is not embraced the conventional or customary law, is, that as soon as war is declared, all the property of the enemy or his subjects, wherever found, whether on the land or on the water, is lawful prize. This position, it is presumed, will not be contested. It is laid down in terms thus broad by all the late as well as the early publicists. By Grotius, lib. 3, cc. 8, 5; Puffendorf, Law Nat. c. 8; Bynkershoeck, c. 2; Vattel, Law Nat. lib. 3, c. 5; Martens, Law Nat. lib. 8, c. 2. If, then, enemy property under any circumstances be exempt from the rigorous operation of this principle, the exemption must be found in the conventional or customary law. That the rigor of this fundamental law has been relaxed by the express agreement of some nations, the tacit acquiescence and consequent customs of others is freely admitted. The severity of the laws of war, and the stern exercise of many belligerent rights, have been gradually modified and ameliorated as civilization and refinement diffused their influence over the nations of the earth; national humanity has kept pace with the progress of science and religion, which gradually infused the benignity of their principles into the whole system of national intercourse. The enlarged views and intellectual improvements resulting from the one, gave efficacy to the precepts of the other, which taught all people that public, like municipal laws, were to be administered, not only in justice, but in mercy.

It was about the middle of the 17th century that these enlightened views were matured into a decisive and practical influence on the conduct of belligerent powers. That the ferocious and sanguinary spirit which had uniformly distinguished national conflicts began to abate. That war became more a contest between governments, than nations, between monarchs contending for political supremacy, with objects more direct and definite than individual calamity. The petty pillage of a town, and the oppression of individuals, whom accident or the pursuit of fortune had placed within his power, ceased to add to the laurels of the prince, or the splendor of his throne; and this new view of national honor and magnanimity, this revolution in moral feeling, produced a

correspondent revolution in the practice, if not in the laws of war. This, too, was an important epoch in the history of European commerce. Ever since the reign of Elizabeth, England had taken a conspicuous part in the politics of Europe. That active princess entered with spirit into the affairs of the continent, for the express purpose of extending the trade and commercial connections of her kingdom. The impulse generated by her measures continued and extended its influence through the whole of the seventeenth century—and it was soon perceived, that a more liberal policy towards each other's subjects, at the commencement of hostilities, was necessary to the safety and convenience of commercial enterprise. To all the views and feelings, therefore, resulting from the increased wisdom and refinement of the times, were added the powerful motives of direct and evident interest. That commerce might be beneficial, not only to individuals, but to the revenues of the state, it was necessary that those engaged in it should pass freely from one country to another, and dwell with safety wherever their pursuits might lead them. If, in times when princes were as capricious, when wars were as frequent quite, and undertaken for causes as trivial as at present, these excursions were to have been attended with captivity and confiscation, it is easy to perceive the evils that would inevitably interrupt the progress of the commercial system then contemplated and begun.

In the progress of social improvement, therefore, we find the source of the desire to remedy these commercial embarrassments, and in that desire the proximate cause of the practice which now generally prevails among belligerents, of exempting from seizure the persons, and from confiscation the effects of each other's subjects within their respective territories, immediately on the commencement of hostilities. The form in which it first appeared, was that of giving notice to alien enemies to depart with their goods, and stipulations to this effect are first found in treaties made soon after that of Munster, in 1647–8. During the violent and complicated wars, terminated by that convention, the property of hostile individuals, as usual, had been confiscated; but by the 24th article, restitution was agreed upon. And in the treaty made seven years afterwards between Cromwell and Lewis XIV it was agreed, that in case of war, the merchants of the contracting powers should have six months to depart with their effects. This is the first stipulation of the kind I have found in a treaty. I am aware that in England some regulations favorable to the freedom of commercial pursuits had been adopted at an earlier period, as appears by the 30th chapter of Magna Charta, and a statute passed in the reign of Edward III. But these were local and municipal regulations, and failed to produce an immediate or decisive effect on the customs of Europe, although they may have prepared the way for the treaty stipulations to which I have alluded. Notwithstanding the precedent which had been established, and the concurring motives of interest and humanity which demanded an amelioration of the first severities of war, the safety of alien enemies, and their effects, rested for a long time exclusively on the special stipulations of treaties. So late as the period when Bynkershoeck wrote, the beginning of the last century, they received no sort of favor or protection, unless there existed a treaty to that effect between the belligerent states. Even Vattel recognizes the relaxation of the ancient rule as a modern practice. From recent instances, and from finding the provision in question in some of our latest treaties, it is even doubtful now whether it has acquired the force of a national custom, and whether the confiscation of enemies' goods, in the country, at the commencement of hostilities, if not protected by treaty, would be deemed a violation of the law of nations, or a mere departure from a recent practice. In the war in which we are now engaged, it is conceded that the rule is to be applied; and having briefly traced its origin and progress, it remains to examine its extent.

It will appear, I think, from the authorities which must govern us, that no effects belonging to an alien enemy, but such as are under particular circumstances within the country at the commencement of hostilities, have ever been deemed, by the law of nations or the usages of war, under the safeguard of public faith, where special compacts do not vary the general rule. No other property is within the modification of the law. All that comes into the country subsequent to the declaration of war, is still subject to seizure and confiscation, where there is no treaty on the subject. We have none with England that can arrest or suspend the application of this principle. In the treaty between the United States and Prussia, the contracting parties stipulated, that in case of war, the subjects of each other should be allowed nine months to settle their affairs and depart with their effects; and the 26th article of the treaty of 1794, with England, is somewhat similar. Both obviously relate to property in the country at the commencement of hostilities, and therefore under the protection of the government.

In an examination of the present question, but little aid can be derived from early writers on national law. Grotius and Puffendorf, and their cotemporaries, who explain with great minuteness the duties and obligations arising from the primitive laws of war, afford no light on a principle unrecognized in practice, at a period when the physical force of nations was not limited in its exercise by those rules which have since derived authority from the acquiescence of a more refined age. The exemption of enemies' property from confiscation under any circumstances, formed no part of the martial policy of that day. Bynkershoeck, as has already been noticed, states in his seventh chapter, that all enemies' goods in the country at the commencement of war, are confiscated, unless protected by treaty. In chapter 3, when treating of the suspension of commercial intercourse between enemies, he says: "It is clear that the goods of enemies brought into our country, are liable to confiscation." Vattel confines the exemption expressly to goods in the country at the time war was announced. I shall give his words, for I may, perhaps, have occasion to make another remark upon them: "The sovereign declaring war can neither detain those subjects of the enemy who are within his dominions at the time of the declaration, nor their effects—they came into his country on the public faith. By permitting them to enter into his territories, and continue there, he tacitly promised them liberty and security for their return; he is, therefore, to allow them a reasonable time for withdrawing with their effects; and, if they stay beyond the term prescribed, he has a right to treat them as enemies—though as enemies disarmed." This embraces all the law on the subject; for, although recognized, it is nowhere more distinctly stated. Martens, more rigid in the application of the rule, says: "Where there are neither treaties nor laws touching these points, nations continue still to seize on all the property belonging to their enemies' subjects which is carried into their territories after the declaration of war." This goes directly to the point before us—and I shall add an extract from Chitty to the same effect. He says, that "in strict justice, the right of seizure can take effect only on those possessions of a belligerent which have come to the hands of his adversary after the declaration of hostilities." In another place he observes: "The prohibition of Vattel reaches to the exemption only of goods in our hands at the time of the declaration, and does not cover property coming into our territory after that declaration." That the exemption of Vattel embraces only goods in the country at the rupture, is perfectly plain; and I think it open to an inquiry, whether a still more rigid rule may not be fairly extracted from the terms in which it is expressed, which is, whether not only the property, but the owner, the claimant, must not have been within the country before the war, to entitle either to governmental protection. Personal property follows the rights of the person. On general principles, therefore, unless the person claiming is entitled to protection, his property cannot be. The persons, according to Vattel, entitled to protection, are those who were in the country at the declaration of war. They must be permitted to return with their effects. And it seems to me that the exemption of hostile property from seizure is founded entirely on this personal right, and that this right is derived from the circumstance of having come into the country before the war, and therefore on the public faith. In common with all other general rules, this must ever be subservient to the express stipulations of a treaty. As it does not seem necessary, I shall not now examine whether such exist between the United States and Great Britain. These remarks are only the partial result of a general investigation, and not a direct examination of the principle they embrace. They are, therefore, particularly open to correction.

This particular branch of the subject has been examined with some care, for the purpose of ascertaining whether there were any, and if so, what circumstances, that could take enemy property, not in the country, out of the operation of the general rule clearly established by the authorities which have been referred to; and I am constrained to say, that not a single dictum has been found, except that in Azuni, to which I shall have occasion to refer, claiming the safeguard of public faith for property not actually within our territorial limits at the commencement of the war. The inference appears to me irresistible, that no extension of the principle is intended. It would seem to follow, then, under the rule which appears to me to be established by that public law which must control the decisions of this court, that if this must be considered enemy property, it is subject to capture and condemnation as prize. Whether the result of my examinations be correct or otherwise, to attempt to show, after what has been said, that the property in question is not protected because laden, and proceeding in ignorance of the war, would be superfluous and irregular. But indulging, as I do, a proper diffidence in my own opinion of the law, on a subject so novel and important, I must be permitted to fortify it, by attempting to develop what I conceive to be the practice of other nations who profess to be governed by it.

In the doctrines held and enforced by Great Britain, we may, perhaps, find a satisfactory exposition of the law, in cases like this we are discussing. And if, in a war with her, we adopt the construction of her own government, and the practice of her own courts, we can afford no just ground of complaint. In examining these we shall find, not only that the English prize courts are in the constant habit of condemning property brought in ignorant of the war when captured, but property in port at the commencement of hostilities, and even property captured before the war, but in contemplation of that event. The only difficulty and discussion that ever occurred on the subject in that country, was to whose benefit the condemnation should inure: whether to the lord high admiral, or, since the abolition of that office, to the king in his office of admiralty, or to him jure coronae. During the

usurpation of Cromwell the office of lord high admiral was in various ways depressed, and its perquisites reduced. The protector found them valuable, and it became his policy and his interest, not only to engross and direct their application to unusual purposes, but to abolish the office itself. From time immemorial, captures made from the enemy under particular circumstances had been considered as perquisites of the admiral, and, under the name of droights of admiralty, appropriated to support the dignity and splendor of his station. The sinister policy and distracted views of the government, at this period, introduced much confusion as to the distribution of the revenue arising from these sources; and at the restoration, the distinction between droights of admiralty and direct forfeitures to the crown was ill understood, and but little regarded in practice. With the regular settlement of the government, the lord high admiral began to claim what had once been considered the rights and emoluments of his office, which produced much animated discussion between him and the king. The controversy was at length referred to the greatest lawyers and the ablest civilians in the kingdom. From their combined wisdom resulted an order of the privy council, which, with great apparent precision, designated the rights and settled the conflicting pretensions of these worthy brothers. This order in council bears date the 6th of March, 1665. As far as relates to this subject, it remains unaltered, and at this day governs the decisions and practice in the British prize courts. Independent of all other matter, a reference to the terms of this order alone will abundantly show that property coming in, ignorant of the war, is subject, in England, to seizure and confiscation. The part of the order connected with this question is in these words: "All ships and goods belonging to enemies, coming into any port, creek or road of his majesty's kingdom, of England or of Ireland, by stress of weather or other accident, or by mistake of port, or by ignorance not knowing of the war, do belong to the lord high admiral." Enemy's ships and goods, then, coming into a port, creek or road, not knowing of the war, are condemned to the admiral. But the coming in must be voluntary, unconnected, at least, with any circumstances resulting from the war, to constitute a droight of admiralty. But what if it be not so? The answer of Sir William Scott is plain: "When vessels come in, not under any motive arising out of the occasions of war, but from distress of weather or want of provisions, or from ignorance of war, and are seized in port, they belong to the lord high admiral. But where the hand of violence has been exercised upon them, where it arises from acts connected with war, &c., they belong to the crown." Thus far, then, we have an exposition of this order, and therefore of the

British practice, which is still regulated by it, showing conclusively that ignorance of the war does not avert a forfeiture, and that under this part of the order these goods would not be droights of admiralty, because the hand of violence has been upon them; because her coming in arose from acts connected with war.

A practical illustration of those principles will be found in the arguments of counsel and judgments of the court in the cases of The Danckebaar Africaan, 1 C. Rob. Adm. 107, The Herstelder, Id. 114, and The Rebeckah, Id. 227, and The Maria Francoise, 6 C. Rob. Adm. 282. All these vessels, I believe, were captured in ignorance of the war. The word "coming," Mr. Brown says, in his "Civil and Admiralty Law," is worthy of attention; and so, indeed, it is in an English prize court. He goes on to say, in the words of Sir William Scott, extracted verbatim from the case of The Rebeckah: "It has, by usage, been construed to include ships and goods already come into ports, creeks or roads," &c.; and in consequence of this construction he adds, "all vessels detained in port, and found there at the breaking out of hostilities, are condemned jure coronae to the king." This practice of condemning vessels in port, at the breaking out of hostilities, is founded exclusively on this strange construction of the order; and it is remarkable enough that they are condemned jure coronae to the king. The claim of the admiral is defeated, I presume, by the circumstance that they were not enemy's vessels when they came in, as he is entitled only to enemy's vessels coming in. Another part of the order is: "All such ships as shall be seized in any of the ports, creeks or roads of this kingdom or of Ireland, before any declaration of war or reprisal by his majesty, do belong unto his majesty." Under this is probably sanctioned the condemnation of property detained by embargo before war is declared; and hence, also, property captured before the war, under whatever pretence or mistaken motive, will be condemned if hostilities commence before the adjudication. Sir William Scott says, that "the person claiming must not only be entitled to restitution at the time of seizure, but he must be in a capacity to claim at the time of adjudication." This, at first view, would seem to be at variance with the general rule or practice already assented to, that property in the country is not liable to confiscation. But the reason of the distinction no doubt is, that the property thus situated came in by coercion, and furnishes conclusive evidence that the rule exempting hostile property from confiscation must be strictly construed; that under the diversified circumstances and various situations in which it may be placed and captured, the public faith is only pledged for the protection of that which was not only in the power of the adversary, but had been

voluntarily brought within his territory, and placed within his power, before the commencement of hostilities. Thus, then, I think it appears, where there is no reciprocal agreement to prevent it, that property is condemned in England, although captured in ignorance of the war, or lying at liberty in port at the commencement of hostilities, or in any way seized or detained before the declaration of war.

In opposition to this practice, and to what I conceive to be the clear and established laws of war in such cases, a passage from Azuni has been cited in these words: "A merchant vessel that happens to be at sea when the nation to which it belongs enters into a war, cannot be captured on its arriving at an enemy's port, in right of the war which has supervened between the two nations. He ought then to be under the safeguard of the public faith." What he ought to be, and what he is allowed to be, by the usages and customs of nations, are very different things. Each of us might, in our closets, devise many humane and beneficial modifications of the laws of war—but to what purpose? The whims and reveries of authors do not govern nations at this day; it requires the sanction of the civilized world to invest them with the force and authority of laws. The passage is remarkable, because it has neither the opinion of any publicist, nor the practice of any nation to support it. 'Tis true he refers to two treaties for a recognition of this principle, and two individual instances of personal magnanimity: the one extracted from a French newspaper. On this authority he has announced a new law to belligerent nations. Surely the provisions of two treaties are not binding on nations not parties to them, nor can personal magnanimity establish a rule for the government of the world. This principle of Azuni has not yet, and I will venture to predict never will, become part of the law of nations, and it never ought, if wars are, as they should be, commenced only for just causes and with legitimate views. The end of a just war is to obtain a remuneration for some loss sustained or injury received; and after announcing to the world that force will be employed to obtain that which is withheld, can it be necessary, in every individual case of attack, to send a herald to proclaim your intention, that your adversary may be prepared to resist—thus hazarding a loss equal to that which it is sought to repair? On a careful perusal of the work in which this doctrine is advanced, I think it will be found that to whatever consideration it may be entitled as a work of ingenuity and research, it is unworthy of much weight as an authority. It was produced, if not under the dictation of a distracted government, yet in some degree for the purpose of supporting the alterations it proposed in the maritime laws of nations, and under the operation of prejudices too strong to admit of an impartial examination of a national question. It was obviously written under the innovating influence of the times, at a period when the inflamed passions of men, and the convulsed energies of nations, were uprooting the foundations of social and political order; when new systems of policy, of municipal and of public law, were everywhere springing up with a luxuriance that threatened to confound all established principles, and perplexed the soundest understandings; when intellectual efforts were perverted by the captivating novelties and splendid plausibilities, engendered "in that season of fulness which opened" upon the world with the French Revolution; when changes and innovations, eccentric in their nature, and infinitely various in their character, overwhelmed every system of ethics and philosophy which laborious wisdom had devised or time consecrated—absorbed or dissipated all that was fantastic in superstition, or venerable in orthodox opinion, while the victorious eagles of a frenzied people indiscriminately overshadowed or subverted all the monuments of human folly, and all that remained of ancient grandeur. From sources so agitated, if not polluted, nothing satisfactory can be drawn. The oracles of wisdom are seldom uttered amidst scenes of tumult and commotion. We must look back beyond the troubles of these latter days for wise rules, and trace their modifications and present form through the acknowledged and uniform practice of settled and civilized nations. That is at variance with this novel suggestion, and it cannot be admitted on an authority so questionable.

It is alleged, 2dly, that this property was captured within the territorial waters of the United States, and therefore not subject to be made prize. There is something so novel in this position, and in the arguments which it has suggested, that it is difficult to reduce them to a systematic examination. It would be easy to explain the foundation of the jurisdictional right of every nation to those portions of the sea that wash its shores. To show that the source from which it is derived is self-preservation. That this sovereignty is assumed by, and conceded to each, for the preservation of its own peace, to avoid the evils that may result from a warfare between others, prosecuted within its immediate vicinity. But whatever may have been the origin of this claim, or by whatever reasons sustained, the precise nature of this sovereignty is involved in some obscurity. It will, however, be unnecessary to investigate that minutely, in order to explain the difficulty which the argument on this branch of the subject was intended to present. By examining the constitution of the admiralty and prize courts, and the power derived to the captors by the prize commission, it will become obvious that it has no connection at all with the general question of prize—that it affords protection under particular circumstances to a friend, never to an enemy—that

it is an appendage (if I may use the term) to a neutral territory—but does not, and cannot exist between belligerents.

The common admiralty jurisdiction (as Comyn calls it) extends to all things done super altum mare. The prize jurisdiction is not thus limited. It embraces the whole question of prize, unrestrained by the locality of the capture: it takes cognizance of all captures, no matter where made, if made as prize. The validity of the capture depends on the "jus belli" as determined by the law of nations. The effect and ultimate direction of the forfeiture depends on the rights granted by the terms of the commission, as explained by legal definitions, and recognized by universal usage. What, then, does the prize commission grant? To make captures of enemy goods on the high seas, limiting the power intended to be conveyed, by the very terms that limit the common admiralty jurisdiction. By ascertaining the extent of that jurisdiction, we must necessarily discover what is meant by the high seas, and thus the interest derived from this capture. Wood gives the answer of the judges of the realm, to the complaints of the admiral concerning prohibitions granted by the common law courts. In different places, they say: "By the laws of this realm, the court of the admiral has no cognizance or jurisdiction of any manner of contract, plea, &c., within any county of the realm, either upon the land or the water. It is not material whether the place be upon the water, infra fluxum and refluxum aqua, but whether it be upon any water, within any county," "taking that to be the sea wherein the admiral hath jurisdiction, which is before by law described to be out of any county." Comyn says: "The admiralty has jurisdiction in matters on the main sea, or coasts of the sea, not being part of the body of any county. And if it be between high and low-water mark when the sea flows; for then it is super altum mare, though upon the reflux it be infra corpus comitatus." The admiralty, then, has jurisdiction on all waters, not infra corpus comitatus; and how is it given? by the very terms contained in this commission. All waters, therefore, not comprehended within the body of a county, constitute a part of the high sea; unless it can be shown, then, that this capture was made within the limits of a county, it was well made, and vests an interest in the captors.

In analogy to the British practice, it has been contended, that by reason of the locality of the capture, the forfeiture must go to the government, in the nature of a droight of admiralty, because included, I presume, in the terms of the British order, which gives a direction to the forfeiture. But we have neither droights of admiralty, nor such an order; the whole subject must be regulated by the commission and instructions. We can only discover what has been reserved to the government, by ascertaining.

what has been granted. They have authorized captures on the high seas, which I think has been shown to include the spot where this capture was made. If even we had droights of admiralty, and an exact copy of that order in force here, still the forfeiture would go to the captors. The place of capture is not embraced by either of the terms used in it, as appears clearly in 2 Browne, Civ. & Adm. Law, 61, and by the exposition given of them by Sir William Scott, in 1 C. Rob. Adm. 231.

It is insisted, 3dly, that this property is exempt from capture, because proceeding in an American vessel, and under the American flag. This objection would seem to be sufficiently answered by the principles already laid down. The same rules that explain the admiralty jurisdiction, and designate the limits between it and the common law jurisdiction, must determine what, under the law of nations, is to be considered in the territory, so as to exempt it from capture; it must be within the common law jurisdiction, within the body of a county. The notion that vessels must be considered as part of the territory of a nation, is antiquated and exploded. The most strenuous advocates for the freedom of goods in free ships, no longer place the controversy on that ground. The principle first formally promulgated in the Consolato del Mare about the twelfth century, that enemy property was good prize on board free ships, has certainly been contested at different periods. It has sometimes been admitted and rejected by the same and different nations: but the high authority of that celebrated code, has generally prevailed where treaty stipulations did not establish a different rule. Within our own times it has been attempted, with great force and with much spirit, to establish a different principle, but it was lost with the scattered fragments of the armed neutrality. Amidst the uproar of the world, the flag, too, has dwindled into a vain emblem of sovereignty, protecting nothing; nothing certainly but the vessel, and designating only to what portion of the globe she belongs. These are the principles of England. They were recognized by our government in its correspondence with the French minister in the year 1793, and I am not prepared to deny that they are founded in reason.

The additional instructions issued by the president, have been relied on as a ground of defence. These instructions were prepared and dated at the city of Washington, the 26th August. On the 29th they were known here. The privateer Tickler was then at sea, and there is no evidence at all to show, that she had a knowledge of them at the time this capture was made, to wit, the 3d September. Indeed, all presumption is against it. Considering, then, the captain of this privateer as ignorant of these instructions. and under the circumstances of the case he must be so considered, I am of opinion, that they could have no effect or operation on his conduct. There is a material difference between acting in ignorance of a supreme legislative act and of executive orders. The one affords no impunity to the commission of a crime; the publication of a law enacted by the known public authority of the country, which operates upon every member of the community, is the only notice which, in the nature of things, can be given of it. A knowledge of it must be presumed ex necessitate, from the impossibility of giving to it farther publicity. But a private executive instruction, for the government of a certain class of public agents, can be made known to them in a different manner, and must be so, before they can be governed by it. In short, the one is a public, the other a private instrument. Ignorance of the one cannot be alleged, but the other cannot be obeyed unless known. A law operates until repealed with the same solemnity with which it was enacted. An instruction must be obeyed, until revoked with the same formality with which it was given. The original instruction was given and communicated to the commanders of these vessels, and another intended to annul or supersede it, must be given and communicated to them in like manner to produce that effect; until then the first instruction is their only rule of action. Again, this is a warlike operation. Considering, then, these instructions of the president in a military point of view, is not every act done under the one legal and effectual until another is communicated? If the libellants had been instructed to capture property of this description, would they not have been bound to do so until an order interdicting it was received? The case has been likened to captures made after a treaty of peace signed; but there is not the least similitude. To capture enemy property is a right of war. If there be no war, there can be no capture. The right to capture is during war, and is extinguished with it, eo instante. Some publicists have contended, even that a capture is good till notice of peace received. But that is exploded. I am clearly of opinion, therefore, that these instructions can have no weight under the circumstances of this case. But suppose, for a moment, that they were to have effect, that they were known, or though not known, that still they were binding. That, it seems to me, would only raise a question between the government and the captors. If this be enemy property, this court would not restore it. If the captors have no claim, it would be condemned to the government. But from the best view I am able to take of these additional instructions, it appears to me that they were not intended to touch the case of enemy property. It is well known, that at the commencement of the war, American vessels, laden in most cases with

American property, were molested and captured by privateers, with a view to a condemnation, on the ground of being engaged in an illegal trade with the enemy. As these vessels sailed in ignorance of the war, the government thought, that under all the circumstances of the case, they were entitled to consideration and lenity. These instructions, then, were issued to protect American vessels and American property from molestation before their arrival, without intending, in my judgment, to interfere with the question of prize in relation to enemy property. If it were otherwise, it would present the case of the executive abrogating, not only a right already vested by law, but one which is universally given and recognized in modern warfare, to capture enemy property on the high seas; and a proceeding resulting in nothing but drawing the forfeiture to the government; thus frustrating the very objects which had led these people to this species of warfare—to capture hostile property within the limits prescribed by their commission. I cannot give to these orders a construction that will lead to this conclusion.

The last question to be considered is whether Mr. Richardson, in whose behalf this property is claimed, is, for the purposes of this proceeding, entitled to all the rights and immunities of an American citizen. In the prosecution of this inquiry, I shall not stop to examine whether a naturalization, obtained for special and temporary, and not for general and permanent purposes, can be valid and effectual? Whether a government is bound, under any circumstances, to protect a citizen or subject, who not only withdraws voluntarily from the performance of every duty, but who, for nearly "twice the period that ordinary calculation assigns to the continuance of human life," incorporates himself and his resources with the numbers and the wealth of another nation? These, in my judgment, are questions well worthy of consideration, and less easy of solution than seems to be apprehended. But, as I have already exceeded the limits usually observed on occasions of this sort, I shall waive their discussion now, and notice only the more limited difficulties suggested by the course of the argument. The facts relative to Mr. Richardson's naturalization here, and residence abroad, as disclosed by the further proof which was ordered, are these: It appears that he was naturalized as a citizen of the United States in the year 1795, according to the laws then in force on that subject; that in 1797 he went to England; that in 1799 he came again to this country, and returned to England in 1800, where he continued to reside till March, 1813, making a residence of sixteen years in England, with the exception of a visit to this country of a few months. The effect of that will presently be noticed. It is contended by the captors that this residence constitutes a domicil under the law of nations. A commercial residence, within the principles of prize law, investing the claimant with all the characteristics of a British trader, and involving him in all the consequences and all the evils incident to that character.

I think it may be assumed as a principle, that the law of nations, without regarding the municipal regulations prescribed for his admission, views every man as a member of the society in which he is found. Residence is prima facie evidence of national character; susceptible, however, at all times, of explanation. If it be for a special purpose, and transient in its nature, it shall not destroy the original or prior national character. But if it be taken up animus manendi, with the intention of remaining, then it becomes a domicil, superadding to the original or prior character, the rights and privileges, as well as the disabilities and penalties of a citizen or subject of the country in which the residence is established. "The domicil," says Vattel, "is the habitation fixed in any place with an intention of always staying there. A man does not then establish his domicil in any place, unless he makes sufficiently known his intention of fixing there, either tacitly, or by an express declaration." Again: "The natural or original domicil is that given us by birth, where our father had his; and we are considered as retaining it, till we have abandoned it in order to choose another. The domicil acquired, is that where we settle by our own choice." This is the general principle, determining the national character solely by the domicil, whether natural or acquired. As the original domicil is given by birth, it requires no explanation. But what shall constitute an acquired domicil? Although the definition given of it appears, at first view, sufficiently plain, yet in analyzing it we have soon to encounter an important difficulty. When shall the intention to remain be deemed to exist? If it be not openly declared, when, as Vattel expresses it, shall it be deemed to be tacitly made known? What shall be evidence of the animus manendi and determine the intention? In order to ascertain this, we must resort to the exposition of able magistrates, whose duty it has been to expound and apply this public law; we must descend into an examination of the judgments and official acts of tribunals sitting and deciding under the law of nations.

It has been contended that the practical illustration of this doctrine, derived from the course and practice of the prize courts, justifies the following conclusions: 1st. That no residence establishes a domicil to any hostile purpose, or operating a condemnation of goods, but that which is either taken up or continued after the commencement of hostilities. 2d. That on the breaking out of war, a citizen or subject of one belligerent country, has a right to return from the other, and bring with him, or withdraw from thence, his goods and effects. I think the consideration of these propositions will embrace all the arguments, and lead to an examination of all the authorities which are in any way applicable to the merits of this cause. It must be remembered, that the principle laid down by Vattel is general, and must be universal in its application. It has no relation whatever to either a state of war or peace. The different authorities which have been cited, must all be examined with a reference to that.

The most general view which has been taken of this subject by Sir Wm. Scott, is in the case of The Harmony, 2 C. Rob. Adm. 324. "Of the few principles," he says, "that can be laid down generally, I may venture to hold, that time is the grand ingredient in constituting domicil. I think that hardly enough is attributed to its effects; in most cases it is unavoidably conclusive; it is not unfrequently said, that if a person comes only for a special purpose, that shall not fix a domicil. This is not to be taken in an unqualified latitude, and without some respect had to the time which such a purpose may or shall occupy; for if the purpose be of a nature that may, probably, or does actually detain the person for a great length of time, I cannot but think that a general residence might grow upon the special purpose. That against such a long residence, the plea of an original, special purpose could not be averred; it must be inferred, in such a case, that other purposes forced themselves upon him, and mixed themselves with his original design, and impressed upon him the character of the country where he resided." Surely, if terms can be explicit, and language can be plain, this is so. There is in it not the least allusion to a state of hostilities, or to a belligerent country. The terms are as comprehensive as those of Vattel. Showing, that residence alone, wherever it may be, is the source and foundation of domicil, and that from the length of the residence is derived the evidence of an intention to remain. If this be not so, why is time the grand ingredient in constituting domicil? If residence in a hostile country were necessary, that would be the grand ingredient; the characteristic feature in this acquired character which works a forfeiture of goods. But it is said, that the further remarks of this great authority in the same case, furnish an inference unfavorable to the opinion I have expressed: "Suppose a man comes into a belligerent country, at or before the beginning of a war; it is certainly reasonable not to bind him too soon to an acquired character, and to allow him a fair time to disengage himself."

From this, I should draw an argument directly the reverse of that which it has been cited to support; why is it too soon to bind him to an acquired character, who comes into a belligerent country at or before the beginning of a war? Most assuredly, because he had not, by a residence previous to the war, established a domicil, or manifested his intention to remain. His residence had been too short to afford evidence of a determination to fix his habitation there. He shall, therefore, be permitted to make his election to retire, and be allowed a fair time to disengage himself. If this claimant had arrived in England at, or immediately preceding the war, we would have had a very different case to examine. Sir William Scott proceeds: "In proof of the efficacy of mere time, it is not impertinent to remark, that the same quantity of business which would not fix a domicil in a certain space of time, would nevertheless have that effect, if distributed over a larger space of time. Suppose an American comes to Europe, with six temporary cargoes, of which he had the present care and management, meaning to return to America immediately; they would form a different case from that of the same American coming to any particular country of Europe with one cargo, and fixing himself there to receive five remaining cargoes, one in each year successively. I repeat, that time is the great agent in this matter; it is to be taken in a compound ratio of the time and the occupation, with a great preponderance on the article of time; be the occupation what it may, it cannot happen, but with a few exceptions, that mere length of time shall not constitute a domicil." He here supposes an American to go to Europe —not to any particular hostile country—and to remain for five years, intimating distinctly that it would fix on him the national character of the country in which he was thus established. It appears, also, from the same case, that one of the Murrays was considered, by the common law of England, as a British trader, subject to the bankrupt laws of that kingdom. How a British trader? Hostilities did not exist then between that country and this. He had acquired, therefore, the character of a British trader, by a residence in time of peace. It is that character that brought him within the operation of these local laws, and that character that would work a condemnation of his property in the prize courts of a nation at war with England. This case is so replete with information on this subject, that I shall notice one other passage found in the judgment of the court: "Time, I have said, is a great agent in those matters, and I should have been glad to have heard any instance quoted, on the part of Mr. Murray, in which a residence of four years, connected with a former residence, was deemed capable of any explanation." It is true, that the residence of the claimant, in that case, was in a hostile country; but it is equally true, that in the passages to which I have referred, the court lays down the general principle, without any reference whatever to the fact, as is obvious from the context, and his general reasoning on the subject.

The case of The Indian Chief (3 C. Rob. Adm. 17) affords much light on this question. This vessel was seized in a British port where she came for orders, on a voyage from an enemy colony to Hamburgh. The claimant was a native American, and the court, after stating that fact, says:—"He came, however, to this country in 1783, and engaged in trade, and has resided in this country till 1797; during that period he was undoubtedly to be considered as an English trader; for no position is more established than this, that if a person goes into another country and engages in trade, and resides there, he is, by the law of nations, to be considered as a merchant of that country. I should, therefore, have no doubt in pronouncing that Mr. Johnson was to be considered as a merchant of this country at the time of the sailing of this vessel on her outward voyage." The vessel sailed in 1795. The residence in this case was twelve years. In the case of Mr. Miller, the claimant of the cargo of this vessel, the principle under consideration was applied with great rigor. He was an American citizen and American consul, resident in some of the remote possessions of Great Britain, in India. He was for that reason pronounced by the court of admiralty a British merchant, and his property condemned for being engaged in a trade prohibited to British subjects. It is very manifest, therefore, that foreigners who reside in Great Britain, and enter into trade, are considered by the government and courts of that country, in pursuance of the general principle of the law of nations, as British merchants, entitled to all the privileges, and subject to all the restrictions of the native merchants of that kingdom.

It also appears, from other cases, that the principle is impartially and universally applied; that their own subjects, when settled abroad, are allowed all the benefits, and held to all the restraints of the native subjects of the country in which they reside. If resident in a neutral country, they are treated as neutral merchants, and may trade freely, even with the enemies of their native land. This general rule is given by Sir William Scott, in the case of The Emanuel, 1 C. Rob. Adm. 302. "The general rule is, that a person living bona fide in a neutral country, is fully entitled to carry on a trade to the same extent as the native merchants of the country in which he resides." In the case of The Dree Gebroeders, 4 C. Rob. Adm. 233, and The Adriana, 1 C. Rob. Adm. 313, the rule is exemplified. Grant and Boland, the respective claimants, were both native subjects of Great Britain, claiming the American character. It does not appear that they were ever naturalized in this country. The court makes no allusion to that circumstance, with the view, no doubt, if the fact were so, to avoid discussing the question of naturalization. He examines nothing but their residence, and admits that, if they had

sufficiently proved it to have been in this country, they would have been entitled to a neutral character. In the case of La Virginie, 5 C. Rob. Adm. 98, a Frenchman claimed the benefit of the American character; and it is fully admitted by the court, that if he had sufficiently made out his residence to have been in this country, he would have been entitled to restoration as a neutral. So it has been decided, even by the lords on appeal, that a British-born subject, resident at Lisbon, acquires by that circumstance the Portuguese character, and can trade with impunity with the enemies of England. And it would seem, by a recent decision, that the same rights are allowed to British subjects residents in this country. There are a great variety of cases, as well in the common law books as in the admiralty decisions, which have a bearing, in point of principle, on this question; but it cannot be necessary, nor is it now convenient, to analyze them all. From all, I think it appears very conclusively, that residence gives national character, independent of the political state or condition of the country in which it is established. Whether the native country or the adopted country be at war or peace, is perfectly immaterial. By residence, neutrals become belligerents; and belligerents neutrals.

But the question constantly recurs: What is it that constitutes this residence? And it certainly is not easy to answer it with precision. It must be such a residence, however, as will stop the party from saying that he came for a special or temporary purpose, such as will fix upon him the animus manendi, the intention to remain. The residence itself, as I have said, is prima facie evidence of the intention; if continued, it becomes, in process of time, conclusive. In the case of The Indian Chief, twelve years was decided to have that effect. In the case of The Embden [1 C. Rob. Adm. 16], ten years was said to fix the national character. In that of The Harmony, four years was declared not susceptible of explanation. In this case there has been a residence of sixteen years, with the exception of a visit to this country. It is well established that a temporary excursion, either to the place of the original domicil or to any other, shall not be deemed to interrupt the residence; the time previous to the absence shall attach to that subsequent, and constitute a continued residence. But taking the time most favorable to the claimant, there is an uninterrupted residence of thirteen years, which, in my judgment, is unavoidably conclusive. In this case, most especially. Mr. Richardson is a native British subject, and the same authority, so often quoted, says: "It is always to be remembered that the native character easily reverts; and that it requires fewer circumstances to constitute domicil in the case of a native subject, than to impress the national character on one who is originally of another country." La Virginie, 5 C. Rob. Adm.

8. This rule applies here with great force. It does not appear, from any evidence that has been produced, that Mr. Richardson was recognized in England as a citizen of America; and upon the general principles held by the government of that country, we must presume that he mingled again with the mass of its population, as a legitimate, complete British subject, enjoying all the rights and advantages of that character without being subject to any of the restrictions and inconveniences of an American citizen. It does not appear that even after the war he was, by himself, or by others, considered liable to the ordinary evils incident to the citizens of a hostile country. There may be other evidence of the intention than that which mere length of residence affords. The intention may be openly declared, publicly made known; and that, however short the residence may be, shall establish the domicil. Whitehill had been but two days in the enemy country when war was declared; but he had previously avowed his intention to remain, and his property was condemned. It has been alleged that Mr. Richardson was established in Liverpool as a commission merchant only, and that he was not engaged in general commerce. That is wholly immaterial—quoad this shipment, he can only be recognized as a merchant; his domicil is established, and this transaction imparts to it a commercial character.

Having endeavored to show how a domicil is established—how a foreign commercial character is acquired—it will be proper to inquire how it is divested; how a citizen of one country can disengage himself and his property from the effects and consequences of a residence established in another; and this brings me to an examination of the last point which I have proposed to consider. It is insisted that Mr. Richardson, being a naturalized citizen of the United States, had a right to withdraw his property from the hostile country. As a general proposition, I think this cannot be maintained. It is by no means clear that a citizen or subject of one belligerent can, stricti juris, withdraw anything from the territories of the other. It is no doubt true that bona fide cases of this kind are treated with indulgence; and that, from motives of public policy, the general principles of the laws of war are not unfrequently relaxed and accommodated to the sufferings and peculiar circumstances of individuals. But it is of no use to discuss the principle, unless the facts disclosed can bring the case within it. It is both proved and admitted that this property was shipped before the declaration of war was known to the claimant, and it is difficult to conceive how property can be claimed here as withdrawn from the hostile country, when it was sent before the claimant knew that the respective nations were at war. This difficulty is increased by the full proof before the court that these goods were shipped for sales and returns. They were not sent to remain here and wait the arrival of the owner. It is clearly established, by the papers, that they were to be sold as soon as might be convenient, and the avails remitted to him in England. All expectation of success, therefore, from this source, must certainly be ill founded.

It is further urged that Mr. Richardson's affidavit, and others offered as further proof, show that he intended to return to this country. The affidavits which have been produced to this point are those of Robert Falkner, James Mills and John Sill. Their affidavits go to show that Mr. Richardson, while in England, at different times expressed an intention to return to America, if the orders in council, complained of by this country, were not repealed, and the commercial intercourse between the two countries restored. Mr. Richardson himself deposes, that he did make these declarations, and did entertain that intention. These facts are well proved, and the claimant is entitled to the full benefit of them. But however distinctly these declarations were made and repeated, and however earnest and decisive that intention may have been, I hold, on the authority of the judgment in the case of The President, and many others, that it is perfectly immaterial and unavailing in a prize court. "A mere intention to remove," said Sir William Scott, "has never been held sufficient without some overt act, being merely an intention, residing secretly and undistinguishably in the breast of the party, and liable to be revoked every hour. The expressions of the letter in which this intention is said to be found are, I observe, very weak and general, of an intention merely in futuro. Were they even much stronger than they are they would not be sufficient. Something more than mere verbal declaration, some solid fact, showing that the party is in the act of withdrawing, has always been held necessary in such cases." 5 C. Rob. Adm. 280. Besides, the intention which was entertained rested wholly on a contingency, the alternative of which might instantly have obliterated this impression from his mind, and produced a determination not to return. This, in fact, must have been the state of the claimant's mind at the moment this shipment was made. He knew not of the war, and the only assigned cause for his intention to return to America was removed. In his opinion the orders in council were so revoked that the usual commercial intercourse between the two countries would be soon restored. Under that supposition these goods were shipped, and from his own showing, therefore, I am not only authorized, but bound to presume, that the intention to return to this country did not at that moment exist. But if it had so existed, the judgment in the case of The Indian Chief, 3 C. Rob. Adm. 14, shows how insufficient and ineffectual it is considered in the prize courts of England. It is there most decisively stated, that the character acquired by residence ceases only by non-residence; that it ceases only from the time the party turns his back on the country where he has resided, on his way to his own; that it adheres to him till the moment he puts himself in motion, bona fide, to quit the country of his residence, sine animo revertendi. The vessel, in that case, was the property of a Mr. Johnson, a native American, but who had for some time resided in England. She was seized as being engaged in a trade with the enemies of England. The court distinctly determined that, if Johnson had remained in England till the time of seizure, she would have been condemned as the property of a British merchant; but as he had left the country on his way to America, he must be deemed to be in pursuit of and to have revived his native character; and for that reason only she was restored. So in the case of The Curtissos [3 C. Rob. Adm. 21, note]: He had been resident in an enemy colony, but had left it before the capture of his property, and was actually on his way home. The lords, on appeal, decided that as he had put himself in motion towards his own country, as he was in itinere he was entitled to restitution. There are other decisions of these distinguished authorities, showing that the character which residence gives, can only be divested by an actual departure from the country in which it is established, or at least some act that may be deemed an actual commencement of his movement from it, and a real substantial effort to regain his native or prior domicil. The principle of these decisions I shall adopt in this case, because I think it founded in good sense, and furnishing the only practicable application of a rule, intended to ameliorate the strict laws of war. If the rule be not thus restricted, and thus applied, there will be no end to alleged intentions of returning. If a previously declared intention is to justify exportations from the enemy country in every dubious state of things, they will always be made in anticipation of possible consequences, and speculative projects, leading to a long-continued intercourse, the evils of which cannot be foreseen, and which it would certainly be destructive to tolerate.

It is said that Mr. Richardson executed the intention he had expressed, by returning to this country. As he has returned, he is certainly now entitled to the benefit of it; but it cannot have a retrospective operation. Having acquired and established the character of a British trader, it adhered to him until he did return. It is also said, and I admit, that a person in a foreign country, at the commencement of hostilities, may elect to return or remain abroad; but surely that election must be made known. How can it be disclosed? What shall be evidence of his election? We have seen that a mere declaration of his intention to return is insufficient. I should presume that a continuation in the foreign country, is the most conclusive evidence that can be furnished of his election to remain, and in the nature of things nothing can be legal and conclusive evidence of his election to return, but an attempt to carry that election into effect. In every act done to effectuate that, he shall be protected. While he remains, the presumption of law is against him, and can only be repelled by the commencement of his return. He cannot remain in the hostile country sending out as many goods as may suit his convenience, and then claim them upon the ground of a previously-declared intention to return. The shipment and his return must be cotemporaneous acts, or so nearly connected in point of time, as substantially to form but one transaction. It is evident from the facts in the case, that at the time this shipment was made, Mr. Richardson was not in pursuit of his American character. This, then, was an act done as a British trader, and cannot be otherwise considered. Mr. Richardson, moreover, did not leave England till seven or eight months after the capture of the Mary and Susan, and his return is now fairly open to the suggestion that it was produced by the capture of his property. Upon principle, therefore, and upon authority too, it is not entitled to consideration, and must be laid entirely out of the case.

I perceive the necessity of closing this opinion without adverting to a few other topics which the argument presented. I have already been too diffusive, for which the nature of the cause, it is hoped, will be deemed a sufficient apology. I was duly impressed with its novelty and importance, and have felt a solicitude, amidst the pressure of other business, to manifest at least a desire to arrive at a just conclusion. That which has been pronounced has been resisted with all the feelings that human misfortune and individual calamity are calculated to produce; but it has been forced upon me by what I conceive to be clear and explicit, though rigorous rules of law, which imperiously demand the suppression of all personal sympathies. I have, however, the consolation to know that if injustice has been done, relief will be administered in another place, where the skill and profound researches of the judge cannot fail to detect and correct my error.

United States v. La Jeune Eugenie
26 Fed. Cas. 832, No. 15,551 (D. Mass., 1822)

STORY, Circuit Justice. This is a libel brought against the schooner La Jeune Eugenie, which was seized by Lieut. Stockton, on the coast of Africa, for being employed in the slave trade. The allegation asserts the offence in two forms: first, as against the slave trade acts of the United States; and, secondly, as against the general law of nations. A claim has been given in by the French consul, in behalf of the claimants, who are subjects of France, resident in Basseterre, in the island of Guadaloupe, as owners of the schooner; and there is also a protest filed by the French consul against the jurisdiction of the court, upon the ground, that this is a French vessel, owned by French subjects, and, as such, exclusively liable to the jurisdiction of the French tribunals, if she shall turn out, upon the evidence, to have been engaged in this dishonourable traffic.

I am fully aware of the importance and difficulty of this case, considered under some of the aspects, in which it has been presented to the court. The case has already, as we are informed, and truly, become the subject of diplomatic intercourse between our government and that of France; and it is not, perhaps, too much magnifying its grave character to declare, that rarely can a case come before a court of justice more deeply interesting to the cause of general justice and humanity, or more likely to excite the jealousies of a foreign government, zealous to assert its own rights, and, it is to be hoped, not, in the slightest degree, reluctant to fulfil its own plighted faith for the abolition of the African slave trade. Whatever may be my own distress in being called upon to attend to such weighty considerations, and whatever my solicitude to discharge my duty to my own country, to France, and to the world, on the present occasion, it cannot escape the attention of any persons, who hear me, that a court of justice in this country has its path clearly marked out and defined. However delicate or painful may be its predicament, it cannot seek shelter under the wings of executive authority, or bind up its judgment under considerations of mere convenience or comity, or a blind obedience to the wishes of any sovereign, or a desire to extinguish, what it must justly deem, a trade abhorrent to the great principles of Christian morality, mercy, and humanity. It is bound to administer the law, as it finds it, fearlessly and faithfully, according to the dictates of its own judgment, in the hope at least, that errors of law may be corrected by a higher tribunal, and national difficulties may be removed by those, who hold the legislative and executive authorities of the nation

It appears from the evidence in the case, that this vessel is duly documented as a French vessel, and that she sailed on a voyage from Basseterre for the coast of Africa, and was found upon that coast by Lieut. Stockton, under circumstances, which left no doubt on his mind that she was engaged in the slave trade. The master and some of the principal officers were on shore engaged, as it should seem, in collecting slaves at one of the factories established for this purpose. The vessel was equipped in the manner, that is usual for the slave trade. She had two guns, a false or movable deck, and a large quantity of water and provisions, and water casks, quite unusual in ordinary voyages, and indispensable in this particular class of voyages. If there are any persons, who entertain doubts as to the real destination and employment of this vessel, I profess myself not willing to be included in that number. Upon the evidence in the case it is irresistibly established to my mind, that the sole purpose of the voyage was a traffic in slaves; and that the intention was to carry them from Africa to some one of the French colonies, and, in all probability, to the port, in which the enterprise originated. In respect to the ownership, it has been already stated, that the vessel was sailing under the customary documents of France, as a French vessel; and certainly in ordinary cases these would furnish prima facie a sufficient proof that the vessel was really owned by the persons, whose names appear upon the papers. In ordinary times, and under ordinary circumstances, when disguises are not necessary or important to cloak an illegal enterprise, or conceal a real ownership, the ship's papers are admitted to import, if not an absolute verity, at least such proof, as throws it upon persons, asserting a right in contradiction to them, to make out a clear title establishing their falsity. But if the trade is such, that disguises and frauds are common; if it can be carried on only under certain flags with safety or success; it is certainly true, that the mere fact of regular ship's papers cannot be deemed entirely satisfactory to any court accustomed to know, how easily they are procured by fraud and imposition upon public officers, and how eagerly they are sought by those, whose cupidity for wealth is stimulated and schooled by temptations of profit, to all manner of shifts and contrivances. Now upon the face of these very papers it appears, that this schooner is American built, and was American owned, and that within about two years she was naturalized in the French marine in the port of her departure, and her American title either really or nominally divested. At this period France and Portugal alone, of all the nations of Europe, possessed the painful and odious prerogative of covering under their flags a traffic, that all the great states of Europe had concurred in condemning to infamy. And by our own laws, which had been long sedulously directed against it, it was almost impracticable for any citizen to pursue the traffic under the flag of our own country, not only from the penalty of confiscation denounced against it, but from the offence being visited with capital punishment, as a most detestable piracy. Under such circumstances, if American citizens were engaged in the traffic, it is manifest, that they would conceal their interests under a foreign flag and passports, and wear any disguises, which might facilitate their designs, and favour their escape from punishment. And that such disguises might be cheaply bought, and promptly obtained through the instrumentality of private agents in foreign countries, who would be ready to assume a nominal ownership, no one, that has been much acquainted with the real business of this commerce, would be inclined to doubt or deny.

Sitting as I do in a court of the law of nations, accustomed to witness, in many shapes, the artifices of fraud, practised by those, whose interest lies in evading the salutary restraints of the laws, I think, that I should manifest a false, delicacy and unjustifiable tenderness for abstract maxims, if I did not borrow somewhat of the experience of the world, to enable me to disentangle the network, which covers up unlawful enterprises. It is too much to ask a court of justice to shut its eyes against what is passing in the world, and to affect an ignorance, of what every man knows; to deal with the surface of causes, and pronounce them to be innocent, because no stain is permitted to appear there, or because guilt is not ostentatiously displayed to the first glance. It cannot be concealed, however humiliating the fact may be, that American citizens are, and have been, long engaged in the African slave trade, and that much of its present malignity is owing to the new stimulus administered at their hands. I speak what the records of this court show; what the records of the government show; what is loudly and vehemently complained of by that foreign government, which is so zealously enlisted in the cause of its abolition. Under such circumstances it cannot but be supposed, that an American court will have its suspicions alive; and that when it sees, that a vessel, recently American, is found in the traffic under foreign papers, something more will be necessary than the mere formalities of those papers, to establish the fact of a bona fide transfer to the ostensible foreign owners. It is doing no injustice to a foreign owner to require in a traffic of this nature, so little reconcilable with good faith or sound morals, and prohibited by our laws, that he should give affirmative evidence, that the case has no admixture of American interests, when he sets up a title derived from American owners. It appears to me, that I should impose no hardship therefore in requiring the claimants in this case to show the bill of sale, by which they acquired their title, to give the names of the American owners; and to establish to a reasonable extent, that the transfer was for a valuable consideration. It is well known, that a bill of sale is the universal instrument, to which courts of admiralty look to establish the legal interests in ships; and this is equally a part of our own law and the law of France. And I take great pleasure in citing from an enlightened authority a confirmation of this doctrine. "It cannot," says Sir W. Scott, "be considered as any hardship upon the subjects of those countries, which still carry on the slave trade, that it (the court) should possess such a power (of inquiring into the real title of the ship.) It can be no unconstitutional breach of the law of nations to require, that when a claim is offered on the ground, that the property belongs to the subjects of a country, which still permits this trade, the burthen of giving proof of the property should lie upon those, who set it up, &c. It would be a monstrous thing, where a ship, admitted to have been, at one time, British property, is found engaging in this traffic, to say, that however imperfect the documentary evidence of the asserted transfer may be, and however startling the other circumstances of the case, no inquiry shall be made into the real ownership." The Donna Marianna, 1 Dod. 91, 92. Standing, then, as this cause does, I am not satisfied, that the property is owned as claimed; and before it would be restored, even if all other difficulties were overcome, I should feel myself bound to require farther proof of proprietary interest. If there were nothing more in the cause, I should pass such an order without hesitation.

But supposing the vessel to be established to be French, sailing under French papers, and employed in the African slave trade, the more important question is, whether this court is at liberty to entertain jurisdiction of the cause, or is bound to restore the property without any farther inquiry, remitting the party to the domestic forum.

It is contended, on behalf of the plaintiffs, that this court has a right to entertain jurisdiction, and is bound to reject the claim of the defendants: First, because the African slave trade is repugnant to the law of nations, secondly, because it is prohibited by the municipal laws of France. On the other side it is contended, that the trade is not repugnant to the law of nations; and if prohibited by the laws of France, it is a municipal regulation, which the tribunals of France are alone competent to inquire into and punish.

Before I proceed to the consideration of these points, it may be well to dispose of one or two preliminary considerations, which have been thrown out in the argument at the bar, and may assist us in coming to a correct determination as to the duty of the court.

Another objection of a more general cast, and involving more general principles, is, that if this is a French vessel, the seizure was tortious, and no right, and consequently no jurisdiction, over this case can be founded on a wrong. It is said, that Lieut. Stockton could only claim to visit this vessel upon the high seas upon the ground of a right of search, which right never exists in a time of peace, and therefore his seizure was founded on an abuse of power, which cannot authorize an American court to use any evidence acquired in virtue of such abuse. I am free to admit, as a general proposition, that the right of visitation and search of foreign ships on the high seas can be exercised only in time of war, in virtue of a belligerent claim; and that there is no admitted principle or practice, which justifies its exercise in times of peace. It is unnecessary to scan opinions or authorities on the subject, since the point was not controverted at the argument, and it is no part of my duty to re-ascend to the source of its origin. But if from a denial of a right of visitation and search on the high seas, it is meant to be concluded, that there exists no right of seizure of any vessel on the high seas, bearing a foreign flag, under any circumstances, I am not ready to admit the correctness of such a conclusion. The right of visitation and search is, in its nature, distinct from a right of seizure. A belligerent cruiser has a right to search all vessels found on the high seas, for the purpose of ascertaining their real, as well as assumed character, and capturing the property of its enemies. The exercise of such a right, being strictly lawful, involves the cruiser in no trespass or wrong, entitling the party searched to damages, if it shall turn

out upon examination, that there was no ground for the search, and that the property is in all respects neutral. If, indeed, upon such search, the captor proceeds to capture the vessel as prize, and sends her in for adjudication, and there is no probable cause of capture, he is liable to responsibility in costs and damages. But this is not for the search, but for the subsequent capture; which, being without sufficient reason, is treated as a tortious act, and a usurpation of possession. It does not, therefore, by any means follow, that a right of search justifies a capture, so that the latter may not be deemed a gross violation of the rights of a foreign neutral ship. It is, indeed, difficult to perceive, how a tortious capture, jure belli, can clothe a party with any more rights, in any respect, either as to evidence, or grounds of condemnation, than a tortious seizure in time of peace. And the right of search, as such, neither protects nor aids a capture, if considered per se the latter is incapable of justification. But a right of seizure may exist on the high seas independently of any right of search, or the protection from damages, which that right guarantees. For instance, no one can doubt, that vessels and property in the possession of pirates may be lawfully seized on the high seas by any person, and brought in for adjudication. But such a seizure is at the peril of the party. If the property upon examination turns out not to be piratical, or piratically employed, the seizor is a trespasser ab initio, and liable, as such, to damages; and it will be no justification upon the principles of general law, that there was probable cause of seizure. And yet no one will be hardy enough to contend, that the mere right to seize property in the possession of pirates on the high seas, which right exists as well in peace, as in war, draws after it a right of visitation and search of every vessel found on the high seas, to ascertain, whether she be piratical or not, or whether her flag be assumed or genuine. If this example should not be thought unexceptionable, I may be permitted, under the sanction of that high tribunal, whose decisions I am bound to obey, to put one, that has passed in rem judicatem. It is now the settled doctrine of the supreme court, that if a foreign vessel has committed any offence within the territorial jurisdiction of another nation, by which a forfeiture is incurred, she may be seized any where upon the high seas by the ships of the nation, against which she has offended. And it is manifest that, in most cases, it cannot be ascertained, whether a ship descried on the high seas be the offending ship or not, without actual search and visitation. Yet it has never been supposed, that a general right of search grew out of this admitted right of seizure. On the contrary, it is the general understanding, that the seizor visits, in such cases, at his peril, and is excused and justified, not by probable cause, but by the fact, that the seizure is followed by a just condemnation.

It appears to me, also, that every nation has a right to seize the property of its own offending subjects on the high seas, whenever it has become subject to forfeiture; and it cannot, for a moment, be admitted, that the fact, that the property is disguised under a foreign flag, or foreign papers, interposes a just bar to the exercise of that right. What, then, is to be done? If it be said, that foreigners are not to be molested on the high seas, while engaged in their own innocent and lawful trade, it is no less true, that foreigners engaged in the fraudulent cover of the property of your own subjects, and, in concert with them, evading your own laws, are not to be protected in such illegal enterprises. In such a case you do not acquire a right of search which justifies your encroachment upon the private concerns of a foreign ship; but nevertheless, having a right to seize for breach of your own laws, you may seize at your peril; and if the case turns out to be innocent, you are responsible for damages; if guilty, you are justified by the event. Unless such a community of right be conceded to exist for purposes like those alluded to, the ocean would become a sanctuary for all sorts of offences; and evils, at least as alarming as those, with which we are threatened in this case, would afflict the whole commercial world. It is not lightly to be supposed, that any nation would be inclined to abuse any right, which it holds in common only with all other nations; and if it should choose, in the wantonness of power, to abuse it to the serious injury of other nations, the same remedy would exist, and none other, as for like oppressions practised within the range of its ordinary authority.

Having adverted to these preliminary considerations, I may now be permitted to proceed to the great points in controversy. And the first question naturally arising out of the asserted facts is, whether the African slave trade be prohibited by the law of nations; for, if it be so, it will not, I presume, be denied, that confiscation of the property ought to follow; for that is the proper penalty denounced by that law for any violation of its precepts; and the same reasons, which enforce that penalty ordinarily, apply with equal force to employment in this trade. The Fortuna, 1 Dod. 81; Madrazo v. Willes, 3 Barn. & Ald. 353.

I shall take up no time in the examination of the history of slavery, or of the question, how far it is consistent with the natural rights of mankind. That it may have a lawful existence, at least by way of punishment for crimes, will not be doubted by any persons, who admit the general right of society to enforce the observance of its laws by adequate penalties. That it has existed in all ages of the world, and has been tolerated by some, encouraged by others, and sanctioned by most, of the enlightened and civilized nations of the earth in former ages, admits of no reasonable question. That it has interwoven itself into the municipal institutions of some countries, and forms the foundation of large masses of property in a portion of our own country, is known to all of us. Sitting, therefore, in an American court of judicature, I am not permitted to deny, that under some circumstances it may have a lawful existence; and that the practice may be justified by the condition, or wants, of society, or may form a part of the domestic policy of a nation. It would be unbecoming in me here to assert, that the state of slavery cannot have a legitimate existence, or that it stands condemned by the unequivocal testimony of the law of nations. But this concession carries us but a very short distance towards the decision of this cause. It is not, as the learned counsel for the government have justly stated, on account of the simple fact, that the traffic necessarily involves the enslavement of human beings, that it stands reprehended by the present sense of nations; but that it necessarily carries with it a breach of all the moral duties, of all the maxims of justice, mercy and humanity, and of the admitted rights, which independent Christian nations now hold sacred in their intercourse with each other. What is the fact as to the ordinary, nay, necessary course, of this trade? It begins in corruption, and plunder, and kidnapping. It creates and stimulates unholy wars for the purpose of making captives. It desolates whole villages and provinces for the purpose of seizing the young, the feeble, the defenceless, and the innocent. It breaks down all the ties of parent, and children, and family, and country. It shuts up all sympathy for human suffering and sorrows. It manacles the inoffensive females and the starving infants. It forces the brave to untimely death in defence of their humble homes and firesides, or drives them to despair and self-immolation. It stirs up the worst passions of the human soul, darkening the spirit of revenge, sharpening the greediness of avarice, brutalizing the selfish, envenoming the cruel, famishing the weak, and crushing to death the broken-hearted. This is but the beginning of the evils. Before the unhappy captives arrive at the destined market, where the traffic ends, one quarter part at least in the ordinary course of events perish in cold blood under the inhuman, or thoughtless treatment of their oppressors. Strong as these expressions may seem, and dark as is the colouring of this statement, it is short of the real calamities inflicted by this traffic. All the wars, that have desolated Africa for the last three centuries, have had their origin in the slave trade. The blood of thousands of her miserable children has stained her shores, or quenched the dying embers of her desolated towns, to glut the appetite of slave dealers. The ocean has received in its deep and silent bosom thousands more, who have perished from disease and want during their passage from their native homes to the foreign colonies. I speak not from vague rumours, or idle tales, but from authentic documents, and the known historical details of the traffic,—a traffic, that carries away at least 50,000 persons annually from their homes and their families, and breaks the hearts, and buries the hopes, and extinguishes the happiness of more than double that number. See state papers of congress for 1821; report on the slave trade, February 9, 1821, page 59. "There is," as one of the greatest of modern statesmen has declared, "something of horror in it, that surpasses all the bounds of imagination." Mr. Pitt's speech on the slave trade, in 1792. It is of this traffic, thus carried on, and necessarily carried on, beginning in lawless wars, and rapine, and kidnapping, and ending in disease, and death, and slavery,—it is of this traffic in the aggregate of its accumulated wrongs, that I would ask, if it be consistent with the law of nations? It is not by breaking up the elements of the case into fragments, and detaching them one from another, that we are to be asked of each separately, if the law of nations prohibits it. We are not to be told, that war is lawful, and slavery lawful, and plunder lawful, and the taking away of life is lawful, and the selling of human beings is lawful. Assuming that they are so under circumstances, it establishes nothing. It does not advance one jot to the support of the proposition, that a traffic, that involves them all, that is unnecessary, unjust, and inhuman, is countenanced by the eternal law of nature, on which rests the law of nations.

Now the law of nations may be deduced, first, from the general principles of right and justice, applied to the concerns of individuals, and thence to the relations and duties of nations; or, secondly, in things indifferent or questionable, from the customary observances and recognitions of civilized nations; or, lastly, from the conventional or positive law, that regulates the intercourse between states. What, therefore, the law of nations is, does not rest upon mere theory, but may be considered as modified by practice, or ascertained by the treaties of nations at different periods. It does not follow, therefore, that because a principle cannot be found settled by the consent or practice of nations at one time, it is to be concluded, that at no subsequent period the principle can be considered as incorporated into the public code of nations. Nor is it to be admitted, that no principle belongs to the law of nations, which is not universally recognised, as such, by all civilized communities, or even by those constituting, what may be called, the Christian states of Europe. Some doctrines, which we, as well as Great Britain, admit to belong to the law of nations, are of but recent origin and application, and have not, as yet, received any public or general sanction in other nations; and yet they are founded in such a just view of the duties and rights of nations, belligerent and neutral, that we have not hesitated to enforce them by the penalty of con-

fiscation. There are other doctrines, again, which have met the decided hostility of some of the European states, enlightened as well as powerful, such as the right of search, and the rule, that free ships do not make free goods, which, nevertheless, both Great Britain and the United States maintain, and in my judgment with unanswerable arguments, as settled rules in the law of prize, and scruple not to apply them to the ships of all other nations. And yet, if the general custom of nations in modern times, or even in the present age, recognized an opposite doctrine, it could not, perhaps, be affirmed, that that practice did not constitute a part, or, at least, a modification, of the law of nations. But I think it may be unequivocally affirmed, that every doctrine, that may be fairly deduced by correct reasoning from the rights and duties of nations, and the nature of moral obligation, may theoretically be said to exist in the law of nations; and unless it be relaxed or waived by the consent of nations, which may be evidenced by their general practice and customs, it may be enforced by a court of justice, whenever it arises in judgment. And I may go farther and say, that no practice whatsoever can obliterate the fundamental distinction between right and wrong, and that every nation is at liberty to apply to another the correct principle, whenever both nations by their public acts recede from such practice, and admits the injustice or cruelty of it.

Now in respect to the African slave trade, such as it has been described to be, and in fact is, in its origin, progress, and consummation, it cannot admit of serious question, that it is founded in a violation of some of the first principles, which ought to govern nations. It is repugnant to the great principles of Christian duty, the dictates of natural religion, the obligations of good faith and morality, and the eternal maxims of social justice. When any trade can be truly said to have these ingredients, it is impossible, that it can be consistent with any system of law, that purports to rest on the authority of reason or revelation. And it is sufficient to stamp any trade as interdicted by public law, when it can be justly affirmed, that it is repugnant to the general principles of justice and humanity. Now there is scarcely a single maritime nation of Europe, that has not in the most significant terms, in the most deliberate and solemn conferences, acts, or treaties, acknowledged the injustice and inhumanity of this trade; and pledged itself to promote its abolition. I need scarcely advert to the conferences at Vienna, at Aix-la-Chapelle, and at London, on this interesting subject, as they have been cited at the argument of this cause, and authenticated by our own government, to show what may be emphatically called the sense of Europe upon this point. France, in particular, at the conferences at Vienna, in 1815, engaged to use "all the means at her disposal, and to act in the employment of these means with all the zeal and perseverance due to so great and noble a cause" (the abolition of the slave trade). And accordingly, in the treaty of peace between her and Great Britain, France, expressing her concurrence without reserve in the sentiments of his Britannic majesty with respect to this traffic, admits it to be "repugnant to the principles of natural justice, and of the enlightened age, in which we live;" and, at a short period afterwards, the government of France informed the British government, that it had "issued directions in order, that on the part of France the traffic in slaves may cease from the present time everywhere and forever." The conduct and opinions of Great Britain, honorably and zealously, and I may add, honestly, as she has been engaged in promoting the universal abolition of the trade, are too notorious, to require a pointed enumeration. She has through her parliament expressed her abhorrence of the trade in the most marked terms, as repugnant to justice and humanity; she has punished it as a felony, when carried on by her subjects; and she has recognized through her judicial tribunals the doctrine, that it is repugnant to the law of nations. Our own country, too, has firmly and earnestly pressed forward in the same career. The trade has been reprobated and punished, as far as our authority extended, from a very early period of the government; and by a very recent statute, to mark at once its infamy and repugnance to the law of nations, it has been raised in the catalogue of public crimes to the bad eminence of piracy. I think, therefore, that I am justified in saying, that at the present moment the traffic is vindicated by no nation, and is admitted by almost all commercial nations as incurably unjust and inhuman. It appears to me, therefore, that in an American court of judicature, I am bound to consider the trade an offence against the universal law of society and in all cases, where it is not protected by a foreign government, to deal with it as an offence carrying with it the penalty of confiscation. And I cannot but think, notwithstanding the assertion at the bar to the contrary, that this doctrine is neither novel nor alarming. That it stands on principles of sound sense and general policy, and, above all, of moral justice. And I confess, that I should be somewhat startled, if any nation, sincerely anxious for the abolition, and earnest in its duty, should interpose its influence to arrest its universal adoption.

There is an objection urged against the doctrine, which is here asserted, that ought not to be passed over in silence; and that is, if the African slave trade is repugnant to the law of nations, no nation can rightfully permit its subjects to carry it on, or exempt them from obedience to that law; for it is said, that no nation can privilege itself to commit a crime against the law of nations by a mere municipal regulation of its own. In a sense the proposition is true, but not universally so. No nation has a right to infringe the law of nations, so as thereby to produce an injury to any other nation. But if it does, this is understood to be an injury, not against all nations, which all are bound or permitted to redress; but which concerns alone the nation injured. The independence of nations guarantees to each the right of guarding its own honor, and the morals and interests of its own subjects. No one has a right to sit in judgment generally upon the actions of another; at least to the extent of compelling its adherence to all the principles of justice and humanity in its domestic concerns. If a nation were to violate as to its own subjects in its domestic regulation the clearest principles of public law, I do not know, that that law has ever held them amenable to the tribunals of other nations for such conduct. It would be inconsistent with the equality and sovereignty of nations, which admit no common superior. No nation has ever yet pretended to be the custos morum of the whole world; and though abstractedly a particular regulation may violate the law of nations, it may sometimes, in the case of nations, be a wrong without a remedy. Then how stands judicial authority on the subject? It appears to me, speaking with all possible deference for those, who may entertain a different opinion, that the case of The Amedie (1 Act. 240, 1 Dod. 84, note) is directly in point; and, unless the principles there stated can be shaken, they must govern the case now in judgment. Sir Wm. Grant, in delivering the judgment of the court of appeals in The Amedie, after adverting to the former state of the British law on the subject of the African slave trade, uses the following language, which I quote the more readily, as I know not, how in so concise and luminous a manner to convey the sentiments, which on this subject I deliberately entertain. "But," says that eminent judge, "by the alteration, which has since taken place in our law, the question now stands upon very different grounds. We do now, and did at the time of this capture, take an interest in preventing that traffic, in which this ship was engaged. The slave trade has since been totally abolished in this country, and our legislature has declared, that the African slave trade is contrary to the principles of justice and humanity. Whatever opinion, as private individuals, we before might have entertained upon the nature of this trade, no court of justice could with propriety have assumed such a position, as the basis of any of its decisions, whilst it was permitted by our own laws. But we do now lay down as a principle, that this is a trade, which cannot, abstractedly, speaking, be said to have a legitimate existence. I say, abstractedly speaking, because we cannot legislate for other countries; nor has this country, a right to control any foreign legislature, that may think proper to dissent from this doctrine, and give permission to its subjects to prosecute this trade. We cannot certainly compel the subjects of other nations to observe any other, than the first and generally received principles of universal law. But thus far we are now entitled to act according to our law, and to hold that, prima facie, the trade is altogether illegal, and thus to throw on a claimant the burthen of proof, in order to shew, that by the particular law of his own country he is entitled to carry on this traffic. As the case now stands, we think, that no claimant can be heard in an application to a court of prize for the restoration of the human beings he carried unjustly to another country for the purpose of disposing of them as slaves. The consequence of making such a proof it is not now necessary to determine; but where it cannot be made, the party must be considered to have failed in establishing his asserted right. We are of opinion, upon the whole, that persons engaged in such a trade cannot, upon principles of universal law, have a right to be heard upon a claim of this nature in any court."

Such is the doctrine sanctioned by the highest prize court known to British jurisprudence. I consider it, as the high court of admiralty has considered it, as establishing the principle, that any trade contrary to the general law of nations, although not tending to, or accompanied with, any infraction of the belligerent rights of that country, whose tribunals are called to consider it, may subject the vessel employed in that trade to confiscation; and it matters not in what stage of the employment, whether in the inception or the prosecution, or the consummation of it, the vessel is arrested. The Fortuna, 1 Dod. 81, 85, 86. It has been said, that this doctrine first arose in a case of capture, jure belli, and was applied by a court of prize. Be it so; but the doctrine is not limited in its terms or purport to cases of this sort. The capture, as a belligerent capture, was tortious and without any reasonable cause; and the court admitted, that there had been no violation of belligerent rights. But it applied the doctrine upon principles of universal law, and asserted, that it might be applied to a claim of such a nature in any court. The Fortuna, Id., and The Donna Marianna, Id. 91, in which the doctrine was followed, were also cases of capture; but although it is pretty clear, that there were some lurking doubts as to the propriety of the doctrine in the mind of the court, there was not the slightest attempt to place it upon any ground, that limited it to the prize jurisdiction. In the case of The Diana, Id. 95, which, at the interval of nearly a year afterwards, called again for the application of the general doctrine, no such distinction was even alluded to, although that was clearly, in the judgment of the court itself, a case on the instance side of the court, where condemnation was directly sought on an information for a forfeiture for an asserted employment in the slave trade. It turned out upon the investigation of the facts, that the vessel was Swedish; and, as such, upon the supposition, that Sweden permitted the traffic to her subjects, restitution was decreed. But the court unequivocally admitted the propriety of applying the doctrine to the case, if the Swedish law were proved to be deficient. I think, then, I stand firm upon the position, that up to the period of these adjudications, no distinction, like that now contended for, was in the contemplation of the court; and certainly no such distinction can in reason be applied to the doctrine in The Amedie. Whatever, indeed, may be the extent of the belligerent right of search and visitation, it does not authorize a subsequent capture, unless for just cause of suspicion; and if the search be in this respect unproductive, it cannot be, that the capture is less tortious on account of the exercise of this right, than it would be, if no such right existed. The capture is just as wrongful, as a seizure in time of peace would be, and no more. It violates the right of the foreign ship just as much, and no more, than such a seizure; and if, notwithstanding such a tortious capture, the party may avail himself of a ground of condemnation for the breach of universal law, independent of belligerent rights, he may, for the same reason, avail himself of it in case of such a tortious seizure. In truth, however, the law looks not to niceties of this sort. If for any cause, precedent or subsequent, known at the beginning or known at the end, the property is condemned, the party is justified and retroactively for all purposes the capture, or seizure, or forcible possession, call it what you may, is deemed rightful and bona fide.

The case of Le Louis, 2 Dod. 210, which followed after a period of almost four years, has been pressed upon the attention of the court, and certainly is entitled to the most respectful and cautious examination. I will not yield to any person in reverence for the profound learning and talents of the accomplished judge, by whom that decision was pronounced. His judgments have been justly the admiration of Europe and America; and will be read for instruction, for beauty of illustration, for felicity of style, and for unambitious, but lofty principles, long after their illustrious author is gathered to the fathers, who have enlightened and improved mankind; as long indeed, in my humble belief, as the common language of his and our country shall indicate to mankind our common lineage. Still, however, it is my duty, painful and responsible as it may be, and with whatever hesitation and humility, when I am led to differ from other minds, with which I have not the least title to be brought in comparison; I say, it is my duty to follow the dictates of my own judgment in all cases, where my judicial conscience is not already bound by the decisions of the highest appellate court of the government, under which I sit. The case of Le Louis may be distinguished from that before the court in several circumstances. The seizure was made at a time, when no public ordinance of France prohibited the slave trade, and before the recent discussions at Aix-la-Chapelle. Upon the very face of the information the vessel was admitted to be French, and seized as such, and condemnation was sought upon two grounds—First, the resistance of the right of search of a British cruiser in a time of peace; and secondly, because the trade was contrary to the laws of France and the law of nations. The whole ground, therefore, excepting that of forfeiture under the law of nations, was removed from the cause, for no such right of search in point of law existed, and no such law of France in point of fact existed. And it is perfectly clear upon the doctrine of the other cases already cited, that it was necessary, that a prohibitory law of France should concur with the public law of nations, before a foreign tribunal could apply the penalty of confiscation. The cause was therefore on its merits correctly decided in perfect harmony with the former cases. But the learned judge, in a most elaborate and masterly manner, discusses the general question, and comes to the conclusion, that the African slave trade is not a crime against the law of nations; and that the seizure of a foreign ship, engaged in that trade, although it is prohibited by the nation, to which she belongs, cannot be rightfully made by a British cruiser, and that a suit for condemnation of such a ship cannot be rightfully maintained in a British court.

The first observation that I am called upon to make respecting this case is, that I do not find, that the court any where attempts to distinguish between this and the preceding cases, by limiting the doctrine of rejecting claims for illegality of traffic to cases of capture during war, or suits in the prize jurisdiction. Nor does it occur to me, meaning to speak with the greatest diffidence of my own judgment, that a distinction of that nature would be quite consistent with what fell from the court in the case of The Diana, 1 Dod. 95. In the next place, I find myself utterly at a loss to comprehend, how the fundamental doctrine of the case of The Amedie, and the other cases already cited, that the slave trade, abstractedly speaking, cannot have a legal existence, and that it is repugnant to the principles of universal law, and the law of nations, can consist with the unequivocal denial of the same doctrine in the case of Le Louis. I find myself driven, therefore, to the conclusion, that the last case is meant silently to abandon and repudiate the whole doctrine, on which the former cases rest. In this conflict of authority and learning, of matured and deeply weighed decisions, it is no rashness

to follow those, which on the whole seem built on the most solid grounds of justice, public policy, and principle. In the struggle, which my own mind has undergone upon this occasion, I cannot escape from the conclusion, that the reasoning of Sir William Grant has not been overturned, even if it should be thought in any measure shaken; and that if I were to adjudge otherwise, it would be following another authority against the dictates of my deliberate judgment. And I think I may call in aid the opinion of a court of common law, though perhaps not, in general, the best qualified court to entertain the discussion of questions of national law, to show, that the doctrine of the former cases meets the entire approbation of such tribunals. I allude to the case of Madrazo v. Willes, 3 Barn. & Ald. 353, and particularly the opinion of Mr. Justice Best, where, though single expressions may appear to militate with my own views on this subject, the fair result of the opinions stands in perfect consistency with the doctrine of The Amedie.

But supposing, that the opinions already expressed by the court are as erroneous, as the counsel for the claimant contends them to be, and that the law of nations is to be exclusively derived from the practice of nations, and the practice is in favor of the African slave trade; still there remains another obstacle to the recovery of the property by the claimants, which must be displaced before his title is unimpeachable. And that is, that the African slave trade stands prohibited by the positive municipal regulations of France. This has not been denied at the argument, at least to the extent of reaching a case, where the trade is attempted to be carried on to a French colony, which is exactly the case before the court, if any slave voyage was intended by the owners. The French ordinance of the 8th of January, 1817, comes up to this point, and purports to be made in execution of the obligations by treaty to abolish the slave trade, however inadequate it may be justly deemed for this purpose. But I think, independently of this document, (which is admitted to exist) by the general principles already asserted, the onus probandi rests on the claimants to establish the legitimate existence of the trade in France; and more especially since her recent declarations in the face of all Europe, that she had caused it to be everywhere abolished. They have not pretended to offer any proof on this point; and the argument of their counsel proceeds upon the supposition of an actual prohibition.

It is said, that the cognizance of penalties and forfeitures for breaches of municipal regulations exclusively belongs to the tribunals of the nation, by whom they are enacted. And this, in a general sense, with reference to the right to originate proceedings for the sole purpose of enforcing such penalties and forfeitures, may be true. But that any court may take notice of the laws of a foreign country, whether civil or penal, which come incidentally before it in the exercise of its general jurisdiction over persons or property, can admit of as little dispute. We know, that the lex loci is often applied in courts of justice to enforce rights and redress wrongs; and that contracts and titles, which cannot have a legal existence in the country, where they have their origin, are held void every where. In respect to mere municipal regulations, the general rule certainly is, that courts do not take notice of them with a view to their direct enforcement. It is often said, that no country takes notice of the revenue laws of a foreign country, or holds itself bound to repudiate commercial transactions, which violate them. But this is a rule adopted from a motive of policy or comity; and is not an essential ingredient in any system of the law of nations. If any nation were disposed to discountenance any smuggling in violation of the laws of a foreign country, and in cases coming regularly before its own courts were to refuse to recognize any rights of property founded on such violation, I am not able to perceive, what just ground of complaint the offended nation could have against such conduct. It seems to me, that it might with more justice complain of the refusal to enforce such laws, and to discountenance such violations. But where a title to property originates in what a nation deems in its own subjects a public crime, more especially if it be an aggravated crime founded on fraud and rapine; and it finds, that another nation deems it a crime of a like nature, and prohibits it as such, and confiscates the property of its subjects engaged in the commission of it, I do not perceive, why such property, so polluted by crimes, should, if it falls into the custody of a court of the former nation, be so sacred from judicial touch, that it must be restored to the wrong-doer. And I would ask, where is the authority, that requires such a court to act in this manner, when the public policy of its own, as well as of the foreign, government is avowedly engaged in endeavoring to suppress that crime? If in a case before this court, acting in rem, a title to property, founded on theft or other municipal crime, or on a fraud committed in a foreign country, were set up, until my judicial conscience is better instructed, I should have extreme difficulty in recognising such a title, if the property was once legally in the custody of the court.

In the case now before me, on the face of the libel, the court certainly has jurisdiction; for if the allegation, as to the property being engaged in the slave trade against our laws, be well founded, it justifies condemnation. But jurisdiction does not depend upon the event of the suit, but upon the right to entertain the suit, and proceed by inquiry to settle its merits. In this respect the case before me stands differently from that of Le Louis. It is, therefore, in the investigation of the merits of this case, that I am met by the title of French subjects to the property; and that title, if the vessel be engaged in the slave trade, is a title connected with a crime against France, and which, by French law, becomes forfeited. In this posture of the cause, it does not occur to me, that any principle of general justice, or of national comity, or of universal law, requires this court to surrender up the property to the claimants, however well it might be disposed to surrender it to the sovereign of France. If, therefore, this ground alone were before the court, as at present advised, I should incline to reject the claim for the breach of this municipal law of France, which our country recognises as a breach, not of mere positive law, but of the immutable principles of justice.

If I am asked, what would be the predicament of this cause under the views, which have been suggested, I answer, that if the vessel be not American, engaged in a traffic contravening our laws, Lieut. Stockton and his associates can have no title to seek condemnation for any interest of their own, for a share in the forfeiture accrues to them only, when the case is reached by our laws; and the libel, so far as it is founded on these allegations, must be dismissed. Then as to the claimants, their claim being rejected, there would be no person judicially before the court to claim restitution. The property, then, must either be condemned to the United States generally, as unclaimed property, or forfeited property, upon principles analogous to those adopted in The Etrusco, 4 C. Rob. Adm. 262. note 1, or it must remain in the custody of the court, to be delivered up to the sovereign of France, if he should choose to interpose a claim, or assert a right to proceed against it in his own courts for the supposed forfeiture. It appears to me, that the latter is the true course. It enables the foreign sovereign to exercise complete jurisdiction over the case, if he shall prefer to have it remitted to his own courts for adjudication. It enforces the policy, common to both nations, of repressing an odious traffic, which is denounced by both. It makes our own country, not a principal, but an auxiliary, in enforcing the interdict of France, and subserves the great interests of universal justice. I am not aware of any obstacle in the constitution of a court of admiralty, proceeding in rem, to the adoption of such a practice; and I am greatly mistaken, if it does not carry in its bosom the seeds of peace and conciliation, instead of animosity and recrimination.

Thus far I have proceeded in the cause without reference to any other claims, but those asserted in the original libel and answer. But at a late period in this cause, by direction of the president, a suggestion has been filed by the district attorney, expressing a willingness to yield up the vessel to the French government, or its consular agent, for the purpose of remitting the cause for ultimate adjudication to the domestic forum of the sovereign of the owners. To a suggestion of this nature this court is bound to listen with the most respectful attention. It is understood to be, not a direction to the court, for that is beyond the reach of executive authority, but an intimation of the wishes of the government, so far as its own rights are concerned, to spare the court any farther investigation. If it had seemed fit to all the parties, whose interests are before the court, to agree to the course held out by this suggestion, it would have relieved my mind from a weight of responsibility, which has most heavily pressed upon it. But the French claimants resist this course, and require, that the property should be delivered over to their personal possession, and not to the possession of their sovereign. Under such circumstances this court must follow the duty prescribed to it by law, independently of any wishes of our own government or of France. I have been compelled, therefore, reluctantly to travel over the whole merits of the cause, and to decide it with reference to the French owners upon the great principles, on which it has been argued.

After listening to the very able, eloquent, and learned arguments delivered at the bar on this occasion—after weighing the authorities, which bear on the case, with mature deliberation,—after reflecting anxiously and carefully upon the general principles, which may be drawn from the law of nations to illustrate or confirm them, I have come to the conclusion, that the slave trade is a trade prohibited by universal law, and by the law of France, and that, therefore, the claim of the asserted French owners must be rejected. That claim being rejected, I feel myself at perfect liberty, with the express consent of our own government, to decree, that the property be delivered over to the consular agent of the king of France, to be dealt with according to his own sense of duty and right. No one can be more sensible than myself of the real magnitude and intricacy of the questions involved in this cause. It becomes me, therefore, to speak with great distrust and diffidence of my own judgment respecting its merits. But I think, I have a right to say, that the American courts of judicature are not hungry after jurisdiction in foreign causes, or desirous to plunge into the endless perplexities of foreign jurisprudence. If I could have had my choice of causes, this class is not that, which would have been selected from peculiar favour. But it is to be remembered, that while the court is not rashly to engage in asserting jurisdiction over foreign causes from the odium, which is justly attached to a traffic conceived in atrocious and unfeeling cruelty, and stained and sealed with blood; it has also a public duty to perform, from which it dare not shrink, to pronounce its own judgment of the law, and to leave it to more wise and learned minds to correct any errors, into which it may inadvertently have fallen.

Polydore v. Prince
19 Fed. Cas. 950, No. 11, 527 (D. Mass., 1837)

This was a libel for an assault and battery committed by the master on a passenger, on a voyage from Guadaloupe to Portland. It appeared from the evidence that the libellant was a slave in Guadaloupe, that he was put on board the vessel by his master, Mons. Bercier, in company with his son, Eugene, a youth of about seventeen years of age, whom he was to attend during his residence in this country, as his servant. One morning, some days after they had been at sea, the captain ordered Polydore to clean out a hen-coop, in which there were some live fowls. Polydore refused, and the captain in his answer, says, that he behaved otherwise insolently to him, and the testimony of some of the witnesses confirms his statement. But it is also in proof, that Polydore did not understand a word of English, nor did the master understand much more of French. It is also alleged by the master that in consequence of his taking Polydore at a low rate of passage money, he receiving sixty francs for Polydore and one hundred and fifty for Eugene, that Polydore was to perform such service in relation to Bercier, and also such service on board the vessel as might be properly required of him; that the fowls were for Eugene, and that it was Polydore's business to attend to them. But there is no proof in support of the first part of this allegation, and it appears in point of fact, that the fowls instead of being exclusively for Eugene, were used as a common stock on board the vessel. Upon the refusal of Polydore to do the service that he was ordered, the captain gave him a pretty severe flogging with a piece of dry twisted cowhide; some days afterwards, the cowhide was abstracted from the cabin and not to be found; on the captain's inquiring for it, he was told that Polydore had taken it and thrown it overboard, when in fact it had been taken and secreted by Eugene for the purpose of bringing it to this country and exhibiting it in court, as the instrument with which Polydore had been flogged. Both Eugene and Polydore concurred in deceiving the captain. The captain then gave Polydore another flogging with a small rope.

WARE, District Judge. Several objections have been taken and learnedly argued by the counsel for the respondent, to the libellant's right to maintain this action.

Another objection has been raised and learnedly argued by the respondent's counsel, which requires a more grave and mature consideration. It is founded on the supposed personal incapacity of the libellant to maintain any action in a court of justice, under any circumstances. It is alleged in the answer as a substantive ground of defence, and the fact is admitted on the other side that the libellant, in his own country, is a slave, and as such, incapable of appearing as a party in any court of justice; and it is contended that this personal incapacity upon the received principles of the jus gentium, or at least on the principles of national comity, follows him into whatever country he may voluntarily go or be carried by his master. The argument is, that the institution of personal servitude, however contrary it may be to natural right, is an institution admitted and acknowledged by the law of nations; that every nation having the exclusive right to regulate its own internal polity, and to determine the personal state or capacity of its members, all other nations are bound by the jus gentium, or by national comity, to take notice of, and recognize this personal status as it would be recognized in the forum of their original domicil, while they remain members of that community; that personal qualities impressed upon them by the law of their original domicil as to their civil capacities, or incapacities, travel with them wherever they go, until their legal connection with that country is dissolved.

I have stated the position of the counsel in its broadest and most comprehensive terms, and it is not to be disguised that it involves questions of serious difficulty, upon which there is no little diversity of opinion among the most eminent jurists, and on which there is not certainly an entire agreement in the practice of different nations. The whole subject is examined with all the learning which belongs to it by Mr. Justice Story, in his very learned and profound treatise on the Conflict of Laws (chapter 4). It may there be seen how many curious and perplexing questions may arise out of the conflicting laws of different nations, relating to the state or capacity of persons; questions which must often occur for discussion in the forum, and judicial decision, in au age of such constant intercourse and intercommunication for the purpose of business and pleasure among all civilized and commercial nations as the present. It may also be seen how much diversity and contrariety of opinion exists among the most celebrated and learned jurists on this subject. It is a large chapter, says Lord Stowell, and full of many difficult questions, that treats of such diversities in the writings of the civilians.

The general doctrine of foreign jurists seems to be, that the state of the person, that is, his legal capacity to do, or not to do, certain acts is to be determined by the law of his domicil, so that if he has by that law, the free administration of his goods, or the right to maintain an action in a court of justice there, he has the same capacity everywhere; and if that capacity is denied to him by the law of his domicil, it is denied everywhere; that the laws determining the civil qualities of the person, called by the foreign jurists personal statutes, follow the person wherever he goes, as the shadow follows the body, and adhere to him like the color of the skin which is impressed by the climate. Personal statutes are those which relate primarily to the person, and determine the civil privileges and disabilities, the legal capacity or incapacity of the individual, and do not affect his goods, but as they are accessory to the person. Such are those which relate to birth, legitimacy, freedom, majority or minority, capacity to enter into contracts, to make a will, to be a party to an action in a court of justice, with others of the like kind. Repertoire de Jurisprudence, mot "Statut." According to this principle, a person who is a major or a minor, a slave or a freeman, has, or has not a capacity to appear as a party to an action in a court of justice, stare in judicio, in his own country, has the same capacities and disabilities wherever he may be. The Code Napoleon has erected what seems to be the prevailing doctrine among the continental civilians into a positive law. "The laws concerning the state or capacity of persons govern Frenchmen, even when residing in a foreign country." Code Civile, art. 3. If this general principle is to be received without qualification, it would seem to decide the present case at once, for it is admitted that in Guadaloupe where the libellant has his domicil, he can maintain no action in a court of justice. But though the principle is stated in these broad and general terms, yet when it is brought to a practical application in its various modifications, in the actual business of life, it is found to be qualified by so many exceptions and limitations, that the principle itself is stripped of a great part of its imposing authority. No nation, it is believed, ever gave it effect in its practical jurisprudence, in its whole extent. Among these personal statutes, for which this ubiquity is claimed, are those which formerly over the whole of Europe, and still over a large part of it, divide the people into different castes, as nobles and plebeians, clergy and laity. The favored classes were entitled to many personal privileges and immunities particularly beneficial and honorable to themselves. It cannot be supposed that these immunities would be allowed in a country which admitted no such distinctions in its domestic policy. If a bill in equity were filed in one of our courts against an English nobleman temporarily resident here, would he be allowed to put in an answer upon his honor, and not under oath, because he was entitled to that personal privilege in the forum of his domicil? I apprehend not. In like manner the disqualification and incapacities, by which persons may be affected by the municipal institutions of their own country, will not be recognized against them in countries by whose laws no such disqualifications are acknowledged. In England a person who has incurred the penalties of a premunire, or has suffered the process of outlawry against him, can maintain no action for the recovery of a debt, or the redress of a personal wrong. But would it be contended that because he could not maintain an action in the forum of his domicil he could have no remedy on a contract entered into, or a tort done to him within our jurisdiction? The reasons upon which an action is denied him in the forum of his domicil are peculiar to that country, and have no application within another jurisdiction. The incapacity is created for causes that relate entirely to the domestic and internal polity of that country. As soon as he has passed beyond its territorial limits, the reason of his incapacity ceases to operate, and in justice the incapacity should cease also.

Every nation has a perfect right to establish for itself its own forms of internal polity, and to determine the state and condition, the civil capacities and incapacities of its own members. Besides these personal laws determining the state and condition of individuals which are founded on natural relations and qualities, and such as are universally recognized among civilized communities, as those of parent and child, those resulting from marriage, from intellectual imbecility, and the like they may and in point of fact do establish distinctions which are not founded in nature, but relate only to the peculiarities of their own social organization, to their own municipal laws, and to the artificial forms of society, which are established among themselves. Now it is freely admitted that other nations are bound by the jus gentium to admit the validity of all those personal statutes of other communities establishing such distinctions among their members, whether natural or artificial, to a certain extent. Their validity will be admitted, and they will be enforced by the tribunals of other countries, as to acts which are done, and rights which are acquired within the territorial limits of the community where these laws are estab-

lished. There they have a legal, and other nations are bound to admit, certainly as a general rule, a rightful authority. But it is by no means so clear that those personal distinctions which are not founded in nature, and are the result of mere civil institutions, can be allowed to accompany them, and give them personal immunities, or affect them with personal incapacities in other countries in which they may be temporarily resident or transiently passing, whose laws acknowledge no such distinction. The law of the place where a person is for the time being, as to acts done, or rights acquired within that jurisdiction, it would seem, ought to prevail so far as his civil rights depend on his personal status. For these personal statutes, establishing distinctions between individuals as to their civil qualities, have a direct relation to public order, and, as is remarked by one of the most eminent living jurists in continental Europe, "every person who establishes his dwelling in a country, or it may be added who is transiently within it, is bound to conform to the measures which the local law prescribes, in the interest of public decorum and good morals." Merl. Repert. "Effet Retroactif," sect. 3, § 2, art. 5. The observation is applied to the case of a married woman. If by the law of her domicil she is authorized to make valid contracts, and to maintain an action in a court of justice in her own name without the authorization of her husband, and she removes to a country by whose laws this power is denied to married women, she will not carry with her into her new residence the capacity to contract, to plead, and to be impleaded in a court of justice as she is allowed by the law of her domicil, this capacity being denied by the local law, as offensive to good-manners. If a person happens to transfer his residence to a country where the same personal distinctions are established, as are allowed in his own domestic forum, it is not intended to be denied, but that the tribunals of this country may allow him his personal immunities or affect him with the personal incapacity of his domicil; but it will, I apprehend, be according to the local law, and not according to the law of his domicil. If a Turkish or Hindoo husband were travelling in this country with his wife, or temporarily resident here, we should, without hesitation, acknowledge the relation of husband and wife between them; but the legal pre-eminence of the husband as to acts done here, would be admitted only to the extent that the marital rights are recognized by our laws, and not as they are recognized by the law of his domicil. If a Roman father, or a father from any country which had adopted the Roman law of paternal power, were travelling in this country with a minor child, we should acknowledge the relation of parent and child, but we should admit, I presume, as a general rule, the exercise of the paternal power no further than as it is authorized by our own law. If a foreigner, in whose country slavery is established, were temporarily resident in Virginia, where slavery also exists, and had brought with him a slave as a servant, a court sitting in Virginia might, I suppose, recognize the relation of master and slave, because that is a relation known to the local law, but it would limit the exercise of the master's authority over his slave, by their own law, and not by the law of the master's domicil.

It is among the first maxims of the jus gentium that the legislative power of every nation is confined to its own territorial limits. This is a principle which results directly and necessarily from the independence of nations. Whatever may be the nature of the law, whether it relates purely to persons and their civil qualities, or to things, it can, proprio vigore, have no force within the territorial limits of another nation. It follows that the peculiar personal status, as to his capacities or incapacities, which an individual derives from the law of his domicil, and which are imparted only by that law, is suspended when he gets beyond the sphere in which that law is in force. And when he passes into another jurisdiction his personal status becomes immediately affected by a new law, and he has those personal capacities only which the local law allows. The civil capacities and incapacities with which he is affected by the law of his domicil, cannot avail either for his benefit or to his prejudice, any further than as they are coincident with those recognized by the local law, or as that community may, on principles of national comity, choose to adopt the foreign law. Though the civilians, as has been observed, generally, hold that the law of the domicil should govern as to the personal status, it is by no means true that they are universally agreed. Voët, one of the most eminent, of whom it has been said that by his clearness and logic he merits the title of the geometer of jurisprudence (Merl. Quest. de Droit Confession, § 2, note 1), after stating that such is the opinion of the majority, "plurium opinio," gives his own opinion in decisive terms, that personal statutes, as well as those relating to things, are limited in their operation to the country by which they are established; and he supports his opinion by the authority of the Roman law, as well as by that plain and obvious axiom of the jus gentium, that the legislative power of every government is confined to its own territorial limits. Ad Pand. lib. 1, tit. 4, pt. 2, notes 5, 7, 8. Gail, who has been styled the Papinian of Germany, maintains the same opinion in terms equally positive. Pract. Obs. lib. 8, Obs. 122, note 11.

The inconveniences which would result from a practical adoption of the principle that the law of the domicil must prevail, which determines the personal status of the individual, wherever he may be, would be found to be very great. If we admit that a foreigner has all those personal capacities and civil qualities in this country which the law of his domicil allows, to be consistent and follow out the principle we must adopt all those subsidiary laws of his domicil which regulate and protect him in the enjoyment of his personal status. If, for example, we acknowledge the relation of master and slave, our law should, in consistency, arm the master with the authority to govern his slave, with the power of disposing of his person and labor, which he enjoys by the law of his own country. It would be a mockery to acknowledge the relation of master and slave and to deny all the legal consequences which that relation imports. If we adopt the artificial distinctions of other nations with regard to their subjects, when they are temporarily resident among us, it would seem that we must also adopt that part of their laws which regulate those artificial relations, and the rights and duties which result from them. Natural relations of foreigners, and such as are established by our own domestic institutions, we recognize in foreigners who are temporarily resident among us; but the rights and obligations which flow from them must, as a general rule at least, be determined by our own law, and be enforced by such means only as the local law allows. But those merely artificial distinctions, those capacities and disqualifications of mere positive institution, established by different communities among their members, which are not founded in nature but which relate to their own domestic economy, their municipal institutions, and their peculiar social organization, cannot be admitted to follow them into other nations in whose laws such distinctions are unknown, without disturbing the whole order of society, and introducing into communities privileged castes of persons, each governed to a considerable extent by different laws and affected by personal privileges peculiar to themselves, and totally at variance with the habits, social order, and the laws of the community among whom they reside.

I have thus far considered the subject as it was presented in one branch of the argument, as purely a question of the jus gentium, to which the same considerations will apply whether it be raised in one country or another, and I come to the conclusion that the libellant is not disqualified from maintaining an action for a personal tort committed within our jurisdiction, merely because he is by the laws of his own country rendered incapable of maintaining an action in the forum of his domicil. And that conclusion will be fortified by recurring to our own domestic jurisprudence. It is stated by Mr. Justice Story as one of the rules which appear to be best established by the jurisprudence of this country and England, that personal disqualifications, not arising from the law of nature but from the principles of the positive or customary law of a foreign country, are not generally regarded in other countries where the like disqualifications do not exist. Confl. Laws, 97. It is now fully settled in England, though it was once a doubtful question, that if a minor, who is disqualified from entering into the marriage contract without the consent of his guardian, goes into Scotland, where a minor has that capacity without such consent, and is married conformably to the laws of Scotland, the contract will be held valid and binding by the law of England. Compton v. Bearscroft, Bull. N. P. 115. The same principle is fully established in this country. 2 Kent, Comm. 92, 93; Story, Confl. Laws, 115, 116; Medway v. Needham, 16 Mass. 157; Inhabitants of West Cambridge v. Inhabitants of Lexington, 1 Pick. 506; Putnam v. Putnam, 8 Pick. 433. And though the considerations on which such marriages have been held valid in the domestic forum of the parties, where there has been a studied evasion of the law of their domicil, is the hardship and the mischief which would arise to society by bastardizing the issue of such marriages, yet it is not the less a distinct recognition of the principle that the legal capacity of a person to do an act depends on the law of the place where the act is done. Huber (De Conflictu Legum, 1–8) denies that the magistrate in the forum of the domicil is bound by the jus gentium to admit the validity of such marriages in direct evasion of the law of the parties' own country, yet no doubt can be entertained that they would be held valid in every other forum. And in a case where two British subjects, being minors, were in France for the purpose of education, and intermarried there, it was held that the validity of the marriage, and of course the capacity of the parties to enter into the contract, was to be determined by the law of France, and not by that of England, although the English domicil remained unchanged, and the marriage being a nullity by the law of France, was held to be void in England. Confl. Laws, 77; 2 Hagg. Consist. 407, 408. It has been decided in Massachusetts, after the most deliberate consideration, that a person who has been convicted of an infamous crime which rendered him incapable of being received as a witness in the country where the conviction took place, is a competent witness when in another jurisdiction. Com. v. Green, 17 Mass. 515. This is another application of the general principle that the personal status of an individual is to be determined by the law of the place where he is, as to acts done within that jurisdiction, and that the civil incapacities which attach to him in one country do not follow him into another. By the law of France a man does not attain to the age of legal majority until the age of twenty-five. If a Frenchman entered into a contract in this state, where the age of major-

ity is twenty-one, between the ages of twenty-one and twenty-five would he be allowed to avoid it on the plea of minority? The supreme court of Louisiana has said that in such a case the contract would be binding, and that the capacity of the person would depend on the law of the place where the contract was made, and not on that of the person's domicil. Confl. Laws, 73; Saul v. His Creditors, 7 Mart. [N. S.] 596. And though that court does not appear to have a settled opinion on the general question how far the personal status of an individual, as it is fixed by the law of his domicil, may be changed by the law of the place where the act is done, it is apprehended that the opinion here expressed would be followed in this state.

But the clearest and most distinct recognition of the principle that the civil capacities and incapacities of an individual are to be determined by the law of the place where the person is, and not by that of his domicil, is found in the decisions upon the very subject which is involved in this case—that of slavery. It was decided in 1772, in Sommersett's Case, that a slave who was carried by his master to England, from any of the colonies, became free as soon as he stepped on English ground. 1 Black. 425, note; Loftt, 1; 11 State Tr. 340. A similar decision, some years after, was made in Scotland. 2 Hagg. Adm. 118. It is supposed, indeed, that a different rule prevailed before that decision. It is said that the traffic in slaves had for a long series of years been as public and notorious in London as in the colonies, and that the legality of it had been sustained by the most eminent lawyers in the kingdom. The Slave Grace, 2 Hagg. Adm. 105–114. However that may be, the law as it was then declared, has never since been brought into doubt; and whether the real grounds of the decision are to be found, as intimated by Lord Stowell, in the "increased refinement of the sentiments and manners of the age," or in the maxims of the ancient common law relating to villanage (2 Hagg. Adm. 109), it seems to me that it may be well vindicated upon those principles of the jus gentium which have already been frequently mentioned, and which are indicated by Lord Stowell in another part of the same opinion. "The entire change of the legal character of individuals, produced by a change of local situation, is far from being a novelty in the law. A residence in a new country introduces a change of legal condition, which imposes rights and obligations totally inconsistent with the former rights and obligations of the same persons. Persons bound by particular contracts which restrain their liberty, debtors, apprentices, and others, lose their character and condition for the time, when they reside in another country, and are entitled as persons totally free, though they return to their original servitude and obligations upon coming back to the country they had quitted." 2 Hagg. Adm. 113. But if the decision in Sommersett's Case did not entirely approve itself to the judgment of that eminent magistrate, we may set against his doubts the opinion of another learned judge, although he also may be thought to trace the decision to the improved moral perceptions of the age, and the more full development of the principles of natural equity and universal justice, than to any ancient maxims of the common law, considered as a mere municipal code. "It is matter of pride to me," says Mr. Justice Best, "to recollect that while economists and politicians were recommending to the legislature the protection of this traffic, and senators were framing statutes for its promotion, and declaring it a benefit to the country, the judges of the land, above the age in which they lived, standing on the high ground of natural right, and disdaining the lower doctrine of expediency, declared that slavery was inconsistent with the genius of the English constitution, and that human beings could not be the subject-matter of property. As a lawyer, I speak of that early determination, when a different doctrine was prevailing in the senate, with a considerable degree of professional pride." Forbes v. Cochrane, 2 Barn. & C. 448. But to whatever cause is to be ascribed this change of the common law of England, if change it was, it has since that time been considered the settled law, that a slave on being introduced into England becomes free. And the law as it was then declared by Lord Mansfield, is believed to be generally adopted by the non-slaveholding states, in this country. Confl. Laws, 92; Case of Francisco, 9 Am. Jur. 490. The question was very fully considered by the supreme court of Massachusetts, in the recent Case of the Slave Med (Com. v. Aves, 18 Pick. 193; Aug., 1836), and it was decided, that a slave on coming into that state became free, except in a case falling within the provisions of the constitution of the United States, and the act of congress of Feb. 12, 1793, by which provision is made for delivering up persons who are held to labor or service in one of the United States on their escaping into another. If the owner voluntarily brings his slave into the state, the case does not come within the provisions of the law, and he becomes free. The same doctrine was held by Mr. Justice Washington in the case of Butler v. Hooper [Case No. 2,241], and again in Ex parte Simmons [Id. 12,863]. And it appears from the cases of Lunsford v. Coquillon, 2 Mart. [N. S.] 404, and Rankin v. Lydia, 2 A. K. Marsh. 470, that the principle has been fully recognized in Louisiana and Kentucky, that the relation of master and slave is founded exclusively on municipal law for which the courts in those states do not claim any extra-territorial force.

All these cases stand upon the principle that slavery, and with it as a necessary consequence, all the civil incapacities which are peculiar to that servile state, depend entirely on the local law. It follows of course that when a slave passes into a country, by whose laws slavery is not recognized, his civil condition is changed from a state of servitude, to that of freedom, and he becomes invested with those civil capacities which the law of the place imparts to all who stand in the same category. It is, indeed, said by Chief Justice Shaw, in delivering the opinion of the court, in the Case of the Slave Med, that "slaves in such case become free, not so much because any alteration is made in their status or condition, as because there is no law which will warrant, but there are laws, if they choose to avail themselves of them, which prohibit their forcible detention, or forcible removal." If by this is meant there is no change in the personal state of a slave in relation to the law of the country he has left, it may well be admitted to be correct. The law of that country, notwithstanding he is for the time withdrawn from its direct and immediate control, would hold him to be a slave until he acquired his freedom in some of the forms of emancipation known to that law. His mere transit into a country whose law declared him free, within its jurisdictional limits would not per se liberate him from the incapacities and obligations resulting from the law of his domicil within the legitimate sphere of that law's operation, and if he were to return to that country the condition of servitude would reattach to him precisely as when he left it. So it was decided by Lord Stowell, in the Case of the Slave Grace, and the same principle is distinctly established by the case of Williams v. Brown, 3 Bos. & P. 69. But it by no means follows that because the law of his domicil holds him to be a slave, he has not, while within a jurisdiction which declares him to be free, all the faculties which belong to a state of freedom. It is difficult to understand what the law does, by declaring him free, if it does not invest him with the rights and capacities of a free man; and if it does, it confers upon him a personal state very different from that of slavery; and there is no absurdity or contradiction in supposing a man to be a free man in one country and a slave in another. Both result from the same principle, the absolute supremacy of the laws of every state within its own territorial limits. And though Lord Stowell rather sarcastically remarks, that the law of England, by adopting this principle, puts the liberty of a man, as it were, into a parenthesis, it is nothing different from what occurs in many other cases, in which an individual is affected by the law of his domicil with peculiar capacities and disqualifications, which are recognized either in his favor or against him while resident within another jurisdiction. When he returns to his own country he becomes reinvested with his original personal status, and the capacities and disqualifications of the law of his domicil attach. Take a case of familiar and daily occurrence. A man is a magistrate in the place of his domicil. He passes out of that jurisdiction, and he can exercise no authority as a magistrate. He becomes a private person, but on his return to the place of his domicil he reassumes his personal status as a magistrate. The law which declares a slave free on his introduction into this country, by necessary consequences, if it be not an identical proposition, declares him to be possessed of the civil qualities of a freeman, and confers on him the faculty of vindicating his rights, and claiming redress for wrongs in the ordinary course of justice; and this general proposition is an answer to another part of the argument, that the libellant in this case, was put under the government of the respondent who stood loco domini, the owner having delegated to him his authority. That authority when the slave was within the jurisdiction of this country, could be exercised only under the restrictions of our law. Years before the decision of Sommersett's Case, it was said by Lord Chancellor Northington, that a negro might maintain an action in England, against his master for ill usage. Shanley v. Harvey, 2 Eden, 126, quoted, 2 Hagg. Adm. 116.

It was supposed in the argument that a distinction might be made, founded on the circumstance that the tort was committed on the high seas, which are within the common jurisdiction of all nations. It is true that no nation can claim an exclusive jurisdiction over any part of the high seas, but all nations can, and do claim an exclusive jurisdiction over their own vessels that float on the high seas. A foreigner who is a passenger on board an American vessel, when the vessel has left the port, and is beyond the jurisdiction of his own country, is amenable to the laws of this country and is under their protection. If he commits a crime he may be indicted in our courts, and punished by our laws. If he commits a tort, he is personally liable to answer for it in our courts, and if he suffers a wrong he may appeal to the laws of this country for redress, as much as though the wrong had been done him on land. If the libellant would not be precluded from maintaining an action for a tort done on land, he may equally maintain one for a tort done in an American vessel on the high seas. Forbes v. Cochrane, 2 Barn. & C. 448.

It was supposed at the argument that the capacity of the libellant to maintain this action in the courts of the United States may stand on grounds somewhat different from what it would in the state courts; that slavery existing in some of the individual states, and not being prohibited by the constitution and laws of the United States, the national courts might be bound by the principles of the jus gentium to recognize the incapacities of slaves having a foreign domicil, even where it would not be done by the state courts, and that the national tribunals are under the same obligations in this respect, whether sitting in a state where slavery is admitted, or where it is prohibited. If this were conceded, and in the view which I take of the case I do not think it necessary to give an opinion upon the question, the answer is, that a court sitting in Louisiana is no more bound, than one sitting in Maine, to recognize as to any acts, or rights acquired, within the exclusive jurisdiction of the United States, the artificial incapacities of persons resulting from a foreign law. The question in both cases, would be, whether the party could by the laws of the United States, have a standing in court. The court certainly is not bound to enforce against him, a personal incapacity derived from the law of his domicil, because that law can have no force in this country any further than our law on the principles of comity chooses to adopt it; and every nation will judge for itself how far it is consistent with its own interest and policy to extend its comity in this respect. If the legislative power has prescribed no rule, the courts must of necessity decide in each individual case as it is presented, and however embarrassing and perplexing the case may sometimes be, the courts cannot escape them. If the incapacity alleged were slavery, it is not for me to say what would be the judgment of a court sitting within a jurisdiction where slavery is allowed, but sitting as this court does, in a place where slavery by the local law is prohibited, I do not feel myself called upon to allow that disqualification when it is alleged by a wrongdoer, as attaching to the libellant by the laws of a foreign power, for the purpose of withdrawing himself from responsibility for his own wrong.

The Lusitania
251 Fed. 715 (S.D., N.Y., 1918)

(The Cunard Steamship Co., owner of the steamship
Lusitania, sunk by German submarine without warning on
May 7, 1915, with a loss of nearly 2000 lives, petitioned
in admiralty for limitation of its liability. In granting the
petition and dismissing claims against Cunard, the Court
said, per MAYER, District Judge:)

Claimants contend strongly that the case at bar comes within Holladay v. Kennard, 12 Wall. 254, 20 L. Ed. 390, where Mr. Justice Miller, who wrote the opinion, carefully stated that that case was
not to be construed as laying down a rule different from that of Railroad Co. v. Reeves, supra. An elaborate analysis of the Holladay
and other cases will not be profitable. Suffice it to say, neither that
nor any other case has changed the rule of law, above stated, as to
the legal import of an intervening illegal act of a third party. The
question, then, is whether the act of the German submarine commander was an illegal act.
The United States courts recognize the binding force of international law. As was said by Mr. Justice Gray in The Paquete Habana,
175 U. S. 677, 700, 20 Sup. Ct. 290, 299 (44 L. Ed. 320):

"International law is part of our law, and must be ascertained and administered by the courts of justice of appropriate jurisdiction as often as
questions of right depending upon it are duly presented for their determination."

At least, since as early as June 5, 1793, in the letter of Mr. Jefferson, Secretary of State, to the French minister, our government has
recognized the law of nations as an "integral part" of the laws of the
land. Moore's International Law Digest, I, p. 10; The Scotia, 14
Wall. 170, 187, 20 L. Ed. 822; The New York, 175 U. S. 187, 197,
20 Sup. Ct. 67, 44 L. Ed. 126; Kansas v. Colorado, 185 U. S. 125,
146, 22 Sup. Ct. 552, 46 L. Ed. 838; Kansas v. Colorado, 206 U. S.
46, 27 Sup. Ct. 655, 51 L. Ed. 956. To ascertain international law:

"Resort must be had to the customs and usages of civilized nations, and, as
evidence of these, to the works of commentators and jurists. * * * Such
works are resorted to by judicial tribunals * * * for trustworthy evidence of what the law really is." The Paquete Habana, 175 U. S. 677, 20 Sup.
Ct. 290, 44 L. Ed. 320 (and authorities cited).

Let us first see the position of our government, and then ascertain
whether that position has authoritative support. Mr. Lansing, in his

official communication to the German government, dated June 9, 1915, stated:

"But the sinking of passenger ships involves principles of humanity which throw into the background any special circumstances of detail that may be thought to affect the cases—principles which lift it, as the Imperial German government will no doubt be quick to recognize and acknowledge, out of the class of ordinary subjects of diplomatic discussion or of international controversy. Whatever be the other facts regarding the Lusitania, the principal fact is that a great steamer, primarily and chiefly a conveyance for passengers, and carrying more than a thousand souls, who had no part or lot in the conduct of the war, was torpedoed and sunk without so much as a challenge or a warning, and that men, women, and children were sent to their death in circumstances unparalleled in modern warfare. The fact that more than one hundred American citizens were among those who perished made it the duty of the government of the United States to speak of these things, and once more, with solemn emphasis, to call the attention of the Imperial German government to the grave responsibility which the government of the United States conceives that it has incurred in this tragic occurrence, and to the indisputable principle upon which that responsibility rests. The government of the United States is contending for something much greater than mere rights of property or privileges of commerce. It is contending for nothing less high and sacred than the rights of humanity, which every government honors itself in respecting, and which no government is justified in resigning on behalf of those under its care and authority. Only her actual resistance to capture, or refusel to stop when ordered to do so for the purpose of visit, could have afforded the commander of the submarine any justification for so much as putting the lives of those on board the ship in jeopardy. This principle the government of the United States understands the explicit instructions issued on August 3, 1914, by the Imperial German Admiralty to its 'commanders at sea, to have recognized and embodied, as do the naval codes of all other nations, and upon it every traveler and seaman had a right to depend. It is upon this principle of humanity, as well as upon the law founded upon this principle, that the United States must stand. * * * The government of the United States cannot admit that the proclamation of a war zone from which neutral ships have been warned to keep away may be made to operate as in any degree an abbreviation of the rights either of American shipmasters or of American citizens bound on lawful errands as passengers on merchant ships of belligerent nationality. It does not understand the Imperial German government to question those rights. It understands it, also, to accept as established beyond question the principle that the lives of noncombatants cannot lawfully or rightfully be put in jeopardy by the capture or destruction of an unresisting merchantman, and to recognize the obligation to take sufficient precaution to ascertain whether a suspected merchantman is in fact of belligerent nationality, or is in fact carrying contraband of war under a neutral flag. The government of the United States, therefore, deems it reasonable to expect that the Imperial German government will adopt the measures necessary to put these principles into practice in respect of the safeguarding of American lives and American ships, and asks for assurances that this will be done." White Book of Department of State, entitled "Diplomatic Correspondence with Belligerent Governments Relating to Neutral Rights and Duties, European War No. 2," at page 172. Printed and distributed October 21, 1915.

The German government found itself compelled ultimately to recognize the principle insisted upon by the government of the United States, for, after considerable correspondence, and on May 4, 1916 (after the Sussex had been sunk), the German government stated:

"The German submarine forces have had, in fact, orders to conduct submarine warfare in accordance with the general principles of visit and search and destruction of merchant vessels as recognized by international law; the sole exception being the conduct of warfare against the enemy trade carried on enemy freight ships that are encountered in the war zone surrounding Great Britain. * * * The German government, guided by this idea, notifies the government of the United States that the German naval forces have received the following orders: In accordance with the general principles of visit and search and destruction of merchant vessels recognized by international law, such vessels, both within and without the area declared as naval war zone, shall not be sunk without warning and without saving human lives, unless these ships attempt to escape or offer resistance."

See Official Communication by German Foreign Office to Ambassador Gerard, May 4, 1916 (White Book No. 3 of Department of State, pp. 302, 305).

There is, of course, no doubt as to the right to make prize of an enemy ship on the high seas, and, under certain conditions, to destroy her, and equally no doubt of the obligation to safeguard the lives of all persons aboard, whether passengers or crew. Phillemore on International Law (3d Ed.) vol. 3, p. 584; Sir Sherston Baker on First Steps in International Law, p. 236; G. B. Davis on Elements of International Law, pp. 358, 359; A. Pearce Higgins on War and the Private Citizen, pp. 33, 78, referring to proceedings of Institute of International Law at Turin in 1882; Creasy on International Law, p. 562, quoting Chief Justice Cockburn in his judgment in the Geneva Arbitration; L. A. Atherby-Jones on Commerce in War, p. 529; Professor Holland's article, Naval War College, 1907, p. 82; Oppenheim on International Law (2d Ed.) vol. 2, pp. 244, 311; Taylor on International Law, p. 572; Westlake on International Law (2d Ed.) p. 309, part II; Halleck on International Law, vol. 2, pp. 15, 16; Vattel's Law of Nations (Chitty's Ed.) 362.

Two quotations from this long list may be given for convenience; one stating the rule and the other the attitude which obtains among civilized governments. Oppenheim sets forth as among violations of the rules of war:

"(12) Attack on enemy merchantmen without previous request to submit to visit."

The observation in Vattel's Law of Nations is peculiarly applicable to the case of the Lusitania:

"Let us never forget that our enemies are men. Though reduced to the disagreeable necessity of prosecuting our right by force of arms, let us not divest ourselves of that charity which connects us with all mankind. Thus shall we courageously defend our country's rights without violating those of human nature. Let our valor preserve itself from every stain of cruelty and the luster of victory will not be tarnished by inhuman and brutal actions."

In addition to the authorities supra are the regulations and practices of various governments. In 1512, Henry VIII issued instructions to the Admiral of the Fleet which accord with our understanding of modern international law. Hosack's Law of Nations, p. 168. Such has been England's course since. 22 Geo. II, c. 33, § 2, subsec. 9 (1749); British Admiralty Manual of Prize Law 188, §§ 303, 304.

Substantially the same rules were followed in the Russian and Japanese regulations, and probably in the codes or rules of many other nations. Russian Prize Regulations, March 27, 1895 (cited in Moore's Digest, vol. 7, p. 518); Japanese Prize Law of 1894, art. 22 (cited in Moore, supra, vol. 7, p. 525); Japanese Regulations, March 7, 1904 (see Takahashi's Cases on International Law during Chino-Japanese War).

The rules recognized and practiced by the United States, among other things, provide:

"(10) In the case of an enemy merchantman it may be sunk, but only if it is impossible to take it into port, and provided always that the persons on board are put in a place of safety." U. S. White Book, European War, No. 3, p. 192.

These humane principles were practiced, both in the War of 1812 and during our own war of 1861–1865. Even with all the bitterness (now happily ended and forgotten) and all the difficulties of having no port to which to send a prize, Capt. Semmes, of the Alabama, strictly observed the rule as to human life, even going so far as to release ships because he could not care for the passengers. But we are not confined to American and English precedents and practices.

While acting contrary to its official statements, yet the Imperial German government recognized the same rule as the United States, and, prior to the sinking of the Lusitania, had not announced any other rule. The war zone proclamation of February 4, 1915, contained no warning that the accepted rule of civilized naval warfare would be discarded by the German government. Indeed, after the Lusitania was sunk, the German government did not make any such claim, but, in answer to the first American note in reference to the Lusitania, the German Foreign Office, per Von Jagow, addressed to Ambassador Gerard a note, dated May 18, 1915, in which, inter alia, it is stated in connection with the sinking of the British steamer Falaba:

"In the case of the sinking of the English steamer Falaba, the commander of the German submarine had the intention of allowing passengers and crew ample opportunity to save themselves. It was not until the captain disregarded the order to lay to and took to flight, sending up rocket signals for help, that the German commander ordered the crew and passengers by signals and megaphone to leave the ship within 10 minutes. As a matter of fact he allowed them 23 minutes, and did not fire the torpedo until suspicious steamers were hurrying to the aid of the Falaba." White Book No. 2, U. S. Department of State, p. 169.

Indeed, as late as May 4, 1916, Germany did not dispute the applicability of the rule, as is evidenced by the note written to our government by Von Jagow, of the German Foreign Office, an extract from which has been quoted supra.

Further, section 116 of the German Prize Code (Huberich & Kind translation, p. 68), in force at the date of the Lusitania's destruction, conformed with the American rule. It provided:

"Before proceeding to a destruction of the vessel, the safety of all persons on board, and, so far as possible, their effects, is to be provided for, and all ship's papers and other evidentiary material, which, according to the views of the persons at interest, is of value for the formulation of the judgment of the prize court, are to be taken over by the commander."

Thus, when the Lusitania sailed from New York, her owner and master were justified in believing that, whatever else had theretofore happened, this simple, humane, and universally accepted principle would not be violated. Few, at that time, would be likely to construe the warning advertisement as calling attention to more than the perils to be expected from quick disembarkation and the possible rigors of the sea, after the proper safeguarding of the lives of passengers by at least full opportunity to take to the boats.

It is, of course, easy now, in the light of many later events, added to preceding acts, to look back and say that the Cunard Line and its captain should have known that the German government would authorize or permit so shocking a breach of international law and so foul an offense, not only against an enemy, but as well against peaceful citizens of a then friendly nation. But the unexpected character of the act was best evidenced by the horror which it excited in the minds and hearts of the American people.

The fault, therefore, must be laid upon those who are responsible for the sinking of the vessel, in the legal as well as moral sense. It is therefore not the Cunard Line, petitioner, which must be held liable for the loss of life and property. The cause of the sinking of the Lusitania was the illegal act of the Imperial German government, acting through its instrument, the submarine commander, and violating a cherished and humane rule observed, until this war, by even the bitterest antagonists. As Lord Mersey said:

"The whole blame for the cruel destruction of life in this catastrophe must rest solely with those who plotted and with those who committed the crime."

But while, in this lawsuit, there may be no recovery, it is not to be doubted that the United States of America and her Allies will well remember the rights of those affected by the sinking of the Lusitania, and, when the time shall come, will see to it that reparation shall be made for one of the most indefensible acts of modern times.

The petition is granted, and the claims dismissed, without costs.

(2) SUBJECTS OF INTERNATIONAL LAW -- STATES AS INTERNATIONAL PERSONS

(a) Sovereignty, Independence, Equality

Williams v. The Suffolk Insurance Co.
38 U.S. (13 Peters) 415 (1839)

Mr. Justice M'LEAN delivered the opinion of the Court:—

Two actions were commenced by the plaintiffs against the defendant, in the Circuit Court of the United States for the state of Massachusetts, on policies of insurance dated 19th August, 1830; whereby the plaintiffs caused to be insured by the defendants, for nine per centum per annum premium, warranting twelve per centum lost or not lost, forty-nine hundred and nineteen dollars on fifteen-sixteenths of schooner Harriet; and eighteen hundred and seventy-five dollars on board said vessel, at and from Stonington, Connecticut, commencing the risk on the 12th August instant at noon, to the southern hemisphere; with liberty to stop for salt at the Cape de Verd islands, and to go round Cape Horn, and to touch at all islands, ports and places, for the purpose of taking seals, and for information and refreshments; with liberty to put his skins on board of any other vessel or vessels, until she returns to her port of discharge in the United States: it being understood that the value of the interest hereby insured, as it relates to this insurance, is not to be diminished thereby, &c.

On the same day there was a similar policy of thirty-five hundred dollars on the schooner Breakwater; and two thousand dollars on outfits on board, at the same premium, &c.

And on the trial the following points were raised in the case, on which the opinions of the judges were opposed, and on which the case-is certified to this Court.

1. Whether, inasmuch as the American government has insisted, and does still insist, through its regular executive authority, that the Falkland islands do not constitute any part of the dominions within the sovereignty of the government of Buenos Ayres; and that the seal fishery at those islands is a trade free and lawful to the citizens of the United States, and beyond the competency of the Buenos Ayres government to regulate, prohibit, or punish; it is competent for the Circuit Court in this cause, to inquire into, and ascertain by other evidence, the title of said government of Buenos Ayres to the sovereignty of the said Falkland islands; and if such evidence satisfies the Court, to decide against the doctrines and claims set up and supported by the American government on this subject: or whether the action of the American government on this subject is binding and conclusive on this Court, as to whom the sovereignty of those islands belongs.

2. Whether, if the seizure of the Harriet by the authority of the Buenos Ayrean government, for carrying on the seal fishery at the Falkland islands, was illegal and contrary to the law of nations, on account of the said islands not being within the territorial sovereignty of the said Buenos Ayrean government; and the master of the Harriet had warning from the governor of the said islands under the government of Buenos Ayres, that he should seize the said Harriet if she should engage in the seal fishery; and after such warning the master of the Harriet engaged in the seal fishery, and the Harriet was illegally seized and condemned therefor; the loss by such seizure and condemnation was a loss for which the plaintiff is entitled to recover in this case, if the master of the Harriet acted in engaging in such seal fishery bona fide, and with a sound and reasonable discretion, and under a belief that he was bound so to do as a matter of duty to his owners and all others interested in the voyage; and in the vindication of the rights recognised and claimed by the American government: or whether he was bound by law to abandon the voyage under such a threat and warning of such illegal seizure.

As the fact is stated in the first point certified, that there is a controversy between this government and that of Buenos Ayres, whether the jurisdiction is rightful, which is assumed to be exercised over the Falkland islands by the latter; and that this right is asserted on the one side and denied by the other, it will not be necessary to look into the correspondence between the two governments on the subject.

To what sovereignty any island or country belongs, is a question which often arises before Courts in the exercise of a maritime jurisdiction; and also in actions on policies of insurance.

Prior to the revolution in South America, it is known that the Malvinas, or Falkland islands, were attached to the vice-royalty of La Plata, which included Buenos Ayres. And if this were an open question, we might inquire whether the jurisdiction over these islands did not belong to some other part, over which this ancient vice-royalty extended, and not to the government of Buenos Ayres: but we are saved from this inquiry by the attitude of our own government, as stated in the point certified.

And can there be any doubt, that when the executive branch of the government, which is charged with our foreign relations, shall in its correspondence with a foreign nation assume a fact in regard to the sovereignty of any island or country, it is conclusive on the judicial department? And in this view it is not material to inquire, nor is it the province of the Court to determine, whether the executive be right or wrong. It is enough to know, that in the exercise of his constitutional functions, he has decided the question. Having done this under the responsibilities which belong to him, it is obligatory on the people and government of the Union.

If this were not the rule, cases might often arise in which, on the most important questions of foreign jurisdiction, there would be an irreconcilable difference between the executive and judicial departments. By one of these departments, a foreign island or country might be considered as at peace with the United States; whilst the other would consider it in a state of war. No well regulated government has ever sanctioned a principle so unwise, and so destructive of national character.

In the cases of Foster *vs.* Neilson, 2 Peters, 253. 307, and Garcia *vs.* Lee, 12 Peters, 511, this Court have laid down the rule, that the action of the political branches of the government in a matter that belongs to them, is conclusive.

And we think in the present case, as the executive, in his message, and in his correspondence with the government of Buenos Ayres, has denied the jurisdiction which it has assumed to exercise over the Falkland islands; the fact must be taken and acted on by this Court as thus asserted and maintained.

The decision of the first point materially affects the second, which turns upon the conduct of the master.

If these islands are not within the jurisdiction of the Buenos Ayrean government, the power assumed and exercised by Governor Vernet was unauthorized, and the master was not bound to regard it. He was not necessarily to be diverted from the objects of his voyage, and the exercise of rights which belonged in common to the citizens of the United States by an unauthorized threat of the seizure of his vessel. He might well consider the prohibition of Vernet as influenced by personal and sinister motives, and would not be enforced. If the principle were admitted, that the assured were bound to regard every idle threat of any individual who might assume to exercise power, as in this case, it would be most injurious, and in many cases destructive, to commercial rights.

The inquiry is, whether the master, under all the circumstances of the case, acted in good faith, and with ordinary prudence.

If he acted fraudulently, he was guilty of barratry; and the underwriters are discharged.

In 4 Taunton, 858, Mr. Justice Gibbs, in giving the opinion of the Court, lays down the true rule. " The master," says he, " being asked why he had not British colours and British papers, said, I cannot have them, because I have not a British register. He stands on his strict rights. He says, I will do nothing to endanger my owners; I am a neutral, and I have a right to enter your port. The master really communicated the true facts of the case when she was searched; and says, I cannot go off, because of my charter-party. The other says: Then I will seize you. We think, then, each party stands on his strict rights; and we are now to consider the strict point of law, not the question whether it would have been more prudent for him to go to Tercera, but whether he acted bona fide."

And so in the present case, the question is not whether the master of the Harriet would not have acted with more prudence had he yielded to the inhibition of Vernet; but whether, in placing himself upon his strict rights, he did not exercise a proper discretion.

He violated no regulation which he was bound to respect. In touching at the Falkland islands, for the purpose of taking seal, he acted strictly within the limits of his commercial enterprise; and did not voluntarily incur a risk which should exonerate the insurers.

It was the duty of the master to prosecute his voyage, and attain the objects of it, for the benefit of his owners: and, in doing this, he was not bound to abandon the voyage by any threat of illegal seizure. We think, therefore, that the underwriters are not discharged from liability, by the conduct of the master, as stated in the second point.

The other case depending upon the same principles, the same certificate will be affixed to that case.

This cause came on to be heard on the transcript of the record from the Circuit Court of the United States, for the district of Massachusetts, and on the points and questions on which the judges of the said Circuit Court were opposed in opinion, and which were certified to this Court for its opinion, agreeably to the act of Congress in such case made and provided, and was argued by counsel. On consideration whereof, it is the opinion of this Court, 1st, That, inasmuch as the American government has insisted and still does insist, through its regular executive authority, that the Falkland islands do not constitute any part of the dominions within the sovereignty of the government of Buenos Ayres, the action of the American government on this subject is binding on the said Circuit Court, as to whom the sovereignty of those islands belongs. And, secondly: That the seizure and condemnation of the Harriet was a loss for which the plaintiff is entitled to recover in this case, under the circumstances as stated in the second point certified. Whereupon, it is ordered and adjudged by this Court, that it be so certified to the said Circuit Court, accordingly.

The Sapphire v. Napoleon III
78 U.S. (11 Wallace) 164 (1871)

Mr. Justice BRADLEY delivered the opinion of the court.

The first question raised is as to the right of the French Emperor to sue in our courts. On this point not the slightest difficulty exists. A foreign sovereign, as well as any other foreign person, who has a demand of a civil nature against any person here, may prosecute it in our courts. To deny him this privilege would manifest a want of comity and friendly feeling. Such a suit was sustained in behalf of the King of Spain in the third circuit by Justice Washington and Judge Peters in 1810.† The Constitution expressly extends the judicial power to controversies between a State, or citizens thereof, and *foreign States*, citizens, or subjects, without reference to the subject-matter of the controversy. Our own government has largely availed itself of the like privilege to bring suits in the English courts in cases growing

† King of Spain v. Oliver, 2 Washington's Circuit Court, 431.

out of our late civil war. Twelve or more of such suits are enumerated in the brief of the appellees, brought within the last five years in the English law, chancery, and admiralty courts. There are numerous cases in the English reports in which suits of foreign sovereigns have been sustained, though it is held that a sovereign cannot be forced into court by suit.*

The next question is, whether the suit has become abated by the recent deposition of the Emperor Napoleon. We think it has not. The reigning sovereign represents the national sovereignty, and that sovereignty is continuous and perpetual, residing in the proper successors of the sovereign for the time being. Napoleon was the owner of the Euryale, not as an individual, but as sovereign of France. This is substantially averred in the libel. On his deposition the sovereignty does not change, but merely the person or persons in whom it resides. The foreign state is the true and real owner of its public vessels of war. The reigning Emperor, or National Assembly, or other actual person or party in power, is but the agent and representative of the national sovereignty. A change in such representative works no change in the national sovereignty or its rights. The next successor recognized by our government is competent to carry on a suit already commenced and receive the fruits of it. A deed to or treaty with a sovereign as such enures to his successors in the government of the country. If a substitution of names is necessary or proper it is a formal matter, and can be made by the court under its general power to preserve due symmetry in its forms of proceeding. No allegation has been made that any change in the real and substantial ownership of the Euryale has occurred by the recent devolution of the sovereign power. The vessel has always belonged and still belongs to the French nation.

If a special case should arise in which it could be shown that injustice to the other party would ensue from a contin-

---

* King of Spain v. Hullett, 1 Dow & Clarke, 169; S. C., 1 Clarke & Finelly, 833; S. C., 2 Bligh, N. S. 31; Emperor of Brazil, 6 Adolphus & Ellis, 801; Queen of Portugal, 7 Clarke & Finelly, 466; King of Spain, 4 Russell, 225; Emperor of Austria, 3 De Gex, Fisher & Jones, 174; King of Greece, 6 Dowling's Practice Cases, 12; S. C., 1 Jurist, 944; United States, Law Reports, 2 Equity Cases, 659; Ditto, Ib. 2 Chancery Appeals, 582; Duke of Brunswick v. King of Hanover, 6 Beavan, 1; S. C., 2 House of Lords Cases, 1; De Haber v. Queen of Portugal, 17 Q. B. 169; also 2 Phillimore's International Law, part vi, chap. i; 1 Daniel's Chancery Practice, chap. ii, § ii.

uance of the proceedings after the death or deposition of a
sovereign, the court, in the exercise of its discretionary
power, would take such order as the exigency might require
to prevent such a result.

Decree of the Circuit Court REVERSED, and the cause remitted to that court with directions to enter a decree

IN CONFORMITY WITH THIS OPINION.

Frelinghuysen v. Key

110 U.S. 63; 3 S. Ct. 462 (1884)

These causes originated in petitions to the Supreme Court of
the District of Columbia, for mandamus upon the Secretary of
State to compel him to pay to the petitioners (representing claims
proved before the commission established under the Claims Convention of July 4th, 1868, with Mexico), their distributive
shares of certain payments made by Mexico to the United
States in accordance with the terms of that convention. The
following are the facts as recited by the court, and on which
the opinion is based.

On the 4th of July, 1868, a convention between the United
States and the Republic of Mexico, providing for the adjustment of the claims of citizens of either country against the
other, was concluded, and, on 1st of February, 1869, proclaimed by the President of the United States, by and with
the advice and consent of the Senate. By this convention
(Art. I.):

" All claims on the part of corporations, companies, or private
individuals, citizens of the United States, upon the government
of the Mexican Republic, arising from injuries to their persons or
property by authorities of the Mexican Republic, and all claims
on the part of corporations, companies, or private individuals,
citizens of the Mexican Republic, upon the government of the
United States, arising from injuries to their persons or property by
authorities of the United States, which may have been presented
to either government for its interposition with the other since
the signature of the treaty of Guadalupe Hidalgo, . . . and
which yet remain unsettled, as well as any other such claims which
may be presented within," a specified time, were to " be referred

to two commissioners, one to be appointed by the President of the United States, by and with the advice and consent of the Senate, and one by the President of the Mexican Republic."

Provision was then made for the appointment of an umpire. Arts. II., IV., and V., are as follows :

ART. II. " The commissioners shall then conjointly proceed to the investigation and decision of the claims which shall be presented to their notice, . . . but upon such evidence or information only as shall be furnished by or on behalf of their respective governments. They shall be bound to receive and peruse all written documents or statements which may be presented to them by or on behalf of their respective governments in support of, or in answer to any claim, and to hear, if required, one person on each side on behalf of each government on each and every separate claim. Should they fail to agree in opinion upon any individual claim, they shall call to their assistance the umpire . .; and such umpire, after having examined the evidence adduced for and against the claim, and after having heard, if required, one person on each side as aforesaid, and consulted with the commissioners, shall decide thereupon finally and without appeal. . . It shall be competent for each government to name one person to attend the commissioners as agent on its behalf, to present and support claims on its behalf and to answer claims made upon it, and to represent it generally in all matters connected with the investigation and decision thereof. The President of the United States . . . . and the President of the Mexican Republic hereby solemnly and sincerely engage to consider the decisions of the commissioners conjointly, or of the umpire, as the case may be, as absolutely final and conclusive upon each claim decided upon by them or him respectively, and to give full effect to such decision without any objection, evasion, or delay whatsoever. . . ."

ART. IV. " When decisions shall have been made by the commissioners and the arbiter in every case which shall have been laid before them, the total amount awarded in all the cases decided in favor of the citizens of the one party shall be deducted from the total amount awarded to the citizens of the other party, and the balance, to the amount of $300,000, shall be paid at the city of Mexico or at the city of Washington, . . . within twelve months from the close of the commission, to the government in favor of whose citizens the greater amount may have been awarded, without interest. . . . The residue of the said balance shall be paid in annual instalments to an amount not exceeding $300,000 . . . in any one year until the whole shall have been paid."

ART. V. " The high contracting parties agree to consider the result of the proceedings of this commission as a full, perfect, and final settlement of every claim upon either government arising out of any transaction of a date prior to the exchange of the ratifications of the present convention ; and further engage that every such claim, whether or not the same may have been presented to the notice of, made, preferred, or laid before the said commission, shall, from and after the conclusion of the proceedings of the said commission, be considered and treated as finally settled, barred, and thenceforth inadmissible." 15 Stat. 679.

Under this convention commissioners were appointed who entered on the performance of their duties. Benjamin Weil and the La Abra Silver Mining Company, citizens of the United States, presented to their government certain claims against Mexico. These claims were referred to the commissioners, and finally resulted in an award, on the 1st of October, 1875, in favor of Weil and against Mexico for $489,810.68, and on the 27th of December, 1875, in favor of La Abra Silver Mining Company for $683,041.32. On the adjustment of balances under the provisions of Art. IV. of the convention it was found that the awards against Mexico exceeded largely those against the United States, and the government of Mexico has promptly and in good faith met its annual payments, though it seems from the beginning to have desired a re-examination of the Weil and La Abra claims.

On the 18th of June, 1878, Congress passed an act (c. 262, 20 Stat. 144), secs. 1 and 5 of which are as follows :

SEC. 1. " That the Secretary of State be, and he is hereby authorized and required to receive any and all moneys which may be paid by the Mexican Republic under and in pursuance of the convention between the United States and the Mexican Republic for the adjustment of claims ; . . . and, whenever and as often as any instalments shall have been paid by the Mexican Republic on account of said awards, to distribute the moneys so received in ratable proportions among the corporations, companies, or private individuals respectively in whose favor awards have been made by said' commissioners, or by the umpires, or to their legal representatives or assigns, except as in this act otherwise limited or provided, according to the proportion which their respective awards shall bear to the whole amount of such moneys then held by him, and to pay the same, without other charge or deduction than is hereinafter provided, to the parties respectively entitled thereto." . . .

Sec. 5. "And whereas the government of Mexico has called the attention of the government of the United States to the claims hereinafter named, with a view to a rehearing, therefore be it enacted that the President of the United [States] be, and he is hereby, requested to investigate any charges of fraud presented by the Mexican government as to the cases hereinafter named, and if he shall be of the opinion that the honor of the United States, the principles of public law or considerations of justice and equity require that the awards in the cases of Benjamin Weil and La Abra Silver Mining Company, or either of them, should be opened and the cases retried, it shall be lawful for him to withhold payment of said awards, or either of them, until such case or cases shall be retried and decided in such manner as the governments of the United States and Mexico may agree, or until Congress shall otherwise direct. And in case of such retrial and decision, any moneys paid or to be paid by the Republic of Mexico in respect of said awards respectively shall be held to abide the event, and shall be disposed of accordingly ; and the said present awards shall be set aside, modified, or affirmed, as may be determined on such retrial : *provided* that nothing herein shall be construed as an expression of any opinion of Congress in respect to the character of said claims, or either of them."

During the year 1879, President Hayes caused an investigation to be made of the charges of fraud presented by the Mexican government, and the conclusion he reached is thus stated in the report of Mr. Evarts, the then Secretary of State:

"I conclude, therefore, that neither the principles of public law nor considerations of justice or equity require or permit, as between the United States and Mexico, that the awards in these cases should be opened and the cases retried before a new international tribunal or under any new convention or negotiation respecting the same between the United States and Mexico.

"Second. I am, however, of opinion that the matters brought to the attention of this government on the part of Mexico do bring into grave doubt the substantial integrity of the claim of Benjamin Weil and the sincerity of the evidence as to the measure of damages insisted upon and accorded in the case of the La Abra Silver Mining Company, and that the honor of the United States does require that these two cases should be further investigated by the United States to ascertain whether this government has been made the means of enforcing against a friendly power claims of our citizens based upon or exaggerated by fraud.

"If such further investigation should remove the doubts which have been fairly raised upon the representations of Mexico, the honor of the United States will have been completely maintained.

If, on the other hand, the claimants shall fail in removing these doubts, or they should be replaced by certain condemnation, the honor of the United States will be vindicated by such measures as may then be dictated.

"Third. The executive government is not furnished with the means of instituting and pursuing methods of investigation which can coerce the production of evidence or compel the examination of parties and witnesses. The authority for such an investigation must proceed from Congress. I would advise, therefore, that the proofs and the conclusions you shall come to thereon, if adverse to the immediate payment on these awards of the instalments received from Mexico, be laid before Congress for the exercise of their plenary authority in the matter."

This action of the President was communicated to Congress under date of April 15th, 1880, by his forwarding a copy of the report of the Secretary of State, which concludes as follows :

"Unless Congress should now make this disposition of the matter, and furnish thereby definite instructions to the Department to reserve further payments upon these awards till the conclusion of such investigation, and to take such further order with the same thereafter as Congress might direct, it would appear to be the duty of the Executive to accept these awards as no longer open to reconsideration, and proceed in the payment of the same pro rata with all other awards under the convention."

No definitive instructions were given by Congress in respect to the matter during that session, and after the close of the session payments were made on these awards by the direction of the President the same as on the others. Another instalment was paid by the Mexican government and distributed to these claimants with the rest during President Garfield's administration. In this way five instalments were distributed. After President Arthur came into office he examined the cases further, and, "believing that said award was obtained by fraud and perjury," negotiated a treaty with Mexico providing for a rehearing. This treaty is now pending before the Senate for ratification. On the 31st of January, 1882, the sixth instalment was paid by Mexico to Mr. Frelinghuysen, the present Secretary of State. A distribution of this instalment to these claimants has been withheld by order of the President on account of the pending treaty.

These suits were brought in the Supreme Court of the District of Columbia to obtain writs of mandamus requiring the Secretary of State to pay to the several relators the amounts distributable to them respectively upon their disputed awards from the instalment of 1882. The relator, Key, is the assignee of part of the Weil claim. In this case the Secretary filed an answer setting up the action of President Arthur in respect to this claim and the negotiation of the new treaty. To this the relator demurred. Upon the hearing the court below sustained the demurrer and awarded a peremptory writ as prayed for.

In the case of the La Abra Company a petition substantially like that of the relator Key was demurred to by the Secretary. Upon the hearing this demurrer was sustained and the petition dismissed. In this case, therefore, the action of President Arthur does not appear affirmatively on the face of the record, but it was conceded on the argument that it might properly be considered.

The writ of error in the Key case was brought by the Secretary of State, and in the other by the La Abra Company.

MR. CHIEF JUSTICE WAITE delivered the opinion of the court.

If we understand correctly the positions assumed by the different counsel for the relators, they are:

1. That the awards under the convention vested in the several claimants an absolute right to the amounts awarded them respectively, and that this right was property which neither the United States alone, nor the United States and Mexico together, could take away; and,

2. That, if this were not so, the action of President Hayes, under the 5th section of the act of 1878, was conclusive on President Arthur, and deprived him of any right he might otherwise have had to investigate the charges of fraud presented by the Mexican government, or to withhold from the relators their distributive shares of any moneys thereafter paid to the Secretary of State under the authority of the first section.

1. There is no doubt that the provisions of the convention as to the conclusiveness of the awards are as strong as language can make them. The decision of the commissioners, or the umpire, on each claim, is to be " absolutely final and conclusive " and " without appeal." The President of the United States and the President of the Mexican Republic are " to give full effect to such decisions, without any objection, evasion, or delay whatsoever," and the result of the proceedings of the commission is to be considered " a full, perfect, and final settlement of every claim upon either government arising out of transactions prior to the exchange of the ratifications of the . . . . convention." But this is to be construed as language used in a compact of two nations "for the adjust-

ment of the claims of the citizens of either . . . against the other," entered into "to increase the friendly feeling between" republics, and "so to strengthen the system and principles of republican government on the American continent." No nation treats with a citizen of another nation except through his government. The treaty, when made, represents a compact between the governments, and each government holds the other responsible for everything done by their respective citizens under it. The citizens of the United States having claims against Mexico were not parties to this convention. They induced the United States to assume the responsibility of seeking redress for injuries they claimed to have sustained by the conduct of Mexico, and as a means of obtaining such redress the convention was entered into, by which not only claims of citizens of the United States against Mexico were to be adjusted and paid, but those of citizens of Mexico against the United States as well. By the terms of the compact the individual claimants could not themselves submit their claims and proofs to the commission to be passed upon. Only such claims as were presented to the governments respectively could be "referred" to the commission, and the commissioners were not allowed to investigate or decide on any evidence or information except such as was furnished by or on behalf of the governments. After all the decisions were made and the business of the commission concluded, the total amount awarded to the citizens of one country was to be deducted from the amount awarded to the citizens of the other, and the balance only paid in money by the government in favor of whose citizens the smaller amount was awarded, and this payment was to be made, not to the citizens, but to their government. Thus, while the claims of the individual citizens were to be considered by the commission in determining amounts, the whole purpose of the convention was to ascertain how much was due from one government to the other on account of the demands of their respective citizens.

As between the United States and Mexico, the awards are final and conclusive until set aside by agreement between the two governments or otherwise. Mexico cannot, under the terms of the treaty, refuse to make the payments at the times agreed on if required by the United States. This she does not now seek to do. Her payments have all been made promptly as they fell due, as far as these records show. What she asks is the consent of the United States to her release from liability under the convention on account of the particular awards now in dispute, because of the alleged fraudulent character of the proof in support of the claims which the United States were induced by the claimants to furnish for the consideration of the commission.

As to the right of the United States to treat with Mexico for a retrial, we entertain no doubt. Each government, when it entered into the compact under which the awards were made, relied on the honor and good faith of the other for protection as far as possible against frauds and impositions by the individual claimants. It was for this reason that all claims were excluded from the consideration of the commission except such as should be referred by the several governments, and no evidence in support of or against a claim was to be submitted except through or by the governments. The presentation by a citizen of a fraudulent claim or false testimony for reference to the commission was an imposition on his own government, and if that government afterwards discovered that it had in this way been made an instrument of wrong towards a friendly power, it would be not only its right but its duty, to repudiate the act and make reparation as far as possible for the consequences of its neglect if any there had been. International arbitration must always proceed on the highest principles of national honor and integrity. Claims presented and evidence submitted to such a tribunal must necessarily bear the impress of the entire good faith of the government from which they come, and it is not to be presumed that any government will for a moment allow itself knowingly to be made the instrument of wrong in any such proceeding. No technical rules of pleading as applied in municipal courts ought ever to be allowed to stand in the way of the national power to do what is right under all the circumstances. Every citizen who asks the intervention of his own government against another for the redress of his personal grievances must necessarily subject himself and his claim to these requirements of international comity. None of the cases cited by counsel are in opposition to this. They all relate to the disposition to be made of the proceeds of international awards after they have passed beyond the reach of the governments and into the hands of private parties. The language of the opinions must be construed in connection with this fact. The opinion of the Attorney-General in *Gibbes'* *Case*, 13 Opinions, 19, related to the authority of the executive officers to submit the claim of Gibbes to the second commission after it had been passed on by the first, without any new treaty between the governments to that effect; not to the power to make such a treaty.

2. The first section of the act of 1878 authorizes and requires

the Secretary of State to receive the moneys paid by Mexico under the convention, and to distribute them among the several claimants, but it manifests no disposition on the part of Congress to encroach on the power of the President and Senate to conclude another treaty with Mexico in respect to any or even all the claims allowed by the commission, if in their opinion the honor of the United States should demand it. At most, it only provides for receiving and distributing the sums paid without a protest or reservation, such as, in the opinion of the President, is entitled to further consideration. It does not undertake to set any new limits on the powers of the Executive.

The fifth section, as we construe it, is nothing more than an expression by Congress in a formal way of its desire that the President will, before he makes any payment on the Weil or La Abra claims, investigate the charges of fraud presented by Mexico,

" and if he shall be of the opinion that the honor of the United States, the principles of public law, or considerations of justice and equity require that the awards, ... or either of them, should be opened and the cases retried," that he will " withhold payment . . . . until the case or cases shall be retried and decided in such manner as the governments of the United States and Mexico may agree, or until Congress may otherwise direct."

From the beginning to the end it is, in form even, only a request from Congress to the Executive. This is far from making the President for the time being a *quasi* judicial tribunal to hear Mexico and the implicated claimants and determine once for all as between them, whether the charges which Mexico makes have been judicially established. In our opinion it would have been just as competent for President Hayes to have instituted the same inquiry without this request as with it, and his action with the statute in force is no more binding on his successor than it would have been without. But his action as reported by him to Congress is not at all inconsistent with what has since been done by President Arthur. He was of opinion that the disputed " cases should be further investigated by the United States to ascertain whether this government has been made the means of enforcing against a friendly power claims of our citizens based upon or exaggerated by fraud," and, by implication at least, he asked Congress to provide him the means " of instituting and furnishing methods of investigation which can coerce the production of evidence or compel the examination of parties or witnesses." He did report officially that he had "grave doubt as to the substantial integrity of the Weil claim" and the "sincerity of the evidence as to the measure of damages insisted upon and accorded in the case of La Abra . . . Company." The report of Mr. Evarts cannot be read without leaving the conviction that if the means had been afforded, the inquiries which Congress asked for would have been further prosecuted. The concluding paragraph of the report is nothing more than a notification by the President that unless the means are provided, he will consider that the wishes of Congress have been met, and that he will act on such evidence as he has been able to obtain without the help he wants. From the statements in the answer of Secretary Frelinghuysen in the Key case, it appears that further evidence has been found, and that President Arthur, upon this and what was before President Hayes, has become satisfied that the contested decisions should be opened and the claims retried. Consequently, the President, believing that the honor of the United States demands it, has negotiated a new treaty providing for such a re-examination of the claims, and submitted it to the Senate for ratification. Under these circumstances it is, in our opinion, clearly within the discretion of the President to withhold all further payments to the relators until the diplomatic negotiations between the two governments on the subject are finally concluded. That discretion of the Executive Department of the government cannot be controlled by the judiciary.

The United States, when they assumed the responsibility of presenting the claims of their citizens to Mexico for payment, entered into no contract obligations with the claimants to assume their frauds and to collect on their account all that, by their imposition of false testimony, might be given in the awards of the commission. As between the United States and the claimants, the honesty of the claims is always open to inquiry for the purposes of fair dealing with the government against which, through the United States, a claim has been made.

Of course, in what we have said we express no opinion on the merits of the controversy between Mexico and the relators. Of that we know nothing. All we decide is, that it was within the discretion of the President to negotiate again with Mexico in respect to the claims, and that as long as the two governments are treating on the questions involved, he may properly withhold from the relators their distributive shares of the moneys now in the hands of the Secretary of State.

*The judgment in the case of the La Abra Company is af-
firmed with costs, and that in the case of Key is reversed
with costs, and the cases remanded with instructions to dismiss the petition of Key.*

Editor's Note. The treaty between the U.S. and Mexico cited by the Court, is the Claims Convention, July
4, 1869, (15 Stat. 679; 1 Malloy, p. 1128). The award
referred to, in the Benjamin Weil claim, is 2 Moore
Digest of International Arbitrations, p. 1326.

Great Western Insurance Co. v. United States
19 Ct. Cl. 206 (1884)
aff'd. 112 U.S. 193, 5 S. Ct. 99 (1884)

DRAKE, Ch. J., delivered the opinion of the court:

This is a motion to dismiss the following petition, for want
of jurisdiction in the court to entertain it:

"The petition of the Great Western Insurance Company
showeth:

"FIRST. That the petitioner, the Great Western Insurance
Company, is a corporation duly organized and established in
accordance with the laws of the State of New York, and having its principal place of business in the city, county, and State
of New York, and that it is duly authorized to make insurance
upon all matters appertaining to, or connected with, marine
risks or transportation.

"SECOND. That at sundry times, for a valuable consideration, said petitioner did make insurance and issue policies upon
various vessels, cargoes, and freights, set forth in schedule 'A'
hereto annexed and made part of this petition. Said insurance covering risks of capture or seizure, restraint or detention
or the consequences of any attempt thereat, by or under the
authority of the so-called Confederate States, or any one or
more of the seceding or revolting States of the United States.

"THIRD. That the said several vessels named in said schedule 'A' were severally captured or destroyed by the so-called
Confederate privateers Alabama and Florida, by said vessels,
respectively, at the dates and times as set forth in schedule 'B'
hereto annexed and made part of this petition.

"FOURTH. That the petitioner did at sundry times, and in
pursuance of its contracts of insurances, as heretofore set forth,
pay to citizens of the United States losses arising from the capture or destruction of said vessels, to the amount upon the said
several vessels as set forth in schedule 'A' hereto annexed and
made part of this petition, to the parties entitled thereto, and
amounting in the aggregate to the sum of $309,635; that in
each and every case the money so paid was paid to American

citizens, and the payment in each and every case of loss set forth in said schedule was less than the value of the property captured or destroyed as heretofore alleged.

" FIFTH. That upon payment of aforesaid losses as heretofore set out each and every party to whom such payment was made assigned to the petitioner his right to recover for such capture and destruction from any and all persons and governments whatsoever. The petitioner further avers that in consequence of its payment of the losses heretofore set forth it became, independently of said assignment, subrogated to the rights of the assured in the aforesaid vessels, and thereby became entitled to demand and recover from any person or government liable for such losses full payment therefor, to the extent of its payments and interest thereon.

" SIXTH. That the kingdom of Great Britain, by the laches of Her Britannic Majesty's government in permitting the so-called Confederate privateers Alabama and Florida to escape from its ports, did incur obligations and become liable for the payment of the losses accruing by reason of the capture or destruction of the vessels or cargoes heretofore specified, by the aforesaid Alabama and Florida, to the owners of said vessels and cargoes and to their assigns.

" SEVENTH. The petitioner made claim as aforesaid against the government of Great Britain, and in obedience to a request from the Department of State, dated Washington, September 22, 1865, requesting citizens of the United States having claims against foreign governments not founded on contract to forward to said department statements of the same under oath, accompanied by proper proof, did furnish full and detailed statements, in accordance with the rules of said department, appended to said request, of its aforesaid claim against the government of Great Britain, and did request the said United States to present said claims against Her Britannic Majesty's government and demand payment therefor for the benefit of the petitioner.

" EIGHTH. That the United States did present said claims of the petitioner, with those of many other citizens and other similar claims, to Her Britannic Majesty's government, and together with proof thereof as furnished by your petitioner, and that the amount of said claims and of the liability of Her Britannic Majesty's government therefor were duly considered by a tribunal of arbitration sitting at Geneva, the claims of your petitioner being presented and urged by the duly accredited agents of the United States to said tribunal.

" NINTH. That said tribunal did, on or about the 14th day of September, 1872, award, as its judgment and opinion, a sum in gross and the cancellation of all claims upon Great Britain considered and allowed by said tribunal, amounting to fifteen million five hundred thousand dollars ($15,500,000), the payment by Great Britain and the acceptance of said sum by the United States to be the surrender and extinguishment of all claims upon the kingdom of Great Britain and Her Britannic Majesty's goverment for all losses growing out of the various matters which had been presented for the consideration of said tribunal, both on the part of the United States and its citizens. The petitioner avers that its claims, as heretofore set forth, were included among these claims.

"TENTH. That Her Britannic Majesty's government and the kingdom of Great Britain acted on and accepted the judgment and report of said tribunal, and on or about the 26th day of May, 1873, appropriated the necessary money, and in September of the same year paid over, in satisfaction and extinguishment of its liability by reason of the claims aforesaid, said sum of fifteen and one-half million dollars to the United States, and the same was received by the Secretary of State of the United States, and during the fiscal year ending June 30, 1874, was invested in the 5 per cent. funded loan of 1881, and a registered bond therefor was issued to the Secretary of State in trust.

"ELEVENTH. That prior to March 31, 1877, portions of said fund had been used in payment and settlement of the claims of individuals presented by the United States as aforesaid, and included in said sum of fifteen million five hundred thousand dollars, but that on that day the balance of said bonds, amounting to nine million five hundred and fifty-three thousand eight hundred dollars ($9,553,800), including interest at 5 per cent. up to that date, were canceled and destroyed, and the value thereof covered into the Treasury of the United States, and that said amount, together with the sum of twenty-two thousand three hundred and fifty dollars and eighteen cents ($22,350.18), being a premium on the sale of bonds over and above the amount theretofore paid to other claimants, which was also at that date covered into the Treasury, constitute a fund now in the Treasury of the United States, and undistributed, for the purposes for which it was awarded and paid by Great Britain as aforesaid, of nine million five hundred and seventy-six thousand one hundred and fifty dollars and eighteen cents ($9,576,150.18), without reckoning any interest thereon since the 1st day of March, 1877. That, as your petitioner is informed and verily believes, the claim of your petitioner, presented in its behalf by the United States as aforesaid, and which were allowed as forming a part of said sum of fifteen million five hundred thousand dollars, with the interest allowed thereon, amounted in the aggregate to four hundred and seventy-one thousand four hundred and nineteen dollars and twenty-nine cents, and that by force of the payment by Her Britannic Majesty's government, as aforesaid, to the United States, the claim of your petitioner to that amount against the Kingdom of Great Britain and her Britannic Majesty's government was canceled and discharged, and that thenceforth the claim of the petitioner for its losses, as aforesaid, to that amount, became a claim against the United States, and the United States, by reason of its presentation of said claims to the government of Great Britain, and its acceptance of said sum of fifteen million five hundred thousand dollars ($15,500,-000) in cancellation and discharge of Great Britain from its liability for such claims as the United States had presented to it, thereby became the trustee of this petitioner to the extent aforesaid, and liable to pay to it said sum of four hundred and seventy-one thousand four hundred and nineteen dollars and twenty-nine cents ($471,419.29), together with such interest as it might receive upon said trust fund.

"TWELFTH. That of the interest accruing upon said trust fund up to the time of its being covered into the Treasury,

March 31, 1877, the proportionate share of your petitioner is seventy-five thousand five hundred and forty-six dollars and fifty-one cents ($75,546.51).

"THIRTEENTH. That the government of the United States refuses, and at all times has refused, to pay or to make any provision for the payment of the claims of your petitioner in the premises. either of the sum of three hundred and nine thousand and six hundred and thirty-five dollars ($309,635), its original claim, without interest, against Her Britannic Majesty's government, the sum of four hundred and seventy-one thousand four hundred and nineteen dollars and twenty-nine cents ($471,419.29), being the amount as allowed, with interest, and paid by her Britannic Majesty's government to the United States for the use and benefit of your petitioner in September, 1873, as aforesaid, or the sum of five hundred and forty-six thousand nine hundred and sixty-five dollars and eighty cents ($546,965.80), the amount of said last-mentioned sum, with interest accruing thereon at 5 per cent., covered into the Treasury March 31, 1877.

" FOURTEENTH. That your petitioner, the Great Western Insurance Company, and each and every one of its stockholders, have at all times borne true allegiance to the government of the United States, and have not in any way voluntarily aided, abetted, or given encouragement to rebellion against the said government.

" FIFTEENTH. The petitioner further states that there has been no assignment or transfer of its said claim, or of any part thereof, or interest therein; and that said claimant is justly entitled to the amount claimed from the United States, hereinafter allowing all just credits and offsets, and that it believes the facts as stated in this petition to be true.

"SIXTEENTH. That by reason of the premises there is justly due to your petitioner from the United States the sum of five hundred and forty-six thousand nine hundred and sixty-five dollars and eighty cents ($546,965.80), as aforesaid, with interest from March 31, 1877.

" Wherefore your petitioner prays judgment against the defendant for the sum of five hundred and forty-six thousand nine hundred and sixty-five dollars and eighty cents ($546,965.80), with interest from the 31st day of March, 1877."

We have set out the petition at large in order that its exact terms may appear in full; but the case can be substantially stated in a few words.

The treaty of Washington, of May 8, 1871, between Great Britain and the United States, authorized a tribunal of arbitration, to which should be referred " all the claims growing out of acts committed by the aforesaid vessels [Alabama and Florida], and generically known as the 'Alabama claims.'"

Among the claims which went before that tribunal were those of the present claimant for losses to the amount of $309,635 paid on twenty vessels it had insured, and which had been destroyed by the Alabama and the Florida.

The tribunal of arbitration awarded nothing on any indi-

vidual claim, but a gross sum of $15,500,000 to be paid to the
United States "for the satisfaction of all the claims referred
to the consideration of the tribunal"; and that sum was paid
by Great Britain to the United States.

The claimant demands payment of its losses out of that
money, asserting that the United States, in presenting its claim
before the tribunal of arbitration, acted as its agent, and in
receiving the amount of the award became its trustee to the
extent of the amount of its losses; and therefore that the United
States have received so much money for its use and benefit.

The claimant admits that its right to demand payment of its
claim out of that money was subject to the authority of Congress to hold the money as a separate fund, set apart from all
other funds, and to subject the same to a course of administration for the purpose of applying it to the claims entitled
thereto.   While the money was invested in United States registered bonds, in pursuance of the *Act March* 3, 1873 (17 Stat.
L., 601, ch. 261), and while the first Court of Commissioners of
Alabama Claims was in existence, the claimant concedes that
it had no right to sue in this court; but that its right to sue
here accrued when that court ceased to be, and the bonds in
which the money was invested were canceled, and so much
of the money as remained was covered into the Treasury.

The motion to dismiss presents the question whether this
court can, under the laws defining its jurisdiction, take cognizance of such an action.   We have not been able to find anything to authorize it.

The petition seems to us to proceed upon an entirely erroneous and indefensible view of the relations between the government and the citizens of the United States in reference to
the matter of the claims of the latter against foreign governments.

It assumes that when that government seeks from another
government reparation for injuries to a citizen of the United
States, it thereby becomes the agent of the citizen.

If this be true, then it necessarily follows that the government derives from the citizen the power to act as his agent, is
subject to the citizen's instructions, is liable to revocation of its
authority by the citizen, and is accountable to the citizen for
the due exercise of its agency.

When it is remembered that the national government, not
only at home but over the whole earth, embodies, represents, and
wields the sovereignty of the American nation, so far as authorized by the Constitution of the United States; and that when
it speaks to or treats with another nation it does so in no character but that of a sovereign, and is not known nor would be

recognized in any other; it seems quite impossible to conceive of there being underneath its apparent sovereignty an agency for a man or a company of men, to whom it is to look for authority and instructions, and to whom it may become answerable in court on an implied *assumpsit,* for money had and received in its sovereign capacity from another sovereign.

It seems to us to be equally impossible to hold the United States to be a trustee for any one when it receives a sum of money from a foreign government, paid in pursuance of a treaty, for the satisfaction of claims of American citizens against such government, unless the trust is declared and created by the terms of the treaty or by an act of Congress. As between the United States and an individual there can be no such thing as an implied or constructive trust, irrespective of written law.

We do not mean to affirm that under no circumstances could the national government become an agent of or trustee for an individual; but that it cannot become such except by a law made conformably to the Constitution, either by the treaty-making or the legislative power. As no such law exists in regard to the money paid by Great Britain under the treaty of Washington, the United States cannot be considered as either an agent or trustee for the claimant. So far from that, the United States never had any relation whatever to private claimants against Great Britain, or to Great Britain, except that of a sovereign state.

When those claimants invoked the aid of the national government in reference to their reclamations on Great Britain, they sought an exercise by that government of the sovereign power through which alone this nation speaks to and acts upon other nations.

When the national government urged upon Great Britain the demands of American citizens on account of the depredations of the rebel cruisers, those demands became reclamations by the sovereignty of this nation against the British sovereign, and passed out of the region of mere private right into the domain of international law, and out of the hands of the citizen into those of his government.

When they so passed, the authority of the national government over them became immovable and supreme, not only as between it and the citizen, but as between it and Great Britain. If not so, it was impossible for the United States to have treated honorably with Great Britain in regard to them; for it was Great Britain's high and undoubted right to know that the United States had sovereign power, absolute and unimpeachable, to do what they saw fit in regard to the claims which were the subject-matter of the treaty, and that there was nothing behind to impair or weaken that power.

When the United States appeared before the tribunal of arbitration created by the treaty, they appeared not as an agent advancing private claims, but as a sovereign seeking satisfaction of its own demands for injuries done to its subjects; and when the tribunal awarded $15,500,000 to be paid to the United States, it was to the United States as a sovereign, "for the satisfaction of all the claims referred to the consideration of the tribunal"; and the United States received that sum, and gave acquittance therefor, as a sovereign, and not otherwise. Thenceforth there existed no private claims of American citizens against Great Britain for the depredations of the rebel cruisers; they were all obliterated by the act of the United States as a sovereign, in demanding and receiving satisfaction therefor. Nor were there, in law, any such claims against the United States. That sum was received by the United States in their sovereign capacity, unmixed, in law, with any private right, and unaffected by any legal obligation to pay out any part of it to any one. None of it could ever go out of the Treasury to any individual except "in consequence of appropriations made by law." If private claimants sought access to it for the payment of their claims, they could obtain it only through an act of Congress; to which body alone it belonged to say whether any, and if any, what, descriptions of the claims "generically known as the 'Alabama claims'" should ever be paid out of that money, and when, where, and how their payments should be authorized and provided for. No failure on the part of Congress to authorize payment of those claims, or any of them, could ever authorize judicial recourse against the United States in this or any other court.

But, inasmuch as the money was paid for private claims, and was a gross sum paid for all such claims, without mention of any individual one, there was a necessity for an official and authoritative ascertainment of those which should be paid. I was the sovereign right of the United States, of their own voli tion, when and how they pleased, to provide, by law, for that ascertainment; and no such right could possibly exist else where. From sovereign inaction or delay, from sovereign par tiality or even injustice in selecting the claims to be allowed, there was no appeal, except to the conscience and good will of Congress. It was to every intent a case where without written law there could be no legal right.

The Congress, without unnecessary delay, met the wishes of those interested by passing, June 23, 1874, (18 Stat. L., part 3, p. 245, ch. 459,) an *Act for the creation of the "Court of Commissioners of Alabama Claims,"* "for the adjudication and dis-

position of the moneys received into the Treasury under the
award of the tribunal of arbitration by virtue of the * * *
treaty aforesaid." That court was revived and re-established
by the *Act June* 10, 1882, (22 Stat. L., 98, ch. 195,) and is now
in existence. The claimant now seeking relief here has never
appeared as a suitor in that tribunal, because its claim does
not belong to any description of demands which those acts authorized to be presented there; and hence its appeal to this
court to take cognizance of its claim under our general jurisdiction of "all claims founded upon any contract, expressed or implied, with the government of the United States." But we
cannot entertain its appeal, for the plain and incontrovertible
reason that the sovereign authority of the nation has created
another tribunal for the investigation and adjudication of the
"Alabama claims," so far as that authority wills to have them
investigated and adjudicated; and by so doing has totally excluded from all other tribunals or authorities any right to take
official action upon the allowance of any claim on the money
received by the United States under the treaty. It matters
not that Congress did not open the door of that court wide
enough to let this claimant in: that was for Congress to do
or not as it saw fit; and we are not here to sit as a court of appeals from the decision of that body, in a matter in which its
power is supreme and we have none at all.

The motion to dismiss the petition is sustained.

Editor's Note. The treaty between the U.S. and
Great Britain, cited by the Court, was the treaty concerning the Alabama claim, May 8, 1871 (17 Stat. 873;
1 Malloy, p. 700). The arbitral award rendered pursuant to that treaty, is printed in 1 Malloy, p. 717.

The Chinese Exclusion Case
Chae Chan Ping v. United States
130 U.S. 581; 9 S. Ct. 623 (1889)

THE court stated the case as follows in its opinion:

This case comes before us on appeal from an order of the
Circuit Court of the United States for the Northern District of
California refusing to release the appellant, on a writ of *habeas
corpus*, from his alleged unlawful detention by Captain Walker,

master of the steamship Belgic, lying within the harbor of San Francisco. The appellant is a subject of the Emperor of China and a laborer by occupation. He resided at San Francisco, California, following his occupation, from some time in 1875 until June 2, 1887, when he left for China on the steamship Gaelic, having in his possession a certificate, in terms entitling him to return to the United States, bearing date on that day, duly issued to him by the collector of customs of the port of San Francisco, pursuant to the provisions of section four of the restriction act of May 6, 1882, as amended by the act of July 5, 1884. 22 Stat. 58, c. 126; 23 Stat. 115, c. 220.

On the 7th of September, 1888, the appellant, on his return to California, sailed from Hong Kong in the steamship Belgic, which arrived within the port of San Francisco on the 8th of October following. On his arrival he presented to the proper custom-house officers his certificate, and demanded permission to land. The collector of the port refused the permit, solely on the ground that under the act of Congress, approved October 1, 1888, supplementary to the restriction acts of 1882 and 1884, the certificate had been annulled and his right to land abrogated, and he had been thereby forbidden again to enter the United States. 25 Stat. 504, c. 1064. The captain of the steamship, therefore, detained the appellant on board the steamer. Thereupon a petition on his behalf was presented to the Circuit Court of the United States for the Northern District of California, alleging that he was unlawfully restrained of his liberty, and praying that a writ of *habeas corpus* might be issued directed to the master of the steamship, commanding him to have the body of the appellant, with the cause of his detention, before the court at a time and place designated, to do and receive what might there be considered in the premises. A writ was accordingly issued, and in obedience to it the body of the appellant was produced before the court. Upon the hearing which followed, the court, after finding the facts substantially as stated, held as conclusions of law that the appellant was not entitled to enter the United States, and was not unlawfully restrained of his liberty, and ordered that he be remanded to the custody of the master of the steamship from which he had been taken under the writ. From this order an appeal was taken to this court.

Mr. Justice Field delivered the opinion of the court.

The appeal involves a consideration of the validity of the act of Congress of October 1, 1888, prohibiting Chinese laborers from entering the United States who had departed before its passage, having a certificate issued under the act of 1882 as amended by the act of 1884, granting them permission to return. The validity of the act is assailed as being in effect an expulsion from the country of Chinese laborers, in violation of existing treaties between the United States and the government of China, and of rights vested in them under the laws of Congress.

It will serve to present with greater clearness the nature and force of the objections to the act, if a brief statement be made of the general character of the treaties between the two countries and of the legislation of Congress to carry them into execution.

The first treaty between the United States and the Empire of China was concluded on the 3d of July, 1844, and ratified in December of the following year. 8 Stat. 592. Previous to that time there had been an extensive commerce between the two nations, that to China being confined to a single port. It was not, however, attended by any serious disturbances between our people there and the Chinese. In August, 1842, as the result of a war between England and China, a treaty was concluded stipulating for peace and friendship between them, and, among other things, that British subjects, with their families and establishments, should be allowed to reside for the purpose of carrying on mercantile pursuits at the five principal ports of the empire. 6 Hertslet's Commercial Treaties, 221; 3 Nouveau Recueil Général de Traités (1842), 484. Actuated by a desire to establish by treaty friendly relations between the United States and the Chinese Empire, and to secure to our people the same commercial privileges which had been thus conceded to British subjects, Congress placed at the disposal of the President the means to enable him to establish future commercial relations between the two countries "on terms of national equal reciprocity." Act of March, 1843, c. 90, 5 Stat. 624. A mission was accordingly sent by him to China, at the head of which was placed Mr. Caleb Cushing, a gentleman of large experience in public affairs. He found the Chinese government ready to concede by treaty to the United States all that had been reluctantly yielded to England through compulsion. As the result of his negotiations the treaty of 1844 was concluded. It stipulated, among other things, that there should be a "perfect, permanent and universal peace, and a sincere and cordial amity" between the two nations; that the five principal ports of the empire should be opened to the citizens of the United States, who should be permitted to reside with their families and trade there, and to proceed with their vessels and merchandise to and from any foreign port and either of said five ports; and while peaceably attending to their affairs should receive the protection of the Chinese authorities. Senate Document No. 138, 28th Cong. 2d Sess.

The treaty between England and China did not have the effect of securing permanent peace and friendship between those countries. British subjects in China were often subjected not only to the violence of mobs, but to insults and outrages from local authorities of the country, which led to retaliatory measures for the punishment of the aggressors. To such an extent were these measures carried, and such resistance offered to them, that in 1856 the two countries were in open war. England then determined, with the cooperation of France, between which countries there seemed to be perfect accord, to secure from the government of China, among other things, a recognition of the right of other powers to be represented there by accredited ministers, an extension of commercial intercourse with that country, and stipulations for religious freedom to all foreigners there, and for the suppression of piracy. England requested of the President the concurrence and active co-operation of the United States similar to that which France had accorded, and to authorize our naval and political authorities to act in concert with the allied forces. As this proposition involved a participation in existing hostilities, the request could not be acceded to, and the Secretary of State in his communication to the English government explained that the war-making power of the United States was not vested in the President but in Congress, and that he had no authority, therefore, to order aggressive hostilities to be undertaken. But as the rights of citizens of the United States might be seriously affected by the results of existing hostilities, and commercial intercourse between the United States and China be disturbed, it, was deemed advisable to send to China a minister plenipotentiary to represent our government and watch our interests there. Accordingly, Mr. William B. Reed, of Philadelphia, was appointed such minister, and instructed, whilst abstaining from any direct interference, to aid by peaceful coöperation the objects the allied forces were seeking to accomplish. Senate Document No. 47, 35th Cong. 1st Sess. Through him a new treaty was negotiated with the Chinese government. It was concluded in June, 1858, and ratified in August of the following year. 12 Stat. 1023. It reiterated the pledges of peace and friendship between the two nations, renewed the promise of protection to all citizens of the United States in China peaceably attending to their affairs, and stipulated for security to Christians in the profession of their religion. Neither the treaty of 1844, nor that of 1858, touched upon the migration and emigration of the citizens and subjects of the two nations respectively from one country to the other. But in 1868 a great change in the relations of the two nations was made in that respect. In that year a mission from China, composed of distinguished functionaries of that empire, came to the United States with the professed object of establishing closer relations between the two countries and their peoples. At its head was placed Mr. Anson Burlingame, an eminent citizen of the United States, who had at one time represented this country as commissioner to China. He resigned his office under our government to accept the position tendered to him by the Chinese government. The mission was hailed in the United States as the harbinger of a new era in the history of China — as the opening up to free intercourse with other nations and peoples a country that for ages had been isolated and closed against foreigners, who were allowed to have intercourse and to trade with the Chinese only at a few designated places; and the belief was general, and confidently expressed, that great benefits would follow to the world generally and especially to the United States. On its arrival in Washington, additional articles to the treaty of 1858 were agreed upon, which gave expression to the general desire that the two nations and their peoples should be drawn closer together. The new articles, eight in number, were agreed to on the 28th of July, 1868, and ratifications of them were exchanged at Pekin in November of the following year. 16 Stat. 739. Of these articles the 5th, 6th and 7th are as follows:

"ARTICLE V. The United States of America and the Emperor of China cordially recognize the inherent and inalienable right of man to change his home and allegiance, and also the mutual advantage of the free migration and emigration of their citizens and subjects respectively from the one country to the other for purposes of curiosity, of trade, or as permanent residents. The high contracting parties, therefore, join in reprobating any other than an entirely voluntary emigration for these purposes. They consequently agree to pass laws making it a pénal offence for a citizen of the United States or Chinese subjects to take Chinese subjects either to the United States or to any other foreign country, or for a Chinese subject or citizen of the United States to take citizens of the United States to China or to any other foreign country without their free and voluntary consent, respectively.

"Article VI. Citizens of the United States visiting or residing in China shall enjoy the same privileges, immunities or exemptions in respect to travel or residence as may there be enjoyed by the citizens or subjects of the most favored nation. And, reciprocally, Chinese subjects visiting or residing in the United States shall enjoy the same privileges, immunities and exemptions in respect to travel or residence as may there be enjoyed by the citizens or subjects of the most favored nation. But nothing herein contained shall be held to confer naturalization upon citizens of the United States in China, nor upon the subjects of China in the United States.

"Article VII. Citizens of the United States shall enjoy all the privileges of the public educational institutions under the control of the government of China; and, reciprocally, Chinese subjects shall enjoy all the privileges of the public educational institutions under the control of the government of the United States, which are enjoyed in the respective countries by the citizens or subjects of the most favored nation. The citizens of the United States may freely establish and maintain schools within the Empire of China at those places where foreigners are by treaty permitted to reside; and, reciprocally, Chinese subjects may enjoy the same privileges and immunities in the United States."

But notwithstanding these strong expressions of friendship and good will, and the desire they evince for free intercourse, events were transpiring on the Pacific Coast which soon dissipated the anticipations indulged as to the benefits to follow the immigration of Chinese to this country. The previous treaties of 1844 and 1858 were confined principally to mutual declarations of peace and friendship and to stipulations for commercial intercourse at certain ports in China and for protection to our citizens whilst peaceably attending to their affairs. It was not until the additional articles of 1868 were adopted that any public declaration was made by the two nations that there were advantages in the free migration and emigration of their citizens and subjects respectively from one country to the other; and stipulations given that each should enjoy in the country of the other, with respect to travel or residence, the "privileges, immunities, and exemptions" enjoyed by citizens or subjects of the most favored nation. Whatever modifications have since been made to these general provisions have been caused by a well-founded apprehension — from the experience of years — that a limitation to the immigration of certain classes from China was essential to the peace of the community on the Pacific Coast, and possibly to the preservation of our civilization there. A few words on this point may not be deemed inappropriate here, they being confined to matters of public notoriety, which have frequently been brought to the attention of Congress. Report of Committee of H. R. No. 872, 46th Cong. 2d Sess.

The discovery of gold in California in 1848, as is well known, was followed by a large immigration thither from all parts of the world, attracted not only by the hope of gain from the mines, but from the great prices paid for all kinds of labor. The news of the discovery penetrated China, and laborers came from there in great numbers, a few with their own means, but by far the greater number under contract with employers, for whose benefit they worked. These laborers readily secured employment, and, as domestic servants, and in various kinds of out-door work, proved to be exceedingly useful. For some years little opposition was made to them except when they sought to work in the mines, but, as their numbers increased, they began to engage in various mechanical pursuits and trades, and thus came in competition with our artisans and mechanics, as well as our laborers in the field.

The competition steadily increased as the laborers came in crowds on each steamer that arrived from China, or Hong Kong, an adjacent English port. They were generally industrious and frugal. Not being accompanied by families, except in rare instances, their expenses were small; and they were content with the simplest fare, such as would not suffice for our laborers and artisans. The competition between them and our people was for this reason altogether in their favor, and the consequent irritation, proportionately deep and bitter, was followed, in many cases, by open conflicts, to the great disturbance of the public peace.

The differences of race added greatly to the difficulties of the situation. Notwithstanding the favorable provisions of the new articles of the treaty of 1868, by which all the privileges, immunities, and exemptions were extended to subjects of China in the United States which were accorded to citizens or subjects of the most favored nation, they remained strangers in the land, residing apart by themselves, and adhering to the customs and usages of their own country. It seemed impossible for them to assimilate with our people or to make any change in their habits or modes of living. As they grew in numbers each year the people of the coast saw, or believed they saw, in the facility of immigration, and in the crowded millions of China, where population presses upon the means of subsistence, great danger that at no distant day that portion of our country would be overrun by them unless prompt action was taken to restrict their immigration. The people there accordingly petitioned earnestly for protective legislation.

In December, 1878, the convention which framed the present constitution of California, being in session, took this subject up, and memorialized Congress upon it, setting forth, in substance, that the presence of Chinese laborers had a baneful effect upon the material interests of the State, and upon public morals; that their immigration was in numbers approaching the character of an Oriental invasion, and was a menace to our civilization; that the discontent from this cause was not confined to any political party, or to any class or nationality, but was well-nigh universal; that they retained the habits and customs of their own country, and in fact constituted a Chinese settlement within the State, without any interest in our country or its institutions; and praying Congress to take measures to prevent their further immigration. This memorial was presented to Congress in February, 1879.

So urgent and constant were the prayers for relief against existing and anticipated evils, both from the public authorities of the Pacific Coast and from private individuals, that Congress was impelled to act on the subject. Many persons, however, both in and out of Congress, were of opinion that so long as the treaty remained unmodified, legislation restricting immigration would be a breach of faith with China. A statute was accordingly passed appropriating money to send commissioners to China to act with our minister there in negotiating and concluding by treaty a settlement of such matters of interest between the two governments as might be confided to them. 21 Stat. 133, c. 88. Such commissioners were appointed, and as the result of their negotiations the supplementary treaty of November 17, 1880, was concluded and ratified in May of the following year. 22 Stat. 826. It declares in its first article that "Whenever, in the opinion of the Government of the United States, the coming of Chinese laborers to the United States, or their residence therein, affects or threatens to affect the interests of that country, or to endanger the good order of the said country or of any locality within the territory thereof, the Government of China agrees that the Government of the United States may regulate, limit, or suspend such coming or residence, but may not absolutely prohibit it. The limitation or suspension shall be reasonable and shall apply only to Chinese who may go to the United States as laborers, other classes not being included in the limitations. Legislation taken in regard to Chinese laborers will be of such a character only as is necessary to enforce the regulation, limitation, or suspension of immigration, and immigrants shall not be subject to personal maltreatment or abuse." In its second article it declares that "Chinese subjects, whether proceeding to the United States as teachers, students, merchants, or from curiosity, together with their body and household servants, and Chinese laborers who are now in the United States shall be allowed to go and come of their own free will and accord, and shall be accorded all the rights, privileges, immunities and exemptions which are accorded to the citizens and subjects of the most favored nation."

The government of China thus agreed that notwithstanding the stipulations of former treaties, the United States might regulate, limit, or suspend the coming of Chinese laborers, or their residence therein, without absolutely forbidding it, whenever in their opinion the interests of the country, or of any part of it, might require such action. Legislation for such regulation, limitation, or suspension was entrusted to the discretion of our government, with the condition that it should only be such as might be necessary for that purpose, and that the immigrants should not be maltreated or abused. On the 6th of May, 1882, an act of Congress was approved, to carry this supplementary treaty into effect. 22 Stat. 58, c. 126. It is entitled "An act to execute certain treaty stipulations relating to Chinese." Its first section declares that after ninety days from the passage of the act, and for the period of ten years from its date, the coming of Chinese laborers to the United States is suspended, and that it shall be unlawful for any such laborer to come, or, having come, to remain within the United States. The second makes it a misdemeanor, punishable by fine, to which imprisonment may be added, for the master of any vessel knowingly to bring within the United States from a foreign country, and land, any such Chinese laborer. The third provides that those two sections shall not apply to Chinese laborers who were in the United States November 17, 1880, or who should come within ninety days after the passage of the act. The fourth declares that, for the purpose of identifying the laborers who were here on the 17th of November, 1880, or who should come within the ninety days mentioned, and to furnish them with "the proper evidence" of their right to go from and come to the United States, the "collector of customs of the district from which any such Chinese laborer shall depart from the United States shall, in person or by deputy, go on board each vessel having on board any such Chinese laborer and cleared or about to sail from his district for a foreign port, and on such vessel make a list of all such Chinese laborers, which shall be entered in registry books to be kept for that purpose, in which shall be stated the name, age, occupation, last place of residence, physical marks or peculiarities and all facts necessary for the identification of each of such Chinese laborers, which books shall be safely kept in the custom-house;" and each laborer thus departing shall be entitled to receive, from the collector or his deputy, a certificate containing such particulars, corresponding with the registry, as may serve to identify him. "The certificate herein provided for," says the section, "shall entitle the Chinese laborer to whom the same is issued to return to and re-enter the United States upon producing and delivering the same to the collector of customs of the district at which such Chinese laborer shall seek to re-enter."

The enforcement of this act with respect to laborers who were in the United States on November 17, 1880, was attended with great embarrassment, from the suspicious nature, in many instances, of the testimony offered to establish the residence of the parties, arising from the loose notions entertained by the witnesses of the obligation of an oath. This fact led to a desire for further legislation restricting the evidence receivable, and the amendatory act of July 5, 1884, was accordingly passed. 23 Stat. 115, c. 220. The committee of the House of Representatives on foreign affairs, to whom the original bill was referred, in reporting it back, recommending its passage, stated that there had been such manifold evasions, as well as attempted evasions, of the act of 1882, that it had failed to meet the demands which called it into existence. Report in H. R. No. 614, 48th Cong. 1st Sess. To obviate the difficulties attending its enforcement the amendatory act of 1884 declared that the certificate which the laborer must obtain "shall be the only evidence permissible to establish his right of re-entry" into the United States.

This act was held by this court not to require the certificate from laborers who were in the United States on the 17th of November, 1880, who had departed out of the country before May 6, 1882, and remained out until after July 5, 1884. *Chew Heong* v. *United States*, 112 U. S. 536. The same difficulties and embarrassments continued with respect to the proof of their former residence. Parties were able to pass successfully the required examination as to their residence before November 17, 1880, who, it was generally believed, had never visited our shores. To prevent the possibility of the policy of excluding Chinese laborers being evaded, the act of

October 1, 1888, the validity of which is the subject of consideration in this case, was passed. It is entitled "An act a supplement to an act entitled 'An act to execute certain treaty stipulations relating to Chinese,' approved the sixth day of May, eighteen hundred and eighty-two." 25 Stat. 504, c. 1064. It is as follows :

"*Be it enacted by the Senate and House of Representatives of the United States of America in Congress assembled*, That from and after the passage of this act, it shall be unlawful for any Chinese laborer who shall at any time heretofore have been, or who may now or hereafter be, a resident within the United States, and who shall have departed, or shall depart therefrom, and shall not have returned before the passage of this act, to return to, or remain in, the United States.

"Sec. 2. That no certificates of identity provided for in the fourth and fifth sections of the act to which this is a supplement shall hereafter be issued ; and every certificate heretofore issued in pursuance thereof is hereby declared void and of no effect, and the Chinese laborer claiming admission by virtue thereof shall not be permitted to enter the United States.

"Sec. 3. That all the duties prescribed, liabilities, penalties, and forfeitures imposed, and the powers conferred by the second, tenth, eleventh and twelfth sections of the act to which this is a supplement, are hereby extended and made applicable to the provisions of this act.

"Sec. 4. That all such part or parts of the act to which this is a supplement as are inconsistent herewith are hereby repealed.

"Approved October 1, 1888."

The validity of this act, as already mentioned, is assailed, as being in effect an expulsion from the country of Chinese laborers in violation of existing treaties between the United States and the government of China, and of rights vested in them under the laws of Congress. The objection that the act is in conflict with the treaties was earnestly pressed in the court below, and the answer to it constitutes the principal part of its opinion. 36 Fed. Rep. 431. Here the objection made is, that the act of 1888 impairs a right vested under the treaty of 1880, as a law of the United States, and the statutes of 1882 and of 1884 passed in execution of it. It must be conceded that the act of 1888 is in contravention of express stipulations of the treaty of 1868 and of the supplemental treaty of 1880, but it is not on that account invalid or to be restricted in its enforcement. The treaties were of no greater legal obligation than the act of Congress. By the Constitution, laws made in pursuance thereof and treaties made under the authority of the United States are both declared to be the supreme law of the land, and no paramount authority is given to one over the other. A treaty, it is true, is in its nature a contract between nations and is often merely promissory in its character, requiring legislation to carry its stipulations into effect. Such legislation will be open to future repeal or amendment. If the treaty operates by its own force, and relates to a subject within the power of Congress, it can be deemed in that particular only the equivalent of a legislative act, to be repealed or modified at the pleasure of Congress. In either case the last expression of the sovereign will must control.

The effect of legislation upon conflicting treaty stipulations was elaborately considered in *The Head Money Cases*, and it was there adjudged " that so far as a treaty made by the United States with any foreign nation can become the subject of judicial cognizance in the courts of this country, it is subject to such acts as Congress may pass for its enforcement, modification, or repeal." 112 U. S. 580, 599. This doctrine was affirmed and followed in *Whitney* v. *Robertson*, 124 U. S. 190, 195. It will not be presumed that the legislative department of the government will lightly pass laws which are in conflict with the treaties of the country; but that circumstances may arise which would not only justify the government in disregarding their stipulations, but demand in the interests of the country that it should do so, there can be no question. Unexpected events may call for a change in the policy of the country. Neglect or violation of stipulations on the part of the other contracting party may require corresponding action on our part. When a reciprocal engagement is not carried out by one of the contracting parties, the other may also decline to keep the corresponding engagement. In 1798 the conduct towards this country of the government of France was of such a character that Congress declared that the United States were freed and exonerated from the stipulations of previous treaties with that country. Its act on the subject was as follows:

" *An Act to declare the treaties heretofore concluded with France, no longer obligatory on the United States.*

" Whereas the treaties concluded between the United States and France have been repeatedly violated on the part of the French government; and the just claims of the United States for reparation of the injuries so committed have been refused, and their attempts to negotiate an amicable adjustment of all complaints between the two nations have been repelled with indignity ; And whereas, under authority of the French government, there is yet pursued against the United States a system of predatory violence, infracting the said treaties, and hostile to the rights of a free and independent nation :

"*Be it enacted by the Senate and House of Representatives of the United States of America in Congress assembled,* That the United States are of right freed and exonerated from the stipulations of the treaties, and of the consular convention, heretofore concluded between the United States and France ; and that the same shall not henceforth be regarded as legally obligatory on the government or citizens of the United States." 1 Stat. 578, c. 67.

This act, as seen, applied in terms only to the future. Of course, whatever of a permanent character had been executed or vested under the treaties was not affected by it. In that respect the abrogation of the obligations of a treaty operates, like the repeal of a law, only upon the future, leaving transactions executed under it to stand unaffected. The validity of this legislative release from the stipulations of the treaties was of course not a matter for judicial cognizance. The question whether our government is justified in disregarding its engagements with another nation is not one for the determination of the courts. This subject was fully considered by Mr. Justice Curtis, whilst sitting at the circuit, in *Taylor* v. *Morton,* 2 Curtis, 454, 459, and he held that whilst it would always be a matter of the utmost gravity and delicacy to refuse to execute a treaty, the power to do so was prerogative, of which no nation could be deprived without deeply affecting its independence; but whether a treaty with a foreign sovereign had been violated by him, whether the consideration of a particular stipulation of a treaty had been voluntarily withdrawn by one party so as to no longer be obligatory upon the other, and whether the views and acts of a foreign sovereign, manifested through his representative, had given just occasion to the political departments of our government to withhold the execution of a promise contained in a treaty or to act in direct contravention of such promise, were not judicial questions; that the power to determine them has not been confided to the judiciary, which has no suitable means to execute it, but to the executive and legislative departments of the government; and that it belongs to diplomacy and legislation, and not to the administration of existing laws. And the learned justice added, as a necessary consequence of these conclusions, that if Congress has this power, it is wholly immaterial to

inquire whether it has, by the statute complained of, departed
from the treaty or not; or, if it has, whether such departure
was accidental or designed; and if the latter, whether the
reasons therefor were good or bad.   These views were reas-
serted and fully adopted by this court in *Whitney* v. *Robertson*,
124 U. S. 190, 195.   And we may add to the concluding observation of the learned justice, that if the power mentioned
is vested in Congress, any reflection upon its motives, or the
motives of any of its members in exercising it, would be entirely uncalled for.   This court is not a censor of the morals
of other departments of the government; it is not invested
with any authority to pass judgment upon the motives of their
conduct.   When once it is established that Congress possesses
the power to pass an act, our province ends with its construction, and its application to cases as they are presented for determination.   Congress has the power under the Constitution
to declare war, and in two instances where the power has
been exercised — in the war of 1812 against Great Britain,
and in 1846 against Mexico — the propriety and wisdom and
justice of its action were vehemently assailed by some of the
ablest and best men in the country, but no one doubted the
legality of the proceeding, and any imputation by this or any
other court of the United States upon the motives of the members of Congress who in either case voted for the declaration,
would have been justly the cause of animadversion.   We do
not mean to intimate that the moral aspects of legislative acts
may not be proper subjects of consideration.   Undoubtedly
they may be, at proper times and places, before the public, in
the halls of Congress, and in all the modes by which the public
mind can be influenced.   Public opinion thus enlightened,
brought to bear upon legislation, will do more than all other
causes to prevent abuses; but the province of the courts is to
pass upon the validity of laws, not to make them, and when
their validity is established, to declare their meaning and apply
their provisions.   All else lies beyond their domain.

There being nothing in the treaties between China and the
United States to impair the validity of the act of Congress of
October 1, 1888, was it on any other ground beyond the competency of Congress to pass it?   If so, it must be because it was
not within the power of Congress to prohibit Chinese laborers
who had at the time departed from the United States, or should
subsequently depart, from returning to the United States.
Those laborers are not citizens of the United States; they are
aliens.   That the government of the United States, through the
action of the legislative department, can exclude aliens from its

territory is a proposition which we do not think open to controversy. Jurisdiction over its own territory to that extent is an
incident of every independent nation. It is a part of its independence. If it could not exclude aliens it would be to that
extent subject to the control of another power. As said by this
court in the case of *The Exchange*, 7 Cranch, 116, 136, speaking by Chief Justice Marshall : "The jurisdiction of the nation
within its own territory is necessarily exclusive and absolute.
It is susceptible of no limitation not imposed by itself. Any
restriction upon it, deriving validity from an external source,
would imply a diminution of its sovereignty to the extent of
the restriction, and an investment of that sovereignty to the
same extent in that power which could impose such restriction.
All exceptions, therefore, to the full and complete power of a
nation within its own territories, must be traced up to the consent of the nation itself. They can flow from no other legitimate source."

While under our Constitution and form of government the
great mass of local matters is controlled by local authorities,
the United States, in their relation to foreign countries and
their subjects or citizens are one nation, invested with powers
which belong to independent nations, the exercise of which
can be invoked for the maintenance of its absolute independence and security throughout its entire territory. The powers
to declare war, make treaties, suppress insurrection, repel invasion, regulate foreign commerce, secure republican governments to the States, and admit subjects of other nations to
citizenship, are all sovereign powers, restricted in their exercise only by the Constitution itself and considerations of public
policy and justice which control, more or less, the conduct of
all civilized nations. As said by this court in the case of
Cohens v. *Virginia*, 6 Wheat. 264, 413, speaking by the same
great Chief Justice : " That the United States form, for many,
and for most important purposes, a single nation, has not yet
been denied. In war, we are one people. In making peace
we are one people. In all commercial regulations, we are one
and the same people. In many other respects, the American
people are one ; and the government which is alone capable of
controlling and managing their interests in all these respects,
is the government of the Union. It is their government, and
in that character they have no other. America has chosen to
be in many respects, and to many purposes, a nation ; and for
all these purposes her government is complete ; to all these objects, it is competent. The people have declared, that in the
exercise of all powers given for these objects, it is supreme. It

can then in affecting these objects legitimately control all individuals or governments within the American territory. The constitution and laws of a State, so far as they are repugnant to the Constitution and laws of the United States, are absolutely void. These States are constituent parts of the United States. They are members of one great empire — for some purposes sovereign, for some purposes subordinate." The same view is expressed in a different form by Mr. Justice Bradley, in *Knox* v. *Lee*, 12 Wall. 457, 555, where he observes that "the United States is not only a government, but it is a national government, and the only government in this country that has the character of nationality. It is invested with power over all the foreign relations of the country, war, peace and negotiations and intercourse with other nations; all which are forbidden to the state governments. It has jurisdiction over all those general subjects of legislation and sovereignty which affect the interests of the whole people equally and alike, and which require uniformity of regulations and laws, such as the coinage, weights and measures, bankruptcies, the postal system, patent and copyright laws, the public lands and interstate commerce, all which subjects are expressly or impliedly prohibited to the state governments. It has power to suppress insurrections, as well as to repel invasions, and to organize, arm, discipline and call into service the militia of the whole country. The President is charged with the duty and invested with the power to take care that the laws be faithfully executed. The judiciary has jurisdiction to decide controversies between the States, and between their respective citizens, as well as questions of national concern; and the government is clothed with power to guarantee to every State a republican form of government, and to protect each of them against invasion and domestic violence."

The control of local matters being left to local authorities, and national matters being entrusted to the government of the Union, the problem of free institutions existing over a widely extended country, having different climates and varied interests, has been happily solved. For local interests the several States of the Union exist, but for national purposes, embracing our relations with foreign nations, we are but one people, one nation, one power.

To preserve its independence, and give security against foreign aggression and encroachment, is the highest duty of every nation, and to attain these ends nearly all other considerations are to be subordinated. It matters not in what form such aggression and encroachment come, whether from the foreign nation acting in its national character or from vast hordes of its people crowding in upon us. The government, possessing the powers which are to be exercised for protection and security, is clothed with authority to determine the occasion on which the powers shall be called forth; and its determination, so far as the subjects affected are concerned, are necessarily conclusive upon all its departments and officers. If, therefore, the government of the United States, through its legislative department, considers the presence of foreigners of a different race in this country, who will not assimilate with us, to be dangerous to its peace and security, their exclusion is not to be stayed because at the time there are no actual hostilities with the nation of which the foreigners are subjects. The existence of war would render the necessity of the proceeding only more obvious and pressing. The same necessity, in a less pressing degree, may arise when war does not exist, and the same authority which adjudges the necessity in one case must also determine it in the other. In both cases its determination is conclusive upon the judiciary. If the government of the country of which the foreigners excluded are subjects is dissatisfied with this action it can make complaint to the executive head of our government, or resort to any other measure which, in its judgment, its interests or dignity may demand; and there lies its only remedy.

The power of the government to exclude foreigners from the country whenever, in its judgment, the public interests require such exclusion, has been asserted in repeated instances, and never denied by the executive or legislative departments. In a communication made in December, 1852, to Mr. A. Dudley Mann, at one time a special agent of the Department of State in Europe, Mr. Everett, then Secretary of State under President Fillmore, writes: "This government could never give up the right of excluding foreigners whose presence it might deem a source of danger to the United States." "Nor will this government consider such exclusion of American citizens from Russia necessarily a matter of diplomatic complaint to that country." In a dispatch to Mr. Fay, our minister to Switzerland, in March, 1856, Mr. Marcy, Secretary of State under President Pierce, writes: "Every society possesses the undoubted right to determine who shall compose its members, and it is exercised by all nations, both in peace and war." "It may always be questionable whether a resort to this power is warranted by the circumstances, or what department of the government is empowered to exert it; but there can be no doubt that it is possessed by all nations, and that each may decide for itself when the occasion arises demanding its exercise." In a communication in September, 1869, to Mr. Washburne, our minister to France, Mr. Fish, Secretary of State under President Grant, uses this language: "The control of the people within its limits, and the right to expel from its territory persons who are dangerous to the peace of the State, are too clearly within the essential attributes of sovereignty to be seriously contested. Strangers visiting or sojourning in a foreign country voluntarily submit themselves to its laws and customs, and the municipal laws of France, authorizing the expulsion of strangers, are not of such recent date, nor has the exercise of the power by the government of France been so infrequent, that sojourners within her territory can claim surprise when the power is put in force." In a communication to Mr. Foster, our minister to Mexico, in July, 1879, Mr. Evarts, Secretary of State under President Hayes, referring to the power vested in the constitution of Mexico to expel objectionable foreigners, says: "The admission that, as that constitution now stands and is interpreted, foreigners who render themselves harmful or objectionable to the general government must expect to be liable to the exercise of the power adverted to, even in time of peace, remains, and no good reason is seen for departing from that conclusion now. But, while there may be no expedient basis on which to found objection, on principle and in advance of a special case thereunder, to the constitutional right thus asserted by Mexico, yet the manner of carrying out such asserted right may be highly objectionable. You would be fully justified in making earnest remonstrances should a citizen of the United States be expelled from Mexican territory without just steps to assure the grounds of such expulsion, and in bringing the fact to the immediate knowledge of the Department." In a communication to Mr. W. J. Stillman, under date of August 3, 1882, Mr. Frelinghuysen, Secretary of State under President Arthur, writes: "This government cannot contest the right of foreign governments to exclude, on police or other grounds, American citizens from their shores." Wharton's International Law Digest, § 206.

The exclusion of paupers, criminals and persons afflicted with incurable diseases, for which statutes have been passed, is only an application of the same power to particular classes of persons, whose presence is deemed injurious or a source of danger to the country. As applied to them, there has never been any question as to the power to exclude them. The power is constantly exercised; its existence is involved in the

right of self-preservation. As to paupers, it makes no difference by whose aid they are brought to the country. As Mr.
Fish, when Secretary of State, wrote, in a communication
under date of December 26, 1872, to Mr. James Moulding, of
Liverpool, the government of the United States "is not willing and will not consent to receive the pauper class of any
community who may be sent or may be assisted in their immigration at the expense of government or of municipal authorities." As to criminals, the power of exclusion has always been
exercised, even in the absence of any statute on the subject.
In a despatch to Mr. Cramer, our minister to Switzerland, in
December, 1881, Mr. Blaine, Secretary of State under President Arthur, writes: "While, under the Constitution and
the laws, this country is open to the honest and industrious
immigrant, it has no room outside of its prisons or almshouses
for depraved and incorrigible criminals or hopelessly dependent
paupers who may have become a pest or burden, or both, to
their own country." Wharton's Int. Law Dig., *supra*.

The power of exclusion of foreigners being an incident of
sovereignty belonging to the government of the United States,
as a part of those sovereign powers delegated by the Constitution, the right to its exercise at any time when, in the judgment of the government, the interests of the country require
it, cannot be granted away or restrained on behalf of any one.
The powers of government are delegated in trust to the United
States, and are incapable of transfer to any other parties.
They cannot be abandoned or surrendered. Nor can their
exercise be hampered, when needed for the public good, by
any considerations of private interest. The exercise of these
public trusts is not the subject of barter or contract. Whatever license, therefore, Chinese laborers may have obtained,
previous to the act of October 1, 1888, to return to the United
States after their departure, is held at the will of the government, revocable at any time, at its pleasure. Whether a
proper consideration by our government of its previous laws,
or a proper respect for the nation whose subjects are affected
by its action, ought to have qualified its inhibition and made
it applicable only to persons departing from the country after
the passage of the act, are not questions for judicial determination. If there be any just ground of complaint on the part of
China, it must be made to the political department of our
government, which is alone competent to act upon the subject.
The rights and interests created by a treaty, which have
become so vested that its expiration or abrogation will not
destroy or impair them, are such as are connected with and

lie in property, capable of sale and transfer or other disposition, not such as are personal and untransferable in their character. Thus in *The Head Money Cases*, the court speaks of certain rights being in some instances conferred upon the citizens or subjects of one nation residing in the territorial limits of the other, which are "capable of enforcement as between private parties in the courts of the country." "An illustration of this character," it adds, "is found in treaties which regulate the mutual rights of citizens and subjects of the contracting nations in regard to rights of property by descent or inheritance, when the individuals concerned are aliens." 112 U. S. 580, 598. The passage cited by counsel from the language of Mr. Justice Washington in *Society for the Propagation of the Gospel* v. *New Haven*, 8 Wheat. 464, 493, also illustrates this doctrine. There the learned justice observes that "if real estate be purchased or secured under a treaty, it would be most mischievous to admit that the extinguishment of the treaty extinguished the right to such estate. In truth, it no more affects such rights than the repeal of a municipal law affects rights acquired under it." Of this doctrine there can be no question in this court; but far different is this case, where a continued suspension of the exercise of a governmental power is insisted upon as a right, because, by the favor and consent of the government, it has not heretofore been exerted with respect to the appellant or to the class to which he belongs. Between property rights not affected by the termination or abrogation of a treaty, and expectations of benefits from the continuance of existing legislation, there is as wide a difference as between realization and hopes.

During the argument reference was made by counsel to the alien law of June 25, 1798, and to opinions expressed at the time by men of great ability and learning against its constitutionality. 1 Stat. 570, c. 58. We do not attach importance to those opinions in their bearing upon this case. The act vested in the President power to order all such aliens as he should judge dangerous to the peace and safety of the United States, or should have reasonable grounds to suspect were concerned in any treasonable or secret machination against the government, to depart out of the territory of the United States within such time as should be expressed in his order. There were other provisions also distinguishing it from the act under consideration. The act was passed during a period of great political excitement, and it was attacked and defended with great zeal and ability. It is enough, however, to say that it is entirely different from the act before us, and the validity of its provisions was never brought to the test of judicial decision in the courts of the United States.

Order affirmed.

Editor's Note. The treaties between the U.S. and China, cited by the Court, were: the Treaty of Peace, Amity and Commerce, July 3, 1844 (8 Stat. 592; 1 Malloy, p. 196); the Treaty of Peace, Friendship and Commerce, June 18, 1858 (12 Stat. 1023; 1 Malloy, p. 211); Additional Articles to the Treaty of 1858, July 28, 1868 (16 Stat. 739; 1 Malloy, p. 234); and the Treaty regarding Chinese Immigration into the U.S., November 17, 1880 (22 Stat. 826; 1 Malloy, p. 239.

Burthe v. Denis
133 U.S. 514; 10 S. Ct. 335 (1890)

At the commencement of the late civil war L. F. Foucher, a citizen of France and a resident of the city of Paris, and bearing the title of Marquis de Circé, was the owner of a plantation situated on the east bank of the Mississippi River, a few miles above the centre of the city of New Orleans, though within its corporate limits. A portion of it was known as Exposition Park or Audubon Park. When the city was occupied by the Federal troops in 1862 they took possession of the plantation. Some of its fields were used for pasture; some were converted into camping ground; and upon part a hospital for the soldiers was built. The whole was in the military occupation and control of the United States, to the entire exclusion of the owner. In 1865 a claim for reimbursement of the damages sustained was presented on behalf of the owner to the Military Claims Commission sitting at New Orleans. General Canby, as commanding general of the district embracing that city, and the head of the commission, made a report upon the claim, recommending, upon the advice of his chief quartermaster, its settlement by the payment of $36,433.33. This report was addressed to the Adjutant General's Department, and forwarded to Washington in June, 1866.

No part of this claim, was, however, paid, for the reason, as
stated by counsel, that before action was had upon it the act
of Congress of February 21, 1867, was passed, forbidding the
settlement of any claim for the occupation of or injury to real
estate by the military authorities or troops of the United
States where such claim originated during the war. 14 Stat.
397, c. 57.

In 1869 Foucher died, leaving a will, in which he made his
widow, also a citizen of France, his universal legatee, and she
was put in possession of his estate. In 1877 she died, leaving
a will by which she devised her entire estate to her nephews
and nieces, who were appointed her universal legatees, jointly.
After some litigation to determine the true construction of
this will, the legatees went into possession of her estate. 31
La. Ann. 568. The estates both of Foucher and of his widow
were settled and the property distributed among the legatees
of the latter or their heirs. The executors were discharged
and the successions considered as finally closed. Neither the
estate of Foucher nor of his widow had received any moneys
upon the claim which had been presented on behalf of Foucher
in 1865, for the damage sustained by the occupation and use
of his plantation by the Federal troops, the payment of which
had been recommended by General Canby; nor was any mention made of the claim in the distribution of the estate of
either.

In January, 1880, a convention was concluded between the
United States and France, 21 Stat. 673, by which it was agreed
that "all claims on the part of corporations, companies, or private individuals, citizens of the United States, upon the government of France, arising out of acts committed against the
persons or property of citizens of the United States not in the
service of the enemies of France, or voluntarily giving aid and
comfort to the same, by the French civil or military authorities, upon the high seas or within the territory of France, its
colonies and dependencies, during the late war between France
and Mexico, or during the war of 1870–'71, between France
and Germany, and the subsequent civil disturbances known as
the 'Insurrection of the Commune;' and on the other hand,
all claims on the part of corporations, companies or private
individuals, citizens of France, upon the government of the
United States, arising out of acts committed against the persons or property of citizens of France not in the service of the
enemies of the United States, or voluntarily giving aid and
comfort to the same, by the civil or military authorities of
the government of the United States, upon the high seas or

within the territorial jurisdiction of the United States, during the period comprised between the thirteenth day of April, eighteen hundred and sixty-one, and the twentieth day of August, eighteen hundred and sixty-six, shall be referred to three commissioners, one of whom shall be named by the President of the United States, and one by the French government, and the third by His Majesty the Emperor of Brazil." The convention also provided that the commission thus constituted should be competent and obliged to examine and decide upon all claims of the above character presented to them by the citizens of either country, except such as had been already diplomatically, judicially or otherwise by competent authorities previously disposed of by either government; but that no claim or item of damage or injury based upon the emancipation or loss of slaves should be entertained. The convention also provided that the commission should, without delay, after its organization, proceed to examine and determine the claims specified, and that the concurring decisions of the commissioners or of any two of them should be conclusive and final; and the contracting parties especially engaged so to consider them, and to give full effect to such decisions, without any objections, evasions, or delay whatever.

The commission thus provided for was organized and proceeded to the hearing of claims at the city of Washington. The claim of Foucher was for acts committed against his property within the period prescribed, and the parties interested in that claim were desirous of presenting it to the commission for consideration. That commission, as it was authorized to do under the act of June 16, 1880, providing for carrying the treaty into effect, had adopted rules for the conduct of its business, among which was one that, if the claimant were dead, his executor or administrator, or legal representatives, must appear for him, and that each claimant should file in the office of the commission a statement of his claim, in the form of a memorial addressed to the commission. 21 Stat. 296, c. 253, § 4. The successions of Mr. and Mrs. Foucher were accordingly reopened, and Arthur Denis was appointed dative testamentary executor in both, that is, an executor to take the place of the one named in the wills of the deceased.

Soon afterwards Mr. Denis filed in the office of the commission a memorial entitled " Arthur Denis, dative testamentary executor of Foucher vs. The United States." In this memorial he presented the claim in the right of Foucher, deceased, and joined with him as claimants all parties interested in the successions of Mr. and Mrs. Foucher, all of whom were citizens of the United States, except Paul Louis Burthe and Dominique François Burthe, who were citizens of France; and he filed a power of attorney showing that he appeared as their agent. Subsequently these latter parties filed a separate petition or memorial, in which they appeared in person. They are heirs each of one-eighth of the estate of Mrs. Foucher.

In June, 1883, the commission rendered its award as follows:

" Arthur Denis
  vs.   } No. 603.
The United States.

" We allow this claim at the sum of nine thousand and two hundred dollars, with interest at five per cent from April 1st, 1865."

Of this award Mr. Denis collected $8229.18, from which he reserved $114.98 for future costs, and deducted $2834.20 for charges and expenses, which are conceded to have been correct, leaving a balance of $5280. This sum as dative executor he proposed to distribute among all the heirs and legatees of Mrs. Foucher precisely as he would have done had this amount been moneys possessed by her as part of her estate at the time of her death. All the parties, except the plaintiffs in error, are citizens of the United States, and were such citizens at the time of the award. The plaintiffs in error being the only heirs who were at the time citizens of France, insisted that they were entitled to the whole award. Mr. Denis presented the matter to the Civil District Court for the Parish of Orleans for determination, showing the respective proportions the heirs and legatees would be entitled to receive if the sum mentioned was to be distributed among them in the same proportion as the original estates. Accompanying this showing — tableau of distribution as it is termed — he made the following statement:

" The undersigned, testamentary executor, understands that the French and American Claims Commission established the uniform jurisprudence for its decisions that it could not hear and determine any claims against the United States except those of claimants and beneficiaries who were French citizens, and that the said commission rejected all claims of persons not French citizens, even when they represented the claim of a deceased French person.

" In claim No. 603, of the succession of L. F. Foucher de Circé, the actual claimants are all American citizens except Paul Louis Burthe and Dominique François Burthe, who are French citizens. Under the said jurisprudence of the commission, and considering the status of the American claimants, the executor felt great doubt and hesitation as to the distribution to be made under this tableau. On the one hand it seemed as if the commission, under its rulings, could not have made any award in favor of the American claimants, and that the award as allowed must have been intended for the French claimants only; but, on the other side, the commission not having in express terms excluded the American claimants, the executor concluded, in making the tableau, to allow to the several legatees their recognized proportions of interest in the estates, leaving the French heirs to come by oppositions and assert their rights, if any they have, to the entire award."

To this representation, or tableau of distribution, the plaintiffs in error made opposition, alleging that they were entitled to the whole award, being the only heirs and legatees who were French citizens at the time the claim was presented and when the award was rendered; and that no award under the treaty could have been made in favor of the other heirs and legatees, they being citizens of the United States at that time, and that no executor, administrator or person representing the succession of a person who was not a French citizen at the time the damage was suffered and award rendered could have any standing before the commission. The District Court of the parish, the court of original jurisdiction, maintained the position of the plaintiffs in error, and decreed that the entire fund, $5280, should go to them, one-half to each. From this judgment the executor appealed to the Supreme Court of Louisiana, which tribunal reversed the decree below, giving judgment in favor of the executor, to the effect that the entire fund in his possession from the award, less the charges and expenses incurred and the amount retained for future costs, should be distributed proportionally among the legatees and heirs of Mrs. Foucher, according to the tableau of distribution presented by him. From this latter judgment the case was brought to this court on writ of error.

MR. JUSTICE FIELD, after stating the case, delivered the opinion of the court.

As the contention of the plaintiffs in error that they are entitled to the entire award rendered by the French and American Claims Commission, after deducting from it the conceded charges and expenses, is founded upon the stipulations of the treaty of 1880, the refusal of the Supreme Court of Louisiana to recognize the right thus asserted by them presents a question for the jurisdiction of this court, within the express terms of the 25th section of the Judiciary Act of 1789, which is reproduced, somewhat enlarged in its provisions, in the Revised Statutes, § 709. The decision was against the right specially claimed under the treaty in question.

The position of the plaintiffs in error was, in our judgment, well taken, and should have been sustained. Independently of the express provisions of the treaty it could not reasonably be urged that the award should inure to the benefit of citizens of the United States. It would be a remarkable thing, and we think without precedent in the history of diplomacy, for the government of the United States to make a treaty with another country to indemnify its own citizens for injuries received from its own officers. To any suggestion of that kind from a foreign country the government of the United States would probably answer that it was entirely competent to deal with its own citizens and to do justice to them without the interposition of any other country.

But the express language of the treaty here limits the jurisdiction of the commission to claims by citizens of one country against the government of the other. It matters not by whom the claim may have been presented to the commission. That body possessed no authority to consider any claims against the government of either the United States or of France, except as held, both at the time of their presentation and of judgment thereon, by citizens of the other country.

There is no ambiguity in the language of the treaty on this subject; it is entirely free from doubt. It is true Arthur Denis presented the claim as dative testamentary executor of Mr. Foucher's succession, and he joined, in his memorial to the commission, all the legatees and heirs under the will of Madame Foucher, to whom the estate of her husband had been left, appearing also for the plaintiffs in error under a power of attorney from them, they subsequently appearing in person. This memorial only gave the commission full knowledge of the origin and condition of the claim. It could not enlarge its power or bring within its jurisdiction any claim against the United States of other parties than citizens of France. When the award was made it could lawfully be intended for no other than such citizens. The right of the plaintiffs in error to the award arises from the treaty, to which any rules for the distribution of estates under the law of Louisiana must give way, the treaty being of superior authority in the case. They were entitled, each to one-eighth of any property coming to them as legatees of Mrs. Foucher, and that proportion of the whole claim shown to exist against the

United States for damages to the property of her husband and for its use was all that the commission could allow, as it could not consider the interests of their co-legatees or co-heirs, they not being citizens of France. The amount of the whole claim as set forth in the memorial presented by Denis exceeded $100,000. The amount which General Canby, in 1865, recommended to be paid, as already stated, exceeded $36,000. Whatever the damages sustained by Foucher as estimated by the commission, that body could allow only one-fourth thereof, the proportion due to the plaintiffs in error. Any award to their co-legatees would have been invalid and void. They may be entitled to an equal share in the whole claim against the government of the United States; but if so they must resort to remedies provided by the laws of the United States for the prosecution of claims against them, or, if those remedies are inadequate to give this relief, they must apply to Congress. Relief by the commission under the treaty could be given only to those legatees who were at the time citizens of France.

On the hearing before the District Court, the brief of counsel for the French government, and of private counsel filed with the commission for the claimants, and letters of the latter counsel, were produced to show that no claim was pressed by them except on behalf of the plaintiffs in error; and also a letter of one of the commissioners, to show that no other claim was considered by the commission. Objection was taken to this evidence on the ground that the decision of the commission could not be interpreted by subsequent testimony, or by the arguments of counsel before it, or the opinions of attorneys employed in the case. As we understand the objection, it went to the competency of the testimony, rather than to its sufficiency. As a general rule, the judgment of a court or commission is to be interpreted by its own language and the pleadings or proceedings upon which it is founded. Extrinsic evidence to aid in its interpretation is inadmissible unless after reference to the pleadings and proceedings there remains some ambiguity or uncertainty in it. In such cases resort may be had to other evidence, as where, from the generality of the language in the pleadings, or proceedings as well as in the decision, it becomes necessary to ascertain and limit the extent of the judgment intended. Thus where a former judgment is pleaded in bar of a second action upon the same demand, it is competent to show by extrinsic evidence the identity of the demands in the two cases, if this does not appear on the face of the pleadings. *Washington, Alexandria & Georgetown Steam Packet Co.* v. *Sickles*, 24 How. 333; *Miles* v. *Caldwell*, 2 Wall.

35; *Cromwell* v. *County of Sac*, 94 U. S. 351, 355.

If it had been necessary to limit the effect of the award of the commission in the present case, we do not perceive any valid objection to extrinsic evidence for that purpose. The brief of counsel for the claimants would show the character and extent of their contention before that body. But letters of counsel and the letter of one of the commissioners can hardly be considered as competent evidence. Their declarations, if receivable at all, could only be so in the form of testimony given by them as witnesses in the case, and not in any *ex parte* written communication. But, though received as evidence, they could not have had any effect upon the decision as to the claim of the plaintiffs in error. Their claim rested on the treaty, which authorized no award in favor of any other parties before the commission. It is therefore immaterial that such evidence was received. The nature and extent of the award, and the parties entitled to it, depended upon considerations which such evidence could in no way affect.

It follows that the judgment of the Supreme Court of Louisiana must be

Reversed and the cause remanded, with directions to take further proceedings in accordance with this opinion; and it is so ordered.

Editor's Note.   The treaty between the U.S. and France, cited by the Court, was the Claims Convention, January 15, 1880 (21 Stat. 673; 1 Malloy, p. 535).

Nishimura Ekiu v. United States
142 U.S. 651; 12 S. Ct. 336 (1892)

HABEAS CORPUS, sued out May 13, 1891, by a female subject of the Emperor of Japan, restrained of her liberty and detained at San Francisco upon the ground that she should not be permitted to land in the United States. The case, as appearing by the papers filed, and by the report of a commissioner of the Circuit Court, to whom the case was referred by that court "to find the facts and his conclusions of law, and to report a judgment therein," and by the admissions of counsel at the argument in this court, was as follows:

The petitioner arrived at the port of San Francisco on the steamship Belgic from Yokohama, Japan, on May 7, 1891. William H. Thornley, commissioner of immigration of the State of California, and claiming to act under instructions from and contract with the Secretary of the Treasury of the United States, refused to allow her to land; and on May 13, 1891, in a "report of alien immigrants forbidden to land under the provisions of the act of Congress approved August 3, 1882, at the port of San Francisco, being passengers upon the steamer Belgic, Walker, master, which arrived May 7, 1891, from Yokohama," made these statements as to the petitioner: "Sex, female. Age, 25." "Passport states that she comes to San Francisco in company with her husband, which is not a fact. She states that she has been married two years, and that her husband has been in the United States one year, but she does not know his address. She has $22, and is to stop at some hotel until her husband calls for her."

With this report Thornley sent a letter to the collector, stating that after a careful examination of the alien immigrants on board the Belgic he was satisfied that the petitioner and five others were "prohibited from landing by the existing immigration laws," for reasons specifically stated with regard to each; and that, pending the collector's final decision as to their right to land, he had "placed them temporarily in the Methodist Chinese Mission, as the steamer was not a proper place to detain them, until the date of sailing." On the same day the collector wrote to Thornley, approving his action.

Thereafter, on the same day, this writ of *habeas corpus* was issued to Thornley, and he made the following return thereon: "In obedience to the within writ I hereby produce the body of Nishimura Ekiu, as within directed, and return that I hold her in my custody by direction of the customs authorities of the port of San Francisco, California, under the provisions of the immigration act; that by an understanding between the United States attorney and the attorney for petitioner, said party will remain in the custody of the Methodist Episcopal Japanese and Chinese Mission pending a final disposition of the writ." The petitioner remained at the mission house until the final order of the Circuit Court.

Afterwards, and before a hearing, the following proceedings took place: On May 16 the District Attorney of the United States intervened in opposition to the writ of *habeas corpus*, insisting that the finding and decision of Thornley and the collector were final and conclusive, and could not be reviewed by the court. John L. Hatch, having been appointed

on May 14, by the Secretary of the Treasury, inspector of
immigration at the port of San Francisco, on May 16 made
the inspection and examination required by the act of March
3, 1891, c. 551, entitled "An act in amendment to the various
acts relative to immigration and the importation of aliens
under contract or agreement to perform labor," (the material
provisions of which are set out in the margin,[1]) and refused to

---

[1] SEC. 1. " The following classes of aliens shall be excluded from admission into the United States, in accordance with the existing acts regulating immigration, other than those concerning Chinese laborers : All idiots, insane persons, paupers or persons likely to become a public charge, persons suffering from a loathsome or a dangerous contagious disease, persons who have been convicted of a felony or other infamous crime or misdemeanor involving moral turpitude," &c.

By sections 3 and 4, certain offences are defined and subjected to the penalties imposed by the act of February 26, 1885, c. 164, § 3, namely, penalties of $1000, " which may be sued for and recovered by the United States, or by any person who shall first bring his action therefor," " as debts of like amount are now recovered in the Circuit Courts of the United States, the proceeds to be paid into the Treasury of the United States." 23 Stat. 333.

SEC. 6. " Any person, who shall bring into or land in the United States by vessel or otherwise, or who shall aid to bring into or land in the United States by vessel or otherwise, any alien not lawfully entitled to enter the United States, shall be deemed guilty of a misdemeanor, and shall, on conviction, be punished by a fine not exceeding one thousand dollars, or by imprisonment for a term not exceeding one year, or by both such fine and imprisonment."

SEC. 7. " The office of superintendent of immigration is hereby created and established, and the President, by and with the advice and consent of the Senate, is authorized and directed to appoint such officer, whose salary shall be four thousand dollars per annum, payable monthly. The superintendent of immigration shall be an officer in the Treasury Department, under the control and supervision of the Secretary of the Treasury, to whom he shall make annual reports in writing of the transactions of his office, together with such special reports in writing as the Secretary of the Treasury shall require."

SEC. 8. " Upon the arrival by water at any place within the United States of any alien immigrants it shall be the duty of the commanding officer and the agents of the steam or sailing vessel by which they came to report the name, nationality, last residence and destination of every such alien, before any of them are landed, to the proper inspection officers, who shall thereupon go or send competent assistants on board such vessel and there inspect all such aliens, or the inspection officers may order a temporary removal of ఒ ich aliens for examination at a designated time and place, and then and there detain them until a thorough inspection is made. But such removal shall not be considered a landing during the pendency of such examination. The medical examination shall be made by surgeons of the marine hospital service. In cases where the services of a marine hospital surgeon cannot be obtained without causing unreasonable delay the inspector may cause an alien to be examined by a civil surgeon, and the Secretary of the Treasury shall fix the compensation for such examination. The inspection officers

allow the petitioner to land, and made a report to the collector in the very words of Thornley's report, except in stating the date of the act of Congress, under which he acted, as

and their assistants shall have power to administer oaths, and to take and consider testimony touching the right of any such aliens to enter the United States, all of which shall be entered of record. During such inspection after temporary removal the superintendent shall cause such aliens to be properly housed, fed and cared for, and also, in his discretion, such as are delayed in proceeding to their destination after inspection. All decisions made by the inspection officers or their assistants touching the right of any alien to land, when adverse to such right, shall be final unless appeal be taken to the superintendent of immigration, whose action shall be subject to review by the Secretary of the Treasury. It shall be the duty of the aforesaid officers and agents of such vessel to adopt due precautions to prevent the landing of any alien immigrant at any place or time other than that designated by the inspection officers; and any such officer or agent or person in charge of such vessel, who shall either knowingly or negligently land or permit to land any alien immigrant at any place or time other than that designated by the inspection officers, shall be deemed guilty of a misdemeanor, and punished by a fine not exceeding one thousand dollars, or by imprisonment for a term not exceeding one year, or by both such fine and imprisonment."

" The Secretary of the Treasury may prescribe rules for inspection along the borders of Canada, British Columbia and Mexico so as not to obstruct or unnecessarily delay, impede or annoy passengers in ordinary travel between said countries: Provided, that not exceeding one inspector shall be appointed for each customs district, and whose salary shall not exceed twelve hundred dollars per year.

" All duties imposed and powers conferred by the second section of the act of August third, eighteen hundred and eighty-two, upon state commissioners, boards or officers acting under contract with the Secretary of the Treasury, shall be performed and exercised, as occasion may arise, by the inspection officers of the United States."

SEC. 10. " All aliens who may unlawfully come to the United States shall, if practicable, be immediately sent back on the vessel by which they were brought in. The cost of their maintenance while on land, as well as the expense of the return of such aliens, shall be borne by the owner or owners of the vessel on which such aliens came; and if any master, agent, consignee or owner of such vessel shall refuse to receive back on board the vessel such aliens, or shall neglect to detain them thereon, or shall refuse or neglect to return them to the port from which they came, or to pay the cost of their maintenance while on land, such master, agent, consignee or owner shall be deemed guilty of a misdemeanor, and shall be punished by a fine not less than three hundred dollars for each and every offence; and any such vessel shall not have clearance from any port of the United States while any such fine is unpaid."

Sec. 11 provides for the return within one year of any alien coming into the United States in violation of law.

Sec. 12 saves all prosecutions and proceedings, criminal or civil, begun under any act hereby amended.

By sec. 13 the Circuit and District Courts of the United States are " invested with full and concurrent jurisdiction of all causes, civil and criminal, arising under any of the provisions of this act;" and the act is to go into effect on April 1, 1891. 26 Stat. 1084–1086.

March 3, 1891, instead of August 3, 1882; and on May 18, Hatch intervened in opposition to the writ of *habeas corpus*, stating these doings of his, and that upon said examination he found the petitioner to be "an alien immigrant from Yokohama, Empire of Japan," and "a person without means of support, without relatives or friends in the United States," and "a person unable to care for herself, and liable to become a public charge, and therefore inhibited from landing under the provisions of said act of 1891, and previous acts of which said act is amendatory;" and insisting that his finding and decision were reviewable by the superintendent of immigration and the Secretary of the Treasury only.

At the hearing before the commissioner of the Circuit Court, the petitioner offered to introduce evidence as to her right to land; and contended that the act of 1891, if construed as vesting in the officers named therein exclusive authority to determine that right, was in so far unconstitutional, as depriving her of her liberty without due process of law; and that by the Constitution she had a right to the writ of *habeas corpus*, which carried with it the right to a determination by the court as to the legality of her detention, and therefore, necessarily, the right to inquire into the facts relating thereto.

The commissioner excluded the evidence offered as to the petitioner's right to land; and reported that the question of that right had been tried and determined by a duly constituted and competent tribunal having jurisdiction in the premises; that the decision of Hatch as inspector of immigration was conclusive on the right of the petitioner to land, and could not be reviewed by the court, but only by the commissioner of immigration and the Secretary of the Treasury; and that the petitioner was not unlawfully restrained of her liberty.

On July 24, 1891, the Circuit Court confirmed its commissioner's report, and ordered "that she be remanded by the marshal to the custody from which she has been taken, to wit, to the custody of J. L. Hatch, immigration inspector for the port of San Francisco, to be dealt with as he may find that the law requires upon either the present testimony before him, or that and such other as he may deem proper to take." The petitioner appealed to this court.

Mr. Justice Gray, after stating the case as above, delivered the opinion of the court.

As this case involves the constitutionality of a law of the United States, it is within the appellate jurisdiction of this court, notwithstanding the appeal was taken since the act establishing Circuit Courts of Appeals took effect. Act of March 3, 1891, c. 517, § 5; 26 Stat. 827, 828, 1115.

It is an accepted maxim of international law, that every sovereign nation has the power, as inherent in sovereignty, and essential to self-preservation, to forbid the entrance of foreigners within its dominions, or to admit them only in such cases and upon such conditions as it may see fit to prescribe. Vattel, lib. 2, §§ 94, 100; 1 Phillimore (3d ed.) c. 10, § 220. In the United States this power is vested in the national government, to which the Constitution has committed the entire control of international relations, in peace as well as in war. It belongs to the political department of the government, and may be exercised either through treaties made by the President and Senate, or through statutes enacted by Congress, upon whom the Constitution has conferred power to regulate commerce with foreign nations, including the entrance of ships, the importation of goods and the bringing of persons into the ports of the United States; to establish a uniform rule of naturalization; to declare war, and to provide and maintain armies and navies; and to make all laws which may be necessary and proper for carrying into effect these powers and all other powers vested by the Constitution in the government of the United States or in any department or officer thereof. Constitution, art. 1, sec. 8; *Head Money Cases*, 112 U. S. 580; *Chae Chan Ping* v. *United States*, 130 U. S. 581, 604–609.

The supervision of the admission of aliens into the United States may be entrusted by Congress either to the Department of State, having the general management of foreign relations, or to the Department of the Treasury, charged with the enforcement of the laws regulating foreign commerce; and Congress has often passed acts forbidding the immigration of particular classes of foreigners, and has committed the execution of these acts to the Secretary of the Treasury, to collectors of customs and to inspectors acting under their authority. See, for instance, acts of March 3, 1875, c. 141; 18 Stat. 477; August 3, 1882, c. 376; 22 Stat. 214; February 23, 1887, c. 220; 24 Stat. 414; October 19, 1888, c. 1210; 25 Stat. 566; as well as the various acts for the exclusion of the Chinese.

An alien immigrant, prevented from landing by any such officer claiming authority to do so under an act of Congress, and thereby restrained of his liberty, is doubtless entitled to a writ of *habeas corpus* to ascertain whether the restraint is lawful. *Chew Heong* v. *United States*, 112 U. S. 536; *United States* v. *Jung Ah Lung*, 124 U. S. 621; *Wan Shing* v. *United States*, 140 U. S. 424; *Lau Ow Bew, Petitioner*, 141 U. S. 583. And Congress may, if it sees fit, as in the statutes in question in *United States* v. *Jung Ah Lung*, just cited, authorize the courts to investigate and ascertain the facts on which the right to land depends. But, on the other hand, the final determination of those facts may be entrusted by Congress to executive officers; and in such a case, as in all others, in which a statute gives a discretionary power to an officer, to be exercised by him upon his own opinion of certain facts, he is made the sole and exclusive judge of the existence of those facts, and no other tribunal, unless expressly authorized by law to do so, is at liberty to reëxamine or controvert the sufficiency of the evidence on which he acted. *Martin* v. *Mott*, 12 Wheat. 19, 31; *Philadelphia & Trenton Railroad* v. *Stimpson*, 14 Pet. 448, 458; *Benson* v. *McMahon*, 127 U. S. 457; *In re Oteiza*, 136 U. S. 330. It is not within the province of the judiciary to order that foreigners who have never been naturalized, nor acquired any domicil or residence within the United States, nor even been admitted into the country pursuant to law, shall be permitted to enter, in opposition to the constitutional and lawful measures of the legislative and executive branches of the national government. As to such persons, the decisions of executive or administrative officers, acting within powers expressly conferred by Congress, are due process of law. *Murray* v. *Hoboken Co.*, 18 How. 272; *Hilton* v. *Merritt*, 110 U. S. 97.

The immigration act of August 3, 1882, c. 376, which was held to be constitutional in the *Head Money Cases*, above cited, imposed a duty of fifty cents for each alien passenger coming by vessel into any port of the United States, to be paid to the collector of customs, and by him into the Treasury, to constitute an immigrant fund; by § 2, the Secretary of the Treasury was charged with the duty of executing the provisions of the act, and with the supervision of the business of immigration to the United States, and, for these purposes, was empowered to make contracts with any state commission, board or officers, and it was made their duty to go on board vessels and examine the condition of immigrants, "and if on such examination there shall be found among such passengers any convict, lunatic, idiot or any person unable to take care of himself or herself without becoming a public charge, they shall report the same in writing to the collector of such port, and such persons shall not be permitted to land;" and by § 3, the Secretary of the Treasury was authorized to establish rules and regulations, and to issue instructions, to carry out this and other immigration laws of the United States. 22 Stat. 214.

The doings of Thornley, the state commissioner of immigration, in examining and detaining the petitioner, and in reporting to the collector, appear to have been under that act, and would be justified by the second section thereof, unless that section should be taken to have been impliedly repealed by the last paragraph of section 8 of the act of March 3, 1891, c. 551, by which all duties imposed and powers conferred by that section upon state commissions, boards or officers, acting under contract with the Secretary of the Treasury, "shall be performed and exercised, as occasion may arise, by the inspection officers of the United States." 26 Stat. 1085.

But it is unnecessary to express a definite opinion on the authority of Thornley to inspect and detain the petitioner.

Putting her in the mission house, as a more suitable place than the steamship, pending the decision of the question of her right to land, and keeping her there, by agreement between her attorney and the attorney for the United States, until final judgment upon the writ of *habeas corpus*, left her in the same position, so far as regarded her right to land in the United States, as if she never had been removed from the steamship.

Before the hearing upon the writ of *habeas corpus*, Hatch was appointed by the Secretary of the Treasury inspector of immigration at the port of San Francisco, and, after making the inspection and examination required by the act of 1891, refused to allow the petitioner to land, and made a report to the collector of customs, stating facts which tended to show, and which the inspector decided did show, that she was a "person likely to become a public charge," and so within one of the classes of aliens "excluded from admission into the United States" by the first section of that act. And Hatch intervened in the proceedings on the writ of *habeas corpus*, setting up his decision in bar of the writ.

A writ of *habeas corpus* is not like an action to recover damages for an unlawful arrest or commitment, but its object is to ascertain whether the prisoner can lawfully be detained in custody; and if sufficient ground for his detention by the government is shown, he is not to be discharged for defects in the original arrest or commitment. *Ex parte Bollman & Swartwout*, 4 Cranch, 75, 114, 125; *Coleman* v. *Tennessee*, 97 U. S. 509, 519; *United States* v. *McBratney*, 104 U. S. 621, 624; *Kelley* v. *Thomas*, 15 Gray, 192; *The King* v. *Marks*, 3 East,

157; *Shuttleworth's Case*, 9 Q. B. 651.

The case must therefore turn on the validity and effect of the action of Hatch as inspector of immigration.

Section 7 of the act of 1891 establishes the office of superintendent of immigration, and enacts that he "shall be an officer in the Treasury Department, under the control and supervision of the Secretary of the Treasury." By § 8 "the proper inspection officers" are required to go on board any vessel bringing alien immigrants and to inspect and examine them, and may for this purpose remove and detain them on shore, without such removal being considered a landing; and "shall have power to administer oaths, and to take and consider testimony touching the right of any such aliens to enter the United States, all of which shall be entered of record;" "all decisions made by the inspection officers or their assistants touching the right of any alien to land, when adverse to such right, shall be final unless appeal be taken to the superintendent of immigration, whose action shall be subject to review by the Secretary of the Treasury;" and the Secretary of the Treasury may prescribe rules for inspection along the borders of Canada, British Columbia and Mexico, "provided that not exceeding one inspector shall be appointed for each customs district."

It was argued that the appointment of Hatch was illegal because it was made by the Secretary of the Treasury, and should have been made by the superintendent of immigration. But the Constitution does not allow Congress to vest the appointment of inferior officers elsewhere than "in the President alone, in the courts of law or in the heads of departments;" the act of 1891 manifestly contemplates and intends that the inspectors of immigration shall be appointed by the Secretary of the Treasury; and appointments of such officers by the superintendent of immigration could be upheld only by presuming them to be made with the concurrence or approval of the Secretary of the Treasury, his official head. Constitution, art. 2, sec. 2; *United States* v. *Hartwell*, 6 Wall. 385; *Stanton* v. *Wilkeson*, 8 Ben. 357; *Price* v. *Abbott*, 17 Fed. Rep. 506.

It was also argued that Hatch's proceedings did not conform to section 8 of the act of 1891, because it did not appear that he took testimony on oath, and because there was no record of any testimony or of his decision. But the statute does not require inspectors to take any testimony at all, and allows them to decide on their own inspection and examination the question of the right of any alien immigrant to land. The provision relied on merely empowers inspectors to administer oaths and to take and consider testimony, and requires only testimony so taken to be entered of record.

The decision of the inspector of immigration being in conformity with the act of 1891, there can be no doubt that it was final and conclusive against the petitioner's right to land in the United States. The words of section 8 are clear to that effect, and were manifestly intended to prevent the question of an alien immigrant's right to land, when once decided adversely by an inspector, acting within the jurisdiction conferred upon him, from being impeached or reviewed, in the courts or otherwise, save only by appeal to the inspector's official superiors, and in accordance with the provisions of the act. Section 13, by which the Circuit and District Courts of the United States are " invested with full and concurrent jurisdiction of all causes, civil and criminal, arising under any of the provisions of this act," evidently refers to causes of judicial cognizance, already provided for, whether civil actions in the nature of debt for penalties under sections 3 and 4, or indictments for misdemeanors under sections 6, 8 and 10. Its intention was to vest concurrent jurisdiction of such causes in the Circuit and District Courts ; and it is impossible to construe it as giving the courts jurisdiction to determine matters which the act has expressly committed to the final determination of executive officers.

The result is, that the act of 1891 is constitutional and valid ; the inspector of immigration was duly appointed ; his decision against the petitioner's right to land in the United States was within the authority conferred upon him by that act ; no appeal having been taken to the superintendent of immigration, that decision was final and conclusive ; the petitioner is not unlawfully restrained of her liberty ; and the

Order of the Circuit Court is affirmed.

Mr. Justice Brewer dissented.

———— · ————

Fong Yue Ting v. United States
149 U.S. 698; 13 S. Ct. 1016 (1893)

(There were three writs of Habeas corpus , granted by the Circuit Court, Southern District of New York, upon petitions of Chinese laborers, arrested and held by the marshal for not having certificates of residence as required by the Congressional Act of May 5, 1892, which prohibited the entry of certain Chinese nationals into the U.S. Each petition alleged that the petitioner was arrested and detained without due process of law, and that the relevant Section 6 of the Act was unconstitutional. The Circuit Court dismissed all three petitions, but allowed appeal to the Supreme Court, and admitted petitioners to bail pending the appeal.)

Mr. Justice Gray, after stating the facts, delivered the opinion of the court.

The general principles of public law which lie at the foundation of these cases are clearly established by previous judgments of this court, and by the authorities therein referred to.

In the recent case of *Nishimura Ekiu* v. *United States*, 142 U. S. 651, 659, the court, in sustaining the action of the executive department, putting in force an act of Congress for the exclusion of aliens, said: " It is an accepted maxim of international law, that every sovereign nation has the power, as inherent in sovereignty, and essential to self-preservation, to forbid the entrance of foreigners within its dominions, or to admit them only in such cases and upon such conditions as it may see fit to prescribe. In the United States, this power is vested in the national government, to which the Constitution has committed the entire control of international relations, in peace as well as in war. It belongs to the political department of the government, and may be exercised either through treaties made by the President and Senate, or through statutes enacted by Congress."

The same views were more fully expounded in the earlier case of *Chae Chan Ping* v. *United States*, 130 U. S. 581, in which the validity of a former act of Congress, excluding Chinese laborers from the United States, under the circumstances therein stated, was affirmed.

In the elaborate opinion delivered by Mr. Justice Field, in behalf of the court, it was said: " Those laborers are not citizens of the United States; they are aliens. That the government of the United States, through the action of the legislative department, can exclude aliens from its territory is a proposition which we do not think open to controversy. Jurisdiction over its own territory to that extent is an incident of every independent nation. It is a part of its independence. If it could not exclude aliens, it would be to that extent subject to the control of another power." " The United States, in their relation to foreign countries and their subjects or citizens, are one nation, invested with powers which belong to independent nations, the exercise of which can be invoked for the maintenance of its absolute independence and security throughout its entire territory." 130 U. S. 603, 604.

It was also said, repeating the language of Mr. Justice Bradley in *Knox* v. *Lee*, 12 Wall. 457, 555 : " The United States is not only a government, but it is a national government, and the only government in this country that has the character of nationality. It is invested with power over all the foreign relations of the country, war, peace, and negotiations and intercourse with other nations ; all of which are forbidden to the state governments." 130 U. S. 605. And it was added : " For local interests the several States of the Union exist ; but for international purposes, embracing our relations with foreign nations, we are but one people, one nation, one power." 130 U. S. 606.

The court then went on to say : " To preserve its independence, and give security against foreign aggression and encroachment, is the highest duty of every nation, and to attain these ends nearly all other considerations are to be subordinated. It matters not in what form such aggression and encroachment come, whether from the foreign nation acting in its national character, or from vast hordes of its people crowding in upon us. The government, possessing the powers which are to be exercised for protection and security, is clothed with authority to determine the occasion on which the powers shall be called forth ; and its determination, so far as the subjects affected are concerned, is necessarily conclusive upon all its departments and officers. If, therefore, the government of the United States, through its legislative department, considers the presence of foreigners of a different race in this country, who will not assimilate with us, to be dangerous to its peace and security, their exclusion is not to be stayed because at the time there are no actual hostilities with the nation of which the foreigners are subjects. The existence of war would render the necessity of the proceeding only more obvious and pressing. The same necessity, in a less pressing degree, may arise when war does not exist, and the same authority which adjudges the necessity in one case must also determine it in the other. In both cases, its determination is conclusive upon the judiciary. If the government of the country of which the foreigners excluded are subjects is dissatisfied with this action, it can make complaint to the executive head of our government, or resort to any other measure which, in its judgment, its interests or dignity may demand; and there lies its only remedy. The power of the government to exclude foreigners from the country, whenever, in its judgment, the public interests require such exclusion, has been asserted in repeated instances, and never denied by the executive or legislative departments." 130 U. S. 606, 607. This statement was supported by many citations from the diplomatic correspondence of successive Secretaries of State, collected in Wharton's International Law Digest, § 206.

The right of a nation to expel or deport foreigners, who have not been naturalized or taken any steps towards becoming citizens of the country, rests upon the same grounds, and is as absolute and unqualified as the right to prohibit and prevent their entrance into the country.

This is clearly affirmed in dispatches referred to by the court in *Chae Chan Ping's case*. In 1856, Mr. Marcy wrote: "Every society possesses the undoubted right to determine who shall compose its members, and it is exercised by all nations, both in peace and war. A memorable example of the exercise of this power in time of peace was the passage of the alien law of the United States in the year 1798." In 1869, Mr. Fish wrote: "The control of the people within its limits, and the right to expel from its territory persons who are dangerous to the peace of the State, are too clearly within the essential attributes of sovereignty to be seriously contested." Wharton's International Law Digest, § 206; 130 U. S. 607.

The statements of leading commentators on the law of nations are to the same effect.

Vattel says: "Every nation has the right to refuse to admit a foreigner into the country, when he cannot enter without putting the nation in evident danger, or doing it a manifest injury. What it owes to itself, the care of its own safety, gives it this right; and in virtue of its natural liberty, it belongs to the nation to judge whether its circumstances will or will not justify the admission of the foreigner." "Thus, also, it has a right to send them elsewhere, if it has just cause to fear that they will corrupt the manners of the citizens; that they will create religious disturbances, or occasion any other disorder, contrary to the public safety. In a word, it has a right, and is even obliged, in this respect, to follow the rules which prudence dictates." Vattel's Law of Nations, lib. 1, c. 19, §§ 230, 231.

Ortolan says : " The government of each state has always the right to compel foreigners who are found within its territory to go away, by having them taken to the frontier. This right is based on the fact that, the foreigner not making part of the nation, his individual reception into the territory is matter of pure permission, of simple tolerance, and creates no obligation. The exercise of this right may be subjected, doubtless, to certain forms by the domestic laws of each country ; but the right exists none the less, universally recognized and put in force. In France, no special form is now prescribed in this matter ; the exercise of this right of expulsion is wholly left to the executive power." Ortolan, Diplomatie de la Mer, lib. 2, c. 14, (4th ed.) p. 297.

Phillimore says : " It is a received maxim of international law, that the government of a state may prohibit the entrance of strangers into the country, and may therefore regulate the conditions under which they shall be allowed to remain in it, or may require and compel their departure from it." 1 Phillimore's International Law, (3d ed.) c. 10, § 220.

Bar says : " Banishment and extradition must not be confounded. The former is simply a question of expediency and humanity, since no state is bound to receive all foreigners, although, perhaps, to exclude all would be to say good-bye to the international union of all civilized states ; and although in some states, such as England, strangers can only be expelled by means of special acts of the legislative power, no state has renounced its right to expel them, as is shown by the alien bills which the government of England has at times used to invest itself with the right of expulsion." " Banishment is regulated by rules of expediency and humanity, and is a matter for the police of the state. No doubt the police can apprehend any foreigner who refuses to quit the country in spite of authoritative orders to do so, and convey him to the frontier." Bar's International Law, (Gillespie's ed. 1883) 708 note, 711.

In the passages just quoted from Gillespie's translation of Bar, " banishment " is evidently used in the sense of expulsion or deportation by the political authority on the ground of expediency, and not in the sense of transportation or exile by way of punishment for crime. Strictly speaking, " transportation," " extradition " and " deportation," although each has the effect of removing a person from the country, are different things, and have different purposes. " Transportation " is by way of punishment of one convicted of an offence against the laws of the country. " Extradition " is the surrender to another country of one accused of an offence against its laws, there to be tried, and, if found guilty, punished. "Deportation" is the removal of an alien out of the country, simply because his presence is deemed inconsistent with the public welfare, and without any punishment being imposed or contemplated, either under the laws of the country out of which he is sent, or under those of the country to which he is taken.

In England, the only question that has ever been made in regard to the power to expel aliens has been whether it could be exercised by the King without the consent of Parliament. It was formerly exercised by the King, but in later times by Parliament, which passed several acts on the subject between 1793 and 1848. 2 Inst. 57; 1 Chalmers Opinions, 26; 1 Bl. Com. 260; Chitty on the Prerogative, 49; 1 Phillimore, c. 10, § 220 and note; 30 Parl. Hist. 157, 167, 188, 217, 229; 34 Hansard Parl. Deb. (1st series) 441, 445, 471, 1065–1071; 6 Law Quart. Rev. 27.

Eminent English judges, sitting in the Judicial Committee of the Privy Council, have gone very far in supporting the exclusion or expulsion, by the executive authority of a colony, of aliens having no absolute right to enter its territory or to remain therein.

In 1837, in a case arising in the Island of Mauritius, which had been conquered by Great Britain from France in 1810, and in which the law of France continued in force, Lord Lyndhurst, Lord Brougham and Justices Bosanquet and Erskine, although considering it a case of great hardship, sustained the validity of an order of the English governor, deporting a friendly alien who had long resided and carried on business in the island, and had enjoyed the privileges and exercised the rights of a person duly domiciled, but who had not, as required by the French law, obtained from the colonial government formal and express authority to establish a domicil there. *In re Adam*, 1 Moore P. C. 460.

In a recent appeal from a judgment of the Supreme Court of the Colony of Victoria, a collector of customs, sued by a Chinese immigrant for preventing him from landing in the colony, had pleaded a justification under the order of a colonial minister claiming to exercise an alleged prerogative of the Crown to exclude alien friends, and denied the right of a court of law to examine his action, on the ground that what he had done was an act of state; and the plaintiff had demurred to the plea. Lord Chancellor Halsbury, speaking for himself, for Lord Herschell (now Lord Chancellor) and for other lords, after deciding against the plaintiff on a question of statutory construction, took occasion to observe: "The facts appearing on the record raise, quite apart from the

statutes referred to, a grave question as to the plaintiff's right
to maintain the action. He can only do so if he can establish
that an alien has a legal right, enforceable by action, to enter
British territory. No authority exists for the proposition that
an alien has any such right. Circumstances may occur in
which the refusal to permit an alien to land might be such an
interference with international comity as would properly give
rise to diplomatic remonstrance from the country of which he
was a native; but it is quite another thing to assert that an
alien, excluded from any part of her Majesty's dominions by
the executive government there, can maintain an action in a
British court, and raise such questions as were argued before
their lordships on the present appeal — whether the proper
officer for giving or refusing access to the country has been
duly authorized by his own colonial government, whether the
colonial government has received sufficient delegated authority
from the Crown to exercise the authority which the Crown
had a right to exercise through the colonial government if
properly communicated to it, and whether the Crown has the
right without parliamentary authority to exclude an alien.
Their lordships cannot assent to the proposition that an alien
refused permission to enter British territory can, in an action
in a British court, compel the decision of such matters as these,
involving delicate and difficult constitutional questions affecting the respective rights of the Crown and Parliament, and
the relations of this country to her self-governing colonies.
When once it is admitted that there is no absolute and unqualified right of action on behalf of an alien refused admission to British territory, their lordships are of opinion that
it would be impossible, upon the facts which the demurrer
admits, for an alien to maintain an action." *Musgrove* v. *Chun
Teeong Toy*, App. Cas. (1891) 272, 282, 283.

The right to exclude or to expel all aliens, or any class of
aliens, absolutely or upon certain conditions, in war or in
peace, being an inherent and inalienable right of every sovereign and independent nation, essential to its safety, its independence and its welfare, the question now before the court
is whether the manner in which Congress has exercised this
right in sections 6 and 7 of the act of 1892 is consistent with
the Constitution.

The United States are a sovereign and independent nation,
and are vested by the Constitution with the entire control of
international relations, and with all the powers of government necessary to maintain that control and to make it
effective. The only government of this country, which other
nations recognize or treat with, is the government of the

Union; and the only American flag known throughout the world is the flag of the United States.

The Constitution of the United States speaks with no uncertain sound upon this subject. That instrument, established by the people of the United States as the fundamental law of the land, has conferred upon the President the executive power; has made him the commander-in-chief of the army and navy; has authorized him, by and with the consent of the Senate, to make treaties, and to appoint ambassadors, public ministers and consuls; and has made it his duty to take care that the laws be faithfully executed. The Constitution has granted to Congress the power to regulate commerce with foreign nations, including the entrance of ships, the importation of goods and the bringing of persons into the ports of the United States; to establish a uniform rule of naturalization; to define and punish piracies and felonies committed on the high seas, and offences against the law of nations; to declare war, grant letters of marque and reprisal, and make rules concerning captures on land and water; to raise and support armies, to provide and maintain a navy, and to make rules for the government and regulation of the land and naval forces; and to make all laws necessary and proper for carrying into execution these powers, and all other powers vested by the Constitution in the government of the United States, or in any department or officer thereof. And the several States are expressly forbidden to enter into any treaty, alliance or confederation; to grant letters of marque and reprisal; to enter into any agreement or compact with another State, or with a foreign power; or to engage in war, unless actually invaded, or in such imminent danger as will not admit of delay.

In exercising the great power which the people of the United States, by establishing a written Constitution as the supreme and paramount law, have vested in this court, of determining, whenever the question is properly brought before it, whether the acts of the legislature or of the executive are consistent with the Constitution, it behooves the court to be careful that it does not undertake to pass upon political questions, the final decision of which has been committed by the Constitution to the other departments of the government.

As long ago said by Chief Justice Marshall, and since constantly maintained by this court: " The sound construction of the Constitution must allow to the national legislature that discretion, with respect to the means by which the powers it confers are to be carried into execution, which will enable that body to perform the high duties assigned to it, in the manner most beneficial to the people. Let the end be legitimate, let it be within the scope of the Constitution, and all means which are appropriate, which are plainly adapted to that end, which are not prohibited, but consistent with the letter and spirit of the Constitution, are constitutional." " Where the law is not prohibited, and is really calculated to effect any of the objects intrusted to the government, to undertake here to inquire into the degree of its necessity would be to pass the line which circumscribes the judicial department, and to tread on legislative ground. This court disclaims all pretensions to such a power." *McCulloch* v. *Maryland*, 4 Wheat. 316, 421, 423; *Juilliard* v. *Greenman*, 110 U. S. 421, 440, 450; *Ex parte Yarbrough*, 110 U. S. 651, 658; *In re Rapier*, 143 U. S. 110, 134; *Logan* v. *United States*, 144 U. S. 263, 283.

The power to exclude or to expel aliens, being a power affecting international relations, is vested in the political departments of the government, and is to be regulated by treaty or by act of Congress, and to be executed by the executive authority according to the regulations so established, except so far as the judicial department has been authorized by treaty or by statute, or is required by the paramount law of the Constitution, to intervene.

In *Nishimura Ekiu's case*, it was adjudged that, although Congress might, if it saw fit, authorize the courts to investigate and ascertain the facts upon which the alien's right to land was made by the statutes to depend, yet Congress might intrust the final determination of those facts to an executive officer, and that, if it did so, his order was due process of law, and no other tribunal, unless expressly authorized by law to do so, was at liberty to reëxamine the evidence on which he acted, or to controvert its sufficiency. 142 U. S. 660.

The power to exclude aliens and the power to expel them rest upon one foundation, are derived from one source, are supported by the same reasons, and are in truth but parts of one and the same power.

The power of Congress, therefore, to expel, like the power to exclude aliens, or any specified class of aliens, from the country, may be exercised entirely through executive officers; or Congress may call in the aid of the judiciary to ascertain any contested facts on which an alien's right to be in the country has been made by Congress to depend.

Congress, having the right, as it may see fit, to expel aliens of a particular class, or to permit them to remain, has undoubtedly the right to provide a system of registration and identification of the members of that class within the country, and to take all proper means to carry out the system which it provides.

It is no new thing for the law-making power, acting either through treaties made by the President and Senate, or by the more common method of acts of Congress, to submit the decision of questions, not necessarily of judicial cognizance, either to the final determination of executive officers, or to the decision of such officers in the first instance, with such opportunity for judicial review of their action as Congress may see fit to authorize or permit.

For instance, the surrender, pursuant to treaty stipulations, of persons residing or found in this country, and charged with crime in another, may be made by the executive authority of the President alone, when no provision has been made by treaty or by statute for an examination of the case by a judge or magistrate. Such was the case of Jonathan Robbins, under article 27 of the Treaty with Great Britain of 1794, in which the President's power in this regard was demonstrated in the masterly and conclusive argument of John Marshall in the House of Representatives. 8 Stat. 129; Wharton's State Trials, 392; Bee, 286; 5 Wheat. appx. 3. But provision may be made, as it has been by later acts of Congress, for a preliminary examination before a judge or commissioner; and in such case the sufficiency of the evidence on which he acts cannot be reviewed by any other tribunal, except as permitted by statute. Act of August 12, 1848, c. 167, 9 Stat. 302; Rev. Stat. §§ 5270–5274; *Ex parte Metzger*, 5 How. 176; *Benson* v. *McMahon*, 127 U. S. 457; *In re Oteiza*, 136 U. S. 330.

So claims to recover back duties illegally exacted on imports may, if Congress so provides, be finally determined by the Secretary of the Treasury. *Cary* v. *Curtis*, 3 How. 236; *Curtis* v. *Fiedler*, 2 Black, 461, 478, 479; *Arnson* v. *Murphy*, 109 U. S. 238, 240. But Congress may, as it did for long periods, permit them to be tried by suit against the collector of customs. Or it may, as by the existing statutes, provide for their determination by a board of general appraisers, and allow the decisions of that board to be reviewed by the courts in such particulars only as may be prescribed by law. Act of June 10, 1890, c. 407, §§ 14, 15, 25, 26 Stat. 137, 138, 141; *In re Fassett*, 142 U. S. 479, 486, 487; *Passavant* v. *United States*, 148 U. S. 214.

To repeat the careful and weighty words uttered by Mr. Justice Curtis, in delivering a unanimous judgment of this court upon the question what is due process of law: "To avoid misconstruction upon so grave a subject, we think it proper to state that we do not consider Congress can either withdraw from judicial cognizance any matter which, from its nature, is the subject of a suit at the common law, or in equity, or admiralty ; nor, on the other hand, can it bring under the judicial power a matter which, from its nature, is not a subject for judicial determination. At the same time, there are matters, involving public rights, which may be presented in such form that the judicial power is capable of acting on them, and which are susceptible of judicial determination, but which Congress may or may not bring within the cognizance of the courts of the United States, as it may deem proper." *Murray* v. *Hoboken Co.*, 18 How. 272, 284.

Before examining in detail the provisions of the act of 1892 now in question, it will be convenient to refer to the previous statutes, treaties and decisions upon this subject.

The act of Congress of July 27, 1868, c. 249, (reënacted in sections 1999–2001 of the Revised Statutes,) began with these recitals : " Whereas the right of expatriation is a natural and inherent right of all people, indispensable to the enjoyment of the rights of life, liberty, and the pursuit of happiness; and whereas in the recognition of this principle this government has freely received emigrants from all nations, and invested them with the rights of citizenship." It then declared that any order or decision of any officer of the United States to the contrary was inconsistent with the fundamental principles of this government; enacted that " all naturalized citizens of the United States, while in foreign states, shall be entitled to and shall receive from this government the same protection of persons and property that is accorded to native-born citizens in like situations and circumstances ; " and made it the duty of the President to take measures to protect the rights in that respect of " any citizen of the United States." 15 Stat. 223, 224.

That act, like any other, is subject to alteration by Congress whenever the public welfare requires it. The right of protection which it confers is limited to citizens of the United States. Chinese persons not born in this country have never been recognized as citizens of the United States, nor authorized to become such under the naturalization laws. Rev. Stat. (2d ed.) §§ 2165, 2169 ; Acts of April 14, 1802, c. 28, 2 Stat. 153; May 26, 1824, c. 186, 4 Stat. 69; July 14, 1870, c. 254, § 7, 16 Stat. 256; February 18, 1875, c. 80, 18 Stat. 318; *In re Ah Yup*, 5 Sawyer, 155; Act of May 6, 1882, c. 126, § 14, 22 Stat. 61.

The treaty made between the United States and China on July 28, 1868, contained the following stipulations :

" ARTICLE V. The United States of America and the

Emperor of China cordially recognize the inherent and inalienable right of man to change his home and allegiance, and also the mutual advantage of the free migration and emigration of their citizens and subjects, respectively, from one country to the other, for purposes of curiosity, of trade, or as permanent residents."

"ARTICLE VI. Citizens of the United States visiting or residing in China," "and reciprocally, Chinese subjects visiting or residing in the United States, shall enjoy the same privileges, immunities and exemptions, in respect to travel or residence, as may there be enjoyed by the citizens or subjects of the most favored nation. But nothing herein contained shall be held to confer naturalization upon citizens of the United States in China, nor upon the subjects of China in the United States."

After some years' experience under that treaty, the government of the United States was brought to the opinion that the presence within our territory of large numbers of Chinese laborers, of a distinct race and religion, remaining strangers in the land, residing apart by themselves, tenaciously adhering to the customs and usages of their own country, unfamiliar with our institutions, and apparently incapable of assimilating with our people, might endanger good order, and be injurious to the public interests; and therefore requested and obtained from China a modification of the treaty. *Chew Heong* v. *United States*, 112 U. S. 536, 542, 543; *Chae Chan Ping* v. *United States*, 130 U. S. 581, 595, 596.

On November 17, 1880, a supplemental treaty was accordingly concluded between the two countries, which contained the following preamble and stipulations:

"Whereas the government of the United States, because of the constantly increasing immigration of Chinese laborers to the territory of the United States, and the embarrassments consequent upon such immigration, now desires to negotiate a modification of the existing treaties which shall not be in direct contravention of their spirit:"

"ARTICLE I. Whenever, in the opinion of the government of the United States, the coming of the Chinese laborers to the United States, or their residence therein, affects or threatens to affect the interests of that country, or to endanger the good order of the said country, or of any locality within the territory thereof, the government of China agrees that the government of the United States may regulate, limit or suspend such coming or residence, but may not absolutely prohibit it. The limitation or suspension shall be reasonable, and shall apply only to Chinese who may go to the United States as laborers, other classes not being included in the limitations. Legislation taken in regard to Chinese laborers will be of such a character only as is necessary to enforce the regulation, limitation or suspension of immigration, and immigrants shall not be subject to personal maltreatment or abuse.

"ARTICLE II. Chinese subjects, whether proceeding to the United States as teachers, students, merchants or from curiosity, together with their body and household servants, and Chinese laborers who are now in the United States, shall be allowed to go and come of their own free will and accord, and shall be accorded all the rights, privileges, immunities and exemptions which are accorded to the citizens and subjects of the most favored nation.

"ARTICLE III. If Chinese laborers, or Chinese of any other class, now either permanently or temporarily residing in the territory of the United States, meet with ill treatment at the hands of any other persons, the government of the United States will exert all its power to devise measures for their protection, and to secure to them the same rights, privileges, immunities and exemptions as may be enjoyed by the citizens or subjects of the most favored nation, and to which they are entitled by treaty." 22 Stat. 826, 827.

The act of May 6, 1882, c. 126, entitled "An act to execute certain treaty stipulations relating to Chinese," and amended by the act of July 5, 1884, c. 220, began with the recital that, "in the opinion of the government of the United States, the coming of Chinese laborers to this country endangers the good order of certain localities within the territories thereof;" and, in section 1, suspended their coming for ten years, and enacted that it should "not be lawful for any Chinese laborer to come from any foreign port or place, or, having so come, to remain within the United States;" in section 3, that this provision should not apply to Chinese laborers who were in the United States on November 17, 1880, or who came here within ninety days after the passage of the act of 1882, and who should produce evidence of that fact, as afterwards required by the act, to the master of the vessel and to the collector of the port; and, in section 4, that "for the purpose of properly identifying Chinese laborers who were in the United States" at such time, "and in order to furnish them with the proper evidence of their right to go from and come to the United States," as provided by that act and by the treaty of November 17, 1880, the collector of customs of the district, from which any Chinese laborers should depart from the United States by sea, should go on board the vessel, and make and register a list of them, with all facts necessary for their identity, and should give to each a corresponding certificate, which should entitle him " to return to and reënter the United States, upon producing and delivering the same to the collector of customs," to be cancelled. The form of certificate prescribed by the act of 1884 differed in some particulars from that prescribed by the act of 1882; and the act of 1884 added that "said certificate shall be the only evidence to establish his right of reëntry." Each act further enacted, in section 5, that any such Chinese laborer, being in the United States and desiring to depart by land, should be entitled to a like certificate of identity; and in section 12, that no Chinese person should be permitted to enter the United States by land, without producing such a certificate, and that "any Chinese person found unlawfully within the United States shall be caused to be removed therefrom to the country from whence he came, and at the cost of the United States, after being brought before some justice, judge or commissioner of a court of the United States, and found to be one not lawfully entitled to be or remain in the United States." The act of 1884 further enacted, in section 16, that a violation of any of the provisions of the act, the punishment of which was not therein otherwise provided for, should be deemed a misdemeanor, and be punishable by fine not exceeding $1000, or by imprisonment for not more than one year, or by both such fine and imprisonment. 22 Stat. 58–60; 23 Stat. 115–118.

Under those acts, this court held, in *Chew Heong* v. *United States*, 112 U. S. 536, that the clause of section 4 of the act of 1884, making the certificate of identity the only evidence to establish a right to reënter the United States, was not applicable to a Chinese laborer who resided in the United States at the date of the treaty of 1880, departed by sea before the passage of the act of 1882, remained out of the United States until after the passage of the act of 1884, and then returned by sea; and in *United States* v. *Yung Ah Lung*, 124 U. S. 621, that a Chinese laborer, who resided in the United States at the date of the treaty of 1880, and until 1883, when he left San Francisco for China, taking with him a certificate of identity from the collector of the port in the form provided by the act of 1882, which was stolen from him in China, was entitled to land again in the United States in 1885, on proving by other evidence these facts, and his identity with the person described in the register kept by the collector of customs as the one to whom that certificate was issued.

Both those decisions proceeded upon a consideration of the various provisions of the acts of 1882 and 1884, giving weight to the presumption that they should not, unless unavoidably, be construed as operating retrospectively, or as contravening the stipulations of the treaty. In the first of those cases Justices Field and Bradley, and in the second case Justices Field, Harlan and Lamar, dissented from the judgment, being of opinion that the necessary construction of those acts was against the Chinese laborer. And in none of the opinions in either case was it suggested that the acts in question, if construed as contended by the United States, and so as to contravene the treaty, would be unconstitutional or inoperative.

In our jurisprudence, it is well settled that the provisions of an act of Congress, passed in the exercise of its constitutional authority, on this, as on any other subject, if clear and explicit, must be upheld by the courts, even in contravention of express stipulations in an earlier treaty. As was said by this court in *Chae Chan Ping's case*, following previous decisions: " The treaties were of no greater legal obligation than the act of Congress. By the Constitution, laws made in pursuance thereof and treaties made under the authority of the United States are both declared to be the supreme law of the land, and no paramount authority is given to one over the other. A treaty, it is true, is in its nature a contract between nations, and is often merely promissory in its character, requiring legislation to carry its stipulations into effect. Such legislation will be open to future repeal or amendment. If the treaty operates by its own force, and relates to a subject within the power of Congress, it can be deemed in that particular only the equivalent of a legislative act, to be repealed or modified at the pleasure of Congress. In either case, the last expression of the sovereign will must control." " So far as a treaty made by the United States with any foreign nation can become the subject of judicial cognizance in the courts of this country, it is subject to such acts as Congress may pass for its enforcement, modification or repeal." 130 U. S. 600. See also *Foster* v. *Neilson*, 2 Pet. 253, 314; *Edye* v. *Robertson*, 112 U. S. 580, 597–599; *Whitney* v. *Robertson*, 124 U. S. 190.

By the supplementary act of October 1, 1888, c. 1064, it was enacted, in section 1, that " from and after the passage of this act, it shall be unlawful for any Chinese laborer, who shall at any time heretofore have been, or who may now or hereafter be, a resident within the United States, and who shall have departed or shall depart therefrom, and shall not have returned before the passage of this act, to return to, or remain in, the United States;" and in section 2, that " no certificates of identity, provided for in the fourth and fifth sections of the act to which this is a supplement, shall hereafter be issued; and every certificate heretofore issued in pursuance thereof is hereby declared void and of no effect, and the Chinese laborer claiming admission by virtue thereof shall not be permitted to enter the United States." 25 Stat. 504.

In the case of *Chae Chan Ping*, already often referred to, a Chinese laborer, who had resided in San Francisco from 1875 until June 2, 1887, when he left that port for China, having in his possession a certificate issued to him on that day by the collector of customs, according to the act of 1884, and in terms entitling him to return to the United States, returned to the same port on October 8, 1888, and was refused by the collector permission to land, because of the provisions of the act of October 1, 1888, above cited. It was strongly contended in his behalf, that by his residence in the United States for twelve years preceding June 2, 1887, in accordance with the fifth article of the treaty of 1868, he had now a lawful right to be in the United States, and had a vested right to return to the United States, which could not be taken from him by any exercise of mere legislative power by Congress; that he had acquired such a right by contract between him and the United States, by virtue of his acceptance of the offer, contained in the acts of 1882 and 1884, to every Chinese person then here, if he should leave the country, complying with specified conditions, to permit him to return; that, as applied to him, the act of 1888 was unconstitutional, as being a bill of attainder and an *ex post facto* law; and that the depriving him of his right to return was punishment, which could not be inflicted except by judicial sentence. The contention was thus summed up at the beginning of the opinion: "The validity of the act is assailed as being in effect an expulsion from the country of Chinese laborers, in violation of existing treaties between the United States and the government of China, and of rights vested in them under the laws of Congress." 130 U. S. 584–589.

Yet the court unanimously held that the statute of 1888 was constitutional, and that the action of the collector in refusing him permission to land was lawful; and, after the passages already quoted, said: "The power of exclusion of foreigners being an incident of sovereignty belonging to the government of the United States, as a part of those sovereign powers delegated by the Constitution, the right to its exercise at any time when, in the judgment of the government, the interests of the country require it, cannot be granted away or restrained on behalf of any one. The powers of government are delegated in trust to the United States, and are incapable of transfer to any other parties. They cannot be abandoned or surrendered. Nor can their exercise be hampered, when needed for the public good, by any considerations of private interest. The exercise of these public trusts is not the subject of barter or contract. Whatever license, therefore, Chinese laborers may have obtained, previous to the act of October 1, 1888, to return to the United States after their departure, is held at the will of the government, revocable at any time, at its pleasure." "The rights and interests created by a treaty, which have become so vested that its expiration or abrogation will not destroy or impair them, are such as are connected with and lie in property, capable of sale and transfer or other disposition, not such as are personal and untransferable in their character." "But far different is this case, where a continued suspension of the exercise of a governmental power is insisted upon as a right, because, by the favor and consent of the government, it has not heretofore been exerted with respect to the appellant or to the class to which he belongs. Between property rights not affected by the termination or abrogation of a treaty, and expectations of benefits from the continuance of existing legislation, there is as wide a difference as between realization and hopes." 130 U. S. 609, 610.

It thus appears that in that case it was directly adjudged, upon full argument and consideration, that a Chinese laborer, who had been admitted into the United States while the treaty of 1868 was in force, by which the United States and China "cordially recognize the inherent and inalienable right of man to change his home and allegiance, and also the mutual advantage of the free migration and emigration of their citizens and subjects, respectively, from one country to the other," not only for the purpose of curiosity or of trade, but "as permanent residents;" and who had continued to reside here for twelve years, and who had then gone back to China, after receiving a certificate, in the form provided by act of Congress, entitling him to return to the United States; might be refused re-admission into the United States, without judicial trial or hearing, and simply by reason of another act of Congress, passed during his absence, and declaring all such certificates to be void, and prohibiting all Chinese laborers who had at any time been residents in the United States, and had departed therefrom and not returned before the passage of this act, from coming into the United States.

In view of that decision, which, as before observed, was a unanimous judgment of the court, and which had the concurrence of all the justices who had delivered opinions in the cases arising under the acts of 1882 and 1884, it appears to be impossible to hold that a Chinese laborer acquired, under any of the treaties or acts of Congress, any right, as a denizen or otherwise, to be and remain in this country, except by the license, permission and sufferance of Congress, to be withdrawn whenever, in its opinion, the public welfare might require it.

By the law of nations, doubtless, aliens residing in a country, with the intention of making it a permanent place of abode, acquire, in one sense, a domicil there; and, while they are permitted by the nation to retain such a residence and domicil, are subject to its laws, and may invoke its protection against other nations. This is recognized by those publicists who, as has been seen, maintain in the strongest terms the right of the nation to expel any or all aliens at its pleasure. Vattel, lib. 1, c. 19, § 213; 1 Phillimore, c. 18, § 321; Mr. Marcy, in *Koszta's case*, Wharton's International Law Digest, § 198. See also *Lau Ow Bew* v. *United States*, 144 U. S. 47, 62; Merlin, Repertoire de Jurisprudence, Domicile, § 13, quoted in the case, above cited, of *In re Adam*, 1 Moore P. C. 460, 472, 473.

Chinese laborers, therefore, like all other aliens residing in the United States for a shorter or longer time, are entitled, so long as they are permitted by the government of the United States to remain in the country, to the safeguards of the Constitution, and to the protection of the laws, in regard to their rights of person and of property, and to their civil and criminal responsibility. But they continue to be aliens, having taken no steps towards becoming citizens, and incapable of becoming such under the naturalization laws; and therefore remain subject to the power of Congress to expel them, or to order them to be removed and deported from the country, whenever in its judgment their removal is necessary or expedient for the public interest.

Nothing inconsistent with these views was decided or suggested by the court in *Chy Lung* v. *Freeman*, 92 U. S. 275, or in *Yick Wo* v. *Hopkins*, 118 U. S. 356, cited for the appellants.

In *Chy Lung* v. *Freeman*, a statute of the State of California, restricting the immigration of Chinese persons, was held to be unconstitutional and void, because it contravened the grant in the Constitution to Congress of the power to regulate commerce with foreign nations.

In *Yick Wo* v. *Hopkins*, the point decided was that the Fourteenth Amendment of the Constitution of the United States, forbidding any State to deprive any person of life, liberty or property without due process of law, or to deny to any person within its jurisdiction the equal protection of the laws, was violated by a municipal ordinance of San Francisco, which conferred upon the board of supervisors arbitrary power, without regard to competency of persons or to fitness of places, to grant or refuse licenses to carry on public laundries, and which was executed by the supervisors by refusing licenses to all Chinese residents, and granting them to other persons under like circumstances. The question there was of the power of a State over aliens continuing to reside within its jurisdiction, not of the power of the United States to put an end to their residence in the country.

The act of May 5, 1892, c. 60, is entitled " An act to prohibit the coming of Chinese persons into the United States "; and provides, in section 1, that "all laws now in force, prohibiting and regulating the coming into this country of Chinese persons and persons of Chinese descent, are hereby continued in force for a period of ten years from the passage of this act."

The rest of the act (laying aside, as immaterial, section 5, relating to an application for a writ of *habeas corpus* " by a Chinese person seeking to land in the United States, to whom that privilege has been denied,") deals with two classes of Chinese persons, first, those " not lawfully entitled to be or remain in the United States," and second, those " entitled to remain in the United States." These words of description neither confer nor take away any right; but simply designate the Chinese persons who were not, or who were, authorized or permitted to remain in the United States under the laws and treaties existing at the time of the passage of this act, but subject, nevertheless, to the power of the United States, absolutely or conditionally, to withdraw the permission and to terminate the authority to remain.

Sections 2–4 concern Chinese "not lawfully entitled to be or remain in the United States;" and provide that, after trial before a justice, judge or commissioner, a " Chinese person, or person of Chinese descent, convicted and adjudged to be not lawfully entitled to be or remain in the United States," shall be imprisoned at hard labor for not more than a year, and be afterwards removed to China or other country of which he appears to be a citizen or subject.

The subsequent sections relate to Chinese laborers " entitled to remain in the United States " under previous laws. Sections 6 and 7 are the only sections which have any bearing on the cases before us, and the only ones, therefore, the construction or effect of which need now be considered.

The manifest objects of these sections are to provide a system of registration and identification of such Chinese laborers, to require them to obtain certificates of residence, and, if they do not do so within a year, to have them deported from the United States.

Section 6, in the first place, provides that "it shall be the duty of all Chinese laborers, within the limits of the United States at the time of the passage of this act, and who are entitled to remain in the United States, to apply to the collector of internal revenue of their respective districts, within one year after the passage of this act, for a certificate of residence." This provision, by making it the duty of the Chinese laborer to apply to the collector of internal revenue of the district for a certificate, necessarily implies a correlative duty of the collector to grant him a certificate, upon due proof of the requisite facts. What this proof shall be is not defined in the statute, but is committed to the supervision of the Secretary of the Treasury by section 7, which directs him to make such rules and regulations as may be necessary for the efficient execution of the act, to prescribe the necessary forms, and to make such provisions that certificates may be procured in localities convenient to the applicants, and without charge to them; and the Secretary of the Treasury has, by such rules and regulations, provided that the fact of residence shall be proved by "at least one credible witness of good character," or, in case of necessity, by other proof. The statute and the regulations, in order to make sure that every such Chinese laborer may have a certificate, in the nature of a passport, with which he may go into any part of the United States, and that the United States may preserve a record of all such certificates issued, direct that a duplicate of each certificate shall be recorded in the office of the collector who granted it, and may be issued to the laborer upon proof of loss or destruction of his original certificate. There can be no doubt of the validity of these provisions and regulations, unless they are invalidated by the other provisions of section 6.

This section proceeds to enact that any Chinese laborer within the limits of the United States, who shall neglect, fail or refuse to apply for a certificate of residence within the year, or who shall afterwards be found within the jurisdiction of the United States without such a certificate, "shall be deemed and adjudged to be unlawfully within the United States." The meaning of this clause, as shown by those which follow, is not that this fact shall thereupon be held to be conclusively established against him, but only that the want of a certificate shall be *prima facie* evidence that he is not entitled to remain in the United States; for the section goes on to direct that he " may be arrested by any customs official, collector of internal revenue or his deputies, United States marshal or his deputies, and taken before a United States judge;" and that it shall thereupon be the duty of the judge to order that the laborer "be deported from the United States" to China, (or to any other country which he is a citizen or subject of, and which does not demand any tax as a condition of his removal to it,) "unless he shall establish clearly, to the satisfaction of said judge, that by reason of accident, sickness or other unavoidable cause, he has been unable to procure his certificate, and to the satisfaction of the court, and by at least one credible white witness, that he was a resident of the United States at the time of the passage of this act ; and if, upon the hearing, it shall appear that he is so entitled to a certificate, it shall be granted upon his paying the cost. Should it appear that said Chinaman had procured a certificate which has been lost or destroyed, he shall be detained and judgment suspended a reasonable time to enable him to procure a duplicate from the officer granting it; and in such cases the cost of said arrest and trial shall be in the discretion of the court."

For the reasons stated in the earlier part of this opinion, Congress, under the power to exclude or expel aliens, might have directed any Chinese laborer, found in the United States without a certificate of residence, to be removed out of the country by executive officers, without judicial trial or examination, just as it might have authorized such officers absolutely to prevent his entrance into the country. But Congress has not undertaken to do this.

The effect of the provisions of section 6 of the act of 1892 is that, if a Chinese laborer, after the opportunity afforded him to obtain a certificate of residence within a year, at a convenient place, and without cost, is found without such a certificate, he shall be so far presumed to be not entitled to remain within the United States, that an officer of the customs, or a collector of internal revenue, or a marshal, or a deputy of either, may arrest him, not with a view to imprisonment or punishment, or to his immediate deportation without further inquiry, but in order to take him before a judge, for the purpose of a judicial hearing and determination of the only facts which, under the act of Congress, can have a material bearing upon the question whether he shall be sent out of the country, or be permitted to remain.

The powers and duties of the executive officers named being ordinarily limited to their own districts, the reasonable inference is that they must take him before a judge within the same judicial district ; and such was the course pursued in the cases before us.

The designation of the judge, in general terms, as "a United States judge," is an apt and sufficient description of a judge of a court of the United States, and is equivalent to or synonymous with the designation, in other statutes, of the judges authorized to issue writs of *habeas corpus*, or warrants to arrest persons accused of crime. Rev. Stat. §§ 752, 1014.

When, in the form prescribed by law, the executive officer, acting in behalf of the United States, brings the Chinese laborer before the judge, in order that he may be heard, and the facts upon which depends his right to remain in the country be decided, a case is duly submitted to the judicial power; for here are all the elements of a civil case — a complainant, a defendant and a judge — *actor, reus et judex.* 3 Bl. Com. 25 ; *Osborn* v. *Bank of United States*, 9 Wheat. 738, 819. No formal complaint or pleadings are required, and the want of them does not affect the authority of the judge, or the validity of the statute.

If no evidence is offered by the Chinaman, the judge makes the order of deportation, as upon a default. If he produces competent evidence to explain the fact of his not having a certificate, it must be considered by the judge ; and if he thereupon appears to be entitled to a certificate, it is to be granted to him. If he proves that the collector of internal revenue has unlawfully refused to give him a certificate, he proves an "unavoidable cause," within the meaning of the act, for not procuring one. If he proves that he had procured a certificate which has been lost or destroyed, he is to be allowed a reasonable time to procure a duplicate thereof.

The provision which puts the burden of proof upon him of rebutting the presumption arising from his having no certificate, as well as the requirement of proof, " by at least one credible white witness, that he was a resident of the United States at the time of the passage of this act," is within the acknowledged power of every legislature to prescribe the evidence which shall be received, and the effect of that evidence, in the courts of its own government. *Odgen* v. *Saunders*, 12 Wheat. 213, 262, 349 ; *Pillow* v. *Roberts*, 13 How. 472, 476 ; *Cliquot's Champagne*, 3 Wall. 114, 143 ; *Ex parte Fisk*, 113 U. S. 713, 721 ; *Holmes* v. *Hunt*, 122 Mass. 505, 516–519. The competency of all witnesses, without regard to their color, to testify in the courts of the United States, rests on acts of Congress, which Congress may at its discretion modify or repeal. Rev. Stat. §§ 858, 1977. The reason for requiring a Chinese alien, claiming the privilege of remaining in the United States, to prove the fact of his residence here, at the time of the passage of the act, " by at least one credible white witness," may have been the experience of Congress, as mentioned by Mr. Justice Field in *Chae Chan Ping's case*, that the enforcement of former acts, under which the testimony of Chinese persons was admitted to prove similar facts, " was attended with great embarrassment, from the suspicious nature, in many instances, of the testimony offered to establish the residence of the parties, arising from the loose notions entertained by the witnesses of the obligation of an oath." 130 U. S. 598. And this requirement, not allowing such a fact to be proved solely by the testimony of aliens in a like situation, or of the same race, is quite analogous to the provision, which has existed for seventy-seven years in the naturalization laws, by which aliens applying for naturalization must prove their residence within the limits and under the jurisdiction of the United States, for five years next preceding, " by the oath or affirmation of citizens of the United States." Acts of March 22, 1816, c. 32, § 2, 3 Stat. 259; May 24, 1828, c. 116, § 2, 4 Stat. 311; Rev. Stat. § 2165, cl. 6; 2 Kent Com. 65.

The proceeding before a United States judge, as provided for in section 6 of the act of 1892, is in no proper sense a trial and sentence for a crime or offence. It is simply the ascertainment, by appropriate and lawful means, of the fact whether the conditions exist upon which Congress has enacted that an alien of this class may remain within the country. The order of deportation is not a punishment for crime. It is not a banishment, in the sense in which that word is often applied to the expulsion of a citizen from his country by way of punishment. It is but a method of enforcing the return to his own country of an alien who has not complied with the conditions upon the performance of which the government of the nation, acting within its constitutional authority and through the proper departments, has determined that his continuing to reside here shall depend. He has not, therefore, been deprived of life, liberty or property, without due process of law; and the provisions of the Constitution, securing the right of trial by jury, and prohibiting unreasonable searches and seizures, and cruel and unusual punishments, have no application.

The question whether, and upon what conditions, these aliens shall be permitted to remain within the United States being one to be determined by the political departments of the government, the judicial department cannot properly express an opinion upon the wisdom, the policy or the justice of the measures enacted by Congress in the exercise of the powers confided to it by the Constitution over this subject.

The three cases now before us do not differ from one another in any material particular.

In the first case, the petitioner had wholly neglected, failed and refused to apply to the collector of internal revenue for a certificate of residence, and, being found without such a certificate after a year from the passage of the act of 1892, was arrested by the United States marshal, with the purpose, as the return states, of taking him before a United States judge within the district; and thereupon, before any further proceeding, sued out a writ of *habeas corpus*.

In the second case, the petitioner had likewise neglected, failed and refused to apply to the collector of internal revenue for a certificate of residence, and, being found without one, was arrested by the marshal and taken before the District Judge of the United States, who ordered him to be remanded to the custody of the marshal, and to be deported from the United States, in accordance with the provisions of the act. The allegation in the petition, that the judge's order was made "without any hearing of any kind," is shown to be untrue by the recital in the order itself, (a copy of which is annexed to and made part of the petition,) that he had failed to clearly establish to the judge's satisfaction that by reason of accident, sickness or other unavoidable cause, he had been unable to procure a certificate, or that he had procured one and it had been lost or destroyed.

In the third case, the petitioner had, within the year, applied to a collector of internal revenue for a certificate of residence, and had been refused it, because he produced and could produce none but Chinese witnesses to prove the residence necessary to entitle him to a certificate. Being found without a certificate of residence, he was arrested by the marshal, and taken before the United States District Judge, and established to the satisfaction of the judge, that, because of the collector's refusal to give him a certificate of residence he was without one by unavoidable cause; and also proved, by a Chinese witness only, that he was a resident of the United States at the time of the passage of the act of 1892. Thereupon the judge ordered him to be remanded to the custody of the marshal, and to be deported from the United States, as provided in that act.

It would seem that the collector of internal revenue, when applied to for a certificate, might properly decline to find the requisite fact of residence upon testimony which, by an express provision of the act, would be insufficient to prove that fact at a hearing before the judge. But if the collector might have received and acted upon such testimony, and did, upon any ground, unjustifiably refuse a certificate of residence, the only remedy of the applicant was to prove by competent and sufficient evidence at the hearing before the judge the facts requisite to entitle him to a certificate. To one of those facts, that of residence, the statute, which, for the reasons already stated, appears to us to be within the constitutional authority of Congress to enact, peremptorily requires at that hearing the testimony of a credible white witness. And it was because no such testimony was produced, that the order of deportation was made.

Upon careful consideration of the subject, the only conclusion which appears to us to be consistent with the principles of international law, with the Constitution and laws of the United States, and with the previous decisions of this court, is that in each of these cases the judgment of the Circuit Court, dismissing the writ of *habeas corpus*, is right and must be

Affirmed.

MR. JUSTICE BREWER dissenting.

I dissent from the opinion and judgment of the court in these cases, and the questions being of importance, I deem it not improper to briefly state my reasons therefor.

I rest my dissent on three propositions: First, that the persons against whom the penalties of section 6 of the act of 1892 are directed are persons lawfully residing within the United States; secondly, that as such they are within the protection of the Constitution, and secured by its guarantees against oppression and wrong; and, third, that section 6 deprives them of liberty and imposes punishment without due process of law, and in disregard of constitutional guarantees, especially those found in the Fourth, Fifth, Sixth, and Eighth Articles of the Amendments.

And, first, these persons are lawfully residing within the limits of the United States. By the treaty of July 28, 1868, 16 Stat. 739, 740, commonly known as the "Burlingame Treaty," it was provided, article 5: "The United States of America and the Emperor of China cordially recognize the inherent and inalienable right of man to change his home and allegiance, and also the mutual advantage of the free migration and emigration of their citizens and subjects, respectively, from the one country to the other, for purposes of curiosity, of trade, or as permanent residents." And article 6: "Citizens of the United States visiting or residing in China shall enjoy the same privileges, immunities, or exemptions in

respect to travel or residence, as may there be enjoyed by
the citizens or subjects of the most favored nation. And,
reciprocally, Chinese subjects visiting or residing in the United
States shall enjoy the same privileges, immunities, and exemptions in respect to travel or residence, as may there be enjoyed
by the citizens or subjects of the most favored nation." At
that time we sought Chinese emigration. The subsequent
treaty of November 17, 1880, 22 Stat. 826, which looked to a
restriction of Chinese emigration, nevertheless contained in
article 2 this provision :

" ARTICLE II. Chinese subjects, whether proceeding to the
United States as teachers, students, merchants, or from curiosity, together with their body and household servants, and
Chinese laborers who are now in the United States shall be
allowed to go and come of their own free will and accord,
and shall be accorded all the rights, privileges, immunities,
and exemptions which are accorded to the citizens and subjects of the most favored nation."

While subsequently to this treaty, Congress passed several
acts — May 6, 1882, 22 Stat. 58, c. 126 ; July 5, 1884, 23 Stat.
115, c. 220 ; October 1, 1888, 25 Stat. 504, c. 1064 — to restrict the entrance into this country of Chinese laborers, and
while the validity of this restriction was sustained in the
Chinese Exclusion case, 130 U. S. 581, yet no act has been
passed denying the right of those laborers who had once lawfully entered the country to remain, and they are here not as
travellers or only temporarily. We must take judicial notice
of that which is disclosed by the census, and which is also a
matter of common knowledge. There are 100,000 and more
of these persons living in this country, making their homes
here, and striving by their labor to earn a livelihood. They
are not travellers, but resident aliens.

But, further, this section six recognizes the fact of a lawful
residence, and only applies to those who have such ; for the
parties named in the section, and to be reached by its provisions, are " Chinese laborers within the limits of the United
States at the time of the passage of this act, and who are
entitled to remain in the United States." These appellants,
therefore, are lawfully within the United States, and are here
as residents, and not as travellers. They have lived in this
country, respectively, since 1879, 1877, and 1874 — almost as
long a time as some of those who were members of the Congress that passed this act of punishment and expulsion.

That those who have become domiciled in a country are
entitled to a more distinct and larger measure of protection
than those who are simply passing through, or temporarily in

it, has long been recognized by the law of nations. It was said by this court, in the case of *The Venus*, 8 Cranch, 253, 278: " The writers upon the law of nations distinguish between a temporary residence in a foreign country, for a special purpose, and a residence accompanied with an intention to make it a permanent place of abode. The latter is styled by Vattel, *domicil*, which he defines to be ' a habitation fixed in any place, with an intention of always staying there.' Such a person, says this author, becomes a member of the new society, at least as a permanent inhabitant, and is a kind of citizen of an inferior order from the native citizens; but is, nevertheless, united and subject to the society, without participating in all its advantages. This right of domicil, he continues, is not established, unless the person makes sufficiently known his intention of fixing there, either tacitly or by an express declaration. (Vatt. pp. 92, 93.) Grotius nowhere uses the word *domicil*, but he also distinguishes between those who stay in a foreign country by the necessity of their affairs, or from any other temporary cause, and those who reside there from a permanent cause. The former he denominates strangers, and the latter subjects." The rule is thus laid down by Sir Robert Phillimore: " It has been said that these rules of law are applicable to naturalized as well as native citizens. But there is a class of persons which cannot be, strictly speaking, included under either of these denominations, namely, the class of those who have ceased to reside in their native country, and have taken up a permanent abode . . . in another. These are domiciled inhabitants; they have not put on a new citizenship through some formal mode enjoined by the law of the new country. They are *de facto* though not *de jure* citizens of the country of their domicil." 1 Phillimore, International Law, Chap. XVIII, p. 347.

In the *Koszta case* it was said by Secretary Marcy: " This right to protect persons having a domicil, though not native-born or naturalized citizens, rests on the firm foundation of justice, and the claim to be protected is earned by considerations which the protecting power is not at liberty to disregard. Such domiciled citizen pays the same price for his protection as native-born or naturalized citizens pay for theirs. He is under the bonds of allegiance to the country of his residence, and if he breaks them incurs the same penalties; he owes the same obedience to the civil laws . . .; his property is in the same way and to the same extent as theirs liable to contribute to the support of the government. . . . In nearly all respects his and their condition as to the duties and burdens of government are undistinguishable." 2 Wharton Int. Law Digest, § 198.

And in *Lau Ow Bew* v. *United States*, 144 U. S. 47, 61, this court declared that "by general international law, foreigners who have become domiciled in a country other than their own, acquire rights and must discharge duties in many respects the same as possessed by and imposed upon the citizens of that country, and no restriction on the footing upon which such persons stand by reason of their domicil, . . . is to be presumed."

Indeed, there is force in the contention of counsel for appellants, that these persons are "denizens" within the true meaning and spirit of that word as used in the common law. The old definition was this:

"A denizen of England by letters patent for life, in tayl or. in fee, whereby he becomes a subject in regard of his person." *Craw* v. *Ramsey*, Vaughan's Reports, 278.

And again:

"A denizen is an alien born, but who has obtained *ex donatione regis* letters patent to make him an English subject, . . . A denizen is in a kind of middle state, between an alien and a natural-born subject, and partakes of both of them." 1 Bl. Com. 374.

In respect to this, after quoting from some of the early constitutions of the States, in which the word "denizen" is found, counsel say: "It is claimed that the appellants in this case come completely within the definition quoted above. They are alien born, but they have obtained the same thing as letters patent from this country. They occupy a middle state between an alien and a native. They partake of both of them. They cannot vote, or, as it is stated in Bacon's Abridgment, they have no 'power of making laws,' as a native-born subject can, nor are they here as ordinary aliens. An ordinary alien within this country has come here under no prohibition, and no invitation, but the appellants have come under the direct request and invitation and under the 'patent' of the Federal government. They have been guaranteed 'the same privileges, immunities, and exemptions in respect to . . . residence' (Burlingame Treaty concluded July 28, 1868) as that enjoyed in the United States by the citizens and subjects of the most favored nation. They have been told that if they would come here they would be treated just the same as we treat an Englishman, an Irishman, or a Frenchman. They have been invited here, and their position is much stronger than that of an alien, in regard to whom there is no guarantee from the government, and who has come not in response to any invitation, but has simply drifted here because there is no prohibition to keep him out. They certainly come within the meaning of 'denizen' as used in the constitutions of the States."

But whatever rights a resident alien might have in any other nation, here he is within the express protection of the Constitution, especially in respect to those guarantees which are declared in the original amendments. It has been repeated so often as to become axiomatic, that this government is one of enumerated and delegated powers, and, as declared in Article 10 of the amendments, " the powers not delegated to the United States by the Constitution, nor prohibited by it to the States, are reserved to the States respectively, or to the people."

It is said that the power here asserted is inherent in sovereignty. This doctrine of powers inherent in sovereignty is one both indefinite and dangerous. Where are the limits to such powers to be found, and by whom are they to be pronounced? Is it within legislative capacity to declare the limits? If so, then the mere assertion of an inherent power creates it, and despotism exists. May the courts establish the boundaries? Whence do they obtain the authority for this? Shall they look to the practices of other nations to ascertain the limits? The governments of other nations have elastic powers — ours is fixed and bounded by a written constitution. The expulsion of a race may be within the inherent powers of a despotism. History, before the adoption of this Constitution, was not destitute of examples of the exercise of such a power ; and its framers were familiar with history, and wisely, as it seems to me, they gave to this government no general power to banish. Banishment may be resorted to as punishment for crime ; but among the powers reserved to the people and not delegated to the government is that of determining whether whole classes in our midst shall, for no crime but that of their race and birthplace, be driven from our territory.

Whatever may be true as to exclusion, and as to that see *Chinese Exclusion case*, 130 U. S. 581, and *Nishimura Ekiu* v. *United States*, 142 U. S. 651, I deny that there is any arbitrary and unrestrained power to banish residents, even resident aliens. What, it may be asked, is the reason for any difference? The answer is obvious. The Constitution has no extraterritorial effect, and those who have not come lawfully within our territory cannot claim any protection from its provisions. And it may be that the national government, having full control of all matters relating to other nations, has the power to build, as it were, a Chinese wall around our borders' and absolutely forbid aliens to enter. But the Constitution has potency everywhere within the limits of our territory, and the powers which the national government may exercise within such limits are those, and only those, given to it by that instrument. Now, the power to remove resident aliens is, confessedly, not expressed. Even if it be among the powers implied, yet still it can be exercised only in subordination to the limitations and restrictions imposed by the Constitution. In the case of *Monongahela Navigation Company* v. *United States*, 148 U. S. 312, 336, it was said: "But like the other powers granted to Congress by the Constitution, the power to regulate commerce is subject to all the limitations imposed by such instrument, and among them is that of the Fifth Amendment we have heretofore quoted. Congress has supreme control over the regulation of commerce; but if, in exercising that supreme control, it deems it necessary to take private property, then it must proceed subject to the limitations imposed by this Fifth Amendment, and can take only on payment of just compensation." And if that be true of the powers expressly granted, it must as certainly be true of those that are only granted by implication.

When the first ten amendments were presented for adoption they were preceded by a preamble stating that the conventions of many States had at the time of their adopting the Constitution expressed a desire, "in order to prevent misconception or abuse of its powers, that further declaratory and restrictive clauses should be added." It is worthy of notice that in them the word "citizen" is not found. In some of them the descriptive word is "people," but in the Fifth it is broader, and the word is "person," and in the Sixth it is the "accused," while in the Third, Seventh, and Eighth there is no limitation as to the beneficiaries suggested by any descriptive word.

In the case of *Yick Wo* v. *Hopkins*, 118 U. S. 356, 369, it was said: "The Fourteenth Amendment to the Constitution is not confined to the protection of citizens. It says: 'Nor shall any State deprive any person of life, liberty, or property without due process of law; nor deny to any person within its jurisdiction the equal protection of the laws.' These provisions are universal in their application to all persons within the territorial jurisdiction, without regard to any differences of race, of color, or of nationality; and the equal protection of the laws is a pledge of the protection of equal laws." The matter considered in that case was of a local nature, a municipal ordinance for regulating the carrying on of public laundries, something fairly within the police power of a State; and yet because its provisions conflicted with the guarantees of the Fourteenth Amendment, the ordinance was declared void.

If the use of the word "person" in the Fourteenth Amendment protects all individuals lawfully within the State, the use of the same word "person" in the Fifth must be equally comprehensive, and secures to all persons lawfully within the territory of the United States the protection named therein; and a like conclusion must follow as to the Sixth.

I pass, therefore, to the consideration of my third proposition: Section 6 deprives of "life, liberty, and property without due process of law." It imposes punishment without a trial, and punishment cruel and severe. It places the liberty of one individual subject to the unrestrained control of another. Notice its provisions: It first commands all to register. He who does not register violates that law, and may be punished; and so the section goes on to say that one who has not complied with its requirements, and has no certificate of residence, "shall be deemed and adjudged to be unlawfully within the United States," and then it imposes as a penalty his deportation from the country. Deportation is punishment. It involves first an arrest, a deprival of liberty; and, second, a removal from home, from family, from business, from property. In Rapalje & Lawrence's Law Dictionary, (vol. 1, page 109,) "banishment" is thus defined: "A punishment by forced exile, either for years or for life; inflicted principally upon political offenders, 'transportation' being the word used to express a similar punishment of ordinary criminals." In 4 Bl. Com. 377, it is said: "Some punishments consist in exile or banishment, by abjuration of the realm, or transportation." In Vattel we find that "banishment is only applied to condemnation in due course of law." Note to § 228, Book 1, c. 19, in 1 Vattel.

But it needs no citation of authorities to support the proposition that deportation is punishment. Every one knows that to be forcibly taken away from home, and family, and friends, and business, and property, and sent across the ocean to a distant land, is punishment; and that oftentimes most severe and cruel. Apt and just are the words of one of the framers of this Constitution, President Madison, when he says (4

Elliot's Debates, 555): "If the banishment of an alien from a country into which he has been invited as the asylum most auspicious to his happiness — a country where he may have formed the most tender connections; where he may have invested his entire property, and acquired property of the real and permanent, as well as the movable and temporary kind; where he enjoys, under the laws, a greater share of the blessings of personal security and personal liberty than he can elsewhere hope for; . . . if, moreover, in the execution of the sentence against him he is to be exposed, not only to the ordinary dangers of the sea, but to the peculiar casualties incident to a crisis of war and of unusual licentiousness on that element, and possibly to vindictive purposes, which his immigration itself may have provoked — if a banishment of this sort be not a punishment, and among the severest of punishments, it will be difficult to imagine a doom to which the name can be applied."

But punishment implies a trial: "No person shall be deprived of life, liberty, or property, without due process of law." Due process requires that a man be heard before he is condemned, and both heard and condemned in the due and orderly procedure of a trial as recognized by the common law from time immemorial. It was said by this court in *Hagar* v. *Reclamation District*, 111 U. S. 701, 708, "undoubtedly where life and liberty are involved, due process requires that there be a regular course of judicial proceedings, which imply that the party to be affected shall have notice and an opportunity to be heard." And by Mr. Justice Bradley, in defining "due process of law" in *Davidson* v. *New Orleans*, 96 U. S. 97, 107, "if found to be suitable or admissible in the special case, it will be adjudged to be 'due process of law,' but if found to be arbitrary, oppressive, and unjust, it may be declared to be not 'due process of law.'" And no person who has once come within the protection of the Constitution can be punished without a trial. It may be summary, as for petty offences and in cases of contempt, but still a trial, as known to the common law. It is said that a person may be extradited without a previous trial, but extradition is simply one step in the process of arresting and securing for trial. He may be removed by extradition from California to New York, or from this country to another, but such proceeding is not oppressive or unjust, but suitable and necessary, and, therefore, due process of law. But here, the Chinese are not arrested and extradited for trial, but arrested and, without a trial, punished by banishment.

Again, it is absolutely within the discretion of the collector to give or refuse a certificate to one who applies therefor. Nowhere is it provided what evidence shall be furnished to the collector, and nowhere is it made mandatory upon him to grant a certificate on the production of such evidence. It can not be due process of law to impose punishment on any person for failing to have that in his possession, the possession of which he can obtain only at the arbitrary and unregulated discretion of any official. It will not do to say that the presumption is that the official will act reasonably and not arbitrarily. When the right to liberty and residence is involved, some other protection than the mere discretion of any official is required. Well was it said by Mr. Justice Matthews, in the case of *Yick Wo* v. *Hopkins, supra*, on page 369 : " When we consider the nature and the theory of our institutions of government, the principles upon which they are supposed to rest, and review the history of their development, we are constrained to conclude that they do not mean to leave room for the play and action of purely personal and arbitrary power."

Again, a person found without such certificate may be taken before a United States Judge. What judge? A judge in the district in which the party resides or is found? There is no limitation in this respect. A Chinese laborer in San Francisco may be arrested by a deputy United States marshal, and taken before a judge in Oregon; and when so taken before that judge, it is made his duty to deport such laborer unless he proves his innocence of any violation of the law, and that, too, by at least one credible white witness. And how shall he obtain that witness? No provision is made in the statute therefor. Will it be said that Article 6 of the amendments gives to the accused a right to have a compulsory process for obtaining witnesses in his favor? The reply is, that if he is entitled to one part of that article, he is entitled to all ; and among them is the right to a speedy and public trial by an impartial jury of the State and district. The only theory upon which this proceeding can be sustained is that he has no right to any benefits of this Article 6 ; and if he has no right thereto, and the statute has made no provision for securing his witnesses or limiting the proceeding to a judge of the district where he resides, the result follows inevitably, as stated, that he may be arrested by any one of the numerous officials named in the statute, and carried before any judge in the United States that such official may select, and, then, unless he proves that which he is given no means of proving, be punished by removal from home, friends, family, property, business, to another country.

It is said that these Chinese are entitled, while they remain, to the safeguards of the Constitution and to the protection of the laws in regard to their rights of person and of property; but that they continue to be aliens, subject to the absolute power of Congress to forcibly remove them. In other words, the guarantees of "life, liberty, and property," named in the Constitution, are theirs by sufferance and not of right. Of what avail are such guarantees?

Once more: Supposing a Chinaman from San Francisco, having obtained a certificate, should go to New York or other place in pursuit of work, and on the way his certificate be lost or destroyed. He is subject to arrest and detention, the cost of which is in the discretion of the court, and judgment of deportation will be suspended a reasonable time to enable him to obtain a duplicate from the officer granting it. In other words, he cannot move about in safety without carrying with him this certificate. The situation was well described by Senator Sherman in the debate in the Senate: "They are here ticket-of-leave men; precisely as, under the Australian law, a convict is allowed to go at large upon a ticket-of-leave, these people are to be allowed to go at large and earn their livelihood, but they must have their tickets-of-leave in their possession." And he added: "This inaugurates in our system of government a new departure; one, I believe, never before practised, although it was suggested in conference that some such rules had been adopted in slavery times to secure the peace of society."

It is true this statute is directed only against the obnoxious Chinese; but if the power exists, who shall say it will not be exercised to-morrow against other classes and other people? If the guarantees of these amendments can be thus ignored in order to get rid of this distasteful class, what security have others that a like disregard of its provisions may not be resorted to? Profound and wise were the observations of Mr. Justice Bradley, speaking for the court in *Boyd* v. *United States*, 116 U. S. 616, 635: "Illegitimate and unconstitutional practices get their first footing in that way, namely, by silent approaches and slight deviations from legal modes of procedure. This can only be obviated by adhering to the rule that constitutional provisions for the security of person and property should be liberally construed. A close and literal construction deprives them of half their efficacy, and leads to gradual depreciation of the right, as if it consisted more in sound than in substance. It is the duty of the courts to be watchful for the constitutional rights of the citizen, and against any stealthy encroachments thereon. Their motto should be *obsta principiis*."

In the *Yick Wo case*, in which was presented a municipal ordinance, fair on its face, but contrived to work oppression to a few engaged in a single occupation, this court saw no difficulty in finding a constitutional barrier to such injustice. But this greater wrong, by which a hundred thousand people are subject to arrest and forcible deportation from the country, is beyond the reach of the protecting power of the Constitution. Its grievous wrong suggests this declaration of wisdom, coming from the dawn of English history : " Verily he who dooms a worse doom to the friendless and the comer from afar than to his fellow, injures himself." (The Laws of King Cnut, 1 Thorpe's Ancient Laws and Institutes of England, p. 397.)

In view of this enactment of the highest legislative body of the foremost Christian nation, may not the thoughtful Chinese. disciple of Confucius fairly ask, Why do they send missionaries here ?

Mr. Justice Field dissenting.[1]

I also wish to say a few words upon these cases and upon the extraordinary doctrines announced in support of the orders of the court below.

With the treaties between the United States and China, and the subsequent legislation adopted by Congress to prevent the immigration of Chinese laborers into this country, resulting in the Exclusion Act of October 1, 1888, the court is familiar. They have often been before us and have been considered in almost every phase. The act of 1888 declared that after its passage it should be unlawful for any Chinese laborer — who might then or thereafter be a resident of the United States, who should depart therefrom and not return before the passage of the act — to return or remain in the United States. The validity of this act was sustained by this court. 130 U. S. 581. In the opinion announcing the decision we considered the treaties with China, and also the legislation of Congress and the causes which led to its enactment. The court cited numerous instances in which statesmen and jurists of eminence had held that it was the undoubted right of every indepen-

---

[1] Mr. Justice Field's dissenting opinion bears the titles of the three cases, Nos. 1345, 1346, and 1347, and is further generally entitled " Chinese Deportation Cases."

dent nation to exclude foreigners from its limits whenever in
its judgment the public interests demanded such exclusion.

"The power of exclusion of foreigners," said the court,
"being an incident of sovereignty belonging to the government of the United States as a part of those sovereign powers
delegated by the Constitution, the right to its exercise at any
time when, in the judgment of the government the interests
of the country require it, cannot be granted away or restrained
on behalf of any one. The powers of government are delegated in trust to the United States and are incapable of transfer to any other parties. They cannot be abandoned or
surrendered. Nor-can their exercise be hampered, when
needed for the public good, by any considerations of private
interest. The exercise of these public trusts is not the subject of barter or contract. Whatever license, therefore,
Chinese laborers may have obtained previous to the act of
October 1, 1888, to return to the United States after their departure, is held at the will of the government, revocable at
any time at its pleasure. Whether a proper consideration by
our government of its previous laws, or a proper respect for
the nation whose subjects are affected by its action, ought to
have qualified its inhibition and made it applicable only to
persons departing from the country after the passage of the
act, are not questions for judicial determination. If there be
any just ground of complaint on the part of China it must be
made to the political department of our government, which is
alone competent to act upon the subject."   p. 609.

I had the honor to be the organ of the court in announcing
this opinion and judgment. I still adhere to the views there
expressed in all particulars; but between legislation for the
exclusion of Chinese persons — that is, to prevent them from
entering the country — and legislation for the deportation of
those who have acquired a residence in the country under a
treaty with China, there is a wide and essential difference.
The power of the government to exclude foreigners from this
country, that is, to prevent them from entering it, whenever
the public interests in its judgment require such exclusion, has
been repeatedly asserted by the legislative and executive departments of our government and never denied ; but its power
to deport from the country persons lawfully domiciled therein
by its consent, and engaged in the ordinary pursuits of life,
has never been asserted by the legislative or executive departments except for crime, or as an act of war in view of existing
or anticipated hostilities, unless the alien act of June 25, 1798,
can be considered as recognizing that doctrine. 1 Stat. 570.

c. 58. That act vested in the President power to order all such aliens as he should adjudge dangerous to the peace and safety of the United States, or should have reasonable grounds to suspect were concerned in any treasonable or secret machinations against the government, to depart out of the territory of the United States within such time as should be expressed in his order. And in case any alien when thus ordered to depart should be found at large within the United States after the term limited in the order, not having obtained a license from the President to reside therein, or having obtained such license should not have conformed thereto, he should on conviction thereof be imprisoned for a term not exceeding three years, and should never afterwards be admitted to become a citizen of the United States; with a proviso that if the alien thus ordered to depart should prove to the satisfaction of the President, by evidence to be taken before such person or persons as he should direct, that no injury or danger to the United States would arise from suffering him to reside therein, the President might grant a license to him to remain within the United States for such time as he should judge proper and at such place as he should designate. The act also provided that the President might require such alien to enter into a bond to the United States in such penal sum as he might direct, with one or more sureties to the satisfaction of the person authorized by the President to take the same, conditioned for his good behavior during his residence in the United States, and not to violate his license, which the President might revoke whenever he should think proper. The act also provided that it should be lawful for the President, whenever he deemed it necessary for the public safety, to order to be removed out of the territory of the United States any alien in prison in pursuance of the act, and to cause to be arrested and sent out of the United States such aliens as may have been ordered to depart, and had not obtained a license, in all cases where, in the opinion of the President, the public safety required a speedy removal. And that if any alien thus removed or sent out of the United States should voluntarily return, unless by permission of the President, such alien, being convicted thereof, should be imprisoned so long as in the opinion of the President the public safety might require.

The passage of this act produced great excitement throughout the country and was severely denounced by many of its ablest statesmen and jurists as unconstitutional and barbarous, and among them may be mentioned the great names of Jefferson and Madison, who are throughout our country

honored and revered for their lifelong devotion to principles
of constitutional liberty.   It was defended by its advocates as
a war measure.   John Adams, the President of the United
States at the time, who approved the bill and against whom
the responsibility for its passage was charged, states in his
correspondence that the bill was intended as a measure of
that character.   9 John Adams's Works, 291.   The State of
Virginia denounced it in severe terms.   Its general assembly
passed resolutions upon the act and another act of the same
session of Congress known as the " sedition act."   Upon the first
— the alien act — one of the resolutions declared that it exercised a power nowhere delegated to the Federal government,
and which, by uniting legislative and judicial powers to those
of executive, subverted the general principles of free government as well as the particular organization and positive provisions of the Federal Constitution.   4 Elliot's Deb. 528.   The
resolutions upon both acts were transmitted to the legislatures of different States, and their communications in answer
to them were referred to a committee of the general assembly of Virginia, of which Mr. Madison was a member, and
upon them his celebrated report was made.   With reference
to the alien act, after observing that it was incumbent in this,
as in every other exercise of power by the Federal government, to prove from the Constitution that it granted the particular power exercised; and also that much confusion and
fallacy had been thrown into the question to be considered by
blending the two cases of aliens, *members of a hostile nation,
and aliens, members of friendly nations*, he said: " With
respect to alien enemies, no doubt has been intimated as to
the Federal authority over them; the Constitution having
expressly delegated to Congress the power to declare war
against any nation, and, of course, to treat it and all its members as enemies.   With respect to aliens who are not enemies,
but members of nations in peace and amity with the United
States, the power assumed by the act of Congress is denied to
be constitutional; and it is accordingly against this act that
the protest of the general assembly is expressly and exclusively directed."   4 Elliot's Deb. 554.

" Were it admitted, as is contended, that the ' act concerning aliens ' has for its object, not a *penal*, but a *preventive*
justice, it would still remain to be proved that it comes within
the constitutional power of the Federal legislature; and, if
within its power, that the legislature has exercised it in a constitutional manner. . . .   It can never be admitted that
the removal of aliens, authorized by the act, is to be con-

sidered, not as punishment for an offence, but as a measure of precaution and prevention. If the banishment of an alien from a country into which he has been invited as the asylum most auspicious to his happiness — a country where he may have formed the most tender connections ; where he may have invested his entire property, and acquired property of the real and permanent as well as the movable and temporary kind ; where he enjoys, under the laws, a greater share of the blessings of personal security and personal liberty, than he can elsewhere hope for ; . . . if a banishment of this sort be not a punishment, and among the severest of punishments, it would be difficult to imagine a doom to which the name can be applied. And, if it be a punishment, it will remain to be inquired whether it can be constitutionally inflicted, on mere suspicion, by the single will of the executive magistrate, on persons convicted of no personal offence against the laws of the land, nor involved in any offence against the law of nations, charged on the foreign state of which they are members." 4 Elliot's Deb. 554, 555. . . . It does not follow, because aliens are not parties to the Constitution, as citizens are parties to it, that, whilst they actually conform to it, they have no right to its protection. Aliens are not more parties to the laws than they are parties to the Constitution ; yet it will not be disputed that, as they owe, on one hand, a temporary obedience, they are entitled, in return, to their protection and advantage.

If aliens had no rights under the Constitution, they might not only be banished, but even capitally punished without a jury or the other incidents to a fair trial. But, so far has a contrary principle been carried, in every part of the United States, that, except on charges of treason, an alien has, besides all the common privileges, the special one of being tried by a jury of which one-half may be also aliens.

" It is said, further, that, by the law and practice of nations, aliens may be removed, at discretion, for offences against the law of nations ; that Congress is authorized to define and punish such offences ; and that to be dangerous to the peace of society is, in aliens, one of those offences.

" The distinction between alien enemies and alien friends is a clear and conclusive answer to this argument. Alien enemies are under the law of nations, and liable to be punished for offences against it. Alien friends, except in the single case of public ministers, are under the municipal law, and must be tried and punished according to that law only." 4 Elliot's Deb. 556. Massachusetts, evidently considering the alien act as a war measure, adopted in anticipation of probable hostilities, said, in answer to the resolutions of Virginia, among other things, that "the removal of aliens is the usual preliminary of hostility, and is justified by the invariable usages of nations. Actual hostility had, unhappily, been long experienced, and a formal declaration of it the government had reason daily to expect." 4 Elliot's Deb. 535.

The duration of the act was limited to two years, and it has ever since been the subject of universal condemnation. In no other instance, until the law before us was passed, has any public man had the boldness to advocate the deportation of friendly aliens in time of peace. I repeat the statement, that in no other instance has the deportation of friendly aliens been advocated as a lawful measure by any department of our government. And it will surprise most people to learn that any such dangerous and despotic power lies in our government — a power which will authorize it to expel at pleasure, in time of peace, the whole body of friendly foreigners of any country domiciled herein by its permission, a power which can be brought into exercise whenever it may suit the pleasure of Congress, and be enforced without regard to the guarantees of the Constitution intended for the protection of the rights of all persons in their liberty and property. Is it possible that Congress can, at its pleasure, in disregard of the guarantees of the Constitution, expel at any time the Irish, German, French, and English who may have taken up their residence here on the invitation of the government, while we are at peace with the countries from which they came, simply on the ground that they have not been naturalized?

Notwithstanding the activity of the public authorities in enforcing the exclusion act of 1888, it was constantly evaded. Chinese laborers came into the country by water and by land; they came through the open ports and by rivers reaching the seas, and they came by way of the Canadas and Mexico. New means of ingress were discovered, and in spite of the vigilance of the police and customs officers great numbers clandestinely found their way into the country. Their resemblance to each other rendered it difficult, and often impossible, to prevent this evasion of the laws. It was under these circumstances that the act of May 5, 1892, c. 60, was passed. It had two objects in view. There were two classes of Chinese persons in the country, those who had evaded the laws excluding them and entered clandestinely, and those who had entered lawfully and resided therein under the treaty with China.

The act of 1892 extended, for the period of ten years from its passage, all laws then in force prohibiting and regulating the coming into the country of Chinese persons, or persons of Chinese descent; and it provided that any person, when convicted or adjudged under any of those laws of not legally being or remaining in the United States, should be removed therefrom to China, or to such other country as it might appear he was a subject of, unless such other country should demand a tax as a condition of his removal thereto, in which case he should be removed to China. The act also provided that a Chinese person arrested under its provisions, or the provisions of the acts extended, should be adjudged to be unlawfully within the United States, unless he should establish by affirmative proof his lawful right to remain within the United States; and that any Chinese person, or person of Chinese descent, "convicted and adjudged not lawfully entitled to be or remain in the United States, should be imprisoned at hard labor for a period not exceeding one year, and thereafter removed from the United States." With this class of Chinese, and with the provisions of law applicable to them, we have no concern in the present case. We have only to consider the provisions of the act applicable to the second class of Chinese persons, those who had a lawful right to remain in the United States. By the additional articles to the treaty of 1858, adopted in 1868, generally called the Burlingame treaty, the governments of the two countries recognized "the inherent and inalienable right of man to change his home and allegiance, and also the mutual advantage of free migration and emigration of their citizens and subjects, respectively, from the one country to the other for purposes of curiosity, of trade, or as permanent residence;" and accordingly the treaty in the additional articles provided that citizens of the United States visiting or residing in China, and Chinese subjects visiting or residing in the United States, should reciprocally enjoy the same privileges, immunities, and exemptions in respect to travel or residence as should be enjoyed by citizens or subjects of the most favored nation, in the country in which they should, respectively, be visiting or residing. 16 Stat. 739, 740. The supplemental treaty of November 17, 1880, providing for the limitation or suspension of the emigration of Chinese laborers, declared that "the limitation or suspension shall be reasonable and apply only to Chinese who may go to the United States as laborers, other classes not being included in the limitation," and that "Chinese subjects, whether residing in the United States as teachers, students, merchants, or from curiosity, together with their body and household servants, and Chinese laborers who were then in the United States, shall be allowed to go and come of their own free will and accord, and shall be accorded all rights, privileges, immunities, and exemptions, which are accorded to the citizens and subjects of the most favored nation."

There are many thousands of Chinese laborers who came to the country and resided in it under the additional articles of the treaty adopted in 1868, and were in the country at the time of the adoption of the supplemental treaty of November, 1880. To these laborers thus lawfully within the limits of the United States section six of the act of May 5, 1892, relates. That section, so far as applicable to the present cases, is as follows:

"SEC. 6. And it shall be the duty of all Chinese laborers within the limits of the United States at the time of the passage of this act and *who are entitled to remain in the United States,* to apply to the collector of internal revenue of their respective districts, within one year after the passage of this act, for a certificate of residence, and any Chinese laborer within the United States, who shall neglect, fail or refuse to comply with the provisions of this act, or who, after one year from the passage hereof, shall be found within the jurisdiction of the United States without such certificate of residence, shall be deemed and adjudged to be unlawfully within the United States, and may be arrested by any United States customs official, collector of internal revenue or his deputies, United States marshal or his deputies, and taken before a United States judge, whose duty it shall be to order that he be deported from the United States, as hereinbefore provided, unless he shall establish clearly to the satisfaction of the said judge that by reason of accident, sickness or other unavoidable cause, he has been unable to procure his certificate, and to the satisfaction of the court, and by at least one credible white witness, that he was a resident of the United States at the time of the passage of this act; and if upon the hearing it shall appear that he is so entitled to a certificate, it shall be granted upon his paying the cost. Should it appear that said Chinaman had procured a certificate which has been lost or destroyed, he shall be detained and judgment suspended a reasonable time to enable him to procure a duplicate from the officer granting it, and in such cases the cost of said arrest and trial shall be in the discretion of the court."

The purpose of this section was to secure the means of readily identifying the Chinese laborers present in the country and entitled to remain, from those who may have clandestinely entered the country in violation of its laws. Those entitled to remain, by having a certificate of their identification, would enable the officers of the government to readily discover and bring to punishment those not entitled to enter but who are excluded. To procure such a certificate was not a hardship to the laborers, but a means to secure full protection to them, and at the same time prevent an evasion of the law.

This object being constitutional, the only question for our consideration is the lawfulness of the procedure provided for its accomplishment, and this must be tested by the provisions of the Constitution and laws intended for the protection of all persons against encroachment upon their rights. Aliens from countries at peace with us, domiciled within our country by its consent, are entitled to all the guaranties for the protection of their persons and property which are secured to native-born citizens. The moment any human being from a country at peace with us comes within the jurisdiction of the United States, with their consent — and such consent will always be implied when not expressly withheld, and in the case of the Chinese laborers before us was in terms given by the treaty referred to — he becomes subject to all their laws, is amenable to their punishment and entitled to their protection. Arbitrary and despotic power can no more be exercised over them with reference to their persons and property, than over the persons and property of native-born citizens. They differ only from citizens in that they cannot vote or hold any public office. As men having our common humanity, they are protected by all the guaranties of the Constitution. To hold that they are subject to any different law or are less protected in any particular than other persons, is in my judgment to ignore the teachings of our history, the practice of our government, and the language of our Constitution. Let us test this doctrine by an illustration. If a foreigner who resides in the country by its consent commits a public offence, is he subject to be cut down, maltreated, imprisoned, or put to death by violence, without accusation made, trial had, and judgment of an established tribunal following the regular forms of judicial procedure? If any rule in the administration of justice is to be omitted or discarded in his case, what rule is it to be? If one rule may lawfully be laid aside in his case, another rule may also be laid aside, and all rules may be discarded. In such instances a rule of evidence may be set aside in one case, a rule of pleading in another; the testimony of eye-witnesses may be rejected and hearsay adopted, or no evidence at all may be received, but simply an inspection of the accused, as is often the case in tribunals of Asiatic countries where personal caprice and not settled rules prevail. That would be to establish a pure, simple, undisguised despotism and tyranny with respect to foreigners resident in the country by its consent, and such an exercise of power is not permissible under our Constitution. Arbitrary and tyrannical power has no place in our system. As said by this court, speaking by Mr. Justice Matthews, in *Yick Wo* v. *Hopkins*, 118 U. S. 356, 369: "When we consider the nature and theory of our institutions of government, the principles upon which they are supposed to rest, and view the history of their development, we are constrained to conclude they do not mean to leave room for the play and action of purely personal and arbitrary power. . . . The fundamental rights to life, liberty, and the pursuit of happiness as individual possessions are secured by those maxims of constitutional law which are the monuments, showing the victorious progress of the race in securing to man the blessings of civilization under the reign of just and equal laws." What once I had occasion to say of the protection afforded by our government I repeat: "It is certainly something in which a citizen of the United States may feel a generous pride that the government of his country extends protection to all persons within its jurisdiction; and that every blow aimed at any of them, however humble, come from what quarter it may, is 'caught upon the broad shield of our blessed Constitution and our equal laws.'" *Ho Ah Kow* v. *Nunan*, 5 Sawyer, 552, 563.

I utterly dissent from and reject the doctrine expressed in the opinion of the majority, that "Congress, under the power to exclude or expel aliens, might have directed any Chinese laborer found in the United States without a certificate of residence to be removed out of the country by executive officers, without judicial trial or examination, just as it might have authorized such officers absolutely to prevent his entrance into the country." An arrest in that way for that purpose would not be a reasonable seizure of the person within the meaning of the Fourth Article of the amendments to the Constitution. It would be brutal and oppressive. The existence of the power thus stated is only consistent with the admission that the government is one of unlimited and despotic power so far as aliens domiciled in the country are concerned. According to its theory, Congress might have ordered executive officers to take the Chinese laborers to the ocean and put them into a boat and set them adrift; or to take them to the borders of Mexico and turn them loose there; and in both cases without any means of support; indeed, it might have sanctioned towards these laborers the most shocking brutality conceivable. I utterly repudiate all such notions, and reply that brutality, inhumanity, and cruelty cannot be made elements in any procedure for the enforcement of the laws of the United States.

The majority of the court have, in their opinion, made numerous citations from the courts and the utterances of individuals upon the power of the government of an independent nation to exclude foreigners from entering its limits, but none, beyond a few loose observations, as to its power to expel and deport from the country those who are domiciled therein by its consent. The citation from the opinion in the recent case of *Nishimura Ekiu* v. *United States*, (the Japanese case,) 142 U. S. 651; the citation from the opinion in *Chae Chan Ping* v. *United States*, (the Chinese Exclusion case,) 130 U. S. 581, 604, 606; the citation in the case before the judiciary committee of the Privy Council — all have reference to the exclusion of foreigners from entering the country. They do not touch upon the question of deporting them from the country after they have been domiciled within it by the consent of its government, which is the real question in the case. The citation from Vattel is only as to the power of exclusion, that is, from coming to the country. The citation from Phillimore is to the same effect. As there stated, the government allowing the introduction of aliens may prescribe the conditions on which they shall be allowed to remain, the conditions being imposed whenever they enter the country. There is no dispute about the power of Congress to prevent the landing of aliens in the country; the question is as to the power of Congress to deport them without regard to the guaranties of the Constitution. The statement that in England the power to expel aliens has always been recognized and often exercised, and the only question that has ever been as to this power is whether it could be exercised by the King without the consent of Parliament, is, I think, not strictly accurate. The citations given by Mr. Choate in his brief show conclusively, it seems to me, that deportation from the realm has not been exercised in England since Magna Charta, except in punishment for crime, or as a measure in view of existing or anticipated hostilities. But even if that power were exercised by every government of Europe, it

would have no bearing in these cases. It may be admitted
that the power has been exercised by the various governments
of Europe. Spain expelled the Moors; England, in the reign
of Edward I, banished fifteen thousand Jews;[1] and Louis
XIV, in 1685, by revoking the Edict of Nantes, which gave
religious liberty to Protestants in France, drove out the
Huguenots. Nor does such severity of European governments belong only to the distant past. Within three years
Russia has banished many thousands of Jews, and apparently
intends the expulsion of the whole race — an act of barbarity
which has aroused the indignation of all Christendom. Such
was the feeling in this country that, friendly as our relations
with Russia had always been, President Harrison felt compelled to call the attention of Congress to it in his message in
1891 as a fit subject for national remonstrance. Indeed, all the
instances mentioned have been condemned for their barbarity
and cruelty, and no power to perpetrate such barbarity is to
be implied from the nature of our government, and certainly
is not found in any delegated powers under the Constitution.

The government of the United States is one of limited and
delegated powers. It takes nothing from the usages or the
former action of European governments, nor does it take any
power by any supposed inherent sovereignty. There is a
great deal of confusion in the use of the word "sovereignty"
by law writers. Sovereignty or supreme power is in this
country vested in the people, and only in the people. By
them certain sovereign powers have been delegated to the
government of the United States and other sovereign powers
reserved to the States or to themselves. This is not a matter
of inference and argument, but is the express declaration of
the Tenth Amendment to the Constitution, passed to avoid
any misinterpretation of the powers of the general government. That amendment declares that "The powers not
delegated to the United States by the Constitution, nor prohibited by it to the States, are reserved to the States, respectively, or to the people." When, therefore, power is exercised
by Congress, authority for it must be found in express terms
in the Constitution, or in the means necessary or proper for
the execution of the power expressed. If it cannot be thus
found, it does not exist.

It will be seen by its provisions that the sixth section recognizes the right of certain Chinese laborers to remain in the

---

[1] The Jews during his reign were cruelly despoiled, and in 1290 ordered,
under penalty of death, to quit England forever before a certain day. —
American Encyclopædia, vol. 6, p. 434.

United States, but to render null that right it declares that if within one year after the passage of the act any Chinese laborer shall have neglected, failed, or refused to comply with the provisions of the act to obtain a certificate of residence, or shall be found within the jurisdiction of the United States without a certificate of residence, he shall be deemed and adjudged to be unlawfully within the United States, and may be arrested by any United States customs official, collector of internal revenue or his deputies, a United States marshal or his deputies, and taken before a United States judge, whose duty it shall be to order that he be deported from the United States, unless he shall establish clearly to the satisfaction of the judge that by reason of accident, sickness, or other unavoidable cause he has been unable to secure his certificate, and to the satisfaction of the judge by at least one credible white witness that he was a resident of the United States at the time of the passage of the act. His deportation is thus imposed for neglect to obtain a certificate of residence, from which he can only escape by showing his inability to secure it from one of the causes named. That is the punishment for his neglect, and that being of an infamous character can only be imposed after indictment, trial, and conviction. If applied to a citizen, none of the justices of this court would hesitate a moment to pronounce it illegal. Had the punishment been a fine, or anything else than of an infamous character, it might have been imposed without indictment; but not so now, unless we hold that a foreigner from a country at peace with us, though domiciled by the consent of our government, is withdrawn from all the guaranties of due process of law prescribed by the Constitution, when charged with an offence to which the grave punishment designated is affixed.

The punishment is beyond all reason in its severity. It is out of all proportion to the alleged offence. It is cruel and unusual. As to its cruelty, nothing can exceed a forcible deportation from a country of one's residence, and the breaking up of all the relations of friendship, family, and business there contracted. The laborer may be seized at a distance from his home, his family and his business, and taken before the judge for his condemnation, without permission to visit his home, see his family, or complete any unfinished business. Mr. Madison well pictures its character in his powerful denunciation of the alien law of 1798 in his celebrated report upon the resolutions, from which we have cited, and concludes, as we have seen, that *if a banishment of the sort described be not a punishment, and among the severest of punishments, it will be difficult to imagine a doom to which the name can be applied.*

Again, when taken before a United States judge, he is required, in order to avoid the doom declared, to establish clearly to the satisfaction of the judge that by reason of accident, sickness, or other unavoidable cause, he was unable to secure his certificate, and that he was a resident of the United States at the time, *by at least one credible white witness.* Here the government undertakes to exact of the party arrested the testimony of a witness of a particular color, though conclusive and incontestible testimony from others may be adduced. The law might as well have said, that unless the laborer should also present a particular person as a witness who could not be produced, from sickness, absence, or other cause, such as the archbishop of the State, to establish the fact of residence, he should be held to be unlawfully within the United States.

There are numerous other objections to the provisions of the act under consideration. Every step in the procedure provided, as truly said by counsel, tramples upon some constitutional right. Grossly it violates the Fourth Amendment, which declares that: "The right of the people to be secure in their persons, . . . against unreasonable searches and seizures, shall not be violated, and no warrant shall issue but upon probable cause, supported by oath or affirmation, and particularly describing the . . . persons . . . to be seized."

The act provides for the seizure of the person without oath or affirmation or warrant, and without showing any probable cause by the officials mentioned. The arrest, as observed by counsel, involves a search of his person for the certificate which he is required to have always with him. Who will have the hardihood and effrontery to say this is not an "unreasonable search and seizure of the person"? Until now it has never been asserted by any court or judge of high authority that foreigners domiciled in this country by the consent of our government could be deprived of the securities of this amendment; that their persons could be subjected to unreasonable searches and seizures, and that they could be arrested without warrant upon probable cause supported by oath or affirmation.

I will not pursue the subject further. The decision of the court and the sanction it would give to legislation depriving resident aliens of the guaranties of the Constitution fills me with apprehensions. Those guaranties are of priceless value to every one resident in the country, whether citizen or alien. I cannot but regard the decision as a blow against constitutional liberty, when it declares that Congress has the right to disregard the guaranties of the Constitution intended for the protection of all men, domiciled in the country with the consent of the government, in their rights of person and property. How far will its legislation go? The unnaturalized resident feels it to-day, but if Congress can disregard the guaranties with respect to any one domiciled in this country with its consent, it may disregard the guaranties with respect to naturalized citizens. What assurance have we that it may not declare that naturalized citizens of a particular country cannot remain in the United States after a certain day, unless they have in their possession a certificate that they are of good moral character and attached to the principles of our Constitution, which certificate they must obtain from a collector of internal revenue upon the testimony of at least one competent witness of a class or nationality to be designated by the government?

What answer could the naturalized citizen in that case make to his arrest for deportation, which cannot be urged in behalf of the Chinese laborers of to-day?

I am of the opinion that the orders of the court below should be reversed, and the petitioners should be discharged.

MR. CHIEF JUSTICE FULLER dissenting.

I also dissent from the opinion and judgment of the court in these cases.

If the protection of the Constitution extends to Chinese laborers who are lawfully within and entitled to remain in the United States under previous treaties and laws, then the question whether this act of Congress so far as it relates to them is in conflict with that instrument, is a judicial question, and its determination belongs to the judicial department.

However reluctant courts may be to pass upon the constitutionality of legislative acts, it is of the very essence of judicial duty to do so when the discharge of that duty is properly invoked.

I entertain no doubt that the provisions of the Fifth and Fourteenth Amendments, which forbid that any person shall be deprived of life, liberty, or property without due process of law, are in the language of Mr. Justice Matthews, already quoted by my brother Brewer, "universal in their application to all persons within the territorial jurisdiction, without regard to any differences of race, of color, or of nationality,"

and although in *Yick Wo's case* only the validity of a municipal ordinance was involved, the rule laid down as much
applies to Congress under the Fifth Amendment as to the
States under the Fourteenth. The right to remain in the
United States, in the enjoyment of all the rights, privileges,
immunities, and exemptions accorded to the citizens and subjects of the most favored nation, is a valuable right, and certainly a right which cannot be taken away without taking
away the liberty of its possessor. This cannot be done by
mere legislation.

The argument is that friendly aliens, who have lawfully
acquired a domicil in this country, are entitled to avail themselves of the safeguards of the Constitution only while permitted to remain, and that the power to expel them and the
manner of its exercise are unaffected by that instrument. It
is difficult to see how this can be so in view of the operation
of the power upon the existing rights of individuals ; and to
say that the residence of the alien, when invited and secured
by treaties and laws, is held in subordination to the exertion
against him, as an alien, of the absolute and unqualified power
asserted, is to import a condition not recognized by the fundamental law. Conceding that the exercise of the power to
exclude is committed to the political department, and that the
denial of entrance is not necessarily the subject of judicial
cognizance, the exercise of the power to expel, the manner in
which the right to remain may be terminated, rest on different ground, since limitations exist or are imposed upon the
deprivation of that which has been lawfully acquired. And
while the general government is invested, in respect of foreign countries and their subjects or citizens, with the powers
necessary to the maintenance of its absolute independence and
security throughout its entire territory, it cannot, in virtue of
any delegated power, or power implied therefrom, or of a supposed inherent sovereignty, arbitrarily deal with persons lawfully within the peace of its dominion. But the act before us
is not an act to abrogate or repeal treaties or laws in respect
of Chinese laborers entitled to remain in the United States, or
to expel them from the country, and no such intent can be
imputed to Congress. As to them, registration for the purpose of identification is required, and the deportation denounced for failure to do so is by way of punishment to
coerce compliance with that requisition. No euphuism can
disguise the character of the act in this regard. It directs
the performance of a judicial function in a particular way,
and inflicts punishment without a judicial trial. It is, in

effect, a legislative sentence of banishment, and, as such, absolutely void. Moreover, it contains within it the germs of the assertion of an unlimited and arbitrary power, in general, incompatible with the immutable principles of justice, inconsistent with the nature of our government, and in conflict with the written Constitution by which that government was created and those principles secured.

Editor's Note. The treaties between the U.S. and China, cited by the Court are: Additional Articles supplementing the Treaty of Commerce of June 18, 1858, concluded July 28, 1868 (16 Stat. 739; 1 Malloy, p. 234); and the Treaty on Chinese Immigration into the U.S., November 17, 1880 (22 Stat. 826; 1 Malloy, p. 239.

Turner v. Williams
194 U.S. 279; 24 S. Ct. 719 (1904)
For opinion see infra VI (2)

United States v. Curtiss-Wright Export Corp.
299 U.S. 304; 57 S. Ct. 216 (1936)

MR. JUSTICE SUTHERLAND delivered the opinion of the Court.

On January 27, 1936, an indictment was returned in the court below, the first count of which charges that appellees, beginning with the 29th day of May, 1934, conspired to sell in the United States certain arms of war, namely fifteen machine guns, to Bolivia, a country then engaged in armed conflict in the Chaco, in violation of the Joint Resolution of Congress approved May 28, 1934, and the provisions of a proclamation issued on the same day by the President of the United States pursuant to authority conferred by § 1 of the resolution. In pursuance of the conspiracy, the commission of certain overt acts was alleged, details of which need not be stated. The Joint Resolution (c. 365, 48 Stat. 811) follows:
"Resolved by the Senate and House of Representatives of the United States of America in Congress assembled, That if the President finds that the prohibition of the sale of arms and munitions of war in the United States to those countries now engaged in armed conflict in the Chaco may contribute to the reëstablishment of peace be-

tween those countries, and if after consultation with the governments of other American Republics and with their coöperation, as well as that of such other governments as he may deem necessary, he makes proclamation to that effect, it shall be unlawful to sell, except under such limitations and exceptions as the President prescribes, any arms or munitions of war in any place in the United States to the countries now engaged in that armed conflict, or to any person, company, or association acting in the interest of either country, until otherwise ordered by the President or by Congress.

"Sec. 2. Whoever sells any arms or munitions of war in violation of section 1 shall, on conviction, be punished by a fine not exceeding $10,000 or by imprisonment not exceeding two years, or both."

The President's proclamation (48 Stat. 1744), after reciting the terms of the Joint Resolution, declares:

"Now, therefore, I, Franklin D. Roosevelt, President of the United States of America, acting under and by virtue of the authority conferred in me by the said joint resolution of Congress, do hereby declare and proclaim that I have found that the prohibition of the sale of arms and munitions of war in the United States to those countries now engaged in armed conflict in the Chaco may contribute to the reëstablishment of peace between those countries, and that I have consulted with the governments of other American Republics and have been assured of the coöperation of such governments as I have deemed necessary as contemplated by the said joint resolution; and I do hereby admonish all citizens of the United States and every person to abstain from every violation of the provisions of the joint resolution above set forth, hereby made applicable to Bolivia and Paraguay, and I do hereby warn them that all violations of such provisions will be rigorously prosecuted.

"And I do hereby enjoin upon all officers of the United States charged with the execution of the laws thereof, the utmost diligence in preventing violations of the said joint resolution and this my proclamation issued thereunder, and in bringing to trial and punishment any offenders against the same.

"And I do hereby delegate to the Secretary of State the power of prescribing exceptions and limitations to the application of the said joint resolution of May 28, 1934, as made effective by this my proclamation issued thereunder."

On November 14, 1935, this proclamation was revoked (49 Stat. 3480), in the following terms:

"Now, therefore, I, Franklin D. Roosevelt, President of the United States of America, do hereby declare and proclaim that I have found that the prohibition of the sale of arms and munitions of war in the United States to Bolivia or Paraguay will no longer be necessary as a contribution to the reëstablishment of peace between those countries, and the above-mentioned Proclamation of May 28, 1934, is hereby revoked as to the sale of arms and munitions of war to Bolivia or Paraguay from and after November 29, 1935, provided, however, that this action shall not have the effect of releasing or extinguishing any penalty, forfeiture or liability incurred under the aforesaid Proclamation of May 28, 1934, or the Joint Resolution of Congress approved by the President on the same date; and that the said Proclamation and Joint Resolution shall be treated as remaining in force for the purpose of sustaining any proper action or prosecution for the enforcement of such penalty, forfeiture or liability."

Appellees severally demurred to the first count of the indictment on the grounds (1) that it did not charge facts sufficient to show the commission by appellees of any offense against any law of the United States; (2) that this count of the indictment charges a conspiracy to violate the joint resolution and the Presidential proclamation, both of which had expired according to the terms of the joint resolution by reason of the revocation contained in the Presidential proclamation of November 14, 1935, and were not in force at the time when the indictment was found. The points urged in support of the demurrers were, first, that the joint resolution effects an invalid delegation of legislative power to the executive; second, that the joint resolution never became effective because of the failure of the President to find essential jurisdictional facts; and third, that the second proclamation operated to put an end to the alleged liability under the joint resolution.

The court below sustained the demurrers upon the first point, but overruled them on the second and third points. 14 F. Supp. 230. The government appealed to this court under the provisions of the Criminal Appeals Act of March 2, 1907, 34 Stat. 1246, as amended, U. S. C. Title 18, § 682. That act authorizes the United States to appeal from a district court direct to this court in criminal cases where, among other things, the decision sustaining a demurrer to the indictment or any count thereof is based upon the invalidity or construction of the statute upon which the indictment is founded.

First. It is contended that by the Joint Resolution, the going into effect and continued operation of the resolution was conditioned (a) upon the President's judgment as to its beneficial effect upon the reëstablishment of peace between the countries engaged in armed conflict in the Chaco; (b) upon the making of a proclamation, which was left to his unfettered discretion, thus constituting an attempted substitution of the President's will for that of Congress; (c) upon the making of a proclamation putting an end to the operation of the resolution, which again was left to the President's unfettered discretion; and (d) further, that the extent of its operation in particular cases was subject to limitation and exception by the President, controlled by no standard. In each of these particulars, appellees urge that Congress abdicated its essential functions and delegated them to the Executive.

Whether, if the Joint Resolution had related solely to internal affairs it would be open to the challenge that it constituted an unlawful delegation of legislative power to the Executive, we find it unnecessary to determine. The whole aim of the resolution is to affect a situation entirely external to the United States, and falling within the category of foreign affairs. The determination which we are called to make, therefore, is whether the Joint Resolution, as applied to that situation, is vulnerable to attack under the rule that forbids a delegation of the law-making power. In other words, assuming (but not deciding) that the challenged delegation, if it were confined to internal affairs, would be invalid, may it nevertheless be sustained on the ground that its exclusive aim is to afford a remedy for a hurtful condition within foreign territory?

It will contribute to the elucidation of the question if we first consider the differences between the powers of the federal government in respect of foreign or external affairs and those in respect of domestic or internal affairs. That there are differences between them, and that these differences are fundamental, may not be doubted.

The two classes of powers are different, both in respect of their origin and their nature. The broad statement that the federal government can exercise no powers except those specifically enumerated in the Constitution, and such implied powers as are necessary and proper to carry into effect the enumerated powers, is categorically true only in respect of our internal affairs. In that field, the primary purpose of the Constitution was to carve from the general mass of legislative powers *then possessed by the states* such portions as it was thought desirable to vest in the federal government, leaving those not included in the enumeration still in the states. *Carter* v. *Carter Coal Co.*, 298 U. S. 238, 294. That this doctrine applies only to powers which the states had, is self evident. And since the states severally never possessed international powers, such powers could not have been carved from the mass of state powers but obviously were transmitted to the United States from some other source. During the colonial period, those powers were possessed exclusively by and were entirely under the control of the Crown. By the Declaration of Independence, "the Representatives of the United States of America" declared the United [not the several] Colonies to be free and independent states, and as such to have "full Power to levy War, conclude Peace, contract Alliances, establish Commerce and to do all other Acts and Things which Independent States may of right do."

As a result of the separation from Great Britain by the colonies acting as a unit, the powers of external sovereignty passed from the Crown not to the colonies severally, but to the colonies in their collective and corporate capacity as the United States of America. Even before the Declaration, the colonies were a unit in foreign affairs, acting through a common agency—namely the Continental Congress, composed of delegates from the thirteen colonies. That agency exercised the powers of war and peace, raised an army, created a navy, and finally adopted the Declaration of Independence. Rulers come and go; governments end and forms of government change; but sovereignty survives. A political society cannot endure without a supreme will somewhere. Sovereignty is never held in suspense. When, therefore, the external sovereignty of Great Britain in respect of the colonies ceased, it immediately passed to the Union. *See Penhallow* v. *Doane,* 3 Dall. 54, 80–81. That fact was given practical application almost at once. The treaty of peace, made on September 23, 1783, was concluded between his Brittanic Majesty and the "United States of America." 8 Stat.—European Treaties—80.

The Union existed before the Constitution, which was ordained and established among other things to form "a more perfect Union." Prior to that event, it is clear that the Union, declared by the Articles of Confederation to be "perpetual," was the sole possessor of external sovereignty and in the Union it remained without change save in so far as the Constitution in express terms qualified its exercise. The Framers' Convention was called and exerted its powers upon the irrefutable postulate that though the states were several their people in respect of foreign affairs were one. Compare *The Chinese Exclusion Case,* 130 U. S. 581, 604, 606. In that convention; the entire absence of state power to deal with those affairs was thus forcefully stated by Rufus King:

"The states were not 'sovereigns' in the sense contended for by some. They did not possess the peculiar features of sovereignty,—they could not make war, nor peace, nor alliances, nor treaties. Considering them as political beings, they were dumb, for they could not speak to any foreign sovereign whatever. They were deaf, for they could not hear any propositions from such sovereign. They had not even the organs or faculties of defence or offence, for they could not of themselves raise troops, or equip vessels, for war." 5 Elliott's Debates 212.[1]

It results that the investment of the federal government with the powers of external sovereignty did not depend upon the affirmative grants of the Constitution. The powers to declare and wage war, to conclude peace, to make treaties, to maintain diplomatic relations with other sovereignties, if they had never been mentioned in the Constitution, would have vested in the federal

---

[1] In general confirmation of the foregoing views, see 1 Story on the Constitution, 4th ed., §§ 198–217, and especially §§ 210, 211, 213, 214, 215 (p. 153), 216.

government as necessary concomitants of nationality. Neither the Constitution nor the laws passed in pursuance of it have any force in foreign territory unless in respect of our own citizens (see *American Banana Co.* v. *United Fruit Co.,* 213 U. S. 347, 356); and operations of the nation in such territory must be governed by treaties, international understandings and compacts, and the principles of international law. As a member of the family of nations, the right and power of the United States in that field are equal to the right and power of the other members of the international family. Otherwise, the United States is not completely sovereign. The power to acquire territory by discovery and occupation (*Jones* v. *United States,* 137 U. S. 202, 212), the power to expel undesirable aliens (*Fong Yue Ting* v. *United States,* 149 U. S. 698, 705 *et seq.*), the power to make such international agreements as do not constitute treaties in the constitutional sense (*Altman & Co.* v. *United States,* 224 U. S. 583, 600–601; Crandall, Treaties, Their Making and Enforcement, 2d ed., p. 102 and note 1), none of which is expressly affirmed by the Constitution, nevertheless exist as inherently inseparable from the conception of nationality. This the court recognized, and in each of the cases cited found the warrant for its conclusions not in the provisions of the Constitution, but in the law of nations.

In *Burnet* v. *Brooks,* 288 U. S. 378, 396, we said, "As a nation with all the attributes of sovereignty, the United States is vested with all the powers of government necessary to maintain an effective control of international relations." Cf. *Carter* v. *Carter Coal Co., supra,* p. 295.

Not only, as we have shown, is the federal power over external affairs in origin and essential character different from that over internal affairs, but participation in the exercise of the power is significantly limited. In this vast external realm, with its important, complicated, delicate and manifold problems, the President alone has the power to speak or listen as a representative of the nation. He *makes* treaties with the advice and consent of the Senate; but he alone negotiates. Into the field of negotiation the Senate cannot intrude; and Congress itself is powerless to invade it. As Marshall said in his great argument of March 7, 1800, in the House of Representatives, "The President is the sole organ of the nation in its external relations, and its sole representative with foreign nations." Annals, 6th Cong., col. 613. The Senate Committee on Foreign Relations at a very early day in our history (February 15, 1816), reported to the Senate, among other things, as follows:

"The President is the constitutional representative of the United States with regard to foreign nations. He manages our concerns with foreign nations and must necessarily be most competent to determine when, how, and upon what subjects negotiation may be urged with the greatest prospect of success. For his conduct he is responsible to the Constitution. The committee consider this responsibility the surest pledge for the faithful discharge of his duty. They think the interference of the Senate in the direction of foreign negotiations calculated to diminish that responsibility and thereby to impair the best security for the national safety. The nature of transactions with foreign nations, moreover, requires caution and unity of design, and their success frequently depends on secrecy and dispatch." U. S. Senate, Reports, Committee on Foreign Relations, vol. 8, p. 24.

It is important to bear in mind that we are here dealing not alone with an authority vested in the President by an exertion of legislative power, but with such an authority plus the very delicate, plenary and exclusive power of the President as the sole organ of the federal government in the field of international relations—a power which does not require as a basis for its exercise an act of Congress, but which, of course, like every other governmental power, must be exercised in subordination to the applicable provisions of the Constitution. It is quite apparent that if, in the maintenance of our international relations, embarrassment—perhaps serious embarrassment—is to be avoided and success for our aims achieved, congressional legislation which is to be made effective through negotiation and inquiry within the international field must often accord to the President a degree of discretion and freedom from statutory restriction which would not be admissible were domestic affairs alone involved. Moreover, he, not Congress, has the better opportunity of knowing the conditions which prevail in foreign countries, and especially is this true in time of war. He has his confidential sources of information. He has his agents in the form of diplomatic, consular and other officials. Secrecy in respect of information gathered by them may be highly necessary, and the premature disclosure of it productive of harmful results. Indeed, so clearly is this true that the first President refused to accede to a request to lay before the House of Representatives the instructions, correspondence and documents relating to the negotiation of the Jay Treaty—a refusal the wisdom of which was recognized by the House itself and has never since been doubted. In his reply to the request, President Washington said:

"The nature of foreign negotiations requires caution, and their success must often depend on secrecy; and even when brought to a conclusion a full disclosure of all the measures, demands, or eventual concessions which may have been proposed or contemplated would be extremely impolitic; for this might have a pernicious influence on future negotiations, or produce immediate inconveniences, perhaps danger and mischief, in relation to other powers. The necessity of such caution and secrecy was one cogent reason for vesting the power of making treaties in the President, with the advice and consent of the Senate, the principle on which that body was formed confining it to a small number of members. To admit, then, a right in the House of Representatives to demand and to have as a matter of course all the papers respecting a negotiation with a foreign power would be to establish a dangerous precedent." 1 Messages and Papers of the Presidents, p. 194.

The marked difference between foreign affairs and domestic affairs in this respect is recognized by both houses of Congress in the very form of their requisitions for information from the executive departments. In the case of every department except the Department of State, the resolution *directs* the official to furnish the information. In the case of the State Department, dealing with foreign affairs, the President is *requested* to furnish the information "if not incompatible with the public interest." A statement that to furnish the information is not compatible with the public interest rarely, if ever, is questioned.

When the President is to be authorized by legislation to act in respect of a matter intended to affect a situation in foreign territory, the legislator properly bears in mind the important consideration that the form of the President's action—or, indeed, whether he shall act at all—

may well depend, among other things, upon the nature
of the confidential information which he has or may thereafter receive, or upon the effect which his action may have
upon our foreign relations. This consideration, in connection with what we have already said on the subject,
discloses the unwisdom of requiring Congress in this field
of governmental power to lay down narrowly definite
standards by which the President is to be governed. As
this court said in *Mackenzie* v. *Hare,* 239 U. S. 299, 311,
"As a government, the United States is invested with
all the attributes of sovereignty. As it has the character
of nationality it has the powers of nationality, especially
those which concern its relations and intercourse with
other countries. *We should hesitate long before limiting
or embarrassing such powers.*" (Italics supplied.)

In the light of the foregoing observations, it is evident
that this court should not be in haste to apply a general
rule which will have the effect of condemning legislation
like that under review as constituting an unlawful delegation of legislative power. The principles which justify
such legislation find overwhelming support in the un-
broken legislative practice which has prevailed almost
from the inception of the national government to the
present day.

Let us examine, in chronological order, the acts of legislation which warrant this conclusion:

The Act of June 4, 1794, authorized the President to
lay, regulate and revoke embargoes. He was "authorized" "whenever, in his opinion, the public safety shall so
require" to lay the embargo upon all ships and vessels in
the ports of the United States, including those of foreign
nations "under such regulations as the circumstances of
the case may require, and to continue or revoke the same,
whenever he shall think proper." C. 41, 1 Stat. 372. A
prior joint resolution of May 7, 1794 (1 Stat. 401), had
conferred *unqualified* power on the President to grant
clearances, notwithstanding an existing embargo, to ships
or vessels belonging to citizens of the United States bound
to any port beyond the Cape of Good Hope.

The Act of March 3, 1795 (c. 53, 1 Stat. 444), gave the
President authority to permit the exportation of arms,
cannon and military stores, the law prohibiting such exports to the contrary notwithstanding, the only prescribed guide for his action being that such exports

should be in "cases connected with the security of the commercial interest of the United States, and for public purposes only."

By the Act of June 13, 1798 (c. 53, § 5, 1 Stat. 566), it was provided that if the government of France "shall clearly disavow, and shall be found to refrain from the aggressions, depredations and hostilities" theretofore maintained against vessels and property of the citizens of the United States, "in violation of the faith of treaties, and the laws of nations, and shall thereby acknowledge the just claims of the United States to be considered as in all respects neutral, . . . it shall be lawful for the President of the United States, being well ascertained of the premises, to remit and discontinue the prohibitions and restraints hereby enacted and declared; and he shall be, and is hereby authorized to make proclamation thereof accordingly."

By § 4 of the Act of February 9, 1799 (c. 2, 1 Stat. 615), it was made "lawful" for the President, "if he shall deem it expedient and consistent with the interest of the United States," by order to remit certain restraints and prohibitions imposed by the act with respect to the French Republic, and also to revoke any such order "whenever, in his opinion, the interest of the United States shall require."

Similar authority, qualified in the same way, was conferred by § 6 of the Act of February 7, 1800, c. 10, 2 Stat. 9.

Section 5 of the Act of March 3, 1805 (c. 41, 2 Stat. 341), made it lawful for the President, whenever an armed vessel entering the harbors or waters within the jurisdiction of the United States and required to depart therefrom should fail to do so, not only to employ the land and naval forces to compel obedience, but "if he shall think it proper, it shall be lawful for him to forbid, by proclamation, all intercourse with such vessel, and with every armed vessel of the same nation, and the officers and crew thereof; to prohibit all supplies and aid from being furnished them" and to do various other things connected therewith. Violation of the President's proclamation was penalized.

On February 28, 1806, an act was passed (c. 9, 2 Stat. 351) to suspend commercial intercourse between the

United States and certain parts of the Island of St. Domingo. A penalty was prescribed for its violation. Notwithstanding the positive provisions of the act, it was by § 5 made "lawful" for the President to remit and discontinue the restraints and prohibitions imposed by the act at any time "if he shall deem it expedient and consistent with the interests of the United States" to do so. Likewise in respect of the Non-intercourse Act of March 1, 1809, (c. 24, 2 Stat. 528); the President was "authorized" (§ 11, p. 530), in case either of the countries affected should so revoke or modify her edicts "as that they shall cease to violate the neutral commerce of the United States," to proclaim the fact, after which the suspended trade might be renewed with the nation so doing.

Practically every volume of the United States Statutes contains one or more acts or joint resolutions of Congress authorizing action by the President in respect of subjects affecting foreign relations, which either leave the exercise of the power to his unrestricted judgment, or provide a standard far more general than that which has always been considered requisite with regard to domestic affairs. Many, though not all, of these acts are designated in the footnote.[2]

It well may be assumed that these legislative precedents were in mind when Congress passed the joint resolutions of April 22, 1898, 30 Stat. 739; March 14, 1912, 37 Stat. 630; and January 31, 1922, 42 Stat. 361, to prohibit the export of coal or other war material. The resolution of 1898 authorized the President "in his discretion, and with such limitations and exceptions as shall seem to him expedient" to prohibit such exportations. The striking identity of language found in the second resolution mentioned above and in the one now under review will be

---

[2] Thus, the President has been broadly "authorized" to suspend embargo acts passed by Congress, "if in his judgment the public interest should require it" (Act of December 19, 1806, c. 1, § 3, 2 Stat. 411), or if, "in the judgment of the President," there has been such suspension of hostilities abroad as may render commerce of the United States sufficiently safe. Act of April 22, 1808, c. 52, 2 Stat. 490. See, also, Act of March 3, 1817, c. 39, § 2, 3 Stat. 361. Compare, but as to reviving an embargo act, the Act of May 1, 1810, c. 39, § 4, 2 Stat. 605.

Likewise, Congress has passed numerous acts laying tonnage and other duties on foreign ships, in retaliation for duties enforced on

seen upon comparison. The resolution of March 14, 1912, provides:

"That whenever the President shall find that in any American country conditions of domestic violence exist which are promoted by the use of arms or munitions of war procured from the United States, and shall make proclamation thereof, it shall be unlawful to export except under such limitations and exceptions as the President shall prescribe any arms or munitions of war from any place in the United States to such country until otherwise ordered by the President or by Congress.

United States vessels, but providing that if the President should be satisfied that the countervailing duties were repealed or abolished, then he might by proclamation suspend the duties as to vessels of the nation so acting. Thus, the President has been "authorized" to proclaim the suspension. Act of January 7, 1824, c. 4, § 4, 4 Stat. 3; Act of May 24, 1828, c. 111, 4 Stat. 308; Act of July 24, 1897, c. 13, 30 Stat. 214. Or it has been provided that the suspension should take effect whenever the President "shall be satisfied" that the discriminating duties have been abolished. Act of March 3, 1815, c. 77, 3 Stat. 224; Act of May 31, 1830, c. 219, § 2, 4 Stat. 425. Or that the President "may direct" that the tonnage duty shall cease to be levied in such circumstances. Act of July 13, 1832, c. 207, § 3, 4 Stat. 578. And compare Act of June 26, 1884, c. 121, § 14, 23 Stat. 53, 57.

Other acts, for retaliation against discriminations as to United States commerce, have placed broad powers in the hands of the President, "authorizing" even the total exclusion of vessels of any foreign country so offending (Act of June 19, 1886, c. 421, § 17, 24 Stat. 79, 83), or the increase of duties on its goods or their total exclusion from the United States (Act of June 17, 1930, c. 497, § 388, 46 Stat. 590, 704), or the exclusion of its goods or the detention, in certain circumstances, of its vessels, or the exclusion of its vessels or nationals from privileges similar to those which it has denied to citizens of the United States (Act of September 8, 1916, c. 463, §§ 804–806, 39 Stat. 756, 799–800). As to discriminations by particular countries, it has been made lawful for the President, by proclamation, which he "may in his discretion, apply . . . to any part or all" of the subjects named, to exclude certain goods of the offending country, or its vessels. Act of March 3, 1887, c. 339, 24 Stat. 475. And compare Act of July 26, 1892, c. 248, 27 Stat. 267. Compare, also, authority given the Postmaster General to reduce or enlarge rates of foreign postage, among other things, for the purpose of counteracting any adverse measures affecting our postal intercourse with foreign countries. Act of March 3, 1851, c. 20, § 2, 9 Stat. 587, 589.

The President has been "authorized" to suspend an act providing for the exercise of judicial functions by ministers, consuls and other officers of the United States in the Ottoman dominions and Egypt whenever he "shall receive satisfactory information" that the govern-

"SEC. 2. That any shipment of material hereby declared unlawful after such a proclamation shall be punishable by fine not exceeding ten thousand dollars, or imprisonment not exceeding two years, or both."

The third resolution is in substantially the same terms, but extends to any country in which the United States exercises extraterritorial jurisdiction, and provides for the President's action not only when conditions of domestic violence exist which *are* promoted, but also when such conditions *may be* promoted, by the use of such arms or munitions of war.

We had occasion to review these embargo and kindred acts in connection with an exhaustive discussion of the general subject of delegation of legislative power in a recent case, *Panama Refining Co.* v. *Ryan,* 293 U. S. 388, 421–422, and in justifying such acts, pointed out that they confided to the President "an authority which was cognate to the conduct by him of the foreign relations of the government."

The result of holding that the joint resolution here under attack is void and unenforceable as constituting an unlawful delegation of legislative power would be to stamp this multitude of comparable acts and resolutions as likewise invalid. And while this court may not, and should not, hesitate to declare acts of Congress, however many times repeated, to be unconstitutional if beyond all rational doubt it finds them to be so, an impressive

---

ments concerned have organized tribunals likely to secure to United States citizens the same impartial justice enjoyed under the judicial functions exercised by the United States officials. Act of March 23, 1874, c. 62, 18 Stat. 23.

Congress has also passed acts for the enforcement of treaties or conventions, to be effective only upon proclamation of the President. Some of them may be noted which "authorize" the President to make proclamation when he shall be "satisfied" or shall receive "satisfactory evidence" that the other nation has complied: Act of August 5, 1854, c. 269, §§ 1, 2, 10 Stat. 587; Act of March 1, 1873, c. 213, §§ 1, 2, 17 Stat. 482; Act of August 15, 1876, c. 290, 19 Stat. 200; Act of December 17, 1903, c. 1, § 1, 33 Stat. 3. *Cf.* Act of June 11, 1864, c. 116, § 1, 13 Stat. 121; Act of February 21, 1893, c. 150, 27 Stat. 472.

Where appropriate, Congress has provided that violation of the President's proclamations authorized by the foregoing acts shall be penalized. See, *e. g.,* Act of June 19, 1886; Act of March 3, 1887; Act of September 8, 1916; Act of June 17, 1930—all *supra.*

array of legislation such as we have just set forth, enacted by nearly every Congress from the beginning of our national existence to the present day, must be given unusual weight in the process of reaching a correct determination of the problem. A legislative practice such as we have here, evidenced not by only occasional instances, but marked by the movement of a steady stream for a century and a half of time, goes a long way in the direction of proving the presence of unassailable ground for the constitutionality of the practice, to be found in the origin and history of the power involved, or in its nature, or in both combined.

In *The Laura*, 114 U. S. 411, 416, this court answered a challenge to the constitutionality of a statute authorizing the Secretary of the Treasury to remit or mitigate fines and penalties in certain cases, by repeating the language of a very early case (*Stuart* v. *Laird*, 1 Cranch 299, 309) that the long practice and acquiescence under the statute was a "practical exposition . . . too strong and obstinate to be shaken or controlled. Of course, the question is at rest, and ought not now to be disturbed." In *Burrow-Giles Lithographic Co.* v. *Sarony*, 111 U. S. 53, 57, the constitutionality of R. S. § 4952, conferring upon the author, inventor, designer or proprietor of a photograph certain rights, was involved. Mr. Justice Miller, speaking for the court, disposed of the point by saying: "The construction placed upon the Constitution by the first act of 1790, and the act of 1802, by the men who were contemporary with its formation, many of whom were members of the convention which framed it, is of itself entitled to very great weight, and when it is remembered that the rights thus established have not been disputed during a period of nearly a century, it is almost conclusive."

In *Field* v. *Clark*, 143 U. S. 649, 691, this court declared that " . . . the practical construction of the Constitution, as given by so many acts of Congress, and embracing almost the entire period of our national existence, should not be overruled, unless upon a conviction that such legislation was clearly incompatible with the supreme law of the land." The rule is one which has been stated and applied many times by this court. As examples, see

Ames v. *Kansas,* 111 U. S. 449, 469; *McCulloch* v. *Maryland,* 4 Wheat. 316, 401; *Downes* v. *Bidwell,* 182 U. S. 244, 286.

The uniform, long-continued and undisputed legislative practice just disclosed rests upon an admissible view of the Constitution which, even if the practice found far less support in principle than we think it does, we should not feel at liberty at this late day to disturb.

We deem it unnecessary to consider, *seriatim,* the several clauses' which are said to evidence the unconstitutionality of the Joint Resolution as involving an unlawful delegation of legislative power. It is enough to summarize by saying that, both upon principle and in accordance with precedent, we conclude there is sufficient warrant for the broad discretion vested in the President to determine whether the enforcement of the statute will have a beneficial effect upon the reëstablishment of peace in the affected countries; whether he shall make proclamation to bring the resolution into operation; whether and when the resolution shall cease to operate and to make proclamation accordingly; and to prescribe limitations and exceptions to which the enforcement of the resolution shall be subject.

Second. The second point raised by the demurrer was that the Joint Resolution never became effective because the President failed to find essential jurisdictional facts; and the third point was that the second proclamation of the President operated to put an end to the alleged liability of appellees under the Joint Resolution. In respect of both points, the court below overruled the demurrer, and thus far sustained the government.

The government contends that upon an appeal by the United States under the Criminal Appeals Act from a decision holding an indictment bad, the jurisdiction of the court does not extend to questions decided in favor of the United States, but that such questions may only be reviewed in the usual way after conviction. We find nothing in the words of the statute or in its purposes which justifies this conclusion. The demurrer in the present case challenges the validity of the statute upon three separate and distinct grounds. If the court below had sustained the demurrer without more, an appeal by the government necessarily would have brought here for our determination all of these grounds, since in that case the record would not have disclosed whether the court considered the statute invalid upon one particular ground or upon all of the grounds alleged. The judgment of the lower court is that the statute is invalid. Having held that this judgment cannot be sustained upon the particular ground which that court assigned, it is now open to this court to inquire whether or not the judgment can be sustained upon the rejected grounds which also challenge the validity of the statute and, therefore, constitute a proper subject of review by this court under the Criminal Appeals Act. *United States* v. *Hastings,* 296 U. S. 188, 192.

In *Langnes* v. *Green,* 282 U. S. 531, where the decree of a district court had been assailed upon two grounds and the circuit court of appeals had sustained the attack upon one of such grounds only, we held that a respondent in certiorari might nevertheless urge in this court in support of the decree the ground which the intermediate appellate court had rejected. That principle is applicable here.

We proceed, then, to a consideration of the second and third grounds of the demurrers which, as we have said, the court below rejected.

1. The Executive proclamation recites, "I have found that the prohibition of the sale of arms and munitions of war in the United States to those countries now engaged in armed conflict in the Chaco may contribute to the reëstablishment of peace between those countries, and that 1 have consulted with the governments of other American Republics *and have been assured of the coöperation of such governments as I have deemed necessary as contemplated by the said joint resolution.*" This finding satisfies every requirement of the Joint Resolution. There is no suggestion that the resolution is fatally uncertain or indefinite; and a finding which follows its language, as this finding does, cannot well be challenged as insufficient.

But appellees, referring to the words which we have italicized above, contend that the finding is insufficient because the President does not declare that the coöperation of such governments as he deemed necessary included any American republic and, therefore, the recital contains no affirmative showing of compliance in this respect with the Joint Resolution. The criticism seems to us wholly wanting in substance. The President recites that he has consulted with the governments of other American republics, and that he has been assured of the coöperation of such governments as he deemed necessary *as contemplated by the joint resolution*. These recitals, construed together, fairly include within their meaning American republics.

2. The second proclamation of the President, revoking the first proclamation, it is urged, had the effect of putting an end to the Joint Resolution, and in accordance with a well-settled rule, no penalty could be enforced or punishment inflicted thereafter for an offense committed during the life of the Joint Resolution in the absence of a provision in the resolution to that effect. There is no doubt as to the general rule or as to the absence of a saving clause in the Joint Resolution. But is the case presented one which makes the rule applicable?

It was not within the power of the President to repeal the Joint Resolution; and his second proclamation did not purport to do so. It "revoked" the first proclamation; and the question is, did the revocation of the proclamation have the effect of abrogating the resolution or of precluding its enforcement in so far as that involved the prosecution and punishment of offenses committed during the life of the first proclamation? We are of opinion that it did not.

Prior to the first proclamation, the Joint Resolution was an existing law, but dormant, awaiting the creation of a particular situation to render it active. No action or lack of action on the part of the President could destroy its potentiality. Congress alone could do that. The happening of the designated events—namely, the finding of certain conditions and the proclamation by the President—did not call the law into being. It created the occasion for it to function. The second proclamation did not put an end to the law or affect what had been done in violation of the law. The effect of the proclamation was simply to remove for the future, a condition of affairs which admitted of its exercise.

We should have had a different case if the Joint Resolution had expired by its own terms upon the issue of the second proclamation. Its operative force, it is true, was limited to the period of time covered by the first proclamation. And when the second proclamation was issued, the resolution ceased to be a rule for the future. It did not cease to be the law for the antecedent period of time. The distinction is clearly pointed out by the Superior Court of Judicature of New Hampshire in *Stevens* v. *Dimond*, 6 N. H. 330, 332, 333. There, a town by-law provided that if certain animals should be found going at large between the first day of April and the last day of October, etc., the owner would incur a prescribed penalty. The trial court directed the jury that the by-law, being in force for a year only, had expired so that the defendant could not be called upon to answer for a violation which occurred during the designated period. The state appellate court reversed, saying that when laws "expire by their own limitation, or are repealed, they cease to be the law in relation to the past, as well as the future, and can no longer be enforced in any case. No case is, however, to be found in which it was ever held before that they thus ceased to be law, unless they expired by express limitation in themselves, or were repealed. It has never been decided that they cease to be law, merely because the time they were intended to regulate had expired. . . . A very little consideration of the subject will convince any one that a limitation of the time to which a statute is to apply, is a very different thing from the limitation of the time a statute is to continue in force."

The first proclamation of the President was in force from the 28th day of May, 1934, to the 14th day of November, 1935. If the Joint Resolution had in no way depended upon Presidential action, but had provided explicitly that, at any time between May 28, 1934, and November 14, 1935, it should be unlawful to sell arms or munitions of war to the countries engaged in armed conflict in the Chaco, it certainly could not be successfully contended that the law would expire with the passing of the time fixed in respect of offenses committed during the period.

The judgment of the court below must be reversed and the cause remanded for further proceedings in accordance with the foregoing opinion.

Reversed.

MR. JUSTICE McREYNOLDS does not agree. He is of opinion that the court below reached the right conclusion and its judgment ought to be affirmed.

MR. JUSTICE STONE took no part in the consideration or decision of this case.

The Ambrose Light
25 Fed. 408 (S.D.N.Y., 1885)
For opinion see <u>infra</u> VIII (1)

Medvedieff v. Cities Service Oil Co.
35 F. Supp. 999 (S.D.N.Y., 1940)

HULBERT, District Judge.

By his motion to remand plaintiff challenges statements set forth in the removal petition and the issues thus raised must be determined by this court; the petitioning defendant has the burden of proof. Wilson v. Republic Iron Co., 257 U.S. 92, 42 S.Ct. 35, 66 L.Ed. 144; see also, McNutt v. General Motors Acceptance Corp., 298 U.S. 178, at page 189, 56 S.Ct. 780, 80 L.Ed. 1135.

Plaintiff brought a prior action in *this court* against the same defendant, a Pennsylvania corporation, and an associated Delaware corporation, and alleged in his complaint that the Pennsylvania corporation had acquired the assets and assumed the obligations and liabilities of the Delaware corporation, including a contract wherein the Delaware corporation had appointed plaintiff General Exclusive Representative in Italy and its colonies, Germany, France, Switzerland, Roumania, Czechoslovakia, Yugoslavia, Austria and Hungary, to negotiate the sale of its petroleum products in that territory, and demanded judgment for $1,000,000 for alleged breach of said contract. In that action plaintiff described himself as: "an alien, presently residing at the Hotel Waldorf Astoria, 301 Park Avenue, Borough of Manhattan, City of New York."

Thus plaintiff sought to protect his rights and pursue his remedy in this court, but he did not allege facts to establish a controversy "between a State, or the *Citizens* thereof, and foreign States, Citizens *or Subjects.*" (Italics for emphasis) U.S. Constitution, Article 3, Section 2, (see Judicial Code Sec. 24(1), Title 28 U.S. C.A. § 41(1), McNutt v. General Motors Acceptance Corp., supra; Alexander, et al. v. Westgate-Greenland Oil Co., et al., 9 Cir., 111 F.2d 769, and cases there cited. After service by the Pennsylvania corporation of various notices of motion addressed to the insufficiency of the complaint, plaintiff filed a notice of voluntary dismissal.

Thereupon the present action was brought in the New York Supreme Court, New York County. The allegations of the complaint are substantially the same except for omissions accountable to the elimination of the Delaware corporation.

Defendant's amended petition for removal alleged that plaintiff was a native of Russia who by naturalization had become, and still is, a citizen of the Kingdom of Italy. The state court was required to accept this allegation as true. Wilson v. Republic Iron Co., supra.

Plaintiff concedes his Russian nativity of Jewish parents; he migrated to Italy in 1914, traveling on a Russian passport, and has never since returned to Russia; on May 3, 1934 he became a naturalized *subject* of the King of Italy. If he had not already forfeited his Russian citizenship, his naturalization terminated it and made him an Italian citizen or subject.

However, plaintiff alleges that on or about September 7, 1938, a royal decree was proclaimed by the King of Italy entitled "Provisions relative to foreign Hebrews", which provided that from the date of publication thereof, September 12, 1938, "whoever was born of parents both of Hebrew race is considered a Hebrew even though he follows a religion other than the Hebrew" and "the grants of Italian citizenship however bestowed upon alien Hebrews after January 1st, 1919, are intended for all purposes hereby revoked" and all alien Hebrews "who began their residence therein after January 1, 1919, must leave the territory of the Kingdom, of Libia and of the Aegean possessions, within six months following the publication of the present decree."

In support of the motion the plaintiff submits an affidavit of Luigi Dionisi, an Italian by birth, admitted to the practice of law at the Bar of Rome, Italy, in 1919, where he practiced his profession for a period of 8 years. For the past 12 years he has resided in the City of New York and rendered opinions on Italian law and testified in various courts in this country with respect thereto. Upon the facts disclosed by the motion papers, Mr. Dionisi states that plaintiff "for all purposes has lost the Italian citizenship previously conferred upon him."

Plaintiff also submits an affidavit of Michael J. Petchkovsky, who was admitted to the Russian Bar in St. Petersburg in 1909, and actively engaged there in the practice of law until 1917; he is now a citizen of the United States and since 1924 his principal occupation has been giving advice upon pre-Soviet and Soviet Russian law for various law firms and testifying in the courts of this country with respect thereto. In his opinion the plaintiff is not a citizen of the Union of Soviet Socialist Republics.

Defendant's only effort to meet this evidence is set forth in a replying affidavit by Joseph M. Sullivan, one of its attorneys, in which he states: "The affidavit of the plaintiff is conspicuously silent as to the fact that he remained in Italy after the decree dated September 12, 1938, canceling his Italian citizenship and did not come to the United States until March 30, 1939, arriving here on the Normandie. Plaintiff at that time was traveling on an Italian passport or permit, which is an admission by plaintiff of Italian citizenship."

Defendant cites Blumen v. Haff, 9 Cir., 78 F.2d 833.

As the plaintiff had resided in Italy *prior to January 1, 1919*, revocation of his citizenship did not forbid him the right to remain in Italy. His arrival in the United States in possession of an Italian passport does not establish his Italian citizenship. It does not appear when the passport was issued or when it expires; it is presumptively regular on its face, but there is nothing in the record to show that a naturalized Italian whose citizenship has been revoked, but still remains a lawful resident of the country, may not be entitled to a passport or permit to visit another country. If the passport was obtained by fraud that would be a matter of concern to the United States but not a ground for relief available to the defendant.

In Blumen v. Haff, supra, the appellants (aliens) were extradited to the United States from England to answer a criminal charge alleged to have been committed on a previous visit, and it was held that in the absence of proof as to the law of the country of their alleged citizenship, and of proof of the acts of the appellants in obtaining and presenting Polish passports for the purpose of entering the United States, the tender thereof was an admission that appellants were subjects of Poland and sustained the conclusion of the Secretary of Labor and her warrant of deportation, but that does not sustain the contention of the defendant here.

The defendant surprisingly asserts that the recognition of the decree of the King of Italy opens the door to irrational discrimination against aliens prohibited by the Fourteenth Amendment of the Constitution of the United States and repugnant to our principles of public policy and good government.

However revolting the acts of a sovereign state may be to a free people accustomed to our way of life, our courts must recognize the comity established by International Law and leave the solution of political questions of an international character to those upon whom the Constitution devolves that duty.

The published records containing Official State Papers are replete with expressions of the policy of the United States toward foreign nations from the inception of the Government (copious excerpts will be found in Moore on International Law) but it should suffice to quote from the opinion of Mr. Chief Justice Fuller in the case of Underhill v. Hernandez, 168 U.S. 250, at page 252, 18 S.Ct. 83, at page 84, 42 L.Ed. 456: "Every sovereign state is bound to respect the independence of every other sovereign state, and the courts of one country will not sit in judgment on the acts of the government of another, done within its own territory. Redress of grievances by reason of such acts must be obtained through the means open to be availed of by sovereign powers as between themselves."

Mr. Justice Holmes, in American Banana Co., v. United Fruit Co., 213 U.S. 347, at page 358, 29 S.Ct. 511, at page 513, 53 L.Ed. 826, 16 Ann.Cas. 1047, said: "The very meaning of sovereignty is that the decree of the sovereign makes law."

In Inglis v. Sailor's Snug Harbour, 3 Pet. 99, at page 162, 7 L.Ed. 617, Mr. Justice Story wrote: "Each government had a right to decide for itself who should be admitted or deemed citizens."

It might be that some distinction exists in Italy between a "citizen" and a "subject." This observation is prompted by the fact that the framers of the Constitution employed the phrase "between a State, or the *citizens* thereof, and foreign States, *citizens* or *subjects.*"

It is to be remembered that the Colonials were "subjects" until their independence was established. The word was doubtless opprobrious to them. They took the word "citizen" from the Latin "civis" which means "freeman of a city." 11 C.J. p. 772, Note 1, 14 C.J.S., Citizens, § 1. They recognized all aliens as "citizens" or "subjects."

The law of Italy is a question of fact and no proof has been offered by the defendant to establish whether there is a distinction between "citizen" and "subject." Therefore, the decisions of our own courts must be applied.

"Subject and citizen are, in a degree, convertible terms as applied to natives, and though the term citizen seems to be appropriate to republican freemen, yet we are, equally with the inhabitants of all other countries, subjects, for we are equally bound by allegiance and subjection to the government and law of the land." 2 Kent Com. 258.

"The term 'citizen,' as understood in our law, is precisely analogous to the term subject in the common law, and the change of phrase has entirely resulted from the change of government. The sovereignty has been transferred from one man to the collective body of the people—and he who before was a 'subject of the king' is now 'a citizen of the State.'" State v. Manuel, 1838, 20 N.C. 144, 4 Dev. & B. 20, 24–26, cited with approval in United States v. Wong Kim Ark, 169 U.S. 649, at page 668, 18 S.Ct. 456, at page 464, 42 L.Ed. 890, where the court said: "Nor can it be doubted that it is the inherent right of every independent nation to determine for itself, and according to its own constitution and laws, what classes of persons shall be entitled to its citizenship."

Moreover, it is well settled that a presumption exists against jurisdiction of any cause by a United States District Court and that in a diversity of citizenship case the essential element of jurisdiction must be affirmatively established. Grace v. American Central Ins. Co., 109 U.S. 278, 3 S.Ct. 207, 27 L.Ed. 932.

[8] In the discharge of its burden, the defendant has failed to establish that the plaintiff is a citizen or subject of a foreign state, and the motion to remand must be granted.

Sevilla v. Elizalde
112 Fed. 2d. 29 (U.S.C.A.; Dist. of Co., 1946)

Before STEPHENS, EDGERTON, and RUTLEDGE, Associate Justices.

STEPHENS, Associate Justice.

In this case the appellant, suing as a citizen of the Commonwealth of the Philippine Islands, sought a determination in equity by the District Court of the United States for the District of Columbia that the appellee does not possess the qualifications requisite to holding the office of Resident Commissioner of the Commonwealth to the United States; and the appellant sought an injunction restraining the appellee from exercising the powers of the office mentioned. The trial court, upon a motion of the appellee, dismissed the complaint upon the grounds that it raised a political question over which the court had no jurisdiction, that it showed insufficient interest in the plaintiff to warrant equitable intervention, and that it stated no controversy between the parties.

From the order of dismissal this appeal was taken.

As a foundation for the relief sought the appellant's complaint alleged that, under the statute by virtue of which the Commonwealth came into existence— the Independence Act of March 24, 1934 (48 Stat. 456), 48 U.S.C.A. § 1231 et seq., under the Constitution of the Commonwealth and of the Ordinance appended thereto, and under "Chapter 390, Section 4, 48 Stat. 879," 48 U.S.C.A. § 1091, the Resident Commissioner to the United States must be a bona fide elector of the Commonwealth, must owe allegiance to the United States, be more than thirty years of age, able to read and write the English language, and must be appointed by the President of the Commonwealth with the consent of the Commission on Appointments, a body created by the Constitution.[1] The complaint charged that

[1] The complaint cites "Chapter 390, Section 4, 48 Stat. 879" as authority for its allegation that the Resident Commissioner must be a bona fide elector, owing allegiance to the United States, over the age of thirty, and able to read and write the English language. The statute referred to is an Act of June 5, 1934, amending Section 20 of Chapter 416 of the Act of August 29, 1916, 39 Stat. 545. The Act of August 29, 1916, prescribes the qualifications of the Resi-

the appellee does not possess the qualifications mentioned and in particular that the Commission on Appointments had not given its consent to his appointment. Therefore, it was asserted, the exercise by the appellee of the powers or the enjoyment of the privileges or immunities of the office in question would be a usurpation and an encroachment upon the right of the citizens of the Commonwealth to be represented by a Resident Commissioner possessing the requisite qualifications. And it was further charged that at the time of the commencement of the action the appellee was purporting to be the Resident Commissioner of the Commonwealth to the United States, and it was alleged that, unless it was judicially determined that he had not the lawful right to hold and exercise the office of Resident Commissioner, the appellee would, upon the convening of the United States Congress in January of 1939, attempt to take a seat in the House of Representatives, to participate in the debates of the House, and to

enjoy the privileges and immunities ordinarily attaching to the office of a member of the House.

The Independence Act provides, in paragraph 5 of Section 7:

"(5) The government of the Commonwealth of the Philippine Islands shall provide for the selection of a Resident Commissioner to the United States, and shall fix his term of office. He shall be the representative of the government of the Commonwealth of the Philippine Islands and shall be entitled to official recognition as such by all departments upon presentation to the President of credentials signed by the Chief Executive of said government. He shall have a seat in the House of Representatives of the United States, with the right of debate, but without the right of voting. His salary and expenses shall be fixed and paid by the government of the Philippine Islands. . . ." [48 Stat. 462]

And the Ordinance appended to the Constitution of the Commonwealth of the

dent Commissioners under the former Philippine government, prior to the Commonwealth. The Act of June 5, 1934, amends the Act of August 29, 1916, only in respect of the date of the commencement of the term of office of the Resident Commissioners, changing the same from the fourth of March to the third of January. The Act of August 29, 1916, as thus amended, has been superseded by the provisions of the Independence Act and of the Ordinance appended to the Constitution of the Commonwealth, and by the provisions of Commonwealth Act No. 10, First National Assembly, approved December 31, 1935 (Messages of the President, Vol. 1 (Revised Edition, Manila Bureau of Printing, 1938) 177). (Although the Independence Act was approved March 24, 1934, it did not take effect until May 1, 1934, the date of the concurrent resolution of the Philippine Legislature (Messages of the President, id. at 300, Appendix H) accepting the Independence Act in accordance with the provisions of Section 17 thereof; and the new Commonwealth government was not established until November 15, 1935, the date of the promulgation by the Secretary of War of the United States of the proclamation of the President of the United States pursuant to Section 4 of the Independence Act announcing the results of the election of officers provided for under the Constitution. For the text of the President's proclamation see

49 Stat. 3481; and for the text of the promulgation of the proclamation by the Secretary of War see Messages of the President, id. at 311, Appendix J. Until November 15, 1935, therefore, the provisions of the Act of August 29, 1916, as amended by the Act of June 5, 1934, were in effect, although the Independence Act had been approved prior to the date of the June 5, 1934 amendment.) Since the Act of August 29, 1916, as amended, has been superseded by the Independence Act and the Ordinance appended to the Constitution of the Commonwealth, and by the provisions of Commonwealth Act No. 10, above referred to, it obviously has nothing to do with the qualifications of any Resident Commissioner representing the present Commonwealth government.

Under the pertinent provisions of the Independence Act and of the Ordinance appended to the Constitution of the Commonwealth and under the provisions of Commonwealth Act No. 10, the Resident Commissioner to the United States must possess the following qualifications: he must be appointed by the President of the Commonwealth with the consent of the Commission on Appointments of the National Assembly; he must have been a citizen and resident of the Philippines for five years before his appointment, and must be thirty years of age or over and a qualified elector of the Philippines.

Philippines provides, in Section 2:

"Sec. 2. Pending the final and complete withdrawal of the sovereignty of the United States over the Philippines, there shall be a Resident Commissioner of the Philippines to the United States who shall be appointed by the President of the Commonwealth of the Philippines with the consent of the Commission on Appointments. The powers and duties of the Resident Commissioner shall be as provided in section seven, paragraph five of Public Act Numbered One hundred and twenty-seven of the Congress of the United States, approved March twenty-four, nineteen hundred and thirty-four, together with such other duties as the National Assembly may determine. The qualifications, compensation, and expenses of the Resident Commissioner shall be fixed by law." [Ordinance Appended to the Constitution of the Philippines (Manila Bureau of Printing, 1935), p. 32]

The theory of the appellant's complaint is that since under Newman v. United States ex rel. Frizzell, 1915, 238 U. S. 537, 35 S.Ct. 881, 59 L.Ed. 1446, an action at law, in quo warranto, against the putative incumbent of a public office, may not be maintained in the District of Columbia, and since—as the appellant contends—the Congress has no power, the appellee not being a member of Congress, to judge of his qualifications, it necessarily follows that there is a remedy, in equity, to determine whether or not the appellee possesses the qualifications legally requisite to the office of Resident Commissioner, and to oust him from office if the determination is in the negative.

But we think that the appellant's theory overlooks the proposition that "in order to entitle the party to the remedy, a case must be presented appropriate for the exercise of judicial power; the rights in danger . . . must be rights of persons or property, not merely political rights, which do not belong to the jurisdiction of a court, either in law or equity." State of Georgia v. Stanton, 1867, 6 Wall. 50, 76, 18 L.Ed. 721. We think that the trial court properly dismissed the complaint upon the ground that it presented a political, not a judicial, question and one therefore of which the court had no jurisdiction. The other grounds of dismissal it is not necessary to discuss.

[4] Courts have no jurisdiction to decide political questions. These are such as have been entrusted by the sovereign for decision to the so-called political departments of government, as distinguished from questions which the sovereign has set to be decided in the courts. Even under a government where there is no express constitutional delegation of powers, this limitation upon judicial authority has long been recognized. It was suggested in The Duke of York's Claim to the Crown, 5 Rotuli Par. 375 (House of Lords, 1460), Wambaugh, Cases on Constitutional Law (1915) 1, 3, where, in respect of the claim of the Duke of York, the "Kyngs Justices" decided that they "durst not enter into eny communication thereof, for it perteyned to the Lordes of the Kyngs blode . . . ."[2] And in Nabob of the Carnatic v. East India Company, 1 Ves.Jr. 371

---

[2] "The matter was thus: On October 16, 1460, the counsel of the Duke of York brought into Parliament a written claim to the crown, desiring speedy answer thereto. It being so resolved, the petition was read, and the chancellor asked what was to be done. The lords answered, 'that the matier was so high and of such wyght, that it was not to eny of the Kynges Subgetts to enter into communication thereof, withoute his high commaundement, agreement and assent had therto.' So all went to the king in person and declared their predicament. He commanded them 'that they shuld serche for to fynde in asmuch as in them was, all such thyngs as myght be objecte and leyde ayenst the cleyme and title of the seid Duc.' The lords, not to be outdone in courtesy, 'besaught the Kyng, that he wuld remember hym, yf he myght fynde any reasonable mater that myght be objected ayenst the seid cleyme and title, in so moche as his seid Highnes had seen and understouden many dyvers writyngs and Cronicles.' Now followed the commission to the judges and their reply:

" 'Weruppon . . . the forseid Lordes sent for the Kyngs Justices . . . and in the Kyngs name gave theym straitely in commaundement, sadly to take avisament therin, and to serche and fynde all such objections as myght be leyde ayenst the same, in fortefying of the Kynges right.

" 'Whereunto the same Justices . . . for their answere upon the seid writyng to theym delyvered seiden, that they were

(1791), 2 Ves.Jr. 56 (1793), in which stems a series of authorities in England (see West Rand Central Gold Mining Company, Ltd. v. The King, [1905] 2 K.B. 391), the distinction between judicial and political power was recognized. See also Penn. v. Lord Baltimore, 1 Ves.Sen. 444 (1750). In the United States as early as Ware v. Hylton, 1796, 3 Dall. 199, 260, 1 L.Ed. 568, it was held "incompetent to the examination and decifion of a Court of Juftice" to determine whether a treaty between England and the United States had been broken by one of the parties to it.

And from that day until the present time, the decisions in the Federal courts recognize and apply this principle of judicial self-limitation in so-called political cases. Thus courts have refused to: Determine whether or not the constitutional guaranty to every state of a republican form of government has been satisfied;[3] or determine the conditions of peace or war;[4] or determine the beginning and end of war;[5] or determine whether or not aliens shall be excluded or expelled;[6] or determine governmental title to or jurisdiction over a territory;[7] or determine the status of

---

the Kyngs Justices, and have to determyne such maters as com before theym in the lawe, betwene partie and partie, and in such maters as been betwene partie and partie they may not be of Counseill; and sith this mater was betwene the Kyng and the seid Duc of York as two parties, and also it hath not be accustumed to calle the Justices to Counseill in such maters, and in especiall the mater was so high, and touched the Kyngs high estate and regalie, which is above the lawe and passed ther lernyng, wherfore they durst not enter into eny communication thereof, for it perteyned to the Lordes of the Kyngs blode, and th' apparage of this his lond, to have communication and medle in such maters; and therfore they humble besought all the Lordes, to have theym utterly excused of eny avyce or Counseill, by theym to be yeven in that matier. . . .' " Quoted from Weston, Political Questions (1925) 38 Harv.L.Rev. 296, 302–303; and see the further discussion of this case, pages 303 et seq.

[3] Pacific States Telephone Co. v. Oregon, 1912, 223 U.S. 118, 32 S.Ct. 224, 56 L.Ed. 377; Luther v. Borden, 1849, 7 How. 1, 42, 12 L.Ed. 581: "Under this article of the Constitution it rests with Congress to decide what government is the established one in a State. For as the United States guarantee to each State a republican government, Congress must necessarily decide what government is established in the State before it can determine whether it is republican or not. And when the senators and representatives of a State are admitted into the councils of the Union, the authority of the government under which they are appointed, as well as its republican character, is recognized by the proper constitutional authority. And its decision is binding on every other department of the government, and could not

be questioned in a judicial tribunal. It is true that the contest in this case did not last long enough to bring the matter to this issue; and as no senators or representatives were elected under the authority of the government of which Mr. Dorr was the head, Congress was not called upon to decide the controversy. Yet the right to decide is placed there, and not in the courts."

[4] United States v. One Hundred and Twenty-Nine Packages, D.C.E.D.Mo., 1862, 27 Fed.Cas. 284, 288, No. 15,941: "The condition of peace or war, public or civil, in a legal sense, must be determined by the political department, not the judicial. The latter is bound by the decision thus made."

[5] The Protector, 1871, 12 Wall. 700. 20 L.Ed. 463.

[6] The Chinese Exclusion Case, 1889, 130 U.S. 581, 9 S.Ct. 623, 32 L.Ed. 1068; The Japanese Immigrant Case, 1903, 189 U.S. 86, 23 S.Ct. 611, 47 L.Ed. 721; Nishimura Ekiu v. United States, 1892, 142 U.S. 651, 660, 12 S.Ct. 336, 35 L. Ed. 1146: The power to exclude or expel aliens "belongs to the political department of the government . . . . * * * It is not within the province of the judiciary to order that foreigners who have never been naturalized, nor acquired any domicil or residence within the United States, nor even been admitted into the country pursuant to law, shall be permitted to enter it, in opposition to the constitutional and lawful measures of the legislative and executive branches of the national government. . . ."

[7] Watts v. United States, 1870, 1 Wash. T. 288; Jones v. United States, 1890, 137 U.S. 202, 11 S.Ct. 80, 34 L.Ed. 691; Foster & Elam v. Neilson, 1829, 2 Pet. 253, 309, 7 L.Ed. 415: "After these acts of sovereign power over the territory in dispute, asserting the American construction of the treaty by which the govern-

Indian tribes;[8] or recognize the existence of states or governments;[9] or enforce the provisions of a treaty when the sovereign chooses to disregard them;[10] or determine whether a treaty has been terminated;[11] or inquire into the constitutional powers of representatives of foreign nations.[12] While the boundaries of the field of de-

ment claims it, to maintain the opposite construction in its own courts would certainly be an anomaly in the history and practice of nations. If those departments which are entrusted with the foreign intercourse of the nation, which assert and maintain its interests against foreign powers, have unequivocally asserted its rights of dominion over a country of which it is in possession, and which it claims under a treaty; if the legislature has acted on the construction thus asserted, it is not in its own courts that this construction is to be denied. A question like this respecting the boundaries of nations, is, as has been truly said, more a political than a legal question; and in its discussion, the courts of every country must respect the pronounced will of the legislature. . . ."

[8] Cherokee Nation v. State of Georgia, 1831, 5 Pet. 1, 8 L.Ed. 25; Kansas Indians, 1866, 5 Wall. 737, 755, 756, 18 L. Ed. 667: "If the tribal organization of the Shawnees is preserved intact, and recognized by the political department of the government as existing, then they are a 'people distinct from others,' capable of making treaties, separated from the jurisdiction of Kansas, and to be governed exclusively by the government of the Union. . . . the action of the political department of the government settles, beyond controversy, that the Shawnees are as yet a distinct people, with a perfect tribal organization. . . ."

[9] Rose v. Himely, 1808, 4 Cranch 241, 2 L.Ed. 608; The Nereide, 1815, 9 Cranch 388, 3 L.Ed. 769; Oetjen v. Central Leather Co., 1918, 246 U.S. 297, 302, 38 S.Ct. 309, 62 L.Ed. 726: "The conduct of the foreign relations of our Government is committed by the Constitution to the Executive and Legislative— 'the political'—Departments of the Government, and the propriety of what may be done in the exercise of this political power is not subject to judicial inquiry or decision. [Citing authorities] It has been specifically decided that 'Who is the sovereign, *de jure* or *de facto*, of a territory is not a judicial, but is a political question, the determination of which by the legislative and executive departments of any government conclusively binds the judges, as well as all other officers, citizens and subjects of that government. This principle has always been upheld by this court, and has been affirmed under a great variety of circumstances.' . . ."

[10] Botiller v. Dominguez, 1889, 130 U. S. 238, 9 S.Ct. 525, 32 L.Ed. 926.

[11] Ware v. Hylton, supra; Taylor v. Morton, C.C.Mass., 1855, 23 Fed.Cas. 784, 787, No. 13,799, affirmed, 1862, 2 Black 481, 17 L.Ed. 277: "Is it a judicial question whether a treaty with a foreign sovereign has been violated by him [the foreign sovereign] . . . ? I [Curtis, Associate Justice, United States Supreme Court, sitting in circuit] apprehend not. These powers have not been confided by the people to the judiciary, which has no suitable means to exercise them; but to the executive and the legislative departments of our government. They belong to diplomacy and legislation, and not to the administration of existing laws. . . ."

[12] Doe v. Braden, 1853, 16 How. 635, 657, 14 L.Ed. 1090: "And it would be impossible for the executive department of the government to conduct our foreign relations with any advantage to the country, and fulfill the duties which the Constitution has imposed upon it, if every court in the country was authorized to inquire and decide whether the person who ratified the treaty on behalf of a foreign nation had the power, by its constitution and laws, to make the engagements into which he entered."

See also on the subject of political questions in the Federal courts: Field, The Doctrine of Political Questions in the Federal Courts (1924) 8 Minn.L.Rev. 485; Weston, Political Questions (1925) 38 Harv.L.Rev. 296. Weston lists the following considerations influencing judicial negation of power: "(a) The fundamental powers and duties in question have distinctly not been delegated to the courts by the Constitution, but rather to the other departments. (b) These fundamental powers and duties are of the sort ordinarily performed by what we understand as political rather than judicial action. The process of legislation is assertion, not decision; foreign affairs are conducted by negotiations, not by pleading and proof; political integrity is maintained by diplomacy or arms, not by injunctions. (c) From another aspect, these powers and duties relate, not to the ordinary matters of law which form the main bulk of controversy between pricision which lies outside the authority of the courts are not wholly definite—this because the question to which department a power has been delegated is often a difficult problem of interpretation. "According as the commission is precise" or "is inexact"[13]—it is not necessary in the instant case to attempt to mark out with precision all points on the boundary, because the instant case clearly falls well within the field of political, rather than judicial action. The Resident Commissioner partakes in part of the characteristics of a diplomatic representative of a foreign power and in part of those of a delegate from a territory. And the determination of the qualifications of such officers lies obviously outside judicial authority and within the field of political action.

As will have been noted from the provisions of the Independence Act which have been set out above, the Resident Commissioner "shall be the representative of the government of the Commonwealth of the Philippine Islands and shall be entitled to official recognition as such by all departments upon presentation to the President of credentials signed by the Chief Executive of said government. . . . His salary and expenses shall be fixed and paid by the government of the Philippine Islands." Moreover the political organization which the Resident Commissioner represents itself presently partakes—during the interim period between the coming into existence of the Commonwealth and the date when it may in the manner provided in the Independence Act acquire complete independence[14]—in some part of

---

vate persons, not to the incidence of the police power upon the workaday world, but to the maintenance, furtherance, and functioning of government, to the exigencies of the state's existence, external and internal. (d) In every instance where a question of fact is to be decided, it is one which the persons executing the power or performing the duty must decide as the very basis of their own not merely ministerial conduct. (e) In those matters which relate to foreign affairs and to military action abroad and at home, the circumstances will often be such as to leave no chance to await the result of test litigation, while the consequences of the action may be so far-reaching that any uncertainty as to its validity becomes intolerable. (f) Other practical considerations come to the fore, which we cannot assume were not adverted to by the framers of the Constitution and which are indicated upon the face of that instrument itself. Unity; certainty; respect and orderliness; efficiency; all are desiderata." 38 Harv.L.Rev. at 327–8.

13 "According as the commission is precise, there is less room for a confusion of the various senses of 'judicial' or 'political' in connection with any given problem of the division of power. According as the commission is inexact, there is more opportunity for such confusion, but the confounding is none the less unjustified in legal thought. Judicial questions, in what may be thought the more useful sense, are those which the sovereign has set to be decided in the courts. Political questions, similarly, are those which the sovereign has entrusted to the

so-called political departments of government or has reserved to be settled by its own extra-governmental action. As to the courts, the question is always the same, whether the method has been that of clear express delegation at the outset of a court's creation, or that of obscure delegation through a centuries-long process, in part of authority given in advance, and in part of approval, express or tacit, given in arrears of jurisdiction already assumed. . . . The problem is one of interpretation in a very well understood sense, and it is only the factors of interpretation which will be for the moment in doubt. . . ." Weston, Political Questions, id. at 301.

14 Sec. 10. (a) of the Independence Act provides that "On the 4th day of July immediately following the expiration of a period of ten years from the date of the inauguration of the new government under the constitution provided for in this Act, the President of the United States shall by proclamation withdraw and surrender all right of possession, supervision, jurisdiction, control, or sovereignty then existing and exercised by the United States in and over the territory and people of the Philippine Islands . . . and, on behalf of the United States, shall recognize the independence of the Philippine Islands as a separate and self-governing nation and acknowledge the authority and control over the same of the government instituted by the people thereof, under the constitution then in force." As explained in footnote 1, the new Commonwealth government was established November 15, 1935. Under present laws,

the characteristics, under international law, of a state.[15] It has a people permanently occupying a fixed territory, bound together by common laws into a body politic, with an organized government exercising powers within the territory and capable, subject to limitations mentioned below, of entering into relations with other states. See 1 Hyde, International Law (1922) § 7; 1 Moore, International Law Digest (1906) § 3. The Commonwealth does not fully satisfy the definition of a state at international law because it does not possess independent treaty making power by virtue of which it may enter into direct relations with other powers.[16] But to the extent that the Commonwealth is like a foreign state, its Resident Commissioner is like a diplomatic representative.

But the Resident Commissioner partakes also of the characteristics of a delegate from a dependent territory. By virtue of paragraph 5 of Section 7 of the Independence Act, above set forth, "He shall have a seat in the House of Representatives of the United States, with the right of debate, but without the right of voting." And although the government which he represents has, as just demonstrated, in some part the characteristics of a foreign state, it also has some of the characteristics of a dependent territory.[17]

The law is settled that the courts have no jurisdiction to pass upon the qualifications of a diplomatic representative of a foreign power. Section 3 of Article II of the United States Constitution express-

---

therefore, the Philippine Islands will achieve complete independence July 4, 1946.

[15] According to the Independence Act (and the Constitution and Ordinance adopted pursuant thereto): All property rights which have been acquired by the United States government in the Philippines are granted to the government of the Commonwealth (except certain properties reserved for military and other purposes) (Sec. 5.). The Commonwealth is obliged to assume and pay the obligations of the old government of the Philippines (Sec. 2. (a) (7)). The United States is relieved from any liability to meet obligations of the Commonwealth which come into existence during the interim period (Sec. 9). The Philippines are to be considered a "separate country" for the purposes of immigration, and for the same purposes the citizens of the Philippines are to be considered aliens (Sec. 8. (a) (1)). A foreign service officer of the United States stationed in the Philippines "shall be considered as stationed in a foreign country" (Sec. 8. (a) (3)). The Commonwealth, subject to the final approval of the President of the United States has power to enact laws affecting currency, coinage, imports, exports and immigration (Sec. 2. (a) (9)). The Commonwealth, subject to the approval of the President of the United States, may contract loans in foreign countries (Sec. 2. (a) (6)). And, subject to the supervision and control of the United States the Commonwealth is to have foreign affairs (Sec. 2. (a) (10)).

[16] For a discussion of the "semi-sovereign" political status of the Common-

wealth government during the interim period, see Fisher, The Status of the Philippine Islands under the Independence Act (1933), 19 Am.Bar Ass'n J. 465.

[17] According to the Independence Act (and the Constitution and Ordinance adopted pursuant thereto): All citizens and every officer of the Commonwealth government shall owe allegiance to the United States (Sec. 2. (a) (1), (2)). All acts passed by the Legislature of the Commonwealth shall be reported to the United States Congress (Sec. 2. (a) (11)). The United States has the right to expropriate Philippine property for public uses, to maintain military reservations and armed forces in the Philippines, and to call into service all military forces organized by the Commonwealth government (Sec. 2. (a) (12)). Decisions of the courts of the Commonwealth are subject to review by the Supreme Court of the United States (Sec. 2. (a) (13)), and appeals from the decisions of the insular auditor may be taken to the President of the United States (Sec. 7. (4)). Citizens and corporations of the United States shall enjoy in the Philippines all the rights of citizens and corporations thereof (Sec. 2. (a) (16)). The Constitution of the Commonwealth when drafted was subject to the final approval of the President of the United States (Sec. 3.) and until final withdrawal of the United States sovereignty every amendment to the Constitution is to be submitted to the President of the United States for approval (Sec. 7. (1)). The President of the United States has authority to suspend the taking effect of any law, contract or executive order of the Common-

ly delegates to the executive branch of the government the power to receive ambassadors: the President "shall receive ambassadors and other public ministers . . . ." From this it follows that in him is the authority to determine the authenticity of the credentials of diplomatic representatives, and whether this government will recognize them as the qualified representatives of a foreign power.

In Re Baiz, 1890, 135 U.S. 403, 10 S.Ct. 854, 34 L.Ed. 222, an action was commenced in the United States District Court for the Southern District of New York to recover damages for the publication by one Baiz of an alleged libel. Upon the ground that this had been published in the course of his representation of the Republic of Guatemala and that in this diplomatic status he was a privileged person, Baiz applied to the Supreme Court for a writ of prohibition to restrain the District Court from exercising jurisdiction. Correspondence between Baiz and the Secretary of State of the United States showed that the State Department had refused to recognize him as an accredited representative of Guatemala. The Supreme Court held, therefore, that the District Court had jurisdiction and refused to issue the writ. It accepted as final and binding upon the courts the refusal of the State Department to recognize Baiz. The Court said:·

"We ought to add that while we have not cared to dispose of this case upon the mere absence of technical evidence, we do not assume to sit in judgment upon the decision of the executive in reference to the public character of a person claiming to be a foreign minister, and therefore have the right to accept the certificate of the State Department that a party is or is not a privileged person, and cannot properly be asked to proceed upon argumentative or collateral proof." [135 U.S. at pages 431, 432, 10 S.Ct. at page 862, 34 L.Ed. 222]

Again in Agency of Canadian Car & F. Co. v. American Can Co., 2 Cir., 1919, 258 F. 363, 6 A.L.R. 1182, it appeared that in 1917 the Russian government had, through officials recognized by the United States government, assigned to the plaintiff Agency all of its interest in certain claims due from the defendant American Can Company. These claims had matured and were the subject of the suit. The defendant raised, among other questions, one as to whether the officials who executed the assignment for the Russian government authentically represented it. The court held that it would not assume to examine into this question for the reason that "who represents and acts for a foreign sovereign or nation in its relation with the United States is determined, not by the judicial department, but exclusively by the political branch of the government," and held that the authority of the officials in question was conclusively established for the court by the fact of their recognition by the United States government. This point was decided upon the authority of In re Baiz, supra. To the same effect see The Rogday, D.C.N.D.Cal., 1920, 279 F. 130.

We think it clear also that the courts have no authority to pass upon the qualifications of a delegate from a territory. Article I, section 5 of the Constitution provides that "each house shall be the judge of the elections, returns, and qualifications of its own members . . . ." And the Supreme Court has recognized that although these powers are judicial, as distinguished from legislative or executive, in type, they have nevertheless been lodged in the legislative branch by the Constitution. In Barry v. United States ex rel. Cunningham, 1929, 279 U.S. 597, 49 S.Ct. 452, 73 L.Ed. 867, an inquiry was instituted by the United States Senate, through a committee thereof, into the validity of the election of a Senator from Pennsylvania. In respect of the committee's action in ordering a witness taken into custody for contumacy, the question whether the Senate was engaged in an inquiry which it had constitutional power to make, was

wealth which in his judgment will result in the failure of the government to fulfill its contracts, or to meet its financial obligations, or which in his judgment will violate international obligations of the United States to other powers (Sec. 7. (2)). The Chief Executive of the Commonwealth shall make annual reports to the President and Congress of the United States (Sec. 7. (3)). The United States High Commissioner is given access to all records of the Commonwealth government and must be furnished by the Chief Executive of the Commonwealth with such information as he requests (Sec. 7. (4)).

presented to the Supreme Court in a habeas corpus proceeding. The Court ruled that it was, saying:

". . . Generally, the Senate is a legislative body, exercising in connection with the House only the power to make laws. But it has had conferred upon it by the Constitution certain powers which are not legislative but judicial in character. Among these is the power to judge of the elections, returns and qualifications of its own members. Art. I, § 5, cl. 1. . . . Exercise of the power necessarily involves the ascertainment of facts, the attendance of witnesses, the examination of such witnesses, with the power to compel them to answer pertinent questions, to determine the facts and apply the appropriate rules of law, and, finally, *to render a judgment which is beyond the authority of any other tribunal to review. . . .*" [279 U.S. at page 613, 49 S.Ct. at page 455, 73 L.Ed. 867] [Italics supplied]

See also the remark in Keogh v. Horner, D.C.S.D.Ill., 1934, 8 F.Supp. 933, 935, that "the power of the respective Houses of Congress with reference to the qualification and legality of the election of its members is supreme. . . . this court has no authority to be the judge of the manner in which such members were elected. . . ." And see Note (1937) 107 A.L.R. 205, 206.

We are cited to no cases, and we find none, in which the Federal courts have even been asked to determine the qualifications of a member of Congress. Apparently it has been fully recognized that that power is lodged exclusively in the legislative branch. Under parallel provisions in state constitutions giving state legislatures the power to determine the qualifications of their members, it is ruled that the legislative power is exclusive—that the courts have no jurisdiction. Reif v. Barrett, 1933, 355 Ill. 104, 188 N.E. 889; Greenwood v. Board of Registrars of Voters of City of Fitchburg, 1933, 282 Mass. 74, 184 N.E. 390; Dinan v. Swig, 1916, 223 Mass. 516, 112 N.E. 91; Covington v. Buffett, 1900, 90 Md. 569, 45 A. 204, 47 L.R.A. 622; Attorney General v. Board of

Canvassers of Seventh Senatorial District, 1908, 155 Mich. 44, 118 N.W. 584; Dalton v. State, 1885, 43 Ohio St. 652, 3 N.E. 685; and see Note (1937) 107 A.L.R. 205, 209.

It is patent, of course, that the Resident Commissioner of the Philippines is not in a full sense of the term a "member of Congress." Neither, however, are delegates to Congress from the various territories. They, like the Resident Commissioner, have some but not all of the characteristics of members, i. e., they have a seat, and they may participate in debate, but they may not vote.[18] In Territory ex rel. Sulzer v. Canvassing Board, 1st Div., 1917, 5 Alaska 602, there was a petition in the territorial court brought by the Territory of Alaska on the relation of one Sulzer for an alternative writ of mandamus to compel a Canvassing Board to reject the alleged votes from certain precincts for the office of delegate to Congress from Alaska, or to issue to Sulzer a certificate of election. The petition was granted, the court holding that mandamus was the proper remedy to compel the Canvassing Board to issue a certificate. But the court recognized that "this certificate of election is not final. The House of Representatives is the tribunal before which the contest of election comes. . . . it is clothed with plenary power to seat whomsoever it pleases—certificate or no certificate." (5 Alaska at pages 631–632) And Congress has, in respect of persons claiming a right to sit as delegates from territories, consistently claimed and exercised power to determine their qualifications. See for example: The Florida Election Case of David Levy, 1 Hinds, Precedents of the House of Representatives (1907) 394 (1841); The Utah Election Case of Campbell v. Cannon, id. at 500 (1882).

[7] We do not assume to rule, because it is not necessary to do so, whether the action of the executive department alone is conclusive of the qualifications of the Resident Commissioner—because he partakes in some part of the characteristics of a diplomatic representative and presents his credentials to the President; or whether the action of the legislative department

---

[18] In respect of the powers of various delegates to Congress see the following: Act of May 7, 1906, c. 2083, § 1, 34 Stat. 169, 48 U.S.C.A. § 131, and Rev.Stat. § 1862 (1873-4)—Alaska; Act of April 30, 1900, c. 339, § 85, 31 Stat. 158, as amended by the Act of June 28, 1906, c. 3582, § 85, 34 Stat. 550, 48 U.S.C.A. § 651—Hawaii.

alone is conclusive of his qualifications— because he partakes in part of the characteristics of a delegate; or whether the ultimate authority to determine the Resident Commissioner's qualifications is in the joint action of the two political departments. It is sufficient for the determination of this case that, under the Constitutional provisions, judicial decisions and reasoning above set forth, the power to determine the qualifications of the Resident Commissioner is exclusively in either the President or the House of Representatives, or both, as political departments of the government, and not in the courts.

Affirmed.

United States v. New York Trust Co.
75 F. Supp. 583 (S.D.N.Y., 1946)
For opinion see <u>infra</u> III (2) (a) (iii) (bb)

Republic Aviation Corporation v. LOWE
69 F. Supp. 472 (S.D.N.Y., 1946)
affirmed 164 F. 2d. 18 (2d. Cir., 1947)
cert. denied 333 U.S. 845; 68 S. Ct. 663 (1948)

(Plaintiff and its insurer sued defendant, Deputy Commissioner of the U.S. Employees Compensation Commission and Mrs. Parker, widow of a U.S. test pilot, for a permanent injunction setting aside a compensation award to Mrs. Parker, ordering payment by plaintiffs death benefits by reason of her husband's death, the award having been made pursuant to the Defense Bases Compensation Act of 1941, (55 Stat. 622) as amended in 1942 (56 Stat. 1035). The Defense Bases Act provided compensation for disability or death resulting from injury to persons employed at military, air, and naval bases, "acquired by the United States from foreign countries, and on lands occupied or used by the United States for military or naval purposes outside the continental limits of the United States..." The deceased was employed by Republic Aviation Corp. and he was made available to the U.S. Government as a test pilot under Republic's contract with the War Department. Assigned to the Far East Air Force at IA SHIMA, an island in the Pacific Ocean, formerly a Japanese possession, but acquired by the U.S. by conquest prior to August 20, 1945. While testing a P-47, Parker crashed and died. Defendants moved for summary judgment.)

LEIBELL, District Judge . ***

Territory of a foreign government may be acquired by cession or by conquest. Hackworth's "Digest of International Law" (1940) Vol. 1, defines acquisition by cession and acquisition by conquest.

"Cession of territory involves the transfer of sovereignty by means of an agreement between the ceding and the acquiring states". p. 421.

"Conquest is the taking of possession of territory of an enemy state by force; it becomes a mode of acquisition of territory —and hence of transfer of sovereignty— only if the conquered territory is effectively reduced to possession and annexed by the conquering state". p. 427.

In the case of Fleming v. Page, 9 How. 603, 614, 50 U.S. 603, 614, 13 L.Ed. 276, involving the legality of duties levied upon the cargo of a schooner which sailed from Tampico, Mexico, to the United States while Tampico was in the possession of the United States and governed by its military authorities as a result of the Mexican War, Chief Justice Taney delivered the opinion of the Court, from which the following is quoted:

"A war, therefore, declared by Congress, can never be presumed to be waged for the purpose of conquest or the acquisition of territory; nor does the law declaring the war imply an authority to the President to enlarge the limits of the United States by subjugating the enemy's country. The United States, it is true, may extend its boundaries by conquest or treaty, and may demand the cession of territory as the condition of peace, in order to indemnify its citizens for the injuries they have suffered, or to reimburse the government for the expenses of the war. But this can be done only by the treaty-making power or the legislative authority, and is not a part of the power conferred upon the President by the declaration of war. * * *

It is true, that, when Tampico had been captured, and the State of Tamaulipas subjugated, other nations were bound to regard the country, while our possession continued, as the territory of the United States, and to respect it as such. * * * As regarded all other nations it was a part of the United States, and belonged to them as exclusively as the territory included in our established boundaries.

But yet it was not a part of this Union. For every nation which acquires territory by treaty or conquest holds it according to its own institutions and laws. And the relation in which the Port of Tampico stood to the United States while it was occupied by their arms did not depend upon the laws of nations, but upon our own Constitution and acts of Congress."

The court concluded that Tampico was a foreign port and that cargoes shipped from Tampico were subject to our revenue laws and were liable to the duty charged upon them.

If we give to the words "acquired * * * from any foreign government" the meaning which they would have in international law, the United States had not "acquired" Ia Shima from Japan by conquest because Ia Shima had not been formally annexed to the United States. It was occupied by the military forces of the United States. If the word "acquire" is given its ordinary meaning—to gain, to come into the possession of—then Ia Shima was a military air base acquired from a foreign government. In which sense did Congress use the word "acquire", considering the situation that existed when the Defense Bases Act was enacted? The United States was not then at war. Defense Bases had been acquired from Great Britain by treaty or agreement. I do not believe that Congress contemplated at that time the acquisition of defense bases by conquest.

Plaintiffs argue that the type of project in connection with the war effort, intended to be covered by the statute, was a work project involving some form of construction, alteration, removal or repair, such as the work specified in § 1651(b), construction work that contributed to the building of the defense base, and that the service contract of Republic did not come within the statutory definition of "public work". But in that definition are expressly included "projects in connection with the war effort". That is a very broad term and should be liberally construed in line with the public policy of protection for the employees, a policy embodied in the Longshoremen's and Harbor Workers' Compensation Act (South Chicago Co. v. Bassett, 309 U.S. 251, 60 S.Ct. 544, 84 L.Ed. 732) which was extended to projects in connection with the war effort by the Defense Bases Act. The project on which Parker was engaged was a design or plan in connection with the war effort. The Congress defined "public work" in this statute and the courts should follow that definition. Fox v. Standard Oil Co., 294 U.S. 87 at page 96, 55 S.Ct. 333, 79 L.Ed. 780.

The Circuit Court of Appeals, First Circuit, discussed the purposes of the Defense Bases Act as originally passed, August 16, 1941, in the case of Royal Indemnity Co. v. Puerto Rico Cement Corp., 142 F.2d 237, at page 239, as follows: "The history of the Defense Bases Act clearly shows the intention of Congress to extend the provisions of the Longshoremen's Act to defense bases without regard to local compensation laws. It was stated in House Report No. 1070, 77th Congress, First Session, that the purpose of the bill was to provide substantially the same relief to outlying territories, including and mentioning Puerto Rico, as the existing law affords employees in the United States, and to assist contractors employing labor at such bases to obtain compensation insurance at reasonable rates."

The weight to be given to administrative interpretation of the Defense Bases Act should be the same as that which the Courts are required to give to administrative interpretations of the Longshoremen's and Harbor Workers' Compensation Act. In Norton, Deputy Comm. v. Warner Co., 321 U.S. 565, 64 S.Ct. 747, 750, 88 L.Ed. 931, the Court held that the judicial review permitted to the courts under § 21 (b) "Does not give authority to the courts to set aside awards because they are deemed to be against the weight of the evidence. More is required. The error must be one of law, such as the misconstruction of a term of the Act."

In Davis v. Department of Labor, 317 U.S. 249, 63 S.Ct. 225, 229, 87 L.Ed. 246, the Court held that the conclusions of the administrative agency "That a case falls within the federal jurisdiction is therefore entitled to great weight and will be rejected only in cases of apparent error".

I have concluded that the interpretation given to the Defense Bases Act by the Deputy Commissioner who heard the Parker claim was correct; that Parker was covered by the Act at the time of his death; and that the award of the Deputy Commissioner was in accordance with law. It follows therefore that the defendants' motion for summary judgment dismissing the complaint herein on the merits should be granted. Settle order accordingly.

Kuniyuki v. Acheson
94 F. Supp. 353 (W.D. Wash., 1950)

HALL, District Judge.

The American born plaintiff seeks in this action a judgment that she is a citizen of the United States.

The first thing to take into consideration is the jurisdiction of the Court.

I will now find that under Section 903 of Title 8 U.S.C.A., this Court has jurisdiction to hear and try this case and make a judicial determination as to whether or not the plaintiff in this case was deprived of her citizenship by voting in the elections in Japan according to the evidence in the case.

The Section involved on the merits is 401(e) of the United States Nationality Act, 801(e), Title 8, U.S.C.A., and reads as follows: "A person who is a national of the United States, whether by birth or naturalization, shall lose his nationality, by * * * voting in a political election in a foreign state or participating in an election or plebiscite to determine the sovereignty over foreign territory".

The first clause is the one that is involved here, that is "voting in a political election in a foreign state". It calls for a judicial determination of several words; and also some factual determination. In the first place, from the facts in the case, there isn't any doubt but what the plaintiff in the case voted, that is, she cast her ballot in two elections, at least, in Japan in the years 1946 and 1947 (although the State Department rests its position upon the claim that she has expatriated herself under the provisions of Section 401(e), by voting in the Japanese political elections of April 1946).

The words which require judicial construction and determination as to their meaning, are three,—"Political election", "foreign" and "State". Taking them in the order which they are easiest to determine, I will take the word "foreign", first. There isn't any doubt but what Japan is foreign to the United States in the sense that it is the opposite of, and is intended to have the opposite meaning of, the word "domestic", which includes the territory of the United States. So whether Japan is or was during that period of time a foreign "state" or not, it nevertheless was foreign.

The main question is whether or not it was a "State". It is the contention of the defendant, here, the Secretary of State, that Japan was a State. As to the definition of the word "State", a great many text books and writers on International Law have dealt with the word for many years; but actually its meaning has not changed much, since it was defined by Vattel in his French work published about

1773. That definition is continued on through Moore's Digest of International Law, Revere, Hackworth and others. I do not wish to ever be in the position of citing simply myself in rulings but in the case, U. S. v. Kusche, D.C., 56 F.Supp. 201, the question was raised whether or not Hitler's Third Reich was a State; that is to say, whether or not it was the same German State as that from which the person involved there had renounced his allegiance. I held that it was; but the case reviewed the elements necessary to constitute a State, and I came to the conclusion, to which I still adhere, that a State comprehends a body of people living in a territory, who are not subject to any external rule but who have the power within themselves to have any form of government which they choose and have the power to deal with other States. In other words, they have sovereignty. That is the first essential, in a State; and I think that is recognized by the cases on which the government relies, e. g.—Jones v. U. S., 137 U.S. 202 at page 212, 11 S.Ct. 80 at page 83, 34 L.Ed. 691. The Court says, "Who is the sovereign, de jure or de facto, of a territory, is not a judicial, but a political, question, the determination of which by the legislative and executive departments of any government conclusively binds the judges", and so forth. But the kernel of the definition, as included there, is sovereignty. Likewise, in the Venustiano Carranza case—Oetjen v. Central Leather Company—, 246 U.S. 297, 38 S.Ct. 309, 62 L.Ed. 726, the Government of the United States acting through the regularly elected officials had officially recognized,—that is to say, the President of the United States had officially recognized the Government of Carranza as the Government of Mexico, and this is certainly quite different than the situation which has obtained here.

In an effort to determine whether or not Japan has any sovereignty and the other attributes which make for the creation or existence of a State, we refer to the plaintiff's Exhibit 2, here, "Occupation of Japan", the official book put out by the

State Department of the United States containing the text of the various documents which relate to Japan prior to the surrender and subsequent to the surrender. I don't think it is necessary to review the Potsdam Declaration, the Emperor's reply thereto and the acceptance thereof. But to start with, the Instrument of Surrender, itself, which is found on page 62 of this document, recites, "We"—now, that is not only the Japanese but also Douglas MacArthur who has signed as Supreme Commander for the Allied Powers.

Incidentally, I can take judicial notice of the fact that prior to this date he had been designated the Supreme Commander for the Allied Powers by the various Allied Powers to act for and on behalf of all of them in connection with the surrender and all subsequent matters. That document is not in this book. However, it is available and it is a matter of which the Court can take judicial notice. The Instrument of Surrender is signed by the Japanese Government and also by the United States Representatives, and Representatives of the Republic of China, the United Kingdom, Soviet Russia, Australia, Dominion of Canada, French Republic, the Netherlands and New Zealand.

With further reference to its text, it recites: "We hereby command all Civil, Military and Naval authorities to obey and enforce all proclamations, orders and directives deemed by the Supreme Commander for the Allied Powers to be proper to effectuate this surrender and issued by him or under his authority and we do direct that all such officials remain at their posts and to continue to perform their non-combatant duties unless specifically relieved by him or under his authority."

And, further: "The authority of the Emperor in the Japanese Government to Rule the State shall be subject to the Supreme Commander for the Allied Powers who will take such steps as he deems proper to effectuate those terms of surrender."

Some suggestion is made, on behalf of the Secretary of State, that the Far Eastern Commission superseded and supplanted the Supreme Commander for the Allied Powers in the Government of Japan. But the original proposal was only that the Allied Commission should act as an advisory body; and that is all it finally amounted to actually, in the agreement which I think was effectuated at Moscow and promulgated December 27, 1945. The Far Eastern Commission is given power to formulate the policies, principles and standards. It has the power to review, on the request of any member, any directive issued by the Supreme Commander and the like, and the functions of the United States Government are defined and outlined. But as I indicated to counsel during the course of the argument, there is a subdivision B to that and that is the, "Allied Council for Japan"; and under that: "The Supreme Commander shall issue all orders for the implementation of the Terms of Surrender." So that the Terms of Surrender— and I am satisfied it has been so regarded by the Supreme Commander in Japan and by the United States Government in supporting the Supreme Commander for the Allied Powers in various disputes which have arisen with the Far Eastern Commission—were that he is the one who effectuates the instrument of surrender; and under the instrument of surrender the authority of the Emperor and the Japanese Government to rule shall be subject to the Supreme Commander for the Allied Powers, and not to any Far Eastern Commission. So actually, in my judgment, and I so hold, this agreement of the Foreign Ministers to establish the Far Eastern Commission did not take away the power of the Supreme Commander which, as I indicated, was complete authority over the Emperor and the Japanese Government.

Returning again to "Occupation of Japan", we find here the document of August 29, 1945. I think it was promulgated on September 6, 1945. On page 75 of "Occupation of Japan" under the subject "Allied Authority," we read: "Although every effort will be made, by consultation and by constitution of appropriate advisory bodies, to establish policies for the conduct of the occupation and the control of Japan which will satisfy"—not the Japanese Government but—"The Principal Allied powers, in the event of any differences of opinion among them, the policies of the United States will govern."

Also,

"Relationship to Japanese Government."

"The authority of the Emperor and the Japanese Government will be subject to the Supreme Commander, who will possess all powers necessary to effectuate the surrender terms, and to carry out the policies established for the conduct of the occupation and the control of Japan."

"The Japanese Government will be permitted, under his instructions, to exercise the normal powers of government in matters of Domestic Administration."

Mind you, it says, that it will be permitted, under his instructions. I have no idea how many directives have been issued, but I will call attention to one or two (and that is a matter of which I can take judicial notice) that the Japanese Government is run by receiving a directive from the Supreme Commander to the Allied Powers addressed to the Japanese Government; and then followed, in turn, by some action on the part of the Japanese Government; or if the matter is initiated by the Japanese Government, it becomes a proposal. And when the proposal is approved it then becomes a directive.

But, continuing: "This policy, however, will be subject to the right and duty of the Supreme Commander to require changes in Governmental machinery or personnel or to act directly if the Emperor or other Japanese authority does not satisfactorily meet the requirements of the Supreme Commander in effectuating the surrender terms. This policy, moreover, does not commit the Supreme Commander to support the Emperor or any other Japanese Governmental authority in opposition to evolutionary changes looking toward the attainment of United States objectives."

And here is the key phrase: "The policy is to use the existing form of government in Japan, not to support it."

Then it goes on further, suggesting methods of change. In Part III * * * Political, (of that Directive) on page 76: "High officials of the Japanese Imperial General Headquarters, and General Staff, other high military and naval officials of the Japanese Government, leaders of ultra-Nationalists and militarist organizations and other important exponents of militarism and aggression will be taken into custody and held for future disposition."

There you are taking the people, whom the Japanese people or the Japanese Government exercising its power as a State had selected as its officials to run it, and you are wiping them out entirely. There is certainly no evidence of independent action or sovereignty there.

Furthermore it says: "Laws, decrees and regulations which establish discriminations on ground of race, nationality, creed or political opinion shall be abrogated; those which conflict with the objectives and policies outlined in this document shall be repealed, suspended or amended as required; and agencies charged specifically with their enforcement shall be abolished or appropriately modified. Persons unjustly confined by Japanese authority on political grounds shall be released. The judicial, legal and police systems shall be reformed as soon as practicable to conform to the policies set forth in Article I and III"—and so forth.

The next document is important, "Economic Demilitarization." They take away the army and navy and the air force. The Japanese were not allowed these. Furthermore, they take away the number and limit the size of ships. The Japanese were not allowed to engage in their ordinary method of banking. Over on page 79: "To this end it shall be the policy of the Supreme Commander: (a) To prohibit the retention in or selection for places of importance in the economic field of individuals who do not direct future Japanese economic effort solely towards peaceful ends; and (b) To favor a program for the dissolution of the large industrial and banking combinations which have exercised control of a great part of Japan's trade and industry."

And pursuant to that, the banks were dissolved,—large corporations which had theretofore existed, were dissolved; their properties were taken and distributed to the Japanese people.

Continuing further on page 79: "The Japanese authorities will be expected, and if necessary directed, to maintain, develop and enforce programs that serve the following purposes"—and it sets forth some of the requirements and aims of the Occupation of Japan.

And, at Page 81:

"International Trade and Financial Relations."

"Japan shall be permitted eventually to resume normal trade relations with the rest of the world. During occupation and under suitable controls, Japan will be permitted to purchase from foreign countries raw materials and other goods that it may need for peaceful purposes, and to export goods to pay for approved imports.

"Control is to be maintained over all imports and exports of goods, and foreign exchange and financial transactions. Both the policies followed in the exercise of these controls and their actual administration shall be subject to the approval and supervision of the Supreme Commander in order to make sure that they are not contrary to the policies of the occupying authorities, and in particular that all foreign purchasing power that Japan may acquire is utilized only for essential needs."

All Japanese property abroad was taken away. Every vestige of sovereignty, as exercised by a nation or state, was taken away. The Japanese did keep their government. As indicated here, it was to be used and not to be supported; and to be used for the purpose of carrying out the policies of the Instrument of Surrender, and of the following document which still remains the principal document of outline.

Further, on page 88: "Authority of General MacArthur as Supreme Commander for the Allied Powers."

And on page 89: "The Authority of the Emperor and the Japanese Government

to rule the State is subordinate to you as Supreme Commander for the Allied powers. You will exercise your authority as you deem proper to carry out your mission. Our relations with Japan do not rest on a contractual basis, but on an unconditional surrender. Since your authority is Supreme, you will not entertain any question on the part of the Japanese as to its scope."

Here not only is a government that has no independence or has no supremacy; but they are not even allowed to question any act of the Supreme Commander for the Allied Powers.

Attention must be given in this connection to Appendix 18, page 94, of "Occupation of Japan", reporting the Japanese "Bill of Rights". You will notice there that that is a SCAP[1] directive of October 4, 1945. In other words, this was an order from the Supreme Commander of the Allied powers to the Japanese Government; and it deals with many, many subjects. But I will not take time to review them, in this oral statement from the bench as they are in front of each of you.

Another SCAP Directive, of January 4, 1946, provides for: "Removal and Exclusion of Undesirable personnel from public office."

It goes on,—well, it just practically cleans out the entire Japanese Government. I am not going to take time to review them but it starts out with war criminals, career persons, and persons influential in activity in certain political associations,—the control associations which exercised power over the various industries in Japan, and particularly with relation to their financial and ordinary, economic business life; that is to say, the private lives of the people. Subdivision "E" of the Appendix, abolishes officers of financial and development organizations involving Japanese expansion; and gives a long list, beginning with the "South Manchurian Railway Company" and so forth and it says,

"Any other bank, development company or institution whose foremost purpose has been the financing of colonization and de-

1. Abbreviation for the term "Supreme Commander for the Allied Powers."

velopment activities in colonial and Japa-nese-occupied territory," and so forth.

And again the SCAP Directive of January 4, 1946, Appendix 21, provides for "Abolition of Certain Political Parties, Associations, Societies, and other Organizations," and gives a list of organizations to be abolished.

The "Japanese Draft Constitution," Appendix 23, appears on page 117. It is to be noted that the draft was submitted by the Japanese Government to SCAP for SCAP's approval; and subsequently the Supreme Commander for the Allied Powers did approve it, and this is the only thing which gave it life or vitality at all.

I think that I perhaps should observe that Appendix number 25 originated with the Emperor, himself—namely, The "Imperial Rescript Denying Divinity of Emperor."

Appendix 27, is another SCAP Directive. And while that says: "You are hereby authorized to hold a general election," it will be noticed that that is entitled a "Directive" from the Supreme Commander from the Allied Powers to the Japanese Government. That is on page 136.

And General MacArthur's reply to the Far Eastern Commission is certainly indicative of the extent to which he regarded his power to go. He says,—well, he indicates at page 138 where it refers to his purge directive, "90 percentum of the members of the present Diet, as well as many other persons holding high government office in the war administration, have been removed from government service and barred from public office or activity as officers of political parties."

He indicates that if the election should go wrong: "The remedy is always in my power to require the dissolution of the Diet and the holding of a new election under such provisions as are deemed necessary."

Again he says the same thing on page 140, in his answer to the Commission's question number 3; and the nature of the elections are indicated by his approval of the elections in Appendix number 30.

I think from what I have said that it is clear that my opinion is that Japan did not exercise any sovereignty. And whatever else it may be called, in the rather mixed up international situation as it is today, it cannot be called a foreign State within the contemplation and meaning of the terms of Section 801(e) of Title 8 of the U.S.C.A.

There is another word, I think, that needs definition and that is "Political Election." In view of the fact that the election was called at the direction of General MacArthur, that all of the candidates had to be screened, that General MacArthur had the power to dissolve the Diet, call a new election and effectuate any purge —that is to say put everybody out of public office who might have been elected—it seems to me that the election held in Japan does not come within the meaning of a political election as used in 801(e). It is more in the nature of a plebiscite.

I think the words "Political Election", as used in 801(e) mean an election by which the people do not just exert or express their wish; but actually exercise a command that certain people shall hold certain public office. Now, actually, what the elections were in Japan were not a command by the people, which they were capable of enforcing, that certain persons should hold certain public offices; but merely, in view of the power of the Commander to negate it, they were merely the expression of a wish, or, at best, merely a plebiscite. I think probably we call them "Polls" in this country today. So I don't think that the election at which this lady voted in Japan, or the elections held were the type of elections that were contemplated by Section 801(e) or meant by that section. That disposes of that feature of the case.

Before coming to the other feature of the case, I would like to say in that connection that I think I am supported in my views here, not only by Arikawa v. Acheson, U.S.D.C.S.D.Cal., 83 F.Supp. 473;

but Hatsuye Ouye v. Acheson, U.S.D.C. Hawaii, 91 F.Supp. 129; Yamamoto v. Acheson, U.S.D.C.Ariz., 93 F.Supp. 346; Brehm v. Acheson, U.S.D.C.Tex., 90 F. Supp. 662, and Fujizawa v. Acheson, U.S. D.C.C.S.D.Cal., 85 F.Supp. 674, all heretofore decided by various United States District Courts.

That disposes of the case and the plaintiff is entitled to judgment on the law. But if I should be in error in the conclusions I have just announced, there remains one other question.

The other question is one of fact and is whether or not the act of the plaintiff in voting was a voluntary act. In the first place, I am satisfied that the statute is not meant to be and was not meant by Congress to be an arbitrary deprivation of a person's citizenship in the United States by doing an act which he did not know the meaning of at the time he did it. In other words, the act has to be knowingly done, and it has to be voluntarily done.

I don't think I would be justified, from any evidence in this case, in holding that there was any duress, that there was any physical threat of bodily harm; or physical threat of the deprivation of her liberty, her home, her job, her food or her clothing or any other of the many various means which modern civilization (and I guess ancient as well) has of hurting people physically in order to coerce them to do things. There is no question as to that at all.

The question is whether her voting was voluntary on her part. We have here a woman who was born in the United States; and when she was two or three years old, was taken to Japan where she lived all of her life except for eight months just prior to the commencement of the war in 1941. She went back to Japan; and remained there until 1950. She was a Japanese citizen. There is no doubt but what she had dual nationality both in the United States and in Japan; and that as a Japanese citizen she was subject to the Japanese laws which regulated and ruled Japanese citizens. I recall, in reading one of the documents here in evidence that the

directive either from SCAP or a publicity release was that all Japanese citizens should vote. Now, certainly, she was a Japanese citizen.

I think in her situation, with the fact that great emphasis in that election in Japan was placed upon the rather subordinate place which women had had in that country theretofore, and the fact they were now to be given an equality of rights, that she did not do a voluntary act.

I think at the time she had, as she has indicated in her testimony in this case, admiration for the conduct of the occupation of Japan by the Supreme Commander for the Allied Powers. I do not think she would have willingly or knowingly done any act at all, which might ever possibly have endangered her American citizenship.

I don't know, perhaps I would not be justified in drawing on my own personal experience in Japan, in going there after the war; but perhaps it is a matter of which we can now take judicial notice, that is, the willingness of the Japanese people generally, and their anxiety to please the Supreme Commander for the Allied Powers and the Occupying Authorities; their great eagerness to actually learn the ways of democracy; their disappointment at having been misled for so many years in the program for world conquest; which the Military Caste in control of Japan had launched upon; and their avid appetite to learn and adopt Democratic ways and institutions. I notice, that in one of these documents in evidence here, it is rather wryly remarked that it may take some time. Of course it will. But in the meantime, certainly, I do not think that this woman should be penalized by a denial of her citizenship, on the ground that she voluntarily and freely voted in these elections, when there was so much confusion in Japan; and when, quite obviously, she did not know that she would be losing her United States citizenship. And on that point I am constrained to hold, and do hold, that the Plaintiff did not voluntarily vote in the elections in Japan, which the evidence shows she did.

The plaintiff will prepare the findings of fact and conclusions of law.

Cobb v. United States
191 F. 2d. 604 (9th Cir., 1951)
Cert. denied 342 U.S. 913; 72 S.Ct. 360 (1952)

Before STEPHENS, ORR and POPE, Circuit Judges.

ORR, Circuit Judge.

The controlling question on this appeal is whether the federal government has, by virtue of the Federal Tort Claims Act, 28 U.S.C.A. §§ 2671–2680, consented to be sued on a tort claim arising out of an accident which took place in October, 1948, on the island of Okinawa. In brief, the question is whether Okinawa was at that time a "foreign country" within the meaning of 28 U.S.C.A. § 2680(k) which excludes from the scope of the Act: "Any claim arising in a foreign country."

Appellant brought this action in the United States District Court for the Northern District of California to recover damages from the United States for personal injuries suffered in an automobile accident in Okinawa, where he was then employed by a contractor engaged in military construction. The accident allegedly resulted from the negligence of an unknown employee of the United States in leaving an unlighted crane parked on the road after dark.

Okinawa is an island in the Ryukyu Archipelago, south of the main Japanese islands and south of 30° north latitude. Prior to World War II, according to the Department of State, Japan was "acknowledged internationally to be the sovereign" of the Ryukyus.[1] During World War II the United States conquered Okinawa, and has continuously occupied the island since that time. In September, 1945, the Department of State announced the policy of limiting "Japan's sovereignty" to the home islands.[2] In furtherance of this policy the Supreme Commander, Allied Powers, in 1946 promulgated an order reading in part as follows: "1. The Imperial Japanese Government is directed to cease exercising, or attempting to exercise, governmental or administrative authority over any area outside of Japan, or over any government officials and employees or any other persons within such areas."[3] "Japan" was defined to exclude those of the Ryukyus south of 30° north latitude, such as Okinawa.

Since its conquest Okinawa has had no independent legislative, executive or judicial government except the United States Military Government, which still

---

1. The quotation is taken from a letter to appellant's counsel dated April 12, 1949, from the Acting Legal Adviser of the Department of State.

2. Exhibit 6 purports to be a copy of a statement entitled: "8. United States Initial Post Surrender Policy for Japan, Advance Echelon, APO 500, 23 September 1945, Department of State Radio News Bulletin, 22 September 1945 (Intercepted by GHQ Signal Service) White House." This statement of policy sets forth the ultimate objectives of the United States as being, in general, to establish a peaceful and responsible Japanese government. The statement proceeds: "The objectives will be achieved by the following principal means: a. Japan's sovereignty will be limited to the islands of Honshu, Hokkaido, Kyushu, Shikoku, and such minor outlying islands as may be determined in accordance with the Cairo Declaration and other agreements to which the United States is or may be a party * * *."

3. Order of Supreme Commander, Allied Powers, entitled: "189. Memorandum concerning Governmental and Administrative Separation of Certain Outlying Areas from Japan," dated 29 Jan. 1946.

controls the island.[4] The United States operates naval, military and air bases on Okinawa, and a congressional committee has expressed a purpose of the United States to maintain these bases indefinitely.[5] Yet the ultimate fate of the island is not settled.[6] The United States has expressed no intention to annex the island, to return it to Japan, or to establish it as an independent state. The island is not under United Nations trusteeship, or the Far Eastern Commission.[7] No peace treaty has yet been concluded with the former sovereign, Japan.

On these facts the District Court held that Okinawa was a "foreign country," relying on three District Court decisions,[8] and on United States v. Spelar, 1949, 338 U.S. 217, 70 S.Ct. 10, 94 L.Ed. 3. In the Spelar case the Supreme Court held that the Tort Claims Act did not grant governmental consent to be sued for a tort which occurred on Newfoundland territory leased by the United States. The court rested this conclusion on two tests applied to the Spelar claim: (1) Whether the leased territory was "territory subject to the sovereignty of another nation", 338 U.S. 217, 219, 70 S.Ct. 10, 11, and, (2) whether the liability asserted was one "depending upon the laws of a foreign power", 338 U.S. at page 221, 70 S.Ct. at page 12. We think it appropriate here to apply these tests to plaintiff's claim:

1. The Sovereignty of Another Nation.

In defining the term "foreign country," as used in 28 U.S.C.A. § 2680(k), the Supreme Court observed: "We know of no more accurate phrase in common English usage than 'foreign country' to denote territory subject to the sovereignty of another nation." 338 U.S. 217, 219, 70 S.Ct. 10, 11. In support of this definition the Court quoted with approval the statement of the Court in De Lima v. Bidwell, 1901, 182 U.S. 1, 180, 21 S.Ct. 743, 746, 45 L.Ed. 1041: "A foreign country was defined by Mr. Chief Justice Marshall and Mr. Justice Story to be one exclusively within the sovereignty of a foreign nation,

---

4. See Rubenstein, Magistrate Courts in Okinawa: A Contribution to Justice in the Ryukyus, 36 A.B.A.J. 1011 (1950).

5. Report of Committee on Armed Services, House of Representatives, 81st Congress, 1st Sess.

6. A letter to appellant's counsel dated April 12, 1949, from the Acting Legal Adviser of the Department of State, states in part: "No formal determination has been reached concerning the final disposition of Okinawa. No treaty of peace with Japan has yet been concluded, nor has any action been taken to place Okinawa under the International trusteeship system established under the Charter of the United Nations."

7. The letter cited in note states in addition: "Okinawa is not controlled by the Far Eastern Commission, which was established pursuant to the Agreement of Foreign Ministers at Moscow on December 27, 1945; the United States has been in charge of the military occupation of the Ryukyus."

A letter to appellant's counsel dated April 20, 1949, from the Political Affairs Officer, Trusteeship Division, United Nations, states in part: "I am directed to inform you that the question of placing Okinawa under trusteeship has not been raised in any organ of the United Nations, and, as far as is known, there have been no representations or statements to the United Nations on this question by any representative of the United States."

8. Brewer v. United States, D.C.N.D.Cal. 1948, 79 F.Supp. 405 (Okinawa); Brunell v. United States, D.C.S.D.N.Y.1948, 77 F.Supp. 68 (Saipan); Straneri v. United States, D.C.E.D.Pa.1948, 77 F. Supp. 240 (Belgium);

Appellee cites for additional support two other cases allegedly decided by the District Courts: Dunn v. United States, N.D.Cal., and Smith v. United States, No. 28865. Appellee cites no report of these decisions and fails to state when they were decided, or what court decided the Smith case, which allegedly dealt with Saipan. Appellee does not state what was involved in the Dunn case.

It does not appear that any of these cases were appealed.

and without the sovereignty of the United States." Since Newfoundland was unquestionably subject exclusively to the "sovereignty" of Great Britain, the leased territory in Newfoundland was held to be part of a "foreign country."

When applied to Okinawa, however, the test of "sovereignty" affords no such satisfactory conclusion. At the outset, it must be assumed that "sovereignty is never held in suspense." [9] The question, therefore, is whether Japan has lost her sovereignty over Okinawa and, if so, to what power that sovereignty has passed. In the event the United States' occupation of Okinawa were of a clearly provisional character designed simply to maintain order on the island until Okinawa could be returned to a responsible Japanese government, it could be said that Japan did not lose her "sovereignty" over the island but had been merely deprived temporarily of the power to exercise some of the rights of sovereignty. [10] This theory would be particularly applicable to the Japanese home islands because in those islands a native Japanese government has been permitted to exercise most of the normal powers of government in matters of domestic administration, subject to the supervision of the Supreme Commander. However, the United States has expressed no intention of returning Okinawa to a Japanese government. On the contrary, the announced policy of the State Department is to place the island outside the "sovereignty" of Japan, and the Supreme Commander has ordered that the Japanese government refrain from attempting to exercise any governmental or administrative authority there. These circumstances divest Japan of all sovereignty over the island. [11]

Sovereignty, therefore, must have passed to some other people. Had the United States announced the objective of establishing an independent state of Okinawa it could be said that, in a sense, sovereignty passed to the people of Okinawa, the government being administered for the people by the occupant as a sort of trustee. [12] The record indicates, however, that no such policy has been adopted. The ultimate fate of Okinawa has not yet been decided. It cannot be said that the loss of "sovereignty" over the island by Japan vests the "de jure sovereignty," in the traditional sense, in the natives of Okinawa.

By evicting the Japanese and affirmatively withdrawing Okinawa from the sovereignty of Japan, the belligerent occupants acquired the exclusive power to control and govern the island. This power, although perhaps acquired in the name of the Allied Powers, is lodged exclusively in the United States. The United States Military Government now governs, and will continue indefinitely to govern, the island of Okinawa, free from interference by other powers. [13] The will of the United States is in fact the "supreme will" [14] on Okinawa. The United States has therefore acquired, and still retains, what may be termed a "de facto sovereignty." [15]

9. United States v. Curtiss-Wright Export Corp., 1936, 299 U.S. 304, 317, 57 S.Ct. 216, 219, 81 L.Ed. 255.

10. See telegram from Secretary Hughes to Ambassador Herrick, dated March 5, 1923, quoted in part in 1 Hackworth, Digest of International Law (1940) p. 146; Cf. De Lima v. Bidwell, 1901, 182 U.S. 1, 194, 21 S.Ct. 743, 45 L.Ed. 1041, citing Fleming v. Page, 1850, 9 How. 603, 13 L.Ed. 276;

Mr. Justice Hunt, concurring in City of New Orleans v. Steamship Co., 1874, 20 Wall. 387, 396, 399, 22 L.Ed. 354.

11. Cf. United States v. Rice, 1819, 4 Wheat. 246, 254, 4 L.Ed. 562.

12. See 1 Hackworth, Digest of International Law, 156–57 (1940); Cf. Neely v. Henkel (No. 1), 1901, 180 U.S. 109, 21 S.Ct. 302, 45 L.Ed. 448.

13. In addition to the letters cited in note 7, supra, appellant's counsel introduced a letter dated (apparently) May 5, 1949, from the Executive Secretary of the Office of the Secretary of Defense, stating in part: "Whereas Japan is occupied and controlled by the Allies, Okinawa is governed solely by the United States."

14. United States v. Curtiss-Wright Export Corp., 1936, 299 U.S. 304, 317, 57 S.Ct. 216, 81 L.Ed. 255.

15. Cf. Thorington v. Smith, 1868, 8 Wall.

However, the traditional "de jure sovereignty" has not passed to the United States. The conqueror does not acquire the full rights of sovereignty merely by occupying and governing the conquered territory without a formal act of annexation or at least an expression of intention to retain the conquered territory permanently.[16] It does not necessarily follow, therefore, that Okinawa is not a "foreign country" within the meaning of the Tort Claims Act. So long as the ultimate disposition of that island remains uncertain, it offers a persuasive illustration of the observation that "the very concept of 'sovereignty' is in a state of more or less solution these days."[17]

In short, the traditional test of sovereignty, when applied to the status of Okinawa, admits of no conclusive answer. While the traditional test furnishes a useful tool of construction in the usual case it cannot control the interpretation of § 2680(k) in the unusual case. Whether the term "foreign country" in the Tort Claims Act includes Okinawa must be decided in the way that accords more clearly with the central purpose of the Act.

2. The Laws of a Foreign Power.

The Federal Tort Claims Act was the product of an effort to reform the cumbersome private bill procedure which has encumbered congressional activities in the past. Despite the desirability of relieving Congress as far as possible of the responsibility for compensating private persons for damages caused by governmental activities, wherever the damages might occur, Congress explicitly excluded from the coverage of the Act claims "arising in a foreign country." The Supreme Court, after studying the congressional hearings and reports, has concluded that the purpose of this exception was to avoid subjecting "the United States to liabilities depending upon the laws of a foreign power."[18] Since liability under the Act is to be determined under the law of the place where the tort occurs, 28 U.S.C.A. § 1346(b), the exception of § 2680(k) was phrased in terms of the place where the claim arises. To decide whether Okinawa is a "foreign country," as the term is used in the statute, it is necessary to determine whether the

---

1, 19 L.Ed. 361; Cross v. Harrison, 16 How. 164, 189, 14 L.Ed. 889; Fleming v. Page, 1850, 9 How. 603, 614, 13 L. Ed. 276; United States v. Rice, 1819, 4 Wheat. 246, 254, 4 L.Ed. 562; 1 Hackworth, Digest of International Law 128 (1940); 1 Moore, International Law Digest 14; 1 Foulke, International Law § 57 (1920); Colby, Occupation under the Laws of War, 26 Col.L.Rev. 146, 158 (1926).

Since "de facto sovereignty," as the term is used here, arises out of the bare power of the occupying authority, the possible interest of the other Allied Powers in the government of Okinawa does not affect this conclusion.

16. See 1 Hyde, International Law § 106 (1922); 2 id. § 907; 1 Hackworth, Digest of International Law 427 (1940); Rules of Land Warfare 273, 275, Basic Field Manual (FM 27–10, 1940) 73–74, quoted in part in 6 Hackworth, Digest of International Law, pp. 385 and 389 (1943). Cf. 2 Garner, International Law and the World War 77 (1920); Ochoa v. Hernandez, 1913, 230 U.S. 139, 154, 33 S.Ct. 1033, 57 L.Ed. 1427. But, cf. United States v. Rice, 1819, 4 Wheat. 246, 254, 4 L.Ed. 562.

17. Mr. Justice Frankfurter, concurring in United States v. Spelar, 1949, 338 U.S. 217, 222, 224, 70 S.Ct. 10, 13, 94 L.Ed. 3. See 1 Foulke, International Law 69, n. 11 (1920); 1 Oppenheim, International Law 101–08 (1905); 1 Hackworth, Digest of International Law § 11 (1940); Aufricht, On Relative Sovereignty, 30 Cornell L.Q. 137 (1944); Colby, op. cit. supra, note 14, p. 155.

18. United States v. Spelar, 1949, 338 U. S. 217, 221, 70 S.Ct. 10, 12, 94 L.Ed. 3. In an article entitled Suits on Tort Claims against the United States, 1948, 7 F.R.D. 689, 695, Judge Hulen, without citing authority, has suggested that this exception was provided "probably because of the difficulty of obtaining evidence and necessity of providing rules of law to govern such liability." These points, if they were to be given weight despite the Spelar opinion, would not be very helpful in deciding whether Okinawa should be treated like Guam or like leased property in Newfoundland, at

law of Okinawa, which controls this claim, is the law "of a foreign power."

Prior to World War II, the law of Okinawa was Japanese law, administered and promulgated by the Japanese sovereign. Regardless of invasion, occupation,[19] or cession,[20] that law continues in force until it is changed.[21] The parties have failed to show any change and it must be presumed that the original Japanese law is still in effect.

However, Okinawa law is not the law "of a foreign power" in the sense that Newfoundland law is the law of another nation. The law of Okinawa cannot now be modified in any way by any government but the United States.[22] By the law of nations, it may be said that the United States has the right—and certainly the United States has the power—to abrogate all the existing tort law of Okinawa and substitute an entirely new tort law.[23] Indeed, the argument might be advanced that the law of Okinawa at the time of conquest owes its continued existence to the will of the United States, which has impliedly adopted that law.[24] In this view the law of Okinawa is not the law "of a foreign power," but the law of the United States; the congressional objection to subjecting the United States to unforeseeable liability based on the laws of other sovereigns, over which the United States has no control, would be inapplicable.

The power of the belligerent occupant is not relevant in this proceeding, however, if the rights and duties are clear. Assuming that the United States once had an unlimited right to revise the tort law of occupied countries, that right was abandoned with the Hague Convention of 1907, to which the United States was a signatory. Article 43, as translated in the United States statutes-at-large, provides:

"The authority of the legitimate power having in fact passed into the hands of the occupant, the latter shall take all

---

least if the burden of proving the applicable law falls on the plaintiff. See United States v. Spelar, 1949, 338 U.S. 217, 218, note 3, 70 S.Ct. 10.

19. Cf. Philippine Sugar Estates Development Co. v. United States, 1904, 39 Ct. Cl. 225, 247, quoted in part in 1 Hackworth, Digest of International Law (1940), p. 156; Colby, op. cit. supra, note 14, p. 151.

20. Panama Railroad Co. v. Bosse, 1919, 249 U.S. 41, 44, 39 S.Ct. 211, 63 L.Ed. 466; American Insurance Co. v. Canter, 1828, 1 Pet. 511, 542, 7 L.Ed. 242.

21. Vilas v. Manila, 1911, 220 U.S. 345, 357, 31 S.Ct. 416, 55 L.Ed. 491; Ortega v. Lara, 1906, 202 U.S. 339, 342, 26 S. Ct. 707, 50 L.Ed. 1055; Mitchel v. United States, 1835, 9 Pet. 711, 734, 9 L. Ed. 283; 1 Hyde, International Law § 122 (1922); 1 Hackworth, Digest of International Law, § 79 (1940).

22. See the Order of the Supreme Commander quoted at note 3, supra; United States v. Rice, 1819, 4 Wheat. 246, 254, 4 L.Ed. 562; City of New Orleans v. Steamship Co., 1874, 20 Wall. 387, 393–394, 22 L.Ed. 354; Mr. Justice Hunt,

concurring, 20 Wall. at page 397, quoting Halleck on International Law; 2 Hyde, International Law § 690 (1922); Cf. 6 Hackworth, Digest of International Law, 398 (1943).

23. Dooley v. United States, 1901, 182 U. S. 222, 230–231, 21 S.Ct. 762, 45 L.Ed. 1074, quoting Halleck on International Law; General Order No. 101, War Department, Adjutant General's Office, July 18, 1898, quoted in Ochoa v. Hernandez, 1913, 230 U.S. 139, 155, note 1, 33 S. Ct. 1033, 57 L.Ed. 1427. Cf. 26 Ops. Att'y Gen. 113, 118 (1907); Opinion of Legal Adviser of Department of State, May 7, 1936, quoted in part in 1 Hackworth, Digest of International Law (1940), p. 156; Colby, Occupation under the Laws of War, 25 Col.L.Rev. 904, 916 (1925).

24. Cf. 26 Ops. Att'y Gen. 113, 118 (1907); Shapleigh v. Mier, 5 Cir., 1936, 83 F.2d 673, 676; Cross v. Harrison, 16 How. 164, 193, 14 L.Ed. 889; Apparently a military proclamation formally adopted the existing civil law of Germany, except as modified by the occupation authorities. Fahy, Legal Problems of German Occupation, 47 Mich.

the measures in his power to restore, and ensure, as far as possible, public order and safety, while respecting, unless absolutely prevented, the laws in force in the country." [25]

In signing this treaty the United States has undertaken a duty, in cases to which the Hague Convention is applicable, to maintain the tort law of the occupied country.[26] It appears to be generally conceded that this Article was originally applicable to the occupation of Okinawa by the United States.[27] Despite the fact that hostilities have long since ceased, that occupation cannot be regarded as anything but a "belligerent occupation," within the scope of Article 43, until the terms of

peace have been finally settled by treaty, proclamation, or otherwise.[28]

But if we assume, as has been ably argued, that Article 43 did not in terms restrict the legislative authority of the United States Military Government in Okinawa in 1948, that article merely expresses "the modern usage of nations, which has become law * * * that sense of justice and of right which is acknowledged and felt by the whole civilized world." [29] At least until the occupant has determined upon the ultimate disposition of the occupied territory, the occupant has the right to legislate only in the interest of the safety of the occupying power or in the interest of the wel-

---

L.Rev. 11, 14, citing U.S.M.G. Proclamation 2, Sept. 19, 1945, Military Gazette, Issue A, p. 2 (1946). The parties to this case have not referred to any comparable proclamation concerning Okinawa.

25. 36 Stat. 2277, 2306; 2 Malloy, Treaties 1910, 2269, 2288. The French text, described by Schwenk as "authoritative," is: "L'autorité du pouvoir légal ayant passé de fait entre les mains de l'occupant, celui-ci prendra toutes les mesures qui dépendent de lui en vue de rétabl'r et d'assurer, autant qu'ilest possible, l'ordre et la vie publics en respectant, sauf empêchement absolu, les lois en vigueur dans le pays." The words "public order and safety," in the "semi-official" translation, have always been inaccurate, for the French appears to contemplate restoring all the aspects of the daily civil life of the occupied country, including presumably the duties imposed by the local law of torts. See Schwenk, Legislative Power of the Military Occupant under Article 43, Hague Regulations, 54 Yale L.J. 393, n. 1.

26. See Schwenk, op. cit. supra, note 24, pp. 399–402; 2 Hyde, International Law § 690 (1922); 2 Oppenheim, International Law § 169 (1906); 6 Hackworth, Digest of International Law § 587 (1943); 2 Garner, International Law and the World War 77, 85, (1920); Colby, Occupation under the Laws of War, 26 Col.L.Rev. 146, 151 (1926).

Cf. Rules of Land Warfare 285–88, Basic Field Manual (FM 27–10, 1940), discussed in the foregoing treatises.

27. Schwenk, writing in 1945, seems to

assume that Article 43 applies generally to belligerent occupations arising out of military operations in World War II. See 54 Yale L.J., pp. 407–08. Both Fahy and Rheinstein appear to assume that Article 43 governed the United States occupation of Germany at least until the unconditional surrender of the German forces. Fahy, Legal Problems of German Occupation, 47 Mich.L.Rev. 11; Rheinstein, The Legal Status of Occupied Germany, 47 Mich.L.Rev. 23, 27 (1948).

28. American Insurance Co. v. Canter, 1828, 1 Pet. 511, 542, 7 L.Ed. 242; Rheinstein, The Legal Status of Occupied Germany, 47 Mich.L.Rev. 23, 27 (1948); Colby, Occupation Under the Laws of War, 25 Col.L.Rev. 904, 905, 910 et seq.; 2 Hyde, International Law § 689 (1922), relying upon Rule 294 of the Rules of Land Warfare; Cf. id. at § 904 et seq.; 2 Oppenheim, International Law § 231 (1906); 6 Hackworth, Digest of International Law § 590 (1943).

Contra: Fahy, Legal Problems of German Occupation, 47 Mich.L.Rev. 11, 13 (1948).

See United States v. Huckabee, 1872, 16 Wall. 414, 434–435, 21 L.Ed. 457.

29. United States v. Percheman, 1833, 7 Pet. 51, 86–87, 8 L.Ed. 604. Cf. Opinion dated March 17, 1947, printed in 7 Selected Opinions of the Office of Military Government for Germany (U.S.) 115, 122; Stein, Application of the Law of the Absent Sovereign in Territory under Belligerent Occupation: The Schio Massacre, 1948, 46 Mich.L.Rev. 341; Rheinstein, loc. cit. supra, note 27.

fare of the inhabitants of the occupied territory; the occupant lacks authority to legislate at will, in disregard of the spirit and traditions of the occupied territory. For example, suppose that the pre-war tort law of Okinawa was based on a doctrine of "strict" liability without fault, and that the United States Military Government, fearing excessive liability under the Federal Tort Claims Act, attempted to abrogate that principle and substitute a doctrine of liability based on fault. Such a change, in disregard of the legitimte interests of the inhabitants, would violate the "dictates of the public conscience," [30] as well as the spirit, if not the letter, of Article 43.

It follows that the United States Military Government was not free to alter the tort law of Okinawa at will, but was bound to maintain the pre-existing "foreign" law. Since Congress was unwilling to subject the United States to liability based on that sort of law, the action was properly dismissed.

Judgment affirmed.

On Rehearing

The petition for rehearing is denied.

POPE, Circuit Judge.

I concur in the action of the Court in denying the petition for rehearing. The petition for rehearing calls to our attention the necessity of a re-examination of our former conclusion as to the applicability of Article 43 of the Hague Convention of 1907 upon which our decision of June 11, 1951, was predicated. The sources of information mentioned in the petition would indicate that in the Ryukyu Islands, as well as in Germany and in Japan, the United States Military Government, with the approval of the State Department, has promulgated regulations relating to traffic and operation of motor and other vehicles. Thus, departments of the Government, whose judgment we are not authorized to review, have taken a position with respect to Article 43 contrary to that suggested in our first opinion.

The majority of the Court have now proposed to amend the opinion to eliminate the reliance upon Article 43 and to substitute other language, and upon this amendment of the opinion to deny the petition for rehearing. I cannot bring myself to believe that the opinion in the amended form establishes a sound reason for the conclusion reached.

The case presents, I think, much more difficulty than did United States v. Spelar, 338 U.S. 217, 70 S.Ct. 10, 11, 94 L.Ed. 3. There the court was able to say: "Sufficient basis for our conclusion lies in the express words of the statute." The court proceeded to conclude that the accident on the Newfoundland airfield was one "arising in a foreign country", because the territory there was clearly subject to the sovereignty of another nation.

It was pointed out in our original opinion that as concerns Okinawa, this "test of sovereignty" furnishes no solution here. The court therefore proceeded to consider some of the other things said in the Spelar case where the court, after consideration of some of the legislative history of the Federal Tort Claims Act came to the conclusion that the exception here applied was inserted in order to avoid subjecting "the United States to liabilities dependent upon the laws of a foreign power." The court then proceeded to test the application of the Tort Claims Act by this summarization of the Congressional motive which the Supreme Court evolved from the legislative history.

---

30. Foreseeing the possibility that the Hague Regulations might be narrowly construed in particular cases, the contracting parties provided in the preamble to the Regulations: "Until a more complete code of the laws of war has been issued, the High Contracting Parties deem it expedient to declare that, in cases not included in the Regulations adopted by them, the **inhabitants** and the **belligerents** **remain under the protection** and the rule of the principles **of the law of nations** as they result from the usages established among civilized peoples, from the laws of humanity, and the dictates of the public conscience." 36 Stat. 2279–80, 2 Malloy, Treaties 1910, p. 2272. [Emphasis added]

I feel that the application of this test has led the court into unnecessary difficulties. What we are doing is not applying the precise language of the Act, but rather a summarization of the legislative history. I have in mind all that Mr. Justice Jackson said in his concurring opinion in Schwegmann Bros. v. Calvert Distillers Corp., 1951, 341 U.S. 384, 71 S.Ct. 745, 751, that "Resort to legislative history is only justified where the face of the Act is inescapably ambiguous * * *."

I am of the opinion that the conclusion at which we have arrived is the only possible one here for the simple reason that I think it is impossible to conclude that Okinawa was anything other than a "foreign country" within the meaning of the exception here involved. Plainly, the term "foreign country" is not self-defining, and it is not as definite as a description of weights and measures. It does not mean the same thing today that it meant in generations past, but I think that any person charged with the specific question here involved cannot arrive at any conclusion other than that Okinawa must be held to be within the meaning of the words "foreign country" as used in the Tort Claims Act.

In arriving at that conclusion, it is not easy to call to mind any pat test. It seems to me that arriving at this conclusion is merely a matter of common sense. I am impressed by what Judge Yankwich said in Hichino Uyeno v. Acheson, D.C., 96 F. Supp. 510, 515, as follows: " * * * it is obvious that the words 'foreign state' are not words of art. In using them, the Congress did not have in mind the fine distinctions as to sovereignty of occupied and unoccupied countries which authorities on international law may have formulated. They used the word in the sense of 'otherness'. When the Congress speaks of 'foreign state', it means a country which is not the United States or its possession or colony,—an alien country,—other than our own. bearing in mind that the average American, when he speaks of a 'foreigner' means an alien, non-American. * * * So here, the interpretation called for is that of common speech and not that derived from abstract speculation on sovereignty as affected by foreign military occupation."

Since I assume that Congress was using the words here involved as those "of common speech", and that so considered the Island of Okinawa would come within them, I think that this action cannot be maintained for the simple reason that it is excluded by the express terms of the Act.

United States v. Ushi Shiroma
123 F. Supp. 145 (D. Hawaii, 1954)

McLAUGHLIN, Chief Judge.

As in this criminal case it became necessary to decide whether, under the Treaty of Peace with Japan, Okinawa, Ryukyu Islands, is an area in the Pacific to which our nation's sovereignty has been extended, the Findings and Conclusions orally made on July 27, 1954, are here recorded.

On May 6, 1954, an information was filed against the defendant, wherein he was charged with violating 8 U.S.C.A. § 1306(b), a misdemeanor. The information alleged that the defendant was an alien and that he failed "to notify the Attorney General in writing of his current address and furnish such additional information as is by regulations required by the Attorney General" within thirty days following January 1, 1954, See 8 U.S.C.A. § 1305. To this charge, the defendant pleaded not guilty on June 3, 1954.

This case was tried jury-waived. Following the hearing of the evidence, argument was deferred until after briefs were filed, and on July 27, 1954, the Court pronounced the defendant guilty as charged.

Findings of Fact.

Under Rule 23(c) of the Federal Rules of Criminal Procedure, 18 U.S.C.A., the Court finds the facts specially as follows:

1. The defendant was born at Aza Onaga, Nishihara Mura, Nakagami Gun, Okinawa, Ryukyu Islands, on August 14, 1897.

2. His father and mother were Okinawans, born in Okinawa.

3. He came to the Territory of Hawaii on January 9, 1913, and has been a legal resident of the Territory since that date.

4. Since his entry in 1913, he has never been naturalized as a citizen of the United States.

5. In 1940, he registered as an alien as required by the Alien Registration Act 1940, 54 Stat. 670.

6. On January 1, 1954, he resided in the County of Honolulu, Territory of Hawaii. Such residence continued to June 28, 1954, the date of trial.

7. He failed to notify the Attorney General in writing of his current address and furnish such additional information as is by regulations required by the Attorney General within thirty days following January 1, 1954.

Conclusions of Law.

From the above findings of fact, the Court concludes as follows:

1. The Court has jurisdiction in this case.

2. The defendant was an alien on January 1, 1954. Consequently, he was required by 8 U.S.C.A. § 1305 to notify the Attorney General in writing of his current address within thirty days following January 1, 1954.

3. Having failed to do so, he is guilty as charged in the information of violating 8 U.S.C.A. § 1306(b).

Opinion.

A novel defense interjected at trial raised the legal question of whether the defendant was an alien in January 1954, the time of the alleged offense.

The defendant ingeniously argued that, because of events occurring subsequent to World War II, Okinawa became a possession of the United States. Thus, being a native of Okinawa, although residing in Hawaii, the defendant became a national of the United States. Consequently, not being an alien, he was legally incapable of committing the offense charged in the information.

Initially, the definitions found in the Immigration and Nationality Act of 1952, 8 U.S.C.A. § 1101 et seq., are helpful. Section 1101(a)(3) provides:

"The term 'alien' means any person not a citizen or national of the United States."

The term "national of the United States" is defined in Section 1101(a) (22) as follows:

"The term 'national of the United States' means (A) a citizen of the United States, or (B) a person who, though not a citizen of the United States, owes permanent allegiance to the United States."

Although the defendant admits that he is not a citizen of the United States, the question remains whether he is a national of the United States. In other words, does the defendant owe permanent allegiance to the United States?

Permanent allegiance is a correlative of the concept of sovereignty. Whether the defendant owes permanent allegiance to the United States depends on whether American sovereignty extends over Okinawa.

Sovereignty may be defined broadly as the "supreme will." See United States

v. Curtiss-Wright Export Corp., 1936, 299 U.S. 304, 317, 57 S.Ct. 216, 81 L.Ed. 255; Cobb v. United States, 9 Cir., 1951, 191 F.2d 604, 608, certiorari denied, 1952, 342 U.S. 913, 72 S.Ct. 360, 96 L. Ed. 683. This case, indeed, lends support to the statement that the "concept of 'sovereignty' is in a state of more or less solution these days." United States v. Spelar, 1949, 338 U.S. 217, 224, 70 S.Ct. 10, 13, 94 L.Ed. 3. Recently, the Ninth Circuit endorsed this observation in Cobb v. United States, supra, 191 F.2d at page 608. Be that as it may, sovereignty *is*, and this justiciable controversy requires a judicial determination.

Okinawa is an island in the Ryukyu Archipelago. It can be judicially noticed that, prior to World War II, Japan had sovereignty over the Ryukyus. During World War II, the United States conquered and occupied Okinawa. Such occupation continued and was effective at the time the Treaty of Peace with Japan was signed on September 8, 1951. U.S.Code Cong. & Adm. Service, 1951, pp. 2730–2748. The Treaty of Peace was subsequently ratified by the United States Senate on March 20, 1952. 98 Cong.Rec. 2594.

Prior to the signing of the Treaty of Peace, the courts deemed Okinawa a "foreign country" within the meaning of the Federal Tort Claims Act, 28 U.S.C. §§ 1346(b), 2671–2680. See Cobb v. United States, supra; Brewer v. United States, D.C.N.D.Cal.1948, 79 F. Supp. 405. In the Cobb case, the court stated, 191 F.2d at page 608, as follows:

"The United States has * * * acquired, and still retains, what may be termed a 'de facto sovereignty' [over Okinawa].

"However, the traditional 'de jure sovereignty' has not passed to the United States. The conqueror does not acquire the full rights of sovereignty merely by occupying and governing the conquered territory without a formal act of annex-

ation or at least an expression of intention to retain the conquered territory permanently."

The question then is whether the United States acquired the traditional "de jure sovereignty" over Okinawa under the Treaty of Peace. Our concern is solely with "de jure sovereignty," because only this time-tested yardstick of international law should be applied in determining the status of a geographical area and its inhabitants. In other words, permanent allegiance is owed only to a "de jure sovereign."

The pertinent part of the Treaty of Peace is Article 3, which reads as follows:

"Japan will concur in any proposal of the United States to the United Nations to place under its trusteeship system, with the United States as the sole administering authority, Nansei Shoto south of 29° north latitude (including the Ryukyu Islands and the Daito Islands), Nampo Shoto south of Sofu Gan (including the Bonin Islands, Rosario Island and the Volcano Islands) and Parece Vela and Marcus Island. Pending the making of such a proposal and affirmative action thereon, the United States will have the right to exercise all and any powers of administration, legislation and jurisdiction over the territory and inhabitants of these islands, including their territorial waters."

The defendant baldly contends that under Article 3 the United States acquired sovereignty over Okinawa, Ryukyu Islands. To this, the Court cannot subscribe.

Sovereignty over a territory may be transferred by an agreement of cession. See 1 Hackworth, Digest of International Law 421 (1940). Here neither in Article 3 nor in any other article of the Treaty of Peace does Japan *cede* Okinawa to the United States. In

Article 2, Japan formally "renounces all right, title and claim" to certain specified territories, including Korea, Formosa and the Kurile Islands. However, there is no such renunciation as to the territories named in Article 3.

On September 5, 1951, John Foster Dulles, who as a consultant to the Secretary of State was instrumental in negotiating the treaty, made a speech at the Conference for the Conclusion and Signature of the Peace Treaty with Japan. See 25 Dept. State Bulletin 452–9 (1951). At that time, Mr. Dulles in explaining the principal provisions of the treaty made the following statement:

"Article 3 deals with the Ryukyus and other islands to the south and southeast of Japan. These, since the surrender, have been under the sole administration of the United States.

"Several of the Allied Powers urged that the treaty should require Japan to renounce its sovereignty over these islands in favor of United States sovereignty. Others suggested that these islands should be restored completely to Japan.

"In the face of this division of Allied opinion, the United States felt that the best formula would be to permit Japan to retain *residual sovereignty*, while making it possible for these islands to be brought into the U.N. trusteeship system, with the United States as administering authority." (Emphasis added.) Id. at p. 455.

The reasonable construction of treaty terms by the State Department, acquiesced in by the other signatory powers, is entitled to great weight. United States v. Reid, 9 Cir., 1934, 73 F.2d 153, 156, certiorari denied, 1936, 299 U.S. 544, 57 S.Ct. 44, 81 L.Ed. 400. Thus Mr. Dulles' construction of Article 3, as opposed to defendant's contentions, is very persuasive.

Furthermore, to the Government's reply brief is attached a copy of a letter dated May 14, 1952, addressed to a Mr. Overton from the Legal Adviser of the Department of State.

The letter states in part as follows:

"1. A legal opinion is requested on the request of the Japanese Vice Minister for Foreign Affairs dated 10 December 1951, that the United States confirm that the 'Southern Islands' (the Ryukyus and the Bonins) remain under the sovereignty of Japan and that their inhabitants remain Japanese nationals.

*   *   *   *   *   *

"6. It is concluded that sovereignty over the Ryukyu and Bonin Islands remains in Japan, and that the inhabitants thereof are Japanese nationals."

"Residual sovereignty" referred to by Mr. Dulles is a concept difficult to define. The defendant analogizes "residual sovereignty" to a "future interest" and conceives it to mean that sovereignty is to arise *in futuro*. Therefore, he argues, under Article 3, "present sovereignty," the antithesis of "residual sovereignty," is in the United States, making him a "national." However, under the law of property, a holder of a "future interest" presently has a bundle of rights, privileges and duties, although the right of possession or enjoyment is postponed until the future. See 1 Simes, Law of Future Interest 2–3 (1936). Moreover, the importation of the niceties from the law of property into the field of international law confuses rather than aids in resolving the instant problem. See Justice Frankfurter's comments concerning the application of the "unwitty diversities of the law of property" in estate tax cases in Helvering v. Hallock, 1940, 309 U.S. 106, 118, 60 S.Ct. 444, 450, 84 L.Ed. 604.

The adjective "residual" means of the nature of something left as residue.

Thus the concept of "residual sovereignty" starts with the assumption that sovereignty is capable of division.

Under Article 3 of the Treaty of Peace, Japan which previously had full sovereignty over Okinawa transferred a part of that sovereignty, while retaining the residue. That portion of the sovereignty which gives the United States "the right to exercise all and any powers of administration, legislation and jurisdiction" under Article 3 may be labeled "de facto sovereignty." The residue or "residual sovereignty" retained by Japan is the traditional "de jure sovereignty." What the situation will be when the United States, under Article 3, makes a proposal to the United Nations to place Okinawa under its trusteeship system and affirmative action is taken thereon is not presently material.

Japan, and not the United States, having "de jure sovereignty" over Okinawa since the ratification of the Treaty of Peace, the defendant is not a national of the United States. Being therefore an alien, he was required to give the Attorney General written notice of his current address within a specified time as directed by 8 U.S.C.A. § 1305.

For the reasons stated above, the defendant was adjudged guilty of violating 8 U.S.C.A. § 1306(b). However, due to his age and the fact that he belatedly met the requirements of 8 U.S.C.A. § 1305 on April 28, 1954, imposition of sentence was suspended and the defendant granted probation, as reflected by the judgment.

Editor's Note.   The Treaty of Peace with Japan, September 8, 1951, cited by the Court, was concluded between the Allied Powers, including the U.S., and published in 3 UST 3169; TIAS #2490; 136 UNTS 45.)

Fifield v. Insurance Co.
47 Pa. St. 166 (1864)
For opinion see infra   VIII (1)

Price v. Poynter
64 Ky. 387 (1867)
For opinion see infra VIII (1)

Matter of Flaum
180 Misc. 1025 (Surr. Ct. Bronx County, 1943)
For opinion see infra IV (3)

Confederation Life Insurance Association v. Ugdale
151 So. 2d. 315 (Dist. Ct. of App., Fla., 1963)
reversed 164 So. 2d 1 (Sup. Ct. of Fla., 1964)
cert. denied 379 U.S. 915; 85 S. Ct. 263 (1964)

Before PEARSON, TILLMAN, C. J., and CARROLL and HORTON, JJ.

CARROLL, Judge.

This is an appeal by the defendant below from an adverse summary judgment. Ap-

pellant, a Canadian corporation, had issued a $20,000 life insurance policy to a resident of Havana, Cuba, in 1948. Some thirteen years later, when requested to pay the cash surrender value, the company offered to pay in Cuban pesos in Havana, but refused to pay in United States dollars. The insured sued the company in Dade County, Florida. Both parties moved for summary judgment. Plaintiff's motion was not augmented by evidentiary matter. Defendant's motion was supported by an affidavit of an expert to the effect that under Cuban law the defendant was authorized and required to pay the obligation in Cuban currency legal tender. Summary judgment was entered against the defendant for $13,825.52,[1] plus certain costs.

The determinative question in the trial court as on this appeal was whether the defendant's obligation under the insurance policy to pay the cash surrender value, at the time demanded, was to be measured in United States dollars, or, as the defendant contended, in Cuban pesos.[2]

The material facts as disclosed by the pleadings were not in dispute. The application for the life insurance policy was made by the appellee in 1948 in Cuba. Both in the application and in the policy which was written in Spanish it was stated that the policy would become effective upon payment of the first premium. The insured received delivery and paid the first premium in Havana. The policy provided that all payments were to be made in United States dollars, and the place for making payments under the policy was specified to be Havana, Cuba.

Subsequent to the issuance of the insurance policy, the Cuban government made certain laws and decrees which removed United States dollars as legal tender and substituted the Cuban currency of legal tender, for discharge of obligations payable in Cuba. Cuban Law No. 13 of December 23, 1948, provided that beginning one year after the Banco Nacional de Cuba should commence operations the currency of the United States of America would cease to be legal tender and to have debt redeeming force in Cuba. The Bank began its operations on April 27, 1950. The one year grace period previously imposed, which would have ended April 26, 1951, was extended to June 30, 1951, by an executive order, Decree No. 1384 of April 19, 1951. That decree provided that after the end of such extended grace period obligations could be discharged in Cuban currency regardless of contract provisions for payment in United States dollars. The provisions of Decree No. 1384 pertinent to that feature were as follows:

"Second. Beginning on the date on which the United States currency shall cease to be legal tender and have debt redeeming force in the territory of the Nation, all obligations contracted or payable in the national territory shall be expressed and settled in national currency pursuant to the provisions of Law No. 13, of December 23, 1948, subject to no exception other than those specified in Articles 96, 98 and 113 thereof.

"The debtors of obligations not included in said exceptions and the payment whereof in United States currency has been stipulated or agreed upon prior to the cessation of such legal tender status and such debt redeeming force, may settle such obligations at par through the delivery of national currency in the same amounts as those previously expressed in United States dollars."

Thereupon the company notified its policy holders in Cuba that under said Decree No. 1384 amounts theretofore provided to

---

1. That sum represented the amount of the cash surrender value under the policy, in dollars. It was stipulated that "The total cash surrender value of the policy as at March 15th, 1962 was 13,825.53." Plaintiff claimed and received judgment for United States dollars in that amount.

Defendant demanded the right to pay only in Cuban pesos.

2. This case does not present any question or problem of expropriation, such as concerned the court in Banco Nacional De Cuba v. Sabbatino, 2 Cir., 1962, 307 F. 2d 845.

be payable in United States dollars would be paid "in Cuban pesos one for one." The plaintiff made subsequent premium payments in Cuban pesos, and the company accepted them at par with the dollar as it was required to do by the Cuban law.

On October 2, 1959, the government of Cuba, under the rule of the dictatorship of Fidel Castro, enacted Law No. 568, which forbade the export of currency or transfer of funds abroad except for cases authorized by the Currency Stabilization Fund of Cuba. Unauthorized transfers were made felonies and it was provided that companies which are "presumed to have infringed the provisions of this law" may be "intervened." Thereafter, on February 23, 1961, the Cuban government enacted Law No. 930, which provided that the Banco Nacional de Cuba should regulate the issuance of currency, and such currency (Cuban pesos) was to be the only legal tender and was to be accepted in payment of any obligation payable in Cuba, and further provided that obligations which by agreement were made payable in another currency must be settled and paid in Cuban legal tender. The demand for payment of the cash surrender value was made October 11, 1961, after enactment of the laws referred to above. The complaint in this suit was filed November 3, 1961.

The appellant contends that the contract is controlled by Cuban law, and that payments thereunder may and in fact must be with Cuban pesos at par with the dollar.

Appellee argues that the contract is governed by the law of Florida, and that it would be against the public policy of the State of Florida to recognize and enforce in behalf of the defendant insurance company the right, as conferred by Cuban law, to discharge the obligation in pesos.

The policy did not specify the law of any particular jurisdiction to govern it. The contract was made in Cuba [3] and by its terms was to be performed there.[4] Neither Florida nor any jurisdiction other than Cuba had any significant contacts with regard to the obligations of the insurance policy so as to justify or require the contract to be governed by the law of Florida or such other jurisdiction.[5] Under the above conditions, it is held uniformly, and in Florida, that when the place of the making and the place of the performance are the same, the law of that jurisdiction determines and controls the validity, interpretation, and the rights and obligations under such a contract. Thomson v. Kyle, 39 Fla. 582, 23 So. 12, 16; Connor v. Elliott, 79 Fla. 513, 85 So. 164, cert. den. 254 U.S. 665, 41 S.Ct. 148, 65 L.Ed. 465 (1920); Brown v. Case, 80 Fla. 703, 86 So. 684; In the Matter of Magnus Harmonica Corporation, 3 Cir., 1959, 262 F.2d 515, 518, note 8; Annot., 50 A.L.R.2d 254, 257; 11 Am.Jur., Conflict of Laws, § 117, p. 401; Restatement, Conflict of Laws, §§ 346, 358.

In the instant case, the defendant asserted as a defense its right to pay in Cuban pesos at par and the obligation of the insured to accept payment in such form, as provided for in the insurance contract as modified by the laws and executive decrees of Cuba. The trial court rejected the defense. In so doing, the trial court erred and deprived appellant of due process of law.

As a sovereign nation, Cuba was entitled to establish a national currency

---

3. The policy provided that it became effective upon delivery and payment of the first premium. The first premium was paid in Cuba. That fixed Cuba as the place of the making of the contract. See Equitable Life Assur. Soc. of the United States of America v. McRee, 75 Fla. 257, 78 So. 22; Columbian National Life Insurance Co. v. Lanigan, 154 Fla. 760, 19 So.2d 67.

4. The policy expressly provided that payments thereunder were to be made in Havana, Cuba.

5. There is authority that does not regard as conclusive the place of making or performance but rather lays emphasis upon the law of the place that has the most significant contacts with the matter in dispute. See Auten v. Auten, 308 N.Y. 155, 124 N.E.2d 99, 50 A.L.R.2d 246 (1954).

and require its use in discharge of obligations governed by its law. Guaranty Trust Co. of New York v. Henwood, 307 U.S. 247, 59 S.Ct. 847, 83 L.Ed. 1266 (1939). And Cuba had the power to declare that which was legal tender for the discharge of such obligations. Legal tender cases, Knox v. Lee and Parker v. Davis, 79 U.S. (12 Wall.) 457, 20 L.Ed. 287 (1870); Juilliard v. Greenman, 110 U.S. 421, 448, 4 S.Ct. 122, 130, 28 L.Ed. 204, 214 (1884). That power could be exercised by Cuba in its sovereign capacity even though to do so altered the terms and impaired the obligations of such contracts theretofore made. Norman v. Baltimore & Ohio R. Co., 294 U.S. 240, 55 S.Ct. 407, 79 L.Ed. 885, 95 A.L.R. 1352 (1935); Guaranty Trust Co. of New York v. Henwood, supra. First, the Cuban government in furtherance of its fiscal policy was entitled to and did make laws relating to its currency and legal tender which effectively changed the contract from one payable in dollars to one payable in Cuban legal tender at one unit (peso) per dollar. Second, as a result thereof, under the terms of the insurance contract as so altered, the obligation of the defendant insurance company to pay the cash surrender value under the policy became an obligation to pay in Cuban legal tender.

With apology for unduly extending this opinion by extensive quotations from the Norman case, it is deemed sufficiently enlightening and authoritative on the problem presented in the instant case to quote the ending of the Norman opinion, in which the Supreme Court of United States repeated and summarized its holding that the national power to regulate currency and prescribe legal tender for payment of debts, in furtherance of policies respecting the monetary system, prevails over contrary contract clauses, which, otherwise, would operate to limit or deprive the sovereign of the exercise of that power. In this connection, in ending that important decision, the Supreme

Court said:

"We are not concerned with consequences, in the sense that consequences, however serious, may excuse an invasion of constitutional right. We are concerned with the constitutional power of the Congress over the monetary system of the country and its attempted frustration. Exercising that power, the Congress has undertaken to establish a uniform currency, and parity between kinds of currency, and to make that currency, dollar for dollar, legal tender for the payment of debts. In the light of abundant experience, the Congress was entitled to choose such a uniform monetary system, and to reject a dual system, with respect to all obligations within the range of the exercise of its constitutional authority. The contention that these gold clauses are valid contracts and cannot be struck down proceeds upon the assumption that private parties, and states and municipalities, may make and enforce contracts which may limit that authority. Dismissing that untenable assumption, the facts must be faced. We think that it is clearly shown that these clauses interfere with the exertion of the power granted to the Congress, and certainly it is not established that the Congress arbitrarily or capriciously decided that such an interference existed."

We adopt that reasoning and apply it to this contract. Thus the government of Cuba was entitled to provide by law as it did in 1948 and later for a uniform currency, eliminating United States dollars as legal tender in Cuba, specifying its own currency legal tender and first authorizing then later requiring that obligations payable there be discharged in Cuban pesos at par, one for one with the dollar. This contract between a Cuban national and a Canadian company was indigenous to Cuba. Its provision for payments in United States dollars was eliminated by the sovereign and there were substituted contract provisions that United States dollars would not be legal tender for discharge of the obligations under the policy and that such obligations were payable in Cuban pesos at par. The insured availed himself of that right by paying premiums in Cuban pesos. No lawful basis has been disclosed on which the trial court could reject unliked terms of the contract as modified by the Cuban currency laws or deny to the defendant its asserted right to meet its obligations under the policy in such pesos.

For the reasons stated, the judgment is affirmed in part and reversed in part, and the cause is remanded with directions to the circuit court to enter judgment for the plaintiff in United States dollars for such sum as shall represent and equal the value, based on the rate of exchange on the date of the original demand, of the 13,825.53 Cuban pesos with which under the contract as controlled by Cuban law the defendant insurance company was entitled and required to pay the demanded cash surrender value under the policy.

Affirmed in part, reversed in part, and remanded.

HORTON, Judge (concurring in part and dissenting in part).

Theye y Ajuria v. Pan American Life Insurance Co.
154 So. 2d. 450 (Ct. of App., La., 1963)
reversed 245 La. 755; 161 So. 2d. 70 (1964)
Cert. denied 377 U.S. 997; 84 S. Ct. 1922 (1964)

Before JOHNSON, EDWARDS and DALFERES, JJ.

A. WILMOT DALFERES, Judge ad hoc.

Plaintiff, a Cuban National born in Cuba, applied to Pan American Life Insurance Company for a policy of life insurance in Havana, Cuba, through the Havana representative of defendant insurance company in May of 1928. For several years prior to the issuing date of this policy, defendant was authorized to do business in the Republic of Cuba, after complying with Cuban statutory regulations pertaining to the insurance field.

Plaintiff's application was in due course referred to the Home Office of defendant in New Orleans, Louisiana. Upon approval of the application, the policy in regular form, written in the Spanish language, was forwarded to the Havana agent of defendant who, after having it countersigned by an agency of the Cuban government, delivered same to the plaintiff. The plaintiff paid to defendant fourteen annual installments on the policy and in the year 1942 selected, as one of the alternatives in the policy provisions, to have the policy converted to a paid-up policy.

A payment known as a "persistency bonus" became due under the policy in 1948.

In 1948, the Cuban government adopted Law No. 13, which provided that after 1951 United States currency might no longer be used in Cuba, and the Cuban peso would become the sole form of legal tender there. By the Monetary Law of Cuba of 1951, all contracts payable to or by Cuban Nationals were required to be paid in Cuban pesos only.

In November of 1948, in May of 1950, and in February of 1952, the plaintiff made loans against the policy in varied amounts and in each instance the proceeds of such loan in pesos were paid to plaintiff by a check drawn on the Havana, Cuba, office of the National City Bank of New York. Each of such loans to defendant company was repaid by plaintiff, who likewise made the payment in Cuban pesos. All the payments were made in Cuba to defendant's Cuban agent and deposited in a Cuban bank.

In January of 1959, the Castro government came into power after a revolution. The government of the United States recognized and maintained diplomatic relations with the Cuban government until about October 26, 1960.

From 1928, the date of the issuance of the policy in controversy, until some date subsequent to the date of the nationalization of respondent insurance company, plaintiff continued to live in Cuba as a Cuban National.

Subsequent to the nationalization of respondent's business, plaintiff left Cuba and is now a refugee in the United States. Upon his arrival in the United States, he appeared at the office of defendant's company in New Orleans and demanded the cash surrender value of the policy. Upon the refusal of defendant to pay the same, this action followed.

This matter was submitted to the Court for summary judgment on admissions, interrogatories, and stipulation.

The trial Court rendered judgment in favor of plaintiff and against defendant in the amount of SEVEN THOUSAND NINETY AND NO/100 ($7090.00) DOLLARS. From this judgment defendant has appealed.

It is elementary law that a sovereign government, having a definite interest in insurance contracts, can enact legislation for the protection of its citizens, controlling the insurance business within its bounds.[1] As the United States Supreme Court said in Osborn v. Ozlin, 310 U.S. 53, 60 S.Ct. 758, 84 L.Ed. 1074,

"The state may fix insurance rates, German Alliance Ins. Co. v. Lewis, 233 U.S. 389, 34 S.Ct. 612, 58 L.Ed. 1011, L.R.A.1915C, 1189; it may regulate the compensation of agents, O'Gorman & Young v. Hartford Ins. Co., 282 U.S. 251, 51 S.Ct. 130, 75 L.Ed. 324, 72 A. L.R. 1163; it may curtail drastically the area of free contract, National Union Fire Ins. Co. v. Wanberg, 260 U.S. 71, 43 S.Ct. 32, 67 L.Ed. 136. States have controlled the expenses of insurance companies, New York Insurance Law, Consolidated Laws of New York, c. 28, § 244, and Wisconsin Statutes, § 201.21; and see Report of Joint (Armstrong) Insurance Investigation Committee (N. Y.) pp. 403–418 (1906). They have also promoted insurance through savings banks; see Berman, the Massachusetts System of Savings Bank Life Insurance, Bulletin No. 615, U. S. Bureau of Labor Statistics, and New York Laws of 1938, c. 471. In the light of all these exertions of state power it does not seem possible to doubt that the state could, if it chose, go into the insurance business, just as it can operate warehouses, flour mills, and other business ventures, Green v. Frazier, 253 U.S. 233, 40 S.Ct. 499, 64 L.Ed. 878, or might take 'the whole business of banking under its control.' "

---

1. Buxton v. Mid-Western Insurance Co., D.C., 102 F.Supp. 500; Lewis v. Manufacturers Casualty Insurance Company, D.C., 107 F.Supp. 465; Boring et al. v. Louisiana State Insurance Company, 154 La. 549, 97 So. 856; Strauss v. New York Life Insurance Co., 204 La. 202, 15 So.2d 61.

Our learned brother, the trial Court, resolved the issues as follows:

"The Court is of the opinion that any laws or decrees of the Republic of Cuba passed subsequently to the date upon which the policy became a paid-up policy of insurance could have no effect upon the obligation which existed at that time.[2] Said obligation continued from that date to now to be an obligation under the laws of the State of Louisiana and subject to and governed only by said law, if the beneficiary or the insured under said policy presented himself in the State of Louisiana to enforce the obligations contained therein."

It must be remembered that plaintiff is a Cuban National. It is a well established principle of law, recognized by all appellate Court decisions, that a recognized Sovereign Nation can make laws binding upon its nationals within its bounds. Chief Justice Marshall, in The Antelope, 10 Wheat. 66, 6 L.Ed. 268, said:

"No principle of general law is more universally acknowledged than the perfect equality of Nations. Russia and Geneva have equal rights. It results from this equality that no one can rightfully impose a rule on another. Each legislates for itself, but its legislation can operate on itself alone * * *."

When Castro rose to power, his government was recognized by the United States of America. Diplomatic relations were maintained between the United States and Cuba, until October 26, 1960. Plaintiff did not leave Cuba until November 4, 1960. On September 29, 1959, following Castro's rise to power, Law 568 was promulgated. That law prohibited Corporations doing business in Cuba, from making payments, or even making any entries in their books which

would result in credit being made available to Cuban Nationals, except in Cuba, and without express authorization of the National Bank of Cuba. Violators of said law were subject to criminal penalties.

Further, on October 24, 1960, all of the affairs and assets of Pan American Life Insurance Company in Cuba were nationalized. The investments, properties and reserves of the said Company were taken over by the Cuban Government, which substituted itself as insurer and assumed all liabilities of the Company; in fact, the business of the Company was carried on through a government appointed administrator.

Certainly any Sovereign Nation can and has the power to change the situs of its National's contracts. Further, a nation can and does frequently impair the obligations of contract. Even our own country did this in the Gold Clause Cases, Norman v. Baltimore & O. R. Co., Nortz v. United States, Perry v. United States, 294 U.S. 240, 317, 330, 55 S.Ct. 407, 428, 432, 79 L.Ed. 885, 905, 912. We do have a provision in the United States Constitution preventing the States of the Union from enacting ex post facto law or laws impairing the obligation of contract. (See 10, U. S. Constitution). But it is within the Sovereign power of the United States Government to do these acts if in its National interests it sees fit to do so.

The Courts of this Country can take judicial notice of treaties made between the U. S. Government and foreign governments. United States v. Reynes, 9 Haw. 127, 50 U.S. 127, 13 L.Ed. 74; Lacroix Fils v. Sarrazin, 5 Cir., 15 F. 489. Further, our Courts will take judicial notice of the Acts of Congress and presidential proclamations. Williams v Windham, 3 La.App. 127; Powell-Myers Lumber Co. v. Tremont & Gulf Realty Co., 2 La.App. 164.

---

2. This policy became a paid-up policy in the year 1942, at the election of plaintiff.

With these legal propositions before us, the Court must recognize and give effect to the Bretton Woods Agreement signed by the United States, Cuba, and some ninety-five sovereign Nations in 1945. Each signatory to the Compact, which included an International Monetary Fund, bound itself to take steps to implement the principles of the international accord, as part of its domestic law. Our own Congress honored its commitment by enacting a statute to that effect. (22 U.S.C.A. § 286 et seq.).

Article VIII, Sec. 2(b) of the Agreement, among other things, provided as follows:

"Exchange contracts which involve the currency of any member and which are contrary to the exchange control regulations of that member * * * shall be unenforceable in the territories of any member."

By accepting and implementing the above, our Congress has undertaken to make the above principle, a part of our national law. On June 14, 1949, the International Monetary Fund, binding on all its members, including Cuba and the United States, issued the following interpretation of Art. VIII, Sec. 2(b):

"An obvious result of the foregoing undertaking is that if a party to an exchange contract referred to in Article VIII, Sec. 2(b) seeks to enforce such a contract, the tribunal of the member country before which the proceedings are brought, will not, on the ground that they are contrary to the public policy of the forum, refuse recognition of the exchange control regulations of the other member which are maintained or imposed consistently with the Fund Agreement. It also follows that such contracts will be treated as unenforceable notwithstanding that under private international law of the forum is not the law which governs the exchange contract or its performance * * *"

Cuban Law 568 of September 29, 1959,

required payments between plaintiff and defendant be made in Cuba, regardless of the language of the contract. Despite this, plaintiff attempts to defy the decrees and laws of Cuba, the sovereign to whom he owed allegiance to come into this country and collect his debt in the currency of another nation. This would nullify and frustrate his own sovereign's legislative will and powers.

Prior to the Bretton Woods Agreement, plaintiff's position might have been upheld. Our Courts have held it to be the public policy of the forum State to refuse to give effect to exchange control legislation of a foreign sovereign, where such was labelled by the forum as penal, punitive, confiscatory or violative of fundamental concepts of justice. In this connection, the Court calls attention to the cases and authorities cited therein of Menendez Rodriguez v. Pan American Life Insurance Co., 5 Cir., 311 F.2d 429 and Menandez v. Aetna Insurance Co., 5 Cir., 311 F.2d 437.

This Court believes, and so holds, that the Bretton Woods Agreement and our Acts of Congress (22 U.S.C.A. § 286 et seq.) supersede the principles enunciated in the above authorities, as to parties or nations who signed the agreement or treaty. It is now our national policy to deny enforcement, in the Court of this land, of contracts which would frustrate the exchange control regulations of another member of the agreement. Our Congress gave recognition to the will of the signatories to the agreement, declaring that the public policy of its members would be better served by a measure of collaboration among them designed to give effect to each other's exchange control regulations. The U. S. Supreme Court, in Kolovrat v. Oregon, 366 U.S. 187, 81 S.Ct. 922, 928, 6 L.Ed. 218, decided May 1, 1961, interpreted the Bretton Woods Agreement as follows:

"These treaties and agreements show that this Nation has adopted programs deemed desirable in bringing about, so far as can be done, stability and uniformity in the difficult field of world monetary controls and exchange. * * * Doubtless these agreements may fall short of that goal. But our National Government's powers have been exercised so far as deemed desirable and feasible toward that end, and the power to make policy with regard to such matters is a national one from the compulsion of both necessity and our Constitution."

We find that the Court below disregarded the above treaty accord between the United States and Cuba and our own Congressional enactments to implement this agreement. Our Courts should not and cannot enforce a contract which transcends the sovereign will of Cuba touching on monetary contracts involving its own nationals. Plaintiff demands should have been rejected.

It must also be remembered that this defendant complied with the laws of Cuba in the operation of its Cuban Agency by maintaining reserves in Cuba to insure the payment of its Cuban obligations, including this policy. When the Castro government nationalized the insurance business, it took over those reserves and any other assets of this defendant in Cuba and went into the insurance business, of which this policy was a part. If this judgment by the trial court is enforced against this defendant in Louisiana, it will amount to a payment of the obligation twice, for the reason that this defendant cannot now withdraw the amount of the judgment from its reserves and assets in Cuba which reserves were put up to insure payment of this and other policies in Cuba.

While it may be more advantageous for plaintiff to have sought relief in the Louisiana Courts and to have urged the application of Louisiana law to the terms of the contract as originally written, the selection of the forum does not dictate the application of the law of the forum; nor can the forum ignore the modifications of a contract by a sovereign government under its police powers and its domination over its citizens, especially when that sovereign government has been recognized by the Executive Department of the United States. There can be but one law applicable to this contract, and we hold that the present law of Cuba, which nationalized under Cuba's police powers the insurance business, including defendant's company, at a time when plaintiff was a resident and national of Cuba, is the applicable law.

The judgment of the District Court is reversed and plaintiff's suit is dismissed at his costs.

Reversed and rendered.

Editor's Note.   The Bretton Wood Agreements establishing the International Monetary Fund, December 27, 1945, cited by the Court, is published in 60 Stat. 1401; TIAS # 1501; 2 UNTS 39.

(b)   Recognition of States, Governments, Belligerency

United States v. Palmer
16 U.S. (3 Wheaton) 610 (1818)
For opnion see infra III (3) (b)

The Divina Pastora
17 U.S. (4 Wheaton) 52 (1819)

APPEAL from the Circuit Court of Massachusetts.

The petition or libel, in this cause, by the Consul
of his Catholic Majesty at Boston, alleges and pro-
pounds, 1. That there lately arrived at the port of
New Bedford, in this district, and is now lying in the
said port of N. B., a Spanish vessel, called the Espe-
ranza, otherwise called the Divina Pastora, having
on board a cargo, consisting of cocoa, cotton, indigo,
hides, and horns, of great value, to wit, of the value
of 10,000 dollars ; that the said vessel is navigated
by seven persons, who are all American citizens, as
he is informed, and believes ; and that there are no
other persons on board of said vessel, and none other
were on board when the said vessel arrived at said
port.   That the aforesaid persons say, that the said
vessel was bound on a voyage from Laguira to Cadiz in Spain, and that she was captured by a privateer, or armed vessel, sailing under a flag, which
they denominate, the flag of La Plata ; and that they
did intend to carry said vessel to some port in the
West Indies, but, afterwards, came into the port of
New Bedford.   2. That the said vessel and cargo
purport to have been consigned to Antonio Seris, a
merchant at Cadiz.   3. That the said Consul verily
believes, that the said vessel has been captured and

1819.

The Divina
Pastora.

brought into the aforesaid port, contrary to the law
of nations, and in violation of the rights of the said
Antonio Seris, and that the said Antonio is justly
and lawfully entitled to the possession of the said
vessel and her cargo : concluding with a prayer,
that the process of the Court may issue, directed to
the Marshal of this district, or his deputy, requiring
of them, respectively, to take the said vessel and
cargo into custody, to the end, that due inquiry may
be made into the facts pertaining to this case, and
that the property may be adjudged, decreed, and restored, according to the just rights of whomsoever
may be therein interested, and according to law and
the comity which the United States have always manifested towards foreign nations.

The plea and answer of "Don Daniel Utley, a
citizen of the free and independent United Provinces
of Rio de la Plata, &c., in behalf of himself and all
concerned, in the capture of the Spanish polacre brig
Divina Pastora and her cargo, to the libel and petition exhibited by Don Juan Stoughton, Consul of his
Catholic Majesty, &c.," sets forth, that the said Utley,
by protestation, and not confessing or acknowledging
any of the matters and things in the libellant's petition and libel contained, to be true, in such manner
and form as the same are therein and thereby alleged,
for plea to the said libel and petition, says, that
the United Provinces of Rio de la Plata in South
America, are free and independent states, and, as
such, have the power to levy war and make peace,
raise armies and navies, &c. And that the Supreme
Provisional Director of said Provinces, at the fort of
Buenos Ayres, on the 25th day of October, 1815,
commissioned a certain schooner, called the Mangoree, to cruize against the vessels and effects of the
kingdom of Spain, and the subjects thereof, excepting only the Spanish Americans who defend their
liberty, and authorized one James Barnes to act as
commander of said schooner, and to seize and capture the vessels and effects of European Spaniards,

and bring them within the government of the United
Provinces, for adjudication, according to the law of nations, Ferdinand VII., king of Spain, then being at
war with said provinces, and general reprisals having been granted by said provisional government
against the European subjects of the said king.
That said schooner Mangoree, bearing the flag of
the said independent Provinces, sailed on a cruise
from the harbour of Buenos Ayres, within the said
Provinces, on or about the first day of January, 1816,
by virtue of said commission. And having touched
at Port au Prince, in the island of Hispaniola, sailed
again on said cruise, and on the 31st of October,
1816, on the high seas, &c. captured the polacre brig
Divina Pastora, belonging to the said king, or to his
European subjects, on board of which brig said
Utley was put as prize-master. And the original
crew of said prize was taken out by the said Barnes,
&c., and put on board of said schooner Mangoree,
and a prize crew sent on board the Pastora. And
the said Barnes, &c., then appointed said Utley to
the command of the said prize, and delivered to him
a copy of his commission, &c., which the said Utley
now brings with him, and respectfully submits to the
inspection of this honourable Court. And thereupon, the said Utley proceeded to navigate the said
prize from the place where she was captured to Port-
au-Prince, in the island of Hispaniola, for the purpose of there procuring supplies and provisions, and
thence proceeding to the port of Buenos Ayres. The
plea then proceeds to state, that in the prosecution of
the voyage, the prize vessel was compelled, by stress
of weather, and want of provisions and water, to put
into the port of New Bedford ; and concludes with
alleging, that by the law of nations, and the comity
and respect due from one independent nation to another, it doth not pertain to this Court, nor is it within
its cognizance, at all to interfere, or hold plea respecting said brig or goods on board, so taken as
prize of war, and a prayer for restitution, with costs

and damages.

The replication of the Spanish Consul states, that inasmuch as the said Utley, in his plea, admits that the said vessel, and the cargo laden on board, were, on the 31st day of October, 1816, the property of a subject or subjects of his majesty Ferdinand VII., the said consul claims the same, as the property of such subject or subjects, the names of whom are to him, at present, unknown; excepting that he verily believes the same to be the lawful property of Antonio Seris, as he, in his petition, hath set forth: And avers, that the same ought to be restored and delivered up for the use of the Spanish owner or owners. The replication then proceeds to aver, that as the said vessel is stated in the plea to have been captured on the high seas by a certain armed vessel called the Mangoree, commanded by one James Barnes, which armed vessel is stated to have been commissioned under a certain authority called the United Provinces of Rio de La Plata in South America, the said capture and seizure, &c. were piratical, or tortious, and contrary to the lawful and well known rights of the faithful subjects of his said majesty, to whom the same belonged at the time of such capture, &c., and that no right of property thereby vested in the said Barnes or Utley, or any other person or persons who were navigating and sailing in the said armed vessel called the Mangoree: 1st. Because, at the time when the said pretended capture as prize of war was made, &c., the several provinces situate in South America, and near to the river called Rio de la Plata, were provinces and colonies of his said majesty Ferdinand VII., and now are provinces and colonies of his said majesty; and that the same had been, for a long course of years, provinces and colonies of the successive kings of Spain; and that all the people, persons, and inhabitants dwelling therein, were, on the 21st day of October, 1815, and for a long time before had been, and now are Spanish subjects, and did at the aforesaid times, and now do owe allegiance and fidelity to his said majesty. 2dly. Because the said subjects and persons, dwelling in the said provinces and colonies in South America, had not, on the 25th day of October, 1815, nor had any, or either of the said subjects and persons, then, or at any other time, any lawful right, power, or authority, to commission any vessel or vessels, or any person or persons whomsoever, to wage war against him, the said Ferdinand VII., nor against his subjects, or their persons, or property, by sea, or elsewhere; and that no person or persons whomsoever, could lawfully receive, and take from any person or persons in any of the said colonies or provinces, any commission, power, or authority, of right, to wage war, and make captures of any property on the high seas. 3dly. Because all captures made on the high seas, under the pretence of power or authority derived from, or in virtue of any such commission as set forth in said plea, is unlawful and piratical; and that all pretended captures and seizures, as prize of war, of property belonging to the subjects of his said majesty when made under such commissions as aforesaid, are cognizable by the Courts of nations at peace and in amity with his said majesty, which hold pleas of admiralty and maritime jurisdiction, and take cognizance of cases arising under the law of nations, whenever the property so captured is found within their respective jurisdictions. And as a further ground for the claim of restitution to the original Spanish owners, the replication recites the 6th, 9th, and 14th articles of the treaty of 1795, between the United States and Spain. And as a further ground for the claim, it alleges, that the papers, exhibited with the plea, and by which the capture is pretended to be justified, are false and colourable; that the prize crew did not speak the Spanish language, and were shipped at Port-au-Prince; that one of the crew stated in his affidavit that the flag of the privateer was obtained at that place; and that all of them stated, that the Divina Pastora, from the time of her capture, was ordered for, and bound to the same place, all the captured persons having been previously taken out of her, and put on board the privateer. And concludes with renewing the averments of the piratical and tortious capture, and praying that restitution of the property may be decreed to him, the Spanish consul, to be held for the right owners or owner thereof, who are subjects, or a subject of the king of Spain.

Upon these pleadings, further proceedings were had in the District Court, under which a decree was pronounced of restitution of the vessel and cargo to the libellant, for the benefit of the original Spanish owners. This decree was affirmed, *pro forma*, in the Circuit Court, and the cause was brought by appeal to this Court.

Mr. Chief Justice MARSHALL delivered the opinion of the Court. The decision at the last term, in the case of the United States v. Palmer,[c] establishes the principle that the government of the United States, having recognized the existence of a civil war between Spain and her colonies, but remaining neutral, the Courts of the Union are bound to consider as lawful, those acts which war authorizes, and which the new governments in South America may direct against their enemy. Unless the neutral rights of the United States, as ascertained by the law of nations, the acts of congress, and treaties with foreign powers, are violated by the cruizers sailing under commissions from those governments, captures by them are to be regarded by us as other captures, *jure belli*, are regarded; the legality of which cannot be determined in the courts of a neutral country. If, therefore, it appeared in this case, that the capture was made under a regular commission from the government established at Buenos Ayres, by a vessel which had not committed any violation of our neutrality, the captured property must be restored to the possession of the captors. But if, on the other hand, it was shown, that the capture was made in violation of our neutral rights and duties, restitution would be decreed to the original owners. But the pleadings in this case are too informal and defective to pronounce a final decree upon the merits. The proceedings in the admiralty must always contain at least a general allegation of such a nature as will apply to the case, as of prize, &c. The Court has always endeavoured to keep these proceedings within some kind of rule, though not requiring the same technical strictness as at common law. Here the pleadings present a case which may be consistent with the demand of the former owners for restitution, but which is tied up to such a state of facts as, if proved, will not authorize it; and will not admit the introduction of evidence varying from the facts alleged. The decree of the Circuit Court must, therefore, be reversed, and the cause remanded to that Court, with directions to permit the pleadings to be amended, and for farther proceedings.

1819.

The Divina Pastora.

Cause remanded.

Underhill v. Hernandez
168 U.S. 250; 18 S. Ct. 83 (1894)
For opinion see <u>infra</u> III (2) (b)

Oetjen v. Central Leather Co.
246 U.S. 297, 38 Sup. Ct. 309 (1918)

Mr. Justice Clarke delivered the opinion of the court,

These two cases involving the same question, were argued and will be decided together. They are suits in replevin and involve the title to two large consignments of hides, which the plaintiff in error claims to own as assignee of Martinez & Company, a partnership engaged in business in the city of Torreon, Mexico, but which the

defendant in error claims to own by purchase from the
Finnegan-Brown Company, a Texas corporation, which
it is alleged purchased the hides in Mexico from General
Francisco Villa, on January 3, 1914.

The cases were commenced in a Circuit Court of New
Jersey, in which judgments were rendered for the defendants, which were affirmed by the Court of Errors and
Appeals, and they are brought to this court on the theory,
that the claim of title to the hides by the defendant in
error is invalid because based upon a purchase from General Villa, who, it is urged, confiscated them contrary to
the provisions of the Hague Convention of 1907 respecting
the laws and customs of war on land; that the judgment
of the state court denied to the plaintiff in error this right
which he "set up and claimed" under the Hague Convention or treaty; and that this denial gives him the right of
review in this court.

A somewhat detailed description will be necessary of
the political conditions in Mexico prior to and at the
time of the seizure of the property in controversy by the
military authorities. It appears in the record, and is a
matter of general history, that on February 23, 1913,
Madero, President of the Republic of Mexico, was assas-
sinated; that immediately thereafter General Huerta
declared himself Provisional President of the Republic
and took the oath of office as such; that on the twenty-
sixth day of March following General Carranza, who was
then Governor of the State of Coahuila, inaugurated a
revolution against the claimed authority of Huerta and
in a "Manifesto addressed to the Mexican Nation" proclaimed the organization of a constitutional government
under "The Plan of Guadalupe," and that civil war was
at once entered upon between the followers and forces of
the two leaders. When General Carranza assumed the
leadership of what were called the Constitutionalist forces
he commissioned General Villa his representative, as
"Commander of the North," and assigned him to an independent command in that part of the country. Such
progress was made by the Carranza forces that in the
autumn of 1913 they were in military possession, as the
record shows, of approximately two-thirds of the area of
the entire country, with the exception of a few scattered
towns and cities, and after a battle lasting several days
the City of Torreon in the State of Coahuila was captured

by General Villa on October 1 of that year. Immediately after the capture of Torreon, Villa proposed levying a military contribution on the inhabitants, for the support of his army, and thereupon influential citizens, preferring to provide the required money by an assessment upon the community to having their property forcibly seized, called together a largely attended meeting and, after negotiations with General Villa as to the amount to be paid, an assessment was made on the men of property of the city, which was in large part promptly paid. Martinez, the owner from whom the plaintiff in error claims title to the property involved in this case, was a wealthy resident of Torreon and was a dealer in hides in a large way. Being an adherent of Huerta, when Torreon was captured Martinez fled the city and failed to pay the assessment imposed upon him, and it was to satisfy this assessment that, by order of General Villa, the hides in controversy were seized and on January 3, 1914, were sold in Mexico to the Finnegan-Brown Company. · They were paid for in Mexico, and were thereafter shipped into the United States and were replevied, as stated.

This court will take judicial notice of the fact that, since the transactions thus detailed and since the trial of this case in the lower courts, the Government of the United States recognized the Government of Carranza as the *de facto* government of the Republic of Mexico, on October 19, 1915, and as the *de jure* government on August 31, 1917. *Jones* v. *United States*, 137 U. S. 202; *Underhill* v. *Hernandez*, 168 U. S. 250.

On this state of fact the plaintiff in error argues that the "Regulations" annexed to the Hague Convention of 1907 "Respecting Laws and Customs of War on Land" constitute a treaty between the United States and Mexico; that these "Regulations" forbid such seizure and sale of property as we are considering in this case; and that, therefore, somewhat vaguely, no title passed by the sale made by General Villa and the property may be recovered by the Mexican owner or his assignees when found in this country.

It would, perhaps, be sufficient answer to this contention to say that the Hague Conventions are international in character, designed and adapted to regulate international warfare, and that they do not, in terms or in purpose, apply to a civil war. Were it otherwise, however, it might be effectively argued that the declaration relied upon that "private property cannot be confiscated" contained in Article 46 of the Regulations does not have the scope claimed for it, since Article 49 provides that "money contributions" . . . "for the needs of the army" may be levied upon occupied territory, and Article 52 provides that "Requisitions in kind and services shall not be demanded . . . except for the needs of the army of occupation," and that contributions in kind shall, as far as possible, be paid for in cash, and when not so paid for a receipt shall be given and payment of the amount due shall be made as soon as possible. And also for the reason that the "Convention" to which the "Regulations" are annexed, recognizing the incomplete character of the results arrived at, expressly provides that until a more complete code is agreed upon, cases not provided for in the "Regulations" shall be governed by the principles of the law of nations.

But, since claims similar to the one before us are being made in many cases in this and in other courts, we prefer to place our decision upon the application of three clearly settled principles of law to the facts of this case as we have stated them.

The conduct of the foreign relations of our Government is committed by the Constitution to the Executive and Legislative—"the political"—Departments of the Government, and the propriety of what may be done in the exercise of this political power is not subject to judicial inquiry or decision. *United States* v. *Palmer*, 3 Wheat. 610; *Foster* v. *Neilson*, 2 Pet. 253, 307, 309; *Garcia* v. *Lee*, 12 Pet. 511, 517, 520; *Williams* v. *Suffolk Ins. Co.*, 13 Pet. 415, 420; *In re Cooper*, 143 U. S. 472, 499. It has been specifically decided that "Who is the sovereign, *de jure* or *de facto*, of a territory is not a judicial, but is a political question, the determination of which by the legislative and executive departments of any government conclusively binds the judges, as well as all other officers, citizens and subjects of that government. This principle has always been upheld by this court, and has been affirmed under a great variety of circumstances." *Jones* v. *United States*, 137 U. S. 202, 212.

It is also the result of the interpretation by this court

of the principles of international law that when a government which originates in revolution or revolt is recognized by the political department of our government as the *de jure* government of the country in which it is established, such recognition is retroactive in effect and validates all the actions and conduct of the government so recognized from the commencement of its existence. *Williams* v. *Bruffy*, 96 U. S. 176, 186; *Underhill* v. *Hernandez*, 168 U. S. 250, 253. See *s. c.* 65 Fed. Rep. 577.

To these principles we must add that: "Every sovereign State is bound to respect the independence of every other sovereign State, and the courts of one country will not sit in judgment on the acts of the government of another done within its own territory. Redress of grievances by reason of such acts must be obtained through the means open to be availed of by sovereign powers as between themselves." *Underhill* v. *Hernandez*, 168 U. S. 250, 253; *American Banana Co.* v. *United Fruit Co.*, 213 U. S. 347.

Applying these principles of law to the case at bar, we have a duly commissioned military commander of what must be accepted as the legitimate government of Mexico, in the progress of a revolution, and when conducting active independent operations, seizing and selling in Mexico, as a military contribution, the property in controversy, at the time owned and in the possession of a citizen of Mexico, the assignor of the plaintiff in error. Plainly this was the action, in Mexico, of the legitimate Mexican government when dealing with a Mexican citizen, and, as we have seen, for the soundest reasons, and upon repeated decisions of this court such action is not subject to reëxamination and modification by the courts of this country.

The principle that the conduct of one independent government cannot be successfully questioned in the courts of another is as applicable to a case involving the title to property brought within the custody of a court, such as we have here, as it was held to be to the cases cited, in which claims for damages were based upon acts done in a foreign country, for it rests at last upon the highest considerations of international comity and expediency. To permit the validity of the acts of one sovereign State to be reëxamined and perhaps condemned by the courts of another would very certainly "imperil the amicable relations between governments and vex the peace of nations."

It is not necessary to consider, as the New Jersey court did, the validity of the levy of the contribution made by the Mexican commanding general, under rules of international law applicable to the situation, since the subject is not open to reëxamination by this or any other American court.

The remedy of the former owner, or of the purchaser from him, of the property in controversy, if either has any remedy, must be found in the courts of Mexico or through the diplomatic agencies of the political department of our Government. The judgments of the Court of Errors and Appeals of New Jersey must be

Affirmed.

Editor's Note. The Hague Convention No. IV, respecting laws and customs of war on land and the regulations annexed thereto, cited by the Court, October 18, 1907 (36 Stat. 2277; T.S. # 539; 2 Malloy p. 1910) is still in force.

Ricaud v. American Metal Co.
246 U.S. 304; 38 Sup. Ct. 312 (1918)

MR. JUSTICE CLARKE delivered the opinion of the court.

In this suit in equity, commenced in the United States District Court for the Western District of Texas, the plaintiff in that court claims to be the owner of and entitled to a large consignment of lead bullion held in bond by the Collector of Customs at El Paso, Texas. An injunction was granted restraining the Collector until further order from delivering the bullion to either of the other defendants.

Barlow, one of the defendants in the District Court, claims to be the owner of the property by purchase from the defendant Ricaud, who it is claimed purchased it from General Pereyra, who in the year 1913 was the commander of a brigade of the Constitutionalist Army of Mexico of which Venustiano Carranza was then First Chief.

It is not seriously disputed that General Pereyra, in his capacity as a commanding officer, in September, 1913, demanded this bullion from the Penoles Mining Company, a Mexican corporation doing business at Bermejillo, Mexico; that when it was delivered to him he gave a receipt which contains a promise to pay for it "on the triumph of the revolution or the establishment of a legal government"; that Pereyra sold the bullion to defendant Ricaud, who sold it to the defendant Barlow; that the proceeds of the sale were devoted to the purchase of arms, ammunition, food and clothing for Pereyra's troops, and that Pereyra in the transaction represented and acted for the Government of General Carranza, which has since been recognized by the United States Government as the *de jure* Government of Mexico.

The plaintiff, appellee here, claims to have purchased the bullion from the Penoles Mining Company in June, 1913.

The District Court rendered a decree in favor of the plaintiff from which defendants appealed to the Circuit Court of Appeals for the Fifth Circuit, and that court certifies three questions as to which it desires the instruction of this court.

The sufficiency of the certificate of the Circuit Court of Appeals is challenged at the threshold.

There is no denying that there is much of merit in the objection to the form of this certificate, including the form of the questions, for the reason that the certificate, instead of containing a "proper statement of the facts on which the questions and propositions of law arise," as is required by Rule 37 of this court, contains a statement of what is "alleged and denied" by the parties plaintiff and defendant in their pleadings, with the additional statement that there was evidence "tending to establish the facts as claimed by each party," but without any finding whatever as to what the evidence showed the facts to be, and the first question, on which the other two depend, is in terms based entirely on an "assumed" statement of facts.

If this certificate had not been supplemented by the recognition by the United States Government of the Government of Carranza, first as the *de facto*, and later as the *de jure* Government of Mexico, of which facts this court will take judicial notice, (*Jones* v. *United States*, 137 U. S. 202; *Underhill* v. *Hernandez*, 168 U. S. 250) it would be our duty to declare the certificate insufficient and to return it to the Circuit Court of Appeals without answering the questions. *Cincinnati, Hamilton & Dayton R. R. Co.* v. *McKeen*, 149 U. S. 259; *Graver* v. *Faurot*, 162 U. S. 435; *Cross* v. *Evans*, 167 U. S. 60; *Stratton's Independence* v. *Howbert*, 231 U. S. 399, 422.

But this recognition of the government under which General Pereyra was acting, as the legitimate Government of Mexico, makes the answers to the questions so certain and its effect upon the case is so clear, that, for the purpose of making an end of the litigation, we will proceed to answer the questions.

The first question is:

"I. Assuming that the bullion in suit was seized, condemned, and sold for war supplies by the Constitutionalist forces in revolution in Mexico, acting under authority from General Carranza, claiming to be the Provisional President of the Republic of Mexico, had the District Court of the Western District of Texas, into which the said bullion had been imported from Mexico, jurisdiction to try and adjudge as to the validity of the title acquired by and through the said seizure, appropriation, and sale by the Carranza forces as against an American citizen claiming ownership of the said bullion prior to its seizure?"

There can be no doubt that the required diversity of citizenship to give the District Court jurisdiction of the case was stated in the petition for injunction. The certificate shows that it was alleged in the petition that the bullion was the property of the plaintiff and that it had been forcibly taken from its possession in Mexico by unknown persons but without any reference being made to a state of war prevailing therein at the time; that it was consigned to defendant Barlow at El Paso, Texas, and was in a bonded warehouse in the possession of the defendant Cobb, as Collector of Customs, who, unless restrained by the court, would deliver it to the other defendants.

This form of petition brought the case within the jurisdiction of the District Court (*United States* v. *Arredondo*, 6 Pet. 691, 709; *Grignon's Lessee* v. *Astor*, 2 How. 319; *Minnesota Co.* v. *St. Paul Co.*, 2 Wall. 609, 632), and the question is, whether the circumstance that the bullion was seized, condemned and sold under the conditions stated in the question deprived the court of jurisdiction to go forward and adjudge as to the validity of the title acquired by the seizure and sale by the Carranza forces.

The answer which should be given to this question has been rendered not doubtful by the fact that, as we have said, the revolution inaugurated by General Carranza against General Huerta proved successful and the government established by him has been recognized by the political department of our Government as the *de facto* and later as the *de jure* Government of Mexico, which decision binds the judges as well as all other officers and citizens of the Government. *United States* v. *Palmer*, 3 Wheat. 610; *In re Cooper*, 143 U. S. 472; *Jones* v. *United States*, 137 U. S. 202. This recognition is retroactive in effect and validates all the actions of the Carranza Government from the commencement of its existence (*Williams* v. *Bruffy*, 96 U. S. 176, 186; *Underhill* v. *Hernandez*, 168 U. S. 250, 253), and the action of General Pereyra complained of must therefore be regarded as the action, in time of civil war, of a duly commissioned general of the legitimate Government of Mexico.

It is settled that the courts will take judicial notice of such recognition, as we have here of the Carranza Government, by the political department of our Government (*Jones* v. *United States*, 137 U. S. 202), and that the courts of one independent government will not sit in judgment on the validity of the acts of another done within its own territory (*Underhill* v. *Hernandez*, 168 U. S. 250, 253; *American Banana Co.* v. *United Fruit Co.*, 213 U. S. 347; *Oetjen* v. *Central Leather Co., ante*, 297). This last rule, however, does not deprive the courts of jurisdiction once acquired over a case. It requires only that, when it is made to appear that the foreign government has acted in a given way on the subject-matter of the litigation, the details of such action or the merit of the result cannot be questioned but must be accepted by our courts as a rule for their decision. To accept a ruling authority and to decide accordingly is not a surrender or abandonment of jurisdiction but is an exercise of it. It results that the title to the property in this case must be determined by the result of the action taken by the military authorities of Mexico and that giving effect to this rule is an exercise of jurisdiction which requires that the first question be answered in the affirmative.

The second question reads:

"II. If [the first question is answered in the affirmative,] does the subsequent recognition by the United States Government of Carranza as the legitimate President of the Republic of Mexico and his government as the only legitimate government of the Republic of Mexico deprive this court of jurisdiction on this appeal to decide and adjudge the case on its merits?"

Our answer to the first requires a negative answer to this second question.

The third question reads:

"III. If question two is answered in the negative, did the seizure, condemnation, and sale of the bullion in the manner and for the purposes stated to be assumed in question one have the effect of divesting the title to or ownership of it of a certain citizen of the United States of America not in or a resident of Mexico when such seizure and condemnation occurred?"

The answer to this question must be in the affirmative for the reasons given and upon the authorities cited in the opinion recently announced in cases Nos. 268 and 269, *Oetjen* v. *Central Leather Co.* The fact that the title to the property in controversy may have been in an American citizen, who was not in or a resident of Mexico at the time it was seized for military purposes by the legitimate Government of Mexico, does not affect the rule of law that the act within its own boundaries of one sovereign State cannot become the subject of reëxamination and modification in the courts of another. Such action, when shown to have been taken, becomes, as we have said, a rule of decision for the courts of this country. Whatever rights such an American citizen may have can be asserted only through the courts of Mexico or through the political departments of our Government. The first and third questions will be answered in the affirmative and the second in the negative.

And it is so ordered.

Editor's Note.   See Monte Blanco Real Estate Corp. v. Wolvin Line, 147 La. 563, 85 So. 242 (1920), decided on the authority of the principal case.

Russian Volunteer Fleet v. United States
282 U.S. 481; 51 S. Ct. 229 (1931)
For opinion see infra VI (2)

United States v. Bank of New York and Trust Co.
296 U.S. 463; 56 S. Ct. 343 (1936)

MR. CHIEF JUSTICE HUGHES delivered the opinion of the Court.

The United States, claiming to be the owner of certain funds which originally had belonged to Russian insurance companies, brought these suits for accounting and delivery. The companies had made deposits with the Superintendent of Insurance of the State of New York in order to obtain authority to transact business within the State. The complaints alleged that in 1917, or 1918, the companies had been dissolved, and their properties had been "confiscated and appropriated," by decrees of the Russian State. The claim of the United States is based upon an assignment made by the Russian Government, on November 16, 1933, in connection with the recognition of that Government. Defendants hold the funds in question under orders and judgments of the state court in New York, providing for liquidation and distribution.

In each case, defendants moved to dismiss the complaint for insufficiency and, in opposition to complainant's motion for an interlocutory injunction restraining distribution, set up the proceedings of the state court. The District Court denied the motions for injunction and dismissed the complaints upon the grounds (1) that the Russian decrees, by reason of their confiscatory character, were ineffective to vest in the Russian Government the title to these funds situated in New York, and (2) that these funds were not covered by the assignment to the United States, 10 F. Supp. 269. The Circuit Court of Appeals held that the jurisdiction of the state court should be respected, and in that view affirmed the decrees of the District Court. 77 F. (2d) 866, 880, 881. Because of the nature and importance of the questions presented, we granted writs of certiorari, October 14, 1935.

The special facts of the three cases are these:

(1) The case against the Bank of New York and Trust Company (No. 195) relates to the deposit made by the Moscow Fire Insurance Company. By order of the Supreme Court of the State of New York, in 1925, the Superintendent of Insurance was appointed liquidator of the United States branch of the company pursuant to § 63 of the state insurance law and creditors were enjoined from pursuing their legal remedies against the assets so sequestered. The Superintendent of Insurance took possession of the assets and proceeded in the course of liquidation to satisfy the claims of domestic creditors and policyholders. There remained a substantial surplus.

Similar results followed the Superintendent's liquidation of the branches of other Russian companies, and the disposition of the surplus assets was brought before the Court of Appeals of New York. Creditors and policyholders with claims arising out of foreign business insisted that the time had come when their claims should be enforcible. The insurance companies insisted that they were still "juristic persons," that they were represented by boards of directors competent to act, and were entitled to possession subject to the remedies of creditors. The court declined to sustain the position of the Superintendent that the surplus should be left in his hands indefinitely,—until the recognition of a Russian government. As the Superintendent had fulfilled the statutory trust, the court considered it to be no part of his duty to ascertain the validity of the claims that would be paid out of the surplus "unless inequity would be done if the claimants were remitted to a remedy at law." Exceptions were recognized where attachments or executions had been levied before the date of liquidation and also where proofs of claim had been filed and diligently pressed while the Superintendent was still in charge and the injunction was still in force. As the creditors so proving were acting in response to an invitation—published in accordance with the order of liquidation—to submit claims of every kind without reference to the place of origin, and were meanwhile stayed, the court thought that there would be manifest inequity if at that late day they were remitted to their legal remedies and compelled to prove anew. A court of equity having assumed control over a fund might continue to grant relief if justice so required. But the court took the view that after the liquidator had made provision for the payment of claims already filed, the surplus then remaining "should be paid to the corporations, represented by directors, a quorum of the board." *Matter of People (Russian Reinsurance Co.)*, 255 N. Y. 415, 420-424; 175 N. E. 114, 117.

The Moscow Fire Insurance Company, however, had been left with but one director; and although he might be treated as a "conservator" of the property of his company when there were assets within the State "that might otherwise be lost," the Court of Appeals was of the opinion that a measure of discretion should be exercised by a court of equity "before surrendering possession." Exercising that discretion the court directed that the delivery of the assets in the case of that company should be conditioned upon the execution of a bond to the People of the State in a sum equal to the value of the assets delivered, with a condition that the director should faithfully apply the assets to the use of the corporation, its creditors and shareholders. In the event of inability or failure to give the bond, the court directed that delivery should be made to a trust company "as agent or depositary" upon the stipulation of the insurance company and its "conservator" that the fund would "not be withdrawn except upon the order of a court of competent jurisdiction." *Matter of People (Moscow Fire Insurance Co.)*, 255 N. Y. 433, 435; 175 N. E. 120, 121. On the remittitur of the Court of Appeals, judgment was entered in the Supreme Court of the State on August 11, 1931, and provided, in the stated alternative, that the Superintendent should deliver the surplus assets to the Bank of New York and Trust Company. The Moscow Company and Paul Lucke, "its sole surviving director and conservator," took advantage of this alternative and gave the required stipulation, whereupon the Trust Company received the surplus assets, of about $1,000,000, on April 18, 1933.

Immediately—on April 19, 1933—the Moscow Company and Lucke brough suit in the Supreme Court of the State to determine the disposition of these assets, including the determination of the claims of creditors. A second suit was brought in June, 1933, by a shareholder of the Moscow Company. In October, 1933, the first of these suits was referred to a referee to hear and determine, and later the two suits were consolidated. Trial was had before the referee and proofs of claims of various creditors and shareholders of the Moscow Company were submitted. On August 13, 1934, when the referee was about to file his report, the United States Attorney presented to the referee a proof of claim of the United States to the entire fund,—based upon the assignment of November 16, 1933, by the Russian Government. Apparently the claim was not pressed and an understanding was reached that the referee would withhold his report until August 21, 1934, and that the United States would meanwhile determine in what manner it would assert its claim, whether by intervention in a proceeding in the state court or by suit in the federal court. The referee made no mention of the claim in his report, which was filed on August 22, 1934. Judgment was at once entered upon the report directing payment of the claims of creditors as allowed by the referee and, after making reservation for future claims and expenses, ordering the distribution of the residue in liquidating dividends to the shareholders of the Moscow Company. There was also provision that any shareholder, or any party to the action, or successor in interest, might apply at the foot of the judgment for further directions. On the same day the United States brought the present suit.

(2) The case against the President and Directors of the Manhattan Company (No. 196) relates to the Northern Insurance Company of Moscow. Under an order of the state court, in 1926, the Superintendent of Insurance took possession of the assets of the United States branch of the company. The statutory liquidation was completed. But as the company was left with but two directors, provision was made in April, 1931—under the decision of the Court of Appeals of New York—for the delivery of the surplus assets to a trust company, in case the required bond was not given. *Matter of People (Northern Insurance Co.)*, 255 N. Y. 433, 435; 175 N. E. 120. In the following year an assignment for the benefit

of creditors was made on behalf of the Northern Insurance Company to the Bank of Manhattan Trust Company, the predecessor in interest of the defendant in the present suit. Pursuant to a decision of the Court of Appeals on reargument (*Matter of People (Northern Insurance Co.*), 262 N. Y. 453; 188 N. E. 17) judgment was entered, on June 6, 1933, in the Supreme Court of the State directing the Superintendent of Insurance to deliver the surplus assets to the Bank of Manhattan Trust Company "as agent or depositary" to be held subject to the order of a court of competent jurisdiction. The delivery was made, the amount being upwards of $245,000. On November 13, 1933, the state court directed the President and Directors of the Manhattan Company, as successor in interest, to transfer the fund to itself "as assignee for the benefit of creditors of the Northern Insurance Company of Moscow." In July, 1934, the state court appointed a referee to take and state the account of the assignee, and to take proof and report as to the claims of creditors and those entitled to share in the disposition of the fund. That proceeding was in progress when the present suit by the United States was begun on August 25, 1934.

(3) The third case (No. 197) relates to the assets of the United States branch of the First Russian Insurance Company, which the state court, in 1925, placed in the hands of the Superintendent of Insurance as liquidator. This case differs from the others in that the Superintendent is still in possession. After the payment of domestic creditors, the surplus assets were retained by the Superintendent under the order of the state court for the purpose of satisfying valid claims founded upon foreign business, where proofs of claim had been filed with him during the statutory liquidation. *Matter of People (First Russian Insurance Co.*), 255 N. Y. 415, 423; 175 N. E. 114. It appears that some of these foreign claims had been allowed by the liquidator and payments on account had been made under orders of the state court, and that other claims which the liquidator had disallowed were being heard before a referee appointed by the state court, when the United States brought the present suit on November

14, 1934. The Government states that the fund then held by the Superintendent amounted to over $1,000,000.

First. When the state court directed the Superintendent of Insurance to take possession of the assets of the United States branches, and to conserve those assets until its further order, the court took jurisdiction of the *res.* While the superintendent was a statutory liquidator, he took possesion under the direction of the court and the fund was at all times subject to the court's control. The proceeding was essentially one *in rem* and the Superintendent was protected by a sweeping injunction in the unimpeded liquidation of the sequestered property. *Matter of People (Russian Reinsurance Co.) supra,* p. 420. Under § 63 of the state statute (Insurance Law; Cons. Laws, c. 28), the liquidator had rights and duties such as had previously "been exercised by and imposed upon ancillary receivers of foreign corporations." *Id.,* p. 424.

When the statutory trust was satisfied by the payment of domestic creditors and policyholders, it did not follow that the remaining assets were automatically released and the state court was *ipso facto* shorn of its jurisdiction. The court still had control of the property and necessarily had the pertinent equitable jurisdiction to decide what should be done with it. In such a case, the court might direct that the surplus assets should be remitted to a domiciliary receiver—if there were one—on appropriate conditions. *Matter of People (Norske Lloyd Insurance Co.),* 242 N. Y. 148; 151 N. E. 159. Or the court might direct further liquidation, in order to provide for the payment of other claims, if that course appealed to the sense of equity in the particular circumstances. *Matter of People (Russian Reinsurance Co.), supra,* p. 423. The latter action was taken and the Superintendent of Insurance was continued in possession of the assets subject to the control of the court. He was virtually its receiver for the purposes specified. In No. 197, the Superintendent still holds possession by virtue of that authorization and the *res* thus remains under the court's jurisdiction.

In the other two cases (Nos. 195 and 196) the Superintendent completed the additional liquidation and turned over the remaining assets to the designated depositaries. To safeguard all rights in the funds, they were not to be withdrawn from the depositaries except upon a court order. We need not pause to inquire as to the effect of that limitation, for, if jurisdiction was relinquished, it was soon resumed. On the very next day, in the case of the Moscow Fire Insurance Company, suit was brought in its name, and by the sole surviving director and conservator, against the depositary and those alleged to be creditors and shareholders of the insurance company, to determine the disposition of the fund. Claims of creditors and shareholders were in course of adjudication in that proceeding when the present suit was brought. At that time, also, in the case of the Northern Insurance Company, the depositary—which had received an assignment for the benefit of creditors—was accounting in the state court for the fund in its hands and the claims of creditors and of those entitled to share in the fund were being heard.

In both these cases the proceedings in the state court were *quasi in rem.* Control of the funds was essential to the exercise of the court's jurisdiction to protect the rights of claimants. It was not necessary for the court to appoint receivers, as the funds were already in the hands of depositaries appointed by the court and subject to its direction. The principle, applicable to both federal and state courts, that the court first assuming jurisdiction over property may maintain and exercise that jurisdiction to the exclusion of the other, is not restricted to cases where property has been actually seized under judicial process before a second suit is instituted. It applies as well where suits are brought to marshal assets, administer trusts, or liquidate estates, and in suits of a similar nature, where, to give effect to its jurisdiction, the court must control the property. *Farmers' Loan & Trust Co.* v. *Lake Street Elevated R. Co.,* 177 U. S. 51, 61. If the two suits are *in rem* or *quasi in rem,* so that the court must have possession or control of the *res* in order to proceed with the cause and to grant the relief sought, the jurisdiction of one court must of necessity yield to that of the other. *Penn General Casualty Co.* v. *Pennsylvania,* 294 U. S. 189, 195. This principle is applied in the discharge of the long recognized duty of this court to give effect to such "methods of procedure as shall serve to conciliate the distinct and independent tribunals of the States and of the Union, so that they may coöperate as harmonious members of a judicial system coextensive with the United States." *Taylor* v. *Carryl*, 20 How. 583, 595. See also, *Peck* v. *Jenness*, 7 How. 612, 625; *Buck* v. *Colbath*, 3 Wall. 334, 341; *Wabash R. Co.* v. *Adelbert College*, 208 U. S. 38, 54; *Palmer* v. *Texas*, 212 U. S. 118, 129; *Lion Bonding Co.* v. *Karatz*, 262 U. S. 77, 89; *Harkin* v. *Brundage*, 276 U. S. 36, 43.

The Government urges that the present suits for an accounting are not suits *in rem* but *in personam;* and that to allow the federal court to pass upon the right asserted would not necessarily interfere with the jurisdiction or control by the state court over the *res.* See *Kline* v. *Burke Construction Co.*, 260 U. S. 226, 230. But these suits are not to enforce a personal liability but to obtain possession of the respective funds. The suits are not merely to establish a debt or a right to share in property, and thus to obtain an adjudication which might be had without disturbing the control of the state court. Compare *Waterman* v. *Canal-Louisiana Bank Co.*, 215 U. S. 33, 44–46; *Riehle* v. *Margolies*, 279 U. S. 218, 223, 224. Complainant demands that the depositaries account and pay over to the complainant, as "the sole and exclusive owner," the entire funds in their hands. Thus the object of the suits is to take the property from the depositaries and from the control of the state court, and to vest the property in the United States to the exclusion of all those whose claims are being adjudicated in the state proceedings.

The Government also insists that the courts of the State had lost jurisdiction of the funds, prior to the time when the present suits were begun, by reason of the fact that the funds were the property of the Russian Government which our Government had recognized. But, whatever the effect of recognition, it is manifest that it did not terminate the state proceedings. The state court still had control of the property and questions as to the rights of the parties who were before it, or of those who might come before it, were legal questions which the court had jurisdiction to decide.

Second. The fact that the complainant in these suits is the United States does not justify a departure from the rule which would otherwise be applicable. The Government invokes § 24 (1) of the Judicial Code (28 U. S. C. 41) which confers jurisdiction upon the District Court to entertain all suits of a civil nature brought by the United States. The Government insists that the United States is entitled to have its claim determined in its own courts. But the grant of jurisdiction to the District Court in suits brought by the United States does not purport to confer exclusive jurisdiction. It is a general rule that the grant of jurisdiction to one court does not, of itself, imply that the jurisdiction is to be exclusive. See *Gittings* v. *Crawford,* Taney's Dec. 1; *Ames* v. *Kansas,* 111 U. S. 449, 464; *Plaquemines Fruit Co.* v. *Henderson,* 170 U. S. 511, 517, 518; *Merryweather* v. *United States,* 12 F. (2d) 407, 409, 410. Upon the state courts, equally with the courts of the Union, rests the obligation to guard and enforce every right secured by the Constitution and laws of the United States whenever those rights are involved in any suit or proceedings before them. *Robb* v. *Connolly,* 111 U. S. 624, 637. In this instance it cannot be doubted that the United States is free to invoke the jurisdiction of the state court for the determination of its claim, and the decision of the state court of any federal question which may be presented upon such an invocation, may be reviewed by this Court and thus all the questions which the Government seeks to raise in these suits may be appropriately and finally decided. Jud. Code, § 237, 28 U. S. C. 344.

The statutory grant of jurisdiction to the District Court leaves open the question of the propriety of its exercise in particular circumstances. Even where the District Court has acquired jurisdiction prior to state proceedings, the character and adequacy of the latter proceedings in relation to the administration of assets within the State, and the status of those assets, may require in the proper exercise of the discretion of the federal court that jurisdiction should be relinquished in favor of the state administration. *Pennsylvania* v. *Williams,* 294 U. S. 176, 185; *Gordon* v. *Ominsky,* 294 U. S. 186, 188; *Penn General Casualty Co.* v. *Pennsylvania, supra,* p. 197. In the instant cases, not only had the state court first acquired jurisdiction, but there are numerous persons whose claims in relation to these funds are in course of adjudication. Whether or not their claims are valid against the claim of ownership by the United States, they are entitled to be heard and they are indispensable parties to any proceeding for the disposition of the property involved. They have not been made parties to the present suits, and this fact in itself would be a sufficient reason for the District Court to refuse to proceed in their absence. Only the stakeholders are defendants. The adverse claimants are parties to the respective proceedings in the state court and from every point of view the principles governing the convenient and orderly administration of justice require that the jurisdiction of the state court should be respected.

There is no merit in the suggestion that the United States, in presenting its claim in the state proceedings, would be compelled to take the position of a defendant,— being sued without its consent. In intervening for the presentation of its claim, the United States would be an actor—voluntarily asserting what it deemed to be its rights—and not a defendant. We cannot see that there would be impairment of any rights the United States may possess, or any sacrifice of its proper dignity as a sovereign, if it prosecuted its claim in the appropriate forum where the funds are held.

As we are dealing simply with the question of the exercise of jurisdiction by the District Court, we intimate no opinion upon the merits.

The decrees are

Affirmed.

United States v. Belmont
301 U.S. 324; 57 Sup. Ct. 758 (1937)

CERTIORARI, 299 U. S. 531, to review the affirmance of a judgment of the District Court dismissing the complaint in an action by the United States to recover from executors a sum of money which had been deposited with their decedent by a Russian corporation and assigned by the Soviet Government, after expropriation, to the United States.

MR. JUSTICE SUTHERLAND delivered the opinion of the Court.

This is an action at law brought by petitioner against respondents in a federal district court to recover a sum of money deposited by a Russian corporation (Petrograd Metal Works) with August Belmont, a private banker doing business in New York City under the name of August Belmont & Co. August Belmont died in 1924; and respondents are the duly-appointed executors of his will. A motion to dismiss the complaint for failure to state facts sufficient to constitute a cause of action was sustained by the district court, and its judgment was affirmed by the court below. 85 F. (2d) 542. The facts alleged, so far as necessary to be stated, follow.

The corporation had deposited with Belmont, prior to 1918, the sum of money which petitioner seeks to recover. In 1918, the Soviet Government duly enacted a decree by which it dissolved, terminated and liquidated the corporation (together with others), and nationalized and appropriated all of its property and assets of every kind and wherever situated, including the deposit account with Belmont. As a result, the deposit became the property of the Soviet Government, and so remained until November 16, 1933, at which time the Soviet Government released and assigned to petitioner all amounts due to that government from American nationals, including the deposit account of the corporation with Belmont. Respondents failed and refused to pay the amount upon demand duly made by petitioner.

The assignment was effected by an exchange of diplomatic correspondence between the Soviet Government and the United States. The purpose was to bring about a final settlement of the claims and counterclaims between the Soviet Government and the United States; and it was agreed that the Soviet Government would take no steps to enforce claims against American na-

tionals; but all such claims were released and assigned
to the United States, with the understanding that the
Soviet Government was to be duly notified of all amounts
realized by the United States from such release and assignment. The assignment and requirement for notice
are parts of the larger plan to bring about a settlement
of the rival claims of the high contracting parties. The
continuing and definite interest of the Soviet Government in the collection of assigned claims is evident; and
the case, therefore, presents a question of public concern, the determination of which well might involve the
good faith of the United States in the eyes of a foreign
government. The court below held that the assignment
thus effected embraced the claim here in question; and
with that we agree.

That court, however, took the view that the situs of
the bank deposit was within the State of New York;
that in no sense could it be regarded as an intangible
property right within Soviet territory; and that the nationalization decree, if enforced, would put into effect
an act of confiscation. And it held that a judgment for
the United States could not be had, because, in view of
that result, it would be contrary to the controlling public policy of the State of New York. The further contention is made by respondents that the public policy of
the United States would likewise be infringed by such a
judgment. The two questions thus presented are the
only ones necessary to be considered.

First. We do not pause to inquire whether in fact there
was any policy of the State of New York to be infringed,
since we are of opinion that no state policy can prevail
against the international compact here involved.

This court has held, *Underhill* v. *Hernandez*, 168 U. S.
250, that every sovereign state must recognize the independence of every other sovereign state; and that the
courts of one will not sit in judgment upon the acts of
the government of another, done within its own territory.

That general principle was applied in *Oetjen* v. *Central
Leather Co.*, 246 U. S. 297, to a case where an action in
replevin had been brought in a New Jersey state court to
recover a consignment of hides purchased in Mexico from

General Villa. The title of the purchaser was assailed on the ground that Villa had confiscated the hides. Villa, it appeared, had seized the hides while conducting independent operations under the Carranza government, which at the time of the seizure had made much progress in its revolution in Mexico. The government of the United States, after the trial of the case in the state court, had recognized the government of Carranza, first as the *de facto* government of the Republic of Mexico, and later as the government *de jure*. This court held that the conduct of foreign relations was committed by the Constitution to the political departments of the government, and the propriety of what may be done in the exercise of this political power was not subject to judicial inquiry or decision; that who is the sovereign of a territory is not a judicial question, but one the determination of which by the political departments conclusively binds the courts; and that recognition by these departments is retroactive and validates all actions and conduct of the government so recognized from the commencement of its existence. "The principle," we said, p. 303, "that the conduct of one independent government cannot be successfully questioned in the courts of another is as applicable to a case involving the title to property brought within the custody of a court, such as we have here, as it was held to be to the cases cited, in which claims for damages were based upon acts done in a foreign country, for it rests at last upon the highest considerations of international comity and expediency. To permit the validity of the acts of one sovereign State to be reëxamined and perhaps condemned by the courts of another would very certainly 'imperil the amicable relations between governments and vex the peace of nations.'" *Ricaud* v. *American Metal Co.*, 246 U. S. 304, 308–309, 310, is to the same effect.

In *A. M. Luther* v. *James Sagor & Co.*, L. R. [1921] 3 K. B. 532, the English Court of Appeal expressly approved and followed our decision in the *Oetjen* case. The English case involved that part of the same decree of the Soviet Government here under consideration which declared certain private woodworking establishments to be the property of the Republic. Under that decree the

Government seized plaintiff's factory in Russia together with a stock of wood therein. Agents of the Republic sold a quantity of the stock so seized to the defendants, who imported it into England. Thereafter, the British Government recognized the Soviet Government as the *de facto* government of Russia. Upon these facts, the court held that, the British Government having thus recognized the Soviet Government, existing at a date before the decree in question, the validity of that decree and the sale of the wood to the defendants could not be impugned, and gave judgment for defendants accordingly. The court regarded the decree as one of confiscation, but was unable to see (Bankes, L. J., p. 546) how the courts could treat the decree "otherwise than as the expression by the de facto government of a civilized country of a policy which it considered to be in the best interest of that country. It must be quite immaterial for present purposes that the same views are not entertained by the Government of this country, are repudiated by the vast majority of its citizens, and are not recognized by our laws." Lord Justice Scrutton, in his opinion, discusses (pp. 557–559) the contention that the courts should refuse to recognize the decree and the titles derived under it as confiscatory and unjust, and concludes that the question is one not for the judges but for the action of the sovereign through his ministers. "I do not feel able," he said, "to come to the conclusion that the legislation of a state recognized by my Sovereign as an independent sovereign state is so contrary to moral principle that the judges ought not to recognize it. The responsibility for recognition or non-recognition with the consequences of each rests on the political advisers of the Sovereign and not on the judges." Further citation of authority seems unnecessary.

We take judicial notice of the fact that coincident with the assignment set forth in the complaint, the President recognized the Soviet Government, and normal diplomatic relations were established between that government and the Government of the United States, followed by an exchange of ambassadors. The effect of this was to validate, so far as this country is concerned, all acts of the Soviet Government here involved from the commencement of its existence. The recognition, establishment of diplomatic relations, the assignment, and agreements with respect thereto, were all parts of one transaction, resulting in an international compact between the two governments. That the negotiations, acceptance of the assignment and agreements and understandings in respect thereof were within the competence of the President may not be doubted. Governmental power over internal affairs is distributed between the national government and the several states. Governmental power over external affairs is not distributed, but is vested exclusively in the national government. And in respect of what was done here, the Executive had authority to speak as the sole organ of that government. The assignment and the agreements in connection therewith did not, as in the case of treaties, as that term is used in the treaty making clause of the Constitution (Art. II, § 2), require the advice and consent of the Senate.

A treaty signifies "a compact made between two or more independent nations with a view to the public welfare." *Altman & Co.* v. *United States*, 224 U. S. 583, 600. But an international compact, as this was, is not always a treaty which requires the participation of the Senate. There are many such compacts, of which a protocol, a modus vivendi, a postal convention, and agreements like that now under consideration are illustrations. See 5 Moore, Int. Law Digest, 210–221. The distinction was pointed out by this court in the *Altman* case, *supra*, which arose under § 3 of the Tariff Act of 1897, authorizing the President to conclude commercial agreements with foreign countries in certain specified matters. We held that although this might not be a treaty requiring ratification by the Senate, it was a compact negotiated and proclaimed under the authority of the President, and as such was a "treaty" within the meaning of the Circuit Court of Appeals Act, the construction of which might be reviewed upon direct appeal to this court.

Plainly, the external powers of the United States are to be exercised without regard to state laws or policies. The supremacy of a treaty in this respect has been recognized from the beginning. Mr. Madison, in the Vir-

ginia Convention, said that if a treaty does not supersede
existing state laws, as far as they contravene its operation, the treaty would be ineffective. "To counteract it
by the supremacy of the state laws, would bring on the
Union the just charge of national perfidy, and involve us
in war." 3 Elliot's Debates 515. And see *Ware* v. *Hylton,*
3 Dall. 199, 236–237. And while this rule in respect of
treaties is established by the express language of cl. 2,
Art. VI, of the Constitution, the same rule would result
in the case of all international compacts and agreements
from the very fact that complete power over international
affairs is in the national government and is not and cannot be subject to any curtailment or interference on the
part of the several states. Compare *United States* v.
Curtiss-Wright Export Corp., 299 U. S. 304, 316, *et seq.*
In respect of all international negotiations and compacts,
and in respect of our foreign relations generally, state
lines disappear. As to such purposes the State of New
York does not exist. Within the field of its powers, whatever the United States rightfully undertakes, it necessarily has warrant to consummate. And when judicial
authority is invoked in aid of such consummation, state
constitutions, state laws, and state policies are irrelevant
to the inquiry and decision. It is inconceivable that any
of them can be interposed as an obstacle to the effective
operation of a federal constitutional power. Cf. *Missouri* v. *Holland,* 252 U. S. 416; *Asakura* v. *Seattle,* 265
U. S. 332, 341.

Second. The public policy of the United States relied
upon as a bar to the action is that declared by the Constitution, namely, that private property shall not be taken
without just compensation. But the answer is that our
Constitution, laws and policies have no extraterritorial
operation, unless in respect of our own citizens. Compare
United States v. *Curtiss-Wright Export Corp., supra,* at
p. 318. What another country has done in the way of
taking over property of its nationals, and especially of
its corporations, is not a matter for judicial consideration
here. Such nationals must look to their own government
for any redress to which they may be entitled. So far
as the record shows, only the rights of the Russian cor-

poration have been affected by what has been done; and it will be time enough to consider the rights of our nationals when, if ever, by proper judicial proceeding, it shall be made to appear that they are so affected as to entitle them to judicial relief. The substantive right to the moneys, as now disclosed, became vested in the Soviet Government as the successor to the corporation; and this right that government has passed to the United States. It does not appear that respondents have any interest in the matter beyond that of a custodian. Thus far no question under the Fifth Amendemnt is involved.

It results that the complaint states a cause of action and that the judgment of the court below to the contrary is erroneous. In so holding, we deal only with the case as now presented and with the parties now before us. We do not consider the status of adverse claims, if there be any, of others not parties to this action. And nothing we have said is to be construed as foreclosing the assertion of any such claim to the fund involved, by intervention or other appropriate proceeding. We decide only that the complaint alleges facts sufficient to constitute a cause of action against the respondents.

Judgment reversed.

Mr. Justice Stone, concurring.

I agree with the result, but I am unable to follow the path by which it is reached. Upon the record before us there is, I think, no question of reëxamining the validity of acts of a foreign state, and no question of the United States' declaring and enforcing a policy inconsistent with one that the State of New York might otherwise adopt in conformity to its own laws and the Constitution.

The United States, by agreement with the Soviet government, has acquired an assignment of all the rights of the latter in a chose in action, against an American citizen, formerly belonging to a Russian national, and confiscated by decree of the Soviet government. If the subject of the transfer were a chattel belonging to an American, but located in Russia, we may assume that the validity of the seizure would be recognized here, *Oetjen* v. *Cen-*

tral Leather Co., 246 U. S. 297; *Ricaud* v. *American Metal Co.*, 246 U. S. 304, 308–310; *Salimoff & Co.* v. *Standard Oil Co.*, 262 N. Y. 220; 186 N. E. 679. Similarly, the confiscation of the present claim, being lawful where made, is upon familiar principles to be regarded as effective in New York, except in so far as that state, by reason of the presence of the debtor there, may adopt and enforce a policy based upon non-recognition of the transfer.

But this Court has often recognized that a state may refuse to give effect to a transfer, made elsewhere, of property which is within its own territorial limits, if the transfer is in conflict with its public policy. *Green* v. *Van Buskirk*, 5 Wall. 307, 311–312; *Hervey* v. *Rhode Island Locomotive Works*, 93 U. S. 664; *Security Trust Co.* v. *Dodd, Mead & Co.*, 173 U. S. 624; *Clark* v. *Williard*, 292 U. S. 112, 122; *Clark* v. *Williard*, 294 U. S. 211. It is likewise free to disregard the transfer where the subject of it is a chose in action due from a debtor within the state to a foreign creditor, especially where, as in the present case, the debtor's only obligation is to pay within the state, on demand. *Harrison* v. *Sterry*, 5 Cranch 289; *Disconto Gesellschaft* v. *Umbreit*, 208 U. S. 570; *Barth* v. *Backus*, 140 N. Y. 230; 35 N. E. 425; *Vladikavkazsky Ry. Co.* v. *New York Trust Co.*, 263 N. Y. 369, 378–379; 189 N. E. 456. The chose in action is so far within the control of the state as to be regarded as located there for many purposes. *Wyman* v. *Halstead*, 109 U. S. 654, 656; *Chicago, R. I. & P. Ry. Co.* v. *Sturm*, 174 U. S. 710; *Harris* v. *Balk*, 198 U. S. 215; *Pennington* v. *Fourth National Bank*, 243 U. S. 269; *Security Savings Bank* v. *California*, 263 U. S. 282, 285; *Corn Exchange Bank* v. *Coler*, 280 U. S. 218; *In re Russian Bank for Foreign Trade*, L. R. 1933, Ch. Div. 745, 767; American Law Institute, Restatement, Conflict of Laws, §§ 108, 213.

It does not appear that the State of New York, at least since our diplomatic recognition of the Soviet government, has any policy which would permit a New York debtor to question the title of that government to a claim of the creditor acquired by its confiscatory decree, and no reason is apparent for assuming that such is its policy.

Payment of the debt to the United States as transferee
will discharge the debtor and impose on him no burden
which he did not undertake when he assumed the position
of debtor. Beyond this he has no interest for the state
to protect. But it is a recognized rule that a state may
rightly refuse to give effect to external transfers of property within its borders so far as they would operate to
exclude creditors suing in its courts. *Harrison* v. *Sterry,
supra; Security Trust Co.* v. *Dodd, Mead & Co., supra;
Disconto Gesellschaft* v. *Umbreit, supra; Clark* v. *Williard, supra; Barth* v. *Backus, supra.*

We recently held, in *Clark* v. *Williard, supra,* that the
full faith and credit clause does not preclude the attachment of property within the state, by a local creditor of
a foreign corporation, all of whose property has been previously transferred, in the state of its incorporation, to a
statutory successor for the benefit of creditors. Due
process under the Fifth Amendment, the benefits of which
extend to alien friends, as well as to citizens, *Russian
Volunteer Fleet* v. *United States,* 282 U. S. 481, does not
require any different result. *Disconto Gesellschaft* v.
Umbreit, supra, 579, 580. The Constitution has no
different application where the property transferred is a
chose in action, later seized by a creditor in the state of
the debtor. *Disconto Gesellschaft* v. *Umbreit, supra.*
See *Harrison* v. *Sterry, supra.* In conformity to this doctrine, New York would have been free to enforce a local
policy, subordinating the Soviet government, as the successor of its national, to local suitors. Its judicial decisions indicate that such may be its policy for the protection of creditors or others claiming an interest in the sum
due. *James & Co.* v. *Second Russian Insurance Co.,* 239
N. Y. 248, 257; 146 N. E. 369; *Matter of People* (City
Equitable Fire Insurance Co.), 238 N. Y. 147, 152; 144
N. E. 484; *Matter of Waite,* 99 N. Y. 433, 448; 2 N. E.
440. See *Vladikavkazsky Ry. Co.* v. *New York Trust
Co., supra.*

It seems plain that, so far as now appears, the United
States does not stand in any better position with respect
to the assigned claim than did its assignor, or any other

transferee of the Soviet government. We may, for present purposes, assume that the United States, by treaty with a foreign government with respect to a subject in which the foreign government has some interest or concern, could alter the policy which a state might otherwise adopt. It is unnecessary to consider whether the present agreement between the two governments can rightly be given the same effect as a treaty within this rule, for neither the allegations of the bill of complaint, nor the diplomatic exchanges, suggest that the United States has either recognized or declared that any state policy is to be overridden.

So far as now relevant, the document signed by the Soviet government, as preparatory to a more general settlement of claims and counterclaims between the two governments, assigns and releases to the United States all amounts "due or that may be found to be due it" from American nationals, and provides that the Soviet government is "to be duly notified in each case of any amount realized by the Government of the United States from such release and assignment." The relevant portion of the document signed by the President is expressed in the following paragraph:

"I am glad to have these undertakings by your Government and I shall be pleased to notify your Government in each case of any amount realized by the Government of the United States from the release and assignment to it of the amounts admitted to be due or that may be found to be due."

There is nothing in either document to suggest that the United States was to acquire or exert any greater rights than its transferor, or that the President, by mere executive action, purported or intended to alter the laws and policy of any state in which the debtor of an assigned claim might reside, or that the United States, as assignee, is to do more than the Soviet government could have done after diplomatic recognition—that is, collect the claims in conformity with those laws. Cf. *Todok* v. *Union State Bank,* 281 U. S. 449.

As respondent debtor may not challenge the effect of the assignment to the United States, the judgment is rightly reversed. But as the reversal is without prejudice to the rights of any other parties to intervene, they should be left free to assert, by intervention or other appropriate procedure, such claims with respect to the amount due as are in accordance with the laws and policy of New York. There is no occasion to say anything now which can be taken to foreclose the assertion by such claimants of their rights under New York law.

MR. JUSTICE BRANDEIS and MR. JUSTICE CARDOZO concur in this opinion.

Guaranty Trust Co. v. United States
304 U.S. 126; 58 Supt. Ct. 785 (1938)

CERTIORARI, 302 U. S. 681, to review the reversal of a judgment dismissing the complaint in an action by the United States to recover from the present petitioner the amount of a bank deposit which the United States claimed as assignee of the Russian Government. The motion was based on the New York statute of limitations.

MR. JUSTICE STONE delivered the opinion of the Court.

The principal questions for decision are whether, in a suit at law brought in a federal district court to recover the deposit of a foreign government with a New York bank, such government is subject to the local statute of limitations as are private litigants; and, if so, whether the assignment of November 16, 1933, by the Russian Soviet Government to the United States of the right of the former to the bank account restricts or overrides the operation of the statute of limitations. A subsidiary question is whether in the circumstances of the case the running of the statute of limitations, if otherwise applicable, was affected by our nonrecognition of the Soviet Government during the interval of approximately sixteen years between recognition of the Provisional Government of Russia and recognition of its successor.

On July 15, 1916, the Imperial Russian Government
opened a bank account with petitioner, the Guaranty
Trust Company, a New York banking corporation. On
March 16, 1917, the Imperial Government was overthrown and was succeeded by the Provisional Government of Russia which was recognized by the United
States on March 22, 1917. On July 5, 1917, Mr. Boris
Bakhmeteff was officially recognized by the President as
the Ambassador of Russia. On July 12, 1917, the account
being overdrawn, $5,000,000 was deposited in the account
by Mr. Serge Ughet, Financial Attache of the Russian
Embassy in the United States. On November 7, 1917,
the Provisional Government was overthrown and was
succeeded by the government of the Union of Soviet
Socialist Republics, which will be referred to as the Soviet
Government. At that time there remained on deposit
in the account the sum of approximately $5,000,000. On
November 28, 1917, the Soviet Government dismissed
Bakhmeteff as Ambassador and Ughet as Financial Attache. But the United States continued to recognize
Bakhmeteff as Ambassador until on June 30, 1922, he
withdrew from his representation of the Russian Government. Thereafter, until November 16, 1933, it continued to recognize the Financial Attache, and after the
retirement of Bakhmeteff as Ambassador it recognized the
former as custodian of Russian property in the United
States.

On November 16, 1933, the United States recognized
the Soviet Government, and on that date took from it an
assignment of all "amounts admitted to be due that may
be found to be due it, as the successor of prior Governments of Russia, or otherwise, from American nationals,
including corporations . . ." After making demand upon
the petitioner for payment of the balance of the account
the United States, on Setember 21, 1934, brought
the present suit in the district court for southern New
York to recover the deposit. Petitioner then moved under
the Conformity Act, 28 U. S. C. § 724; New York Civil
Practice Act, § 307; and Rules 107 and 120 of the New
York Rules of Civil Practice, to dismiss the complaint on
the ground that the recovery was barred by the New
York six year statute of limitations.

In support of the motion petitioner submitted numerous affidavits, two depositions, and other documentary proof tending to show that on February 25, 1918, it had applied the balance of the account as a credit against indebtedness alleged to be due to it by the Russian Government by reason of the latter's seizure of certain ruble deposit accounts of petitioner in Russian private banks; that on that date it had repudiated all liability on the deposit account; and that it had then given notice of such repudiation to the Financial Attache of the Russian Embassy and later both to the Financial Attache and to Bakhmeteff as Ambassador. The United States submitted affidavits and exhibits in opposition. The district court found that petitioner had repudiated liability on the account on February 25, 1918; that it had given due notice of repudiation prior to June 30, 1922 to both the Financial Attache and Ambassador Bakhmeteff; and that recovery was barred by the applicable six year statute of limitations of New York. New York Civil Practice Act, § 48. The Court of Appeals for the second circuit reversed the judgment for petitioner, holding that the New York statute of limitations does not run against a foreign sovereign. 91 F. (2d) 898. Moved by the importance of the questions involved, we granted certiorari.

Respondent argues that the Soviet Government, in a suit brought in the federal courts, is not subject to the local statute of limitations, both because a foreign, like a domestic, sovereign is not subject to statutes of limitations, and its immunity as in the case of a domestic sovereign constitutes an implied exception to that statute and to the Conformity Act; and because in any case, since no suit to recover the deposit could have been maintained in New York by the Soviet Government prior to its recognition by the United States, and since according to New York law the statute does not run during the period when suit cannot be brought, the present suit is not barred. It is insisted further that even though the Soviet Government is bound by the local statute of limitations the United States is not so bound, both because the New York statute which bars the remedy but does not extinguish the right is not applicable to the United States, and because the statute is inoperative and ineffective since it conflicts with and impedes the execution of the Executive Agreement between the Soviet Government and the United States by which the assignment was effected. Finally, the Government assails the finding of fact of the district court that petitioner repudiated the liability upon the deposit account, and contends that notice of the repudiation given by petitioner to representatives of the Provisional Government was ineffective to set the statute running against the Soviet Government and in favor of petitioner.

First. The rule *quod nullum tempus occurrit regi*— that the sovereign is exempt from the consequences of its laches, and from the operation of statutes of limitations— appears to be a vestigial survival of the prerogative of the Crown. See *Magdalen College Case,* 11 Co. Rep. 66b, 74b; Hobart, L. C. J. in *Sir Edward Coke's Case,* Godb. 289, 295; Bracton, De Legibus, Lib. ii, c. 5, § 7. But whether or not that alone accounts for its origin, the source of its continuing vitality where the royal privilege no longer exists is to be found in the public policy now underlying the rule even though it may in the beginning have had a different policy basis. Compare Maine, Ancient Law (10th ed., 1930) 32 *et seq.* "The true reason . . . is to be found in the great public policy of preserving the public rights, revenues, and property from injury and loss, by the negligence of public officers. And though this is sometimes called a prerogative right, it is in fact nothing more than a reservation, or exception, introduced for the public benefit, and equally applicable to all governments." Story, J., in *United States* v. *Hoar,* Fed. Cas. No. 15,373, p. 330. Regardless of the form of government and independently of the royal prerogative once thought sufficient to justify it, the rule is supportable now because its benefit and advantage extend to every citizen, including the defendant, whose plea of laches or limitation it precludes; and its uniform survival in the United States has been generally accounted for and justified on grounds of policy rather than upon any inherited notions of the personal privilege of the king. *United States* v. *Kirkpatrick,* 9 Wheat. 720, 735; *United States* v. *Knight,* 14 Pet. 301, 315; *United*

States v. *Thompson,* 98 U. S. 486, 489; *Fink* v. *O'Neil,* 106 U. S. 272, 281; *United States* v. *Nashville, C. & St. L. R. Co.,* 118 U. S. 120, 125. So complete has been its acceptance that the implied immunity of the domestic "sovereign," state or national, has been universally deemed to be an exception to local statutes of limitations where the government, state or national, is not expressly included; and to the Conformity Act. See *United States v. Thompson, supra.*

Whether the benefit of the rule should be extended to a foreign sovereign suing in a state or federal court is a question to which no conclusive answer is to be found in the authorities. Diligent search of counsel has revealed no judicial decision supporting such an application of the rule in this or any other country. The alleged immunity was doubted in *French Republic* v. *Saratoga Vichy Spring Co.,* 191 U. S. 427, 437, and in *Commissioners of the Sinking Fund* v. *Buckner,* 48 Fed. 533. It was rejected in *Western Lunatic Asylum* v. *Miller,* 29 W. Va. 326, 329; 1 S. E. 740, and was disregarded in *Royal Italian Government* v. *International Committee of Y. M. C. A.,* 273 N. Y. 468; 6 N. E. 2d 407, where neither appellate court delivered an opinion.

The only support found by the court below for a different conclusion is a remark in the opinion of the Court in *United States* v. *Nashville, C. & St. L. R. Co., supra,* where its holding that the United States, suing in a federal court, is not subject to the local statute of limitations, was said to rest upon a great principle of public policy "applicable to all governments alike." The statement is but a paraphrase, which has frequently appeared in judicial opinion,[1] of Mr. Justice Story's statement in *United States* v. *Hoar, supra,* already quoted. His reference to the public policy supporting the rule that limitation does not run against a domestic sovereign as "equally applicable to all governments" was obviously designed to point out that the policy is as applicable to our own as to a monarchical form of government, and is therefore not to be

---

[1] *United States* v. *Knight,* 14 Pet. 301, 315; *Gibson* v. *Chouteau,* 13 Wall. 92, 99; *United States* v. *Thompson,* 98 U. S. 486, 490; *Fink* v. *O'Neil,* 106 U. S. 272, 281.

discarded because of its former identity with the royal prerogative. We can find in that pronouncement and in its later versions no intimation that the policy underlying exemption of the domestic sovereign supports its extension to a foreign sovereign suing in our courts.

It is true that upon the principle of comity foreign sovereigns and their public property are held not to be amenable to suit in our courts without their consent. See *The Exchange,* 7 Cranch 116; *Berizzi Bros. Co.* v. *S. S. Pesaro,* 271 U. S. 562, *Compania Espanola* v. *The Navemar,* 303 U. S. 68. But very different considerations apply where the foreign sovereign avails itself of the privilege, likewise extended by comity, of suing in our courts. See *The Sapphire,* 11 Wall. 164, 167; *Russian S. F. S. Republic* v. *Cibrario,* 235 N. Y. 255; 139 N. E. 259. By voluntarily appearing in the rôle of suitor it abandons its immunity from suit and subjects itself to the procedure and rules of decision governing the forum which it has sought. Even the domestic sovereign by joining in suit accepts whatever liabilities the court may decide to be a reasonable incident of that act. *United States* v. *The Thekla,* 266 U. S. 328, 340, 341; *United States* v. *Stinson,* 197 U. S. 200, 205; *The Davis,* 10 Wall. 15; *The Siren,* 7 Wall. 152, 159.[2] As in the case of the domestic sovereign in like situation, those rules, which must be assumed to be founded on principles of justice applicable to individuals, are to be relaxed only in response to some persuasive demand of public policy generated by the nature of the suitor or of the claim which it asserts. That this is the guiding principle sufficiently appears in the many instances in which courts have narrowly restricted the application of the rule *nullum tempus* in the case of the

---

[2] A foreign sovereign as suitor is subject to the local rules of the domestic forum as to costs, *Republic of Honduras* v. *Soto,* 112 N. Y. 310; 19 N. E. 845; *Emperor of Brazil* v. *Robinson,* 5 Dowl. Pr. 522; *Otho, King of Greece,* v. *Wright,* 6 Dowl. Pr. 12; *The Beatrice,* 36 L. J. Rep. Adm. (N. S.) 10; *Queen of Holland* v. *Drukker,* (1928) Ch. 877, 884, although the local soverign does not pay costs. *United States* v. *Verdier,* 164 U. S. 213, 219. The foreign sovereign suing as a plaintiff must give discovery. *Rothschild* v. *Queen of Portugal,* 3 Y. & C. Ex. 594, 596; *United States* v. *Wagner,* L. R. 2 Ch. App. 582, 592, 595; *Prioleau* v. *United States,* L. R. 2 Eq. 659. A foreign

domestic sovereign.[3] It likewise appears from those cases which justify the rule as applied to the United States suing in a state court, on the ground that it is sovereign within the state and that invocation of the rule *nullum tempus* protects the public interest there as well as in every other state. *United States* v. *Beebe,* 127 U. S. 338; *Swearingen* v. *United States,* 11 Gill. & J. 373; *McNamee* v. *United States,* 11 Ark. 148; cf. *United States* v. *California,* 297 U. S. 175, 186.

We are unable to discern in the case where a foreign sovereign, by suit, seeks justice according to the law of the forum, any of the considerations of public policy which support the application of the rule *nullum tempus* to a domestic sovereign. The statute of limitations is a statute of repose, designed to protect the citizens from stale and vexatious claims, and to make an end to the possibility of litigation after the lapse of a reasonable time. It has long been regarded by this Court and by the courts of New York as a meritorious defense, in itself serving a public interest. *Bell* v. *Morrison,* 1 Pet. 351, 360; *M'Cluny* v. *Silliman,* 3 Pet. 270, 278; *Campbell* v. *Haverhill,* 155 U. S. 610, 617; *United States* v. *Oregon Lumber Co.,* 260 U. S. 290; *Brooklyn Bank* v. *Barnaby,* 197 N. Y. 210, 227; 90 N. E. 834; *Schmidt* v. *Merchants Despatch Transportation Co.,* 270 N. Y. 287, 302; 200 N. E. 824. Denial of its protection against the demand

---

sovereign plaintiff "should so far as the thing can be done be put in the same position as a body corporate." *Republic of Costa Rica* v. *Erlanger,* L. R. 1 Ch. D. 171, 174; *Republic of Peru* v. *Weguelin,* L. R. 20 Eq. 140, 141; cf. *King of Spain* v. *Hullett,* 7 Bligh N. S. 359, 392.

[3] The presumption of a grant by lapse of time will be indulged against the domestic sovereign. *United States* v. *Chaves,* 159 U. S. 452, 464. The rule *nullum tempus* has never been extended to agencies or grantees of the local sovereign such as municipalities, county boards, school districts and the like. *Metropolitan R. Co.* v. *District of Columbia,* 132 U. S. 1; *Boone County* v. *Burlington & Missouri River R. Co.,* 139 U. S. 684, 693. It has been held not to relieve the sovereign from giving the notice required by local law to charge endorsers of negotiable paper, *United States* v. *Barker,* 12 Wheat. 559; cf. *Cooke* v. *United States,* 91 U. S. 389, 398; *Wilber National Bank* v. *United States,* 294 U. S. 120, 124, and in tax cases has been narrowly construed against the domestic sovereign. *Bowers* v. *New York & Albany Lighterage Co.* 273 U. S. 346, 350. Compare *United States* v. *Knight,* 14 Pet. 301; *Fink* v. *O'Neil,* 106 U. S. 272.

of the domestic sovereign in the interest of the domestic community of which the debtor is a part could hardly be thought to argue for a like surrender of the local interest in favor of a foreign sovereign and the community which it represents. We cannot say that the public interest of the forum goes so far.

We lay aside questions not presented here which might arise if the national government, in the conduct of its foreign affairs, by treaty or other appropriate action, should undertake to restrict the application of local statutes of limitations against foreign governments, or if the states in enacting them should discriminate against suits brought by a foreign government. We decide only that in the absence of such action the limitation statutes of the forum run against a foreign government seeking a remedy afforded by the forum, as they run against private litigants.

Second. Respondent, relying on the New York rules that the statute of limitations does not run against a suit to recover a bank account until liability upon it is repudiated, *Tillman* v. *Guaranty Trust Co.,* 253 N. Y. 295; 171 N. E. 61, and that the statute of limitations does not run against a plaintiff who has no forum in which to assert his rights, *Oswego & Syracuse R. Co.* v. *State,* 226 N. Y. 351, 359, 362; 124 N. E. 8; *Cayuga County* v. *State,* 153 N. Y. 279, 291; 47 N. E. 288; *Parmenter* v. *State,* 135 N. Y. 154, 163; 31 N. E. 1035, argues that until recognition of the Soviet Government there was no person to whom notice of petitioner's repudiation could be given and no court in which suit could be maintained to recover the deposit.

It is not denied that, in conformity to generally accepted principles, the Soviet Government could not maintain a suit in our courts before its recognition by the political department of the Government. For this reason access to the federal and state courts was denied to the Soviet Government before recognition. *The Penza,* 277 Fed. 91; *The Rogdai,* 278 Fed. 294; *Russian S. F. S. Republic* v. *Cibrario,* 235 N. Y. 255; *Preobazhenski* v. *Cibrario,* 192 N. Y. Supp. 275./But the argument ignores the principle controlling here and recognized by the courts of New York that the rights of a sovereign state are vested in the state rather than in any particular government which may purport to represent it, *The Sapphire, supra,* 168, and that suit in its behalf may be maintained in our courts only by that government which has been recognized by the political department of our own government as the authorized government of the foreign state. *Jones* v. *United States,* 137 U. S. 202, 212; *Russian Government* v. *Lehigh Valley R. Co.,* 293 Fed. 133, 135, aff'd *sub nom. Lehigh Valley R. Co.* v. *State of Russia,* 21 F. (2d) 396, 409; *Matter of Lehigh Valley R. Co.,* 265 U. S. 573; *Russian S. F. S. Republic* v. *Cibrario, supra;* Moore, International Law Digest, §§ 75, 78.

What government is to be regarded here as representative of a foreign sovereign state is a political rather than a judicial question, and is to be determined by the political department of the government. Objections to its determination as well as to the underlying policy are to be addressed to it and not to the courts. Its action in recognizing a foreign government and in receiving its diplomatic representatives is conclusive on all domestic courts, which are bound to accept that determination, although they are free to draw for themselves its legal consequences in litigations pending before them. *Jones* v. *United States, supra,* 212; *Agency of Canadian Car & F. Co.* v. *American Can Co.,* 258 Fed. 363; *Lehigh Valley R. Co.* v. *State of Russia, supra.*

We accept as conclusive here the determination of our own State Department that the Russian State was represented by the Provisional Government through its duly recognized representatives from March 16, 1917 to November 16, 1933, when the Soviet Government was recognized.[4] There was at all times during that period a recog-

---

[4] The United States accorded recognition to the Provisional Government March 16, 1917 and continued to recognize it until November 16, 1933, when the Soviet Government was recognized. During that period the United States declined to recognize the Soviet Government or to receive its accredited representative, and so certified in litigations pending in the federal courts. *The Penza, supra; The Rogdai, supra.* It recognized Mr. Bakhmeteff as Russian Ambassador from July 5, 1917 until June 30, 1922, when he retired, having designated Mr. Ughet as custodian of Russian property in the United States. Mr. Ughet, after his appointment as Financial Attache April 7, 1917, continued to be recognized as such by the United States until November 16, 1933. He was recognized by the United States as Charge d'Affaires ad interim, during the absence

nized diplomatic representative of the Russian State to whom notice concerning its interests within the United States could be communicated, and to whom our courts were open for the purpose of prosecuting suits in behalf of the Russian State. In fact, during that period suits were brought in its behalf in both the federal and state courts, which consistently ruled that the recognized Ambassador and Financial Attache were authorized to maintain them.[5]

We do not stop to inquire what the "actual" authority of those diplomatic representatives may have been. When the question is of the running of the statute of limitations, it is enough that our courts have been open to suit on behalf of the Russian State in whom the right to sue upon the petitioner's present claim was vested, and that the political department of the Government has accorded recognition to a government of that state, received its diplomatic representatives, and extended to them the privilege of maintaining suit in our courts in behalf of their state. The right and opportunity to sue upon the claim against petitioner was not suspended; and notice of repudiation of the liability given to the duly rec-

---

of the Ambassador from December 3, 1918 to July 31, 1919. Their diplomatic status as stated was certified in the present suit by the Secretary of State, who stated that he considered Mr. Ughet's status unaffected by the termination of the Ambassador's duties.

Their status was certified to by the Department on October 31, 1918 and July 2, 1919, respectively, in *Russian Government* v. *Lehigh Valley R. Co.*, 293 Fed. 133. Mr. Bakhmeteff's status as Ambassador was certified May 18, 1919 in *Agency of Canadian Car & Foundry Co.* v. *American Can Co.*, 258 Fed. 363, 368; on April 6, 1920 in *The Rogdai*, 278 Fed. 294, 295; on June 24, 1919 in *The Penza*, 277 Fed. 91, 93. Certificate with respect to both Mr. Bakhmeteff and Mr. Ughet was given February 19, 1923 and with respect to Mr. Ughet December 22, 1927. On the faith of the two last mentioned certificates the Court, in the *Lehigh Valley Railroad* case, *supra*, as stated by the Government's brief in the present case, ordered to be paid to Mr. Ughet approximately $1,000,000, of which more than $700,000 was paid to the United States Treasurer "on account of interest due on obligations of the Provisional Government of Russia by the Treasurer."

[5] *Russian Government* v. *Lehigh Valley R. Co.*, 293 Fed. 133; 293 Fed. 135, aff'd 21 F. (2d) 396; *State of Russia* v. *Bankers' Trust Co.*, 4 F. Supp. 417, 419, aff'd 83 F. (2d) 236. See also *Agency of Canadian Car & Foundry Co.* v. *American Can Co.*, 258 Fed. 363.

ognized diplomatic representatives must, so far as our own courts are concerned, be taken as notice to the state which they represented.

The Government argues that recognition of the Soviet Government, an action which for many purposes validated here that government's previous acts within its own territory, see *Underhill* v. *Hernandez,* 168 U. S. 250; *Oetjen* v. *Central Leather Co.,* 246 U. S. 297; *Ricaud* v. *American Metal Co.,* 246 U. S. 304; *United States* v. *Belmont,* 301 U. S. 324; *Dougherty* v. *Equitable Life Assurance Society,* 266 N. Y. 71, 84, 85; 193 N. E. 897; *Luther* v. *Sagor & Co.,* [1921] 3 K. B. D. 532, operates to set at naught all the legal consequences of the prior recognition by the United States of the Provisional Government and its representatives, as though such recognition had never been accorded. This is tantamount to saying that the judgments in suits maintained here by the diplomatic representatives of the Provisional Government, valid when rendered, became invalid upon recognition of the Soviet Government. The argument thus ignores the distinction between the effect of our recognition of a foreign government with respect to its acts within its own territory prior to recognition, and the effect upon previous transactions consummated here between its predecessor and our own nationals. The one operates only to validate to a limited extent acts of a *de facto* government which by virtue of the recognition, has become a government *de jure.* But it does not follow that recognition renders of no effect transactions here with a prior recognized government in conformity to the declared policy of our own Government. The very purpose of the recognition by our Government is that our nationals may be conclusively advised with what government they may safely carry on business transactions and who its representatives are. If those transactions, valid when entered into, were to be disregarded after the later recognition of a successor government, recognition would be but an idle ceremony, yielding none of the advantages of established diplomatic relations in enabling business transactions to proceed, and affording no protection to our own nationals in carrying them on.

So far as we are advised no court has sanctioned such

a doctrine. The notion that the judgment in suits maintained by the representative of the Provisional Government would not be conclusive upon all successor governments, was considered and rejected in *Russian Government* v. *Lehigh Valley R. Co., supra.* An application for writ of prohibition was denied by this Court. 265 U. S. 573. We conclude that the recognition of the Soviet Government left unaffected those legal consequences of the previous recognition of the Provisional Government and its representatives, which attached to action taken here prior to the later recognition.

Third. If the claim of the Russian Government was barred by limitation the United States as its assignee can be in no better position either because of the rule *nullum tempus* or by virtue of the terms of the assignment. We need waste no time on refinements upon the suggested distinction between rights and remedies, for we may assume for present purposes that the United States acquired by the assignment whatever rights then survived the running of the statute against the Russian Government, and that it may assert those rights subject to such plea of limitations as may be made by petitioner.

As has already been noted, the rule *nullum tempus* rests on the public policy of protecting the domestic sovereign from omissions of its own officers and agents whose neglect, through lapse of time, would otherwise deprive it of rights. But the circumstances of the present case admit of no appeal to such a policy. There has been no neglect or delay by the United States or its agents, and it has lost no rights by any lapse of time after the assignment. The question is whether the exemption of the United States from the consequences of the neglect of its own agents is enough to relieve it from the consequences of the Russian Government's failure to prosecute the claim. Proof, under a plea of limitation, that the six-year statutory period had run before the assignment offends against no policy of protecting the domestic sovereign. It deprives the United States of no right, for the proof demonstrates that the United States never acquired a right free of a preexisting infirmity, the running of limitations against its assignor, which public policy does not forbid. *United States* v. *Buford*, 3 Pet. 12, 30; *King* v. *Morrall*, 6 Price 24, 28, 30.

Assuming that the respective rights of petitioner and the Soviet Government could have been altered and that petitioner's right to plead the statute of limitations curtailed by force of an executive agreement between the President and the Soviet Government, we can find nothing in the agreement and assignment of November 16, 1933, which purports to enlarge the assigned rights in the hands of the United States, or to free it from the consequences of the failure of the Russian Government to prosecute its claim within the statutory period.

The agreement and assignment are embodied in a letter of Mr. Litvinov, People's Commissar of Foreign Affairs of the Soviet Government, to the President and the President's letter of the same date in reply. So far as now relevant the document signed in behalf of the Soviet Government makes mention of "amounts admitted to be due or that may be found to be due it as the successor of prior governments or otherwise from American nationals, including corporations, companies, partnerships or associations." It purports to "release and assign all such amounts to the Government of the United States" and the Soviet Government agrees, preparatory to final settlement of claims between it and the United States and the claims of their nationals, "not to make any claims with respect to . . . (b) Acts done or settlements made by or with the Government of the United States, or public officials of the United States, or its nationals, relating to property, credits, or obligations of any Government of Russia or nationals thereof." The relevant portion of the document signed by the President is expressed in the following paragraph:

"I am glad to have these undertakings by your Government and I shall be pleased to notify your Government in each case of any amount realized by the Government of the United States from the release and assignment to it of the amounts admitted to be due, or that may be found to be due."

There is nothing in either document to suggest that the United States was to acquire or exert any greater rights than its transferor or that the President by mere executive action purported or intended to alter or diminish the rights of the debtor with respect to any assigned claims, or that the United States, as assignee, is to do more than the Soviet Government could have done after diplomatic recognition—that is, collect the claims in conformity to local law.   Even the language of a treaty wherever reasonably possible will be construed so as not to override state laws or to impair rights arising under them.   *United States* v. *Arredondo,* 6 Pet. 691, 748; *Haver* v. *Yaker,* 9 Wall. 32, 34; *Dooley* v. *United States,* 182 U. S. 222, 230; *Nielsen* v. *Johnson,* 279 U. S. 47, 52; *Todok* v. *Union State Bank,* 281 U. S. 449, 454.   The assignment left unaffected the right of petitioner to set up against the United States the previous running of the statute of limitations.

Fourth.   Respondent assails the finding of the district court that there was an unqualified repudiation by petitioner of its liability on the account, and in support of its contention presents an elaborate review of the evidence.   The evidence is said to establish that petitioner's alleged repudiation was tentative and conditional, to await negotiations with a stable Russian government upon its recognition by the United States.   If this contention be rejected, respondent insists that at least there is a conflict in the evidence and in the inferences which may be drawn from it which, under the local practice, should have been resolved by a full trial rather than summarily on motion.   As these questions were not passed on by the Court of Appeals, the case will be remanded to that court for further proceedings in conformity with this opinion.

Reversed.

MR. JUSTICE CARDOZO and MR. JUSTICE REED took no part in the consideration or decision of this case.

Editor's Note.   The agreement between the U.S. and the U.S.S.R., cited by the Court, is the Arrangement relating to the Establishment of Diplomatic Relations and Claims, November 16, 1933 (Department of State Publication No. 528; Eastern European Series No. 1 (1933).

United States v. Pink
315 U.S. 203; 62 Sup. Ct. 552 (1942)

MR. JUSTICE DOUGLAS delivered the opinion of the Court.

This action was brought by the United States to recover the assets of the New York branch of the First Russian Insurance Co. which remained in the hands of respondent after the payment of all domestic creditors. The material allegations of the complaint were, in brief, as follows:

The First Russian Insurance Co., organized under the laws of the former Empire of Russia, established a New York branch in 1907. It deposited with the Superintendent of Insurance, pursuant to the laws of New York, certain assets to secure payment of claims resulting from transactions of its New York branch. By certain laws, decrees, enactments and orders, in 1918 and 1919, the Russian Government nationalized the business of insurance and all of the property, wherever situated, of all Russian insurance companies (including the First Russian Insurance Co.), and discharged and cancelled all the debts of such companies and the rights of all shareholders in all such property. The New York branch of the First Russian Insurance Co. continued to do business in New York until 1925. At that time, respondent, pursuant to an order of the Supreme Court of New York, took possession of its assets for a determination and report upon the claims of the policyholders and creditors in the United States. Thereafter, all claims of domestic creditors, i.e., all claims arising out of the business of the New York branch, were paid by respondent, leaving a balance in his hands of more than $1,000,000. In 1931, the New York Court of Appeals (255 N. Y. 415, 175 N. E. 114) directed respondent to dispose of that balance as follows: first, to pay claims of foreign creditors who had filed attachment prior to the commencement of the liquidation proceeding, and also such claims as were filed prior to the entry of the order on remittitur of that court; and second, to pay any surplus to a quorum of the board of directors of the company. Pursuant to that mandate, respondent proceeded with the liquidation of the claims of the foreign creditors. Some payments were made thereon. The major portion of the allowed claims, however, were not paid, a stay having been granted pending disposition of the claim of the United States. On November 16, 1933, the United States recognized the Union of Soviet Socialist Republics as the *de jure* Government of Russia and as an incident to that recognition accepted an assignment (known as the Litvinov Assignment) of certain claims.[1] The Litvinov Assignment was in the form of a letter, dated November 16, 1933, to the President of the United States from Maxim Litvinov, People's Commissar for Foreign Affairs, reading as follows:

"Following our conversations I have the honor to inform you that the Government of the Union of Soviet Socialist Republics agrees that, preparatory to a final settlement of the claims and counter claims between the Governments of the Union of Soviet Socialist Republics and the United States of America and the claims of their nationals, the Government of the Union of Soviet Socialist Republics will not take any steps to enforce any decisions of courts or initiate any new litigations for the amounts admitted to be due or that may be found to be due it, as the successor of prior Governments of Russia, or otherwise, from American nationals, including corporations, companies, partnerships, or associations, and also the claim against the United States of the Russian Volunteer Fleet, now in litigation in the United States Court of Claims, and will not object to such amounts being assigned and does hereby release and assign all such amounts to the Government of the United States, the Government of the Union of Soviet Socialist Republics to be duly notified in each case of any amount realized by the Government of the United States from such release and assignment.

"The Government of the Union of Soviet Socialist Republics further agrees, preparatory to the settlement re-

---

[1] See Establishment of Diplomatic Relations with the Union of Soviet Socialist Republics, Dept. of State, Eastern European Series, No. 1 (1933) for the various documents pertaining to recognition.

ferred to above not to make any claims with respect to:

"(a) judgments rendered or that may be rendered by American courts in so far as they relate to property, or rights, or interests therein, in which the Union of Soviet Socialist Republics or its nationals may have had or may claim to have an interest; or,

"(b) acts done or settlements made by or with the Government of the United States, or public officials in the United States, or its nationals, relating to property, credits, or obligations of any Government of Russia or nationals thereof."

This was acknowledged by the President on the same date. The acknowledgment, after setting forth the terms of the assignment, concluded:

"I am glad to have these undertakings by your Government and I shall be pleased to notify your Government in each case of any amount realized by the Government of the United States from the release and assignment to it of the amounts admitted to be due, or that may be found to be due, the Government of the Union of Soviet Socialist Republics, and of the amount that may be found to be due on the claim of the Russian Volunteer Fleet."

On November 14, 1934, the United States brought an action in the federal District Court for the Southern District of New York, seeking to recover the assets in the hands of respondent. This Court held in *United States* v. *Bank of New York & Trust Co.*, 296 U. S. 463, that the well settled "principles governing the convenient and orderly administration of justice require that the jurisdiction of the state court should be respected" (p. 480); and that, whatever might be "the effect of recognition" of the Russian Government, it did not terminate the state proceedings. p. 479. The United States was remitted to the state court for determination of its claim, no opinion being intimated on the merits. p. 481. The United States then moved for leave to intervene in the liquidation proceedings. Its motion was denied "without prejudice to the institution of the time-honored form of action." That order was affirmed on appeal.

Thereafter, the present suit was instituted in the Supreme Court of New York. The defendants, other than respondent, were certain designated policyholders and other creditors who had presented in the liquidation proceedings claims against the corporation. The complaint prayed, *inter alia,* that the United States be adjudged to be the sole and exclusive owner entitled to immediate possession of the entire surplus fund in the hands of the respondent.

Respondent's answer denied the allegations of the complaint that title to the funds in question passed to the United States and that the Russian decrees had the effect claimed. It also set forth various affirmative defenses— that the order of distribution pursuant to the decree in 255 N. Y. 415, 175 N. E. 114, could not be affected by the Litvinov Assignment; that the Litvinov Assignment was unenforceable because it was conditioned upon a final settlement of claims and counterclaims which had not been accomplished; that under Russian law the nationalization decrees in question had no effect on property not factually taken into possession by the Russian Government prior to May 22, 1922; that the Russian decrees had no extraterritorial effect, according to Russian law; that if the decrees were given extraterritorial effect, they were confiscatory and their recognition would be unconstitutional and contrary to the public policy of the United States and of the State of New York; and that the United States, under the Litvinov Assignment, acted merely as a collection agency for the Russian Government and hence was foreclosed from asserting any title to the property in question.

The answer was filed in March, 1938. In April, 1939, the New York Court of Appeals decided *Moscow Fire Ins. Co.* v. *Bank of New York & Trust Co.,* 280 N. Y. 286, 20 N. E. 2d 758. In May, 1939, respondent (but not the other defendants) moved, pursuant to Rule 113 of the Rules of the New York Civil Practice Act and § 476 of that Act, for an order dismissing the complaint and awarding summary judgment in favor of respondent "on the ground that there is no merit to the action and that it is insufficient in law." The affidavit in support of the motion stated that there was "no dispute as to the facts"; that the separate defenses to the complaint "need not now be considered for the complaint standing alone is insufficient in law"; that the facts in the *Moscow* case and the instant one, so far as material, were "parallel" and the Russian decrees the same; and that the *Moscow* case authoritatively settled the principles of law governing the instant one. The affidavit read in opposition to the motion stated that a petition for certiorari in the *Moscow* case was about to be filed in this Court; that the motion was premature and should be denied, or decision thereon withheld pending the final decision of this Court. On June 29, 1939, the Supreme Court of New York granted the motion and dismissed the complaint "on the merits," citing only the *Moscow* case in support of its action. On September 2, 1939, a petition for certiorari in the *Moscow* case was filed in this Court. The judgment in that case was affirmed here by an equally divided Court. 309 U. S. 624. Subsequently, the Appellate Division of the Supreme Court of New York affirmed, without opinion, the order of dismissal in the instant case. The Court of Appeals affirmed with a *per curiam* opinion (284 N. Y. 555, 32 N. E. 2d 552) which, after noting that the decision below was "in accord with the decision" in the *Moscow* case, stated:

"Three of the judges of this court concurred in a forceful opinion dissenting from the court's decision in that case, but the decision left open no question which has been argued upon this appeal. We are agreed that without again considering such questions this court should, in determining title to assets of First Russian Insurance Company, deposited in this State, apply in this case the same rules of law which the court applied in the earlier case in determining title to the assets of Moscow Fire Insurance Company deposited here."

We granted the petition for certiorari because of the nature and public importance of the questions raised.

First. Respondent insists that the complaint in this action was identical in substance and sought the same relief as the petition of the United States in the *Moscow* case, and that his answer set up the same defenses as were successfully sustained against the United States by the defendants in that case. He also maintains that both parties agreed, on the motion for summary judgment, that the decision in the *Moscow* case governed this cause, leaving no issues to be tried. We agree with those contentions. It is in accord not only with the motion papers, but also with the ruling of the New York Court of Appeals that the *Moscow* case "left open no question which has been argued upon this appeal." In view of that ruling, we are not free to inquire, as petitioner suggests, into the propriety under New York practice of grounding the motion for summary judgment on the record in the *Moscow* case. That is distinctly a question of state law, on which New York has the last word.

But it does not follow, as respondent urges, that the writ should be dismissed as improvidently granted. The *Moscow* case is not *res judicata*, since respondent was not a party to that suit. *Stone* v. *Farmers' Bank of Kentucky*, 174 U. S. 409; *Rudd* v. *Cornell*, 171 N. Y. 114, 127–128, 63 N. E. 2d 823; *St. John* v. *Fowler*, 229 N. Y. 270, 274, 128 N. E. 199. Nor was our affirmance of the judgment in that case by an equally divided court an authoritative precedent. While it was conclusive and binding upon the parties as respects that controversy (*Durant* v. *Essex Company*, 7 Wall. 107), the lack of an agreement by a majority of the Court on the principles of law involved prevents it from being an authoritative determination for other cases. *Hertz* v. *Woodman*, 218 U. S. 205, 213–214.

The upshot of the matter is that we now reach the issues in the *Moscow* case insofar as they are embraced in the pleadings in this case. And there is no reason why we cannot take judicial notice of the record in this Court of the *Moscow* case. *Bienville Water Supply Co.* v. *Mobile*, 186 U. S. 212, 217; *Dimmick* v. *Tompkins*, 194 U. S. 540, 548; *Freshman* v. *Atkins*, 269 U. S. 121, 124.

Second. The New York Court of Appeals held in the *Moscow* case that the Russian decrees [2] in question had no extraterritorial effect. If that is true, it is decisive of the present controversy. For the United States acquired, un-

---

[2] The three decrees on which the United States placed primary emphasis (apart from the one set forth in note 3, *infra*) were described in the findings of the referee in the *Moscow* case as follows:

"88. The decree of November 18, 1919 on the annulment of life insurance contracts abolished insurance of life in all its forms in the Republic and annulled all contracts with insurance companies and savings banks with respect to the insurance of life, capital and income.

der the Litvinov Assignment, only such rights as Russia had. *Guaranty Trust Co.* v. *United States,* 304 U. S. 126, 143. If the Russian decrees left the New York assets of the Russian insurance companies unaffected, then Russia had nothing here to assign. But that question of foreign law is not to be determined exclusively by the state court. The claim of the United States based on the Litvinov Assignment raises a federal question. *United States* v. *Belmont,* 301 U. S. 324. This Court will review or independently determine all questions on which a federal right is necessarily dependent. *United States* v. *Ansonia Brass & Copper Co.,* 218 U. S. 452, 462–463, 471; *Ancient Egyptian Order* v. *Michaux,* 279 U. S. 737, 744–745; *Broad River Power Co.* v. *South Carolina,* 281 U. S. 537, 540; *Pierre* v. *Louisiana,* 306 U. S. 354, 358. Here, title obtained under the Litvinov Assignment depends on a correct interpretation of Russian law. As in cases arising under the full faith and credit clause (*Huntington* v. *Attrill,* 146 U. S. 657, 684; *Adam* v. *Saenger,* 303 U. S. 59, 64), these questions of foreign law on which the asserted federal right is based are not peculiarly within the cognizance of the local courts. While deference will be given to the determination of the state court, its conclusion is not accepted as final.

We do not stop to review all the evidence in the voluminous record of the *Moscow* case bearing on the question of the extraterritorial effect of the Russian decrees of nationalization, except to note that the expert testimony tendered by the United States gave great credence to its position. Subsequently to the hearings in that case, how-

"89. The decree of the Soviet of People's Commissars dated March 4, 1919, on the liquidation of obligations of State enterprises, provided that stock certificates and shares of joint stock companies, whose enterprises have been either nationalized or sequestered, are annulled and also provided that such enterprises are free from the payment of all debts to private persons and enterprises which have arisen prior to the nationalization of these enterprises, including payments on bond loans with the exception only of wages due to workers and employees.

"90. The decree of the Soviet of People's Commissars dated June 28, 1918 provides in Article I that the commercial and industrial enterprises enumerated therein, which are located within the boundaries of the Soviet Republic, together with all their capital and property, regardless of what the latter may consist, are declared the property of the Republic."

ever, the United States, through diplomatic channels, requested the Commissariat for Foreign Affairs of the Russian Government to obtain an official declaration by the Commissariat for Justice of the R. S. F. S. R. which would make clear, as a matter of Russian law, the intended effect of the Russian decree [3] nationalizing insurance companies

---

[3] Relevant portions of the Insurance Decree dated November 28, 1918, translated in accordance with the findings of the referee in the *Moscow* case, are:

"603. On the organization of the insurance business in the Russian Republic.

"(1) Insurance in all its forms, such as: fire insurance, insurance on shipments, life insurance, accident insurance, hail insurance, livestock insurance, insurance against failure of crops, etc. is hereby proclaimed as a State monopoly.

"Note. Mutual insurance of movable goods and merchandise by the cooperative organizations is conducted on a special basis.

"(2) All private insurance companies and organizations (stock and share holding, also mutual) upon issuance of this decree are subject to liquidation; former rural* (People's Soviet) and municipal mutual insurance organizations operating within the boundaries of the Russian Republic are hereby proclaimed the property of the Russian Socialist Federated Soviet Republic.

"(3) For the immediate organization of the insurance business and for the liquidation of parts of insurance institutions, which have become the property of the Russian Socialist Federated Soviet Republic, a Commission is established under the Supreme Soviet of National Economy, consisting of representatives of the Supreme Soviet of National Economy, the People's Commissariats of Commerce and Industry, Interior Affairs, the Commissar of Insurance and Fire Prevention, Finances, Labor, and State Control, and of Soviet Insurance Organizations (People's Soviet and Municipal Mutual).

"Note. The same commission is charged with the liquidating of private insurance organizations, all property and assets of which, remaining on hand after their liquidation, shall become the property of the Russian Socialist Federated Soviet Republic.

---

* "zemskie."

The referee in the *Moscow* case found that, upon publication of this decree, all Russian insurance companies were prohibited from engaging in the insurance business in Russia; that they became subject to liquidation and were dissolved; that all of their assets in Russia became the property of the State; that, on publication of the decree, the directors of the companies lost all power to act as directors or conservators of the property, or to represent the companies in any way; and that the Russian Government became the statutory successor and domiciliary liquidator of companies whose property was nationalized.

upon the funds of such companies outside of Russia. The official declaration, dated November 28, 1937, reads as follows:

"The People's Commissariat for Justice of the R. S. F. S. R. certifies that by virtue of the laws of the organs of the Soviet Government all nationalized funds and property of former private enterprises and companies, in particular by virtue of the decree of November 28, 1918 (Collection of Laws of the R. S. F. S. R., 1918, No. 86, Article 904), the funds and property of former insurance companies, constitute the property of the State, irrespective of the nature of the property and irrespective of whether it was situated within the territorial limits of the R.S.F.S.R. or abroad."

The referee in the *Moscow* case found, and the evidence supported his finding, that the Commissariat for Justice has power to interpret existing Russian law. That being true, this official declaration is conclusive so far as the intended extraterritorial effect of the Russian decree is concerned. This official declaration was before the court below, though it was not a part of the record. It was tendered pursuant to § 391 of the New York Civil Practice Act, as amended by L. 1933, c. 690.[4] In New York, it would seem that foreign law must be found by the court (or in case of a jury trial, binding instructions must be

---

"(4) The above-mentioned reorganization and liquidation of existing insurance organizations and institutions shall be accomplished not later than the first day of April 1919.

. . . . .

"(8) The present decree comes into force on the day of its publication."

[4] That section reads:

"A printed copy of a statute, or other written law, of another state, or of a territory, or of a foreign country, or a printed copy of a proclamation, edict, decree or ordinance, by the executive power thereof, contained in a book or publication purporting or proved to have been published by the authority thereof, or proved to be commonly admitted as evidence of the existing law in the judicial tribunals thereof, is presumptive evidence of the statute, law, proclamation, edict, decree or ordinance. The unwritten or common law of another state, or of a territory, or of a foreign country, may be proved as a fact by oral evidence. The books of reports of cases adjudged in the courts thereof must also be admitted as presumptive evidence of the unwritten or common law thereof. The law of such state or territory or foreign country is to be determined by the court or referee and included in the

given), though procedural considerations require it to be presented as a question of fact. *Fitzpatrick* v. *International Railway Co.*, 252 N. Y. 127, 169 N. E. 112; *Petrogradsky M. K. Bank* v. *National City Bank*, 253 N. Y. 23, 170 N. E. 479. And under § 391, as amended, it is clear that the New York appellate court has authority to consider appropriate decisions interpreting foreign law even though they are rendered subsequently to the trial. *Los Angeles Investment Securities Corp.* v. *Joslyn*, 282 N. Y. 438, 26 N. E. 2d 968. We can take such notice of the foreign law as the New York court could have taken.[5] *Adam* v. *Saenger, supra.* We conclude that this official declaration of Russian law was not only properly before the court on appeal, but also that it was embraced within those "written authorities" which § 391 authorizes the court to consider, even though not introduced in evidence on the trial. For, while it was not "printed," it would seem to be "other written law" of unquestioned authenticity and authority, within the meaning of § 391.

We hold that, so far as its intended effect[6] is concerned, the Russian decree embraced the New York assets of the First Russian Insurance Co.

Third. The question of whether the decree should be given extraterritorial effect is, of course, a distinct matter. One primary issue raised in that connection is whether, under our constitutional system, New York law can be allowed to stand in the way.

The decision of the New York Court of Appeals in the *Moscow* case is unequivocal. It held that "under the law of this State such confiscatory decrees do not affect the property claimed here" (280 N. Y. 314, 20 N. E. 2d 769); that the property of the New York branch acquired a

---

findings of the court or referee or charged to the jury, as the case may be. Such finding or charge is subject to review on appeal. In determining such law, neither the trial court nor any appellate court shall be limited to the evidence produced on the trial by the parties, but may consult any of the written authorities above named in this section, with the same force and effect as if the same had been admitted in evidence."

[5] Hence, the denial of the motion of the United States to certify the official declaration as part of the record of the *Moscow* case in this Court (281 N. Y. 818, 24 N. E. 2d 487) would seem immaterial to our right to consult it.

[6] See also note 7, *infra.*

"character of its own" which was "dependent" on the law of New York (p. 310); that no "rule of comity and no act of the United States government constrains this State to abandon any part of its control or to share it with a foreign State" (p. 310); that, although the Russian decree effected the death of the parent company, the situs of the property of the New York branch was in New York; and that no principle of law forces New York to forsake the method of distribution authorized in the earlier appeal (255 N. Y. 415, 175 N. E. 114) and to hold that "the method which in 1931 conformed to the exactions of justice and equity must be rejected because retroactively it has become unlawful" (p. 312).

It is one thing to hold, as was done in *Guaranty Trust Co.* v. *United States, supra,* 304 U. S. at p. 142, that under the Litvinov Assignment the United States did not acquire "a right free of a preëxisting infirmity," such as the running of the statute of limitations against the Russian Government, its assignor. Unlike the problem presented here and in the *Moscow* case, that holding in no way sanctions the asserted power of New York to deny enforcement of a claim under the Litvinov Assignment because of an overriding policy of the State which denies validity in New York of the Russian decrees on which the assigned claims rest. That power was denied New York in *United States* v. *Belmont, supra,* 301 U. S. 324. With one qualification, to be noted, the *Belmont* case is determinative of the present controversy.

That case involved the right of the United States under the Litvinov Assignment to recover, from a custodian or stakeholder in New York, funds which had been nationalized and appropriated by the Russian decrees.

This Court, speaking through Mr. Justice Sutherland, held that the conduct of foreign relations is committed by the Constitution to the political departments of the Federal Government; that the propriety of the exercise of that power is not open to judicial inquiry; and that recognition of a foreign sovereign conclusively binds the courts and "is retroactive and validates all actions and conduct of the government so recognized from the commencement of its existence." 301 U. S. at p. 328. It further held (p. 330) that recognition of the Soviet Government, the establishment of diplomatic relations with it, and the Litvinov Assignment were "all parts of one transaction, resulting in an international compact between the two governments." After stating that, "in respect of what was done here, the Executive had authority to speak as the sole organ" of the national government, it added (p. 330): "The assignment and the agreements in connection therewith did not, as in the case of treaties, as that term is used in the treaty making clause of the Constitution (Art. II, § 2), require the advice and consent of the Senate." It held (p. 331) that the "external powers of the United States are to be exercised without regard to state laws or policies. The supremacy of a treaty in this respect has been recognized from the beginning." And it added that "all international compacts and agreements" are to be treated with similar dignity for the reason that "complete power over international affairs is in the national government and is not and cannot be subject to any curtailment or interference on the part of the several states." p. 331. This Court did not stop to inquire whether in fact there was any policy of New York which enforcement of the Litvinov Assignment would infringe since "no state policy can prevail against the international compact here involved." p. 327.

The New York Court of Appeals, in the *Moscow* case (280 N. Y. 309, 20 N. E. 2d 758), distinguished the *Belmont* case on the ground that it was decided on the sufficiency of the pleadings, the demurrer to the complaint admitting that under the Russian decree the property was confiscated by the Russian Government and then transferred to the United States under the Litvinov Assignment. But, as we have seen, the Russian decree in question was intended to have an extraterritorial effect and to embrace funds of the kind which are here involved. Nor can there be any serious doubt that claims of the kind here in question were included in the Litvinov Assignment.[7] It is broad and inclusive. It should be inter-

---

[7] A clarification of the Litvinov Assignment was made in an exchange of letters between the American Charge d'Affaires and the People's Commissar for Foreign Affairs on January 7, 1937. The letter of the former read:

"I have the honor to inform you that it is the understanding of the Government of the United States that the Government of the Union

preted consonantly with the purpose of the compact to eliminate all possible sources of friction between these two great nations. See *Tucker* v. *Alexandroff,* 183 U. S. 424, 437; *Jordan* v. *Tashiro,* 278 U. S. 123, 127. Strict construction would run counter to that national policy. For,

of Soviet Socialist Republics considers that by and upon the formation of the Union of Soviet Socialist Republics and the adoption of the Constitution of 1923 of the Union of Soviet Socialist Republics, the Union of Soviet Socialist Republics acquired the right to dispose of the property, rights, or interests therein located abroad of all corporations and companies which had theretofore been nationalized by decrees of the constituent republics or their predecessors.

"The Government of the United States further understands that it was the purpose and intention of the Government of the Union of Soviet Socialist Republics to assign to the Government of the United States, among other amounts, all the amounts admitted to be due or that may be found to be due not only the Union of Soviet Socialist Republics but also the constituent republics of the Union of Soviet Socialist Republics or their predecessors from American nationals, including corporations, companies, partnerships, or associations, and also the claim against the United States of the Russian Volunteer Fleet, in litigation in the United States Court of Claims, and that the Government of the Union of Soviet Socialist Republics did release and assign all such amounts to the Government of the United States by virtue of the note addressed by you to the President of the United States on November 16, 1933.

"Will you be good enough to confirm the understanding which the Government of the United States has in this matter, concerning the law of the Russian Socialist Federated Soviet Republic, the Constitution and laws of the Union of Soviet Socialist Republics, and the intention and purpose of the Government of the Union of Soviet Socialist Republics in the above-mentioned assignment?"

The reply of the People's Commissar for Foreign Affairs was:

"In reply to your note of January 7, 1937, I have the honor to inform you that the Government of the Union of Soviet Socialist Republics considers that by and upon the formation of the Union of Soviet Socialist Republics and the adoption of the Constitution of 1923 of the Union of Soviet Socialist Republics, the Union of Soviet Socialist Republics acquired the right to dispose of the property, rights, or interests therein located abroad of all corporations and companies which had theretofore been nationalized by decrees of the constituent republics or their predecessors.

"You are further informed that it was the purpose and intention of the Government of the Union of Soviet Socialist Republics to assign to the Government of the United States, among other amounts, all the amounts admitted to be due or that may be found to be due not only the Union of Soviet Socialist Republics but also the con-as we shall see, the existence of unpaid claims against Russia and its nationals, which were held in this country, and which the Litvinov Assignment was intended to secure, had long been one impediment to resumption of friendly relations between these two great powers.

The holding in the *Belmont* case is therefore determinative of the present controversy, unless the stake of the foreign creditors in this liquidation proceeding and the provision which New York has provided for their protection call for a different result.

Fourth. The *Belmont* case forecloses any relief to the Russian corporation. For this Court held in that case (301 U. S. at p. 332): ". . . our Constitution, laws and policies have no extraterritorial operation, unless in respect of our own citizens. . . . What another country has done in the way of taking over property of its nationals, and especially of its corporations, is not a matter for judicial consideration here. Such nationals must look to their own government for any redress to which they may be entitled."

But it is urged that different considerations apply in case of the foreign creditors [8] to whom the New York Court of Appeals (255 N. Y. 415, 175 N. E. 114) ordered distribu-

---

stituent republics of the Union of Soviet Socialist Republics or their predecessors from American nationals, including corporations, companies, partnerships, or associations, and also the claim against the United States of the Russian Volunteer Fleet, in litigation in the United States Court of Claims, and that the Government of the Union of Soviet Socialist Republics did release and assign all such amounts to the Government of the United States by virtue of the note addressed by me to the President of the United States on November 16, 1933.

"I have the honor, therefore, to confirm the understanding, as expressed in your note of January 7, 1937, which the Government of the United States has in this matter, concerning the law of the Russian Socialist Federated Soviet Republic, the Constitution and laws of the Union of Soviet Socialist Republics, and the intention and purpose of the Government of the Union of Soviet Socialist Republics in the above-mentioned assignment."

[8] In view of the disposition which we make of this case, we express no view on whether these creditors would be barred from asserting their claims here by virtue of the ruling in *Canada Southern Ry. Co.* v. *Gebhard*, 109 U. S. 527, 538, that "anything done at the legal home of the corporation, under the authority of such laws, which discharges it from liability there, discharges it everywhere."

tion of these funds. The argument is that their rights in these funds have vested by virtue of the New York decree; that to deprive them of the property would violate the Fifth Amendment which extends its protection to aliens as well as to citizens; and that the Litvinov Assignment cannot deprive New York of its power to administer the balance of the.fund in accordance with its laws for the benefit of these creditors.

At the outset, it should be noted that, so far as appears, all creditors whose claims arose out of dealings with the New York branch have been paid. Thus we are not faced with the question whether New York's policy of protecting the so-called local creditors by giving them priority in the assets deposited with the State (*Matter of People*, 242 N. Y. 148, 158–159, 151 N. E. 159) should be recognized within the rule of *Clark* v. *Williard,* 294 U. S. 211, or should yield to the Federal policy expressed in the international compact or agreement. *Santovincenzo* v. *Egan,* 284 U. S. 30, 40; *United States* v. *Belmont, supra.* We intimate no opinion on that question. The contest here is between the United States and creditors of the Russian corporation who, we assume, are not citizens of this country and whose claims did not arise out of transactions with the New York branch. The United States is seeking to protect not only claims which it holds but also claims of its nationals. H. Rep. No. 865, 76th Cong., 1st Sess. Such claims did not arise out of transactions with this Russian corporation; they are, however, claims against Russia or its nationals. The existence of such claims and their non-payment had for years been one of the barriers to recognition of the Soviet regime by the Executive Department. Graham, Russian-American Relations, 1917–1933: An Interpretation, 28 Am. Pol. Sc. Rev. 387; 1 Hackworth, Digest of International Law (1940), pp. 302–304. The purpose of the discussions leading to the policy of recognition was to resolve "all questions outstanding" between the two nations. Establishment of Diplomatic Relations with the Union of Soviet Socialist Republics, Dept. of State, Eastern European Series, No. 1 (1933), p. 1. Settlement of all American claims against Russia was one method of removing some of the prior objections to recognition based on the Soviet policy of nationalization. The Litvinov Assignment was not only part and parcel of the new policy of recognition (*id.*, p. 13), it was also the method adopted by the Executive Department for alleviating in this country the rigors of nationalization. Congress tacitly recognized that policy. Acting in anticipation of the realization of funds under the Litvinov Assignment (H. Rep. No. 865, 76th Cong., 1st Sess.), it authorized the appointment of a Commissioner to determine the claims of American nationals against the Soviet Government. Joint Resolution of August 4, 1939, 53 Stat. 1199.

If the President had the power to determine the policy which was to govern the question of recognition, then the Fifth Amendment does not stand in the way of giving full force and effect to the Litvinov Assignment. To be sure, aliens as well as citizens are entitled to the protection of the Fifth Amendment. *Russian Volunteer Fleet* v. *United States,* 282 U. S. 481. A State is not precluded, however, by the Fourteenth Amendment from according priority to local creditors as against creditors who are nationals of foreign countries and whose claims arose abroad. *Disconto Gesellschaft* v. *Umbreit,* 208 U. S. 570. By the same token, the Federal Government is not barred by the Fifth Amendment from securing for itself and our nationals priority against such creditors. And it matters not that the procedure adopted by the Federal Government is globular and involves a regrouping of assets. There is no Constitutional reason why this Government need act as the collection agent for nationals of other countries when it takes steps to protect itself or its own nationals on external debts. There is no reason why it may not, through such devices as the Litvinov Assignment, make itself and its nationals whole from assets here before it permits such assets to go abroad in satisfaction of claims of aliens made elsewhere and not incurred in connection with business conducted in this country. The fact that New York has marshaled the claims of the foreign creditors here involved and authorized their payment does not give them immunity from that general rule.

If the priority had been accorded American claims by treaty with Russia, there would be no doubt as to its validity. Cf. *Santovincenzo* v. *Egan, supra.* The same result obtains here. The powers of the President in the conduct of foreign relations included the power, without consent of the Senate, to determine the public policy of the United States with respect to the Russian nationalization decrees. "What government is to be regarded here as representative of a foreign sovereign state is a political rather than a judicial question, and is to be determined by the political department of the government." *Guaranty Trust Co.* v. *United States, supra,* 304 U. S. at p. 137. That authority is not limited to a determination of the government to be recognized. It includes the power to determine the policy which is to govern the question of recognition. Objections to the underlying policy as well as objections to recognition are to be addressed to the political department and not to the courts. See *Guaranty Trust Co.* v. *United States, supra,* p. 138; *Kennett* v. *Chambers,* 14 How. 38, 50–51. As we have noted, this Court in the *Belmont* case recognized that the Litvinov Assignment was an international compact which did not require the participation of the Senate. It stated (301 U. S. pp. 330–331): "There are many such compacts, of which a protocol, a modus vivendi, a postal convention, and agreements like that now under consideration are illustrations." And see *Monaco* v. *Mississippi,* 292 U. S. 313, 331; *United States* v. *Curtiss-Wright Corp.,* 299 U. S. 304, 318. Recognition is not always absolute; it is sometimes conditional. 1 Moore, International Law Digest (1906), pp. 73–74; 1 Hackworth, Digest of International Law (1940), pp. 192–195. Power to remove such obstacles to full recognition as settlement of claims of our nationals (Levitan, Executive Agreements, 35 Ill. L. Rev. 365, 382–385) certainly is a modest implied power of the President who is the "sole organ of the federal government in the field of international relations." *United States* v. *Curtiss-Wright Corp., supra,* p. 320. Effectiveness in handling the delicate problems of foreign relations requires no less. Unless such a power exists, the power of recognition might be thwarted or seriously diluted. No such obstacle can be placed in the way of rehabilitation of relations between this country and another nation, unless the historic conception of the powers and responsibilities of the President in the conduct of foreign affairs (see Moore, Treaties and Executive Agreements, 20 Pol. Sc. Q. 385, 403–417) is to be drastically revised. It was the judgment of the political department that full recognition of the Soviet Government required the settlement of all outstanding problems including the claims of our nationals. Recognition and the Litvinov Assignment were interdependent. We would usurp the executive function if we held that that decision was not final and conclusive in the courts.

"All constitutional acts of power, whether in the executive or in the judicial department, have as much legal validity and obligation as if they proceeded from the legislature, . . ." The Federalist, No. 64. A treaty is a "Law of the Land" under the supremacy clause (Art. VI, Cl. 2) of the Constitution. Such international compacts and agreements as the Litvinov Assignment have a similar dignity. *United States* v. *Belmont, supra,* 301 U. S. at p. 331. See Corwin, The President, Office & Powers (1940), pp. 228–240.

It is, of course, true that even treaties with foreign nations will be carefully construed so as not to derogate from the authority and jurisdiction of the States of this nation unless clearly necessary to effectuate the national policy. *Guaranty Trust Co.* v. *United States, supra,* p. 143 and cases cited. For example, in *Todok* v. *Union State Bank,* 281 U. S. 449, this Court took pains in its construction of a treaty, relating to the power of an alien to dispose of property in this country, not to invalidate the provisions of state law governing such dispositions. Frequently the obligation of a treaty will be dependent on state law. *Prevost* v. *Greneaux,* 19 How. 1. But state law must yield when it is inconsistent with, or impairs the policy or provisions of, a treaty or of an international compact or agreement. See *Nielsen* v. *Johnson,* 279 U. S. 47. Then, the power of a State to refuse enforcement of rights based on foreign law which runs counter to the public policy of the forum (*Griffin* v. *McCoach,* 313 U. S. 498, 506) must give way before the superior Federal policy evidenced by a treaty or international compact or agreement. *Santovincenzo* v. *Egan, supra,* 284 U. S. 30; *United States* v. *Belmont, supra.*

Enforcement of New York's policy as formulated by the *Moscow* case would collide with and subtract from the Federal policy, whether it was premised on the absence of extraterritorial effect of the Russian decrees, the conception of the New York branch as a distinct juristic personality, or disapproval by New York of the Russian program of nationalization.[9] For the *Moscow* case refuses to give effect or recognition in New York to acts of the Soviet Government which the United States by its policy of recognition agreed no longer to question. Enforcement of such state policies would indeed tend to restore some of the precise impediments to friendly relations which the President intended to remove on inauguration of the policy of recognition of the Soviet Government. In the first place, such action by New York, no matter what gloss be given it, amounts to official disapproval or non-recognition of the nationalization program of the Soviet Government. That disapproval or non-recognition is in the face of a disavowal by the United States of any official concern with that program. It is in the face of the underlying policy adopted by the United States when it recognized the Soviet Government. In the second place, to the extent that the action of the State in refusing enforcement of the Litvinov Assignment results in reduction or non-payment of claims of our nationals, it helps keep alive one source of friction which the policy of recognition intended to remove. Thus the action of New York tends to restore

---

[9] In this connection it should be noted that § 977(b) of the New York Civil Practice Act provides for the appointment of a receiver to liquidate local assets of a foreign corporation where, *inter alia,* it has been dissolved, liquidated, or nationalized. Subdivision 19 of that section provides in part:

" . . . such liquidation, dissolution, nationalization, expiration of its existence, or repeal, suspension, revocation or annulment of its charter or organic law in the country of its domicile, or any confiscatory law or decree thereof, shall not be deemed to have any extra-territorial effect or validity as to the property, tangible or intangible, debts, demands or choses in action of such corporation within the state or any debts or obligations owing to such corporation from persons, firms or corporations residing, sojourning or doing business in the state."

some of the precise irritants which had long affected the relations between these two great nations and which the policy of recognition was designed to eliminate.

We recently stated in *Hines* v. *Davidowitz,* 312 U. S. 52, 68, that the field which affects international relations is "the one aspect of our government that from the first has been most generally conceded imperatively to demand broad national authority"; and that any state power which may exist "is restricted to the narrowest of limits." There, we were dealing with the question as to whether a state statute regulating aliens survived a similar federal statute. We held that it did not. Here, we are dealing with an exclusive federal function. If state laws and policies did not yield before the exercise of the external powers of the United States, then our foreign policy might be thwarted. These are delicate matters. If state action could defeat or alter our foreign policy, serious consequences might ensue. The nation as a whole would be held to answer if a State created difficulties with a foreign power. Cf. *Chy Lung* v. *Freeman,* 92 U. S. 275, 279–280. Certainly, the conditions for "enduring friendship" between the nations, which the policy of recognition in this instance was designed to effectuate,[10] are not likely to flourish where, contrary to national policy, a lingering atmosphere of hostility is created by state action.

Such considerations underlie the principle of *Oetjen* v. *Central Leather Co.,* 246 U. S. 297, 302–303, that when a revolutionary government is recognized as a *de jure* government, "such recognition is retroactive in effect and validates all the actions and conduct of the government so recognized from the commencement of its existence." They also explain the rule expressed in *Underhill* v. *Hernandez,* 168 U. S. 250, 252, that "the courts of one country will not sit in judgment on the acts of the government of another done within its own territory."

The action of New York in this case amounts in substance to a rejection of a part of the policy underlying recognition by this nation of Soviet Russia. Such power is not accorded a State in our constitutional system. To permit

---

[10] Establishment of Diplomatic Relations with the Union of Soviet Socialist Republics, *supra* note 1, p. 20.

it would be to sanction a dangerous invasion of Federal authority. For it would "imperil the amicable relations between governments and vex the peace of nations." *Oetjen* v. *Central Leather Co., supra,* p. 304. It would tend to disturb that equilibrium in our foreign relations which the political departments of our national government had diligently endeavored to establish.

We repeat that there are limitations on the sovereignty of the States. No State can rewrite our foreign policy to conform to its own domestic policies. Power over external affairs is not shared by the States; it is vested in the national government exclusively. It need not be so exercised as to conform to state laws or state policies, whether they be expressed in constitutions, statutes, or judicial decrees. And the policies of the States become wholly irrelevant to judicial inquiry when the United States, acting within its constitutional sphere, seeks enforcement of its foreign policy in the courts. For such reasons, Mr. Justice Sutherland stated in *United States* v. *Belmont, supra,* 301 U. S. at p. 331, "In respect of all international negotiations and compacts, and in respect of our foreign relations generally, state lines disappear. As to such purposes the State of New York does not exist."

We hold that the right to the funds or property in question became vested in the Soviet Government as the successor to the First Russian Insurance Co.; that this right has passed to the United States under the Litvinov Assignment; and that the United States is entitled to the property as against the corporation and the foreign creditors.

The judgment is reversed and the cause is remanded to the Supreme Court of New York for proceedings not inconsistent with this opinion.

Reversed.

MR. JUSTICE REED and MR. JUSTICE JACKSON did not participate in the consideration or decision of this case.

MR. JUSTICE FRANKFURTER:

The nature of the controversy makes it appropriate to add a few observations to my Brother DOUGLAS' opinion.

Legal ideas, like other organisms, cannot survive severance from their congenial environment. Concepts like "situs" and "jurisdiction" and "comity" summarize views evolved by the judicial process, in the absence of controlling legislation, for the settlement of domestic issues. To utilize such concepts for the solution of controversies international in nature, even though they are presented to the courts in the form of a private litigation, is to invoke a narrow and inadmissible frame of reference.

The expropriation decrees of the U. S. S. R. gave rise to extensive litigation among various classes of claimants to funds belonging to Russian companies doing business or keeping accounts abroad. England and New York were the most active centers of this litigation. The opinions in the many cases before their courts constitute a sizeable library. They all derive from a single theme—the effect of the Russian expropriation decrees upon particular claims, in some cases before and in some cases after recognition of the U. S. S. R., either *de jure* or *de facto*. One cannot read this body of judicial opinions, in the Divisional Court, the Court of Appeal and the House of Lords, in the New York Supreme Court, the Appellate Division, and the Court of Appeals, and not be left with the conviction that they are the product largely of casuistry, confusion, and indecision. See Jaffee, Judicial Aspects of Foreign Relations, *passim*. The difficulties were inherent in the problems that confronted the courts. They were due to what Chief Judge Cardozo called "the hazards and embarrassments growing out of the confiscatory decrees of the Russian Soviet Republic," *Matter of People (Russian Reinsurance Co.)*, 255 N. Y. 415, 420, 175 N. E. 114, 115, and to the endeavor to adjust these "hazards and embarrassments" to "the largest considerations of public policy and justice," *James & Co.* v. *Second Russian Insurance Co.*, 239 N. Y. 248, 256, 146 N. E. 369, 370, when private claims to funds covered by the expropriation decrees were before the courts, particularly at a time when non-recognition was our national policy.

The opinions show both the English and the New York courts struggling to deal with these business consequences of major international complications through the application of traditional judicial concepts. "Situs," "jurisdiction," "comity," "domestication" and "dissolution" of corporations, and other legal ideas that often enough in

litigation of a purely domestic nature prove their limitations as instruments for solution or even as means for
analysis, were pressed into service for adjudicating claims
whose international implications could not be sterilized.
This accounts for the divergence of views among the judges
and for such contradictory and confusing rulings as the
series of New York cases, from *Wulfsohn* v. *Russian Republic,* 234 N. Y. 372, 138 N. E. 24, to the ruling now under
review, *Moscow Fire Ins. Co.* v. *Bank of New York &
Trust Co.,* 280 N. Y. 286, 20 N. E. 2d 758, accounts for
Russian Commercial & Industrial Bank v. *Comptoir
d'Escompte de Mulhouse,* [1925] A. C. 112, compared with
Lazard Brothers & Co. v. *Midland Bank,* [1933] A. C. 289,
and for the fantastic result of the decision in *Lehigh Valley
R. Co.* v. *State of Russia,* 21 F. 2d 396, in which the Keren-
sky régime was, in accordance with diplomatic determination, treated as the existing Russian government a decade
after its extinction.

Courts could hardly escape perplexities when citizens asserted claims to Russian funds within the control of the
forum.   But a totally different situation was presented
when all claims of local creditors were satisfied and only
the conflicting claims of Russia and of former Russian
creditors were involved.   In the particular circumstances
of Russian insurance companies doing business in New
York, the State Superintendent of Insurance took possession of the assets of the Russian branches in New York to
conserve them for the benefit of those entitled to them.
Liquidation followed, domestic creditors and policy holders were paid, and the Superintendent found a large surplus on his hands.   As statutory liquidator, the Superintendent of Insurance took the ground that "in view of the
hazards and uncertainties of the Russian situation, the
surplus should not be paid to any one, but should be left
in his hands indefinitely, until a government recognized
by the United States shall function in the territory of what
was once the Russian Empire."   255 N. Y. 415, 421, 175
N. E. 114, 115.   So the Appellate Division decreed.   229
App. Div. 637, 243 N. Y. S. 35.   But the Court of Appeals
reversed and the scramble among the foreign claimants
was allowed to proceed.   255 N. Y. 415, 175 N. E. 114.
The Court of Appeals held that the retention of the sur-

plus funds in the custody of the Superintendent of Insurance until the international relations between the United
States and Russia had been formalized "did not solve the
problem.   It adjourned it *sine die*."   But adjournment, it
may be suggested, is sometimes a constructive interim
solution to avoid a temporizing and premature measure giving rise to new difficulties.   Such I believe to
have been the mischief that was bound to follow the rejection of the Superintendent's policy of conservation of the
surplus Russian funds until recognition.   Their disposition was inescapably entangled in recognition.

In the immediate case the United States sues, in effect,
as the assignee of the Russian government for claims by
that government against the Russian Insurance Company
for monies in deposit in New York to which no American
citizen makes claim.   No manner of speech can change
the central fact that here are monies which belonged to a
Russian company and for which the Russian government
has decreed payment to itself.

And so the question is whether New York can bar
Russia from realizing on its decrees against these funds
in New York after formal recognition by the United States
of Russia and in light of the circumstances that led up to
recognition and the exchange of notes that attended it.
For New York to deny the effectiveness of these Russian
decrees under such circumstances would be to oppose, at
least in some respects, its notions as to the effect which
should be accorded recognition as against that entertained
by the national authority for conducting our foreign
affairs.   And the result is the same whether New York
accomplishes it because its courts invoke judicial views
regarding the enforcement of foreign expropriation decrees, or regarding the survival in New York of a Russian
business which according to Russian law had ceased to
exist, or regarding the power of New York courts over
funds of Russian companies owing from New York creditors.   If this Court is not bound by the construction which
the New York Court of Appeals places upon complicated
transactions in New York in determining whether they
come within the protection of the Constitution against impairing the obligations of contract, we certainly should not
be bound by that court's construction of transactions so

entangled in international significance as the status of New York branches of Russian companies and the disposition of their assets. Compare *Appleby* v. *City of New York,* 271 U. S. 364 and *Irving Trust Co.* v. *Day,* 314 U. S. 556. When the decision of a question of fact or of local law is so interwoven with the decision of a question of national authority that the one necessarily involves the other, we are not foreclosed by the state court's determination of the facts or of the local law. Otherwise, national authority could be frustrated by local rulings. See *Creswill* v. *Knights of Pythias,* 225 U. S. 246; *Davis* v. *Wechsler,* 263 U. S. 22.

It is not consonant with the sturdy conduct of our foreign relations that the effect of Russian decrees upon Russian funds in this country should depend on such gossamer distinctions as those by which courts have determined that Russian branches survive the death of their Russian origin. When courts deal with such essentially political phenomena as the taking over of Russian businesses by the Russian government by resorting to the forms and phrases of conventional corporation law, they inevitably fall into a dialectic quagmire. With commendable candor, the House of Lords frankly confessed as much when it practically overruled *Russian Commercial & Industrial Bank* v. *Comptoir d'Escompte de Mulhouse, supra,* saying through Lord Wright, "the whole matter has now to be reconsidered in the light of new evidence and of the historical evolution of ten years." *Lazard Brothers & Co.* v. *Midland Bank,* [1933] A. C. 289, 300.

For we are not dealing here with physical property— whether chattels or realty. We are dealing with intangible rights, with choses in action. The fact that these claims were reduced to money does not change the character of the claims, and certainly is too tenuous a thread on which to determine issues affecting the relation between nations. Corporeal property may give rise to rules of law which, we have held, even in purely domestic controversies ought not to be transferred to the adjudication of impalpable claims such as are here in controversy. *Curry* v. *McCanless,* 307 U. S. 357, 363 *et seq.*

As between the states, due regard for their respective

governmental acts is written into the Constitution by the Full Faith and Credit Clause (Art. IV, § 1). But the scope of its operation—when may the policy of one state deny the consequences of a transaction authorized by the laws of another—has given rise to a long history of judicial subtleties which hardly commend themselves for transfer to the solution of analogous problems between friendly nations. See *Huntington* v. *Attrill*, 146 U. S. 657; *Finney* v. *Guy*, 189 U. S. 335; *Milwaukee County* v. *White Co.*, 296 U. S. 268; *Pacific Ins. Co.* v. *Industrial Comm'n*, 306 U. S. 493, 502; *Pink* v. *A. A. A. Highway Express*, 314 U. S. 201.

For more than fifteen years, formal relations between the United States and Russia were broken because of serious differences between the two countries regarding the consequences to us of two major Russian policies. This complicated process of friction, abstention from friendly relations, efforts at accommodation, and negotiations for removing the causes of friction, are summarized by the delusively simple concept of "non-recognition." The history of Russo-American relations leaves no room for doubt that the two underlying sources of difficulty were Russian propaganda and expropriation. Had any state court during this period given comfort to the Russian views in this contest between its government and ours, it would, to that extent, have interfered with the conduct of our foreign relations by the Executive, even if it had purported to do so under the guise of enforcing state law in a matter of local policy. On the contrary, during this period of non-recognition New York denied Russia access to her courts and did so on the single and conclusive ground: "We should do nothing to thwart the policy which the United States has adopted." *Russian Republic* v. *Cibrario*, 235 N. Y. 255, 263, 139 N. E. 259, 262. Similarly, no invocation of a local rule governing "situs" or the survival of a domesticated corporation, however applicable in an ordinary case, is within the competence of a state court if it would thwart to any extent "the policy which the United States has adopted" when the President reëstablished friendly relations in 1933.

And it would be thwarted if the judgment below were allowed to stand.

That the President's control of foreign relations includes the settlement of claims is indisputable.   Thus, referring to the adhesion of the United States to the Dawes Plan, Secretary of State Hughes reported that "this agreement was negotiated under the long-recognized authority of the President to arrange for the payment of claims in favor of the United States and its nationals.   The exercise of this authority has many illustrations, one of which is the Agreement of 1901 for the so-called Boxer Indemnity." (Secretary Hughes to President Coolidge, February 3, 1925, MS., Department of State, quoted in 5 Hackworth, Digest of Int. Law, c. 16, § 514.)   The President's power to negotiate such a settlement is the same whether it is an isolated transaction between this country and a friendly nation, or is part of a complicated negotiation to restore normal relations, as was the case with Russia.

That the power to establish such normal relations with a foreign country belongs to the President is equally indisputable.   Recognition of a foreign country is not a theoretical problem or an exercise in abstract symbolism.   It is the assertion of national power directed towards safeguarding and promoting our interests and those of civilization.   Recognition of a revolutionary government normally involves the removal of areas of friction.   As often as not, areas of friction are removed by the adjustment of claims pressed by this country on behalf of its nationals against a new régime.

Such a settlement was made by the President when this country resumed normal relations with Russia.   The two chief barriers to renewed friendship with Russia—intrusive propaganda and the effects of expropriation decrees upon our nationals—were at the core of our negotiations in 1933, as they had been for a good many years.   The exchanges between the President and M. Litvinov must be read not in isolation but as the culmination of difficulties and dealings extending over fifteen years.   And they must be read not as self-contained technical documents, like a marine insurance contract or a bill of lading, but as characteristically delicate and elusive expressions of diplomacy.   The draftsmen of such notes must save sensibilities and avoid the explicitness on which diplomatic negotiations so easily founder.

The controlling history of the Soviet régime and of this country's relations with it must be read between the lines of the Roosevelt-Litvinov Agreement. One needs to be no expert in Russian law to know that the expropriation decrees intended to sweep the assets of Russian companies taken over by that government into Russia's control no matter where those assets were credited. Equally clear is it that the assignment by Russia meant to give the United States, as part of the comprehensive settlement, everything that Russia claimed under its laws against Russians. It does violence to the course of negotiations between the United States and Russia, and to the scope of the final adjustment, to assume that a settlement thus made on behalf of the United States—to settle both money claims and to soothe feelings—was to be qualified by the variant notions of the courts of the forty-eight states regarding "situs" or "jurisdiction" over intangibles or the survival of extinct Russian corporations. In our dealings with the outside world, the United States speaks with one voice and acts as one, unembarrassed by the complications as to domestic issues which are inherent in the distribution of political power between the national government and the individual states.

MR. CHIEF JUSTICE STONE, dissenting:

I think the judgment should be affirmed.

As my brethren are content to rest their decision on the authority of the dictum in *United States* v. *Belmont*, 301 U. S. 324, without the aid of any pertinent decision of this Court, I think a word should be said of the authority and reasoning of the *Belmont* case and of the principles which I think are controlling here.

In the *Belmont* case, the United States brought suit in the federal court to recover a debt alleged to be due upon a deposit account of a Russian national with a New York banker. The complaint set up the confiscation of the account by decrees of the Soviet Government and the transfer of the debt to the United States by the Litvinov assignment, concurrently with our diplomatic recognition of that Government. It was not alleged, nor did it appear, that the New York courts had, subsequent to recognition, refused to give effect to the Soviet decrees as operating to transfer the title of Russian nationals to property located in New York. No such national or any adverse claimant was a party to the suit. In sustaining the complaint against demurrer, this Court said (p. 332): "In so holding, we deal only with the case as now presented and with the parties now before us. We do not consider the status of adverse claims, if there be any, of others not parties to this action. And nothing we have said is to be construed as foreclosing the assertion of any such claim to the fund involved, by intervention or other appropriate proceeding. We decide only that the complaint alleges facts sufficient to constitute a cause of action against the respondents."

The questions thus explicitly reserved are presented by the case now before us. The courts of New York, in the exercise of the constitutional authority ordinarily possessed by state courts to declare the rules of law applicable to property located within their territorial limits, have refused to recognize the Soviet decrees as depriving creditors and other claimants representing the interests of the insurance company of their rights under New York law. Numerous individual creditors and other claimants, and the New York Superintendent of Insurance, who represents all claimants, are parties to the present suit and assert their claims to the exclusion of the United States.

It is true that this Court, in the *Belmont* case, indulged in some remarks as to the effect on New York law of our diplomatic recognition of the Soviet Government and of the assignment of all its claims against American nationals to the United States. Upon the basis of these observations it thought that the New York courts were bound to recognize and apply the Soviet decrees to property which was located in New York when the decrees were promulgated. But all this was predicated upon the mistaken assumption that by disregarding the decrees the New York courts would be giving an extraterritorial effect to New York law. These observations were irrelevant to the decision there announced and, for reasons shortly to be given, I think plainly inapplicable here. They were but *obiter dicta* which, so far as they have not been discredited by our decision in *Guaranty Trust Co.* v. *United States,* 304 U. S. 126, and so far as they now merit it "may be respected, but ought not to control the judgment in a subsequent suit, when the very point is presented for decision." Chief Justice Marshall in *Cohens* v. *Virginia*, 6 Wheat. 264, 399; Mr. Justice Sutherland in *Williams* v. *United States*, 289 U. S. 553, 568.

We have no concern here with the wisdom of the rules of law which the New York courts have adopted in this case or their consonance with the most enlightened principles of jurisprudence. State questions do not become federal questions because they are difficult or because we may think that the state courts have given wrong answers to them. The only questions before us are whether New York has constitutional authority to adopt its own rules of law defining rights in property located in the state, and, if so, whether that authority has been curtailed by the exercise of a superior federal power by recognition of the Soviet Government and acceptance of its assignment to the United States of claims against American nationals, including the New York property.

I shall state my grounds for thinking that the pronouncements in the *Belmont* case, on which the Court relies for the answer to these questions, are without the support of reason or accepted principles of law. No one doubts that the Soviet decrees are the acts of the government of the Russian state, which is sovereign in its own territory, and that in consequence of our recognition of that government they will be so treated by our State Department. As such, when they affect property which was located in Russia at the time of their promulgation, they are subject to inquiry, if at all, only through our State Department and not in our courts. *Underhill* v. *Hernandez*, 168 U. S. 250; *Oetjen* v. *Central Leather Co.*, 246 U. S. 297; *Ricaud* v. *American Metal Co.*, 246 U. S. 304, 308–10; *Salimoff & Co.* v. *Standard Oil Co.*, 262 N. Y. 220, 186 N. E. 679. But the property to which the New York judgment relates has at all relevant times been in New York in the custody of the Superintendent of Insurance as security for the policies of the insurance company, and is now in the Superintendent's custody as Liquidator acting under the direction of the New York courts. *United States* v. *Bank of New York Co.*, 296 U. S. 463, 478–79. In administering and distributing the property thus within their control, the New York courts are free to apply their own rules of law, including their own doctrines of conflict of laws, see *Erie R. Co.* v. *Tompkins,* 304 U. S. 64, 78; *Griffin* v. *McCoach,* 313 U. S. 498; *Kryger* v. *Wilson,* 242 U. S. 171, 176, except insofar as they are subject to the requirements of the full faith and credit clause—a clause applicable only to the judgments and public acts of states of the Union and not those of foreign states. *Aetna Life Insurance Co.* v. *Tremblay,* 223 U. S. 185; cf. *Bank of Augusta* v. *Earle,* 13 Pet. 519, 589–90; *Bond* v. *Hume,* 243 U. S. 15, 21–22.

This Court has repeatedly decided that the extent to which a state court will follow the rules of law of a recognized foreign country in preference to its own is wholly a matter of comity, and that, in the absence of relevant treaty obligations, the application in the courts of a state of its own rules of law rather than those of a foreign country raises no federal question. *Rose* v. *Himely,* 4 Cranch 241; *Harrison* v. *Sterry,* 5 Cranch 289; *United States* v. *Crosby,* 7 Cranch 115; *Oakey* v. *Bennett,* 11 How. 33, 43–46; *Hilton* v. *Guyot,* 159 U. S. 113, 165–66; *Disconto Gesellschaft* v. *Umbreit,* 208 U. S. 570; cf. *Baglin* v. *Cusenier Co.,* 221 U. S. 580, 594–97; *United States* v. *Guaranty Trust Co.,* 293 U. S. 340, 345–47. This is equally the case when a state of the Union refuses to apply the law of a sister state, if there is no question of full faith and credit, *Kryger* v. *Wilson, supra; Finney* v. *Guy,* 189 U. S. 335, 340, 346; *Alropa Corp.* v. *Kirchwehm,* 313 U. S. 549; see *Milwaukee County* v. *White Co.,* 296 U. S. 268, 272–73, or due process, *Home Ins. Co.* v. *Dick,* 281 U. S. 397. So clearly was this thought to be an appropriate exercise of the power of a forum over property within its territorial jurisdiction that this Court, in *Ingenohl* v. *Olsen & Co.,* 273 U. S. 541, 544–45, accepted as beyond all doubt the right of the British courts in Hong Kong to refuse recognition to the American alien property custodian's transfer of exclusive rights to the use of a trademark in Hong Kong, and the Court gave effect here to the Hong Kong judgment.

In the application of this doctrine, this Court has often held that a state, following its own law and policy, may refuse to give effect to a transfer made elsewhere of property which is within its own territorial limits. *Green* v.

Van Buskirk, 5 Wall. 307, 311–12; *Hervey* v. *Rhode Island Locomotive Works*, 93 U. S. 664; *Security Trust Co.* v. *Dodd, Mead & Co.*, 173 U. S. 624; *Clark* v. *Williard*, 292 U. S. 112, 122; *Clark* v. *Williard*, 294 U. S. 211. So far is a state free in this respect that the full faith and credit clause does not preclude the attachment by local creditors of the property within the state of a foreign corporation, all of whose property has been previously transferred in the state of its incorporation to a statutory successor for the benefit of creditors. *Clark* v. *Williard, supra; Fischer* v. *American United Life Ins. Co.*, 314 U. S. 549. Due process under the Fifth Amendment, the benefits of which extend to alien friends as well as to citizens, *Russian Volunteer Fleet* v. *United States*, 282 U. S. 481, does not call for any different conclusion. *Disconto Gesellschaft* v. *Umbreit, supra*, 579–80.

At least since 1797, *Barclay* v. *Russell*, 3 Vesey, Jr., 424, 428, 433, the English courts have consistently held that foreign confiscatory decrees do not operate to transfer title to property located in England, even if the decrees were so intended, whether the foreign government has or has not been recognized by the British Government. *Lecouturier* v. *Rey*, [1910] A. C. 262, 265. Cf. also *Folliott* v. *Ogden*, 1 H. Black. 123, 135–36, affirmed 3 T. R. 726, affirmed, 4 Brown's Cases in Parl., 111; and *Wolff* v. *Oxholm*, 6 M. & S. 92, both of which may have carried the doctrine of non-recognition of foreign confiscatory decrees even further. See Holdsworth, The History of Acts of State in English Law, 41 Columbia L. Rev. 1313, 1325–26. The English courts have applied this rule in litigation arising out of the Russian decrees, holding that they are not effectual to transfer title to property situated in Great Britain. *Sedgwick Collins & Co.* v. *Rossia Insurance Co.*, [1926] 1 K. B. 1, 15, affirmed, [1927] A. C. 95; *The Jupiter (No. 3)*, [1927] P. 122, 144–46, affirmed, [1927] P. 250, 253–55; *In re Russian Bank for Foreign Trade*, [1933] 1 Ch. 745, 767–68. The same doctrine has prevailed in the case of the Spanish confiscatory decrees, *Banco de Vizcaya* v. *Don Alfonso*, [1935] 1 K. B. 140, 144–45, as well as with respect to seizures by the American alien property custodian. *Sutherland* v. *Administrator of German Property*, [1934] 1 K. B. 423; and see the decision of the British court for

Hong Kong discussed in *Ingenohl* v. *Olsen & Co., supra,* and the Privy Council's decision in *Ingenohl* v. *Wing On & Co.,* 44 Patents Journal 343, 359–60. In no case in which there was occasion to decide the question has recognition been thought to have subordinated the law of the forum, with respect to property situated within its territorial jurisdiction, to that of the recognized state. Never has the forum's refusal to follow foreign transfers of title to such property been considered inconsistent with the most friendly relations with the recognized foreign government, or even with an active military alliance at the time of the transfer.

It is plain that under New York law the claimants in this case, both creditors and those asserting rights of the insurance company, have enforcible rights, with respect to the property located there, which have been recognized though not created by the judgments of its courts. The conclusion is inescapable that, had there been no assignment and this suit had been maintained by the Soviet Government subsequent to recognition, or by a private individual claiming under an assignment from it, the decision of the New York court would have presented no question reviewable here.

The only question remaining is whether the circumstances in the present case, that the Russian decrees preceded recognition and that the assignment was to the United States, which here appears in the role of plaintiff, call for any different result. If they do, then recognition and the assignment have operated to give to the United States rights which its assignor did not have. They have compelled the state to surrender its own rules of law applicable to property within its limits, and to substitute rules of Russian law for them. A potency would thus be attributed to the recognition and assignment which is lacking to the full faith and credit clause of the Constitution. See *Clark* v. *Williard, supra; Fischer* v. *American United Life Ins. Co., supra.*

In deciding any federal question involved, it can make no difference to us whether New York has chosen to express its public policy by statute or merely by the common law determinations of its courts. *Erie R. Co.* v. *Tompkins, supra,* 304 U. S. 64; *Skiriotes* v. *Florida,* 313 U. S.

69, 79; *Hebert* v. *Louisiana,* 272 U. S. 312, 316. The state court's repeated declaration of a policy of treating the New York branch of the insurance company as a "complete and separate organization" would permit satisfaction of whatever claims of foreign creditors, as well as those of sister states, that New York deems provable against the local fund. But if my brethren are correct in concluding that all foreign creditors must be deprived of access to the fund, it would seem to follow—since the Soviet decrees have exempted no class of creditors—that the rights of creditors in New York or in sister states, or any other rights in the property recognized by New York law, must equally be ousted by virtue of the extraterritorial effect given to the decrees by the present decision. For, statutory priorities of New York policyholders or New York lienholders, and the common law priorities and system of distribution which the judgment below endeavored to effectuate and preserve intact, must alike yield to the superior force said to have been imparted to the Soviet decrees by the recognition and assignment. Nothing in the Litvinov assignment or in the negotiations for recognition suggests an intention to impose upon the states discriminations between New York and other creditors which would sustain the former's liens while obliterating those of the latter. If the Litvinov assignment overrides state policies which protect foreign creditors, it can hardly be thought to do less to domestic creditors, whether of New York or a sister state.

I assume for present purposes that these sweeping alterations of the rights of states and of persons could be achieved by treaty or even executive agreement, although we are referred to no authority which would sustain such an exercise of power as is said to have been exerted here by mere assignment unratified by the Senate. It is true that, in according recognition and in establishing friendly relations with a foreign country, this Government speaks for all the forty-eight states. But it was never true that recognition alters the substantive law of any state or prescribes uniform state law for the nationals of the recognized country. On the contrary, it does not even secure for them equality of treatment in the several states, or equal treatment with citizens in any state, save as the

Constitution demands it.   *Patsone* v. *Pennsylvania,* 232
U. S. 138; *Terrace* v. *Thompson,* 263 U. S. 197; *Clarke* v.
Deckebach, 274 U. S. 392 and cases cited.   Those are ends
which can be achieved only by the assumption of some
form of obligation expressed or fairly to be inferred from
its words.

Recognition, like treaty making, is a political act, and
both may be upon terms and conditions.   But that fact no
more forecloses this Court, where it is called upon to adju-
dicate private rights, from inquiry as to what those terms
and conditions are than it precludes, in like circumstances,
a court's ascertaining the true scope and meaning of a
treaty.   Of course, the national power may by appropriate
constitutional means override the power of states and the
rights of individuals.   But, without collision between
them, there is no such loss of power or impairment of
rights, and it cannot be known whether state law and
private rights collide with political acts expressed in
treaties or executive agreements until their respective
boundaries are defined.

It would seem, therefore, that in deciding this case some
inquiry should have been made to ascertain what public
policy or binding rule of conduct with respect to state
power and individual rights has been proclaimed by the
recognition of the Soviet Government and the assignment of its claims to the United States.   The mere act of
recognition and the bare transfer of the claims of the
Soviet Government to the United States can, of themselves,
hardly be taken to have any such effect, and they can be
regarded as intended to do so only if that purpose is made
evident by their terms, read in the light of diplomatic
exchanges between the two countries and of the surrounding circumstances.   Even when courts deal with the language of diplomacy, some foundation must be laid for in-
ferring an obligation where previously there was none, and
some expression must be found in the conduct of foreign
relations which fairly indicates an intention to assume it.
Otherwise, courts, rather than the executive, may shape
and define foreign policy which the executive has not
adopted.

We are not pointed to anything on the face of the documents or in the diplomatic correspondence which even

suggests that the United States was to be placed in a better position, with respect to the claim which it now asserts, than was the Soviet Government and nationals. Nor is there any intimation in them that recognition was to give to prior public acts of the Soviet Government any greater extraterritorial effect than attaches to such acts occurring after recognition—acts which, by the common understanding of English and American courts, are ordinarily deemed to be without extraterritorial force, and which, in any event, have never before been considered to restrict the power of the states to apply their own rules of law to foreign-owned property within their territory. As we decided in *Guaranty Trust Co.* v. *United States, supra,* 304 U. S. at 143, and as the opinion of the Court now appears to concede, there is nothing in any of the relevant documents "to suggest that the United States was to acquire or exert any greater rights than its transferor or that the President by mere executive action purported or intended to alter or diminish the rights of the [New York] debtor with respect to any assigned claims, or that the United States, as assignee, is to do more than the Soviet Government could have done after diplomatic recognition—that is, collect the claims in conformity to local law."

Recognition opens our courts to the recognized government and its nationals, see *Guaranty Trust Co.* v. *United States, supra,* 140. It accepts the acts of that government within its own territory as the acts of the sovereign, including its acts as a *de facto* government before recognition, see *Underhill* v. *Hernandez, supra,* 168 U. S. 250; *Oetjen* v. *Central Leather Co., supra,* 246 U. S. 297; *Ricaud* v. *American Metal Co., supra,* 246 U. S. 304. But, until now, recognition of a foreign government by this Government has never been thought to serve as a full faith and credit clause compelling obedience here to the laws and public acts of the recognized government with respect to property and transactions in this country. One could as well argue that by the Soviet Government's recognition of our own Government, which accompanied the transactions now under consideration, it had undertaken to apply in Russia the New York law applicable to Russian property in New York. Cf. *Ingenohl* v. *Olsen & Co., supra,* 273 U. S.

541; *Pacific Ins. Co.* v. *Industrial Comm'n,* 306 U. S. 493, 501–02.

In *Guaranty Trust Co.* v. *United States, supra,* this Court unanimously rejected the contention that the recognition of the Soviet Government operated to curtail or impair rights derived from the application of state laws and policy within the state's own territory. It was argued by the Government that recognition operated retroactively, for the period of the *de facto* government, to set aside rights acquired in the United States in consequence of this Government's prior recognition of the Russian Provisional Government. This argument, we said, p. 140, "ignores the distinction between the effect of our recognition of a foreign government with respect to its acts within its own territory prior to recognition, and the effect upon previous transactions consummated here between its predecessor and our own nationals. The one operates only to validate to a limited extent acts of a *de facto* government which by virtue of the recognition, has become a government *de jure*. But it does not follow that recognition renders of no effect transactions here with a prior recognized government in conformity to the declared policy of our own Government." Even though the two governments might have stipulated for alteration by this Government of its municipal law, and the consequent surrender of the rights of individuals, the substance of the Court's decision was that such an abdication of domestic law and policy is not a necessary or customary incident of recognition or fairly to be inferred from it. No more can recognition be said to imply a deprivation of the constitutional rights of states of the Union, and of individuals arising out of their laws and policy, which are binding on the Federal Government except as the act of recognition is accompanied by some affirmative exercise of federal power which purports to set them aside.

Nor can I find in the surrounding circumstances or in the history of the diplomatic relations of the two countries any basis for saying that there was any policy of either to give a different or larger effect to recognition and the assignment than would ordinarily attach to them. It is significant that the account of the negotiations published by the State Department (Establishment of Diplomatic

Relations with the Union of Soviet Socialist Republics, Eastern European Series No. 1), and the report of subsequent negotiations for adjustment of the claims of the two countries submitted to Congress by the Secretary of State (H. Rep. No. 865, 76th Cong., 1st Sess.) give no intimation of such a policy. Even the diplomatic correspondence between the two countries, of January 7, 1937, to which the opinion of the Court refers, and which occurred long after the United States had entered the Moscow Fire Insurance Company litigation, merely repeated the language of the assignment without suggesting that its purpose had been to override applicable state law.

That the assignment after recognition had wide scope for application without reading into it any attempt to set aside our local laws and rights accruing under them is evident. It was not limited in its application to property alleged to be confiscated under the Soviet decrees. Included in the assignment, by its terms, were all "amounts admitted to be due or that may be found to be due it [the Soviet Government], as the successor of prior Governments of Russia, or otherwise, from American nationals." It included claims of the prior governments of Russia, not arising out of confiscatory decrees, and also claims like that of the Russian Volunteer Fleet, growing out of our own expropriation during the war of the property of Russian nationals. The assignment was far from an idle ceremony if treated as transferring only the rights which it purports to assign. Large sums of money have already been collected under it, and other amounts are in process of collection, without overturning the law of the states where the claims have been asserted.[1]

At the time of the assignment, it was not known what position the courts of this country would take with respect to property here, claimed to have been confiscated by the Soviet decrees. But it must have been known to the two governments that the English courts notwithstanding British recognition of the Soviet Government,

---

[1] By June 30, 1938, the sums collected by virtue of the Litvinov assignment amounted to $1,706,443. Report of the Attorney General for 1938, p. 122. Other claims are apparently still in litigation. See the Report for 1939, p. 99; also H. Rep. No. 865, 76th Cong., 1st Sess., p. 2.

had refused to apply the Soviet decrees as affecting property located in England. *Sedgwick Collins & Co.* v. *Rossia Insurance Co., supra; The Jupiter (No. 3), supra; In re Russian Bank for Foreign Trade, supra.* It must also have been known that the similar views expressed by the New York courts before recognition with respect to property situated in New York raised at least a strong possibility that mere recognition would not alter the result in that state. *Sokoloff* v. *National City Bank,* 239 N. Y. 158, 167–69, 145 N. E. 917; *James & Co.* v. *Second Russian Ins. Co.,* 239 N. Y. 248, 257, 146 N. E. 369; *Joint Stock Co.* v. *National City Bank,* 240 N. Y. 368, 148 N. E. 552; *Petrogradsky M. K. Bank* v. *National City Bank,* 253 N. Y. 23, 29, 170 N. E. 479. The assignment plainly contemplated that this, like every other question affecting liability, was to be litigated in the courts of this country, since the assignment only purported to assign amounts admitted to be due or "that may be found to be due." It was only in the courts where the debtor or the property was located that the amounts assigned would normally be "found to be due." Cf. *United States* v. *Bank of New York Co., supra,* 296 U. S. 463.

By transferring claims of every kind, against American nationals, to the United States and leaving to it their collection, the parties necessarily remitted to the courts of this country the determination of the amounts due upon this Government's undertaking to report the amounts collected as "preparatory to a final settlement of the claims and counterclaims" asserted by the two governments. They thus ended the necessity of diplomatic discussion of the validity of the claims, and so removed a probable source of friction between the two countries. In all this, I can find no hint that the rules of decision in American courts were not to be those afforded by the law customarily applied in those courts. But if it was the purpose of either government to override local law and policy of the states and to prescribe a different rule of decision from that hitherto recognized by any court, it would seem to have been both natural and needful to have expressed it in some form of undertaking indicating such an intention. The only obligation to be found in the assignment and its acknowledgment by the President is that of the United

States, already mentioned, to report the amounts collected. This can hardly be said to be an undertaking to strike down valid defenses to the assigned claims. Treaties, to say nothing of executive agreements and assignments which are mere transfers of rights, have hitherto been construed not to override state law or policy unless it is reasonably evident from their language that such was the intention. *Guaranty Trust Co.* v. *United States, supra,* 304 U. S. at 143; *Todok* v. *Union State Bank,* 281 U. S. 449, 454; *Rocca* v. *Thompson,* 223 U. S. 317, 329–34; *Disconto Gesellschaft* v. *Umbreit, supra,* 208 U. S. at 582; *Pearl Assurance Co.* v. *Harrington,* 38 F. Supp. 411, 413–14; affirmed, 313 U. S. 549; *Patsone* v. *Pennsylvania,* 232 U. S. 138, 145–46; cf. *Liverpool Ins. Co.* v. *Massachusetts,* 10 Wall. 566, 568, 576–77. The practical consequences of the present decision would seem to be, in every case of recognition of a foreign government, to foist upon the executive the responsibility for subordinating domestic to foreign law in conflicts cases, whether intended or not, unless such a purpose is affirmatively disclaimed.

Under our dual system of government, there are many circumstances in which the legislative and executive branches of the national government may, by affirmative action expressing its policy, enlarge the exercise of federal authority and thus diminish the power which otherwise might be exercised by the states. It is indispensable to the orderly administration of the system that such alteration of powers and the consequent impairment of state and private rights should not turn on conceptions of policy which, if ever entertained by the only branch of the government authorized to adopt it, has been left unexpressed. It is not for this Court to adopt policy, the making of which has been by the Constitution committed to other branches of the government. It is not its function to supply a policy where none has been declared or defined and none can be inferred.

MR. JUSTICE ROBERTS joins in this opinion.

The Hornet
12 Fed. Cas. 529 No. 6,705 (D., No. Car. 1870).

Application to interpose a claim, in admiralty. The steamer Hornet was seized upon a libel of information, founded upon a charge of violating the neutrality laws. J. Morales Lemus, as agent of the so-called "Republic of Cuba," now applied to be allowed to intervene and interpose a claim and contest the suit. The only question now made was as to the propriety of allowing such agent to claim.

BROOKS, District Judge. The question submitted to the court is—can this court recognize as existing, any government or organized body of people, or element known as the "Republic of Cuba," to the extent of allowing that as a body politic, or government to come through an agent into court, and be admitted as claimant of the property libeled in this cause?

The capacity of this struggling element in Cuba, styling themselves the "Republic of Cuba," to take and hold property is not a question for consideration. But it is now simply for this court to declare to what extent it may properly go (if to any extent), in declaring how far any revolutionary element or people have succeeded in their efforts to separate and free themselves from any established and acknowledged government.

I feel that I have been aided materially in coming to a correct conclusion upon this question, by the very clear and able arguments of the counsel who addressed the court—both for the United States and for the individual who styles himself the "agent of the Republic of Cuba;" yet I am embarrassed by the importance of this question, in its connection with this cause. Were I satisfied that my opinion would be revised by the supreme court, and be by that body corrected if wrong, I would announce the conclusion to which I have come with less reluctance than I do.

It was contended by Mr. Phelps, the counsel who submitted the argument on the part of the United States—that this court would exceed its power in recognizing to any extent, or for any purpose—the existence of any mere revolutionary body, such as that styling itself the "Republic of Cuba," in the absence of any act, resolution, proclamation of the legislative or executive department of our government, declaring or admitting to any extent, the existence of such a government. That there is no authority to show that such power was designed to be allowed the courts, or was ever exercised by the courts of the United States, but on the contrary there is abundant and conclusive authority—both of our circuit and supreme court, to show that they have not only declined to claim or exercise such power—but declared it to exist with and to have been exercised by the political departments of the government alone. That a power or government must necessarily be recognized to have existence before they can be admitted as claimants to defend or be in any way heard in the court.

Other objections were urged by the counsel to the sufficiency of the evidence offered by J. Morales Lemus, to show that he was authorized to represent and claim for the Republic of Cuba. This, like the question of title, the court regards as not now necessary to be considered.

I listened with care and much interest to the argument of the learned counsel who addressed the court in behalf of the party who asks to be admitted as agent, for the purpose of interposing a claim, and to the authorities read and commented upon by him. I have examined the authorities cited on both sides, and considered these authorities and the arguments with care, and have been forced to the conclusion that this question is with the United States, and I must so declare.

I confess to some degree of hesitancy in so declaring, because, partially considered, it may seem as if it recognized to some extent, a right in the strong to deny justice to the weak. But, if anything should be yielded for such a consideration, it would be altogether unjustifiable on my part. Less defensible for me would such a course be for the reason that I entertain so clearly the opinion that courts have no right to consider any question of law submitted to them, in a policy view. Courts should construe the law—ascertain, and declare the law, as it is, without reference to any opinion of the judge, as to what the law should be. Though no case parallel to this case has been cited, yet cases have been referred to and commented upon by the counsel for the government, which, in my opinion, conclusively settle this question.

I will first refer to the case of U. S. v. Palmer, 3 Wheat. [16 U. S.] 610. This was an indictment against the defendant and others, under the act of congress, for robbery upon the high seas—in the circuit court for the district of Massachusetts. The judges were not agreed, and certified eleven questions for the opinion of the supreme court. That eminent judge, Chief Justice Marshall, delivered the opinion of the court. I will only refer to the remarks of the learned chief justice upon the tenth question so certified. The question was certified in the following language. "Whether any colony, district, or people, who have revolted from their native allegiance, and have assumed upon themselves the exercise of independent and sovereign power, can be deemed in any court of the United States an independent or sovereign nation or government, until they have been acknowledged as such by the government of the United States; and whether such acknowledgment can be proved in a court of the United States otherwise than by some act, resolution, or statute of congress, or by some public proclamation or other public act of the executive authority of the United States, directly containing or announcing such acknowledgment, or by publicly receiving or acknowledging an ambassador or other public minister from such colony, district, or people; and whether such acknowledgment can be proved by mere inference from the private acts or private instructions of the executive of the United States, where no public acknowledgment has ever been made; and whether the courts of the states are bound judicially to take notice of the existing relations of the states as to foreign states and sovereignties, their colonies and dependencies."

That great judge and the supreme court, declare as follows: "Those questions which respect the rights of a foreign empire, which asserts and is contending for its independence, and the conduct which must be observed by the courts of the Union towards the subjects of such sections of an empire who may be brought before the tribunals of this country are equally difficult and delicate. As it is understood that the construction which has been given to the acts of congress will render a particular answer unnecessary, the court will only observe that such questions are generally rather political than legal in their character. They belong more properly to those who can declare what the law shall be; who can place the nation in such a position with respect to foreign powers as to their judgment may seem wise; to whom are entrusted all its foreign relations; than to that tribunal whose power as well as duty is confined to the application of the rule which the legislature may prescribe for it. In such contests the nation may engage itself with one party or the other—may observe absolute neutrality—may recognize the new state absolutely, or may make a limited recognition of it. The proceedings in courts must depend so entirely on the course of the government that it is difficult to give a precise answer to questions which do not refer to a particular nation. This court is of opinion that, when a civil war rages in a foreign nation—one part of which separates itself from the old established government and erects itself into a distinct government—the courts of the Union must view such newly constituted government as it is viewed by the legislative and executive departments of the government of the United States."

Then the same learned judge, in the case of The Divina Pastora, 4 Wheat. [17 U. S.] 52, decided at the next term of the supreme court, says that "the decision at the last term, in U. S. v. Palmer [supra], establishes the principle that the government of the Union having recognized the existence of a civil war between Spain and her colonies, but remaining neutral, the courts of the Union are bound to consider as lawful, those acts which war authorizes, and which the new government in South America may direct against their enemy." Hence I conclude that for the reason that the government of the United States had recognized the existence of a civil war between Spain and her colonies, the courts were forbidden to say that the act of capturing The Divina Pastora was unlawful. That the court could not say, after such an acknowledgment, if the capturing ship had come within the jurisdiction of the United States, that she was a piratical vessel, and treat her as such. That the effect of this acknowledgment was to accord to the new power belligerent rights, so far as the United States were concerned; one of which is to grant letters of marque and reprisal, one of the important advantages arising from which (to such as act under them), is exemption from the penalty for piracy. This is but saying to such a people that we see and understand that you are struggling to separate from the mother country.

That whether a revolted colony is to be treated as a sovereign state, even de facto, is a political question, and to be decided by the government, and not the court, has been decided in effect in several other cases than those before mentioned, as in Kennett v.

Chambers, 14 How. [55 U. S.] 38; Clark v. U. S. [Case No. 2,838].

And in the great case of Luther v. Borden [7 How. (48 U. S.) 1], than in the argument of which the great American constitutional lawyer rarely if ever displayed more learning, the supreme court unmistakably declared, against the view urged by Mr. Webster, that the federal courts have no jurisdiction of the question whether a government, organized in a state, is the duly constituted government in the state. That is a question which belongs to the political, not to the judicial power. In that case any disposition of that question could not have disturbed our relation with any established foreign power. No power with whom the United States was at peace or to whom our government was solemnly pledged to a just and clearly prescribed course, as by our neutrality acts, could or would have complained of a contrary decision in that case—and still that was held not to be a question with the court.

How much the more reason in the conclusion to which our courts have come, and on which they have acted in relation to this subject, where even by possibility their action might involve our country in war with foreign powers. There are other cases to which I might refer establishing in my view this principle.

I do not deem it necessary to refer to the other cases cited by the counsel for the government. It cannot be intended that such power should be vested in the courts. It would be a power dangerous to our government to be so vested, and one which judges could not so well exercise as congress or the executive.

If the courts have the power to do any act which would in effect accord to this new government advantages, I do not see what limits there would be to the benefits which they might so confer, and the result might be that our nation would be involved in a war from the action of one judge, when the people and those who represent the people were disposed to peace.

If the courts, before the political departments had spoken, have the right to take one step in this direction, I do not see any limit to their power, short of declaring perfect freedom and independence. What act has been performed, what resolution, declaration, or proclamation has been made by congress or the executive, indicating an intention on their part to acknowledge, at any time or to any extent, the existence of the Republic of Cuba?

This court knows of no such act, and nothing of that character has been shown or alleged by counsel. Then this court cannot know of the existence of such a government. Such knowledge is essential to the admission of this agent, as claimant for his government.

My time for the examination of this question has not been so ample as I could have desired.

Application denied.

Canadian Car & F. Co. v. American Can Co.
253 Fed. 152 (S.D., N.Y., 1918)
affirmed 258 Fed. 363 (2d. Cir., 1919)

MAYER, District Judge. The suit is to recover $1,500,000 with interest. Defendant concedes, and always has conceded, that it owes $1,500,000 to somebody; but, because of certain transactions and documents, defendant's position is that it cannot safely pay the money to plaintiffs, and that it may hereafter be subject to a judgment or decree in some suit or action which may be brought by some "Russian government."

Two principal propositions are relied upon by plaintiffs:

(1) That under the documents and transactions in the case the

Russian government has not any beneficial interest in the money due from defendant, and therefore that plaintiffs alone are entitled thereto.

(2) That if any beneficial interest in the $1,500,000 existed in favor of the Russian government, a release and assignment executed by authorized representatives of the Russian government disposed of and discharged such beneficial interest. If the plaintiffs prevail, there arises the question of what interest, if any, is due to the respective plaintiffs, i. e., the date from which interest should run and the rate. There is also a minor subsidiary controversy between Can Co. and Recording Co. which was referred to a special master. The master has submitted a clear and concise report in respect of the matter before him. His report is confirmed, and further reference thereto is unnecessary.

1. The basis of the indebtedness owing by Can Co. is the manufacture and delivery of fuses by Recording Co. The liability of Can Co. to pay for fuses manufactured by Recording Co. arose under two agreements dated, respectively, August 23, 1916, and November 21, 1916, the details of which need not be recited. The net result was that Recording Co. manufactured 1,500,000 time fuses which were delivered and accepted. Recording Co., however, was indebted to Agency Co., and Agency Co. had large contracts with the Russian government for the manufacture of munitions.

On October 31, 1916, an arrangement was entered into by Can Co., Recording Co., and Agency Co. which was expressed in the following letter:

"October 31, 1916.

"American Can Company, 120 Broadway, New York City—Dear Sirs: In consideration of your making advances to Recording & Computing Machines Company of the sums provided in your contract, dated August 23, 1916, with that company for the manufacture of 1,250,000 Russian time fuses, and of your making the payments to that company of the purchase price of time fuses, as provided in said contract, out of which the sum of one dollar ($1.00) of the purchase price of each fuse delivered shall be paid by you to us, until all sums which may now or hereafter be due from and payable by that company to us are adjusted and paid or otherwise satisfied:

"We hereby agree that you may take security for such advances on all materials purchased by that company from the sums so advanced, and that we will waive any claim or lien which we may have upon the time fuses manufactured for you by that company under its said contract with you, and that we will not interfere with the delivery to you by that company of the time fuses so manufactured for you by that company under its said contract with you. * * *

"Yours very truly,

"Agency of Canadian Car & Foundry Company,
"C. H. Cahan, Chairman of the Board of Directors.

"Accepted by:
"American Can Company,
"J. R. Harbeck, Vice President.

"Accepted by:
"Recording & Computing Machines Company,
"H. A. Toulmin, Vice President."

The above is the document of primary importance in the case.

On January 2, 1917, an agreement (too long to quote) was entered into between "General A. Zalubovsky, President of the Imperial Russian Supply Committee in America, Acting for and on Behalf of the Chief Artillery Board of the Imperial Russian Government," and Agency Co. The instrument was signed, "For Lieutenant General A. Zalubovsky, President of the Imperial Russian Supply Com-

mittee in America, by Major General Khrabroff, Vice President."
By this agreement, inter alia, Agency Co. assigned to the Russian
government the agreement or order of October 31, 1916, supra, "to
receive from American Can Company all sums of money payable to
the Agency Company under the terms of said agreement," and the
Russian government agreed to make certain payments to Agency Co.

Contemporaneously with the agreement of January 2, 1917, there
was indorsed on the order of October 31, 1916, the following:

"New York City, January 2, 1917.

"For valuable consideration, Agency of Canadian Car & Foundry Company,
limited, hereby assigns to the Imperial Russian Government, all the right, title
and interest of said company in and to all sums of money payable under the
within agreement, dated October 31, 1916.

"Agency of Canadian Car & Foundry Company,
"By C. H. Cahan,
"Chairman of Board of Directors. [Seal.]"

As part of the transaction of January 2, 1917, Recording Co. on
January 11, 1917, entered into an agreement with the Russian government (acting through the same officials) that contractors with
Recording Co. for time fuses (which included defendant) should
deduct $1 from the purchase price of each fuse and pay the same
to the Russian government until payment should be made in full of
the amount which the Russian government was required to pay to
Agency Co. under the agreement of January 2, 1917.

On September 14, 1917, Can Co. agreed with Recording Co. that Can
Co. retain $1,500,000 "for account of Agency of Canadian Car and
Foundry Company or the Imperial Russian government, as their
interests may appear" until such time as there was a final adjustment
of account between the interested parties or a final determination
by law.

Certain differences having arisen, the details of which may be passed
by, matters were finally settled between Recording Co., Agency Co.,
and the Russian government acting through Gen. Khrabroff, now
president of the Russian Supply Committee, and the settlement was
expressed in elaborate detail in an agreement dated December 18,
1917, and executed by the three parties. On the same day, and as a
part of the same transaction, the Russian government, acting through
Gen. Khrabroff as "President of the Russian Supply Committee in
Behalf of the Russian Government" assigned to Agency Co. and Recording Co. all its right, title, and interest, if any, to the $1,500,000
held by Can Co. Under date of December 19, 1917, Gen. Khrabroff,
as president of the Russian Supply Committee in America, also executed and delivered a general release to Recording Co. By an agreement dated December 22, 1917, Recording Co. and Agency Co. stated
and adjusted their accounts as between themselves; the amount due
Agency Co. out of the $1,500,000 being fixed at $713,176.07.

From the foregoing outline of the essential facts and an examination of the documents, it is clear beyond question that the Russian government has not any beneficial interest in the money held
by Can Co. Even if Gen. Khrabroff lacked authority to sign on behalf of the Russian government, that government could not successfully maintain in any court in this country any suit or action
against Can Co. for the $1,500,000, or any part thereof, once Record-
ing Co. and Agency Co. had settled their differences.

2. It would be unnecessary to go further, but for the fact that defendant expresses the fear that in some jurisdiction—possibly foreign—it may be held that under the documents the Russian government has a beneficial interest, and that this it has never relinquished because of lack of proof that Gen. Khrabroff had authority to bind the then existing Russian government by his signature to the settlement agreement of December 18, 1917.

The contention, in effect, is that the Russian Supply Committee originally acted for the Imperial Russian government, of which the Czar was head; that that government has fallen and other governments have followed, and, as a result, the Russian Supply Committee no longer had authority; and that proof is wholly lacking as to the powers or status of Gen. Khrabroff.

The attempt was made to offer lay proof as to who were, at present, in control of the Russian government, or, in other words, who or what the present government of Russia is. This line of testimony was excluded upon the well-settled principle that the question of sovereignty is a political question, the determinaton of which by the political branch or branches of our government, i. e., executive and/or legislative departments, binds the judicial department. Jones v. United States, 137 U. S. 202, 212, 11 Sup. Ct. 80, 34 L. Ed. 691; Pearcy v. Stranahan, 205 U. S. 257, 265, 27 Sup. Ct. 545, 51 L. Ed. 793; Williams v. Suffolk Ins. Co., 13 Pet. 415, 419, 10 L. Ed. 226; The Hornet, Fed. Cas. No. 6705; Kennett v. Chambers, 55 U. S. (14 How.) 38, 14 L. Ed. 316; Phillips v. Payne, 92 U. S. 130, 23 L. Ed. 649; Oetjen v. Central Leather Co., 246 U. S. 297, 38 Sup. Ct. 309, 62 L. Ed. 726; Ricaud v. American Metal Co., 246 U. S. 304, 38 Sup. Ct. 312, 62 L. Ed. 733.

After the date of the beginning of the transactions and before the settlement in December, 1917, the United States had recognized the Russian government which succeeded that of the Czar. In response to a letter of inquiry by one of the counsel for defendant, Mr. Polk, the counselor to the Department of State, replied:

"I find that this government instructed the American Ambassador, under date of March 20, 1917, to recognize the new government of Russia and to state to the proper Russian authorities that the United States will be pleased to continue intercourse with Russia through the medium of the new government."

Shortly thereafter, viz. on July 5, 1917, Boris Bakhmetieff was recognized as the Russian Ambassador, and that recognition still continues, as evidenced by the following certificate of our Secretary of State:

"To All Whom These Presents Shall Come, Greeting:

"Know ye that I, Robert Lansing, Secretary of State of the United States of America, do hereby certify that Boris Bakhmetieff presented his letter of credence to the President of the United States and was officially received by the President as Ambassador Extraordinary and Plenipotentiary of Russia on the fifth day of July, 1917; and that the said Boris Bakhmetieff has accordingly since that date been recognized by the Department of State as Ambassador of Russia and as entitled to all the rights, privileges and immunities of such status.

"In witness whereof, I have hereunto subscribed my name and caused the Seal of the Department of State to be affixed.

"Done in the city of Washington this eighth day of May, one thousand nine hundred and eighteen. Robert Lansing. [Seal.]"

This certificate is controlling upon the courts (In re Baiz, 135 U. S. 405, 10 Sup. Ct. 854, 34 L. Ed. 222; Jones v. United States, 137 U. S. 202, 11 Sup. Ct. 80, 34 L. Ed. 691), and is preliminary to a certificate from Ambassador Bakhmetieff in connection with this suit.

What happened was that Mr. Murray, of Coudert Bros., attorneys for the Russian government, informed the Russian Ambassador of the pendency of this litigation and of a request made of him (Murray) to testify and he asked for the Ambassador's instructions. As a result of this inquiry, Mr. Murray did testify and produced at the trial a certificate of the Russian Ambassador, setting forth the personnel of the Russian Supply Committee, and certifying:

"That the Russian Supply Committee in the United States was organized in October, 1915, for the purpose of purchasing supplies in the United States for Russia, accepting supplies purchased or manufactured in the United States for Russia, and settling all matters relating to contracts for supplies purchased or manufactured in the said United States for Russia; that said committee's authority continued until the first day of March, 1918; that the said committee had full charge of all matters pertaining to the two contracts between Russia and Canadian Car & Foundry Company, Ltd., for 5,000,000 rounds of ammunition, also all the relations between Russia and Agency of Canadian Car & Foundry Company, Ltd., arising from the assignment by Canadian Car & Foundry Company to Agency of Canadian Car & Foundry Company of the contracts for 5,000,000 rounds of ammunition, also of all relations with the Recording & Computing Machines Company of Dayton, Ohio, which company was engaged in the manufacture of Russian time fuses; that the said committee had full power and authority between the date of its organization and the first day of March, 1918, to liquidate and close all accounts with Agency of Canadian Car & Foundry Company, Ltd., Canadian Car & Foundry Company, Ltd., and the Recording & Computing Machines Company."

An ambassador, of course, is not subject to process in a foreign court, and there are, perhaps, some matters in respect of which an ambassador's certificate might not be admissible; but, when he certifies to the law of his country or to the personnel and authority of officials of his government, such certificate is clearly admissible as proof of the facts therein set forth. In the Goods of Klingerman, 3 Sw. & Tr. 18; In the Goods of Anne Downey, 3 Hagg. Ecc. Rep. 767; Goods of Prince Oldenburg, L. R. 9 Prob. Div. 234; The Republic of Mexico v. De Arangoiz, 12 N. Y. Super. Ct. 643, 646. See, also, Wigmore, vol. 2, p. 1820 et seq., §§ 1455, 1456; Chamberlayne, vol. 4, p. 3805 et seq., §§ 2769–2775; 16 Cyc. 1217.

The change in the form of Russian government and the fact that in the original papers that government was described as the "Imperial Russian Government," while the settlement papers are executed on behalf of the "Russian Government," are matters of no significance.

Since the notable precedent of The Sapphire, 78 U. S. (11 Wall.) 164, 20 L. Ed. 127, the principle is firmly established in our courts that the rights and liabilities of a state are unaffected by a change either in the form or personnel of its government, however accomplished, whether by revolution or otherwise. No other doctrine is thinkable, at least among nations which have any conception of international honor. See, also, United States of America v. McRea, L. R. 8 Eq. 69; John Bassett Moore's Digest of International Law, vol. 1, p. 249, and also 251, quoting Secretary Bayard's instructions to the then American Minister to Peru (September 23, 1886).

Other grounds could be stated which, so far as concerns the Russian government, fully support the validity of the settlement of December, 1917; but enough has been pointed out to demonstrate that there is no occasion for further timidity on the part of defendant.

It may, however, be added that the officially responsible character of the Russian Supply Committee as evidenced by the many and, in money, enormous transactions confided to it throughout all the dates relevant to this controversy, should assure defendant that no tribunal in this country will ever subject defendant to a second payment—and we have no concern with remote possibilities as to the action of any foreign tribunal.

It may be further added, in passing, that some cables from Russia were received in evidence, where the proof, because of war conditions, was not in accordance with what defendant regarded as orthodox methods of proving communications of this kind. As I understand, the modern method permits the trier of the facts to determine whether as matter of fact the paper is genuine and was sent as indicated. War exigencies require that the courts shall deal with such situations in a sensible way, not too much fettered by inelastic rules, while at the same time safeguarding against the reception in evidence of fabricated communications.

For the reasons outlined, plaintiffs are entitled to recover.

I note appreciation of the aid of counsel in submitting very helpful briefs, and I am further obliged to Mr. Chrystie for the convenient form in which many of the important exhibits were printed.

Russian Government v. Lehigh Valley R. Co.
293 Fed. 133 (S.D.N.Y., 1919)

MAYER, District Judge. The motion is to dismiss the action, and for such other relief as may be proper, on the ground that there was not in existence "the Russian government," and therefore no plaintiff. Defendant also requests the court to address a communication to the Secretary of State of the United States of America, inquiring as to certain diplomatic matters revolving around the status of the Russian government in its relations with the government of the United States.

In Canadian Car Co. v. American Can Co. (D. C.) 253 Fed. 152, the same procedure was suggested, but the court deemed it inadvisable to comply with the request to inquire of the Executive Department, in respect of public questions affecting the relations of the United States with Russia. In this case the court must pursue the same policy. There may, of course, arise situations of a character which would suggest to the court an inquiry of this nature, but the court will make official inquiry only for reasons of an impelling character, especially where such inquiry may involve pending questions of the greatest delicacy.

Referring to the merits of the motion, the facts, briefly stated, follow:

On July 29, 1916, defendant, a common carrier, had in its possession certain property belonging to the then Imperial Russian government, under bills of lading which restricted the right to sue for loss or damage to two years. On July 29 or 30, 1916, the so-called Black Tom explosion occurred, and the property was destroyed, and therefore any cause of action available to the Russian government expired on July 30, 1918. After vain efforts to obtain an extension of time to commence suit, the attorneys for the Russian government obtained authority from one Boris Bakhmetieff to commence these actions. This is the same person to whom reference is made in Canadian Car Co. v. American Can Co., supra.

The continuing recognition of Bakhmetieff, as ambassador, by the United States, has been brought practically down to date (a) by a certificate of the Secretary of State, dated October 31, 1918; and (b) by a certificate of the Acting Secretary of State, dated January 2, 1919. These are as follows:

"To All to Whom These Present Shall Come—Greeting:
"Know ye, that I, Robert Lansing, Secretary of State of the United States of America, do hereby certify that Boris Bakhmetieff presented his letter of credence to the President of the United States and was officially received by the President as ambassador extraordinary and plenipotentiary of Russia on the fifth· day of July, 1917, and that the said Boris Bakhmetieff has accordingly since that date been recognized by the Department of State as ambassador of Russia, and as entitled to all the rights, privileges and immunities of such status.
"In witness whereof, I have hereunto subscribed my name and caused the seal of the Department of State.to be affixed.
"Done in the city of Washington, this thirty-first day of October, one thousand nine hundred and eighteen.
    "[Seal.]   Robert Lansing."

"To All to Whom These Present Shall Come—Greeting:
"Know ye, that I, Frank L. Polk, Acting Secretary of State of the United States of America, do hereby certify that Boris Bakhmetieff presented his letter of credence to the President of the United States and was officially received by the President as ambassador extraordinary and plenipotentiary of Russia on the fifth day of July, 1917; that the said Boris Bakhmetieff has accordingly since that date been recognized by the Department of State as ambassador of Russia; that on the third day of December, 1918, the said Boris Bakhmetieff officially informed the Department of State that he was proceeding temporarily to France, and was that day turning over the affairs of the embassy to Mr. Serge Ughet, financial attaché of the Russian embassy. who would act as chargé d'affaires during his absence; that since the third day of December, 1918, the said Serge Ughet has been treated by the Department of State as chargé d'affaires ad interim, of Russia.
"In witness whereof I have hereunto subscribed my name and caused the seal of the Department of State to be affixed.
"Done in the city of Washington this second day of January, one thousand nine hundred and nineteen.   Frank L. Polk."

Counsel earnestly presses the arguments which were fully considered in Canadian Car Co. v. American Can Co., supra, and insists that the court may make its independent investigation to determine who and what the Russian government is.

The contentions are further made, in effect: (1) That from the certificates above quoted it cannot be held that Ambassador Bakhmetieff had authority to instruct counsel to bring these actions; and (2) that the court may resort to newspaper reports and comments to inform itself that there is at the moment no recognized Russian government.

First. That the court is bound by the recognition of the political branch of its own government, and can and should look no further, is a proposition so well settled and so well grounded in common sense and in the necessities of orderly procedure that further discussion is unnecessary. Canadian Car Co. v. American Can Co., supra.

It may, however, be observed that the importance of recognizing governmental continuity, quite irrespective of considerations as to the existing form of a foreign government, or as to the human beings in control at any particular time, is well illustrated in this case, where it is sought to deprive a foreign state forever of the opportunity to be heard in an effort to recover for the loss of property which belonged to the foreign state; i. e., the "Russian government," by whatever name called. It may also be noted, in passing, that the executive and judicial branches of the government have recognized "the present government of Russian" in proceedings to naturalize Russian subjects. Since the fall of the Imperial Russian government, such applicants for citizenship forswear allegiance to "the present government of Russia."

Second. In Canadian Car Co. v. American Can Co., supra, it was necessary for the court to go further than is here required in construing the power of an ambassador and the extent to which his certificate could be received as evidence. That a foreign government may sue in our courts is elementary. That its ambassador, on its behalf, has authority to instruct that suit shall be begun, seems one of the simplest incidents of the ambassadorial office. Such authority has nowhere been doubted as matter of law, and it has long since become effective by practical construction in addition to other reasons.

Finally, it may be suggested that it is at least doubtful whether the relief sought by defendant can be reached by a motion such as this, but I have preferred to go to the merits, rather than to decide the motion upon a point of procedure.

Motion denied.

Russian Government v. Lehigh Valley R. Co.
293 Fed. 135 (S.D., N.Y., 1923)

GODDARD, District Judge, The cases are now before this court upon the separate trial of the issues, under stipulations and orders filed in accordance with Rev. St. U. S. § 649 (Comp. St. § 1587). These issues are as to the capacity of the plaintiff to bring and now to prosecute the suits. In addition, the defendant makes several motions, all having for their object the dismissal of the suits, upon the claimed incapacity of the plaintiff to commence them or to proceed with them. The defendant maintains that no cause of action can be enforced under existing conditions, because the only existing government of Russia is not recognized by the United States, and is therefore not entitled to any standing in this court.

[1] The suits were commenced July 23, 1918, to recover $1,675,-042.47, damages for loss of property on July 29, 1916, owned by the then Imperial Russian government, and in the possession of the railroad company. The goods were destroyed in an explosion. The bill of lading under which the goods were shipped restricted the right to sue to two years. The ambassador of the "provisional Russian government" had the capacity to commence the actions, even though that

government may then have fallen, for he was at this time, and continued to be until June 30, 1922, the accredited ambassador of that government, which recognized the government he represented.

As Mayer, C. J., stated in an opinion on another motion in this same litigation (293 Fed. 133), which involved a similar principle:

"That the court is bound by the recognition of the political branch of its own government, and can and should look no further, is a proposition so well settled, and so well grounded in common sense and in the necessities of orderly procedure, that further discussion is unnecessary. Canadian Car Co. v. American Can Co., 253 Fed. 152."

And quoting further from his opinion:

"That a foreign government may sue in our courts is elementary. That its ambassador on its behalf has authority to instruct that suit shall be begun seems one of the simplest incidents of the ambassadorial office. Such authority has nowhere been doubted as matter of law, and it has long since become effective by practical construction in addition to other reasons."

The following official correspondence with the Secretary of State brings up the main questions now for consideration:

"February 17, 1923.
"Hon. Charles E. Hughes, Secretary of State, Washington, D. C.—My Dear Mr. Secretary: I am asking my partner, Mr. Raoul E. Desvernine, to present this letter and secure, if he can, such answers as you deem proper to make to the following questions:

"(1) What is the present government of Russia, and its name?
"(2) Has such government been recognized by the United States?
"(3) What is the extent and nature of such recognition?

"If, through ignorance of the proper procedure, I have not asked the appropriate questions, what I am after is to ascertain whether there is any government in Russia to-day which the United States government has recognized. My reason for asking these questions is that I am defending a case brought by the Russian government against the Lehigh Valley Railroad Company, which is set for trial on Tuesday, and I understand that for the solution of questions of this kind the courts look to the Department of State for information.

"Sincerely yours,   Lindley M. Garrison."

The response:

"Department of State, Washington,

"February 19, 1923.
"My Dear Judge Garrison: In reply to the inquiry contained in your letter of February 17, 1923, and to certain additional inquiries made orally to-day by your partner, Mr. Raoul E. Desvernine, I have to inform you that the so-called provisional government of Russia, which succeeded to authority upon the abdication of the Czar, was recognized by the government of the United States on March 22, 1917. On July 5 of the same year Mr. Boris Bakhmetieff was received by the President as the ambassador extraordinary and plenipotentiary of the newly recognized government.

"Mr. Bakhmetieff continued to be recognized as the ambassador of Russia to the United States until June 30, 1922. The custody of the property of the Russian government in this country, for which Mr. Bakhmetieff had been responsible, was, after the date of his retirement, considered to vest in Mr. Serge Ughet, the financial attaché of the Russian embassy, whose diplomatic status with this government was not considered to be altered by the termination of the ambassador's duties.

"In answer specifically to your questions, I may say that the United States has not recognized any other government in Russia since the fall of the provisional government, to which reference is made above.

"The régime now functioning in Russia, and known as the " 'Soviet Régime,' has not been recognized by the United States.

"Sincerely yours,   Charles E. Hughes.
"Hon. Lindley M. Garrison, No. 24 Broad Street, New York City."

Does the fact that the government to which Mr. Bakhmetieff was accredited has fallen, and that no other government in Russia has been recognized by the United States, cause these actions to be abated? Or does the fact that the custody of the property for which Mr. Bakhmetieff has been responsible was considered by our government to vest in Mr. Ughet, whose diplomatic status was not considered to be altered save them? That the real party in interest is the state of Russia, and that Russia, the state, still lives and is a continuing entity in the contemplation of the law, is true. In The Sapphire Case, 11 Wall. 164, 20 L. Ed. 127, Mr. Justice Bradley says:

"The next question is whether the suit has become abated by the recent deposition of the Emperor Napoleon. We think it has not. The reigning sovereign represents the national sovereignty, and that sovereignty is continuous and perpetual, residing in the proper successors of the sovereign for the time being. Napoleon was the owner of the Euryale, not as an individual, but as sovereign of France. This is substantially averred in the libel. On his deposition the sovereignty does' not change, but merely the person or persons in whom it resides. The foreign state is the true and real owner of its public vessels of war. The reigning emperor, or national assembly, or other actual person or party in power, is but the agent and representative of the national sovereignty. A change in such representative works no change in the national sovereignty or its rights. The next successor recognized by our government is competent to carry on a suit already commenced and receive the fruits of it. A deed to or treaty with a sovereign as such inures to his successors in the government of the country. If a substitution of names is necessary or proper, it is a formal matter, and can be made by the court under its general power to preserve due symmetry in its forms of proceeding. No allegation has been made that any change in the real and substantial ownership of the Euryale has occurred by the recent devolution of the sovereign power. The vessel has always belonged and still belongs to the French nation."

The importance of recognizing governmental continuity, irrespective of considerations as to the existing form of a foreign government, or as to the human beings in control at any particular time, is mentioned in many of the cases and text-books.

The question suggesting itself is: How can Mr. Ughet represent a government which has fallen? The answer is that the provisional government had fallen when Mr. Bakhmetieff began the suits, and they are held to have been properly begun, for the reason that at the time our government recognized him as such ambassador, and the court is bound by the action of our government, and so, regardless as to whether or not that government may have fallen, if our government considers this "financial attaché of the Russian embassy, whose diplomatic status with this government was not considered to be altered," to have become vested with the custody of the property of the Russian government after Mr. Bakhmetieff's retirement, I think that it is conclusive with the court, and that in this capacity the plaintiff may prosecute these suits. No precedent for such a situation has been presented to me, and I have not been able to find one. I feel, however, that our government may have adopted this plan for the purpose of preventing what otherwise would have been a loss of rights to Russia, because of its refusal to recognize the present régime now functioning in Russia, and I come more readily to the conclusion that I do, for I realize how highly important it is that the rights of Russia shall not be lost in this manner.

The motion to amend the complaints, to entitle the plaintiff "the State of Russia" is granted. This is in accordance with the opinion of Mack,

Circuit Judge, upon a motion in this litigation, and also consistent with Mr. Justice Bradley's opinion in The Sapphire Case, supra.

The defendant's motions to dismiss these actions, to have them declared abated, and for judgment on the pleadings, together with its motions for judgment upon the separate issues, are denied.

The plaintiff's motions for judgment upon the separate issues now on trial are granted, with costs.

The motions to supplement the record nunc pro tunc are granted—at the request of the defendant:

"That at the close of the trial the defendant renewed all of its motions made at the opening, that the court indicate its action and allow appropriate exceptions, and that (if the motions are not granted in that form) the defendant thereupon moved for a verdict upon the issues on trial, in its favor, and that the court take similar action as to any then proper exceptions, and that this suggestion be made part of the record of the trial as recorded in the minutes, all without prejudice to any and all exceptions reserved by either party on the trial."

At the request of the plaintiff:

"To note our motions made at the end of the trial for a denial of defendant's motions, and for judgment in favor of plaintiff upon the issues now on trial, and to note our exception to any adverse ruling of the court upon any of our motions, all without prejudice to any of the exceptions urged by either party upon the trial."

Lehigh Valley R. Co. v. State of Russia
21 F. 2d. 396 (2d. Cir., 1927)
cert. denied 275 U.S. 571, 48 S. Ct. 159 (1927)

Before MANTON, L. HAND, and SWAN, Circuit Judges.

MANTON, Circuit Judge. The defendant in error has recovered a judgment against the plaintiff in error for loss of explosives and ammunition while in transit from the United States to Russia and while in its possession as carrier in its freight yards at Jersey City, N. J. The loss is due to a fire and explosion occurring July 30, 1916, and it is admitted that the fire was incendiary in its origin. The action by the defendant in error was instituted by the Russian government, and after the deposition of the then government of Russia, pursuant to an order granted, the action was continued in the name of the state of Russia.

Eight carloads of high explosives were on the same railroad siding, and, separated by a single car, on the same siding were seven cars of benzol and wet nitrocellulose; on an adjoining track were seven cars of ammunition of cannon. In the same vicinity were eight other cars of ammunition of cannon, two cars of combination fuses, and another car of benzol. A fire started in a car of ammunition prior to the first explosion, which occurred on a barge in the North River, which barge was also loaded with explosives, and then another explosion occurred in a car in the terminal. The barge was owned and operated by the Johnson Lighterage Company. After the fire started, no one, because of fear of the result that might follow from the explosive materials, attempted to put out the fire. Neither the railroad men, private detectives, nor the city firemen attempted to apply water or otherwise combat the fire, with one exception, a crew of the railroad-men, who succeeded in removing some cars to a place of safety. Some lost their lives in this act. The railroad company failed to maintain a locomotive at the Black Tom Terminal, and the engine used in removing these cars was brought 2½ miles from Communipaw yards. At the time there was in force regulation No. 1906, which provided that in case of fire, to protect cars marked by placards "Inflammable," they should be quickly isolated. But in any case the explosions occurred before the engines arrived. Liability was imposed below because of the breach of the railroad's obligation as a common carrier, as supplemented by the Carmack Amendment (Comp. St. § 8604a [49 USCA § 20]), under the terms of the bills of lading issued.

There is a companion case (C. C. A.) 21 F.(2d) 406, referred to as action No. 2, but which is based upon the theory of negligence, which was tried at the same time. The trial of this action was suspended, and action No. 2 was begun and concluded before the same judge, but a different jury. It involved the destruction of war materials, aluminum, and other property in a nearby warehouse. The parties in writing stipulated that the specific findings, answering two questions propounded to the jury in action No. 2, might be used as facts in action No. 1. The jury found that the fire originated in the railroad terminal and the first explosion occurred on the barge Johnson No. 17. It also found, in action No. 2, that the railroad company's sole negligence was the proximate cause of the loss of the aluminum in the warehouse.

[1-6] At the outset the railroad company attacks the right of the defendant in error to maintain the suit, and to do so in the courts of the United States. The right to recover damages for breach of this carrier's obligation became the property of the state of Russia on July 30, 1916, when the loss occurred. The government was then the Russian Imperial Government. The right of a foreign government to sue is now well recognized. Oetjen v. Central Leather Co., 246 U. S. 297, 38 S. Ct. 309, 62 L. Ed. 726; The Sapphire, 78 U. S. (11 Wall.) 164, 20 L. Ed. 127. It is equally a settled rule of law that the foreign relations of our government are committed by the Constitution to the executive and legislative departments of our government, and what is done by such departments is not subject to judicial inquiry or decision. In re Cooper, 143 U. S. 472, 12 S. Ct. 453, 36 L. Ed. 232; Williams v. Suffolk Ins. Co., 13

Pet. 420, 10 L. Ed. 226; United States v. Palmer, 3 Wheat. 610, 4 L. Ed. 471; The Penza (D. C.) 277 F. 91. Who may be the sovereign de jure or de facto of a territory is a political question; not judicial. Oetjen v. Central Leather Co., supra; Jones v. United States, 137 U. S. 212, 11 S. Ct. 80, 34 L. Ed. 691. The state is a community or assemblage of men, and the government the political agency through which it acts in international relations. State of Texas v. White, 7 Wall. 700, 19 L. Ed. 227; Cherokee Nation v. Georgia, 5 Pet. 52, 8 L. Ed. 25; Foulke, International Law, vol. 1, pp. 62, 82, 102, 192. The foreign state is the true or real owner of its property, and the agency the representative of the national sovereignty. The Sapphire, supra; The Rogdai (D. C.) 278 F. 294.

On July 5, 1917, Mr. Boris Bakhemeteff was recognized by our State Department as the accredited representative of the Russian government—the provisional Russian Government—as successor to the Imperial Russian Government. He continued as such until July 30, 1922. At that date he retired, and the custody of the property of the Russian government, for which Bakhemeteff was responsible, was recognized by the State Department to vest in Mr. Ughet, the financial attaché of the Russian embassy. The Soviet government, which later secured control of the Russian government, was never recognized by our State Department, and ever since the diplomatic status with our government was never altered by the termination of the ambassador's duties. Therefore the provisional Russian Government is the last that has been recognized, and after its ambassador retired its property was considered by the State Department to vest in its financial attaché. Prior to his retirement, and while the accredited ambassador, Mr. Bakhemeteff authorized the suits here considered, which were commenced July 23, 1918.

Various preliminary attacks by motions to dismiss the complaint have been made, and the District Court has in each instance properly denied them, recognizing the principles of law referred to and their application to the fact that there has been no change recognized in the government or agency for Russia by the political branches of our government. Mr. Ughet, by the State Department's determination, is entitled to the custody in the United States of the property of Russia, and as part of that duty he was authorized to continue the suits for the state of Russia. This duty became obvious. It became important to avoid efforts to destroy the right of action as a basis of keeping its property, when motions to dismiss were made and delays occurred which would give rise to the bar of limitation to sue. The question of Mr. Ughet's power under his agency is generally important, because of the change in name of the plaintiff in the action to the state of Russia in substitution of the Imperial Russian Government. We must judicially recognize that the state of Russia survives.

Abatement of the action or a dismissal could only be sustained by reason of the non-existence of the state, or the action of our government to no longer recognize the agency once accredited and never revoked. The action was properly started by an unquestioned agency. The attorneys and the agency thus employed were obliged to continue until some other government was recognized. It has been recognized that diplomatic agents of one state, while in another, may commence and maintain actions on behalf of their state while they are recognized as such. Republic of Mexico v. De Arangoiz, 12 N. Y. Super. Ct. 643. Proof of the agency or of the diplomat is dependent entirely upon the political fact of the recognition by the political department of the government. The courts may not independently make inquiry as to who should or should not be recognized. The argument of the plaintiff in error is directed entirely toward the court making its own investigation, in expectation that there would be some other government found, either de facto or de jure. This we may not do. Kennett v. Chambers, 14 How. 38, 14 L. Ed. 316; Agency of Canadian Car Co. v. American Can Co. (C. C. A.) 258 F. 363, 6 A. L. R. 1182; Russian Socialist Federated Republic v. Cibrario, 235 N. Y. 255, 139 N. E. 259. If it be a fact that there is a Russian Socialist Federated Republic now in charge of the government of Russia, it would bring no different result here.

Where there is a change of government, foreign states must of necessity judge for themselves whether they will continue their accustomed diplomatic relations with the prince whom they choose to regard as the legitimate sovereign. Wheaton on International Law, p. 332. It matters little whether the recognized state co-operates in it or not. Moore's Digest of International Law, vol. 1, p. 73. It is for the executive and legislative departments to say in what relations any other country stands toward it. Courts of justice cannot make the decision. Agency of Canadian Car Co. v. American Can Co., supra; Moore's International Law, vol. 1, p. 63. Nor does the personal withdrawal of an ambassador affect the relations with the government. Hyde, International Law, vol. 1, p. 731; Moore's Digest of International Law, vol. 4, p. 437. And, unless the political department of our government has decided otherwise, the judiciary recognizes the condition of things with respect to another country which once existed, and is still subsisting because of no other recognition. Phillips v. Payne, 92 U. S. 130, 23 L. Ed. 649; The Ambrose Light (D. C.) 25 F. 412.

"Changes in the government or the internal polity of a state do not as a rule affect its position in international law. A monarchy may be transformed into a republic, or a republic into a monarchy; absolute principles may be substituted for constitutional, or the reverse; but, though the government changes, the nation remains, with rights and obligations unimpaired." Moore, Digest International Law, vol. 1, p. 249.

The granting or refusal of recognition has nothing to do with the recognition of the state itself. If a foreign state refuses the recognition of a change in the form of government of an old state, this latter does not thereby lose its recognition as an international person. Oppenheim, International Law, p. 120; Moore, Digest of International Law, vol. 1, p. 298. The suit did not abate by the change in the form of government in Russia; the state is perpetual, and survives the form of its government. The Sapphire, supra. The recognized government may carry on the suit, at least until the new government becomes accredited here by recognition.

The argument that the plaintiff in error may at some future time, if the Soviet régime is recognized by our government, be compelled to pay again what it is obliged to pay now, is fallacious. It is only the acts performed in its own territory that can be validated by the retroactive effect of recognition. Acts theretofore performed outside its own territory cannot be validated by recognition. The former are illustrated in Underhill v. Hernandez, 168 U. S. 250, 18 S. Ct. 83, 42

L. Ed. 456, where the acts in question were performed in Venezuela; Oetjen v. Central Leather Co., supra, and Ricaud v. American Metal Co., 246 U. S. 304, 38 S. Ct. 312, 62 L. Ed. 733, where there were acts of confiscation in Mexico; and the English case of Luther v. Sagor [1921] 3 K. B. 532, acts performed in Russia. The latter are illustrated by Kennett v. Chambers, supra; U. S. v. Trumbull (D. C.) 48 F. 99; Agency of Canadian Car Co. y. American Can Co., supra. Following these principles, we agree with the contention of the defendant in error that the state of Russia, as a plaintiff, may continue the prosecution through the agency vested in Mr. Ughet, and the plaintiff in error will be protected as against any possible future claims of a subsequent recognized government of Russia, if payment be made as directed in this judgment.

Judgment affirmed, with costs.

For concurring opinion, see following case, 21 F.(2d) 409.

The Rogdai
278 Fed. 294 (N.D., Cal., 1920)

DIETRICH, District Judge. This is an action in rem, brought against and to secure the possession of the Rogdai (or Rogday), a steamer lying in San Francisco Bay, state of California. By the bill it is represented that the libelant "Russian Socialist Federal Soviet Republic" is a sovereign nation, and that it is the owner of the vessel, and that the other libelant, Ludwig C. A. K. Martens, is its agent and representative in the United States, duly authorized to act in its behalf. Process of attachment issued, by virtue of which the steamer was seized and is now held in custody by the marshal. The "Russian Government" and Boris Bakhmeteff, appearing specially, move for an order dissolving the writ of attachment. The motion is supported by "suggestion," signed by Boris Bakhmeteff, and under the seal of the Russian Embassy at Washington, accompanied by a certificate duly executed by the Department of State of the United States, on April 6, 1920, certifying that Boris Bakhmeteff was formally received by the President as the duly accredited Ambassador Extraordinary and Plenipotentiary of Russia to the United States, on July 5, 1917, and that he has continuously since that date been recognized as such by the government of the United States, and further that the government has not received or recognized Ludwig C. A. K. Martens in any representative capacity, "nor has the so-called Russian Socialist Federal Soviet Republic been recognized in any way by the government of the United States."

By the "suggestion" it is shown that the Rogdai is a "Russian naval transport under the command of Mili Gordener, a lieutenant commander in the Russian navy," that she was purchased for Russia in the United States on July 20, 1917, that thereafter under an agreement with the ambassador she was used by the United States government in prosecuting the war with Germany, and that on the 6th day of October, 1919, with the written consent of the Secretary of State of the United States, she was again taken over by the Russian Embassy at Washington, and was in its possession and under its control at the time of her seizure by the marshal. No counter showing is made by the libelants, except in so far as the averments in the libel to the effect that the "Russian Socialist Federal Soviet Republic" is Russia, or the Russian government, may be considered as such.

It will be noted that fundamentally there is no controversy touching the real ownership of the transport; she belongs to Russia; no adverse claim, either public or private, is involved. By Russia, of course, I do not refer to any particular political group or organization, but to the national entity or sovereignty. It follows that the issue is reduced to the simple question whether the Russian nation is represented by Ludwig C. A. K. Martens and the organization back of him or by Boris Bakhmeteff and the group for which he speaks. Plainly, consideration of such an issue upon the merits would of necessity draw us into the realm of international diplomacy; and it is equally plain that no useful purpose could be subserved by such an investigation. If the court assumes the right to make an original inquiry, it logically follows that it must exercise its own independent judgment upon the facts thus disclosed and reach an independent conclusion. In that view it might recognize Martens, while Washington recognizes Bakhmeteff. To state the proposition is to discredit it. True, the Russian sovereignty may speak through different representatives, and it may have business agents as well as diplomatic agents; but all must derive their authority from a single source. The national will must be expressed through a single political organization; two conflicting "governments" cannot function at the same time. By the same token, discordant voices cannot express the sovereign will of the American nation. Either the executive or the judiciary must be supreme in a given sphere.

The question at issue is one of state; it involves international relations, and is primarily for the State Department. If, as contended by libelants, it be granted that a revolution has taken place in Russia, and that the Soviet Republic is in actual control, the question when, if at all, such de facto government shall be recognized, is a political one. It involves considerations of national policy, which are not justiciable, and touching it the voice of the Chief Executive is the voice, not of a branch of the government, but of the national sovereignty, equally binding upon all departments. Accordingly it must be held that the courts are powerless to grant the relief which the libelants seek. It is to be reiterated that we are not here concerned with the claim of a third party, either public or private, to the property in controversy, nor have we a case where the Department of State has failed to act, or where it is sought only to protect a party in actual possession. The case is one where the court is asked to take property conceded to be that of the Russian nation from the actual possession of those whom the State Department unmistakably recognizes as the accredited agents of the Russian government, and turn it over to other persons whom that department has declined to recognize as having any official standing whatsoever.

In assuming the correctness of the facts exhibited by the "suggestion" of the Russian Embassy and the certificate of the Secretary of State, I have not been unmindful of the objection interposed by libelants to the reception and consideration of these documents. The competency of the certificate as proof of the facts therein set forth is hardly open to question, and I have already held the facts to be material. The objections to the "suggestion" are overruled with less confidence. I am inclined to the view that logically the representations made in the "suggestion" should come through the appropriate executive channels of the American government. As we have seen, the gist of the objection to the suit, and particularly to the attachment process, is that the controlling questions involved affect national policies, touching which the authority of the State Department is supreme. But if, in so far as such policies are concerned, the courts are to defer to such authority, they should be advised of the executive will directly and from an authoritative source, and such source the foreign government may call into activity through appropriate diplomatic channels. The Florence H. (D. C.) 248 Fed. 1012, 1017. But the procedure here followed is not without precedent, and in view of the fact that the attitude of the State Department is unmistakably shown, though not approving of the practice, I have thought it proper under the circumstances to receive and give credit to the "suggestion." Whether the statements of fact made therein are or are not conclusive is a question which need not be decided, for libelants have tendered nothing in rebuttal.

In the main the judicial decisions cited in the briefs for both parties are obviously distinguishable, but for convenience of possible reference those thought to be most nearly in point are here noted: The Luigi (D. C.) 230 Fed. 495; The Johnson Lighterage Co. (D. C.) No. 24, 231 Fed. 365; The Attualita, 238 Fed. 909, 152 C. C. A. 43; The Florence H. (D. C.) 248 Fed. 1012; The Roseric (D. C.) 254 Fed. 154; The Adriatic, 258 Fed. 902, 169 C. C. A. 622; Agency of Con. Car & F. Co. v. Am. Car Co. (D. C.) 253 Fed. 155; Id., 258 Fed. 368, 169 C. C. A. 379, 6 A. L. R. 1182; The Conception, 6 Fed. Cas. No. 360; King of Spain v. Oliver, Fed. Cas. No. 7,814, 2 Wash. C. C. 429; Christensen v. Rogday, No. 16,797, this court; [1] The Gagara, [1919] Prob. Div. 95; The Dora, [1919] Prob. Div. 105, 88 L. J. P. [1919] 101, 107; The Exchange v. McFaddon, 11 U. S. (7 Cranch) 116, 3 L. Ed. 287; Thorington v. Smith, 75 U. S. (8 Wall.) 1, 19 L. Ed. 361; The Sapphire, 78 U. S. (11 Wall.) 167, 20 L. Ed. 127; The Davis, 77 U. S. (10 Wall.) 15. 19 L. Ed. 875; Williams v. Bruffy, 96 U. S. 176, 24 L. Ed. 716.

The motion is allowed, and an order will be entered discharging the attachment.

The Rogday
279 Fed. 130 (N.D., Cal., 1920)

VAN FLEET, District Judge. [1] This is an application to release from seizure and attachment in admiralty the above-named vessel, interposed by and on behalf of the Russian government, through its consular office at the port of San Francisco, by a suggestion, in proper form, setting forth that the attached vessel was at the time of seizure the property of the Russian government and engaged in its public service, and that such seizure and detention is an interference with and detrimental to that service.

The application is accompanied by the certificate of the Secretary of State, certifying to the existing recognition by the President and the State Department of Mr. Boris Bakhmeteff as the duly accredited diplomatic representative of Russia to the United States at Washington, and a certificate from the latter that Mr. George Romanovsky, the party presenting the suggestion, is entitled to recognition as the acting Russian consul at San Francisco and authorized to represent the Russian government in the matter pending before the court. These facts bring the case fully within the principles of The Roseric (D. C.) 254 Fed. 154, and the cases therein cited; and under the principles there announced, and in the later case of The Adriatic, 258 Fed. 902, 169 C. C. A. 622, the court is not at liberty to ignore the request of the Russian Government for the release of the vessel.

The question raised by the libelants as to whether the officers making the demand duly represent the present Russian government presents no proper subject of inquiry for the court, that being purely a political question, concluded here by the certificate of the Secretary of State.

The attachment will accordingly be quashed, and the vessel released.

On Motion for Alias Monition.

DOOLING, District Judge. The libelants move for the issuance of an alias monition to seize the steam vessel Rogday in satisfaction of their claim for wages. They are met by the suggestion of the Russian embassy that the Rogday is a Russian vessel in government service. In support of this is presented a certificate of the recognized Russian ambassador, of date August 12, 1920, that the Rogday is a Russian naval transport, and as such a public naval vessel of Russia. This certificate is conclusive, and the situation shows no material change since April, when a former attachment of the vessel was quashed by Judge Van Fleet.

The motion for an alias monition must be denied; and it is so ordered.

Banque de France v. Equitable Trust Co.
33 F. 2d. 202 (S.D., N.Y., 1929)
affirmed without reference to international law
60 F. 2d. 703 (2d. Cir., 1932)

GODDARD, District Judge. These motions are to strike out each of the seven separate defenses contained in the answers to amended complaints upon the ground that each of such defenses is insufficient in law, and to strike out from the denials what is alleged to be "the defense consisting of new matter * * * in so far as it is attempted by such new matter to set up the title of the State Bank of the Union of Soviet Socialist Republics."

There are two actions—one against the Chase National Bank of the City of New York, and one against the Equitable Trust Company of New York—each brought to recover gold of the value of $2,600,500. The pleadings in the actions are substantially similar, and the motions are addressed to the respective actions.

It is averred in the amended complaint that: "Before and at the commencement of this action the defendant had and it thereafter held said chattels in its possession in violation of plaintiff's rights as owner thereof, for the account of persons other than the plaintiff and without the plaintiff's consent; and that the possession of said chattels by the defendant was and remains wrongful, and defendant still detains the same from the plaintiff. • • •"

The answer denies the possession by the defendant of the gold, except the defendant "admits that before and at the commencement of this action, it had, and until on or about April 5, 1928, held, a shipment of what purported and was stated to be bars of gold received from the Garantie und Kreditbank fur den Osten, A. G. Hamburg, Germany, by order and for account of the State Bank of the Union Soviet Socialist Republics."

The answer also denies the making of any demand upon them by the plaintiff or any refusal by the defendants, except each defendant "admits that before the commencement of this action, and on or about March 6, 1928, it received a letter, copy of which is hereto annexed, made a part hereof, and marked 'Exhibit A' from the attorneys for the plaintiff in this action, demanding delivery of certain gold alleged to have been received by the defendant on or about February 21, 1928 from, or for account of the State Bank of the Soviet Union."

This letter, referred to as "Exhibit A," sets forth the grounds of plaintiff's alleged right to the gold:

"Pursuant to the instructions under which we are acting, we give you notice of the following facts:

"Beginning on or about January 14, 1915, and until July 11, 1917, the Bank of France purchased in the open market in Russia various quantities of gold aggregating at par the value of 52,246,988.77 gold francs, or $10,109.26. This gold the Bank of France thereupon entrusted for safekeeping to The State Bank of the Russian Empire at Petrograd, Russia, to be held for account of the Bank of France for delivery to it upon its demand. This gold upon its purchase became part of the metallic reserve of the Bank of France and has been carried as such

ever since to this day. The Bank of France did not consent to the taking over of said gold by the State Bank of the Soviet Union and has duly and repeatedly demanded the return of the same nor has the Bank of France consented to the shipment of said gold to the United States, but since it is in your possession the Bank of France ·claims it as the true owner and entitled to the immediate possession of the same notwithstanding the fact that it may have been commingled with other gold and whether or not the said gold is the identical gold which was held by the State Bank of the Russian Empire prior to the delivery of said gold to the State Bank of the Soviet Union."

The answers set forth matter alleged by way of separate defenses contained in seven separate defenses, several of which are based upon the plaintiff's alleged right to the gold as stated in said letter, Exhibit A.

First. That the gold in possession of the respective defendants is not plaintiff's property, but was the property of the State Bank of the Union Soviet Socialist Republics.

Second. That the shipment was received by the respective defendants as bailee for the account of the State Bank of the Union Soviet Socialist Republics, and that the respective demands upon them preliminary to the suit being instituted did not afford them a reasonable opportunity to investigate and determine the facts relative to the claim or ownership by the plaintiff, and that in any event the defendants, as bailee, had the right after demand to return and did return the gold to their respective bailors.

Third. That assuming the facts stated in the demand to be true, inasmuch as all gold, if any, of the plaintiff intrusted or delivered to the State Bank of the Russian Empire was confiscated under decrees of the Government of the Russian Socialist Federal Soviet Republic, it is now a part of the Union of Soviet Socialist Republics, which government has been recognized de jure by the Republic of France, of which the plaintiff is a citizen, such recognition validated the acts of the Union of Soviet Socialist Republics including the decrees of confiscation.

Fourth. That by the diplomatic correspondence between the Republic of France and the Union of Soviet Socialist Republics, all claims of the Republic of France and its nationals, including that of the plaintiff, became the exclusive subject of negotiation between the two governments and otherwise excluded the maintenance of any legal proceedings for the enforcement of the same.

Fifth. Assumes that the claim set forth in plaintiff's demand is true, and it sets forth facts which the respective defendants contend established the defense that the gold sought to be recovered is immune from judicial processes in this action.

Sixth. Assumes that the facts stated in plaintiff's demand are true, and avers facts which the respective defendants contend establish the defense that the determination of this action will involve an examination of the acts and decrees of each of said governments of Russia with respect to property located in its own territorial jurisdiction at the time of the making and enforcement of the said decrees.

Seventh. Assumes that the plaintiff's demand states the true facts; sets up as a defense that by reason of the recognition de jure accorded to the Union of Soviet Socialist Republics by the Republic of France, the plaintiff, a citizen and inhabitant of France, is not entitled by comity or otherwise to maintain these actions, for to permit it to do so would subject the defendants to the possibility of double liability.

In their denials of the allegations of the complaints, defendants expressly deny that the gold in question was part of or commingled with the gold claimed by plaintiff to have been intrusted by it to the State Bank of the Russian Empire, and in the allegations of the separate defenses, there is no such averment. Thus the ownership of the gold by plaintiff is denied, and in their separate defenses affirmatively allege that the gold was not the property of the plaintiff. The separate defenses contain no admission or averment that any gold was intrusted by the plaintiff to the State Bank of the Russian Empire, but do contain allegations of confiscation by the Soviet Government of all banks including the State Bank of the Russian Empire.

What is averred in the respective separate defenses is merely that whatever gold, if any, of the plaintiff was in possession of the State Bank of the Russian Empire was confiscated by the decrees of the Soviet Government and thus seized along with the gold in all other banks.

The first separate defense avers that the shipment to it "was not the property of the plaintiff, but is the sole and exclusive property of the State Bank of the Union Soviet Socialist Republics." Plaintiff urges that this defense is insufficient because it contends that the State Bank of the Union Soviet Socialist Republics is to be regarded as legally nonexistent, inasmuch as our government does not recognize the Union of Soviet Socialist Republics of which the bank is a part.

Under section 1093 of the Civil Practice Act (N. Y.), a defendant, "by answer, may defend on the ground that a third person was entitled to the chattel, without connecting himself with the latter's title."

Therefore, in so far as this motion to strike out the separate defense on the ground that it is insufficient is concerned, the averment that the shipment is not the property of the plaintiff, and therefore is the property of some one else, is to be regarded as admitted by the plaintiff whether its ownership is in the State Bank of the Union of Soviet Socialist Republics or not. If it be conceded that inasmuch as our government has not recognized the Union of Soviet Socialist Republics, and that as the State Bank is a part of that government, there can be no ownership by the State Bank of the shipments; the averment that the shipments are not the property of the plaintiff still stands, for there is no admission nor allegation in the first separate defense, or in any other part of the answer, that the gold in question was ever a part of any gold that belonged to the plaintiff or had been deposited by it with the State Bank or had been mingled with gold which at any time belonged to the plaintiff. For instance, under this allegation, the defendants might prove that the gold had never been confiscated by the Union of Soviet Socialist Republics; that it had been mined or procured from other sources subsequent to the time any gold had been confiscated.

The separate defenses include allegations of the existence of a de facto government of the Union of Soviet Socialist Republics recognized de jure by many of the civilized nations of the world and existing to the exclusion of any previous government overthrown thereby.

This court should not assume that the

Union of Soviet Socialist Republics acquired title to the gold in question by confiscation or in any manner inconsistent with our accepted standards. If there are any circumstances under which the Soviet Government might acquire title to property which would be recognized, then these defendants, American nationals, should be allowed an opportunity to show the circumstances relating to their source of title.

There is a distinction between the private rights and obligations of an individual and those of a body or a "paramount force" in control of the country wherein that individual resides and where the "paramount force" or government of that state is not recognized by our government. In Russian Reinsurance Co. v. Stoddard, 240 N. Y. 149, on page 158, 147 N. E. 703, 705, Judge Lehman stated: " * * * Until the State Department has recognized the new establishment, the Court may not pass upon its legitimacy or ascribe to its decrees all the effect which inheres in the laws or orders of a sovereign." However, he continues to state on page 158 of 240 N. Y. (147 N. E. 705): "It cannot determine how far the private rights and obligations of individuals are affected by acts of a body not sovereign or with which our Government will have no dealings. That question does not concern our foreign relations. It is not a political question, but a judicial question." See, also, Sokoloff v. National City Bank, 239 N. Y. 158, 145 N. E. 917, 37 A. L. R. 712.

That there is an existing government in Russia Sovereign within its own territory cannot be and is not entirely ignored even by our own country, although it has not recognized such government. For instance, in proceedings to naturalize Russian citizens, the executive and judicial branches of our own government acknowledge the existence of "the present Government of Russia" to the extent of requiring such applicants for citizenship to forswear allegiance to "the present Government of Russia." Russian Government v. Lehigh Valley R. Co. (D. C.) 293 F. 133, 135. See, also, article by Mr. Louis Connick of the Yale Law Journal, vol. 34, No. 5, p. 499. A marriage which is valid under the laws of the present government of Russia is quite universally regarded as valid in this country.

It was stated in Wulfsohn v. Russian, etc., Republic, 234 N. Y. 372, 138 N. E. 24, that except where the actual existence of a government created by rebellion or otherwise "becomes a political question affecting our neutrality laws, the recognition of the decrees of prize courts and similar questions, * * * the fact of the existence of such a Government whenever it becomes material may probably be proved in other ways" than by the determination of the State Department. See, also, James & Co. v. Second Russian Ins. Co., 239 N. Y. 248, 146 N. E. 369, 37 A. L. R. 720.

The Penza (D. C.) 277 F. 91; The Rogdai (D. C.) 278 F. 294, cited by the plaintiff as holding to the contrary, had to do with a situation where the Soviet Government sought to libel ships which were in the jurisdiction of the United States District Courts, and it was merely held that the Soviet Government, not having been recognized by our government, could not bring suit in our courts; and Judge Dietrich in Re The Rogdai, supra, in the opinion of the court, stated: "It will be noted that fundamentally there is no controversy touching the real ownership of the transport; she belongs to Russia; no adverse claim, either public or private, is involved. * * * It is to be reiterated that we are not here concerned with the claim of a third party, either public or private, to the property in controversy, nor have we a case where the Department of State has failed to act, or where it is sought only to protect a party in actual possession."

The courts in this country have not followed the decision of the English Court of Appeal in Luther v. Sagor, 1921 L. R. 1 K. B. 456, 1921 L. R. 3 K. B. 532.

The Supreme Court in the Civil War cases sustained many acts relating to the creation of domestic corporations, the sale of property, and the payment of debts depending upon the validity of the decrees of the Confederate States. Laws necessary to the peace and good order of the country, such as sanctioning and protecting marriage, determining laws of descent, regulating the transfer of property, etc., were generally upheld. The decrees and laws of the Confederate States were recognized as valid by the Supreme Court unless public policy and justice required otherwise. See United States v. Rice, 4 Wheat. (17 U. S.) 246, 4 L. Ed. 563; United States v. Home Ins. Co., 22

Wall. (89 U. S.) 99, 22 L. Ed. 816; Thorington v. Smith, 8 Wall. (75 U. S.) 1, 19 L. Ed. 361; Dalmas v. Ins. Co., 14 Wall. (81 U. S.) 661, 20 L. Ed. 757; Texas v. White, 7 Wall. (74 U. S.) 700, 19 L. Ed. 227; Williams v. Bruffy, 96 U. S. 176, 24 L. Ed. 716; Baldy v. Hunter, 171 U. S. 388, 18 S. Ct. 890, 43 L. Ed. 208.

Later, came the views expressed by Judge Cardozo in Sokoloff v. National City Bank, supra, and there has now developed what I think will be generally regarded as the rule here. It holds to the principle that the refusal of the political department to recognize a government should not be allowed to affect private rights which may depend upon proving the existing conditions in such state. James & Co. v. Second Russian Ins. Co., supra; Russian Reinsurance Co. v. Stoddard, supra; Wulfsohn v. Russian Republic, supra.

Justice requires that effect should be given by our courts, even though we do not recognize the Russian Government, to those acts in Russia upon which the rights of our citizens depend, provided that in so doing our judicial department does not encroach upon or interfere with the political branch of our government. See "Legal Effects of Recognition in International Law," by John G. Hervey, chapter 7.

To deprive these defendants who are American nationals of asserting title to the gold which was shipped to them to be in the State Bank, and to preclude the defendants from showing in what manner such title was acquired, I believe would be doing violence to fundamental justice and would be contrary to the principles which the courts of this country apply. It is quite apparent that if the defendants are not permitted to do this, the probable result would be to subject them to double liability, which the court in Russian Reinsurance Co. v. Stoddard, supra, rightly, in my opinion, held should be avoided.

In so far as the third and fourth defenses are concerned, the defendants set up the defense that if any of the plaintiff's gold was confiscated by the decree of the Soviet Socialist Republics, such acts became valid and binding on all citizens of France upon the recognition by France of the Union of Soviet Socialist Republics as the de jure Government of Russia, and that the plaintiff, a corporation organized under the laws of France, was therefore divested of its ownership to such property and cannot assert such ownership in this jurisdiction, even though the Union of Soviet Socialist Republics has not been recognized de facto or de jure by the United States Government; and that the plaintiff must look to its own Government of France to present this claim, if any, against the Russian Government in their respective negotiations.

By diplomatic communications exchanged between the French Government and the Union of Soviet Socialist Republics, recognition de jure was accorded to the Union of Soviet Socialist Republics by the Republic of France in October, 1924, and apparently the Government of France made all the claims of the Republic of France and its nationals the subject of negotiation between the two governments to the exclusion of legal proceedings for their enforcement. But if such claims as the plaintiff now urges were not expressly reserved for negotiation, and if the law applied by France to the rights of its citizens upon her recognition of the Union of Soviet Socialist Republics as the de jure Government of Russia does differ in effect from that given such recognition by the laws in the jurisdiction where this suit is brought, then the French law is a matter of proof. Latham v. De Loiselle, 3 App. Div. 525, 38 N. Y. S. 270, affirmed 158 N. Y. 687, 53 N. E. 1127, and cases therein cited.

It is settled law in this jurisdiction that recognition of a foreign government, either de jure or de facto, validates all acts of such foreign government from the time it existed. Williams v. Bruffy, supra; Oetgen v. Central Leather Co., 246 U. S. 297, 38 S. Ct. 309, 62 L. Ed. 726; Underhill v. Hernandez, 168 U. S. 250, 18 S. Ct. 83, 42 L. Ed. 456.

I think the position of the defendants is sound and supported by the authorities, and without discussing, but after consideration of, the cases cited in the briefs of the learned counsel for the plaintiff, which seem to be distinguishable, I refer to the following as supporting this view:

Mr. Moore, in his Digest on International Law, volume 6, § 970, states: "A citizen of one nation wronged by conduct of another nation must seek redress through his own government. His government must assume responsibility of presenting his claim or it need not be considered."

See, also, United States v. Diekelman, 92 U. S. 520, at page 524 (23 L. Ed. 742), in which the Supreme Court stated: "Hence, a citizen of one nation wronged by the conduct of another nation, must seek redress through his own government. His sovereign must assume the responsibility of presenting his claim, or it need not be considered. If this responsibility is assumed, the claim may be prosecuted as one nation proceeds against another, not by suit in the courts, as of right, but by diplomacy, or, if need be, by war. It rests with the sovereign against whom the demand is made to determine for himself what he will do in respect to it. He may pay or reject it; he may submit to arbitration, open his own courts to suit, or consent to be tried in the courts of another nation." See, also, 2 Wharton's Digest on International Law. Oliver American Trading Co., Inc., v. Mexico (C. C. A.) 5 F.(2d) 659.

Referring to the fifth and to the sixth separate defenses, the questions of law presented in these are similar. It is to be noted that the answer sets up that the shipments of gold in question were shipped by the State Bank of the Union of Soviet Socialist Republics, and that it appears from the pleadings of the plaintiff that its gold was seized by the Government of Russia and that the State Bank of the Union of Soviet Socialist Republics was a part of said government, so that the plaintiff is here asserting that the gold in question is claimed by the Union of Soviet Socialist Republics in opposition to the plaintiff's rights, and the result is a suit brought in this jurisdiction which involves the title to property claimed by the Russian Government, and that leads to the consideration of the question: Who is the sovereign de facto or de jure in Russia? And this is not a judicial but is a political question, and it is immaterial whether the foreign sovereign has been recognized or not.

Wulfsohn v. Russian Republic, supra; Jones v. United States, 137 U. S. 202, 11 S. Ct. 80, 34 L. Ed. 691.

Furthermore, it is alleged by the plaintiff itself that the Union of Soviet Socialist Republics is a foreign government, so that as in the Wulfsohn Case, it is unnecessary for that fact to be made known to the court by a formal "suggestion" through the State Department. Thus, it appears that this court is not in a position to pass upon the issue, not because of nonrecognition but simply for the reason, as stated by Judge Andrews in Wulfsohn v. Russian, etc., Republic, supra, at page 376 of 234 N. Y. (138 N. E. 26): "They may not bring a foreign sovereign before our bar, not because of comity, but because he has not submitted himself to our laws. Without his consent he is not subject to them."

Therefore, in my judgment both of these alleged defenses should be permitted to stand.

Relative to the seventh separate defense, this should be permitted to stand for the reasons expressed above. While it is true that Russian Reinsurance Co. v. Stoddard, supra, was a case in equity, the same principles of justice apply, namely: That the defendants, who were American nationals, should not be subjected to double liability.

Finally, taking up for consideration the second separate defenses, That the demands served by plaintiff preliminary to instituting suit did not afford defendants an opportunity to ascertain the facts upon which plaintiff based its claim to the gold, and that in any event defendants, as bailees, were entitled to and did return it to their respective bailors.

Accordingly, plaintiff's motions to strike out the separate defenses in the answers are denied, with the exception that they are granted to the extent of striking out that portion of the second separate defense which seeks to set up as a defense that after plaintiff's demand the gold was returned to the defendants' respective bailors.

Republic of China v. Merchant's Fire Assurance Corp. of N.Y.
49 F. 2d. 862 (9th Cir., 1931)

WILBUR, Circuit Judge.

This is an appeal from an order of the United States Court for China refusing to vacate the entry of the satisfaction of a money judgment against appellee and in favor of the republic of China. It appears from the affidavits and records used upon the motion and incorporated in the transcript that the judgment and satisfaction were the result of a compromise arrangement entered into between the appellee and the attorney at law and attorney in fact of the plaintiff in the action upon an obligation of the appellee growing out of a loss sustained upon a fire insurance policy issued by it to the Chinese government telephone administration, Wuchang, upon its telephone building at Wuchang, China, which was destroyed by fire on the 22d day of February, 1926, while the policy was still in force. The amount of the loss had been ascertained in accordance with the terms of the policy to be $66,238.12, Mexican silver dollars. In pursuance of the stipulation for a settlement of the claim, the above-mentioned judgment was entered, and, upon payment being made in accordance with the terms of this stipulation, the satisfaction of judgment was entered. The suit was brought in pursuance of authority thereto by the civil officers purporting to represent the Chinese government at Peking who were co-operating with the military forces under General Chang Tso Ling which had captured the city of Peking and driven out the officers of the Provisional government of the republic of China. In making the settlement and consenting to the judgment and in making a payment thereof, the appellee. dealt with the same attorneys at law and in fact who had brought the suit. After these transactions were completed and the judgment satisfied, the government of the United States, in July, 1928, recognized as the rightful government of China the Nationalist government of China, with headquarters at Nanking, whose military forces had been operating under General Chang Kai Shek. Upon the theory that such recognition related back to the beginning of the Nationalist government, it is contended that the courts must act upon the theory that, at the time this action was brought, and when judgment was rendered and the time of its satisfaction, the present recognized government of China was the only authority authorized to bring and maintain the action, and that the judgment in this action in favor of the republic of China, while actually procured by agents of the Peking government, is nevertheless the property of the Nationalist government, because such government is now recognized as the rightful government of China, and such recognition is binding upon the judicial department of our government. It is therefore contended that the recognized government has a right to the judgment and to claim here that the payment thereof was to persons who were not authorized to represent the republic of China, and that such payment therefor should be ignored and the satisfaction of the judgment vacated.

[1] It should be observed at the outset that this contention is in conflict with the axiom that he who takes benefit must bear the corresponding burden. In this case the benefit which the appellant seeks to appropriate is the judgment in favor of the republic of China. The corresponding burden is the agreement under which the judgment was procured, and this agreement not only provided for the entry of the judgment, but for its satisfaction in the manner and by the payments authorized thereby. This is in accord with the opinion of the trial judge, who stated his views in his opinion given in connection with his ruling upon the motion as follows:.

"The satisfaction of the judgment, for the consideration so specified, was therefore an essential and very important factor in the contract by which the compromise and settlement was to be effected, and but for the agreement to give such satisfaction of judgment no such judgment would ever have been entered.

"To permit the movant, under such circumstances, to reject the satisfaction and compromise of the judgment, which were the very conditions upon which the judgment was procured and entered, and at the same time to take over the judgment as the beneficial owner thereof and have execution thereon for the full amount of the judgment, would in my opinion do violence to the most elementary principles of equity and justice. Such a course of procedure would result in compelling the defendant to pay the judgment a second time, and in an amount of money very much in excess of the consideration for which the judgment had already been compromised and settled."

This consideration alone we think would require us to affirm the action of the trial court in refusing to set aside the satisfaction of the judgment. In view of the somewhat complicated situation presented by the record, we will state some additional facts and consider their applicability to the question involved on this appeal.

At the time of the procurement of the policy on the Telephone Exchange Building in Wuchang, the government telephone administration using the building and procuring the fire insurance policy was the duly recognized Provisional government having its capital at Peking. Thereafter the military forces operating under Chang Kai Shek of the Nationalist government captured the cities of Wuchang and Hangkow, China, across the Yangtse river from Wuchang. The fire which caused the loss sued upon occurred before the capture of Wuchang by the forces of the Nationalist government and during the continuance of the Provisional government recognized by the United States government. The Nationalist government took possession of the Telephone Exchange building, and thereafter operated the exchange. It secured possession of the policy involved in this action, and after the adjustment of the loss brought a suit (No. 3004) upon the policy against the appellee in the name of the republic of China in the United States Court for China at Shanghai, which place was also occupied by the military forces of the Nationalist government. Shortly thereafter, this action (No.

3025), instituted by the authorities at Peking, was brought in the name of the republic of China against the appellee upon the same policy and loss. With these two actions pending before the United States Court for China against the appellee upon the same insurance policy and for the same loss, the jurisdiction of the court was invoked by appropriate motions to have determined which of the two governments or sets of officials was entitled to sue upon the claim of the republic of China, neither government having been expressly recognized by the government of the United States, and the government which had been recognized (the Provisional government at Peking) having been entirely dissipated and dispersed by the military forces operating under Chang Tso Ling. The trial court, recognizing the principle that it lies with the executive and legislative departments of the government to determine which government of China it should recognize, came to the conclusion that the United States government had sufficiently recognized the Peking government to justify that government in prosecuting the action. This decision was based upon a telegram from the American minister at Peking. The court thereafter sustained the authority of the attorneys at law and in fact who were prosecuting this action (by the Peking government), No. 3025, and in action No. 3004 decided against the authority of those who were prosecuting that action in behalf of the republic of China upon authorization from the Nationalist government. The Nationalist government appealed to this court. In the meantime the government of the United States recognized the Nationalist government, and, basing our judgment upon that ground, this court reversed the judgment of dismissal in case No. 3004. Republic of China v. Merchants' Fire Assur. Corp., 30 F.(2d) 278.

In the meantime, the trial court had proceeded to judgment in this action, No. 3025, as hereinbefore stated. When case No. 3004 was remanded for further proceedings by the trial court, the appellant insurance company, defendant in that action, set up the judgment in No. 3025 as a bar to the action. The court rendered judgment in favor of the defendant (appellee herein) sustaining its claim that the judgment in No. 3004 was res judicata. Appellant, in effect, claims that this judgment in action No. 3004 was erroneous. In the absence of an appeal, the judgment is binding, even if erroneous. After the rendition of the judgment in case No. 3004, appellant took the position in action No. 3025 hereinbefore stated, namely, that as the recognized government of China it was entitled to collect the judgment in favor of the republic of China rendered in case No. 3025. The settlement between the parties claiming to represent the republic of China in this case, No. 3025, and the appellee insurance company, provided that the judgment, when rendered, should be satisfied by a payment to the Equitable Eastern Banking Corporation of $43,-029.20, Mexican, and the assignment to said bank of a claim of the appellant against the Russo-Asiatic Bank at Hankow for $25,993.-99, Mexican. The sum of these two amounts represents the total loss due to the fire, with interest thereon. This money was to be paid, and the assignment of' the claim against the Russo-Asiatic Bank was to be made, to the Chinese Electric Company, Limited, the attorney in fact of the Chinese (Peking) government. In the event this court, upon the pending appeal from the judgment of dismissal in case No. 3004, reversed that judgment, it was agreed that the money so paid and the assignment should be deposited with the Equitable Eastern Bank Corporation at Shanghai, China, to be held to await the event of the trial of case No. 3004, and, in case the judgment was rendered against the appellant in that action, the money and assignment were to be returned to the appellee insurance company, to be applied to the satisfaction of any judgment rendered in action No. 3004. It was also agreed that the counsel for the Chinese government (Peking government) should have the right to defend against the action of the Nationalist government (in case No. 3004) and take an appeal to this court in the event of an adverse judgment. No express agreement is made with reference to the disposition of this deposit in the event that the judgment in No. 3004 was adverse to the Nationalist government, as it was.

There seems to be no serious question but that the money paid into the banking company upon this settlement and the assignment is available to the appellant, the recognized government of China. The principal complaint made here is that the appellee insurance company gained an advantage in the settlement because of the transfer of a claim against an insolvent bank in lieu of the corresponding obligation to pay money. It is claimed that the agreement for the satisfaction of the judgment was a collusive one, brought about by the desire on the part of the insurance company to realize upon this claim of doubtful value. This contention, however, is based upon the erroneous theory that the judgment in case No. 3025 belongs to the appellant, and that the appellant is not bound by the acts of the agents who procured that judgment, even though it ratifies their act to the extent of appropriating the fruits of their action in the form of a judgment. This contention we think conflicts with the fundamental principles of agency which is thus stated in 21 Ruling Case Law, 923, 924, § 102:

"If a principal elects to ratify any portion of an unauthorized transaction of his agent he must ratify the whole of it. He cannot avail himself of such acts as are beneficial to him, and repudiate such as are detrimental, whether the ratification be expressed or implied. If, for example, an agent obtains possession of the property of another by making a stipulation or condition which he is not authorized to make, the principal must either return the property, or remain subject to the condition upon which it was parted with by the former owner. Similarly, keeping part of the goods left for a person with an unauthorized agent, who assumed to accept them in discharge of a contract which the other party had the option to discharge either in goods or in money, ratifies the act of the agent in accepting the goods, and prevents the rejection of other portions of the goods. And on the same principle the payee of a renewal note cannot, after knowledge of all the facts, ratify the act of his agent in obtaining such note by suing thereon, and at the same time repudiate as unauthorized the act of his agent in executing contemporaneously therewith an agreement detrimental to him, which contemporaneous agreement was the inducing cause of the execution of the renewal note. (21 R. C. L. 923, 924, § 102 of Principal and Agent.)"

In view of the action of the appellant in

abandoning the suit No. 3004 brought by it and in moving to appropriate the fruits of the action brought by the Peking government, we find it unnecessary to discuss or further consider the perplexing problems growing out of the civil war in China and the conflicting claims of the various civil and military organizations claiming to represent all or a part of China. If the appellant had adhered to its position taken originally on appeal in its case No. 3004, some of these questions pressed upon us for consideration would have required determination, but, for the reasons stated, it is unnecessary to enter into these perplexing questions.

Order affirmed.

SAWTELLE, Circuit Judge, concurs.

State of Russia v. National City Bank of New York
69 F. 2d. 44 (2d. Cir., 1934)

Before MANTON, AUGUSTUS N. HAND, and CHASE, Circuit Judges.

MANTON, Circuit Judge.

This action, brought in the name of the state of Russia July 9, 1928, sought the recovery of a deposit in the National City Bank of New York. A decree for the defendant was entered October 11, 1933, and this appeal was taken by the state of Russia.

Mr. Serge Ughet, the financial attaché of the Russian Embassy under the Russian Provisional Government, in the name of the state of Russia, appealed from the decree October 14, 1933. On October 21, 1933, Mr. Ughet sent a letter to the Department of State expressing a desire to be relieved of his duties as a representative of the state of Russia, and, on November 15, 1933, he made an assignment of this cause of action to the United States. On November 16, 1933, the President of the United States established diplomatic relations with the Union of Soviet Socialist Republics as the de jure government of Russia. Mr. Maxim Litvinoff, the People's Commissar for Foreign Affairs of the Soviet Republics, assigned to the government of the United States the claim in suit and thus ratified the assignment of the claim in suit which had been made by Mr. Ughet. We judicially recognized Mr. Ughet as the financial attaché of the Russian Embassy in the United States. Lehigh Valley R. Co. v. State of Russia, 21 F.(2d) 396 (C. C. A. 2).

The deposit of money, in December, 1917, was in the Bankers' Trust Company in the name of three individuals, and was drawn from the general account of the Russian government and deposited with the National City Bank. These individuals were empowered to sign checks. They were officials of the Russian Railroad Commission in the United States appointed prior to the Soviet Revolution. It was a government account. In 1918 one of these same three officials had transferred allegiance to the Soviet government. The others arranged to transfer to the National City Bank the existing credit balance in the Bankers' Trust Company. Mr. Ughet obtained their check and deposited the same with the bank to a general account for the credit of the Russian government. The account, $115,788.32, remained there until July, 1928, under a special arrangement unnecessary to consider here. This action was then commenced.

Below it was agreed that the money is the sole and exclusive property of the Russian government, but that the government owes the National City Bank $4,435,000, evidenced by a promissory note dated May 1, 1917. The money was used to finance the purchase of railroad cars in the United States for the Russian government. Below the bank successfully offset its claim against the deposit.

The diplomatic letters exchanged, dated November 16, 1933, were as follows:

"The White House, Washington,
November 16, 1933.

"My Dear Mr. Litvinov:

"I am very happy to inform you that as a result of our conversations the Government of the United States has decided to establish normal diplomatic relations with the Government of the Union of Soviet Socialist Republics and to exchange ambassadors.

"I trust that the relations now established between our peoples may forever remain normal and friendly, and that our nations henceforth may cooperate for their mutual benefit and for the preservation of the peace of the world.

"I am, my dear Mr. Litvinov,

"Very sincerely yours,

"Franklin D. Roosevelt

"Mr. Maxim M. Litvinov, People's Commissar for Foreign Affairs, Union of Soviet Socialist Republics."

"Washington, November 16, 1933.

"My dear Mr. President:

"Following our conversations I have the honor to inform you that the Government of the Union of Soviet Socialist Republics agrees that, preparatory to a final settlement of the claims and counter claims between the Governments of the Union of Soviet Socialist Republics and the United States of America and the claims of their nationals, the Government of the Union of Soviet Socialist Republics will not take any steps to enforce any decisions of courts or initiate any new litigations for the amounts admitted to be due or that may be found to be due it, as the successor of prior Governments of Russia, or otherwise, from American nationals, including corporations, companies, partnerships, or associations, and also the claim against the United States of the Russian Volunteer Fleet, now in litigation in the United States Court of Claims, and will not object to such amounts being assigned and does hereby release and assign all such amounts to the Government of the United States, the Government of the Union of Soviet Socialist Republics to be duly notified in each case of any amount realized by the Government of the United States from such release and assignment.

"The Government of the Union of Soviet Socialist Republics further agrees, preparatory to the settlement referred to above not to make any claim with respect to:

"(a) judgments rendered or that may be rendered by American courts in so far as they relate to property, or rights, or interests therein, in which the Union of Soviet Socialist Republics or its nationals may have had or may claim to have an interest; or,

"(b) acts done or settlements made by or with the Government of the United States, or public officials, in the United States, or its nationals, relating to property, credits, or obligations of any Government of Russia or nationals thereof.

"I am, my dear Mr. President,

"Very sincerely yours,

"Maxim Litvinoff,

"People's Commissar for Foreign Affairs, Union of Soviet Socialist Republics.

"Mr. Franklin D. Roosevelt, President of the United States of America, The White House."

Since this exchange of notes, the state of Russia is no longer recognized by this government for any purpose. It may not appear as a litigant, neither on behalf of the assignee or otherwise. The assignee of the claim named in a legally sufficient assignment is now the proper party appellant. A motion is made by the United States as an assignee to be permitted to prosecute this appeal.

The appellee argues that the assignments by Ughet and Litvinoff are ineffectual, and that to bring the United States in as a party now requires a petition in the nature of a supplemental bill in the District Court. It also maintains that the substance of the diplomatic notes of Mr. Litvinoff to the President is tantamount to an abandonment of the appeal.

The United States is in the nature of a corporate entity, and has a common-law right to acquire property. Fay v. United States, 204 F. 559 (C. C. A. 1); United States v. Rubin (D. C.) 227 F. 938. Therefore a lawful assignment to it is effective. One government may transfer property rights to another government. Hijo v. United States, 194 U. S. 315, 24 S. Ct. 727, 48 L. Ed. 994; Herrera

v. United States, 222 U. S. 558, 32 S. Ct. 179, 56 L. Ed. 316.

While specific powers and duties of a secretary or minister for foreign affairs of a nation are generally prescribed and regulated by the municipal law of that nation at home, international law defines his position regarding intercourse with other nations. 1 Oppenheim International Law (3d Ed.) 1920, p. 538.

In United States v. De la Maza Arredondo, 6 Pet. 691, at page 728, 8 L. Ed. 547, the court said: "The grants of colonial governors, before the revolution, have always been, and yet are, taken as plenary evidence of the grant itself, as well as authority to dispose of the public lands. Its actual exercise, without any evidence of disavowal, revocation or denial by the king, and his consequent acquiescence and presumed ratification, are sufficient proof, in the absence of any to the contrary (subsequent to the grant), of the royal assent to the exercise of his prerogative by his local governors. This or no other court can require proof that there exists in every government a power to dispose of its property; in the absence of any elsewhere, we are bound to presume and consider, that it exists in the officers or tribunal who exercises it, by making grants, and that it is fully evidenced by occupation, enjoyment and transfers of property, had and made under them, without disturbance by any superior power, and respected by all co-ordinate and inferior officers and tribunals throughout the state, colony or province where it lies. A public grant, or one made in the name and assumed authority of the sovereign power of the country, has never been considered as a special verdict; capable of being aided by no inference of the existence of other facts than those expressly found or apparent by necessary implication. * * * "

The minister of foreign affairs in his public character is the regular political intermediary between the state and foreign government. He has plenary authority to represent his state at conference and diplomatic negotiations. 3 Genet, Traite de Diplomatie et de Droit Diplomatique 1932, 162; Hall, Treatise on International Law (6th Ed. by Atlay) p. 295.

If the minister is commissioned to undertake special negotiations of a public charac-

ter which require his presence in a foreign jurisdiction, he must and usually is furnished with powers to negotiate. The powers may be embodied either in an ordinary letter of credence or in special letters patent. These powers within reasonable limits define the authority for his acts, which acts will be binding upon his government. Hall, Treatise on International Law (6th Ed. by Atlay) p. 295. While no authority has been found, respecting the principle of public international law or national policy, which conflicts with the recognition in the minister for foreign affairs of a nation of the power to alienate the proprietary rights or interests of his nation by the execution of an assignment in his name, still there are here sufficient reasons upon which we may conclude presumptively that he had such powers.

As to the authority of Foreign Commissar Litvinoff to make the assignment on behalf of his government, there is a presumption of authority in his designation, recognition, and the President's acceptance of the assignment. It is a matter of political action in foreign affairs, and the question of who represents and acts for a sovereign or nation in its relation to the United States is determined, not by the Judicial Department, but exclusively by the political branch of the government. Lehigh V. R. Co. v. State of Russia, supra; Doe ex dem. Clark v. Braden, 16 How. 635, 656, 14 L. Ed. 1090; Hyde on International Law, Vol. 1, p. 368; Terlinden v. Ames, 184 U. S. 270, 288, 22 S. Ct. 484, 491, 46 L. Ed. 534. In Terlinden v. Ames, supra, the court said: "In Doe ex dem. Clark v. Braden, 16 How. 635, 656, 14 L. Ed. 1090, where it was contended that so much of the treaty of February 22, 1819 ceding Florida to the United States, as annulled a certain land grant, was void for want of power in the King of Spain to ratify such a provision, it was held that whether or not the King of Spain had power, according to the Constitution of Spain, to annul the grant, was a political, and not a judicial, question, and was decided when the treaty was made and ratified."

Quoting Chief Justice Taney, it was said: "'And it would be impossible for the Executive Department of the government to conduct our foreign relations with any advantage to the country, and fulfill the duties which the Constitution has imposed upon it, if every court in the country was authorized to inquire and decide whether the person who ratified the treaty on behalf of a foreign nation had the power, by its Constitution and laws, to make the engagements into which he entered.'"

Our courts must accept the assertion of the government of the United States as to the effect of an assignment. Jones v. United States, 137 U. S. 202, 11 S. Ct. 80, 34 L. Ed. 691; Williams v. Suffolk Ins. Co., 13 Pet. 415, 10 L. Ed. 226. Nor is the acceptance of this assignment a treaty in any formal sense. It is clearly within the exclusive powers of the executive and is known as an executive agreement. An ambassador to Russia was appointed by the President, and his appointment confirmed January 11, 1934, by the Senate, and in the debate of the Senate it is said that valid agreements have been "reached between the President and the Representative of the Russian Soviet Union upon which the recognition of the Soviet Government is based," founded upon the exclusively "executive function and prerogative to recognize foreign governments," and there was mentioned "the basis of contractual relationship upon which recognition has been granted. * * *" Congressional Record, vol. 78 (Jan. 11, 1934) p. 440.

The President of the United States is intrusted with the right of conducting all negotiations with foreign governments and is the judge of the expediency of instituting, conducting, or terminating such negotiations in respect to claims against foreign governments. Agreements of such adjustment or settlement of such claims are not submitted to the Senate. J. B. Moore, Treaties and Executive Agreements, Political Science Quarterly, vol. 20, p. 385; Moore's International Law Digest, vol. 5, § 752.

The government of Russia is the agent of the state. Lehigh V. Ry. Co. v. State of Russia, supra. The solicitors representing this application prosecuted the suit below and were recognized by the agent of the plaintiff. They have now been appointed Special Assistants to the Attorney General of the United States to carry on this appeal. This is suf-ficient authorization for them to appear.

The authority of the United States of America, after the lawful assignment, to proceed in this court, is fully established. F. A. Mfg. Co. v. Hayden & Clemons, Inc., 273 F. 374 (C. C. A. 1).

The Litvinoff letter refers to "the amounts admitted to be due or that may be found to be due it [the Soviet Govenment] * * * from American nationals," and states that the Soviet government "will not object to such amounts being assigned and does hereby release and assign all such amounts to the Government of the United States. * * *" This sufficiently, for an assignment, covers the claim alleged to be due, the subject of the appellant's suit. The acknowledgment of the Soviet government further was "not to make any claim with respect to: (a) judgments rendered or that may be rendered by American courts. * * *" This phrase does not mean that the United States shall not continue an appeal already taken from the decree below. The appeal of the cause of action in suit had already been perfected when this assignment was made, and further action respecting it was then a subject for the consideration of the government of the United States and not of the Soviet government. There is no undertaking upon the part of the United States not to prosecute this appeal, and the rights to be obtained by this appeal belong to the United States by virtue of the assignment. Neither party to the exchange of diplomatic notes intended waiving rights of appeal, for they did not say so. Moreover, it is apparent that the intent was to assign all the claims of the Soviet government to the United States, and it agreed to leave undisturbed diplomatically final nonappealable judgments and decrees of the American courts touching Russian affairs and nonjudicial acts done in good faith by and with the officials of the previously recognized government of Russia. This we think was the intention on the part of the governments as stated in this exchange of correspondence. It cannot be that the parties intended to prevent an appeal, the claim of which had been assigned and which was lodged against a third party.

Motion granted.

Amtorg Trading Corporation v. United States
71 F. 2d. 524 (C.C.P.A., 1934)

Before GRAHAM, Presiding Judge, and BLAND, HATFIELD, GARRETT, and LENROOT, Associate Judges.

GRAHAM, Presiding Judge.

Certain matches of the strike-on-box type were exported from the Union of Socialist Soviet Republics and imported at the port of New York, in three entries, under the Tariff Act of 1922 (42 Stat. 858). The last importation was entered on May 28, 1930.

On May 19, 1930, the Secretary of the Treasury made and promulgated a finding of dumping under the Anti-Dumping Act of 1921 (19 USCA §§ 160–173), which finding is known as T. D. 44037, and which is as follows:

"Antidumping—Safety matches from Soviet Russia

"The Secretary of the Treasury makes a finding of dumping in the case of safety matches from Soviet Russia

"Treasury Department, May 19, 1930.

"To Collectors of Customs and Others Concerned:

"After due investigation in accordance with the provisions of section 201, Anti-Dumping Act, 1921, I find that the industry of manufacturing safety matches of the strike-on-box type in the United States is being, and is likely to be, injured by reason of the importation into the United States of safety matches of the strike-on-box type from the Union of Socialist Soviet Republics (Soviet Russia), and that such safety matches of the strike-on-box type are being sold, and are likely to be sold, in the United States at less than their fair value.

"A. W. Mellon,
"Secretary of the Treasury."

Proceeding under the authority of said dumping order, the ordinary appraisements of dutiable value were made, and an ascertainment of anti-dumping duty was made, as to the goods in each entry. Appeals to reappraisement were taken to the United States Customs Court in each case. These included appeals as to the ordinary and usual appraisements of the goods in reappraisements 97872—A and 97991—A, and as to the dumping duty in all three reappraisements. The various reappraisements having been consolidated, were heard by Judge McClelland. Several witnesses were called and examined on the part of both the importer and the Government, including the Secretary of the Treasury and the Commissioner of Customs. During the course of the taking of testimony, a number of so-called "affidavits" were offered in evidence by the importer, and admitted.

During the taking of testimony, a motion was made on behalf of the Government to dismiss the appeal on the grounds that the importer, Amtorg Trading Corporation, was an agency of the Soviet Government, and, inasmuch as the Government of the United States had not, at that time, recognized the Soviet Government, that its agents and representatives had no right to appear in any of the courts of the United States as a party to any litigation therein. As to this matter, the single judge sitting in reappraisement held that the Amtorg Trading Corporation was shown by the record to be a corporation domiciled in and existing under the laws of the state of New York, and that it might legally appear in the United States Customs Court and prosecute its appeals to a conclusion; that no foreign value had been shown for the imported goods, and no cost of production; and that there was no evidence in the record from which it might be deduced that the Secretary of the Treasury was justified in issuing the dumping order complained of. In conclusion, and for the above-stated reasons, the court found that no dumping duty could properly be collected.

Appeals were duly prosecuted from this

judgment to the Third Appellate Division. The division held that the alleged affidavits in the record were not, in fact, affidavits, and that they were not properly received in evidence. The theory upon which this holding was made, as we understand it, is that these affidavits were not upon oath as was, according to the view of the court, required by law. From this conclusion it was considered by the division that there was no evidence before the single judge in support of the proposition that no foreign value existed, and that, therefore, the appeal should have been dismissed upon the authority of United States v. Malhame & Co., 19 C. C. P. A. (Customs) 164, T. D. 45276.

The division also held that the finding of fair value under the Anti-Dumping Act of 1921. was within the discretion of the Secretary of the Treasury, and that his judgment on these matters could not be judicially disturbed. Therefore, the decision of the single judge was reversed, with directions to dismiss the appeal.

Both parties appeal to this court. The importer insists that the judgment of the Third Division was in error in holding that the affidavits might not be received in evidence, in not holding that no foreign value for home consumption in Russia had been shown for the goods in question, and in directing a dismissal of the importer's appeal to reappraisement.

On its part, the Government seeks a reversal upon the grounds of various rulings during the trial, which will sufficiently appear by the discussion of the case hereinafter to be made.

We shall first direct our attention to the argument stressed by amicus curiæ that the importer, appellant Amtorg Trading Corporation, has no right to appeal and sue herein; that said corporation, being an agent of the Union of Socialist Soviet Republics, a Government not recognized by the Government of the United States, had no more right to sue in our courts than did the said nonrecognized Government; that said Government could not so sue; that, therefore, the appeals for reappraisement herein should have been dismissed.

It is conceded by counsel, and the court will take judicial notice of the fact, that, at the time of the importations of the goods in issue, the United States Government had not recognized the Union of Socialist Soviet Republics of Russia, and that there was then no diplomatic interchange between said Governments. Oetjen v. Central Leather Co., 246 U. S. 297, 38 S. Ct. 309, 62 L. Ed. 726; Jones v. United States, 137 U. S. 202, 214, 11 S. Ct. 80, 34 L. Ed. 691; Underhill v. Hernandez, 168 U. S. 250, 18 S. Ct. 83, 42 L. Ed. 456; The Penza (D. C.) 277 F. 91.

As to the representative capacity of the Amtorg Trading Corporation, the record shows that, at the time of entry and hearing, this was a corporation, organized and doing business under the laws of the state of New York, with its domicile and principal place of business in said state; that the capital of the corporation consisted of $3,000,000, represented by 30,000 shares of $100 each; that this stock was held in trust by Peter A. Bogdanov, for the Bank of Foreign Trade of the Union of Socialist Soviet Republics; that said Bank of Foreign Trade was under the control of the Soviet Government; and that its stock was distributed as to ownership between the Commissariat of Foreign Trade, a department of the Soviet Government, and several syndicates, industrial trusts, and mixed corporations. Bogdanov testified that some foreign capital was invested in some of these stocks.

The corporation has a board of seven directors, which are elected at meetings in the New York office. Bogdanov, as the trustee for the stock, is able to, and does, select these directors. In order to comply with the New York law, one of these directors is a citizen of the United States. The other six are citizens of the Soviet Government. Bogdanov was sent from Moscow by the Bank of Foreign Trade to the United States to take charge of the business of the corporation, to relieve one Bron, who had, up to that time, been in management of the corporation. The syndicates, trusts, and mixed organizations mentioned by Bogdanov as owning the stock of the Bank of Foreign Trade, are all generally supervised and regulated by the Soviet Government.

It appears, therefore, that the Amtorg Trading Corporation was under the direct control, through stock ownership, of the Soviet Government at the time the goods herein were imported. It must also be held, under the authorities, that said corporation was a citizen of the state of New York. Chicago & N. W. Railway Co. v. Whitton, 13 Wall. 270, 283, 20 L. Ed. 571; Case of the Sewing Mach. Companies, 18 Wall. 553, 575, 21 L. Ed. 914; Mississippi & R. River Boom Co. v. Patterson, 98 U. S. 403, 407, 25 L. Ed. 206; Doctor v. Harrington, 196 U. S. 579, 586, 25 S. Ct. 355, 357, 49 L. Ed. 606.

We must conclude that the Amtorg Trading Corporation was, in all things, complying with the laws of the state of New York. It was, therefore, a citizen of that state, invested with the right to sue and be sued in the courts of the country.

It is argued, however, that the courts in certain cases may "pierce the veil" and may reach and investigate the character of the incorporators and stockholders. A leading case cited is United States v. Lehigh Valley R. R. Co., 220 U. S. 257, 31 S. Ct. 387, 55 L. Ed. 458.

A very interesting case on the subject is Home Fire Insurance Co. v. Barber, 67 Neb. 644, 93 N. W. 1024, 1032, 60 L. R. A. 927, 108 Am. St. Rep. 716. Discussing the question now before us, the court said:

" * * * Accordingly, courts and textwriters have been in entire agreement that equity will look behind the corporate entity, and consider who are the real and substantial parties in interest, whenever it becomes necessary to do so to promote justice or obviate inequitable results. * * *

"Cases of this kind must be differentiated sharply from those where the proceeding is at law, or where a question of title to the corporate property is involved. There is no question that stockholders, as such, have no title to the corporate property which they can convey or incumber in their own names. * * *

"Hence, we think the rule to apply to such cases is this: Where a corporation is proceeding at law, or where it is asserting a title to property, or the title to property is involved, the corporation is regarded as a person separate and distinct from its stockholders, or any or all of them. But where it is proceeding in equity to assert rights of an equitable nature, or is seeking relief upon rules or principles of equity, the court of equity will not forget that the stockholders are the real and substantial beneficiaries of a recovery,

and if the stockholders have no standing in equity, and are not equitably entitled to the remedy sought to be enforced by the corporation in their behalf and for their advantage, the corporation will not be permitted to recover."

We think it may be safely stated that in those cases where the court has gone behind the corporate entity, and has considered the real parties in interest, there has been some equitable remedy required or some matter of public policy involved. In other cases, the courts have not done so. Stone v. Cleveland, etc., R. Co., 202 N. Y. 352, 95 N. E. 816, 35 L. R. A. (N. S.) 770; Salvin v. Myles Realty Co., 227 N. Y. 51, 124 N. E. 94, 6 A. L. R. 581; Elenkrieg v. Siebrecht, 238 N. Y. 254, 144 N. E. 519, 34 A. L. R. 592; Berkey v. Third Ave. Ry. Co., 244 N. Y. 84, 155 N. E. 58, 50 A. L. R. 599.

It is argued that, inasmuch as various agencies of the Union of Socialist Soviet Republics own the stock and control the operation of the Amtorg Trading Corporation through such ownership, the corporation must be treated as a part of the Soviet Government itself. We cannot, however, come to this conclusion. In this proceeding, which is purely statutory, we are not concerned with the ownership of the stock, nor does it make any difference where the stockholders reside. City of St. Louis v. Wiggins, etc. Co., 40 Mo. 580, 590. The character of the corporation, and its powers and responsibilities, depend upon the place where the charter was granted. Harley v. Charleston Steam-Packet Co., 2 Miles (Pa.) 249.

When a government becomes a stockholder in a corporation, it does not exercise its sovereignty as such. "It acts merely as a corporator, and exercises no other power in the management of the affairs of the corporation than are expressly given by the incorporating act." Bank of Kentucky v. Wister, 2 Pet. 318, 324, 7 L. Ed. 437; Briscoe v. Bank of Kentucky, 11 Pet. 257, 326, 9 L. Ed. 709; Moore v. Board of Trustees, 7 Ind. 462; Bank of U. S. v. Planters' Bank, 9 Wheat. 904, 6 L. Ed. 244. Nor does the fact that the government may own all or a majority of the capital stock take from the corporation its character as such, or make the government the real party in interest. United States ex rel. Skinner & Eddy Corp. v. Mc-

Carl, 275 U. S. 1, 48 S. Ct. 12, 72 L. Ed. 131; Sloan Shipyards Corp. v. U. S. Em. Fleet Corp., 258 U. S. 549, 42 S. Ct. 386, 66 L. Ed. 762; United States v. Strang, 254 U. S. 491, 41 S. Ct. 165, 65 L. Ed. 368; Commercial Pac. Cable Co. v. Philippine Nat. Bank (D. C.) 263 F. 218.

Two cases are cited by amicus curiæ which are thought to support the proposition that the Amtorg Trading Corporation has no right to sue in the courts of the United States. The first of these is Russian Socialist Federated Soviet Republic v. Cibrario et al., 235 N. Y. 255, 139 N. E. 259. There the court held that the unrecognized Soviet Government might not so sue; that a foreign power brings an action in our courts not as a matter of right, but as the result of comity; that where no such comity exists, then such foreign power has no right to appear in our courts as a litigant; that, as a matter of law, there is no such party litigant.

The second case cited is The Penza (D. C.) 277 F. 91. In this case the Russian Socialist Federated Soviet Republic, and one Martens, an agent and representative thereof, filed a libel on behalf of the Soviet Government against two steamers, known as the Penza and Tobolsk, claiming that they were detained illegally from the possession of the libelants. The District Court held, on exception, that the libelant could not sue, the Soviet Government not having been recognized, and dismissed the libel.

These cases do not dispose of the issue here. They simply recognize what seems to be the rule, that only a recognized foreign government has a standing in our courts, as is indicated in cases such as The Sapphire, 11 Wall. 164, 20 L. Ed. 127.

In the two cases above discussed, the suitor was neither a person nor a corporation. In the case before us, the suitor is a corporation and, as such, is, in all legal aspects, a citizen of the state of New York.

An authoritative case is Amtorg Trading Corp. (the appellant here) v. New York Indemnity Co., 256 N. Y. 671, 177 N. E. 187. In that case, suit was brought by the plaintiff to recover for a loss under a policy of burglary insurance. In the trial court, in the answer to the complaint, the defendant pleaded the ownership of plaintiff by the Soviet Government of Russia, and that because such Government was not recognized by the Government of the United States at that time, the plaintiff had no right to sue and recover. The trial judge charged the jury that the plaintiff had a right to so sue. Judgment was rendered for the plaintiff.

The Appellate Division of the Supreme Court affirmed the judgment, without opinion, 229 App. Div. 772, 242 N. Y. S. 811. On further appeal to the Court of Appeals, the judgment was again affirmed without opinion. An examination of the briefs of both counsel in the Court of Appeals discloses that the said right of the plaintiff to sue was fully argued in the Court of Appeals.

The decision in the cited case may, therefore, be considered as in harmony with the views herein expressed.

In Amtorg Trading Corp. v. Commissioner of Internal Revenue, 65 F.(2d) 583, the Circuit Court of Appeals of the Second Circuit exercised jurisdiction to final judgment. It is true, the exact point here at issue does not seem to have been raised there, but the nature and organization of the petitioner, and the nonrecognition of the Soviet Government, were known to the court and freely discussed in the opinion rendered.

Our conclusion upon this phase of the case is that the Amtorg Trading Corporation might properly appeal to reappraisement and seek its remedy in the trial court and here, and that the motion of the Government to dismiss was properly overruled.

In view of these conclusions, the judgement of the United States Customs Court, Third Division, is reversed, and the course is remanded for further proceedings in conformity herewith.

Day-Gormley Leather Co. v. National City Bank
8 F. Supp. 503 (S.D., N.Y., 1934)

CAFFEY, District Judge.

I regret that there has not been earlier opportunity to take up this case since the briefs were submitted in May. Even now lack of time prevents me from treating the matter thoroughly or commenting extensively on the authorities.

At the oral argument in April the plaintiff withdrew its objection to the thirteenth defense and the defendant withdrew the fifth, the sixth, and the seventh defenses. We are concerned, therefore, merely with the sufficiency of the first to the fourth, the eighth, the ninth, the eleventh, and the twelfth defenses. In the view I take, as well apparently as in the view of counsel, the eleventh is the most important. So I shall examine it first.

In testing the sufficiency of a defense, only allegations of facts, either in the complaint or in the defense, which are well pleaded are to be taken as true. Moreover, any material portion of the defense which constitutes a denial of an allegation of the complaint must be discarded.

Looking at the pleadings in the way indicated, the complaint divides itself into two branches. One bases the cause of action asserted exclusively on an obligation undertaken by the Petrograd branch itself; the other (paragraphs 7 and 8 of the complaint), on an assumption of liability by the defendant regardless of what was undertaken by the branch alone. The former will be dealt with in the beginning as if the latter (dealt with later) had not been included in the complaint.

The complaint alleges, in substance, that one term of the deposit contract between the plaintiff and the Petrograd branch was that the branch agreed to repay in Russia, in Russian currency, on demand (paragraph 6); that a revolution occurred November 7, 1917 (paragraph 10); that by reason thereof the branch was closed March 9, 1918, thereupon performance of the terms and conditions of the contract became impossible, among the

phases of impossibility was inability of the plaintiff to demand or to receive payment of its deposit in Russia from the branch and the impossibility of performance still continues (paragraph 11); and that on October 24, 1933, the plaintiff made demand on the defendant in New York City for repayment of the deposit (paragraph 14).

In the eleventh defense, allegations of facts which do not deny allegations of facts in the complaint, in substance, are these: All the transactions between the plaintiff and the Petrograd branch took place in Russia (paragraph I); the deposit agreement provided that it should be performed in Russia and be governed by Russian law (paragraph IX); under Russian law, with respect to stoppage of defendant's operations in Russia, the branch was subject to that law and to the decisions of the Russian government (paragraph II); in November, 1917, the Soviet government decreed a nationalization of all private joint-stock banks operating in Russia and, in carrying out the decree, the Soviet government seized such banks and further decreed that all the liabilities of any private bank so seized were taken over by the State Bank acting for the Soviet government (paragraph V); the Soviet government also decreed that the liability of the Petrograd branch to its depositors was taken over and assumed by the Soviet government acting through the State Bank (paragraph VI); all deposit accounts were confiscated by the Soviet government and credited on the books of the State Bank (paragraph VIII); the Soviet government has now been recognized by the United States government (paragraph XI).

In detail in paragraph VIII, among other things, it is alleged as follows: "By the decrees and regulations of the Soviet Government, the deposit account, if any, referred to in the complaint, was seized and confiscated by the Soviet Government and thereupon became its property; and all right, title and interest of the plaintiff therein and thereto, as against the defendant, became divested."

I have puzzled somewhat as to the meaning of this particular statement by the defendant. At first I was inclined to treat it as a conclusion merely and, therefore, not a well-pleaded allegation of facts which, for the purpose of passing on the eleventh defense, I may take as admitted by the plaintiff. After studying it, however, I have concluded that, when taken in conjunction with the other allegations of the defense, fairness to the pleader requires that I regard it as asserting that in the decrees and regulations of the Soviet government there was a provision which, in terms and effect, confiscated the deposit account here involved and transferred the account to itself. It is upon this interpretation of the defense that I proceed in disposing of the question relating to it. I should make clear, however, that if at the trial the defendant fails in its evidence to establish that the Soviet government issued such a decree or decrees or such a regulation or regulations as I understand the defendant to say it did, then, by the same token, I am not to be deemed by the trial judge to have passed on a defense based on different proof.

From the angle heretofore stated, in order to determine whether the eleventh defense is good, three things will be taken as uncontroverted: (1) All the pertinent transactions between the plaintiff and the defendant occurred in Russia and, according to its laws, were governed thereby. (2) Through the action of a revolutionary government in that country, such government endeavored to confiscate, and if its action was valid did confiscate, the property rights of the plaintiff in the deposit and divested the plaintiff of all interest therein. (3) Subsequent to the attempted or purported confiscation the government of the United States granted full diplomatic recognition to that revolutionary government (the documents covering which are set out in State of Russia v. National City Bank of New York (C. C. A.) 69 F.(2d) 44).

In the light of the circumstances as I have recited them, I think: First, that if the action l the Soviet government be valid, then the plain t has no title to the cause of action sued on; d, secondly, that, irrespective of original invalidity, if it existed, diplomatic recognition by this country of that government has validated the seizure of the deposit (Underhill v. Hernandez, 168 U. S. 250, 18 S. Ct. 83, 42 L. Ed. 456; Oetjen v. Central Leather Co., 246 U. S. 297, 38 S. Ct. 309, 62 L. Ed. 726; Ricaud v. American Metal Co., 246 U. S. 304, 38 S. Ct. 312, 62 L. Ed. 733).

In an oral opinion, on June 5, 1931, in Banque de France v. Chase National Bank, L. 42/63, and Same v. Equitable Trust Company of New York, L. 42/64, I indicated the reasons, largely applicable here, which influenced me to accept the interpretation which I am putting on the Supreme Court decisions cited. A copy of this, in the form of an extract from the stenographic minutes of the trial of those cases, page 4800 et seq., is on file in the clerk's office.

The instance would probably be rare in which the sensibilities of outsiders would not be aroused by accounts given by sufferers from a revolution. In the case at bar, however, upon the undisputed allegations, it seems to me that both the depositor and the bank were victims. The problem is to determine upon which, as between the victims, the law imposes the loss resulting from the catastrophe. So also, as I feel, the solution depends upon international law and, aside from that law, no differentiation can be made between a cause of action, in favor of one victim against the other, for breach of contract and for a tort. It is upon this account that I do not go into the state court decisions. I am bound by the rule laid down by the Supreme Court of the United States as to what is the relevant international law and what is its effect in application. Kunglig Jarnvagsstyrelsen v. Dexter & Carpenter (C. C. A.) 32 F.(2d) 195, 200.

This brings us to the consideration of paragraphs 7 and 8 of the complaint. These will be taken to mean, in substance, that the defendant, as one of the terms of the deposit agreement, subjected all its assets to responsibility for the discharge of any liability (such as for the deposit with which we are here concerned) incurred by its Petrograd branch. That, however, as it seems to me, does not help the plaintiff if the conclusion I have reached as to the effect of diplomatic recognition of the Soviet government be correct. This is so because, as I view the matter, the action of the Soviet government (which diplomatic recognition has rendered lawful and binding as between the parties to this action) completely destroyed the plaintiff's ownership of the deposit account and remitted the plaintiff solely to such remedy, if any, as was provided by the Soviet government itself under its decrees and regulations on the subject, described in the eleventh defense, or otherwise.

As I see it, it makes not the slightest difference that the plaintiff and the defendant are or at the time of the transactions were American corporations. With respect to the transactions both voluntarily had gone into Russia and subjected themselves to Russian law. In consequence, their rights inter sese are, to the extent I have stated, subject to what happened in Russia bearing upon those rights, regardless of the circumstance that the present litigation is in a court of the United States and regardless of how this court may feel as to what are the equities as between the parties. For this court to employ to any other end the judicial power with which it is vested would, as I conceive, be a trespass upon the functions of the political branch of the government of the United States.

Upon the facts alleged in the first and second defenses, let it be assumed that the deposit contract was subject to Russian law and that, under that law, the defendant was excused from performance in Russia (paragraphs III and VI of the first defense). Yet I think that a proper interpretation of paragraphs 7 and 8 of the complaint makes both defenses bad. As I construe those paragraphs of the complaint, it was a part of the deposit agreement that the defendant subjected all its assets to liability for a breach of the agreement. The agreement was breached and thereupon, as I see it, the assets of the defendant outside of Russia, by express terms of the agreement, became available for the satisfaction of the damages which plaintiff suffered by the breach. It would be substituting shadow for substance if the agreement were held to mean that, in these circumstances, there could be no recovery by the plaintiff in a court, outside of Russia, having jurisdiction of the parties.

Even though the deposit agreement permitted the defendant at any time to repay the plaintiff, as alleged in paragraph I of the third defense, nevertheless the defendant does not allege that there was any repayment or even that the rubles owing were tendered to the plaintiff. It seems to me manifest that mere notice, given by the defendant to the plaintiff, to withdraw its deposit did not alter the contract rights of the plaintiff or transfer to the shoulders of the plaintiff any risk flowing from failure to comply with the notice. Accordingly, I think the third defense is bad.

Restriction by Russian law, at the time of the deposit agreement or since, on exportation of rubles or restriction by law of the United States, until 1920, on making payments in this country on account of bank deposits in Russia may or may not affect the measure of recovery by the plaintiff if successful in the present suit. See Zimmerman v. Hicks (C. C. A.) 7 F.(2d) 443; Tillman v. Russo Asiatic Bank, 51 F.(2d) 1023, 80 A. L. R. 1368. In determining whether the complaint states a cause of action, however, we are not concerned with the measure of damages and I leave, as I think I should leave, the question as to what the measure should be for decision at the trial, without being prejudiced (under the law of the case rule) by anything said in this memorandum. Obviously, as I believe, a mere showing that a plaintiff is not entitled to recover as much as he seeks is not a defense, either complete or partial. The fourth defense, therefore, is not good.

The eighth and ninth defenses seem to me bad because—even though bringing the action be not, in and of itself, a sufficient demand, a point which I do not decide—the complaint alleges (paragraph 14) an express demand on the defendant in October, 1933, to repay the rubles sued for. It follows that a provision in the deposit agreement under Russian law that demand should precede suit, as alleged in the eighth defense, does not stand in the way of a recovery by the plaintiff. Whether the measure of recovery be affected by delay in the demand is not a question for present determination, but should be determined only at the trial.

Likewise, as I see it, mere writing off by the Russian government of plaintiff's claim as worthless, because of the depreciation of rubles in which the claim was payable, as alleged in the twelfth defense, could not affect the contract rights as between the plaintiff and the defendant.

Counsel have furnished me elaborate briefs for both sides in Dougherty v. National City Bank, Supreme Court, Nassau County, pending before Harrison Tweed, Esq., referee. From an examination of those briefs I am impressed that the issues of fact in this case may be so extensive and complicated that they ought not in the first instance to be submitted to a jury. Accordingly, I suggest that counsel consider whether or not, on their application, those issues should not be sent, in advance of trial—or at the trial the court

may not, of its own motion, send them—to an auditor for findings which shall have the effect of prima facie evidence, in accordance with the practice approved in Ex parte Peterson, 253 U. S. 300, 40 S. Ct. 543, 64 L. Ed. 919.

Motion to strike out the first, second, third, fourth, eighth, ninth, and twelfth defenses granted and to strike out the eleventh defense denied, with leave to the defendant, within twenty days after service of the order hereon, to amend any of the defenses stricken out and, if desired, to amend the 11th defense in the light of this memorandum.

Settle order on two days' notice.

The Kotkas
35 F. Supp. 983 (E.D., N.Y., 1940)

GALSTON, District Judge.

This is a possessory libel. It appears that the libellant is a resident of the City of Tallinn, Estonia, and alleges that he is the true and lawful owner of S. S. Kotkas, a vessel now lying in the port of New York. It is alleged that Kallas was appointed by the libellant as master of the vessel; that on or about the 1st of September, 1940, the libellant removed Kallas as master and demanded possession of the vessel, but that the demand was refused by Kallas, who likewise refused to deliver possession of the ship's papers. Accordingly the libellant seeks to have the vessel delivered to him.

Kallas's answer admits that he is the master; that he was legally appointed as such; and alleges that the true owners of the vessel are J. Remmelgass, N. Vaino, E. Silberberg, M. Kronstrom and J. Onno, all residents of the port of Tallinn, Estonia. It is alleged that the libel was not filed in good faith, but on the contrary was filed under the instigation, duress or threats of the Russian Government which confiscated the S. S. Kotkas and other ships belonging to the above named owners for the purpose of taking the vessel to the

port of Murmansk, pursuant to a confiscation decree of the Russian Government, promulgated since the annexation of the Republic of Estonia by the Russian Government, without compensation to her real and true owners.

The answer of the claimant Kaiv admits that Kallas is the master legally appointed; alleges that he is the duly accredited Consul General of the Republic of Estonia at the port of New York and recognized as such by the Government of the United States; that under the laws of the Republic of Estonia, at the time before the forceable invasion and annexation by the United Soviet Socialist Republic, the claimant is the constituted trustee of the property of any Estonian National who for any reason is incapable of acting for himself. It is further alleged that the United States has not recognized the forceable annexation of the Republic of Estonia by the United Soviet Socialist Republic.

At the trial the libellant called no witness and offered no competent testimony, and rested subject to an application for the issuance of letters rogatory to prove ownership.

The respondent and claimant went forward with the proof and they established that on July 23, 1940, as appears in the Official Gazette of Estonia for the issue of that day, among other matters were the following: " * * * the Chamber of Deputies proclaims nationalization of banks and large industrial enterprises in the entire territory of Estonia." And: "from now on are proclaimed as property of the people, that is of the State, of banks, together with their treasures, of large industrial enterprises, mines and transportation enterprises." And: "The Chamber of Deputies charges the Government with the duty to draw up and approve without delay a list of enterprises that are subject to nationalization."

In the State Gazette for July 28, 1940, the following provision is noted concerning a list of shipping enterprises subject to nationalization: "The shipping enterprises whose part owners are M. Kronstrom, J. Remmelgass, N. Vaino, E. Silberberg and J. Onno."

The record establishes from the various decrees of the Government after the Russian occupation that the Kotkas was a vessel owned by Kronstrom, Remmelgass, Vaino, Silberberg and Onno, and was among the properties nationalized. It is to be observed also that the name of the libellant, Juri Silberberg, does not appear in any of the documentary evidence. From all the evidence then it appears that there is nothing before the court to show that the libellant is the owner. Moreover, from these governmental decrees it would appear that none of the persons forming the "ship enterprises" could any longer give orders concerning the ships, or powers of attorney relating to any interest in the ships, because, as between them and the Government of Estonia as occupied and controlled by the United Soviet Socialist Republic, the Government became the owner.

So this suit would fail for that reason if for no other. However, there was offered in evidence a communication from our State Department as of October 24, 1940, reciting that this Government does not recognize the absorption of Estonia by the Union of Soviet Socialist Republics and indeed continues to recognize Johannes Kaiv (i. e. the claimant) as acting Consul General of Estonia. Thus there arises a somewhat anomalous situation resulting from the plight of the owners who are residents of Estonia and subject to the compulsion of the decree of July 28, 1940, which provided among other matters: "All ship owners are compelled, in accordance with this regulation, to give immediately the necessary instructions to the masters of vessels by telegraph or radio." And further: "All ship owners are compelled in accordance with this regulation, to refuse to make further voyages, even if respective agreements have been made." And further: "All Estonian ships are compelled to hoist the flag of Russia."

Not only does our Government not recognize the validity of these decrees but also the executive order of the United States Government, No. 6560 of April 10, 1940, supplemented by executive order of July 15, 1940, popularly known as "freezing orders", in effect prevents the transfer of property of nationals of invaded countries so that such property may not inure to the benefit of the aggressors.

At the conclusion of the trial there was no formal motion made to take anybody's deposition, but at a supplementary hearing held on November 15, 1940, the proctor for the libellant sought leave to take the depositions of Juri Silberberg, the libellant, and of Kronstrom, Remmelgass, Vaino and Onno, for the purpose of proving the ownership of the libellant, or for the purpose of showing that he was the duly authorized agent of the libellant. He then sought to have letters-rogatory issued to the Supreme Court of the R. S. F. S. R. of the Soviet Union for the purpose of taking depositions of those individuals in Moscow. Counsel, however, frankly stated that all of the persons named are residents of Tallinn, which is in Estonia.

The motion to amend the libel so as to recite that the libellant is the authorized agent of Kronstrom, Remmelgass, Vaino and Onno is granted but the application to have letters-rogatory issued to a court of the Soviet Republic for the purpose of taking depositions in Moscow of residents of Tallinn, Estonia, must be denied, for under existing relations between this

Government and the Republic of Estonia, no legal process could issue from the Supreme Court of the R. S. F. S. R. of the Soviet Republic to residents of Estonia. See Rule 28 of Rules of Civil Procedure, 28 U.S.C.A. following section 723c, and Title 28, U.S.C.A. Sec. 711.

For all of the foregoing reasons the libel will be dismissed.

Submit findings of fact and conclusions of law in conformity with the foregoing opinion.

Editor's Note. In a similar libel seeking possession of a Latvian ship, the same court denied a motion for letters rogatory to be issued to a competent court of the Soviet Union. The REGENT, 35 F. Supp. 985 (E.D., N.Y. , 1940)

The Signe (renamed Florida)
37 F. Supp. 809 (E.D., La., 1941)

CAILLOUET, District Judge.

Proctors of record for the libelant herein, filed their motion suggesting to the court that they desire to procure the testimony of Oskar Tiedemann, the libelant, who is represented as residing at Vabaduse Valjak 10, Tallinn, Estonia.

It is made to appear by said motion that such testimony can not be secured, save and except by and through means of letters rogatory from this court, requesting the Supreme Court of the Russian Soviet Federated Socialist Republic, Union of Soviet Socialist Republics, at Moscow, to assist this court in obtaining said testimony; and the appropriate order for such letters rogatory, from this court, addressed to said Supreme Court, "or such Court or Courts of competent jurisdiction exercising jurisdiction in the City of Moscow, U.S.S.R.", is accordingly applied for.

Strenuous opposition to the granting of said order is made by the proctors for respondent and claimant, and whilst the court's first natural inclination was to grant the application for letters rogatory since, as it is represented by the movers, the testimony of the libelant may not otherwise be secured, and he should, under normal conditions, be granted the opportunity to present to the court such legal evidence as he deems proper to establish the claimed rights of himself and his alleged principals in and to the S. S. Florida, her engines, tackle, apparel, furniture, appurtenances and equipment, a further and more comprehensive examination into the subject matter, however, has forced the court to the definite conclusion that there would be no justification for the granting of the application for such letters rogatory, in view of existent circumstances, over which, it may nevertheless be true, the libelant has, unfortunately, no control.

Such libelant is represented by the movers to be a resident of Estonia, and Estonia is that autonomous country of which the absorption by and into the Union of Soviet Socialist Republics was sought to be effected by said Union during the year 1940, although the United States of America has never recognized such attempted absorption, and regards as still in force the Treaty of Friendship, Commerce and Consular Rights between said Estonia and themselves, which was signed on December 23, 1925; and said United States of America, as late as December 19, 1940, and unto this very day (the court has no reason to doubt), continues to recognize an Acting Counsel General of Estonia, at New York, as vested with authority to act as such.

Letters rogatory are the medium, in effect, whereby one country, speaking through one of its courts, requests another country, acting through its own courts and by methods of court procedure peculiar thereto and entirely within the latter's control, to assist the administration of justice in the former country; such request being made, and being usually granted, by reason of the comity existing between nations in ordinary peaceful times.

The country so requesting this aid for and on behalf of the orderly administration and dispensing of justice in its courts, first conveys, in its letters rogatory, the official greetings of its governing head to the court, or courts, in the foreign country wherein resides a witness whose testimony it is sought to take by means of the good offices of said court, or courts, and the sustaining authority of the laws therein administered concerning the taking of evidence under letters rogatory. 24 Words and Phrases, Permanent Edition, "Letters Rogatory", pp. 704, 705; Black's Law Dictionary, 3d Edition, p. 1092.

For usual form of letters rogatory, see Benedict on Admiralty, 6th Edition–Knauth, § 400, p. 99; and form used in this court.

"By the law of nations", reads Benedict on Admiralty, § 400, p. 92, "the courts of justice of different countries are bound mutually to aid and assist each other for the furtherance of justice." To secure such aid and assistance, letters rogatory are resorted to (the author continues), and the request to take the desired testimony which is thereby made of the court, or courts, in the foreign country is justified by the offer to do the like, should request therefor ever be made in a similar case, by such foreign court, under authority of the national laws which govern it.

In this case, here at issue, the form of letters rogatory submitted by the applicants therefor is made the medium of conveying the official greetings of His Excellency, the President of the United States, to the Supreme Court, Russian Soviet Federated Socialist Republic, Moscow, U.S.S.R, and of the giving of assurance to said court that "we shall be pleased to do the same for you in a similar case, when required".

This District Court of the United States of America, whose power and authority to function as such within the Eastern District of Louisiana is derived from the Constitution and the Acts of Congress, should not exercise that authority (as for instance in the issuance of letters rogatory now being applied for) in such a manner as to belittle, in the eyes of a foreign court, the very source of the authority which, alone, under normal conditions, would justify this court in seeking the good offices of said foreign court, in the name of said United States of America, to the end that justice may be done in this American court.

This nation does not recognize that the Supreme Court of the Russian Soviet Federated Socialist Republic, Union of Soviet Socialist Republics, at Moscow, is justly vested with legal jurisdiction over any part of Estonia, but, on the contrary, officially deprecates and condemns the action of the Union of Soviet Socialist Republics in attempting to absorb into the Russian Soviet Federated Socialist Republics the hitherto autonomous nation of Estonia.

The letters rogatory applied for and submitted for issuance by this court, however, specifically assert that the libelant is within the jurisdiction of said Supreme Court of the Russian Soviet Federated Socialist Republic, Moscow, Union of Soviet Socialist Republics, and for that reason, request is made of said court by this American court that, "in the furtherance of justice" and "by proper and usual process" of said Supreme Court, the libelant, "who resides at Vabaduse Valjak 10, Tallinn, Estonia," be caused to appear before said Supreme Court, etc.

This court should not, and will not, under the existent circumstances detailed hereinabove, issue any such letters rogatory.

It is true that the motion of counsel for such letters rogatory alleges that the libelant, who is therein represented to be a resident of Estonia, "upon being summoned or notified by said Court (meaning the Supreme Court, to whom it is desired to have the letters rogatory addressed) will voluntarily appear at said tribunal to answer the interrogatories", but neither the United States of America nor this court recognizes any legal authority in said Supreme Court, Russian Soviet Federated Socialist Republic, Union of Soviet Socialist Republics, Moscow, to summon before it a resident of Estonia, at the instance of this American court and by way of assisting it in the doing of justice. How, then, can official request for such summons be made?

The libelant, it must be remembered, carries the burden of making out his case, and the evidence that he would submit, in any event, would be subject to the scrutiny of this court.

Under the Treaty of May 25th, 1926, between Estonia and the United States of America, 44 Stat. 2379, full provision is made for the taking of the testimony of a resident of Estonia, such as is, admittedly, the libelant. By executive agreement, evidenced by the notes exchanged on November 22, 1935, at Moscow, U.S.S.R., between U. S. Ambassador William C. Bullitt and M. Litvinoff, People's Commissar for Foreign Affairs, special procedure covering the delivery of all letters rogatory issued out of the courts of the United States for execution in the Union of Soviet Socialist Republics was provided for, it being specially declared by the Litvinoff note that the Supreme Court of "that constituent republic" of the Union of Soviet Socialist Republics "which is competent to execute such letters rogatory" should be addressed by the American court, or, in case the exact title of such court were unknown, then addressed to "the competent Court of the Union of Soviet Socialist Republics"; the delivery to and from said Supreme Court of said constituent republic, to be effected through diplomatic channels. Benedict on Admiralty, supra, at pp. 96–98.

This convention between the two nations, so evidenced by the exchange of the Bullitt and Litvinoff notes, still exists, and in order for letters rogatory to legally find their way to the Supreme Court of the constituent republic of the Union of Soviet Socialist Republic which would be request-

ed, as a favor, to assist this United States Court in the discharge of its duty to the litigants before it, the usual diplomatic channels would have to be resorted to.

It is unthinkable that, in view of the aforedetailed condition of affairs concerning the status of Estonia in its National relations to the United States, this United States court should now issue letters rogatory in aid of the libelant, the Estonian resident, which could only be executed by the very governmental authority that, contrary to the official views of the United States, asserts jurisdiction over the territory of Estonia.

If the libelant, in good faith, wishes to present to this court his own testimony, and no restrictions are placed upon his journeying beyond the bounds of the territory wherein he resides in order to give such testimony under other circumstances than those involved in the application made for letters rogatory to the Supreme Court at Moscow, and which respondent represents as indicative of a situation necessarily justifying one to look with suspicion upon the whole proceeding, it may be that libelant may find it advantageous and possible to avail himself of the respondent's offer, concerning the giving of such testimony beyond the borders of the territory now under control of the Union of Soviet Socialist Republics, which is presented by the brief of respondent's counsel.

If he may not, for any reason, avail himself of said offer, it may be that it will be found advisable by Mover's counsel to stipulate (in keeping with the additional offer of respondent's counsel) as to what would be libelant's answers to the interrogatories were his testimony taken in the territory controlled by the Union of Soviet Socialist Republics.

If, unfortunately for him and those he claims to represent, libellant finds himself unable to discharge the burden of proof he assumed in coming before this court as libelant, the situation is not one that the court feels justified in ameliorating by the issuance of the letters rogatory applied for.

For which reasons, the application is denied.

Editor's Note.   The treaty between the U.S. and Estonia, cited by the Court, is the treaty of Friendship, Commerce and Consular Rights, December 23, 1925 (44 Stat. 2379; 4 Trentwith, p. 4105; 50 LNTS 13) still in force.

The Florida
133 F. 2d. 719 (5th Cir., 1943)
cert. denied 319 U.S. 774, 63 S. Ct. 1439 (1943)

Before HUTCHESON, HOLMES, and McCORD, Circuit Judges.

McCORD, Circuit Judge.

The appeal is from a final decree dismissing a libel purportedly filed on behalf of Oskar Tiedemann and other Estonian shipowners against the Honduras steamship "Florida" formerly the Estonian steamship "Signe", and against Estoduras Steamship Company, respondent and claimant of the ship. The decree also dismissed an intervening libel filed by the same proctors in the name of Estonia State Cargo and Passenger Steamship Line. The ship was released to Estoduras, and the trustee was discharged. Appeal was taken without the filing of a supersedeas bond, and it appears that the vessel is not now within the territorial jurisdiction of the Court. Cf. The Denny, 3 Cir., 127 F.2d 404.

Prior to June 17, 1940, the Republic of Estonia was a free, independent, sovereign nation recognized as such by the United States of America and other nations. On June 17, 1940, the armies of Soviet Russia invaded Estonia and other Baltic States. Thereafter there was set up in Estonia a Soviet Government, Estonian Soviet Socialist Republic, which was absorbed into the Union of Soviet Socialist Republics. The government thus set up in Estonia nationalized and confiscated all transportation and shipping enterprises including Kasmu Laeva Omanikud, Kasmu Shipowners, owners of the "Signe", now the "Florida".

The United States Government does not recognize the government set up in Estonia after the invasion, but continues to abide by the Treaty of Friendship, Commerce and Consular Rights entered into at Washington, D. C., on December 23, 1925, between it and the Government of Estonia, and continues to recognize Johannes Kaiv as the duly accredited Acting Consul General of the Republic of Estonia and in Charge of Legation.

Immediately after the passage of the nationalization decrees other decrees were passed directing owners of steamships to order their vessels to proceed to Murmansk, Russia, for the purpose of having them reduced to Russian possession. It was further provided that masters who refused to take their ships to Murmansk would be considered traitors to the State and subject to dire penalties, and that their families and near relatives would be held responsible for their disobedience. The "Signe" was in Cuba at the time, and the master, who is also part owner of the ship, refused to sail to Murmansk, and instead brought the ship to the United States in completion of a charter party under which it was then engaged. The master appealed to the recognized Estonian Consul, Kaiv, who declared himself trustee of the ship and assumed control of its affairs. Thereafter, by direction of the Consul, Estoduras Steamship Company, Inc., was organized for the purpose of holding title to the ship and changing its registry from that of Estonia to that of Honduras, and for "the specific purpose of protecting and conserving the property rights of all the co-owners of the said SS. Signe (Renamed "Florida"), as those rights existed prior to June 17, 1940".

The "Florida" was at the Port of New Orleans in December, 1940, engaged in the performance of a charter party, when the libel for possession was filed. The libel was filed in the name of Tiedemann on behalf of himself and some thirty-five other Estonian citizens, including Rudolph Pahlberg and Boris Shivolovitch, claiming that these persons were the true and only lawful owners of the ship. The libel was filed by authority of a cabled power of attorney dated December 1, 1940, and purportedly signed and sent by Oskar Tiedemann, who claimed to have a power of attorney from the other libellants. The intervening libel alleged that Estonian State Steamship Line, a corporation organized under the laws of the Russian-Estonian Government, was then lawfully engaged in taking over the "nationalized" properties of Tiedemann and the other named owners.

The evidence shows that Tiedemann resides in Estonia, and fully supports the finding of the lower court that he was under duress of the Russian authorities when he made and executed the cabled power of attorney authorizing the filing of the libel. Pahlberg and Shivolovitch, who were named by Tiedemann as consenting part owners of the "Signe", and who were beyond the influence and domination of the Russian authorities, testified that they had not authorized anyone to sue for them; that the proctors were not authorized to file the original libel on their behalf; that Tiedemann in ordering the libel to be filed was under the domination of the Union of Soviet Socialist Republics; and that at the time of the passage of the Estonian-Russian decrees, the ship was not under the control of either the libellants or intervening libellant, but was at a port in Cuba and under the control of its master and part owner, Captain Pahlberg.

The record shows clearly enough that before June, 1940, the "Signe" was the property of Tiedemann and his associates. However, the authority of the proctors to represent them is not established. We further find that no credence should be given to the alleged power of attorney of Tiedemann since he was under duress at the time of its execution. Moreover, the intervening libellant, Estonian State Steamship Lines, which is a creature of the Russian Government, disputed the title of Tiedemann and his associates, and claimed title and right to possession of the vessel. Nowhere does the record disclose a right in libellants to possession of the ship. There is nothing save the allegations and proof as to the taking over of Estonia by Russia, and the passage of decrees of nationalization and confiscation. For aught appearing, the Russian Government may no longer possess and control Estonia. We take knowledge of the fact that by force of arms Germany has usurped and taken custody and control of Estonia from Russia, and that the status of Estonia as a nation will be determined by future events. Cf. Cia. Minera Ygnacio Rodriguez Ramos, S. A., v. Bartlesville Zinc Co., 115 Tex. 21, 275 S.W. 388; Terrazas v. Holmes, 115 Tex. 32, 275 S.W. 392.

Without discussion of the many interesting propositions of admiralty and international law posed by the briefs, we deem it sufficient to say that the only certain facts appearing from the record are that Kaiv is recognized as the duly accredited representative of the Republic of Estonia; that the United States still adheres to its treaty with that nation, and does not recognize any other government for Estonia; that Kaiv declared himself trustee for the ship and organized Estoduras to take it over and hold and keep it for its true owners. We are of opinion and so hold that on this record, which lacks clear and convincing proof of ownership by libellants, that neither the original libellants nor intervening libellant should recover, and that the District Court properly allowed Estoduras to retain possession of the vessel in trust for the co-owners. Cf. The Kuressaar, 1941 A. M. C. 1190.

The judgment is affirmed.

Editor's Note. The treaty between the U.S. and Estonia, cited by the Court, is the treaty of Friendship, Commerce and Consular Rights, December 23, 1925 (44 Stat. 2379; 4 Trentwith, p. 4105; 50 LNTS 13) still in force.

The S.S. Denny
40 F. Supp. 92 (D., N.J., 1941)

SMITH, District Judge.

This is a possessory suit brought in the name of Lithuanian Baltic Lloyd Ltd. (hereinafter referred to as Baltic Lloyd), formerly a stockholders association of the Republic of Lithuania, and by Agricultural Cooperative Association of Lithuania Lietukis (hereinafter referred to as Agricultural Cooperative Association), a cooperative association of the Republic of Lithuania, to recover possession of the Steamship Denny, and the cargo, respectively. The libel was filed on behalf of the said libellants by one Charles Recht, as attorney-in-fact.

The subject matter of the suit is at present in the custody and possession of the respondent Lithuanian American Import and Export Corporation (hereinafter referred to as the Import and Export Corporation), a corporation of the State of New York, as trustee, appointed by Jonas Budrys, Consul General of the Republic of Lithuania. The said respondent asserts the right to custody and possession for the use and benefit of the said libellants under the said appointment

The Latvian State Cargo and Passenger Steamship Line (hereinafter referred to as State Steamship Line), a corporation of the Republic of Latvia, Union of Soviet Socialist Republics, has intervened in the suit and claims ownership and right to possession of the vessel. The said claim is founded upon nationalization laws and decrees promulgated thereunder, to which specific reference is hereinafter made.

Findings of Fact.

1. The libellant Baltic Lloyd, prior to November 6, 1940, was a stockholders association or legal entity, organized and existing under the laws of the Republic of Lithuania. It was dissolved on the said date, if not prior thereto, by decree of the Supreme Soviet of the Union of Soviet Socialist Republics, to which specific reference is hereinafter made.

2. The libellant, Agricultural Cooperative Association,' prior to November 6, 1940, was a cooperative association or legal entity, organized and existing under the laws of the Republic of Lithuania. It was dissolved on the said date, if not prior thereto, by decree of the Supreme Soviet of the Union of Soviet Socialist Republics, to which specific reference is hereinafter made.

3. The respondent, Import and Export Corporation, is a corporation organized and existing under the laws of the State of New York, and is, and has been since 1938, the commercial representative of both libellants in the United States of America.

4. The intervenor, State Steamship Line, is a legal entity, the exact nature of which is uncertain, organized and existing under the laws of the Republic of Latvia, Union of Soviet Socialist Republics, having been organized on October 25, 1940, under authority of a decree of the Council of People's Commissars of the Union of Soviet Socialist Republics. It definitely appears, however, that the said intervenor, although designated in the statute as a "separate economic organization having the right of a juridical person", is not an independent entity, but is, in fact, an instrumentality of the government of its creation, organized for the sole purpose of taking custody and possession of the steamship lines nationalized pursuant to and in accordance with the laws and decrees to which reference is hereinafter made. The said intervenor is subject to the exclusive control and supervision of the People's Commissariat of Maritime Fleet (Narkommorflot), a division of the government.

5. On or about March 7, 1940, the li-

bellant Baltic Lloyd purchased the Steamship Denny, and at all times thereafter, prior to June 17, 1940, if not thereafter, was the owner of the said vessel. The respondent, Import and Export Corporation, acted as the agent and representative of the said libellant in the purchase of the vessel.

6. In March and April of 1940 the libellant, Agricultural Cooperative Association, in a series of purchases, purchased the cargo, consisting of gasoline, oil, and other commodities, and at all times thereafter, prior to June 17, 1940, if not thereafter, was the owner of the said cargo. The respondent, Import and Export Corporation, acted as the agent and representative of the said libellant in the said purchases.

7. The vessel and cargo, since the time of their acquisition by the respective libellants, have remained in the United States of America.

8. On or about July 21, 1940 (the exact date is not fixed), the "People's Parliament" established the Lithuanian Soviet Socialist Republic and adopted a soviet government. The Prime Minister assumed the duties of the President of the Republic, and, in a series of decrees promulgated under the authority of the "People's Parliament", announced the nationalization of all commercial and industrial enterprises. It is to be noted, however, that these events were preceded by an invasion of the Republic of Lithuania by the armies of Soviet Russia.

9. Thereafter, on July 26, 1940, pursuant to and in accordance with the Constitution of the Union of Soviet Socialist Republics, there were enacted laws under which all industrial and commercial enterprises were nationalized, and the properties and assets of said nationalized enterprises appropriated by the State. Nationalization decrees were promulgated by the Prime Minister, Acting President of the Republic, pursuant to and in accordance with the said laws.

10. Pursuant to and in accordance with the nationalization decrees, the libellants were divested of all right, title and interest in and to their properties and assets, and commissars were appointed to administer their business affairs.

11. On August 3, 1940, the newly created Lithuanian Soviet Socialist Republic was accepted into the Union of Soviet Socialist Republics.

12. On or about September 5, 1940, pursuant to and in accordance with the nationalization laws, by decree promulgated thereunder, the Council of People's Commissars of the Soviet Socialist Republic of Lithuania directed that the properties and assets, including seagoing vessels, of the libellant Baltic Lloyd, be surrendered and delivered to the People's Commissariat of Maritime Fleet (Narkommorflot), a division of the Government.

13. On or about November 26, 1940, pursuant to and in accordance with the nationalization laws, by resolutions adopted thereunder, the Council of People's Commissars of the Soviet Socialist Republics of Lithuania, organized and established the Organizing Bureau for Lithuanian Republic's Consumers Association Society, which organization appropriated the properties and assets of the libellant Agricultural Cooperative Association and undertook the administration of its business affairs.

14. It is suspiciously significant that the nationalization decrees hereinabove referred to, although they divested the libellants of all right, title and interest in and to their properties and assets, and deprived their officers of all authority in the administration of their business affairs, preserved the "validity" of the signatures of those officers who, prior, thereto, had been authorized to act for and on behalf of the libellants. This observation is made at this time because the libel is filed by one Charles Recht, as attorney-in-fact, whose authority is predicated on powers of attorney, which are offered as instruments "voluntarily" executed by the officers of the libellants.

15. These facts are of further significance when consideration is given to the claim asserted by the State Steamship Line. The right, title and interest of the said claimant is predicated entirely upon the nationalization decrees, hereinabove referred to, and the rights acquired thereunder. This claimant recognizes that the le-

gal title and the right to possession of the vessel may be vested in the libellants, but only for the purpose of insuring surrender and delivery to the said claimant at the conclusion of these proceedings.

The petition for leave to intervene, filed on behalf of this claimant, is likewise filed by the same Charles Recht as attorney-in-fact.

16. On November 6, 1940, by decree of the Supreme Soviet of the Union of Soviet Socialist Republics, the laws of the Republic of Lithuania were superseded by the codes of the Russian Soviet Federated Socialist Republic. The laws, upon which the existence of the libellants as legal entities depended, were abrogated, thereby effecting their dissolution, if, in fact, this result had not been accomplished prior thereto by the nationalization decrees.

17. The acceptance of the Republic of Lithuania into the Union of Soviet Socialist Republics is not recognized by the United States of America. The sovereignty of the state, Lithuanian Soviet Socialist Republic, created on the territory of the Republic of Lithuania, and the newly established soviet government of that state, have not achieved recognition. The Republic of Lithuania is recognized as the sovereign state, and recognition is accorded its duly accredited representatives.

18. On or about February 20, 1941, Jonas Budrys, Consul General of the Republic of Lithuania, under authority of the Minister of Lithuania to the United States of America, pursuant to and in accordance with the Baltic Civil Code and the Consular Statutes, appointed the Import and Export Corporation trustee of the vessel and its cargo. The appointment authorizes the trustee to retain custody and possession of the vessel and its cargo for the use and benefit of the owners thereof; it further authorizes the trustee to operate the vessel and to account to the owners for the proceeds of such operation.

The vessel and cargo are, in effect, in custodia legis, the custody and possession thereof having been taken by the said Consul General of the Republic of Lithuania, pursuant to and in accordance with his power and authority, to protect and conserve the properties and assets of his nationals.

19. The said Consul General of the Republic of Lithuania is the duly accredited representative of the recognized government of the said Republic.

20. It is reasonable to infer from the foregoing facts and circumstances that the powers of attorney, under the authority of which the said attorney-in-fact purports to act, were not voluntarily executed, but were executed under coercion, if not actual, implied. This finding is corroborated by cablegrams, received in evidence over objection, transmitted by the persons whose signatures appear on the said powers of attorney. This evidence, admittedly not the best, is worthy of some consideration, especially when it definitely appears that the best evidence is not available under the existing conditions, of which the Court takes judicial notice.

It cannot be assumed that prudent executives would willfully divest themselves of authority and vest that authority in a stranger, when, as here, the natural and probable consequence of such act would be inimical, not only to the interest of their business organization, but to their personal interest in that organization. It is apparent that at the time the powers of attorney were executed, the properties, assets and business affairs of the libellants were under the administration of the commissars appointed by the newly established Soviet Government. It may be presumed, under these circumstances, that prudent executives, exercising sound business judgment, would permit the physical assets of the business to remain, as in the immediate case, in the custody and possession of a commercial representative of their own selection, Import and Export Corporation, beyond the jurisdiction of those who seek to confiscate them.

21. The present suit is a mere fiction, and the parties, except the respondent, Import and Export Corporation, are mere nominal parties. The libellants, Baltic Lloyd and Agricultural Cooperative Association, no longer exist as juridical persons, having been dissolved by operation of law, as hereinabove stated; their officers have been divested of all authority, and the administration of their business affairs has been entrusted to commissars. The claimant, State Steamship Line, is an instrumentality of the

unrecognized Soviet Government of the Lithuanian Soviet Socialist Republic. The respondent, Import and Export Corporation, is but the servant and agent of the Consul General of the Republic of Lithuania. The vessel is of foreign registry.

The real parties in interest are: First, the Lithuanian Soviet Socialist Republic, and it stands in the anomalous position of being both libellant and claimant; and, second, the Consul General of the Republic of Lithuania, who, at this time, is not within the jurisdiction of the Court. The real controversy is between them.

22. The real parties in interest are neither citizens nor subjects of the United States of America. They are aliens, and, insofar as this Court is concerned, subjects of the Republic of Lithuania. This is equally true of the nominal parties, except Import and Export Corporation.

Conclusions of Law.

1. The libellants, having been dissolved by operation of law, as hereinabove stated, are without the capacity to maintain this suit. They, as legal entities, are no longer in esse within the territorial limits of their former existence.

2. The powers of attorney, under the authority of which this suit was instituted by the purported attorney-in-fact, are void, having been executed under coercion. The attorney-in-fact is, therefore, without authority to maintain this suit for and on behalf of the libellants.

3. This suit may not be maintained by the libellants. A suit in a court of admiralty may be maintained only by the real party in interest. The libellants are mere nominal parties; the real party in interest is the Lithuanian Soviet Socialist Republic.

4. This suit may not be maintained either directly or indirectly by the Soviet Government of the Lithuanian Soviet Socialist Republic. The Soviet Government, never having achieved recognition by the Department of State, may not invoke the jurisdiction of the courts. Its agents and representatives are in no better position, even though they purport to act in the name of nominal parties, who, under ordinary circumstances, would be permitted access to the courts.

5. The claimant, State Steamship Lines, is an instrumentality of the Soviet Government of the Lithuanian Soviet Socialist Republic, and it likewise, may not invoke the jurisdiction of the courts.

6. The determination of sovereignty is a political question committed by the Constitution to the executive and legislative branches of the Government. The decision is binding upon the courts and is not subject to judicial inquiry.

7. The parties to this suit, except the respondents Import and Export Corporation and Ole Hanvorsen, are aliens, and, insofar as this Court is concerned, subjects of the Republic of Lithuania. The aforementioned respondents are mere agents of the Consul General of the Republic of Lithuania, who is in custody and possession of the vessel and its cargo. This suit, therefore, should be regarded as one involving subjects of a foreign country. If so regarded, the Court may decline jurisdiction. The citizenship of a mere nominal party will not deprive the Court of this right.

8. A court of admiralty, although not a court of equity, may proceed on equitable principles. It is bound by its nature and constitution to give judgment upon equitable principles to prevent an obvious injustice. The Consul General has assumed custody and possession of the subject matter of this litigation for the purpose of conservation. It is the opinion of the Court that the rights of the libellants will be adequately protected and their interest in the subject matter of the litigation preserved if the libel is dismissed.

Discussion.

The libellants, having been dissolved by operation of law, as hereinabove stated, are without capacity to maintain this suit. The laws of the Republic of Lithuania, upon which the existence of the libellants as legal entities depended, were superseded by the codes of the Russian Soviet Federated Socialist Republic. The right of the libellants as juridical persons to sue and be sued was thereupon abrogated. They are no longer in esse within the territorial limits of their former existence, and, therefore, should not be granted extraterritorial rights.

The powers of attorney, under the authority of which this suit was instituted by the purported attorney-in-fact, are void, having been executed under coercion. The attorney-in-fact is, therefore, without authority to maintain this suit for and on behalf of the libellants. The trial court may inquire, at any stage of the proceedings, into the authority of the person bringing the suit, where, as in the instant case, the litigation is instituted by one who purports to be acting for and on behalf of another. If it appears upon such inquiry that the suit is not authorized, the court may dismiss it. Pueblo of Santa Rosa v. Fall et al., 273 U.S. 315, 47 S.Ct. 361, 71 L.Ed. 658.

It is apparent that the libellants are not the real parties in interest; they, therefore, may not maintain this suit. The libellants are mere nominal parties; their rights are mere colorable rights evanescent in nature; when, and if, enforced, title in the subject matter of the litigation will pass from them to the Lithuanian Soviet Socialist Republic or its designee, the State Steamship Line. It is evident that the real party in interest is the said Lithuanian Soviet Socialist Republic. It is a well-established rule that a suit in a court of admiralty may be maintained only by the real party in interest. The Trader, D.C., 129 F. 462; The Algic, D.C., 13 F.Supp. 834; The Mandu, D.C., 20 F.Supp. 820. The practice of instituting a suit in the name of one person for the benefit of another does not prevail in admiralty. Fretz et al. v. Bull et al., 12 How. 466, 13 L.Ed. 1068; Goldman v. Furness, Withy & Co., Ltd., D.C., 101 F. 467; Wittig v. Canada S. S. Lines, Ltd., D.C., 59 F.2d 428.

It cannot be disputed that the Lithuanian Soviet Socialist Republic, as the real party in interest, may not maintain this suit either directly or indirectly in the absence of recognition of its sovereignty by the Department of State. It is clearly established by competent evidence, and, in fact, it is not denied that the Lithuanian Soviet Socialist Republic has failed to achieve that recognition. A suit on behalf of a foreign state may be maintained in our courts only after recognition of its sovereignty and only by that government which is recognized as its authorized government. Jones v. United States, 137 U.S. 202, 11 S.Ct. 80, 34 L.Ed. 691; Guaranty Trust Co. v. United States, 304 U.S. 126, 58 S.Ct. 785, 82 L.Ed. 1224; The Penza, D.C., 277 F. 91; The Rogdai, D.C., 278 F. 294. These well-recognized principles cannot be defeated by indirection.

The claimant, State Steamship Line, is an instrumentality of the Soviet Government of the Lithuanian Soviet Socialist Republic, and it, likewise, may not be permitted to invoke the jurisdiction of this court. It is, as hereinabove stated, an arm of the People's Commissariat of Maritime Fleet (Narkommorflot), a division of the said government. If access to the courts must be denied a foreign government because of its failure to achieve recognition, it must likewise be denied an integral part of that government.

The determination of political questions is committed by the Constitution to the executive and legislative branches of the Government, and the propriety of their determination is not subject to judicial inquiry. The question of sovereignty is a political question, the determination of which by the political department of the Government conclusively binds the courts. Oetjen v. Central Leather Co., 246 U.S. 297, 38 S.Ct. 309, 62 L.Ed. 726; United States v. Belmont, 301 U.S. 324, 57 S.Ct. 758, 81 L.Ed. 1134; Agency of Canadian Car & Foundry Co., Ltd., et al. v. American Can Co., 2 Cir., 258 F. 363, 6 A.L.R. 1182; Russian Government v. Lehigh Valley R. Co., D.C., 293 F. 133, and other cases hereinabove cited.

The parties to this suit, except the respondents Import and Export Corporation and Ole Hanvorsen, are aliens, and, insofar as this court is concerned, subjects of the Republic of Lithuania. The said respondents are mere agents of the Consul General, who is in custody and possession of the vessel and its cargo. The suit, therefore, should be regarded as one involving the subjects of a foreign state. If so regarded, this court may decline jurisdiction. The courts of admiralty have complete jurisdiction over suits of a maritime nature between foreigners. The retention of that jurisdiction, however, is discretionary. Charter Shipping Co., Ltd., v. Bowring, Jones & Tidy, Ltd., 281 U.S. 515, 50 S.Ct. 400, 74 L.Ed. 1008; Langnes v. Green, 282 U.S. 531, 51 S.Ct. 243, 75 L.Ed. 520; Canada Malting Co., Ltd., v. Paterson Steamships, Ltd., 285 U.S. 413, 52 S.Ct. 413, 76 L.Ed. 837. The citizenship of a mere nominal party will not deprive the court of the right to decline jurisdiction. United States Merchants' & Shippers' Ins. Co. v. A/S Den Norske Afrika Og Australie Line, 2 Cir., 65 F.2d 392; The Lady Drake, D.C., 1 F. Supp. 317.

The court of admiralty, although not a court of equity, may apply equitable principles in the determination of the rights of parties within its jurisdiction. United States v. Cornell Steamboat Co., 202 U.S. 184, 26 S.Ct. 648, 50 L.Ed. 987; Shoenamsgruber v. Hamburg American Line, 294 U.S. 454, 55 S.Ct. 475, 79 L.Ed. 989; The Gold Digger, D.C., 44 F.2d 660; Rice v. Charles Dreifus Co. et al, 2 Cir., 96 F. 2d 80; Gardner et al. v. Dantzler Lumber & Export Co., Inc., 5 Cir., 98 F.2d 478; Rubin Iron Works, Inc., v. Johnson et al., 5 Cir., 100 F.2d 871. The instant case is one in which equitable principles are peculiarly applicable, and their application can lead to but one result, to wit, the dismissal of the libel. The Court cannot fail to take cognizance of the fact that prior to the events which led to this litigation, and when the libellants were free to exercise their independent judgment, they selected the respondent Import and Export Corporation as their commercial representative in the United States of America. It is our opinion that the libellants, if permitted a free choice at this time, would continue that relationship as it had existed since 1938. The dismissal of the libel will permit the vessel and its cargo to remain in the custody and possession of the said respondent for the use and benefit of the libellants, subject, however, to the supervision of the Consul General, an accredited representative of the Republic of Lithuania. This is the only course which can insure a preservation of the status quo until conditions are more settled.

It is evident that this suit is a mere fiction, and, if for no other reason, should not be countenanced. When the pleadings are considered in the light of the proof, the subterfuge, as well as the necessity for it, become manifest. The actual relief sought is enforcement of the nationalization laws and the decrees promulgated thereunder.

The conclusions of law on first reading would seem to present some inconsistencies; closer study, however, will reveal that this is not the fact. There is a distinction between according recognition to a foreign government and recognizing the effect of its laws upon persons and properties within its jurisdiction. While the courts may not accord recognition to a foreign government which has failed to achieve that status, they are not required to ignore the effect of its laws upon persons and properties within the territorial limits of its jurisdiction.

There are cited in support of the contentions advanced on behalf of the libellants several cases which, except for an outstanding distinguishing fact, would seem to support them. The cited cases involved recognized foreign states and their accredited representatives, and are, therefore, not applicable.

The libel is dismissed.

The Denny
127 F . 2d . 404 (3rd . Cir ., 1942)

Before MARIS, JONES, and GOOD-RICH, Circuit Judges.

MARIS, Circuit Judge.

Baltic Lloyd[1] was organized as a stockholders' association and Lietukis[2] as a cooperative association under the laws of the Republic of Lithuania. These associations were juridical persons with the power to sue and be sued. In 1940 Litamcor[3], American agent for the two corporations, purchased the S. S. Denny for Baltic Lloyd and a large quantity of gasoline, lubricating oil and other cargo for Lietukis. The vessel and cargo remained in the United States in the custody of Litamcor. On February 1, 1941 a libel for possession of the S. S. Denny and her cargo and for damages for their detention was filed in the District Court for the District of New Jersey in the names of Baltic Lloyd and Lietukis by one Charles Recht purporting to act as their attorney-in-fact. The marshal of the district executed the monition and citation by seizing the S. S. Denny and her cargo at Newark, New Jersey and by serving notice upon the respondents, Litamcor and Ole Hanvorsen, the watchman in charge of the vessel. On February 20, 1941 the Consul General of the Republic of Lithuania, under written authority of the Minister of Lithuania to the United States appointed Litamcor trustee of the S. S. Denny and her cargo. On February 24, 1941 Litamcor filed an answer to the libel as claimant. Before the matter came on for trial Charles Recht, purporting to act as attorney-in-fact for the State Steamship Line[4], a corporation of the Soviet Socialist Republic of Latvia obtained leave for that corporation to in-tervene as libellant. On July 28, 1941 the District Court dismissed the libel and the intervening libel. On October 20, 1941 the libellants filed a notice of appeal with bond for costs on appeal. No supersedeas bond has ever been filed. After the expiration of ten days from the entry of the decree of the District Court dismissing the libel the clerk of the court ordered their release to the claimant. Counsel for the claimant stated at bar that the vessel has since engaged in trade between American and Canadian ports. He likewise stated that the cargo has been sold and that the proceeds are in the possession of the claimant. Consequently when the appeal was taken the court had neither actual nor constructive possession of the res.

All parties concede that both title and the right to possession of the vessel are in Baltic Lloyd and of the cargo in Lietukis. Recht maintains that he is the agent authorized by Baltic Lloyd and Lietukis to take possession on their behalf and he relies upon powers of attorney from each of them to substantiate his claim of agency.[5] Litamcor maintains that it is the agent of both and is authorized to retain possession for them and it also offers as proof its appointment as trustee by the Lithuanian consul. It attacks the sufficiency of the powers of attorney to Recht upon three distinct grounds; that they were improperly executed, acknowledged and authenticated; that they were given by the officers of Baltic Lloyd and Lietukis under duress; and that they were given by officers of Baltic Lloyd and Lietukis at a time when those corporations had been nationalized and therefore had no juridical existence

---

[1] Lietuvos Baltijos Lloydas (Lithuanian Baltic Lloyd Ltd.).

[2] Lietuvos Zemes Ujio Kooperatyvu Sajunga Lietukis (Agricultural Cooperative Association of Lithuania Lietukis).

[3] Lithuanian-American Import and Export Corporation.

[4] Latvian State Cargo and Passenger Steamship Line.

[5] In the intervening libel Recht makes the claim that by reason of the nationalization decrees of the Soviet Socialist Republic of Lithuania the right to possession of the S. S. Denny is in Baltic Lloyd solely for the purpose of delivering it to the State Steamship Line, the corporation entrusted with the task of the nationalization of the Lithuanian merchant marine.

in the country of their origin.[6] The district court found that Baltic Lloyd and Lietukis had been dissolved by operation of law and their right as juridical persons to sue had been abrogated and that the powers of attorney to file suit on their behalf had been executed under coercion and therefore conferred no authority upon Recht.

We shall deal first with the contention that the acknowledgment and authentication of the powers of attorney given by Baltic Lloyd and Lietukis were insufficient to authorize their admission in evidence without further proof and that the powers were therefore improperly admitted. . . . . In the present case the acknowledgments of the powers of attorney given by Lietukis and Baltic Lloyd were made before Vilhelmas Burkevicius, a notary of the Kaunas State Notary Office at Kaunas, Lithuania. To both of the powers he appended his certificate and affixed his seal. Lietukis and Baltic Lloyd could of course act only through officers who were authorized to do so. The certificate of the notary to the power of attorney given by Lietukis recites that the power "was stated to me and signed before me by the fully authorized members, who are known to me, of the Executive Board of * * * Lietukis * * *; 1/Jurgis Kriksciunas and 2/Vincas Meilus, * * * acting in the name of * * *, Lietukis, in accordance with the by-laws * * * and in conformity with the protocol of the general annual convention of delegated members of the said association held on May 10th, 1940." The notary's seal and signature were authenticated by the Assistant People's Commissar of Justice of the Lithuanian Soviet Socialist Republic, the signature of that official was authenticated by the Chief of the Consular Bureau of the People's Commissariat for Foreign Affairs for the Union of Soviet Socialist Republics at Moscow, and the latter's signature, seal and official status were in turn authenticated by an American Vice Consul at Moscow. Not only the identity of the persons acting on behalf of the association but also their authority so to act, as evidenced by the by-laws, is vouched for by the notary. . . . . .
. . . We conclude that the certificate of the Lithuanian notary, authenticated as we have indicated, was sufficient evidence of the execution of the power of attorney by the officers of Lietukis and of their authority to act to render the power admissible in evidence in a court of admiralty without other proof. What we have said as to the power of attorney given by Lietukis applies as well to the power of attorney given by Baltic Lloyd.

An entirely different problem, however, is raised by the paper upon which Recht relies for his authority to act as attorney in fact for State Steamship Line. That paper is nothing more than a cablegram, unsigned, instructing Recht to act on behalf of the corporation. There is nothing upon which one could base a finding that the State Steamship Line, taking corporate action through duly authorized officers, had granted to Recht authority to make claim to the S. S. Denny. The paper is clearly insufficient to establish Recht's authority to act for State Steamship Line.

The next contention is that the powers of attorney were void because executed by the officers of Baltic Lloyd and Lietukis under duress. The only evidence presented to the district court [10] having

6 Some historical background is necessary in order to understand these contentions. In June, 1940 the Russian army entered Lithuania. In July, 1940, the conduct of the affairs of the Republic of Lithuania was taken over by the Lithuanian Soviet Socialist Republic. In August, 1940, the application of that regime to be absorbed into the Union of Soviet Socialist Republics was accepted. In September, 1940 the Lithuanian Soviet Socialist Republic passed a number of decrees directed at the nationalization of private commercial enterprises, of industrial enterprises and of the merchant marine. The United States Department of State has not recognized the regime now functioning in Lithuania, the absorption of Lithuania by the Union of Soviet Socialist Republics nor the legality of the nationalization decrees.

10 An appeal in admiralty from the

any bearing upon this issue may be summarized as follows: A witness for the claimant testified that he saw armed Russian troops enter Kaunas, Lithuania in June, 1940. He saw Russian sentries placed at the depots, granaries and warehouses of Lietukis but not at the retail shops. Another witness for the claimant, the president of Litamcor, testified that in May, 1941 Litamcor received a cablegram from Berlin which read:

"1941 May 21 AM 713
"WS1 XA PRD224
"Berlin 46 21 1115
"Urgent Lithuanian American Import Export Corporation
"157 Chambers New York
"At the request of Reklaitis Glemza I inform you that Laivynas was nationalized October 1940 Stop Power of Attorney was given to Recht when the Board of Directors was no more functioning and on the orders of Commissar for Finance Stop Signatures were given under compulsion Stop Now being free revoke the signatures Stop Lietukis reorganized under compulsion name changed Stop Letter follows
                              "Ancevicius"

Reklaites and Glemza, referred to in the cable, were president and secretary of Baltic Lloyd. The witness testified that he was informed that these men were in a Lithuanian refugee camp in Germany. The competency of the evidence is extremely questionable and in our opinion falls short of justifying the fact finding that the powers of attorney were given under duress.

Nor are we persuaded that the powers of attorney are without effect because Lietukis and Baltic Lloyd are no longer in existence. It is at least doubtful whether Lietukis has in fact been nationalized. None of the decrees in evidence bears directly upon the nationalization of agricultural cooperatives. Exhibit C-8 dealing with registration of various enterprises, treats cooperative societies in a separate classification from nationalized enterprises. Exhibit C-9 consists of excerpts from Lithuanian newspaper articles

to the effect that a structural reorganization of Lietukis was in contemplation. This assumes the continued existence of Lietukis as a base for the enlarged organization. There is evidence that commissars were appointed for Lietukis but none that the appointment of commissars meant nationalization. A witness for the libellants, qualified in Russian law, testified that by that law cooperatives are not nationalized. We are therefore confronted with arguments based upon the theory that Lietukis was nationalized but no proof that such is the fact.

The case of Baltic Lloyd is different. It is undisputed that the corporation was nationalized. The dispute is as to the effect of nationalization. From the decree of nationalization, Exhibit C-7, it seems clear that all property of Baltic Lloyd is to be taken over by a designated substitute and that the stockholders of Baltic Lloyd are to be compensated at a fixed rate. The court is not enlightened, however, as to the effect of the nationalization of a corporation upon its continuance in existence so long as is necessary for the collection of its assets. There is no evidence that immediately upon nationalization a corporation ceases to exist for all purposes and no basis for such a fact finding. If Baltic Lloyd continued to exist for the sole purpose of collecting its assets it had capacity to grant a power of attorney to an agent for that purpose.

Finally it is argued that since the government of the Lithuanian Soviet Socialist Republic and its admission to the Union of Soviet Socialist Republics have not been recognized by our government this court may not, by permitting Recht to act under the powers of attorney given to him, recognize or give effect to the decrees of the Soviet Socialist Republic which reorganized Lietukis and nationalized Baltic Lloyd. But these are both Lithuanian associations and the parties in interest, so far as here appears, are all citizens of Lithuania and domiciled therein. The rights of American citizens or residents are not involved. We may not

District Court to the Circuit Court of Appeals opens the entire case for a trial de novo in the appellate court. Brooklyn

Eastern Dist. Terminal v. United States, 1932, 287 U.S. 170, 176, 53 S.Ct. 103, 77 L.Ed. 240.

ignore the fact that the Soviet Socialist government did actually exercise governmental authority in Lithuania at the time the decrees in question were made and the powers of attorney were given, but must treat its acts within its own territory as valid and binding upon its nationals domiciled therein.[11] It follows that the respondents may not question in this court the validity of the Lithuanian decrees insofar as concerns their effect upon the interests of the former members of the associations therein or the validity of the powers of attorney executed by the associations' officers and offered in this proceeding.

We accordingly conclude that the powers of attorney given by the two libellants were sufficiently proved and were effectual to empower Recht to file the libel on their behalf but that his authority to act for State Steamship Line was not established. It follows that the district court erred in dismissing the libel insofar as it set up claims of Lietukis and Baltic Lloyd against the respondents in personam. These claims were for damages for the detention of the vessel and cargo. No fact findings were made by the district court as to these alleged damages. Indeed such fact findings would have had no significance in view of the court's conclusion that the libels were improperly filed. Save for the bill of sale for the S. S. Denny and bills of lading for the cargo the libellants offered no evidence having any bearing on their claims for damages. The course and conduct of the trial were such as practically to preclude such evidence. The parties should, therefore, be accorded a further hearing of these issues.

The decree is reversed and the cause is remanded with directions to reinstate the libel of Lietukis and Baltic Lloyd solely as to the claims therein in personam for damages, and to accord the parties a rehearing upon the issues raised by the pleadings as to those claims.

Union of Soviet Socialist Republic · v. National City Bank of N.Y.
41 F. Supp. 353 (S.D., N.Y., 1941)

MOSCOWITZ, District Judge.

The complaint herein alleges that plaintiff is the successor in interest of the Russian Socialist Federated Soviet Republic which in 1918 entered into an agreement with one Cibrario by reason of which plaintiff's predecessor caused to be deposited with the defendant in New York a million dollars. It further alleges that defendant has failed to pay out and disburse the money in accordance with the terms of said contract and that defendant has failed to pay said deposit or account for it to plaintiff.

Two issues are now before the Court for determination, both of which defendant contends merit the dismissal of the complaint. The first is based upon defendant's claim that plaintiff is not the real owner of the claim, assuming one to exist, and the second that, suit not having been commenced until April 30, 1937, any claim is barred by the six year contract limitation prescribed by New York law. Civil Practice Act, § 48.

It appears that at the time of the recognition of the Soviet Union by the United States on November 16, 1933, there was an exchange of letters between Maxim Litvinoff, the then People's Commissar for Foreign Affairs of the plaintiff and the President of the United States, whereby the Soviet Government assigned to the United States of America the claims which it might have against nationals of the United States. Because of this compact defendant contends that the Soviet Union is no longer the real owner of the claim

---

[11] M. Salimoff & Co. v. Standard Oil Co., 262 N.Y. 220, 186 N.E. 679, 89 A.L.R. 345.

and hence is not entitled to sue thereon. It further appears, however, that the United States speaking through the Secretary of State, in a note dated June 3, 1939 addressed to the Charge d'Affaires of the plaintiff in this country, and dealing with this very cause of action, stated as follows: "In view of the nature of the transaction outlined in your note it is the understanding of my Government that it was not the intention either of the Government of the United States of America or of the Government of the Union of Soviet Socialist Republics to include this deposit within the assignments embodied in the exchange of notes of November 16, 1933 between the President of the United States and Mr. Litvinoff".

Our government, as is well known, is one based upon a separation of powers among three different branches of the government. Subject to the advice and consent of the Senate, the matter of foreign affairs rests in the executive department of our government, U.S.Const. Art. II, Section 2. Here we find that the executive department states conclusively that the United States has no interest in the claim and that it was not intended to be embraced within the compact of November 16, 1933. While, normally, the judicial department has within its particular province the interpretation of laws, yet the interpretation of the scope and extent of an international compact in so far as it relates to the rights of international sovereigns as against each other is a matter in which the executive's interpretation should be accepted as binding by the Courts. In view of the clear expression of opinion by the Secretary of State, in which it might be added the Attorney General concurs, it must be held that the plaintiff is the owner of the claim in question.

There remains for consideration defendant's obligation with respect to the statute of limitations. Since plaintiff's cause of action apparently arose in 1921, it is clearly barred unless there is some basis for regarding the statute as having been tolled. Plaintiff contends that since plaintiff and its predecessor in interest, the Russian Socialist Federated Soviet Republic, were incapable of bringing suit until the recognition of the present Soviet government by the United States in 1933, the statute

of limitations should be regarded as tolled during that period of incapacity. Analogy is drawn to the treatment of infancy, insanity, etc., under the New York law.

Aside from the fact that no specific provision of the New York statute of limitation appears to exempt the case at bar from its scope, there are other fatal defects in plaintiff's position. In Guaranty Trust Co. v. United States, 304 U.S. 126, 58 S.Ct. 785, 82 L.Ed. 1224, a somewhat similar situation came before the United States Supreme Court. In that case the United States, claiming by assignment from the Soviet government, sought to recover certain monies deposited with the Guaranty Trust Company by the old Russian Imperial Government. Since the six year statutory period had elapsed between the time the cause of action had accrued and the time it was assigned to the United States, the statute of limitations was pleaded as a defense. The Court sustained the defense, pointing out that although the Soviet government could not sue, there existed throughout the period in question "a government in exile" recognized by the United States which could sue on behalf of "the Russian State".

The present case varies from the Guaranty Trust Company case only in that the deposit upon which suit is brought was made not by the old Imperial Government but by the unrecognized revolutionary government. If however, the theory of the Guaranty Trust Company case is, as it appears to be, that the claim rests in "the Russian State" and not in any particular government thereof, then the holding of that case should be equally applicable herein.

There is, moreover, a further reason adverted to in the Guaranty Trust Company case which lends support to this conclusion. One of the results of non-recognition of a foreign government is its incapacity to bring suit in our courts. Were it decided that during that period of non-recognition the statute of limitations was merely tolled and did not run, one of the most effective sanctions of non-recognition would lose most of its value. It always rests within the power of a foreign government to secure recognition by complying with the requests of our government. If, under such circumstances, the foreign government chooses to remain unrecognized, it must take with it the consequences in the form of incapacity to sue in our courts which may include loss of substantive rights.

Judgment for defendant. Settle findings and decree on notice.

United States v. Uhl
137 F. 2d. 903 (2d. Cir., 1943)
for opinion see <u>infra</u> VI (1)

Government of France v. Isbrandsten-Moller Co.
48 F. Supp. 631 (S.D., N.Y., 1943)

In admiralty. Action by the Government of France against the Isbrandtsen-Moller Company, Incorporated, to recover demurrage and other charges, wherein the respondent filed a motion to dismiss.

RIFKIND, District Judge.

Respondent moves (1) to dismiss the above entitled action upon the ground that it had not been properly commenced prior to the severance of diplomatic relations between this country and France and could not be commenced thereafter; and (2) to strike from the files of the clerk of this court a verification of the amended libel, signed by the former French Ambassador to this country, upon the ground that it was filed on November 9, 1942, on which date the Government of France did not have access to the courts of this country.

This is an action to recover demurrage and other charges alleged to be due the Government of France. On October 1, 1941, a libel verified by the proctor for the libellant was filed; and an amended libel, verified in the same manner, was filed on March 8, 1942. Thereafter, respondent moved under Rule 12 of the Admiralty Rules of this court for a stay of all proceedings pending the procurement of personal verification of the libellant. This motion was granted; and in the order entered thereon, on October 30, 1942, it was provided that if the personal verification of the libellant was not filed on or before November 30, 1942, the action was to be dismissed.

A verification which purports to have been signed and sworn to by the French Ambassador on October 3, 1942, was filed in this court by proctors for libellant on November 9, 1942, the day after France had severed diplomatic relations with this country and had recalled its ambassador. By letter dated November 18, 1942, the Secretary of State notified the proctors for the respondent that on November 9, 1942, Mr. Gaston Henry-Haye was not the French Ambassador to this country and, because of the German occupation of all of France, the Government of Metropolitan France was no longer recognized by this country. In a telegram dated the same day the Secretary of State informed the proctors for the libellant that at the present time the United States did not recognize the existence of any Government of France. On November 8, 1942, General Ruling No. 11 of the Treasury Department promulgated under the authority of Executive Orders No. 8389 and 9193 of 1942, 12 U.S.C.A. § 95 note, 50 U.S.C.A. Appendix § 6 note and the Trading With the Enemy Act, 50 U.S.C.A. Appendix §§ 1–31 was amended so as to include in the term "enemy territory" all the territory of continental France. It is apparent, therefore, that the verification in question was filed after diplomatic relations with France had been severed, the French Ambassador's authority had ceased, the United States had withdrawn its recognition of the French Government and its territory had become enemy territory.

Upon the basis of these facts the respondent contends that this action had not been properly commenced and the court had not acquired jurisdiction because the Government of France, being a sovereign body, had failed to waive its immunity before the severance of diplomatic relations and was powerless to do so thereafter.

It is undoubtedly true that a foreign sovereign is immune from suit in our courts. Guaranty Trust Co. v. United States, 1938, 304 U.S. 126, 58 S.Ct. 785, 82 L.Ed. 1224; Dexter & Carpenter, Inc., v. Kunglig Jarnvagsstyrelsen, 2 Cir., 1930, 43 F.2d 705, certiorari denied 282 U.S. 896, 51 S.Ct. 181, 75 L.Ed. 789.

In a proper case the courts will take judicial notice of such immunity. Puente v. Spanish Nat. State, 2 Cir., 1940, 116 F. 2d 43, certiorari denied 314 U.S. 627, 62 S.Ct. 57, 86 L.Ed. 504.

However, where it is not apparent that there is sovereign immunity, it must be claimed by the duly accredited representative of the sovereign state involved. In re Muir, 1921, 254 U.S. 522, 41 S.Ct. 185, 65 L.Ed. 383; The Gul Djemal, 1924, 264 U.S. 90, 44 S.Ct. 244, 68 L.Ed. 574.

It is also undoubtedly true that a foreign sovereign, recognized by our Government, may sue in the courts of the United States. Guaranty Trust Co. v. United States, supra; Land Oberoesterreich v. Gude, 2 Cir., 1940, 109 F.2d 635, certiorari denied 311 U.S. 670, 61 S.Ct. 30, 85 L.Ed. 431; Kingdom of Roumania v. Guaranty Trust Co., 2 Cir., 1918, 250 F. 341, Ann. Cas.1918E, 524, certiorari denied 246 U.S. 663, 38 S.Ct. 333, 62 L.Ed. 928. And it may waive its immunity and consent to be sued. Ervin v. Quintanilla, 5 Cir., 1939, 99 F.2d 935, certiorari denied 306 U.S. 635, 59 S.Ct. 485, 83 L.Ed. 1037; People of Porto Rico v. Ramos, 1914, 232 U.S. 627, 34 S.Ct. 461, 58 L.Ed. 763; Dexter & Carpenter v. Kunglig Jarnvagsstyrelsen, supra.

However, immunity against suit is a defense which is available to the sovereign state and its duly accredited representatives only. It cannot be asserted by a private party litigant. Kunglig Jarn-

vagsstyrelsen v. Dexter & Carpenter, 2 Cir., 1929, 32 F.2d 195, certiorari denied 280 U.S. 579, 50 S.Ct. 32, 74 L.Ed. 629. See, The Schooner Exchange v. M'Faddon et al., 1812, 7 Cranch 116, 3 L.Ed. 287.

The foregoing propositions are well established. They are recited here as background for the novel contention advanced by respondent that because libellant is a sovereign and immune to suit, it can not commence a suit unless and until it has waived its immunity through its ambassador. None of the authorities called to my attention supports this view of libellant's capacity to sue. The reliance of respondent upon Colombia v. Rothschild, 1 Simons 106 is misplaced. The significance of that case has been much contracted by the English courts, United States v. Wagner, [1867] L.R. 2 Ch. 582 and its holding repudiated in this country. The Republic of Mexico v. De Arangoiz, 1856, 5 Duer, N.Y., 634. See also State of Yucatan v. Argumedo, 1915, 92 Misc. 547, 157 N.Y.S. 219. In the last cited case the verification of a complaint by attorneys for a sovereign plaintiff was expressly approved. To the same effect is Republic of Mexico v. Arrangoiz, 1856, 5 Duer, N.Y., 643.

This action was properly commenced prior to the severance of diplomatic relations between France and the United States by the filing of a libel duly verified by the proctor for the libellant in accordance with the provisions of Rule 12 of the Admiralty Rules of this court. It was not a pre-requisite to the commencement of this action that the personal verification of the libellant be obtained. However, Rule 12 afforded the respondent the right to move for a stay of all proceedings until the procurement of such personal verification. This the respondent did and the action was stayed, but it was not dismissed, and it was pending when, on November 8, 1942, diplomatic relations were severed. From that day to the present time the United States has recognized no Government of France. This is evident from the two communications from the Secretary of State and the regulations of the Treasury Department referred to above. Accordingly, on November 9, 1942, the Government of France did not have access to our courts. Guaranty Trust Co. v. United

States, 1938, 304 U.S. 126, 58 S.Ct. 785, 82 L.Ed. 1224.

Furthermore, since November 8, 1942, the Government of France has been an "enemy alien" within the purview of the Trading With the Enemy Act, 50 U.S. C.A. Appendix §§ 1–31, and as such it is precluded from suing in our courts. Ex parte Colonna, 1942, 314 U.S. 510, 62 S.Ct. 373, 86 L.Ed. 379. It follows, therefore, that on November 9, 1942, neither the Government of France nor anyone acting on its behalf had power to file in this court the verification of the French Ambassador.

However, that does not mean that the action abates or must be dismissed. It means that the action is suspended until France is no longer an "enemy alien" and a Government of France is again recognized by the United States. This is the rule applicable to actions commenced by enemy aliens. Stumpf v. A. Schreiber Brewing Co., D.C.W.D.N.Y. 1917, 242 F. 80; Plettenberg, Holthaus & Co. v. I. J. Kalmon & Co., D.C.S.D.Ga. 1917, 241 F. 605; Rothbarth v. Herzfeld, 1917, 179 App. Div. 865, 167 N.Y.S. 199, affirmed 223 N.Y. 578, 119 N.E. 1075.

And it should also apply to actions which were properly commenced by foreign Governments prior to such Governments' loss of recognition by this country. To hold otherwise would do violence to the spirit of the rule enunciated by the Supreme Court in The Sapphire, 1871, 78 U.S. 164, at page 168, that: "The reigning Emperor, or National Assembly, or other actual person or party in power, is but the agent and representative of the national sovereignty. A change in such representative works no change in the national sovereignty or its rights. The next successor recognized by our government is competent to carry on a suit already commenced and receive the fruits of it." See Republic of China v. Merchants' Fire Assur. Corp. of N. Y.,. 9 Cir., 1929, 30 F.2d 278.

The motion to dismiss is denied. The motion to strike from the files of this court the verification of the French Ambassador filed on November 9, 1942, is granted. In view of the changed circumstances, however, the libellant's time to file the verification in question or the verification of any other accredited representative of the Government of France is extended until sixty days after the date upon which a French Government is again recognized by the United States. This, of course, is without prejudice to any action which the Alien Property Custodian may see fit to take.

Settle order on notice.

Chemacid S.A. v. Ferrotar Corp.
51 F. Supp. 756 (S.D., N.Y., 1943)

Action by Chemacid, S. A., a foreign corporation, against the Ferrotar Corporation for accounting. On defendant's motion to dismiss the complaint.

CONGER, District Judge.

On April 20, 1942, interlocutory summary judgment was granted in favor of the plaintiff and a Special Master was appointed by this court to take and state the account between the parties. The hearings before the Special Master have been held and closed, but he has not yet rendered his report.

The defendant now moves for a dismissal of the complaint on the ground that the court lacks jurisdiction. The plaintiff, Chemacid, S. A., is a corporation organized under the laws of Belgium. The defendant claims that since Belgium is occupied by the armed forces of Germany, this plaintiff is a non-resident alien enemy within the meaning of the Trading with the Enemy Act, 50 U.S.C.A.Appendix § 1 et seq.

The trading with the Enemy Act, although stating that, "Nothing in this Act shall be deemed to authorize the prosecution of any suit or action at law or in equity in any court within the United States by an enemy or ally of enemy prior to the end of the war, * * *", 50 U.S.C.A. Appendix § 7(b), does not expressly prohibit the institution of a suit or action.

The view that Section 7(b) of the Trading with the Enemy Act does not contain any affirmative prohibition against suits by enemies, but rather that Congress in enacting that section of the Act merely endeavored to make certain that it was to be understood that the common law remained in effect, was expressed by the Solicitor General in his brief for the United States as amicus curiae in Ex parte Kawato, 317 U.S. 69, at page 75, 63 S.Ct. 115, at page 119, 87 L.Ed. ——. Cf. Sommerich, Recent Innovations in Legal and Regulatory Concepts as to the Alien and His Property, (1943) 37 Am.J.Int.L. 58, 61.

The prohibition against the institution or prosecution of suits by enemies rests, therefore, not on statute, but on the common law. "From the language employed in the Act as well as from the evident intent of the framers of the bill and the legislative debates, the general purposes of the Act, in so far as the Act relates to the trade with and the property of enemies, are the following: * * * 4. To leave in force the common law provisions regarding the effect of war on contracts, statutes of limitations, rights to devises and bequests, and rights as parties to actions, except in so far as the Act mitigates the rigor of the common law." Huberich, The Law relating to Trading with the Enemy (1918), p. 46, quoted in Kaufman v. Eisenberg, 177 Misc. 939, 942, 943, 32 N.Y. S.2d 450.

It is well settled that an enemy may not prosecute an action in our courts. Ex parte Colonna, 314 U.S. 510, 62 S.Ct. 373, 86 L.Ed. 379; Rothbarth v. Herzfeld, 179 App.Div. 865, 167 N.Y.S. 199, affirmed 223 N.Y. 578, 119 N.E. 1075. In like manner, the privilege of suing in our courts is withheld from a corporation domiciled in territory occupied by the enemy, since it is also deemed an enemy. Drewry v. Onassis, 266 App.Div. 292, 42 N.Y.S.2d 74.

In the instant case the domicile and registered office of the plaintiff corporation was moved to New York City by resolution of the board of directors on or about June 21, 1940 in accordance with the Belgian Decree-Law of February 2, 1940. The holders of approximately 99.8% of the capital stock of the corporation now reside in the United States or in England.

"The Government of the United States recognizes the Belgian Government now functioning in England as the Government of Belgium * * *." Certificate of the Secretary of State #4062, dated August 5, 1943. Recognition of a foreign government also embodies a recognition of its laws. United States v. Pink, 315 U.S. 203, 62 S.Ct. 552, 86 L.Ed. 796; United States v. Belmont, 301 U.S. 324, 57 S.Ct. 758, 81 L.Ed. 1134.

The Belgian Decree-Laws provide that Belgian corporations may remove their company seat (domicile) to any unoccupied territory or foreign country. Article 8 of the Decree-Law of February 19, 1942, which is a compilation of the earlier Decree-Laws. With respect to all corporate properties and affairs outside Belgium, the powers of stockholders, directors and officers residing in Belgium were and are suspended (Article 14 Decree-Law).

Our courts have accorded full faith and credit to the decrees and laws of the Governments in Exile. Anderson v. N. V. Transandine Handelmaatschappij, 289 N. Y. 9, 43 N.E.2d 502; Koninklijke Lederfabriek "Oisterwijk" N. V. v. Chase National Bank, 177 Misc. 186, 30 N.Y.S.2d 518, affirmed 263 App.Div. 815, 32 N.Y.S.2d 131; Amstelbank, N. V. v. Guaranty Trust Co., 177 Misc. 548, 31 N.Y.S.2d 194.

If we are to recognize and give effect to the Belgian Decree-Laws, we must and do hold that the plaintiff corporation is not a non-resident alien enemy, but rather a resident alien. Whether we consider the plaintiff a resident alien enemy or merely a resident alien is of no import since at common law a resident alien enemy could sue in our courts. Clarke v. Morey, 10 Johns., N.Y. 69. "A lawful residence implies protection, and a capacity to sue and be sued. A contrary doctrine would be repugnant to sound policy, no less than to justice and humanity." Chief Justice, later Chancellor, Kent in Clarke v. Morey, supra, 10 Johns., N.Y., at page 72.

The right of alien enemies lawfully residing in the United States to have access to our courts is unquestioned in the absence of statute or presidential proclamation to the contrary. Ex parte Kawato, 317 U.S. 69, 63 S.Ct. 115, 87 L.Ed. ——; Petition of Bernheimer, 3 Cir., 130 F.2d 396. Cf. Gambera v. Bergoty, 2 Cir., 132 F.2d 414. "The ancient rule against suits by resident alien enemies has survived only so far as necessary to prevent use of the courts to accomplish a purpose which might hamper our own war efforts or give aid to the enemy. This may be taken as the sound principle of the common law today." Ex parte Kawato, supra, 317 U.S. at page 75, 63 S.Ct. at page 118, 87 L.Ed. ——.

In Drewry v. Onassis, supra, a French corporation was considered a non-resident alien enemy since its registered office was located in Paris, France, which is occupied by the enemy. The fact that the principal stockholder was in England was held to be immaterial; the controlling factor was the domicile of the corporation, not the domicile of the stockholder. The court in the Drewry case relied heavily upon the House of Lords decision in V/O Sovfracht v. van Udens Scheepvart, [1943] 1 All Eng. Rep. 76. In that case a company incorporated under the law of the Netherlands and having its principal place of business at Rotterdam instituted an action in the English courts. The court held that at common law a company incorporated under the laws of a neutral or an allied country which has been occupied by the enemy so that that country is provisionally under the effective control of the enemy is, by reason of the mere fact that it continues to carry on its business in that country, to be treated as an enemy alien to the extent that it is incapacitated from taking proceedings in the English courts to recover a trade debt. In the course of the opinion it was said that: "The test (of enemy character) is an objective test, turning on the relation of the enemy power to the territory where the individual voluntarily resides or the company is commercially domiciled or controlled: it is not a question of nationality or of patriotic sentiment." Page 79. "If the enemy power invades and forcibly occupies territory outside his own boundaries, residence in the territory may disqualify from

bringing or maintaining a suit in the King's courts in the like manner as residence in the enemy power's territory would. The same applies to a company commercially domiciled or controlled in occupied territory." Page 79. "* * * the test which has been taken of enemy character in English law is not nationality, but domicil in the sense of settled residence or, in the case of traders, commercial domicil." Page 84. "No doubt both in prize and at common law a person who is engaged in business in a country which becomes hostile, but is not resident there, is given a reasonable time to dissociate himself from the business if he wishes to avoid becoming an alien enemy and, even if he resides in such a country, it may be that he will escape the imputation of hostility by removing himself from it as quickly as is reasonably possible; * * * But there is no suggestion that such a course has been taken on behalf of the respondent company in the present case." Page 93.

A case on all fours with the case under consideration was decided in England a short time after the Sovfracht decision. There a Belgian corporation, under the provisions of the Belgian Decree-Law of February 2, 1940, moved its domicile to the United States. It brought an action in the English courts and the defendant asserted that the action should be stayed on the ground that the plaintiff had become an enemy alien at common law. The court held that the corporation, by the action it took in June, 1940, had established its commercial domicile in the United States and could continue the action even though Belgium had become enemy-occupied territory. The Pamia, [1943] 1 All Eng.Rep. 269. The court said that the only question was whether the plaintiff had succeeded in taking itself out of the decision of the House of Lords in the Sovfracht case. To show that it had, the court referred to the objective test established in the Sovfracht case, i. e. where is the company commercially domiciled or controlled.

It is the opinion of this court that the facts of the case at bar take it out of the decision in the Drewry case, supra, since Chemacid, S. A., is not commercially domiciled in enemy-occupied territory.

Chemacid, S. A., has done all that it could do to sever completely its ties with occupied Belgium and to move its domicile to the United States. Its lawful domicile, at the present time, is in New York. It owes no allegiance to any person or government within the enemy-occupied territory of Belgium, but rather owes allegiance to the exiled Government of Belgium located in England and recognized by the Government of the United States. Both legally and de facto, Chemacid is effectively removed from German influence and subjected to the sovereignty of our own Government and the Belgian Government in Exile.

In all cases of this type, one of the most important aspects to be considered by the court is whether it will aid and comfort the enemy if the plaintiff is allowed to maintain the action and, if successful, recover a judgment. "There is nothing 'mysteriously noxious' * * * in a judgment for an alien enemy. Objection to it in these days goes only so far as it would give aid and comfort to the other side." Holmes, J., in Birge-Forbes Co. v. Heye, 251 U.S. 317, 323, 40 S.Ct. 160, 161, 64 L.Ed. 286. "The object is not to defeat the alien enemy of his right to recover whatever may be owing him, nor to shield the citizen from the enforcement of his just obligations, but to obviate any advantage being derived by the enemy, directly or indirectly, pending hostilities. * * *" Weiditschka v. Supreme Tent Knights of Maccabees, 188 Iowa 183, 191, 170 N.W. 300, 303, 175 N.W. 835. In this case it is difficult to see how the enemy can be aided and comforted since a judgment recovered by Chemacid cannot be enforced without a license from the Treasury Department. Cf. Domke, Trading with the Enemy in World War II (1943), pp. 305–310; Petition of Bernheimer, supra.

Since the English courts have recognized that these so-called "corporations in exile" are friends and have given them access to their courts, there is no reason why we should deny them the right to prosecute an action in our courts in the absence of legislation or executive proclamation to the contrary. We do not close the doors of our courts to individuals who are resident alien enemies, therefore, why should we close them to resident alien corporations? It would be inequitable and unjust to hold that the plaintiff cannot maintain this action.

The motion to dismiss the complaint on the ground that the court lacks jurisdiction is, therefore, denied.